INTERPERSONAL COMMUNICATION

D0207114

Some of us may believe that interpersonal communication is a matter of common sense or that skillful communication is an innate ability that you either have or you don't. In this textbook, Denise Solomon and Jennifer Theiss demonstrate that interpersonal communication skills are not just common sense; nor are they mysterious qualities that defy learning. *Interpersonal Communication: Putting Theory into Practice* draws on theory and research in the interpersonal communication discipline to help you identify strategies to improve your communication skills. Denise and Jen introduce interpersonal communication as a subject of scientific research that has enormous relevance to your daily lives. You will learn to use what researchers have discovered about interpersonal communication to improve your own ability to communicate well. You will also read about contemporary research in interpersonal communication, a foundation for establishing skill-building tips.

In making research accessible, Denise and Jen show that communication scholars tackle important questions that have real-life relevance, and they dispel myths about interpersonal communication. A touchstone throughout this textbook is a commitment to topics and applications that can help you in many different situations and throughout your life. When you have finished reading this textbook, you will be better prepared to communicate effectively in all areas of your world, with skills and understanding that you can use to improve your interactions with the people around you.

Denise Solomon is Professor of Communication Arts and Sciences at the Pennsylvania State University, University Park.

Jennifer Theiss is Associate Professor of Communication at Rutgers University.

INTERPERSONAL COMMUNICATION

Putting Theory into Practice

Denise Solomon and Jennifer Theiss

Routledge
Taylor & Francis Group

NEW YORK AND LONDON

Please visit the companion website at www.routledge.com/cw/solomon

First published 2013
by Routledge
711 Third Avenue, New York, NY 10017

Simultaneously published in the UK
by Routledge
2 Park Square, Milton Park, Abingdon, Oxon OX14 4RN

Routledge is an imprint of the Taylor & Francis Group, an informa business

Library of Congress Cataloging in Publication Data
Solomon, Denise.
  Interpersonal communication : putting theory into practice / Denise Solomon
  and Jennifer Theiss.
    p. cm.
  1. Interpersonal communication. I. Theiss, Jennifer. II. Title.
  P94.7.S65 2013
  302.2—dc23   2012016255

ISBN 13: 978–0–415–80751–7 (hbk)
ISBN 13: 978–0–415–80752–4 (pbk)
ISBN 13: 978–0–203–14783–2 (ebk)

Typeset in Berkeley
by Keystroke, Station Road, Codsall, Wolverhampton.

Publisher: Linda Bathgate
Textbook Development Manager: Rebecca Pearce
Editorial Assistant: Kayley Hoffman
Production Editor: Gail Newton
Marketing Manager: Paul Myatovich
Text Design: Karl Hunt at Keystroke Typesetting and Graphic Design Ltd
Copy-editor: Susan Dunsmore
Proofreader: Rictor Norton
Indexer: Penelope Kent
Cover Design: Gareth Toye
Companion Website Designer: Marie Mansfield

Denise dedicates this book to Melinda, Sara, Carrie, and Ann. Jen dedicates this book to Sarah, Carla, Heather, and Claire. Our best friends, whose loyalty, friendship, and love have been the model for good interpersonal communication in our lives.

Brief Table of Contents

1 WHAT IS INTERPERSONAL COMMUNICATION?   2

2 CULTURE AND INTERPERSONAL COMMUNICATION   38

3 IDENTITY AND INTERPERSONAL COMMUNICATION   68

4 PERCEPTION AND INTERPERSONAL COMMUNICATION   96

5 LANGUAGE AND INTERPERSONAL COMMUNICATION   126

6 NONVERBAL COMMUNICATION   154

7 EMOTIONS AND COMMUNICATION   180

8 LISTENING   206

9 DEVELOPING AND ENDING RELATIONSHIPS   236

10 INTIMACY AND INTERPERSONAL COMMUNICATION   264

11 COMMUNICATION IN FAMILIES   292

12 INTERPERSONAL INFLUENCE   320

13 INTERPERSONAL CONFLICT   346

14 COMMUNICATING SUPPORT AND COMFORT   376

   BIBLIOGRAPHY   401
   INDEX   438

Contents

Preface xiii
Icons Used in this Text xx
Acknowledgments 1

CHAPTER 1   WHAT IS INTERPERSONAL COMMUNICATION?   **2**

WHAT IS INTERPERSONAL COMMUNICATION? 4
PRACTICING INTERPERSONAL COMMUNICATION 16
STUDYING INTERPERSONAL COMMUNICATION 23
INTERPERSONAL COMMUNICATION ETHICS 28
SUMMARY 31
ACTIVITIES FOR EXPLORING COMMUNICATION ETHICS 33
KEY WORDS 34

PART 1   FOUNDATIONS   36

CHAPTER 2   CULTURE AND INTERPERSONAL COMMUNICATION   38

WHAT IS CULTURE? 40
CULTURE AND COMMUNICATION 50
INTERCULTURAL COMMUNICATION 55
SUMMARY 65
ACTIVITIES FOR EXPLORING COMMUNICATION ETHICS 67
KEY WORDS 67

CHAPTER 3   IDENTITY AND INTERPERSONAL COMMUNICATION   68

SELF-CONCEPT: HOW YOU SEE YOURSELF 70
IDENTITY: THE COMMUNICATED SELF 79
IDENTITIES IN TRANSITION 88
SUMMARY 93

ACTIVITIES FOR EXPLORING COMMUNICATION ETHICS 95
KEY WORDS 95

CHAPTER 4 PERCEPTION AND INTERPERSONAL COMMUNICATION 96

STAGES OF PERCEPTION 98
ATTRIBUTION: PERCEIVING AND MISPERCEIVING CAUSES 105
FACTORS THAT AFFECT PERCEPTION 113
SUMMARY 120
ACTIVITIES FOR EXPLORING COMMUNICATION ETHICS 122
KEY WORDS 122

PART 2 INTERPERSONAL INTERACTION 124

CHAPTER 5 LANGUAGE AND INTERPERSONAL COMMUNICATION 126

THE NATURE OF VERBAL COMMUNICATION 128
THE RULES OF LANGUAGE 135
FACTORS THAT AFFECT LANGUAGE USE 142
BIASED LANGUAGE 148
SUMMARY 151
ACTIVITIES FOR EXPLORING COMMUNICATION ETHICS 153
KEY WORDS 153

CHAPTER 6 NONVERBAL COMMUNICATION 154

WHAT IS NONVERBAL COMMUNICATION? 156
THE FUNCTIONS OF NONVERBAL MESSAGES 162
INDIVIDUAL DIFFERENCES 169
COMBINING VERBAL AND NONVERBAL CUES 172
SUMMARY 178
ACTIVITIES FOR EXPLORING COMMUNICATION ETHICS 179
KEY WORDS 179

CHAPTER 7 EMOTIONS AND COMMUNICATION 180

WHAT ARE EMOTIONS? 182
FEELINGS AND COMMUNICATION 190
FACTORS THAT AFFECT EMOTIONS AND COMMUNICATION 193
THE DARK SIDE OF EMOTIONS IN CLOSE RELATIONSHIPS 198
SUMMARY 203

ACTIVITIES FOR EXPLORING COMMUNICATION ETHICS 205
KEY WORDS 205

CHAPTER 8 LISTENING 206

WHAT IS LISTENING? 208
ACTIVE LISTENING 219
LISTENING FOR RELATIONAL MEANINGS 226
SUMMARY 231
ACTIVITIES FOR EXPLORING COMMUNICATION ETHICS 233
KEY WORDS 233

PART 3 INTERPERSONAL RELATING 234

CHAPTER 9 DEVELOPING AND ENDING RELATIONSHIPS 236

FORMING RELATIONSHIPS 239
ESCALATING RELATIONSHIPS 244
ENDING RELATIONSHIPS 251
WHEN THINGS GO WRONG 255
SUMMARY 260
ACTIVITIES FOR EXPLORING COMMUNICATION ETHICS 262
KEY WORDS 262

CHAPTER 10 INTIMACY AND INTERPERSONAL COMMUNICATION 264

THE NATURE OF INTIMACY 266
COMMUNICATION IN INTIMATE RELATIONSHIPS 272
INDIVIDUAL DIFFERENCES IN INTIMACY 277
EXTREMES OF INTIMACY 284
SUMMARY 288
ACTIVITIES FOR EXPLORING COMMUNICATION ETHICS 290
KEY WORDS 290

CHAPTER 11 COMMUNICATION IN FAMILIES 292

WHAT IS A FAMILY? 294
COMMUNICATION IN FAMILY SYSTEMS 299
THE FAMILY LIFESPAN 305
SUMMARY 315
ACTIVITIES FOR EXPLORING COMMUNICATION ETHICS 317
KEY WORDS 317

PART 4	STRATEGIC INTERPERSONAL COMMUNICATION	318

CHAPTER 12   INTERPERSONAL INFLUENCE   320

GOALS	322
INFLUENCE MESSAGES	328
INTERPERSONAL INFLUENCE IN ACTION	334
SUMMARY	343
ACTIVITIES FOR EXPLORING COMMUNICATION ETHICS	345
KEY WORDS	345

CHAPTER 13   INTERPERSONAL CONFLICT   346

WHAT IS CONFLICT?	348
MANAGING CONFLICT	354
CONFLICT DYNAMICS	364
SUMMARY	372
ACTIVITIES FOR EXPLORING COMMUNICATION ETHICS	374
KEY WORDS	375

CHAPTER 14   COMMUNICATING COMFORT AND SUPPORT   376

PROVIDING COMFORT	378
INDIVIDUAL DIFFERENCES IN COMFORTING BEHAVIOR	389
COMFORT WHEN IT COUNTS	394
SUMMARY	398
ACTIVITIES FOR EXPLORING COMMUNICATION ETHICS	400
KEY WORDS	400

Bibliography	401
Index	438

Preface

Students attend college for a variety of reasons: to broaden their minds, to learn a vocation, or to become independent adults. But all students need to master interpersonal communication skills. Everyone, regardless of her or his personal and career goals, benefits from an ability to promote a friendship, to resolve a conflict, to comfort someone in need, and to answer questions clearly. Throughout the course of our lives, the experiences that bring us joy, that define who we are, and that connect us to others are grounded in interpersonal communication.

As active communication researchers, we hope that the studies we conduct will someday offer tangible solutions to complex human problems. As teachers, our greatest professional joys have come from seeing students improve their communication skills in ways that changed their lives. Denise remembers a student who started the semester paralyzed by the thought of interpersonal conflict and who, over the course of the semester, became confident enough to express herself during disagreements. That student wrote a couple of years later to say that she had become the go-to person in her workplace whenever someone had an interpersonal communication problem. Jen has seen how learning strategies for listening and self-disclosure helped a shy and lonely first-year student emerge as a confident campus leader. Like all teachers of interpersonal communication, we have countless stories like these. Because of the impact of interpersonal communication on students' lives, we are inspired to promote the teaching of interpersonal communication.

OUR MISSION

This book introduces students to interpersonal communication as a subject that has enormous relevance to their daily lives. We provide concrete strategies for building communication skills that are firmly grounded in contemporary communication research. We also show that effective interpersonal communication is based on strategies and skills that everybody can learn to do better. Our touchstone throughout is a commitment to topics and applications that can help students in many different situations and throughout their lives.

Improve Quality of Life by Promoting Communication Skills

A central goal of this text is helping students use what researchers have learned about interpersonal communication to improve their own ability to communicate well. To that end, we weave skill-building suggestions throughout every section of every chapter. We frequently invite students to pause and reflect on material in the text, so that they can identify connections between what they are learning and their own life experiences. We suggest activities for applying concepts, and we provide self-assessments to promote personal insight. Each section of every chapter suggests ways that students can practice what they have learned – these recommendations are focused, concrete, and closely tied to the information in the chapter. Then, because good communication is attentive to ethical issues and priorities, each chapter concludes with a set of activities for promoting communication ethics.

Use Contemporary Research to Inform Concrete Skill-Building Tips

As college students, we were both drawn to the study of interpersonal communication because we saw that communication scholars take on important questions that have real-life relevance. For Denise, discovering the inherent biases people bring to conflict interactions motivated her to study how personal relationships develop and survive in the face of threats. Jen wanted to understand how romantic partners express intimacy and establish mutual commitment within relationships. As researchers, we have worked independently and together to understand how romantic partners experience and withstand challenges, such as uncertainty, jealousy, hurtful messages, and conflict. As teachers, we continually draw upon communication research to develop concrete guidelines for building communication skills.

Dispel Myths about Interpersonal Communication

Like many teachers of interpersonal communication, we've been confronted by two persistent myths that students bring to our classrooms. One is that interpersonal communication is just a matter of common sense. Paradoxically, the other myth is that communication skill is an innate gift that you either have or you don't. In translating the richness of the communication discipline for the introductory communication skills course, we show students that interpersonal communication skill isn't just common sense, but neither is it a mysterious quality that defies learning.

To drive home this point, we focus on topics that connect fundamental communication concepts to students' daily lives. We also address communication issues that emerge at different life stages, from childhood and through all the transitions of adolescence and adulthood. These topics give readers insight into communication issues relevant to their own stage of life, the changes that the future may hold, and the experiences of people around them. And throughout every chapter, we help students apply what they discover about these issues so they can become better communicators.

A Text that Reaches Out to Students

Helping students see the complexity of interpersonal communication, as well as how to improve their skills, requires teaching both the fundamental parts of the communication process and how those parts come together. Accordingly, both the order of the chapters and the organization of material within each chapter are designed to meet students at a basic level and then elevate their ability to communicate. We also capitalize on technology as an important part of students' lives by encompassing communication via social media within the scope of interpersonal communication and providing materials to engage course material more deeply on an online companion website, available at: http://www.routledge.com/cw/solomon.

The text begins with a chapter that introduces students to interpersonal communication as a practice that can be skillful and consequential – and as the focus of scientific research designed to reveal and explain the inner workings of this complex phenomenon. The remainder of the text is organized into four parts that accomplish the following important goals:

- Explore the foundations of interpersonal communication: culture, the characteristics of individuals, and the workings of the mind.
- Explore the behaviors and dynamics that unfold in interpersonal interactions.
- Locate interpersonal communication at the heart of developing, intimate, and family relationships.
- Describe how people can use communication to accomplish strategic goals like influencing others, managing conflicts, and comforting each other.

In this way, we help students to master specific facets of interpersonal communication, and we put the pieces together to help students succeed in communication situations they face every day over the course of their lives.

In a similar fashion, each chapter begins with foundational concepts and then layers the nuances of interpersonal communication onto that foundation. People learn by mastering basic ideas and then elaborating their knowledge with specific details. Following a consistent structure for presenting information can also make unfamiliar content easier to understand. Accordingly, students go through the same general sequence in most chapters:

- *Students master key concepts.* The primary goal of the opening section of most chapters is to define key terms and fundamental assumptions. For example:

  - Chapter 2 on communication and culture defines the layers of culture and explains how cultures develop and change.
  - Chapter 5 on verbal communication begins by discussing the nature of language.
  - Chapter 10 on communication in intimate relationships opens by defining intimacy and clarifying the forms it can take.

  Our discussion of these fundamental topics concludes with concrete suggestions for putting knowledge of these core concepts to practical use.

- *Students relate communication to the core concepts.* After we introduce core concepts, we show students how they are relevant to everyday communication experiences. For example:

  - Chapter 2 examines how people use verbal and nonverbal messages to reveal important cultural beliefs and values to others.
  - Chapter 3 considers how people can use communication strategies to enhance self-esteem.
  - Chapter 10 explores the role of communication in maintaining intimacy.

  We draw from research examples to bring these relationships to life, and again we show students how to apply this knowledge to build communication skills.

- *Students probe socially significant issues.* In the final sections of most chapters, we feature real-world issues that affect or are affected by interpersonal communication. For example:

  - Chapter 2 on culture and communication explores how men's and women's different communication experiences over the lifespan can affect relationships.
  - In Chapter 9, the reader learns about the communication challenges created by unrequited love and "friends-with-benefits" relationships.
  - Chapter 11 discusses how improved communication patterns can strengthen family bonds.

  These sections reveal the important research questions and lifespan issues that communication scholars are grappling with, and they point to the real-life situations this text can help students deal with more effectively.

- *Students apply their knowledge.* Each chapter includes a feature called "Putting Theory into Practice." These sections offer students tips for using what they have learned to improve their interpersonal communication. Then, through recommendations, concrete examples, and numerous exercises, we help students apply what they have learned to their day-to-day communication experiences.

HELPING STUDENTS PUT THEORY INTO PRACTICE

Interpersonal communication is an essential life skill that everybody can learn. We include a variety of learning aids to engage students in activities that will help them to understand their own communication experiences and, more importantly, to improve their ability to communicate effectively.

Pause & Reflect

Each chapter poses 8–10 questions that ask students to reflect on their own experiences so that they can see how communication affects them every day. These moments of reflection ask students to think about their own communication practices, experiences that they found rewarding, or situations where skillful communication might have made a difference. For example:

- Which verbal and nonverbal cues make you think that someone is listening to you – or not?
- Which stories are told and retold within your family, and how do they reflect your family's values?
- What happened in a recent conversation that left you feeling loved and supported?

Questions like these invite students to draw connections between the text and their own lives. Instructors might also find them useful as topics for discussion, journal assignments, or themes for extended writing assignments.

Communication in Action

Each chapter includes 3–5 exercises that help students probe or test the chapter's claims and to examine communication in their own world. These activities directly connect course material to students' personal experiences, and they point to situations where skillful communication can make a difference. These exercises take various forms, such as:

- encouraging students to observe and record aspects of the communication that occurs around them;
- asking students to reflect on their own experiences, for example, keeping a diary to chart communication and emotions over the course of a few days;
- providing students with problem-solving tasks, like mapping communication boundaries within their family and identifying ways to revise those boundaries to improve communication.

As with Pause & Reflect questions, Communication in Action exercises can be completed at the student's discretion or integrated into homework assignments. Instructions and forms for Communication in Action exercises are referenced in the text, with supporting materials provided as needed on the companion website.

How Do You Rate?

Each chapter also offers one or two self-report or observational research measures. Using scales provided on the companion website, students can, for example, assess their ability to engage in perspective-taking, their preferred listening style, their competence with computer-mediated communication, the norms for communication within their family, or their preferred types of social support. We consistently find that students enjoy these tools. In addition, these exercises promote insights that are relevant to students' own interpersonal communication experiences.

Real Words

In several chapters, we offer transcripts of conversations to bring concepts and ideas to life. In most cases, the transcripts come from interactions that we video-taped in our communication labs or that were given to us by other researchers. Thus, these dialogues are, in fact, "real words." The transcripts that are showcased include topics such as hurtful conversations, interpersonal conflicts, and comforting interactions. By reading these transcripts, students get a close look at what works and what doesn't work in real conversations between people.

Inside Communication Research

To illustrate how communication research points to strategies for effective communication, each chapter presents one extended description of a particular communication study. We take students inside the research process by reviewing the methods and results of a study. Follow-up questions then direct students to consider both the implications of the findings and the pros and cons of the research procedures. For example, students will learn about research on perceiving flirtatious communication after consuming alcohol, detecting deceit, communicating grief, and communicating in friendships across the lifespan. These boxes seek to make interpersonal communication research accessible and to show students how research findings can inform their own communication practices.

Scholar Spotlights in the Communication Café

We created space within the companion website called the "Communication Café." Here, students will find our video introductions to each unit – our goal with these is to help bring alive the learning objectives for each part of the book. In addition, the Café provides video-recorded interviews with leading scholars in the field of interpersonal communication. We've invited one scholar for each chapter to elaborate on topics covered within that chapter. In the interviews, we also asked these scholars to describe their own journey as interpersonal communication researchers. These videos showcase some of the most influential people in the field of interpersonal communication, and bring alive their experiences as people who practice and advance the science of interpersonal communication.

Exploring Communication Ethics

Ethical issues permeate all facets of interpersonal communication; therefore, we offer them as the capstone to every chapter. Each chapter presents three different types of exercises:

- We ask students to consider an ethical choice in a particular situation.
- We invite students to think about the ethical implications of a line of reasoning or a communication decision.

- ■ We offer students activities for analyzing communication ethics in concrete materials.

Whether completed independently or as a part of classroom assignments, these exercises encourage students to probe the ethical issues that emerge within interpersonal communication contexts.

WHAT'S AHEAD

We are excited to share this journey with teachers and students. We both remember vividly our first introduction to interpersonal communication. We have enjoyed devoting our professional lives to investigating the complexities of interpersonal communication and practicing what we hope is skillful interpersonal communication in our personal lives. We know from our own experiences that interpersonal communication is challenging – even to people like us who spend all their time studying and thinking about it. We also know that everyone can improve their interpersonal communication skills. Improving interpersonal communication skills takes knowledge, opportunities to practice, and believing that interpersonal communication is something one can and should do better. We designed this text to help others on their journey toward more effective and satisfying interpersonal communication, and we hope that everyone who reads this book finds what they need to have more fulfilling interpersonal communication experiences.

Jen & Denise

Icons Used in this Text

Look for these icons throughout the text – they indicate material for you to use, complete, or watch on the companion website.

 Communication Café: When you see this icon, go to the companion website and watch videos of Denise and Jen. They provide introductions to each of the four Parts in the text, and they interview some of the leading scholars in the field of communication in the Scholar Spotlights.

 Communication in Action: A Communication in Action box with this icon indicates an activity on the companion website that will give you the opportunity to probe or test the claims in the text and examine communication in your own world.

 How Do You Rate? When you see this icon, you can complete a self-evaluation exercise on the companion website. It will be related to the topic under discussion and will help you understand your own interpersonal communication experiences.

Acknowledgments

The idea for this book has been with us for a long time, and we are grateful to several people who helped us get from there to here. Rhona Robbins was a tireless fan, whose critical feedback and sense of humor kept us hopeful that our vision for this book would someday be realized. We are also grateful for Rhona's good will when our image for this book required us to move in a direction that she could not go. That path took us to Linda Bathgate! We are so grateful for the enthusiasm with which Linda embraced our goals for this book, and for the professionalism of everyone on Routledge's editorial, production, and marketing team, especially Rebecca Pearce and Mallory Moore. It was such a pleasure to finish this book with people who were the living embodiment of excellent interpersonal communication.

Denise has other people to thank, none more so than Jen. Without Jen's dedication and hard work, this book would have languished on Denise's back burner. Jen was the perfect co-author: an expert in the field, a gifted teacher who so easily translates her pedagogy into writing, and a very good friend. Denise is also grateful to her spouse, Jim, and sons, Jackson and Quincy, who sacrificed time together as a family so that Denise could work on this project, and who were exceptionally creative in devising ways to celebrate the milestones.

Jen is endlessly grateful to Denise for inviting her to be a part of this project. It was a delight to collaborate on a project that we both felt so passionately about. Jen also thanks her husband, Kevin, for his constant support, encouragement, and understanding, and her golden retriever, Riley, for keeping her feet warm while she wrote.

We are also grateful to our colleagues, friends, and family who encouraged and supported us along the way. Particular thanks go to Mandy Goodwin and Victoria Jennings-Kelsall, who test-drove PDF versions of this book, and provided us with very helpful feedback from their classrooms. More generally, we thank our mentors and our many, many students for inspiring us to be better scholars and teachers.

Throughout the development of this book, many reviewers have contributed invaluable suggestions and feedback to the manuscript. We thank all of our reviewers, some of whom elect to remain anonymous, for their contribution to making this a better textbook. We specifically wish to thank Deatra Sullivan-Morgan (Elmhurst College), Charles Veenstra (Dordt College), Kyle Tusing (University of Arizona), Randall Koper (University of the Pacific), Deborah Manning (Monash University), Kristen Froemling-Orlov (Radford University), Kevin Visconti (Northeastern University), and Kenneth Albone (Rowan University).

WHAT IS INTERPERSONAL COMMUNICATION?

1

4   WHAT IS INTERPERSONAL COMMUNICATION?

16 PRACTICING INTERPERSONAL COMMUNICATION

23 STUDYING INTERPERSONAL COMMUNICATION

28 INTERPERSONAL COMMUNICATION ETHICS

31 SUMMARY

33 ACTIVITIES FOR EXPLORING COMMUNICATION ETHICS

34 KEY WORDS

For two years, 2011 and 2012, Aerosmith front-man, Steven Tyler, and pop-diva, Jennifer Lopez, joined Randy Jackson to judge contestants on the popular reality television competition, *American Idol*. The judges on the show are tasked with the sometimes difficult jobs of helping the performers to relax before their audition, communicating rejection to untalented contestants, offering comfort to devastated singers who don't make the cut, and delivering criticism in a way that is constructive and helpful to those in the competition. Steven Tyler quickly earned a reputation as the clown of the group, often resorting to humor and wacky stunts to soften the blow of bad news. Although most of the contestants appreciated his effort to lighten the mood, some of his communication strategies landed him in hot water with the network when his jokes bordered on inappropriate. Jennifer Lopez was often the counterweight to Tyler because her communication demonstrated a great deal of empathy and compassion when dealing with the contestants. She was brought to tears when they had to cut one of her favorite performers and requested that she be the one to deliver the news. The *American Idol* judges have demonstrated how interpersonal communication can be a challenging, but powerful process.

I nterpersonal communication skills are critically important in every facet of life. As the *American Idol* judges have shown, interpersonal communication can be a useful tool for offering constructive criticism, managing conflict, providing comfort and support, or sharing a humorous moment. You will certainly use interpersonal communication for these reasons, but you will find that interpersonal communication skills are also important in a variety of other situations, such as when you converse with a new neighbor, coordinate your schedule with your roommate, or negotiate a raise with a boss. You can use interpersonal communication to build successful relationships in the home, at school, at work, and in public. Because interpersonal communication has always been a part of your life, you may find it difficult to think about it as a topic you can study and learn more about. In this chapter, we'll offer you a deeper understanding of interpersonal communication, explain how you can develop and improve your interpersonal communication skills, describe how researchers study interpersonal communication, and consider what it means to practice ethical interpersonal communication.

WHAT IS INTERPERSONAL COMMUNICATION?

Interpersonal communication is a specific type of communication. **Communication**, in general, is the use of symbols to represent ideas so that meanings can be shared. Street signs, magazines, podcasts, conversations, weblogs, and books are all examples of communication. These forms of communication use some kind of **symbols** – sounds, movements, or images – to represent ideas. During interpersonal communication, you use symbols in the form of talking, gesturing, or writing to represent the complex ideas in your mind. In this part of the chapter, you'll learn the definition of interpersonal communication, the characteristics of interpersonal communication, the types of messages created through interpersonal communication, and some of the contexts in which you experience interpersonal communication.

A Basic Definition

Whereas communication, in general, includes any use of symbols to represent meanings, interpersonal communication refers more specifically to communication that occurs between people and creates a personal bond between them. Let's probe this term by breaking it down into its two parts: "inter" and "personal," as shown in Figure 1.1. The *inter* part of the word highlights how interpersonal communication connects people. In interpersonal communication, one person's actions both affect and reflect another person's actions. This is not the case with all kinds of communication: you can shut down your Internet browser without having an effect on the source of those messages. In contrast, if you don't respond to an instant message, your communication partner will probably have some kind of a reaction. When you engage in interpersonal communication, you and another person become linked together.

Interpersonal communication is also *personal*. This doesn't mean that interpersonal communication always involves private topics or that it only occurs in close relationships. Rather, it means that your unique qualities as a person matter during interpersonal communication. If you are at a restaurant and you are treated only as a customer – someone who needs to place an order and get food – you aren't really experiencing interpersonal communication. This would be considered impersonal communication, because your personal qualities are irrelevant to the interaction. But if your server shows an interest in you as an individual and communicates with you in unique ways because of your characteristics and circumstances, then that conversation is much more personal. In interpersonal communication, you are attentive to the personal qualities that you and your partner bring to the interaction.

What does "interpersonal communication" mean to you? The activity described in the Communication in Action 1.1 box gives you a chance to reflect on your own perceptions of interpersonal communication. You'll find Communication in Action exercises throughout the chapters of this book. Like the activity on "Defining Interpersonal Communication," these exercises give you a chance to explore what you are learning about interpersonal communication by paying attention to your own experiences and the world around you.

Symbols
Sounds, gestures, or images that represent ideas.

Communication
Using symbols to represent ideas so that meanings can be shared.

Interpersonal Communication
Using symbols to represent ideas in order to share meanings and create a personal bond between people.

Impersonal Communication
Using symbols to represent ideas in a manner that ignores personal qualities of the people involved in the interaction.

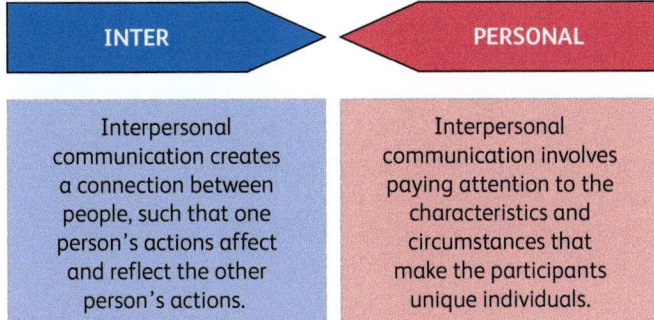

FIGURE 1.1 Defining interpersonal communication

Communication
Using symbols to represent ideas so that meanings can be shared.

COMMUNICATION IN ACTION 1.1

Defining Interpersonal Communication

Make a list of five communication experiences you had in the past week that you consider to be interpersonal communication. Then, list five communication experiences you had that you do NOT consider to be interpersonal communication. Reflecting on those two lists, what features of your experiences seem to define communication episodes as interpersonal?

Dyad

Two people, which is a common context for interpersonal communication.

You might think of interpersonal communication as something that occurs between two people, also known as a **dyad**. A dyad is a common setting for interpersonal communication, because each partner in the interaction is free to focus her or his attention exclusively on the other. Notice, though, that the definition of interpersonal communication can include more than two people. If you communicate with a group of people in ways that are personal and connect everyone involved, interpersonal communication occurs. An example might be a group of friends who regularly hang out together. You might also have dyadic interpersonal communication with a person who is part of a larger group, for example, talking with your best friend while you are both with your larger social group. The key factor in interpersonal communication isn't the number of people present, but personal interaction.

PAUSE & REFLECT

Think about a person with whom you spend time, both one-on-one and as part of a larger group. How are your communication experiences with that person the same in those two situations? How are they different?

Interpersonal communication often occurs in face-to-face interactions. Face-to-face interaction allows partners to communicate both verbally and nonverbally – with words, with gestures, and with body language. Face-to-face interaction also helps each partner attend to the other as an individual. Interpersonal communication doesn't have to occur face-to-face though. When you talk on the phone, exchange text or instant messages, or participate in a chat room, your communication can create a personal connection with another person. Once again, the key is the presence of interaction that is personal, no matter what tools you use to communicate.

Characteristics

Now that you have learned the definition of interpersonal communication, let's examine features that are present in any interaction you might have. Figure 1.2 shows the **transactional model of communication** – this name reflects the fact that people involved in an interpersonal interaction participate together in the act of communicating. The model includes at least two *participants*, who bring personal qualities to the interaction, as well as their own thoughts and their impressions of their partner. Together, these participants create and interpret symbols that represent ideas. The interaction unfolds in a *context* that includes everything from physical characteristics of the setting to the cultural environment. The process of interpersonal communication also unfolds over time. Although we've identified the separate parts of an interaction to help you learn about them, in practice, all of these components come together to create a holistic and dynamic experience that is communication. In this section, we consider five characteristics of interpersonal communication that are implied by this model.

Interpersonal communication is a continuous process. Notice that the model in Figure 1.2 connects the communication partners with a double-headed arrow. This arrow reflects the continuous exchange of messages that occurs during interpersonal communication. Even when one partner is speaking, the other is communicating through body position, eye contact, and facial expressions. This arrow also represents the **channel** or the medium through which messages are exchanged between people. That channel

Transactional Model of Communication
A conception of the components present in an interpersonal interaction and how people participate together in the act of communicating.

Channel
The medium through which messages are exchanged between people.

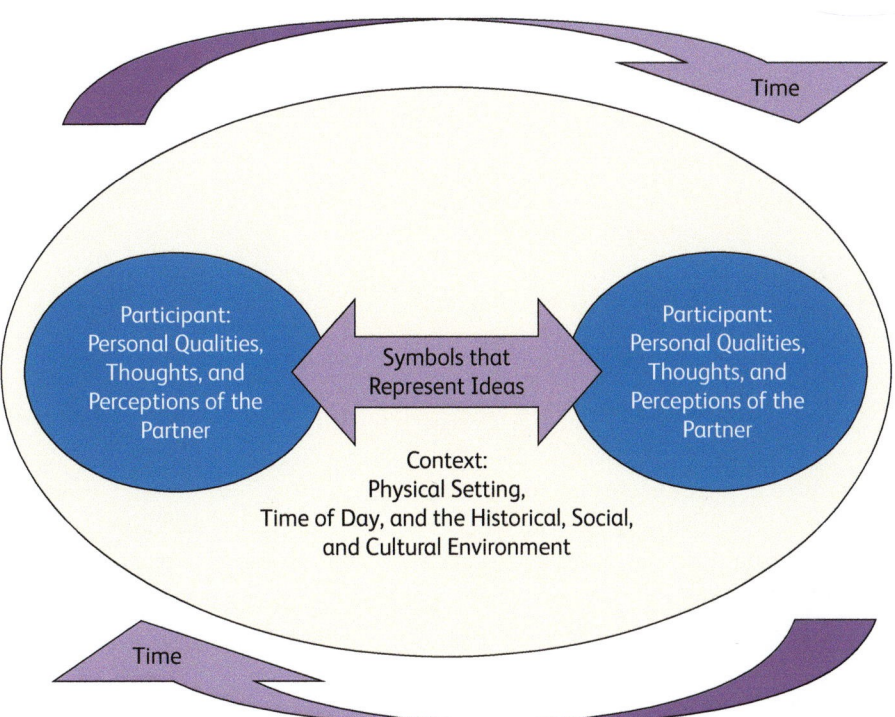

FIGURE 1.2 The transactional model of communication

might be a connection that exists when face-to-face partners give each other their attention, or it could be a cell phone or Internet connection. Sometimes, people don't even have a sense of a communication channel, because they are so thoroughly connected by their mutual engagement in the communication experience. In all cases, the channel allows partners to jointly participate in the continuous creation and interpretation of symbols that represent ideas.

Interpersonal communication is a dynamic process. Interpersonal communication is a dynamic process because meanings change and unfold over time, and previous messages affect how subsequent messages are created and understood. In the Real Words box, you can read a transcript from a conversation that was recorded in Denise's research lab. We'll share dialogs like this one throughout this book to illustrate ideas and concepts using real conversations. In this case, notice how Alicia's assertion that she is hard-working changes as the conversation unfolds. At first, Alicia doesn't realize that Marcus is criticizing her, and she offers more evidence to back up her claim. Over time, though, Alicia starts taking Marcus's comments more to heart. When Alicia repeats that she is hard-working later in the conversation, her statement is more forceful and defensive than it was at the beginning. This example illustrates how messages have different meanings at different times and how meaning depends on prior messages.

REAL WORDS

A HURTFUL CONVERSATION

This transcript was drawn from a study of dating couples (Priem, McLaren, & Solomon, 2010). In the study, the researchers asked one member of the couple to identify a personal trait he or she valued. Then they secretly instructed that person's dating partner to challenge that trait.

ALICIA: I wrote down that I was hard-working, because I had to work really hard to get into this college.

MARCUS: I don't understand; what was so hard about getting into this college?

ALICIA: Well, I always had this goal, and I worked hard toward it.

MARCUS: Like what? You had to finish high school? How is that hard?

ALICIA: Well, I also worked hard at sports too.

MARCUS: Your sports were softball and basketball; how were those hard?

ALICIA: What do you mean? You had to be like in top physical condition – that makes you hard-working. I had to run miles.

MARCUS: For softball?

ALICIA: Yes. That makes me hard-working.

MARCUS: I just don't see that it was all that hard.

ALICIA: What about how hard I work for my classes? How many hours of homework did I do last semester? Like six hours a night.

MARCUS: Steve's in the same major and he doesn't do any work. It's an easy major. It's like playing softball instead of soccer.

ALICIA: I'm sorry that I didn't play soccer and you think that's a better sport. We're not talking about soccer and we're not talking about your major. We're talking about me being hard-working and I am hard-working.

MARCUS: Are you sure?

ALICIA: Why are you putting me down right now?

MARCUS: I just don't think you are any more hard-working than anyone else.

ALICIA: What about the fact that I work 5 days a week waitressing? Do you know how hard waitressing is?

MARCUS: Oh brother, Alicia. Just about everyone we know waits tables.

ALICIA: I guess I don't care what you think. I think I'm hard-working. You shot down everything that I've said, but I still think I'm hard-working.

Interpersonal communication is consequential. Interpersonal communication has consequences – in other words, it produces outcomes. When people actively use interpersonal communication to accomplish a goal, those consequences are deliberate. For example, you might use interpersonal communication to persuade a classmate to help you with a paper, to resolve a conflict with a sibling, or to cheer up a friend. At other times, the consequences are unintentional. For example, without realizing it, you might put down a co-worker, insult a classmate, or hurt a romantic partner. The consequences of interpersonal communication, intended or unintended, can take a variety of forms. Some of the most common consequences of interpersonal communication include the following:

- *Learning*: Interpersonal communication allows you to gather information about yourself, other people, and past, present, or predicted events, beliefs, and attitudes.
- *Helping*: Interpersonal communication allows you to provide information, advice, emotional support, or assistance that can help the recipient deal with a problem.
- *Influencing*: Interpersonal communication allows you to persuade another person to provide help, give advice, share an activity, change an attitude, change a relationship, give permission, or fulfill an obligation.
- *Relating*: Interpersonal communication allows you to experience closeness or distance, agreement or disagreement, and equality or inequality with another person.
- *Playing*: Interpersonal communication allows you to experience humor, camaraderie, celebrations, as well as to pass time and coordinate shared activities.

PAUSE & REFLECT

Think about the last time that an interpersonal interaction made you feel especially strong emotions, such as happiness, anger, or sadness. What was it about the conversation that produced those emotions? In your experience, do communication experiences that occur face-to-face versus using some technology, such as instant messaging, evoke more or less intense emotions?

Interpersonal communication is irreversible. You can't take back messages that you have communicated, and you can't recreate communication opportunities that have passed. If you make hurtful comments, for example, you can apologize, you can explain, you can try to correct a misunderstanding, but all of your future conversations with that partner will include those comments as part of your shared history. Just as you can't "un-say" messages after the fact, you can't deliver messages after their moment has passed. Have you ever been teased or insulted, and thought of a perfect comeback hours after the conversation occurred? As much as you might want to call the person and deliver your zinger, you'll never recapture that moment in the interaction when your response would have been most appropriate.

Interpersonal communication is imperfect. Finally, keep in mind that interpersonal communication is imperfect. Your thoughts can never be completely communicated to another person. You have to use symbols to represent those ideas, and you have to rely on your partner to decipher those symbols. Inevitably, your partner will attach slightly different meanings to the symbols than you did. Sometimes, our different interpretations are noticeable, frustrating, or humorous. When Denise was a child, for example, she thought her father invited her to "sailing," when he actually asked her to go with him to "Salem" (a town 150 miles away) – although her warm clothing wasn't useless, an overnight bag would have been more helpful! Even when you don't notice a misunderstanding, try to keep in mind that there is always some slippage between the ideas in people's minds and the meanings they create through interpersonal communication.

Sometimes, people forget that interpersonal communication is imperfect, and they place too much faith in what communication can do. Table 1.1 corrects some common misconceptions about interpersonal communication. When you keep the limits of interpersonal communication in mind, you can begin to improve your interpersonal communication experiences.

Types of Messages

As you learned previously, interpersonal communication involves creating shared meaning with people. In this section, we describe the two general kinds of meanings created through interpersonal communication: content messages and relational messages.

Content Messages

The literal or typical meanings of the symbols used to communicate.

Content messages are the literal or typical meanings of the symbols used to communicate. Consider the question "Are you using your car this afternoon?" You can attach a dictionary or literal meaning to those words and easily decipher the content meaning – the speaker wants to know if you will be doing something that involves your car. You can probably also recognize the conventional or typical meaning: this question often means that the speaker would like to borrow your car. As this example shows, content messages can be the direct or literal meaning of the words, or they can be the indirect meanings of the symbols that are used.

Relational Messages

The nature of the relationship between communication partners that is implied by the symbols that are used to communicate.

Relational messages are the meanings that symbols have for the relationship between communicators. Let's continue the previous example. What kind of relationship do you think exists between communication partners if one asks the other, "Are you using your car this afternoon?" Notice that you aren't focused on the meanings of the words themselves, but what those words imply about the relationship. The communicators

TABLE 1.1 Correcting misconceptions about interpersonal communication

Interpersonal communication is NOT a natural ability

Although people are born with the ability to learn to communicate, creating and interpreting messages requires self-knowledge, attention to a communication partner's perspective, detailed understanding of how the situation shapes meaning, and an ability to select and sequence messages to achieve particular goals. These abilities take effort and practice to develop.

Interpersonal communication does NOT always solve problems

Sometimes, talking through a problem helps people to understand each other, sheds new light on the situation, and leads to resolution. Sometimes, however, interpersonal communication produces greater misunderstanding, confusion, and an increase in tension. Effective communication can sometimes solve problems, but advice to "just talk about it" overlooks the flaws that are inherent in interpersonal communication.

Interpersonal communication does NOT always build close relationships

Interpersonal communication occurs within personal relationships, and it can help you create a bond with a relationship partner. But interpersonal communication can also be used to damage a relationship, decrease closeness, and avoid intimacy.

Interpersonal communication does NOT always advance pro-social goals

By communicating with other people, you can achieve a variety of desirable goals – for example, you can influence people, resolve conflicts, or provide comfort. But interpersonal communication also has negative consequences that may be intended or unintended. Through messages, people manipulate each other, create and escalate conflicts, and inflict pain. Interpersonal communication can advance positive outcomes, but it doesn't always do so.

probably aren't strangers or enemies, because we don't usually ask strangers or enemies about their cars or their afternoon plans. The speaker's choice of words also suggests that the partners aren't really, really close – if they were, the speaker might just say, "Hey, I need your car." The symbols used to communicate shed some light on the relationship that exists between communication partners. In this case, you might conclude that the communicators have a familiar, but not intimate, relationship.

The relational messages present in an interpersonal interaction might reflect one person's attempt to change the relationship – perhaps by making it more or less close. An acquaintance who asks how you are handling the demands of your new job is showing interest in your life that might suggest a closer bond. On the other hand, a friend from your hometown who doesn't want to hear about your experiences in college may also be telling you that you aren't as close as you used to be. Research shows that people in interpersonal relationships often avoid discussing their relationship explicitly, especially if they aren't sure about whether their relationship is romantic or just friends (Afifi & Burgoon, 1998; Baxter & Wilmot, 1985). How do people negotiate intimacy when they don't talk about it directly? They pay attention to the relational messages that show up when other topics are discussed.

Sometimes, relational messages are easily seen in the words or behaviors used to communicate, as in the case of phrases like "I'm so glad that we're friends," or "I want a divorce." Often, though, relational messages have to be inferred from a communicator's choice of symbols. As we make sense of relational messages, we use the three sources of information summarized in Table 1.2. The symbols themselves are one source of information about a relationship, especially if relationship information is expressed explicitly. Your previous relationship with a communication partner also helps you interpret that person's symbols. Third, the situation offers important clues to the meaning of relational messages. Although relational messages can be hard to decipher, they are an important part of interpersonal communication.

Contexts

Interpersonal communication can unfold between strangers, acquaintances, close friends, or family members. Most often, your communication partners will be people with whom you have a personal relationship. The shared history you have with your friends, family members, or romantic partner makes it easy to form a personal connection when you communicate. Communication is also essential to developing and maintaining closeness in personal relationships. In this section, we remind you of some of the other contexts in which you experience interpersonal communication.

Organizations. The workplace is a venue in which people have many interpersonal interactions. What happens within organizations depends a lot on the characteristics of the particular setting – whether it is formal or casual, whether there is a clear power

TABLE 1.2 Sources of information about relational messages

Source	Examples
The symbols used	"Let's get together more often" "I hope we never work together on another project"
The relationship history	"I love you" spoken for the first time between romantic partners "I love you" spoken at a 50th wedding anniversary
The situation	"I love you" after a fight "I love you" before a long separation

hierarchy, or whether the industry traditionally employs men, or women, or both men and women. Within the organizational structure, people's experiences are also shaped by their interpersonal interactions (Fairhurst & Putnam, 2004). When you and a co-worker chat about your personal lives, when you pitch an idea to your boss, when you influence the decisions made by your team, and when you address a conflict about work schedules, you use interpersonal communication to connect with people. Moreover, interpersonal interactions with co-workers provide important, emotionally fulfilling experiences, and they allow us to express and work through our own personal issues (Miller, Considine, & Garner, 2007). Thus, interpersonal communication is an integral part of organizations.

Health settings. Interpersonal communication also occurs in contexts related to your health and well-being. Communication researchers have shown that giving and receiving affectionate messages decreases physical symptoms of stress and improves people's ability to recover from stressful experiences (Floyd, 2006; Floyd, Mikkelson, Tafoya et al., 2007). In addition, the people in our lives might use interpersonal communication to persuade us to adopt a healthier lifestyle or maybe to engage in behaviors that pose a health risk. Our interactions with medical professionals also affect whether we get the care we need to maintain or regain our health. The study described in the "Inside Communication Research" box shows how interpersonal communication can have important consequences for our immediate and long-term well-being. In every chapter of this book, we'll showcase a communication study like this one to reveal how communication researchers are working to better understand how interpersonal communication unfolds within – and affects – your life.

INSIDE COMMUNICATION RESEARCH

Interpersonal Communication and Health

Giving and receiving affection are fundamental human needs that not only maintain close relationships, but also improve physical and mental health. Communication scholar Kory Floyd has conducted studies indicating that people who express love, appreciation, and affection to another person have reduced symptoms of stress. Because cholesterol levels are affected by stress levels, Floyd and his colleagues wondered if producing affectionate messages would decrease cholesterol levels (Floyd, Mikkelson, Hesse, & Pauley, 2007).

The researchers recruited 34 undergraduate students to participate in the study. At the start of the study, the researchers collected a blood sample from each participant so that they could measure cholesterol levels. Then, the participants were asked to participate in a 20-minute writing activity every Wednesday for the three weeks following their initial visit to the lab. Half of the participants were asked to write about their feelings for the person they love the most, a letter to their best friend expressing how much they care about him or her, and about the most positive qualities of their favorite family member. The other participants were asked to write about mundane topics, such as the things that happened to them in the last week, the layout of their apartment, or qualities of their current job. At the end of the study, the researchers again collected a blood sample to measure cholesterol levels for each participant.

The researchers found that individuals who wrote affectionate messages showed a significant decrease in their cholesterol levels over the course of the study. In contrast, individuals who wrote about mundane topics showed a significant increase in their cholesterol levels after participating in the three writing activities. This study suggests that expressing our affection for others can have a noticeable and positive impact on our health.

THINK ABOUT IT

1. This study asked participants to write about their affection for others. How might the results differ if participants were asked to express their affection orally? How might the results differ if the participants expressed their affection directly to a recipient?
2. The results of this study imply that expressing affection affects physical health. What other kinds of communication experiences do you think might have a positive effect on health? What communication experiences might negatively impact health? Do you think is feasible to recommend that people change their interpersonal communication behavior as part of a healthier lifestyle?

Computer-mediated Communication

Interaction between people that is made possible by computer technology.

Computer-mediated communication. Many interpersonal communication experiences involve computers and technology such as email, instant messaging, text messaging, chat rooms, discussion boards, online social networks (e.g., Facebook), and virtual worlds. Using technology, we are able to create a personal connection with others that transcends the separations imposed by time or space. **Computer-mediated communication** refers generally to the variety of ways in which computer technology allows people to exchange messages with each other. Computer-mediated communication offers a less threatening communication venue for people who get anxious about talking to new acquaintances (Caplan, 2005). In fact, Jen knows two men who prefer to address conflicts about their shared apartment using instant messaging, which they rely on even while they are sitting at computers in the same room! Given the volume of messages that we create and share via technology, our understanding of interpersonal communication necessarily embraces computer-mediated interactions.

FIGURE 1.3 The ubiquity of cell phones

Source: © Mick Stevens/The New Yorker Collection/www.cartoonbank.com.

"Would you mind talking to me for a while? I forgot my cell phone."

PAUSE & REFLECT

What proportion of your interpersonal interactions involves the use of technology? How might your personal and work relationships be different if you didn't have technology to help you stay connected?

Putting Theory into Practice: Thinking Critically

The goal of this first section of the chapter has been to open your eyes to the complexity of interpersonal communication. You can learn to communicate more effectively if you appreciate the nuances of this rich and dynamic process.

Recognize the fallibility of symbols. One of the first steps toward developing your interpersonal communication skills is recognizing that communication is inherently flawed. The symbols you use will always have a different meaning to your interaction partner than they do to you, and you will never get your point across exactly as you intended. If you recognize that interpersonal communication is fallible, you can take steps to reduce miscommunication.

- As you communicate, pay attention to your partner's responses to see if he or she seems to be getting the right idea. Notice whether your partner asks relevant questions, laughs when you meant to be funny, or looks concerned when you express disappointment. Your partner's messages can tell you whether your meanings are coming across.
- If the messages you receive seem out of line, don't assume that your partner disagrees with you. Instead, double-check how well your meaning was understood. Phrases like "Did you understand that I meant . . .?" or "I'm not sure I was clear – what do you think I'm trying to say?" can help you to discover misunderstanding.
- Keep in mind that you have more than one opportunity to express your ideas, then restate, clarify, or elaborate your messages if you need to.

By double-checking your partner's interpretations and addressing points of confusion, you can improve the understanding that you achieve through interpersonal communication.

Pay attention to relational messages. Relational messages are always part of our interpersonal communication experiences, so you'll communicate more effectively if you pay attention to the relational messages that you receive and send to others. The Communication in Action 1.2 exercise is designed to help you become more aware of relational messages.

COMMUNICATION IN ACTION 1.2

Deciphering Relational Messages

This exercise helps you to decipher relational messages so that you can become more attentive to them in your interpersonal interactions. You can download Form 1.1 from the **companion website** to help you complete this activity. For each statement in the table, identify what you think is the content message based on the direct or implied meanings of the words. Then, for each relationship context listed, identify at least one possible relational message.

PRACTICING INTERPERSONAL COMMUNICATION

Interpersonal communication is a necessary and inevitable part of life – you can't avoid exchanging messages with people, and you can engage in interpersonal communication without a lot of practice or knowledge. At the same time, interpersonal communication is a skill: like playing music or soccer, it is the product of human creativity or effort that varies in perceived quality. When we focus on interpersonal communication as a skill, we acknowledge that it can be learned through study, practice, and observation. In this part of the chapter, we examine the characteristics of good interpersonal communication, conditions that promote high-quality communication, and how skillful interpersonal communication varies across contexts.

Communication Competence

Interpersonal Communication Competence

The ability to use symbols appropriately and effectively to create a personal connection with another person.

Fidelity

The extent to which meanings can be correctly inferred from the symbols that are used.

In general, competence is an ability to do something well, as measured against some standard for performance. **Interpersonal communication competence**, then, is the ability to use well the symbols that represent ideas and create a personal connection with another person. Communication competence is measured by six standards: fidelity, appropriateness, satisfaction, effectiveness, efficiency, and ethics (Spitzberg & Cupach, 2002).

    Fidelity. Fidelity refers to the clarity of a message – the extent to which meanings can be correctly inferred from the symbols. Fidelity exists when a receiver can hear the message, understand the symbols, and interpret meanings accurately. Fidelity might be undermined by noise in the environment, such as when the sound of construction equipment outside an office makes it difficult for a teacher and student to hear each other. Fidelity is also reduced when communicators use different kinds of symbols, perhaps due to their distinct cultural backgrounds, educational experiences, or age. Consider, for example, how the abbreviations and acronyms that are common in text messages might be difficult for someone less familiar with communication technology to understand. Although threats to fidelity are often outside a person's control, communication competence is not. Competent communicators adjust their behaviors to overcome the barriers to communication – they eliminate noise or move to a quiet location, or they use less jargon when communicating with someone with a different background. As a result, competent communicators produce messages that are easier for a partner to understand.

Appropriateness. Communication is appropriate when the messages that people produce match the requirements of the situation. How do you know what is appropriate communication? All interpersonal interactions are guided by **social rules**, which are guidelines that specify the actions that are expected, preferred, and off-limits in a given situation. We have rules that apply broadly within a community. For example, online communities often have guidelines specifying that participants will not insult one another. People within close-knit social groups, like families, can also develop rules for communication. For example, blended families – which include remarried spouses and their children from former marriages – often develop rules that prohibit communication about the former spouses (Afifi, 2003; Golish & Caughlin, 2002). Competent communicators notice the social rules that are relevant to a communication situation, and they produce messages appropriate to the circumstances.

Social Rules
Guidelines that specify the actions that are expected, preferred, and off-limits within an interaction.

PAUSE & REFLECT

Consider some of the interactions that you have had in the past week, including those related to school, work, and your personal relationships. What are some of the social rules that guided your communication in those situations? Do you have any distinct rules for communication using various forms of social media?

Satisfaction. Competent communication is also enjoyable. Consider the feelings you have after an especially good conversation – you might be energized, feel happy, and enjoy a sense of connection with your interaction partner. Compare those reactions to how you feel after a conversation where you were ignored, slighted, or misunderstood. What makes a conversation satisfying? Grandparents report that they are more satisfied with communication with their grandchildren when both parties take equal responsibility for initiating interaction (Holladay & Seipke, 2007). In the workplace, communication satisfaction arises from high-quality content messages, which address organizational practices, as well as relational messages that maintain personal connections between people in the organization (Gray & Laidlaw, 2004). In general, competent communicators create satisfying interactions by paying attention to their partner's point of view, being responsive to that partner, and maintaining a positive atmosphere.

Effectiveness. A fourth criterion for communication competence is effectiveness. Remember that interpersonal communication allows you to do many things, including learn, help, influence, relate, and play. Your communication is effective when you are able to produce the outcomes that you want. For example, if your best friend was upset about a conflict with his girlfriend, you might want to help make him feel better. If you choose your messages well ("Let's talk through what happened" or "I can appreciate how you're feeling"), you can make a big difference to your friend. Less competent communicators are less effective because their messages don't allow them to achieve their goals.

Efficiency. Interpersonal communication is efficient if you can produce the outcomes you seek with no more than a reasonable amount of effort. Think about the last time you had to ask for a favor – perhaps you needed time off from work or you wanted to use a friend's computer. How hard did you try to get what you wanted? If your request was granted after just a little effort, your communication was efficient. What if you had to provide a lot of reasons or even beg or threaten before you could get what you were after? Although you might achieve your outcome, your communication would be less efficient, because you had to put out a lot of effort – and maybe even damage your image or relationship – to get what you wanted.

Ethics. Ethics is a consideration of what constitutes right versus wrong or good versus evil. **Ethical communication** involves using values as a moral guide when you interact with other people. Ethical communicators make their values and assumptions clear to others, and they demonstrate a respect for the values and assumptions that other people express. Unethical communication can be tempting at times; for example, it might be easier to get a loan from a relative if you imply that the money is needed for tuition. Although communication strategies that involve lying, false implications, or hostility can be effective and efficient, they fall short of being ethical, because the messages don't represent a person's agenda honestly and they don't treat other people with integrity. This final standard for communication competence requires being true to yourself and others when you participate in interpersonal interactions.

Communication competence can be difficult to achieve because it involves being clear, appropriate, satisfying, effective, efficient, and ethical, and these goals can sometimes conflict. Consider the example of Robyn, who has young children and doesn't want to waste her time dating anyone who doesn't like kids. When Robyn meets someone new and senses a potential romance, she has a few choices. If she wants to be appropriate, she might casually chat about children, eventually mention her own kids, and observe her communication partner's response. This strategy will give Robyn some information about the other person's attitude about her children, but it might not be very precise. Or, Robyn could say right away that she's not interested in seeing anyone who doesn't like kids. This strategy would effectively and efficiently weed out potential partners who don't meet her criteria, but it might be so inappropriate that suitable dating partners would be put off. Being a competent communicator involves balancing all of the different requirements for communication competence.

Promoting Communication Competence

Now that you know the standards for competent interpersonal communication, let's consider some of the conditions that can help you to achieve communication competence. In the following paragraphs, we examine three ingredients for interpersonal communication competence: motivation, knowledge, and skills.

Motivation. Competent communication takes effort – you need to pay attention to what is and is not appropriate and satisfying, weigh your options so that you maximize effectiveness and efficiency, and attend to ethical considerations. As a result, competent communication requires motivation or a desire to communicate well. Consider how you might feel as you prepare for a job interview. You'd probably spend some time thinking

---

Ethical Communication
Using values as a moral guide when you interact with other people.

about the kinds of questions you'll be asked, and how you can answer them in ways that make you look like a good employee. When you have important outcomes that are tied to your communication performance, you'll be motivated to identify clear, appropriate, satisfying, effective, efficient, and ethical conversational strategies. When the consequences of your interpersonal communication are less dire, you'll be less concerned about getting your message just right.

> **PAUSE & REFLECT**
>
> Recall a time when you were especially motivated to achieve a communication goal. How did your desire to achieve that outcome affect what you did before, during, and after that conversation?

Knowledge. All the motivation in the world won't help if you don't know what communication behaviors are best for a given situation. Consider the challenges of comforting another person. As you'll learn in Chapter 14, different people prefer different kinds of comforting. Some people like tangible help that will fix their problem, others want information that will help them figure out a solution on their own, and still others like to discuss their feelings and emotions, rather than fix the problem directly (Xu & Burleson, 2001). If you care about a person and empathize with his or her distress, you'll be motivated to help. To do so, though, also requires knowing what kinds of comfort the other person wants and how to provide it.

You can develop the knowledge you need to communicate competently in the same way that you learn about other topics. Studying interpersonal communication will help you to learn communication strategies and the situations where they can be used. You can also observe other people to see what works or doesn't work for them. And of course, paying attention to your own successes and failures is an important source of knowledge. If you actively seek knowledge, you can become more expert at identifying the interpersonal communication behaviors that are appropriate and effective within particular situations.

Skills. People need skills to act upon their motivation and knowledge in an interpersonal interaction. **Communication skills** are the ability to create symbols and perform behaviors that are appropriate and effective in a given social situation. Skills aren't reflexes or habits – they are learned. When you have learned communication skills, you can enact behaviors intentionally to achieve desired outcomes (Spitzberg, 2003). In particular, a skillful communicator is someone who can do the following tasks (adapted from Wilson & Sabee, 2003, pp. 8–9):

Communication Skills
The ability to create symbols and perform behaviors that are clear, appropriate, satisfying, effective, efficient, and ethical in a given social situation.

- *Identify expectations within a situation and behave in ways that meet or exceed expectations.* For example, when you meet with an instructor to discuss your class project, recognize that your instructor expects you to show enthusiasm about the project, to express ideas of your own, and to ask questions about how to complete the assignment successfully.

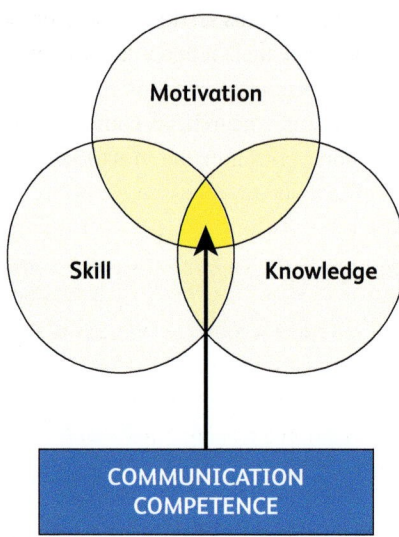

FIGURE 1.4 Communication competence

- *Recognize when obstacles to success are and are not controllable, and respond with behaviors that increase the chance of success.* For example, when you ask your family to excuse you from Thanksgiving dinner because you made other plans, start off by acknowledging the importance of spending holidays together and expressing appreciation for your family.
- *Enact, monitor, and adjust plans for communication.* For example, if your explanation for forgetting your romantic partner's birthday doesn't lead to forgiveness, consider planning a special, though belated, celebration.
- *Adapt quickly and smoothly to changes or new information.* For example, when you discover that someone you are interested in romantically is dating someone else, redirect your messages toward becoming friendly acquaintances – just in case.
- *Enact behaviors that invite and include different perspectives.* For example, if a newcomer to your social group reveals a political affiliation that isn't shared by most of the others, acknowledge the validity of different points of view and try to learn about this person's beliefs.

As the preceding list illustrates, skillful communicators need to be attentive to the situation and to translate their perceptions into a fitting response. When motivation, knowledge, and skills all exist, the possibility for competent communication exists (see Figure 1.4).

The Role of Culture, Setting, and Age

Interpersonal communication competence is always evaluated with respect to the context for communication. Consider how competent communication requires different behaviors depending on whether you're in class or at a party, talking to your professor or a friend, at work or with your family. In this section, we explore some of the ways in which the context for communication can affect standards for competence.

Cultural differences. Cultural differences are one reason that perceptions of communication competence vary. For example, research shows that Hispanic and Anglo-Americans generally do not consider a greeting kiss to be part of good communication in an initial interaction, whereas Spaniards and Chileans rate a greeting kiss as important in this situation (Johnson, Lindsey, & Zakahi, 2001). In addition research supports that, in general Latino friends emphasize concern for the relationship, Asian American friends expect a caring and positive exchange of ideas, African American friends value respect and acceptance, and Anglo-American friends recognize the needs of individuals (Collier, 1996). The cultural context shapes standards for fidelity, rules for appropriateness, factors leading to satisfaction, the priority placed on effectiveness and efficiency, and the values that underlie communication ethics. In other words, culture shapes what it means to communicate competently.

FIGURE 1.5 A family dinner

Source: Getty Images.

PAUSE & REFLECT

What standards for competent communication are most prominent in your own friendships? Do you know people who seem to have different expectations for communication between friends?

Setting. Our perceptions of communication competence also depend on the setting in which the interaction takes place. For example, both doctors and patients see an ability to explain or provide information about medical problems as an important part of communication competence in a medical setting, but neither doctors nor patients consider emotional supportiveness relevant to each other's competence (Cegala, McGhee, & McNeilis, 1996). Even subtle variations between settings can have dramatic consequences for evaluations of messages. For example, a flirtatious message between co-workers is seen as more sexually harassing when it occurs in a meeting room during work hours versus at an after-hours retirement party (Solomon, 2006). In the How Do You Rate? 1.1 exercise, you can test yourself using the features of communication competence in computer-mediated interactions.

Age. Your perceptions of communication competence are also related to your communication partner's age. Young children need to develop both their verbal communication skills and their knowledge about how to use communication (Haslett & Samter, 1997). When we communicate with children, then, we allow them greater latitude for making speech errors, leaving out relevant information, or perhaps sharing more detail than is necessary. By adolescence, we expect communicators to have an understanding of appropriate conversation, but we might accept that teenagers are still developing their ethical standards. As people age, we might expect more wisdom, maturity, authority, or forgetfulness from them (Nussbaum, Pecchioni, Baringer, & Kundrat, 2002). In these ways, perceptions of communication competence are tied to changes that occur over the lifespan.

Putting Theory into Practice: Communicating Competently

Becoming a competent communicator is a never-ending process. If you make interpersonal communication competence a priority, you can become a more effective communicator over the course of your lifetime.

Clarify your communication ethics. Ethical communication involves being responsive to your values and committed to moral behavior, regardless of context. One way you can improve communication competence, then, is to take stock of your values and identify how you can communicate ethically in any communication situation. The Communication in Action 1.3 exercise can help you to do this.

COMMUNICATION IN ACTION 1.3

Identifying Strategies for Ethical Communication

This exercise helps you to identify specific communication strategies that will help you accomplish your ethical goals during interaction. In the table provided on the **companion website**, identify some of the values that are most important to you when you communicate with other people. Then, identify how you can demonstrate those values in your interpersonal interactions. The first two rows provide examples to help get you started.

Practice, practice, practice. Communication is a skill, not unlike playing an instrument or riding a horse. And just as with other skills, you'll get better at it if you practice. Your experiences as a college student give you many opportunities to practice interpersonal communication.

■ If you have trouble talking to new acquaintances, introduce yourself to a classmate, chat with someone you meet at the library, or strike up a conversation with the person waiting in line at the coffee shop. These are low-risk situations that allow you to practice creating appropriate and satisfying conversations.

■ Within your classes, make a commitment to commenting or asking a question at least once a week. Although you might find it uncomfortable to draw attention to yourself, your instructor and your classmates will probably appreciate your contributions. More to the point, the classroom is a better place than the boardroom to develop your ability to be clear, concise, and effective.

■ Are you upset about your roommate's behavior, a class grade, or your family's unwillingness to adjust to your exam schedule? Here's your chance to build your communication competence. Try to express your concerns in ways that are clear ("Here is exactly what is bothering me"), appropriate ("I recognize that you're the final authority in the class"), and ethical ("Nothing is more important to me than my family"). Then, take stock of what worked and what didn't, so you can do better the next time.

Adapt to communication situations. Keep in mind that there isn't one right way to communicate. As you encounter different communication situations, consider a few basic questions to get you thinking about how to best adapt to those circumstances:

- What are the expectations people have for me, given their cultural background? How should I change my expectations given my partner's cultural background?
- What are the expectations people have for me, given the context (personal relationship, work situation, health setting, or computer-mediated interaction)? How should I change my expectations, given the context?
- What are the expectations people have for me, based on my age? How should I change my expectations, based on my communication partner's age?

This list can get you started thinking about how to adapt your communication behaviors to the different kinds of interpersonal interactions you experience.

STUDYING INTERPERSONAL COMMUNICATION

When we think of interpersonal communication as a skill, we focus on how people create and perform messages in ways that are more or less competent. The science of interpersonal communication refers to work conducted by communication researchers to understand how interpersonal communication works. Physicists study the properties of physical substances, such as their molecular structure, how they are affected by forces like heat or radiation, and the effects of one physical substance on other substances. Interpersonal communication researchers study the properties of interaction between people, such as the structure of messages or conversations, how messages and conversations are affected by the characteristics of the participants or the situation, and the outcomes of the interaction. Understanding the scientific study of interpersonal communication can help you to see how the practice of communication is related to the parts of communication and how they work together. In this section of the chapter, you'll learn about theory and research as the two core components of communication science.

> **SCHOLAR SPOTLIGHT**
>
> Visit the **Communication Café** on the **companion website** to view a conversation with Charles Berger, a pioneer in the scientific study of interpersonal communication.

Theory

A **theory** is a description of the relationships among concepts that helps us to understand a phenomenon. In a sense, a theory is just an explanation for why something is the way it is. In science, for example, the theory of gravity explains why things fall down, and the theory of evolution explains the diversity of species that exist on our planet. You create informal theories every time you try to make sense of a situation. Why did your parents divorce? Why do you have such a good time with your best friend? Why did someone else get the job you wanted? Because interpersonal communication theories help you answer questions like these, the following sections help you to understand the parts of a theory.

Theory
A description of the relationships among concepts that promote an understanding of a phenomenon.

PAUSE & REFLECT

Think about the break-up of a marriage or dating relationship that you either experienced or witnessed. How do you explain that break-up? Do you think that other people involved in that relationship would explain the break-up in the same way? If not, how do your theories differ?

A theory highlights specific concepts. How do we understand an event, situation, or experience? We do so by identifying the relevant details. A theory focuses on some parts of a situation and ignores other details. Let's consider the theory you might develop for why you didn't get a job you wanted. You might focus on your lack of training or experience; you might consider the stiff competition; you might think that the interviewer was biased against you for some reason; or you might decide it was just bad luck. Each of these "theories" emphasizes different concepts: training, competition, interviewer bias, and luck. The **concepts** within a theory, then, are the categories of phenomena that are believed to be relevant to understanding an event, situation, or experience. If you think that whether people like you depends on how confident you are when you talk, the concepts in your personal interpersonal communication theory are communication style and liking. Throughout this book, you'll learn about many concepts that can shed light on your communication experiences.

A theory describes how concepts are related. A theory does more than just identify relevant concepts – it describes how those concepts are related to each other. If you decide that you didn't get the job offer because you didn't perform well during your interview, you are linking interpersonal communication competence to getting a job. In particular, you are saying that communication competence and getting a job have a **positive association**: the more competence, the greater the likelihood of getting hired. Your theory, then, would look like the first model in Figure 1.6.

Concepts
Categories of phenomena that are believed to be relevant to understanding an event, situation, or experience.

Positive Association
When an increase in the amount, frequency, or intensity of one phenomenon corresponds with an increase in another phenomenon.

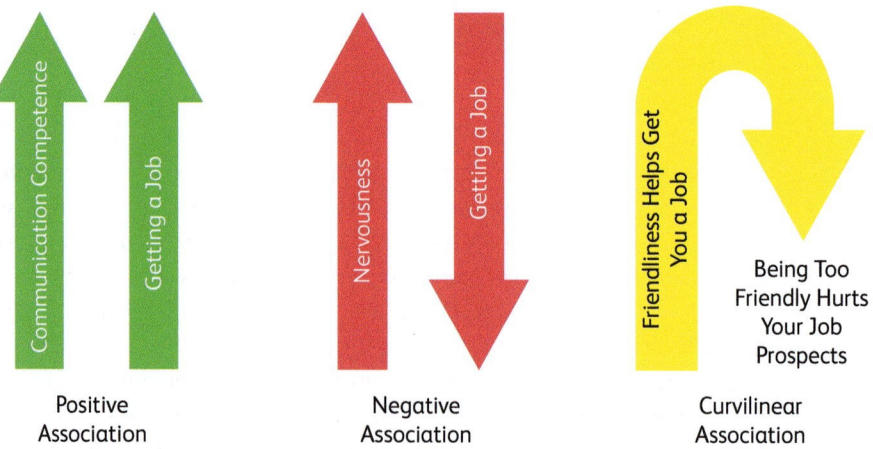

| Positive Association | Negative Association | Curvilinear Association |

FIGURE 1.6 Examples of relationships described by theories

There can be other types of relationships between concepts as well. As illustrated in Figure 1.6, there is a **negative association** between nervousness and getting a job: the more nervous you seem, the less likely you are to get the job. A **curvilinear association** exists when two concepts are positively or negatively related, but only up to a point. For example, communicating friendliness can help you get the job offer, but only up to a point – extremely friendly behavior might be seen as unprofessional and hurt your chances of getting hired. Because phenomena in the world around us are related in many different and complex ways, theories can describe a variety of relationships among concepts.

A theory is always incomplete. Another quality of theories needs to be mentioned: theories are always incomplete. For example, success in an interview is probably based on many different factors – your training and experience, your communication competence, the interviewer's personal biases, and a host of other factors, ranging from the weather that day to economic projections and even including your height. If a theory included every possible relevant concept, it wouldn't be very helpful, because it wouldn't focus attention on the concepts that really matter. In practice, then, a theory emphasizes particular concepts that a communication scholar believes are most important to understanding an event, situation, or experience. Other concepts that might be involved are left out.

A theory is tested against the experiences of people. Communication theories are similar to the explanations you create to understand your own experiences, but there are some important differences. Whereas your private theories focus on understanding your personal experience, a formal theory tries to understand the experiences of people in general. In addition, your private theories are evaluated against your own impressions and beliefs, but formal theories are judged by communication experts based on how accurate or useful they are for understanding interpersonal communication. You might conclude, for example, that you didn't get a job because you were so much taller than the boss – and you might even be right. Your ideas don't rise to the level of interpersonal communication theory unless they are supported by the experiences of many people documented in carefully designed research studies. Because this notion of testing theories through research is an important part of the science of interpersonal communication, we turn to that topic next.

Research

A good theory is accurate, meaning that the explanation it offers more or less matches reality. Thus, interpersonal communication scholars test their theories by observing communication in the real world, and comparing what they observe to the ways that theories describe communication. Interpersonal communication research encompasses the variety of methods that communication scholars use to test theories against real-life experiences.

Broadly speaking, communication research involves observing interpersonal communication and drawing conclusions based on those observations. As summarized in Table 1.3, researchers use a variety of methods to study interpersonal communication.

Negative Association

When a decrease in the amount, frequency, or intensity of one phenomenon corresponds with an increase in another phenomenon.

Curvilinear Association

When the positive or negative association between two phenomena exists only up to a certain point, and then reverses.

TABLE 1.3   Research methods for the study of interpersonal communication

Interviews

The researcher asks people questions about their communication experience, usually following an outline for the interview but also probing topics as they come up. Interviews allow researchers to interact closely with the people they are studying.

Ethnography

The researcher observes a group of people, either as an anonymous bystander or by participating in interpersonal interactions, and takes detailed notes on communication experiences. Researchers draw conclusions from studies like these by reflecting on their observations, looking for patterns that seem especially important or meaningful, and identifying core themes or concepts.

Surveys/questionnaires

The researcher asks participants short-answer or multiple-choice questions by phone, the Internet, or on paper. These tools might also include short answer questions, which the researcher codes with numbers to represent different types of responses. Then, researchers use statistics to evaluate the relationships between scores.

Interaction studies

The researcher records conversations and examines patterns of communication over the course of the dialog. The key characteristic of an interaction study is that it captures actual communication between people. These recordings allow researchers to analyze patterns of communication as they unfold over time.

Experiments

The researcher manipulates some aspect of a situation and records behaviors under those conditions, perhaps using questionnaires or coding behavior to identify different types of actions. Experiments often involve dividing participants into groups and giving each group different experiences – other than the manipulated aspect of the situation, the researcher tries to keep the experiences of the different groups identical.

PAUSE & REFLECT

If a researcher did an ethnographic study of your college or university – in other words, observed what people at your school do, who talks to whom, and what kinds of topics they talk about – what communication practices would stand out?

Let's focus on surveys and questionnaires as one common type of research method. If you have ever taken a phone survey, completed a course evaluation form, or rated your satisfaction with an online shopping tool, you've participated in a survey or questionnaire study. In this approach to research, a lot of people are asked the same set of questions, and they record their answer by choosing among options – not unlike a multiple choice test. Researchers then add up or average responses to different questions to figure out how people score on a topic. The How Do You Rate? 1.2 box demonstrates how questionnaires are used by communication scholars to measure certain features of interaction.

Researchers have a lot of methods available to explore interpersonal communication. These methods all provide ways of observing and analyzing concepts that are relevant to communication experiences. By comparing the results of these studies to communication theories, scholars advance our understanding of how interpersonal communication works.

Putting Theory into Practice: Studying Interpersonal Communication

As a student of interpersonal communication, you will learn about a lot of different theories and hear about a variety of different studies that explain and examine interpersonal communication phenomena. As you read about theories and research in this book and hear about them from your instructor, use the guidelines given in this section to be a smart consumer of information about interpersonal communication.

Think theoretically about interpersonal communication. Theories are helpful because they focus attention on the issues that matter. One way to develop your knowledge of interpersonal communication is to pay attention to the theories you form about your own experiences. What are the concepts or details that you think are most important, and how do you think those concepts relate to each other? The Communication in Action 1.4 exercise can help you become more aware of your own theories about interpersonal communication.

HOW DO YOU RATE? 1.2

Communication Satisfaction

You can probably recall interactions you've had that were extremely enjoyable, as well as ones that were quite unpleasant. Visit the **companion website** to complete a scale that measures communication satisfaction in both European and African-American populations (Larkey & Hecht, 1995). It shows how researchers assess communication concepts using a questionnaire.

COMMUNICATION IN ACTION 1.4

Testing Your Own Theories of Communication

For three days, keep a diary in which you record at least three conversations you have on each day. For each interaction, describe who was present, the setting for the conversation, the background leading up to the event, the content of the interaction, and the reactions that you and your partner had to the conversation. Rate each conversation on a scale of 1 to 5 in terms of how satisfying the interaction was, with 5 being the most satisfying. Then, examine each entry to identify the features of conversations that were especially satisfying or unsatisfying. How might these features be arranged to present your theory of communication satisfaction?

Evaluate research on interpersonal communication. You'll have the opportunity in this book to learn about communication research. Lots of studies report interesting findings, but it is important to think critically about the research methods that are used in those studies. Here are some criteria to apply when you read about studies of interpersonal communication:

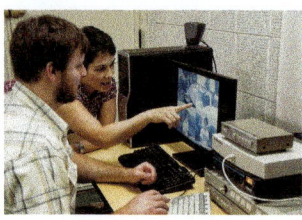

FIGURE 1.7 Denise and Andy High discuss nonverbal cues displayed during a conversation that was recorded in Penn State's Communication Research Laboratory

- Do the findings in this study apply to all people, in general, or are they limited to a certain population or group?
- Do the questions on surveys and questionnaires really measure what the researchers say they do?
- In experimental studies, are the manipulated conditions realistic and ethical, and do they produce the effects that the researcher intended?
- Are the research methods used in the study the best way to answer the researcher's questions, or would a different method have been more appropriate?
- Do the researcher's personal opinions bias his or her research methods or findings?

You can learn a lot more about interpersonal communication research in a class devoted to that topic; in the meantime, you can think critically about whether the research methods in the studies you encounter make sense to you.

INTERPERSONAL COMMUNICATION ETHICS

As you study interpersonal communication – both its practice and the research that informs what we know about interpersonal communication – you will improve your ability to make educated decisions about how you communicate. Earlier in this chapter, you learned that competent communicators engage in ethical communication by using their values as a moral guide when communicating with others. Because all interpersonal communication involves an ethical dimension, we end this first chapter by delving deeper into ethics as they are related to interpersonal communication practice and research.

Communicating Ethically

In general, a consideration of ethics involves questions about *right* and *wrong*, what we value as *good* or *honorable* or *moral,* and how people conduct themselves to promote and protect that which is *good.* Unfortunately, what constitutes *right* and *wrong* isn't always obvious, and people don't always agree about what is *good* and what is *bad.* Understanding ethical communication is further complicated by the fact that an evaluation of *good* and *bad* communication must also consider the specifics of the communication situation. For example, honesty is almost universally valued as *good* communication behavior and hurting someone's feelings is typically viewed as *bad* communication behavior, so what happens when you find yourself in a situation in which your honesty might be hurtful? Should you be honest even though the result might be negative, or should you be dishonest to protect the other person's feelings? In many ways, your decision in this context will depend on which trait – honesty or kindness – you view as most honorable or moral in that situation. Interpersonal interactions can be so automatic and fast that we often don't reflect on the values we want to promote when we communicate with others. One component of ethical communication, then, is being attentive to the values that you want to uphold in a particular situation.

Interpersonal communication occurs between people, and **interpersonal communication ethics** involve a consideration of the moral responsibilities that you have to the

Interpersonal Communication Ethics
Considering moral responsibilities to other people and relationships when making communication decisions.

other person and to your relationship when making communication decisions. As you'll learn throughout this book, your interpersonal communication behaviors have consequences for others – you can affect how people think about themselves and others (and you), the emotions that others experience, the quality of their relationships, and whether they achieve their goals, resolve their conflicts, or find support in times of distress. In their book on communication ethics, communication scholars Ronald Arnett, Janie Harden Fritz, and Leeanne Bell (2009) define ethical interpersonal communication as communication that takes responsibility for the communication partner, as well as the relationship with that person, whatever the personal consequences might be. Thus, another component of ethical interpersonal communication is recognizing the impact of your communication decisions on other people and your relationship with them.

Given that definitions of what is *right* or *wrong* and *good* or *bad* can be hard to pin down, how do you decide which communication choices are ethical? As communicators, we need to avoid assuming that anything goes. Although people have different views of what is *right* and *wrong*, that does not mean that any behavior is acceptable as long as somebody believes it is the right thing to do. But we also need to avoid assuming that there is one single objectively *right* way to communicate. Communication ethics involves an informed consideration of the diverse values that exist in our world as we discover the principles that we want to protect and uphold through our own actions (Arnett et al., 2009). A third component of ethical interpersonal communication is learning about how communication works and how it affects people so that you can make informed decisions about your own communication behavior.

The three elements that contribute to ethical interpersonal communication are summarized in Figure 1.8. You have taken an important step toward improving your communication ethics by choosing to learn more about interpersonal communication.

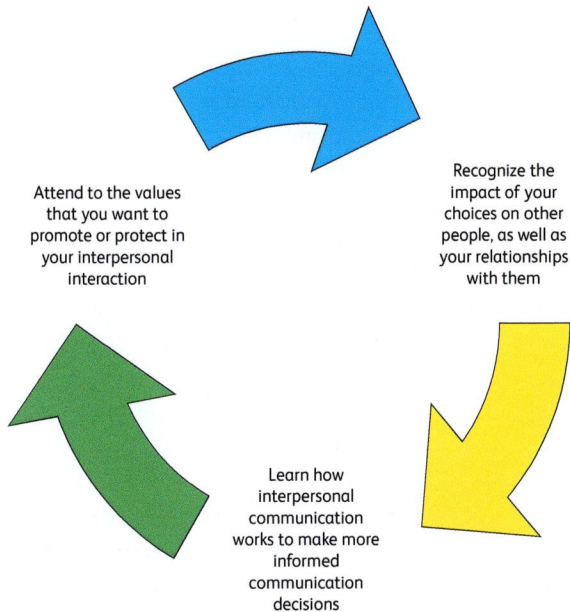

FIGURE 1.8 Components of ethical interpersonal communication

As you study interpersonal communication, work toward identifying the values that are most important to you as a communicator and reflect on how you want to affect others through interpersonal communication.

Ethics in Communication Research

Scholars who conduct research on interpersonal communication also attend to standards for moral behavior within the scientific community. All scientists are expected to be truthful in how they report research findings, to clearly identify the sources that they consulted in developing their thinking, and to credit through authorship the people who played a substantive role in producing a research report. Interpersonal communication researchers also have important ethical obligations that revolve around protecting the people who participate in research studies.

Sometimes, the questions a researcher seeks to answer involve behaving in ways that would be inappropriate outside the research setting. For example, studying very private or sensitive topics, such as conflict within a family, communication about sexual intimacy, or verbally aggressive communication, involves probing into topics that are often only discussed within close relationships. These are important topics to learn about, in part because they are such influential and powerful communication experiences, and we wouldn't want interpersonal communication researchers to neglect questions about sensitive issues. Instead, researchers conduct their investigations into topics such as these in ways that protect the confidentiality of the research participants and the information that they provide. In addition, people are typically given a description of the study in advance so that they can participate – or not – with full knowledge of the issues that will be examined.

Occasionally, studies conducted by interpersonal communication researchers might involve procedures that are only explained to the participant after the fact. Consider, for example, the study conducted in Denise's research lab on hurtful communication, which was featured in the Real Words box earlier in this chapter. Denise and her colleagues were trying to find out how people react emotionally and physically to hurtful messages. To get answers, they couldn't tell people in advance that their romantic partner was going to say something hurtful – if the research participants were forewarned, they wouldn't have been hurt. Instead, Denise's research group took several steps to minimize risks to their participants: (a) they monitored the interactions through a two-way mirror, so that they could interrupt any conversations that were excessively upsetting; (b) they provided specific guidelines to the romantic partners, to gain control over the focus and intensity of the hurtful messages; and (c) they explained the procedures to participants in detail after the study was over, with particular emphasis on the fact that the romantic partner had only been following instructions when he or she said hurtful things. Once partic-ipants knew that the comments were scripted for their partners, they no longer felt hurt.

Interpersonal communication research involves observing people, analyzing mes-sages produced by people, or engaging people in surveys or experiments that focus on their own behavior and their relationships with other people. In other words, the science of interpersonal communication delves into the personal conduct and lives of the people who participate in research studies. Consequently, when scholars seek to advance our understanding of interpersonal communication, ethical considerations are always relevant.

Putting Theory into Practice: Ethical Interpersonal Communication

Every topic that is covered in this book involves questions about ethics. Which values do you want to promote when you communicate with people from other cultures, when you present yourself to others, when you make sense of other people's communication behaviors? Which principles are important to you as you choose your words, display nonverbal messages, experience and act upon emotions, and listen to others? How will you uphold your standards for right and wrong when developing and ending relationships, maintaining intimate bonds, and communicating within your family? And how will you influence other people, manage your conflicts, and give or receive support in ways that are morally sound?

Because ethics are a part of all of the topics you will learn about, we have included opportunities for you to explore communication ethics at the end of every chapter in this book. By considering the questions posed in these exercises, our hope is that you will develop your awareness of the values that inform your interpersonal communication and, in turn, develop an ability to engage in ethical interpersonal communication.

SUMMARY

This chapter begins your study of interpersonal communication. As a foundation for this journey, you learned that interpersonal communication is the use of symbols to represent ideas so that meanings can be shared between people. You also learned that interpersonal communication is a continuous and dynamic process, it has consequences, and it is irreversible and imperfect. We use interpersonal communication to convey both content and relational messages, and we do so in all of the contexts in which our lives unfold.

You also learned that interpersonal communication is a skill, meaning that it is the product of human creative activity, practice, and effort. Just as an artist or athlete can perfect his or her technique through study and practice, you can improve how you communicate with other people. Communication competence involves sending clear messages, being appropriate or responsive to social rules, producing satisfying interactions, achieving your objective both effectively and efficiently, and communicating in ways that are ethical. Although meeting all these criteria can be challenging, your communication competence should increase if you are motivated to communicate well, you improve your knowledge about interpersonal communication, and you develop the skills you need to perform the communication behaviors that fit a given situation. Remember, also, that what counts as competent communication will vary across the many circumstances that you experience over the course of your life.

As you strive to become a better communicator, take advantage of advances in interpersonal communication theory and research. A theory is an effort to explain or understand something by identifying the most relevant concepts and describing how they are related. A theory won't tell you everything you need to know about interpersonal communication, but it can provide some general knowledge that may help you to understand your experiences. Keep in mind that the information you'll learn about interpersonal communication is usually based on research. Through interviews, ethnography, survey and questionnaires, interaction studies, and experiments, communication researchers gather information about interpersonal communication, and they use that information to develop or improve their theories. Just like other fields of study, such as biology, psychology, or economics, interpersonal communication is a discipline filled with people doing studies to advance our knowledge.

Although you're just beginning your exploration of interpersonal communication, you already have some tips you can use to improve your communication experiences. By thinking critically about interpersonal communication, making communication competence a priority, and studying interpersonal communication in the world around you, you can develop the tools you need to use symbols to create a personal connection with other people. Based on what you have learned about interpersonal communication so far, consider the following activities for exploring communication ethics. Activities such as these are included at the end of every chapter, so that you can develop your sense of communication ethics at the same time your build your expertise in interpersonal communication.

ACTIVITIES FOR EXPLORING COMMUNICATION ETHICS

At this end of each chapter in this book, we'll present some opportunities for you to consider communication ethics. Remember that ethical communication involves using values as a moral guide when you interact with other people. The exercises we offer invite you to decide what an ethical communicator would – or should – do in a particular situation, to think about an ethical dilemma, and to collect evidence that can inform a judgment about ethical communication.

What Would You/Should You Do?

Imagine that your good friend is running for office in a student organization on campus. Of course, your friend wants to get enough votes to win. You've been proud of your friend for working hard to connect with people in the organization by describing her priorities and values. As the election draws closer, though, you've noticed that she is offering people rewards for supporting her. For example, you clearly heard her tell someone in the organization that she would make him treasurer if he voted for her. You appreciate that competent communication involves being both effective and efficient, and this strategy is likely to win the election. As you reflect on other standards for competent communication, like appropriateness, you have some concerns. As an ethical communicator, what would you or should you do?

Something to Think About

Communication research involves making observations about communication and comparing those observations to the assumptions made within a communication theory. Sometimes, communication research involves recording conversations that people have in their own homes or videotaping partners as they talk in a communication lab. In fact, some studies involve getting partners to have a conflict or asking one partner to be hurtful, upset, or supportive. These studies can yield information about how people communicate with each other, but they also intrude on the private domain of a relationship. What are the ethical issues involved in conducting research on personal topics like interpersonal communication?

Analyze Communication Ethics Yourself

The college you attend uses symbols to represent itself to both people inside the institution and outsiders, such as potential students, alumni, and the community around the university. Review the home page for your university or college, your major department, and a few programs on your campus such as athletics, theatre, or fraternities and sororities. What are some of the symbols that are used to represent your college and particular organizations within it? How well do these symbols capture qualities of the institution they represent? How do these symbols distort or neglect important, though perhaps less glowing, qualities of your college or the particular organization? What are the ethical issues involved in using symbols to portray your campus to the world?

KEY WORDS

channel	dyad	negative association
communication	ethical communication	positive association
communication skills	fidelity	relational messages
computer-mediated communication	impersonal communication	social rules
concepts	interpersonal communication	symbols
content messages	interpersonal communication competence	theory
curvilinear association	interpersonal communication ethics	transactional model of communication

PART 1 FOUNDATIONS

Visit the Communication Café on the **companion website** to hear Denise and Jen talk about the topics addressed in Part 1 of this book.

In Chapter 1, we described interpersonal communication as a fluid and dynamic process in which communication partners create meanings by sharing messages that they encode and decode – these experiences create bonds between people and have consequences that last beyond a particular interaction. None of the parts of the communication system is more important than the others, and what one person considers the first topics to study when learning about interpersonal communication might not be what another person considers the foundations for this journey. How could communication transpire without understanding how messages work? Or how relationships form and change? Or the goals that we can achieve through communication? While we believe that all the aspects of the communication experience are important to understanding interpersonal communication, we position the communication experience of the individual as the foundation to learning about interpersonal communication. Understanding how one person experiences interactions with others will give you a basis for learning how people work together to create interpersonal communication.

Perhaps the most influential characteristic of a person is his or her culture. The culture that people are born into shapes everything from the kind of family structure they are raised in, the language and nonverbal cues that they learn, the relationships they value, and the goals they pursue through interpersonal communication. We also use evidence of another person's culture as a touchstone for making sense of our encounters with them. Because culture has such a significant influence on interpersonal communication, we begin our exploration of the foundations of interpersonal communication in Chapter 2 by examining the role of culture.

Whereas culture is the framework for making sense of the world that people share with others, people also have personal characteristics that are equally important to understanding how they experience interpersonal communication. Our interactions with other people shape how we see ourselves, and we also use communication to show other people who we are. In Chapter 3, we focus on the individual, and we consider how interpersonal communication relates to a person's self-perception and identity.

The third and final chapter in this unit focuses on the processes by which people see and make sense of the world around them. Somehow, the human body translates all the stimuli collected through the senses of smell, taste, sight, hearing, and touch into a useful portrayal of the environment. This basic human function is an essential part of interpersonal communication, which requires people to make sense of complex and often ambiguous symbols, as well as information in the communication context, often in rapidly unfolding interactions. In Chapter 4, then, we examine how perception works and the aspects of perception that are most relevant to interpersonal communication experiences.

CHAPTER 2

CULTURE AND INTERPERSONAL COMMUNICATION 38

CHAPTER 3

IDENTITY AND INTERPERSONAL COMMUNICATION 68

CHAPTER 4

PERCEPTION AND INTERPERSONAL COMMUNICATION 96

LEARNING OBJECTIVES

After reading this chapter, you should be able to:

1. Understand the different layers of culture.
2. Describe the steps through which cultures form and change.
3. Identify three types of communication that explicitly reflect culture.
4. Recognize barriers to effective intercultural communication.
5. Strengthen your ability to communicate with people of different cultures.

PUTTING THEORY INTO PRACTICE

In this chapter, you will learn how to:

1. Find experiences you and a communication partner have in common.
2. Adapt to new cultural environments.
3. Help others understand your culture.
4. Explore communication practices in different cultures.
5. Explore the rituals and stories of other cultures.
6. Strengthen the culture of relationships you value.
7. Maintain realistic expectations for intercultural communication.
8. Avoid communicating based on stereotypes.
9. Avoid exaggerating sex differences.

CULTURE AND INTERPERSONAL COMMUNICATION

2

40 WHAT IS CULTURE?

50 CULTURE AND COMMUNICATION

55 INTERCULTURAL COMMUNICATION

65 SUMMARY

67 ACTIVITIES FOR EXPLORING COMMUNICATION ETHICS

67 KEY WORDS

In March 2011, Alexandra Wallace posted a YouTube video in which she ranted about the prevalence and mannerisms of Asian students enrolled along with her at the University of California, Los Angeles. In the video, Ms. Wallace complains about Asian students using cell phones in the library, makes fun of the sound of Asian languages, and criticizes the international student community for failing to adopt American practices. The video drew a widespread response, ranging from the university chancellor, who criticized the video as thoughtless and hurtful, to dozens of online messages and videos condemning Ms. Wallace and her attitudes. Ms. Wallace even found herself on the receiving end of death threats. Although UCLA decided not to discipline Ms. Wallace formally, citing her freedom of speech rights, the third-year student ended up leaving the university mid-semester. The story of Ms. Wallace illustrates the consequences that can occur when people disrespect cultural differences in interpersonal communication and violate their own culture's standards for appropriate communication behavior.

People from different races, cultures, religions, and even genders may use and interpret symbols in different ways. The meanings that you create through communication are necessarily influenced by your **culture** – the values, beliefs, and customs that you share with a group of people. An important part of culture is **norms**, or shared expectations for behavior. Cultural norms shape your communication experiences – they influence your nonverbal communication, the words you choose, how you form those words into sentences, and every other aspect of interpersonal communication. Ms. Wallace's frustrations with cultural differences led her to make a demeaning YouTube video that targeted, in particular, Asian students' interpersonal communication behavior. What Ms. Wallace didn't anticipate was that her own community's cultural norms wouldn't tolerate Ms. Wallace's use of communication to attack international students. Although your own experiences with culture and interpersonal communication are hopefully less dramatic and consequential than Ms. Wallace's, it is important to appreciate the role of culture as part of interpersonal communication.

When you create messages, your culture provides guidelines that help you decide what is expected, appropriate, or desirable. For example, your culture helps you know whether you should greet another person with a handshake or a kiss, call a person by his or her first name, and look your interaction partner directly in the eye. At the same time, other people send you messages that are influenced by their perceptions of your culture. From the topics people discuss with you to how formally or informally they speak, the messages you receive are different from those sent to someone who is a different age, a different gender, or a different ethnicity than you. In this chapter, we'll explore how culture provides a framework for all of your interpersonal communication experiences.

WHAT IS CULTURE?

Some cultural differences, such as languages, physical characteristics, or clothing styles, are easy to see. Other cultural boundaries can be hard to define. Would you consider someone with different political values, someone with different musical tastes, or someone attending a different college to be a member of your culture? And would you put yourself in the same cultural group as people who attended your college 20, 40, or 100 years ago? In this section, we probe the complexity of culture by examining different layers of culture, how cultures change over time, and core differences between cultures.

Layers of Culture

A cultural group is a subset of people whose common experiences have led them to develop similar ways of thinking, feeling, and behaving. When we ask students in our classes to identify the cultural groups they belong to, some of them mention only one or two broad ethnic, national, or religious groups (African-American, Vietnamese, Muslim). Others also mention groups defined by gender, sexual orientation, or age (woman, gay, empty-nester). Still others give a lengthy list of affiliations (member of Alpha Tau, varsity lacrosse player, business major). These responses show the many different ways we can identify a cultural group. These layers of culture are illustrated in Figure 2.1, and discussed in the paragraphs that follow.

Cultural institutions. At the broadest level, cultural groups are defined by the members' nationality, religion, or ethnic heritage. Within the boundaries of a nation, the

Culture
The values, beliefs, and customs that we share with a group of people.

Norms
Expectations for behavior that are shared within a cultural group.

FIGURE 2.1 Layers of culture

The columns shown with different ecosystems are a metaphor for different cultures that are distinguished by their cultural institutions. Just as different ecosystems can contain similar components, cultural groups defined by a shared standpoint can cut across cultural institutions, such as when people share a connection because of their similar gender, economic status, or military status. Different ecosystems also contain unique features that are shaped by the specific conditions in the climate. Similarly, speech communities emerge, usually among people from the same cultural institution, when opportunities for interaction promote shared communication patterns.

form of government, the monetary system, holidays, and national heroes and heroines unify people's experiences and create a common culture for billions of people who share the same institutions. For example, when Denise was a college student, she studied abroad in Scotland, where she ended up celebrating the 4th of July with several other U.S. citizens at a youth hostel. Although the travelers were from different parts of the United States, different ages and races, and traveling for different reasons, they were connected by their shared appreciation for the holiday and the rituals used to mark it. Likewise, people who affiliate with a particular religion or an ethnic group, regardless of their nationality, adopt a set of beliefs, perform particular rituals, and celebrate specific holidays. At this broadest level, then, cultures develop because national, religious, or ethnic institutions promote particular beliefs and customs.

PAUSE & REFLECT

What labels do you use to identify your cultural background? What are some of the ways of living, thinking, and feeling that you have in common with other people who share these labels?

Standpoint

The position from which people see the world based on their social or economic status.

Standpoints. A cultural group can also form when people have similar life experiences because of their social or economic circumstances. This kind of group is defined by its members' similar **standpoint** – the position from which people see the world based on their status in society (cf. Hallstein, 2000). Men and women, for example, are treated differently as children, form different kinds of friendships, have different job opportunities, and play distinct roles as parents. Because of these differences, some scholars have suggested that men and women constitute distinct cultures with unique standpoints (e.g., Dougherty, 2001). In the same way, access to education, jobs, health care, or the Internet can create cultural divides based on people's age or economic class (e.g., Rodino-Colocino, 2006). For example, a person brought up in an upper-middle-class family has different experiences from a person brought up in a low-income family; as a result, these two individuals would most likely have very different standpoints. Thus, cultural groups that are created from a similar standpoint can range from just two or three people with a similar perspective to millions of people with shared experiences.

Figure 2.1 shows how cultural groups defined by standpoints often cut across national, ethnic, or religious boundaries. In other words, people in the same cultural institution might have distinct standpoints, and people who are members of different cultural institutions might have a shared standpoint. As an example, consider two women who live in different countries, speak different languages, and have different religions. Despite these differences, these two women might have many experiences in common. Perhaps both experience poverty, have trouble finding work because their societies discriminate against women, and are mothers trying to care for their children. Even though these two women belong to different cultural institutions, they share a culture based on a common standpoint.

Speech Community

A group of people who use and interpret symbols in the same way.

Speech communities. Cultures also arise when people who have regular contact with each other develop shared norms and values. A **speech community** is a group of people who have similar ways of using and interpreting symbols. A speech community arises when people live, study, or work together and therefore have shared experiences, norms, and communication practices (e.g., Baxter & Goldsmith, 1990; Ruud, 2000). The requirement that members of these groups have regular contact means that speech communities have relatively few members. Fraternities and sororities are speech communities: Members display their unique culture by wearing their Greek letters, adopting a mascot, recording the organization's history, and holding private pledge ceremonies. Even two people in a romantic relationship or friendship can create their own speech community, complete with anniversaries, rules, important symbols like wedding rings, and rituals (Baxter, 1987; Bruess & Pearson, 1997).

Speech communities can be considered **subcultures** because they are distinguished from the broader culture by a handful of unique practices. Unlike cultural groups based on a shared standpoint, speech communities develop when people communicate with each other directly. And because we are more likely to have frequent contact with people who live near us and who have the same ethnic or religious practices, speech communities typically form among people who belong to the same cultural institution. For example, parishioners who attend a particular church follow the norms for their religion, and they most likely have a few practices that are unique to the congregation. In this way, speech communities create subcultures within a cultural institution.

Virtual groups or online communities show how communication is at the heart of building speech communities. Millions of people turn to online communities to find people with similar backgrounds and experiences with whom they can provide support, share information, and form social connections. Many people are drawn to virtual communities because they allow connections with other users who may not live nearby and permit the discussion of topics that might be taboo in face-to-face contexts. Even though the individuals who comprise an online community may have diverse cultural backgrounds and belong to different social groups in the physical world, they create a unique speech community in the virtual world through their interactions online. Within virtual groups, traits that foster group cohesion, such as referring to the group as a community, expressing shared goals, and agreeing about discussion topics, tend to increase over time (Cassell & Tversky, 2005). A study focused on an online video gaming community found that participants with more experience create more positive social messages and use more specialized conventions, such as emoticons and abbreviations (Pená & Hancock, 2006). Another study showed that women who participate in discussion boards for breast cancer survivors feel a sense of connection with the online community that increases over time (Rodgers & Chen, 2005). In these ways, virtual groups have many of the same qualities that emerge when members of a speech community interact in person.

Subcultures
Speech communities that share some unique practices within a broader cultural group.

PAUSE & REFLECT

Have you ever been a member of a virtual community? If so, can you identify any beliefs, norms, or communication practices that participants in the community shared?

**HOW DO
YOU RATE?** 2.1

**Ethnic Identity
Salience Scale**

Everybody can be
characterized in terms
of their ethnic heritage,
but people differ in how
important that ethnicity
is to them. To find out
the importance that you
place on your own
ethnicity, complete the
scale on the **companion
website**.

When you consider all the labels you might use to define your own cultural identity, you will probably find that you are a member of many different cultural groups. All of your cultural groups define who you are as an individual, but some may be more important to you than others. For example, you can complete the How Do You Rate? exercise to see how important your ethnic identity is to you. Notably, the cultural groups that are most important to you are the ones you most likely try to emphasize in your interactions with others. As you'll learn throughout this chapter, your cultural identity has a pervasive effect on your interpersonal communication.

How Cultures Form and Change

In general, cultural groups differ based on their members' beliefs, values, and norms, or behavior patterns. Although every culture is unique, three general processes allow cultures to develop, grow, and change over time (see Figure 2.2). Understanding these processes can help you to see how distinct cultures develop different ways of seeing and doing things.

Culture emerges through selectivity. People everywhere perform certain actions that are simply part of being human: we make friends, we love, we dislike or hate, we suffer, we empathize, and we celebrate. Although these activities occur in all cultures, different cultural groups perform them in different ways (Duranti, 2006). How do you communicate your affection for a friend? How do you talk to someone who is older or younger? How do you mark an anniversary or birthday? As a member of a cultural group, you probably enact behaviors that are expected and meaningful within your community. Thus, cultures are distinct because cultural groups have selected different behaviors as meaningful.

For a concrete example, think about how different cultures approach the common task of exchanging greetings. When people greet each other, they acknowledge each

FIGURE 2.2 Cultural dynamics

other's presence, establish whether their conversation will be brief or lengthy, and – in some cases – reconnect with a relationship partner (Duranti, 1997; Sigman, 1991). Although these functions are universal, the behaviors used to perform them depend on culture. For example, telephone greetings vary across nations: in France, people tend to apologize for calling; in England, they identify themselves; in Greece, they dive into the conversation; in Taiwan, they use a formal style (Hopper & Chen, 1996). Likewise, members of speech communities develop unique ways of greeting each other, such as secret handshakes and special words or phrases (Bell & Healey, 1992). Across the vast array of human activities, cultural groups are distinguished by the ways that members communicate with each other.

> ## PAUSE & REFLECT
>
> What are some of the ways that people in your social network or family communicate with each other? How do these communication events set your speech communities apart from other groups?

Culture is shared with new members. The practices that are selected as meaningful within a culture must be taught to new members of the group. Socialization is the process by which newcomers come to understand a culture's assumptions and guidelines. Socialization involves two phases: first, members transmit information about the culture to newcomers, and, second, newcomers adopt the cultural practices. In some cases, socialization includes specific activities designed to teach a culture's rules to a new member. For example, many college campuses have orientation programs for new students that cover everything from how to register for classes to how to cheer at football games. Within dangerous professions, such as fire fighting, new employees may be given subservient tasks (for example, cooking, cleaning, or desk duty) to help them learn respect for experienced co-workers and the importance of being reliable under any circumstances (Myers, 2005). More generally, socialization occurs as newcomers and experts communicate and exchange information about cultural practices (Bullis, 1993).

Socialization
The process by which newcomers to a cultural group come to understand its assumptions and guidelines.

The ways in which interpersonal communication contributes to socialization can be seen in the messages adults use to convey cultural values to children. In one research study, parents from the north-eastern United States or from India made up stories to go with a picture book that shows a boy searching for, and finding, a lost frog (Harkins & Ray, 2004). Parents from the United States emphasized how the boy's hard work achieved his personal goal of finding the frog – their stories revealed the goal-oriented and individualistic cultural values of the United States. In contrast, parents in India described how the boy's recovery of the frog created sadness within the frog's family. In this version of the story, children learn that selfish ambitions can hurt the community. When parents communicate with their children, they guide children toward the cultural values and norms of their community. The Communication in Action activity 2.1 suggests another way that cultural values are taught to children.

COMMUNICATION IN ACTION 2.1

Discovering Cultural Messages

Although communication with parents and caretakers plays a key role in teaching culture to children, the television shows that children watch also convey cultural values. To complete the table provided on the **companion website**, watch a few shows designed for young children – try Nickelodeon, Noggin, or PBS networks that are devoted to children's programs. As you watch the stories, identify the messages or themes that support the values within your culture, and also note any messages that contradict or question your cultural beliefs.

Culture changes over time. The ways of thinking, feeling, and behaving that define a culture evolve over time. As one example, consider some of the changes in marriage and family that have occurred in the United States over the past 50 years (Cherlin, 2004). In the 1950s, only about 5% of unmarried adults lived with their romantic partner, and having children outside of marriage was rare. In the 1970s, living together before marriage and having children outside of marriage gradually became more acceptable. At present in the United States, living together is a viable alternative to marriage, about 1 out of 3 children are born to unmarried parents, and 25% of all stepfamilies are formed by cohabitation rather than marriage. Moreover, single-parent homes, half-siblings, and step-families are common parts of the social landscape. Although there are certainly differences of opinion about the sanctity of marriage, American culture has moved toward more diverse views of marriage and family over the past 50 years.

PAUSE & REFLECT

How has your family grown or shrunk over the years and how has that affected the dynamics in your family? Have the norms for communication in your family changed since you were a child?

Invention
The development of new cultural practices.

One way that culture changes is through **invention** – the development of new cultural practices. When social revolutions, medical breakthroughs, or technological advances create novel situations, societies must create new norms. Consider the cultural inventions made necessary by the explosion in cell phone use in the 1990s. At a practical level, cultures needed to develop rules about where and when cell phones could be used. For example, Connecticut, New Jersey, and New York were the first states to make it illegal to use a hand-held phone while driving, and places such as hospitals, movie theatres, and locker rooms began posting explicit rules against using cell phones. Cell phones have also changed people's basic expectations for social interaction, because they allow us to communicate at any time and in (virtually) any place (Katriel, 1999). In much the same way, access to the Internet, the invention of Facebook, opportunities for telecommuting, and the decoding of human DNA have prompted the invention of new norms for close relationships, employment, and health care (Hylmö, 2006; Silva, 2005; Stafford, Kline, & Dimmick, 1999).

Cultures also change through the process of **diffusion**, which occurs when a society adopts the cultural practices of another group. Because U.S. culture is displayed around the world via the Internet, syndicated television shows, and blockbuster films, some societies have become concerned that their own culture is being overwhelmed by American practices. In fact, Canada, France, and Korea, among other countries, have laws that require their symphonies, theatres, and cinemas to feature at least some national artists or productions. Although cultural heritage is certainly worth protecting, diffusion is inevitable when two groups come into contact. Moreover, the mingling of different cultures is at the root of many wonderful creations, including reggae music, spaghetti with marinara sauce, and New York City.

Diffusion
When the cultural practices of one group are adopted by another society.

Classifying Cultures

A cultural group's communication norms are shaped by the way the group members answer some basic questions about how people relate to each other. Which is more important: the individual or the group? Are all people essentially equal, or do some people have more power than others? Which is more important when communicating: the words that are spoken or the context for them? Is it more important to get things done or to follow a good process? Should we avoid risks or seek out novel experiences? The answers to these questions help us distinguish cultures along five important dimensions (see Table 2.1).

As an example of the effect of cultural dimensions on communication, consider how citizens of the United States and South Korea refer to older members within their society. Korean culture values collectivism, high power distance, and high context communication, whereas U.S. culture values individualism, low power distance, and explicit language. Not coincidentally, Koreans often refer to older members of society using terms that mean "grandma," "grandpa," "uncle," "older brother," etc., even when the other person isn't a relative. In this way, Koreans extend the bonds of family to everyone in the social group and acknowledge the power and status of elders. And notice how using these terms means that you must rely on the social context to figure out if the person actually is the speaker's grandmother, grandfather, uncle, or older brother. In comparison, people from the United States are likely to use first names, which emphasize a person's individuality, and they have only a few words (for example, "sir" or "ma'am") that signal status. Because residents of the United States explicitly name another person, sometimes even going so far as to distinguish "Grandma Jane" from "Grandma Marie," they don't need to rely on the social context to figure out who they are talking about. As this example illustrates, the values of a cultural group have far-reaching effects on interpersonal communication.

TABLE 2.1 Dimensions that distinguish cultures

Individualism	*Collectivism*
Individualistic cultures value independence and autonomy more than the group	Collectivistic cultures put the needs of the community before the needs of the individual
High power distance	*Low power distance*
High power distance cultures respect a rigid hierarchy based on power and status	Low power distance cultures assume that all people have equal rights and opportunities
High context	*Low context*
High context cultures rely on the social situation to give messages meaning	Low context cultures rely on explicit language to make meanings clear
Outcome-oriented	*Process-oriented*
Outcome-oriented cultures value achievement, deadlines, and getting a job done	Process-oriented cultures appreciate the experiences gained by working on a task
Uncertainty-avoidant	*Uncertainty-seeking*
Uncertainty-avoidant cultures prefer stable routines that avoid risks or novel experiences	Uncertainty-seeking cultures prefer diverse, novel, and even risky experiences

Putting Theory into Practice: Finding Common Ground for Communication

When we think about the layers of culture, the dynamics by which culture develops and evolves, and the dimensions that differentiate cultures, we can see that defining a person's cultural affiliation is difficult. You participate in multiple cultural groups defined by cultural institutions, common standpoints, and speech communities. And culture isn't stable – it evolves as new practices are selected, new members are socialized, and time passes. While this view of culture emphasizes its complexity, it also opens doors to improving your interpersonal communication experiences.

Find experiences you and your partner have in common. The multiple layers of culture make it possible for you and a communication partner to belong to similar and different cultures *at the same time*. For example, because you and your parents and siblings are all part of a family speech community, you can understand each other in ways that non-family members cannot. You also belong to cultural groups, such as your university community, your major, and your circle of friends, that the rest of your family might have difficulty understanding. When you are interacting with another person, keep in mind that you have both cultural differences and similarities, and work to find those experiences that provide you with a common foundation for communication.

Finding areas of cultural overlap gives you and your partner a shared framework that can improve your communication experiences. When you start a conversation with a new acquaintance, open with general topics that can point you to things you have in common. Questions like "Where are you from?" allow you to gather information that may direct you to common ground. The key is to follow up by focusing on connections. If your interaction partner answers "I'm from Virginia," your job is to think of something – anything – that connects you to Virginia: "Oh, I have a cousin in Virginia;" "I read a book about Virginia" or "I've always wanted to visit Virginia." You have a lot of options for locating some point of overlap. And if you can't find any way to connect with the information you've received, move quickly to another topic ("What's your major?"). By seeking out common ground with your interaction partners, you can have more fulfilling and effective interpersonal communication experiences.

Socialize yourself in new cultural environments. Socialization often takes place gradually as cultural insiders and outsiders interact. You can also be proactive by using the following strategies to help you to learn the ropes in a new cultural setting:

- *Learn as much as you can about a culture before you interact with its members.* Examine websites, publications, or media coverage to find out how a cultural group presents itself to the public. Any information you can discover can help you to master the culture more quickly.
- *Take notes or keep a journal to record the events that seem particularly meaningful within the culture.* When you reflect on your observations, you may be able to identify patterns that can guide your entry into the culture.
- *Identify someone who can serve as your informant on cultural practices.* Secretaries in an organization, advisors in an academic department, and civil servants in a government office are people who really know the culture, and they can be invaluable resources.
- *Test whether your conclusions about cultural practices are correct.* Ask questions: Should I call professors by their first names? Is it okay to bring my cousin to a fraternity meeting? Also, try out your guesses about the culture – wear jeans to work on Fridays or bring snacks to share at a meeting. People will be especially tolerant of your errors and more willing to help you when you are still a newcomer, so take advantage of this grace period to experiment with your perceptions of the culture and make sure you're on the right track.
- *Openly seek feedback.* Checking whether your conclusions about the culture are accurate can help you learn the ropes more quickly, save you from making mistakes down the road, and show others that you are eager to adapt to the cultural environment.

Using these strategies will help you join the cultural group more quickly and enhance your interpersonal communication experiences.

Help others understand your culture. You have a great deal of expertise about the beliefs and customs that are important to members of your cultural group. Use this knowledge to help others to understand or adapt to your culture. As a first step, make your implicit cultural assumptions explicit; in other words, create a list that identifies or describes assumptions, beliefs, and customs that characterize your culture. Then, make a point of sharing your observations with newcomers. One communication professor we know went so far as to have students in his class create a video for future students in which they explained the challenges of completing the class project and the strategies that helped them along the way. Just as this video helped subsequent students adapt to the demands of the course, you can help cultural newcomers by being explicit about the beliefs, values, and customs of your speech community.

CULTURE AND COMMUNICATION

Speech Codes Theory

A theory that explains how people's culture influences their communication behaviors.

Your culture inevitably shapes your interpersonal communication. One theory that describes the link between culture and communication is **speech codes theory**. According to this theory, people communicate based on their understanding of the meanings, norms, and values that are relevant in a particular context (Phillipsen, 1997; Phillipsen, Coutu, & Covarrubias, 2005). In this section of the chapter, we'll examine the assumptions of speech codes theory and use them to explore how culture shapes communication and communication reflects culture.

Culture Shapes Communication

According to speech codes theory, context always affects communication. Consider the example of Katie, a college student who works at a restaurant. When Katie's friends come in for dinner one evening, her interactions with them involve taking their order, serving their food, checking that they are enjoying everything, and accepting a tip. While the messages exchanged in this context make sense to both Katie and her friends, imagine how out of place they would be if Katie had invited her friends for dinner at her apartment instead! From the orders for food to the offer of a tip, every message would have a quite different (if not insulting) meaning. As this example illustrates, context has a very strong effect on the way we produce and make sense of messages.

Speech Code

The system of symbols, rules, and assumptions that people create to accomplish communication.

The theory defines a **speech code** as the system of symbols, rules, and assumptions that people create to accomplish communication. People create speech codes through social interaction and within particular situations, and their meanings are both complicated and flexible. In fact, a speech code is like a genetic code: it is intricate, it can combine in different ways to produce different effects, and the outcomes produced depend heavily on the environment.

PAUSE & REFLECT

Are there speech codes that you use in some of your social groups that would be complete nonsense in other social groups? How do the symbols and rules that are meaningful in each group set them apart?

Because context affects the meaning of communication behaviors, different cultures have distinct speech codes. For an example, consider the speech codes that shape interpersonal communication and relationships in Bogotá, Colombia (Fitch, 1998). Within this culture, people persuade others to do things by emphasizing social connections ("Be a good brother, and help me with the gardening"), rather than logical arguments ("The gardening needs to be finished before the rain starts") or personal needs ("I can't do the gardening alone"). They also consider making a request to be a sign of closeness, rather than an imposition. In fact, people phrase requests as commands ("Take care of the laundry!") when they want to underscore the strength of their bond with the other person. Although these communication practices show up in other cultures too, citizens of Bogotá use them intentionally to emphasize the value they place on social ties. The speech codes within this Colombian community enable members to appreciate the full meaning of the messages that are exchanged.

Communication Reflects Culture

Speech codes arise from culture, and they are the basis of communication. Consequently, the messages people create reveal their culture. More specifically, acts of communication reflect a cultural group's way of thinking, assumptions about human relationships, and strategies for living. Communication features that reflect culture include boundary markers, myths, and rituals (see Table 2.2).

Members of a cultural group mark activities that are off-limits through a variety of specific communication devices. **Boundary markers** are messages that indicate when an action is inappropriate within the cultural group. For example, participants in a virtual community signal that a message violates norms by ignoring or dismissing it (Vrooman, 2002). In the Real Words box, participants in an online forum for family members of military recruits help a woman who was upset by a comment from someone outside the military culture – the participants' suggestions clearly show how communication can be used to mark boundaries for appropriate behavior. When you consider someone's words or messages to be humorous or obscene, you are also defining the boundaries of acceptable behaviors and attitudes within your cultural group (Harwood & Giles, 1992; Stapleton, 2003). Likewise, when people gossip, they focus on inappropriate behavior

Boundary Markers
Messages that signal that an action is inappropriate or off-limits within a cultural group.

TABLE 2.2 Communicative reflections of culture

Communication device	Description
Boundary markers	Cultures mark the messages or behaviors that are considered inappropriate by ignoring them, defining them as humorous or obscene, or gossiping about the people who perform them
Myths	Cultures communicate core cultural themes by creating sacred stories about heroes and villains
Rituals	Cultures celebrate culturally significant events, ranging from important moments in history to weddings, through carefully scripted public performances

and target people who have violated cultural rules (Baumeister, Zhang, & Vohs, 2004). As these examples show, looking closely at communication can provide insight into the values and customs within a culture.

REAL WORDS

MARKING BOUNDARIES FOR APPROPRIATE COMMUNICATION

This transcript was drawn from an online forum for family and loved ones of military recruits: http://www.recruitparents.com/forums/. Notice the communication behaviors participants suggest the poster use to mark an upsetting message as inappropriate. At the same time, the replies bolster the values shared within this online military community.

POSTER: Today at work someone asked me about my boyfriend, who left for bootcamp about a month ago . . . Then he decided to ask me if I was aware that the marines have the highest death rate? I stayed strong and held my tears until I got home (right now) and I'm having an EXTREMELY hard time keeping myself together after what he said. It just wasn't a good night for me to hear something like that (this isn't the first time and I'm sure comments like these have been made to many of you ladies) . . . I'm just looking for ANY advice from anyone for what to do when this happens . . .

REPLY 1: Unfortunately, you'll more than likely hear comments like these more than once or twice down the road. When I hear them, I feel like decking the person who said it in the face, but obviously, I don't. I keep my composure and kindly tell them that I don't listen to the statistics and I'm proud of what my husband does and support him all the way . . . When people make ignorant comments like that, just be proud that you're a strong woman who's got a great man by her side.

REPLY 2: I have had people say similar stuff, it's hurtful and has almost broken my heart!! But people are ignorant and don't think!!! The best thing is to just hold your head high, pray that your boy will stay safe and ignore those who don't think before they speak!!

REPLY 3: What I tell people when they make comments like that is just "thanks for your input but your negativity isn't welcome . . . I only want positivity surrounding me, so, please, if you feel the need to be negative, do it somewhere private alone." Some people just don't think before they talk. I''m sorry you had to endure that ignorance.

REPLY 4: I have found that the best way to handle people who are clueless is to perfect that look, you know the one that your teacher would give you when you did something wrong and it would stop you in your tracks, you have to just give them that "look" and walk away. These people will never get it.

Myths
Sacred stories in which the characters and their actions embody core cultural themes.

People also reveal their culture through the stories they tell. **Myths** are sacred stories in which the characters and their actions embody core cultural themes. For example, the Anglo-American culture of the eighteenth century was embodied in the myth of Buffalo Bill – stories of this Pony Express rider celebrated masculinity and Whiteness and dismissed violence against Native Americans (Dickinson, Ott, & Aoki, 2005). Likewise, the myth of the evil, greedy wicked stepmother brings to light cultural values that continue to challenge stepmothers (Christian, 2005). Speech communities such as families also develop myths, which take the form of stories about important or revealing family moments (Kellas, 2005). Through historical figures, childhood fairytales, and family stories that are told and retold, myths underscore the beliefs and values shared within a cultural group.

PAUSE & REFLECT

Think about a family story that is told within your family and shared with others. What does that story reveal about your family's speech community?

Culture is also highlighted by **rituals**, which are carefully scripted performances that mark culturally significant events. Public rituals that are common in the United States include fireworks on the 4th of July, the Macy's Thanksgiving Day Parade, and the countdown on New Year's Eve at Times Square. Other cultures celebrate their own unique rituals, such as the running of the bulls in Pamplona, the changing of the guard at Buckingham Palace, and the annual Carnivale celebration in Rio de Janiero. Within interpersonal relationships, rituals are a way of recognizing private events as important within the cultural group. A good example of this is the wedding ceremony, which elevates the private union between romantic partners to the public institution known as marriage.

Rituals
Carefully scripted performances that mark culturally significant events.

Like other forms of communication, rituals reinforce cultural beliefs and social roles. For example, a wedding or baby shower includes specific activities to mark a couple's passage into marriage or parenthood, and participants will explicitly embarrass newcomers who don't follow the rules (Braithwaite, 1995). Within Euro American families, people who are committed to participating in family rituals, such as celebrating birthdays together, also value communication and agreement within their family (Baxter

FIGURE 2.3 Characters from the African folktales about Anansi, the Spiderman of Africa. One popular African folktale tells the story of Anansi, who loves to eat, but is lazy, so he tries to trick other animals out of their food. When Anansi puts his own needs ahead of the needs of his community, he ends up alone and hungry. This folktale reinforces the value that the cultural group places on hard work, honesty, and putting the community's needs ahead of personal needs.

Source: http://www.crabgrasspuppets.com/anansi.html.

& Clark, 1996). In fact, creating new rituals that blend former family customs is one way that step-families can foster their own unique family culture (Braithwaite, Baxter, & Harper, 1998). Thus, rituals can help create solidarity within a speech community.

Putting Theory into Practice: Appreciating Cultural Diversity

In this part of the chapter, we have examined how culture is woven into the very heart of our communication experiences. From the speech codes you use to the cultural events you participate in, you enact your culture in everything you do. Viewed in this light, communication becomes an opportunity to celebrate cultural diversity.

Explore the speech codes of different cultures. Because communication is a reflection of speech codes, the symbols and messages people create may be thought of as folk art: they are unique and sometimes beautiful cultural performances. Become an art connoisseur – someone who appreciates and understands different forms of art – by exploring the speech codes of different cultures. Try this simple exercise to get you started: The next time you're in someone's home, apartment, or dorm room, take a look at the objects that person has on display – artwork, photographs, memorabilia. As you study these cultural artifacts, think about how they symbolize important values, customs, or events within that person's cultural groups. By making a habit of viewing communication practices as cultural symbols, you'll open your eyes to the diversity of cultures around you.

Ask people about their rituals and stories. Knowing the rituals that people perform and the stories that they enjoy can help you to understand what is important to them. Jen has a friend who had formed elaborate plans for her wedding long before she'd even met her spouse. Another friend hadn't given wedding arrangements a moment's thought until she and her partner decided to marry. Whereas the first couple displays photos from their wedding and enjoys retelling how the groom lost the marriage license, the other couple is pressed to remember the date of their anniversary. Which woman do you think has the more conservative view of marriage? Not surprisingly, the "wedding planner" has a more traditional marriage – she is responsible for the house and children (and paperwork!), while her husband pursues his career. In the other couple, both partners work outside the home and play a more equal role in homemaking. As this example illustrates, you can gain insight into people's beliefs and values by asking them about the rituals and stories that are important to them.

COMMUNICATION IN ACTION 2.2

Learning about Others through Rituals and Stories

Asking people about the rituals celebrated within their families and the family stories that they like to tell can help you learn about their cultural values. Talk to two different people as you complete the table on the **companion website**. This exercise can help you see the connection between family ritual and stories and cultural values.

Create rituals and stories within relationships you value. You can also take steps to encourage rituals and stories that promote a sense of community with others. In the interpersonal relationships you value, look for activities that can become special for you and your partners, and turn these into rituals by repeating their key components. For example, you can maintain closeness in a group of old friends by embracing birthday celebrations as a cultural ritual. You might make a point of gathering for each person's birthday, holding an annual reunion where all the birthdays are celebrated, or developing norms for location, food, and gifts that mark your celebration. Likewise, you might signal to a new friend that the relationship is special by turning your occasional lunch together into a regular event at a favorite restaurant. For the most part, the activity itself doesn't matter as much as identifying it as a marker of your relationship culture.

INTERCULTURAL COMMUNICATION

Sometimes the effects of cultural differences on interpersonal interactions are quite obvious. When we ask our students to identify a personal experience with intercultural communication, they usually recall a time when they traveled abroad or talked to an international student. It can be quite easy to identify differences in language and norms when you communicate with someone from a different country. But what about more subtle differences? People who live in or near New York City, for example, recognize the dialects, customs, and rituals that distinguish people from Manhattan versus the other boroughs, north Jersey versus south Jersey, and Mets fans versus Yankees fans. Although these individuals might share the same nationality, ethnicity, or religion, the fact that they come from distinct speech communities means that cultural differences have emerged. In this section, we'll examine what makes interpersonal communication intercultural, as well as some of the barriers to effective intercultural communication.

The Nature of Intercultural Communication

A person's cultural background always shapes interpersonal communication experiences. What sets intercultural communication apart is the extent to which messages reflect a focus on a person's culture. Specifically, **intercultural communication** occurs when interaction is guided by the participants' memberships in different social groups, rather than their unique qualities as individuals (Gudykunst, 2005). In other words, if a person's cultural group membership is very relevant to you and you tailor your messages with that cultural group in mind, you are engaging in intercultural communication. So, intercultural communication occurs when you adjust your word choice and nonverbal behaviors because you are talking to a person who doesn't share the same meaning for words and actions. Intercultural communication also occurs when you adjust your messages based on a partner's gender, age, political views, or favorite baseball team. In each of these cases, you might change the way you communicate based on your knowledge or stereotypes about a partner's cultural group.

> **SCHOLAR SPOTLIGHT**
>
> Visit the Communication Café on the **companion website** to view a conversation with Howard Giles, a leading scholar who studies intercultural and intergroup communication.

Intercultural Communication
Interaction that is guided by a person's membership in a social group, rather than his or her unique qualities as an individual.

Have you ever communicated with someone from Great Britain and started speaking with a British accent? When you talk to your grandparents or other elderly individuals, do you tend to speak more slowly and loudly than usual? **Communication accommodation theory** is a general model of interaction that describes how cultural group memberships influence interpersonal interactions (Gallois, Ogay, & Giles, 2005).

Communication accommodation theory identifies two communication patterns that might emerge over the course of a conversation: characteristics of the participants' speech can become more similar to each other, or they can become more distinct (see Figure 2.4). These communication patterns may be conscious or subconscious, but they reflect a desire either to increase or decrease the connection to a partner. In particular, we tend

Communication Accommodation Theory
A model that describes how cultural group memberships influence interpersonal interactions.

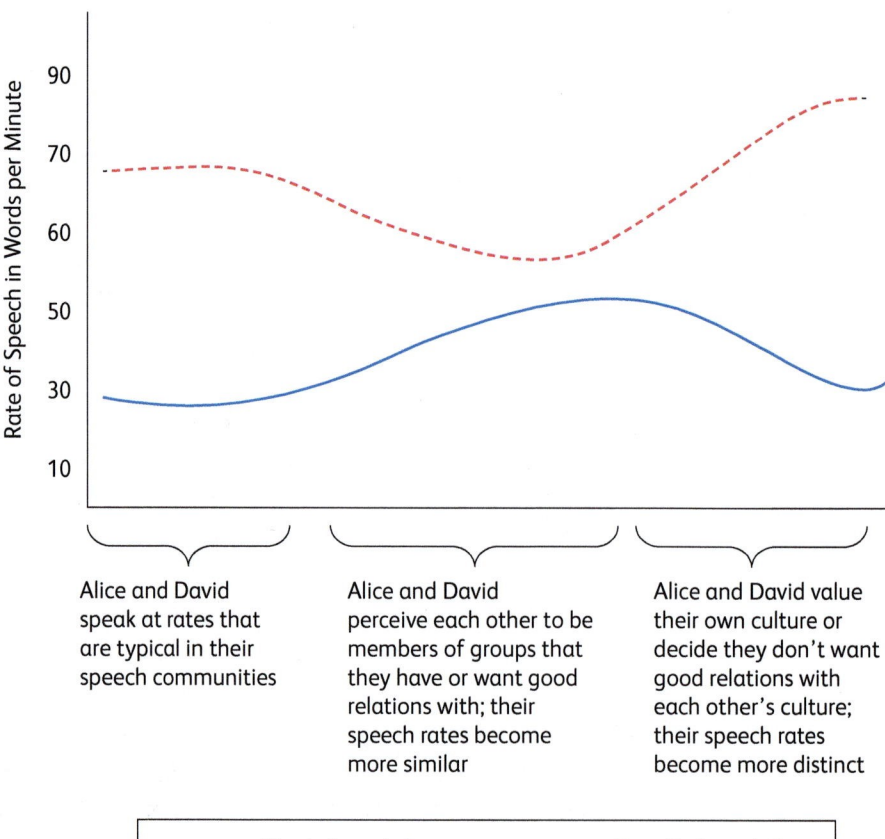

FIGURE 2.4 Communication accommodation theory. Communication accommodation theory describes how two people adjust their communication behaviors to become more similar or more different over the course of an interaction. The graphs show how Alice and David change their rate of speech to signal their desire to be more or less connected with each other's cultural group.

to match the communication behaviors of people we like or feel similar to, and we exaggerate communication patterns that distinguish us from people we don't like (Giles, Mulac, Bradac, & Johnson, 1987). In intercultural interactions, we tend to adopt a partner's communication patterns when we want to promote intergroup relationships or we have had positive interactions with members of this culture in the past. On the other hand, we maintain or exaggerate differences in communication if our own culture is important to us at that moment or we have a bad history with our partner's cultural group.

Communicating in ways similar to an interaction partner has important advantages. Grandchildren and grandparents who pick up each other's speech patterns feel more satisfaction, closeness, and solidarity (Harwood, 2000; see also Lin & Harwood, 2003). Conversely, college students are dissatisfied after conversations with an elderly person when that person doesn't match their communication behaviors (Williams & Giles, 1996). In one research study, Australian undergraduates judged Chinese speakers more favorably when their speech included communication patterns typical for English-speaking Australians (Hornsey & Gallois, 1998). When you adjust your communication behavior for an interaction partner, you can signal your willingness to bridge cultural gaps.

INSIDE COMMUNICATION RESEARCH

Predicting Attraction in Interethnic Interactions

Communication scholars Carmen Lee and William Gudykunst (2001) studied the factors that predict interpersonal attraction in initial interactions between interethnic partners. The researchers predicted that people would be more attracted to members of different ethnic groups when they perceived similarities with the communication style of that group. They also hypothesized that people would be more attracted to an interethnic partner when they had more positive expectations for interaction with members of that ethnic group.

To test these predictions, the researchers asked 283 college students from diverse ethnic backgrounds to interact with a partner from a different ethnic group. Some of the participants interacted with their partner up to three additional times after their initial meeting. About a week after the initial interaction, the participants filled out a questionnaire reporting on their perceptions of their interethnic interaction and their attraction to the interethnic partner.

The results of the study supported the researchers' predictions. Participants who thought they shared a similar communication style with the ethnic group of their partner reported more attraction toward their interethnic interaction partner. In addition, participants who had positive expectations for their interaction with someone of a different cultural background were also more attracted to their partner from that culture. Thus, attraction to members of a different culture is shaped by positive expectations for intercultural communication and perceived similarities between the communication styles of different ethnic groups.

THINK ABOUT IT

1. This study focused on interactions and attraction within interethnic relationships. Do you think these findings generalize to relationships between people of the same ethnicity? Has the perceived similarity of communication styles influenced how attracted you are to people, regardless of their ethnicity?

2. This study found that having positive expectations for intercultural communication is associated with more attraction to members of a different culture. Given this finding, what can be done to enhance intercultural relationships for people who don't have positive expectations for intercultural communication?

Barriers to Intercultural Communication

In our efforts to communicate with partners from different cultures, we face a number of barriers. Have you ever tried to order food, ask for directions, or offer assistance to someone who didn't speak a language you know? When you communicate across cultural boundaries, you confront a number of barriers: different speech codes, different expectations for interaction, and different customs. Beyond these logistical issues, intercultural communication is also complicated by biases and tensions, including ethnocentrism, uncertainty and anxiety, and marginalization (see Table 2.3).

Ethnocentrism. Ethnocentrism refers to seeing one's own cultural beliefs and practices as more correct, appropriate, or moral than those of other cultures. To some extent, culture is inherently ethnocentric, because adopting cultural norms means viewing those practices as right or natural. By comparison, the norms of other cultures seem "deviant," "weird," or even "immoral." To glimpse the power of ethnocentrism, imagine how repulsed you would be if you were invited to dinner at someone's home and served a main course of roasted grasshoppers. A Hindu person from India would probably be just as horrified to be served some juicy roast beef. Because ethnocentrism involves evaluating practices with respect to one's own cultural rules and assumptions, we often find flaws in another culture's practices.

Ethnocentrism can have a powerful impact on our feelings and behavior. In one study, American students completed a self-report measure of ethnocentrism and evaluated a video of a Korean student interviewing for a job in the United States (Neuliep, Hintz, & McCroskey, 2005). People who scored high in ethnocentrism rated the Korean student negatively in terms of social attractiveness, competence, and character, and they didn't recommend hiring him. Similarly, undergraduates who scored high in ethnocentrism rated jokes involving an ethnic victim as funnier than jokes with a non-ethnic

Ethnocentrism

The tendency to see one's own cultural beliefs as more correct, appropriate, and moral than other cultures.

TABLE 2.3 Barriers to intercultural communication

Barrier	Definition
Ethnocentrism	The tendency to see one's own cultural beliefs as more correct, appropriate, and moral than those of other cultures
Uncertainty and anxiety	A lack of knowledge and fear of consequences that can make people unable to predict or enjoy intercultural interactions
Marginalization	The tendency to treat less dominant groups of people in a society as inferior or unimportant

victim (Gallois & Callan, 1985). This research illustrates how a tendency to privilege their own culture can cause people to discriminate against members of other cultural groups.

PAUSE & REFLECT

Have you ever been hurt by another person's ethnocentrism? Can you think of times that ethnocentrism has affected your treatment of another person?

Uncertainty and anxiety. Your communication with someone from a different culture may also be affected by uncertainty and anxiety. *Uncertainty* refers to a lack of knowledge about the person's traits, expectations, and customs. *Anxiety* is a negative emotional state that arises when you feel uneasy, worried, or apprehensive (Stephan & Stephan, 1985). All communication episodes can provoke uncertainty and anxiety. When cultural differences are conspicuous, you may be especially likely to experience uncertainty and anxiety (Gudykunst & Shapiro, 1996; Gudykunst & Nishida, 2001).

Anxiety/uncertainty management theory explains how these forces affect intercultural interactions (Gudykunst, 1993, 2005). According to the theory (Figure 2.5),

Anxiety/Uncertainty Management Theory
A framework that explains how uncertainty and anxiety affect intercultural communication.

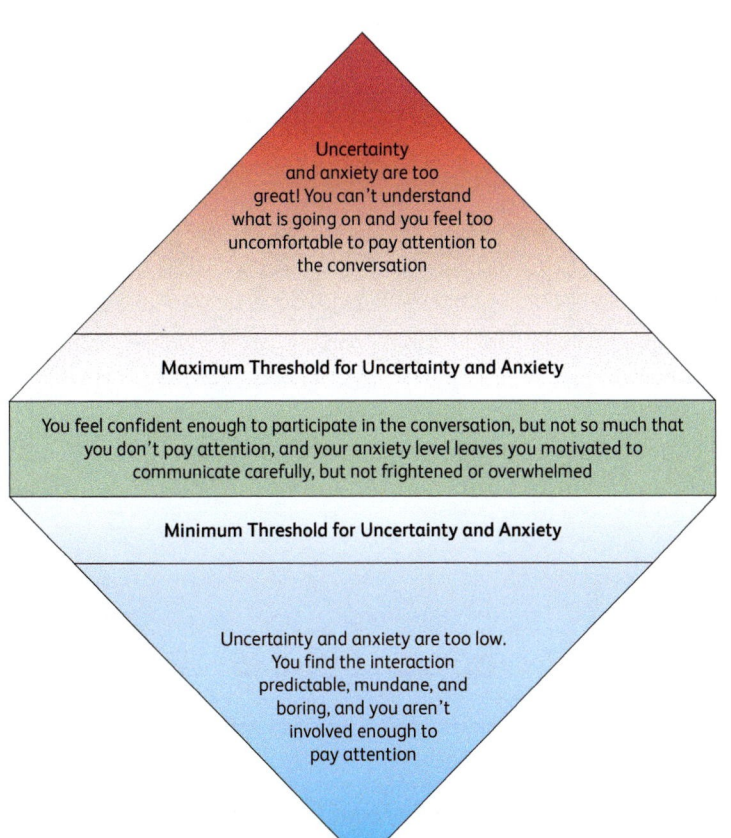

FIGURE 2.5 Anxiety/uncertainty management theory

Marginalization
When less dominant groups of people in a society are treated as inferior or unimportant.

people have maximum and minimum thresholds for uncertainty and anxiety during interpersonal exchanges (see Figure 2.4). The maximum threshold is the highest amount of uncertainty or anxiety you can tolerate, and the minimum threshold is the lowest level you can experience without becoming overconfident, bored, or uninterested. Effective intercultural communication requires that your uncertainty and anxiety remain between the maximum and minimum thresholds. When your uncertainty level is between the two thresholds, you feel comfortable and motivated to interact with others.

Marginalization. Within a diverse society, some cultural groups tend to have more influence than others. In the United States, for example, men, whites, and the wealthy have held more prominent roles historically than women, ethnic minorities, and the poor. Influential cultural groups have the power to determine the communication norms and values for the whole society. Marginalization occurs when less dominant groups are treated as inferior or unimportant. As a stark illustration, consider the images of refugees stranded at the New Orleans Superdome in the aftermath of Hurricane Katrina (Figure 2.6). That crisis demonstrated how this community's evacuation and emergency services left members of marginalized groups to fend for themselves.

Marginalization can be a barrier to effective intercultural communication because it tends to make cultural differences more pronounced. When marginalized members of a society communicate with members of the dominant group, they are forced to adapt to the very values and norms that marginalize them (DeTurk, 2001). Consider an example from an episode of *The Office* where Pam, the receptionist, leaves the company with her

FIGURE 2.6 After Hurricane Katrina, National Guardsmen stand watch at barricades outside the Superdome as emotional refugees driven from their homes by the hurricane await evacuation from the flooded city of New Orleans, La. Shots were fired and a near riot erupted at the arena as thousands who had taken shelter there fought to board the buses for the Astrodome in Houston, Tex.

Source: Photo by Michael Appleton/NY Daily News Archive via Getty Images.

boss, Michael, to start an independent paper company. Although Pam made it clear that she wanted to have a more prominent role in sales, Michael expected her – instead of her male colleague – to complete all of the secretarial duties like photocopying and typing. If Pam wanted to interact with Michael, she was forced to adopt the same role that made her feel marginalized at the old company. On the other hand, people who are in positions of power may be perceived as condescending, inappropriate, or weak if they try to reach out to someone in a marginalized group. On those occasions when Michael asked Pam to help make decisions about the new company, he ended up looking incompetent by revealing that he didn't have a clear plan of action. Perhaps not surprisingly, people who belong to a marginalized group experience greater self-esteem and feel less isolated from society when they can communicate with others who share their marginalized status (McKenna & Bargh, 1998). One of the great challenges to intercultural communication, then, is finding ways to bridge cultural gaps that are magnified by power differences.

COMMUNICATION IN ACTION 2.3

Exploring Marginalized and Dominant Identities

This exercise helps you to identify how the social groups that you belong to may have some benefits, because they are privileged groups in society, or some disadvantages, because they are marginalized in some way. Completing the table on the **companion website** can also help you to think about whether any of the groups you belong to contribute to the marginalization of other cultural groups.

Communication between Men and Women

One intercultural encounter that people have on a daily basis involves interacting with members of the other sex. Whereas **sex** refers to whether a person is biologically male or female, **gender** refers to one's psychological orientation toward masculine or feminine traits, or how one is socialized to be a man or a woman. Often, the words "sex" and "gender" are used interchangeably, because people often infer someone's psychological gender from their biological sex. While people vary in the degree to which they have more masculine or feminine characteristics, regardless of their biological sex, sex differences are often taken as a proxy for gender differences. Cultural differences between men and women aren't as obvious as the differences that can exist between blacks and whites or between U.S. citizens and Pakistanis, but men and women have different life experiences that can foster distinct cultural values and practices. Although the debate about the magnitude and relevance of sex differences in communication is ongoing (Dindia & Canary, 2006), we can illustrate some of the challenges of intercultural communication by exploring the experiences of men and women across the lifespan.

Infancy and childhood. From birth, boys and girls have unique social experiences that can promote distinct ways of seeing the world and relating to others. Mothers tend to talk more to infant daughters than to sons, and they use more supportive and less

Sex
Whether a person is biologically male or female.

Gender
A social construction of one's psychological identity as predominantly masculine or feminine.

FIGURE 2.7 "How to Speak Woman"

Source: www.CartoonStock.com

complex messages when they do; conversely, fathers tend to talk more to infant sons than to daughters, and they use more challenging language with boys (Leaper, Anderson, & Sanders, 1998). When young children begin to socialize with peers, they prefer playing with same-sex friends (Martin, Fabes, Evans, & Wyman, 1999), and boys and girls develop distinct norms for communication and interaction. For example, compared with pairs of male friends, female friends are more likely to disclose and discuss private information as a way of maintaining connection and intimacy (Rawlins, 1993). What happens when boys and girls communicate with each other? Parents and other friends may signal disapproval of a friendship – or at least not encourage the relationship – and the children's distinct communication experiences can make it difficult for them to find common ground.

Dating. When we consider the world of dating, we can point to fundamental similarities between men and women: men and women both engage in dating, and they both seek romantic partners to fulfill personal and social needs. But within heterosexual relationships in the United States, men and women are expected to play distinct roles in the dating game. Here are some conclusions from research studies conducted in the 1990s:

■ Both men and women expected men to initiate first dates, plan the activities, drive, pay for expenses, and initiate sexual intimacy (Rose & Frieze, 1993).

■ 83% of undergraduate men reported that they had been asked out on a first date by a woman, and 63% of undergraduate women reported that they had asked a man out on a first date (Mongeau, Hale, Johnson, & Hillis, 1993).

■ Men tend to form higher expectations for sexual involvement on dates that women initiate (Mongeau & Carey, 1996).

■ Women who initiate dates are seen as more feminist and less attractive than women who wait to be asked out (Mongeau et al., 1993).

Although norms for heterosexual dating have no doubt changed since the 1990s, men and women continue to bring unique perspectives to the dating game.

One difference that may exist between men and women is how they talk about their dating relationships to others. In a study that Jen conducted, an interviewer asked men and women a variety of questions about their romantic relationship – and often got different details from each partner. For one couple describing how they met, the woman had lots of detail to share:

> We met in the beginning of the school year. Ummm, actually, the night before my birthday. I decided that since it was the night before my birthday I wasn't gonna stay in, I planned to go out, so, I . . . and none of my friends on my floor were going out, so . . . I . . . spoke to a different friend who's like, "Okay, fine, we'll go out," and, um, he happened to be a mutual friend, and so we met, he was also going out, so we met through him.

This woman's partner, however, simply answered "September 9th, the night before her birthday, uh, my friend picked us up, and we went to a party. So, we shared the same car, hung out at the party." In Jen's study, men and women in relationships were interviewed separately – can you imagine how the conversation might unfold if the partners were communicating their impressions of their first meeting to each other? The woman in this case might find her boyfriend's focus on the bare bones details disappointing compared to the serendipity she highlights in her answer.

PAUSE & REFLECT

How do your own experiences dating compare to the research findings from the 1990s? Did your interactions with friends during your childhood help you to understand the cultural rules for your sex? What did those interactions teach you?

Work relationships. Men and women also confront unique communication challenges and perceive meanings differently at work. In the United States, many organizations adopt masculine norms for communication: managers are expected to be assertive, to use their dominance to influence decisions and provide leadership, and to talk about their own strengths (Murphy & Zorn, 1996). If a woman follows these norms, she violates the expectations that many people have about women: namely, that her communication style be submissive, polite, and other-focused (Martin, 2004). Even when men and women have similar communication styles, group members respond more favorably to information that is presented by a man (Propp, 1995). Also, men are less likely than women to rate flirtatious or sexual comments that occur in the workplace as sexual harassment (McCabe & Hardman, 2005; Solomon, 2006). These examples show how men and women encounter different expectations in the workplace, and how these differences can complicate communication between the sexes.

Putting Theory into Practice: Improving Your Intercultural Interactions

Although everyone faces barriers to intercultural communication, there are specific skills that will help you have more effective and fulfilling encounters with people from different cultural groups.

Maintain realistic expectations. It would be nice to think that being more sensitive will always allow you to bridge cultural divides. And, no doubt, being mindful of cultural differences can contribute to more effective communication between cultural groups (Gudykunst, 2005). At the same time, intercultural interactions occur within historical and social contexts that place real limits on communication outcomes. When cultural groups have a history of conflict and violence, when power differences have allowed one group to dominate the other, or when two groups are competing for scarce resources, communication will be strained (Gallois, 2003). One way to enhance your intercultural communication experience, then, is to keep those constraints in mind.

When you focus on the challenges to intercultural communication, you can implement strategies that directly target those barriers. For example, at a newly formed multiethnic college, administrators and students confronted the possibility of cultural tension head on. By creating procedures and forums for addressing interethnic conflicts, the emerging speech community was able to overcome historical and social obstacles to unity (Ross, 1999). In the same way, you can tackle intercultural obstacles in your interpersonal interactions. Identify the intercultural tensions, and talk about them with your partner. For example, openly acknowledge the religious differences you have with a roommate, and use that as a foundation for learning about each other's cultures. Or, point out to a classmate that your culture values punctuality to open a discussion about how to coordinate your meeting times. By bringing these constraints out into the open, you can put them in perspective. In doing so, you convey a respect for cultural group membership, a sensitivity to group differences, and an appreciation for how you and your partner are more than just representatives of your cultural groups.

Practice person-centered communication. When you adjust your communication based on assumptions about another person's culture, your behavior is likely to be restricted, rigid, and inadequate. Instead, make an effort to notice the distinct and unique characteristics that your partner reveals, and tailor your communication to those qualities. Does your grandmother really need you to speak more loudly, or are you just doing so because of your stereotypes about the elderly? Is your new acquaintance from Jamaica really laid back, carefree, and forgiving when you're late, or are you acting on your beliefs about island communities? Pay attention to the communication behaviors your partners actually prefer, and avoid letting cultural stereotypes drive your interpersonal communication experiences.

Avoid exaggerating sex differences. When people accept the belief that men and women are wildly different in their attitudes and behaviors, they allow themselves to treat sex differences as unavoidable and insurmountable. At the end of the day, men and women have many overlapping life experiences and many shared communication values. Each of us is a great deal more than just a man or a woman. Be careful about your assumptions and focus on the qualities that your partner actually brings to the exchange.

COMMUNICATION IN ACTION 2.4

Practicing Person-Centered Communication

This exercise can help you to be more thoughtful about how your expectations for a cultural group might be influencing your communication with a member of that cultural group. By completing the table on the **companion website**, you might identify ways you can make your intercultural communication experiences more person-centered.

In your effort to keep sex differences in perspective, you might make a list of the values and norms that you share with relationship partners of the other sex. Then use this list of similarities as a context for discussing the communication practices you prefer. Deborah Tannen (1991) argues that women like to talk at length about their problems and men prefer to search for immediate solutions. If a woman adopts this gendered view, she might fixate on how she wants to go on and on about her problems, while her partner just wants the easy solution. But if both partners can remember their shared goal of decreasing stress in their lives, perhaps the female partner can vent about the problem for 10 minutes and then the male partner can work with her to solve it. The differences between men and women can be subtle, varied, and far from absolute; keep that in mind in your conversations with both men and women.

SUMMARY

This chapter focused on the fundamental role of culture in our interpersonal communication experiences. As a starting point, we examined the complexity of culture by considering the various layers at which culture can be defined, the processes by which cultures develop, are passed on, and change over time, and how cultures can be distinguished from each other. The view of culture offered in this chapter highlighted how it is both nuanced and dynamic. In other words, our culture is a shifting, complicated, and evolving part of our lives.

Culture includes our assumptions about living, thinking, and feeling; therefore, it is inevitably reflected in our communication. Speech codes are culturally grounded systems of symbols and rules for interpretation that make communication possible. Although all of our interpersonal communication reflects cultural speech codes, boundary markers, myths, and rituals make a cultural group's values particularly conspicuous. By examining the communication that occurs between people in a cultural group, you can gain insight into the experiences and beliefs that are meaningful within a culture.

Because culture is always reflected in communication, it always affects interpersonal communication experiences. When cultural differences are especially pronounced, interpersonal communication becomes intercultural communication. Under these circumstances, people adjust their communication behavior to signal either solidarity or disagreement with an interaction partner's cultural group. Communicating based on stereotypical cultural assumptions can lead to rigid and even condescending behavior, whereas attempts to bridge cultural gaps by adopting a partner's communication norms can create more satisfying interactions. You can improve your intercultural interactions by keeping in mind how ethnocentrism, uncertainty and anxiety, and marginalization can be barriers to effective communication. Even interactions between men and women can involve intercultural communication.

Although your membership in cultural groups may be more or less noticeable as you communicate with other people, it is an ever present force in your interactions with others. Now that you understand the impact of culture on interpersonal communication, you may be ready to grapple with the ethical issues that surround culture and interpersonal communication.

ACTIVITIES FOR EXPLORING COMMUNICATION ETHICS

What Would You/Should You Do?

You are at a party when someone starts telling jokes that disparage a particular ethnic group. Many of your friends laugh, but others appear to be uncomfortable. What would you or should you do?

Something to Think About

The opposite of ethnocentrism is *cultural relativism*, the tendency to see all cultural practices as morally equivalent. When you think about some practices that are culturally sanctioned – for example, female genital mutilation or the murder of women who bring shame on their families – culture relativism would seem to have some limits. How do you balance the need to keep ethnocentrism in check with the limits of cultural relativism?

Analyze Communication Ethics Yourself

The last half of the twentieth century saw a dramatic increase in international travel, trade, and communication. One consequence of this increased cultural exchange is a blending of cultures and a concern that the unique qualities that distinguish cultural groups will be lost. As a result, some nations and organizations have taken steps to outlaw foreign cultural practices and promote local culture. Visit the website for the International Network for Cultural Diversity (http://www.incd.net) and examine the concerns expressed by this organization, as well as their tactics for protecting native cultures. Based on your analysis, what are the ethical issues involved in cultural diffusion and protectionism?

KEY WORDS

anxiety/uncertainty management theory	gender	socialization
boundary markers	intercultural communication	speech code
communication accommodation theory	invention	speech codes theory
cultural identity salience	marginalization	speech community
culture	myths	standpoint
diffusion	norms	subcultures
ethnic identity salience	rituals	
ethnocentrism	sex	

LEARNING OBJECTIVES

After reading this chapter, you should be able to:

1. Define self-concept and describe characteristics of the self.
2. Identify sources of self-knowledge.
3. Define, identity, and distinguish among the four layers of identity.
4. Define identity gaps and describe their consequences.
5. Describe the challenges that confront people as identities change in early adulthood and when children move out of the family home.
6. Strengthen your ability to use interpersonal communication to support your own identity, as well as the identities of others.

PUTTING THEORY INTO PRACTICE

In this chapter, you will learn how to:

1. Seek out situations that activate important facets of yourself.
2. Behave in ways that reflect who you want to be.
3. Enhance your self-esteem.
4. Communicate with integrity.
5. Reduce your identity gaps.
6. Find opportunities to represent multiple identities.
7. Confide in others as your identity changes.
8. Embrace diverse identities.
9. Support parents as they empty the nest.

IDENTITY AND INTERPERSONAL COMMUNICATION

3

70 SELF-CONCEPT: HOW YOU SEE YOURSELF

79 IDENTITY: THE COMMUNICATED SELF

88 IDENTITIES IN TRANSITION

93 SUMMARY

95 ACTIVITIES FOR EXPLORING COMMUNICATION ETHICS

95 KEY WORDS

Source: Getty Images.

On the popular television program *What Not to Wear*, men and women get a complete makeover that includes new clothes, hair, and make-up. People who are on the show have been nominated by their friends and family, who feel that the person's style of dressing doesn't reflect his or her true identity. For example, Shannon (Episode 47) was a telephone salesperson, who was embarking on a new position that involved face-to-face sales. Her co-workers nominated her for the show because they thought her penchant for whimsical socks and matching outfits lacked the professional punch she would need when communicating with customers. With help from the show's hosts, Stacey and Clinton, Shannon was able to trash the socks and find a style that would make a good first impression on her clients. The changes to Shannon's wardrobe, hair, and make-up did more than change her look; Shannon ended the show feeling as professional, confident, and competent as she now looked. In show after show, the cast of *What Not to Wear* give participants a new look that raises their self-esteem and gives them greater confidence in their interactions with others.

C an you identify some of the ways that your personal style or appearance might affect how other people perceive you? Do your ways of presenting yourself to others affect or reflect how you see yourself? What might happen to your self-perceptions and communication experiences if you changed how you look, act, or speak? Shannon's experience as a participant on *What Not to Wear,* described above, highlights how our self-perceptions are closely tied to the ways that we present ourselves to others.

Your sense of self both shapes and is shaped by interpersonal communication. You express your personality, goals, and values in every interpersonal interaction. Through interpersonal communication, then, you reveal yourself to others. At the same time, the messages you receive from others affect how you see yourself. By communicating with other people, for example, we learn whether we are interesting, funny, intelligent, or worthy of respect. In this chapter, we examine how the self is formed and performed through interpersonal communication. With a deeper understanding of the self, you will be able to play a more active role in supporting both your own unique identity and the identities of others.

SELF-CONCEPT: HOW YOU SEE YOURSELF

Our personal experiences and interactions with others provide us with substantial information about who we are. When we communicate with other people, we both observe our own behavior and we receive feedback about how others perceive us. That sum total of knowledge that you have about yourself is your **self-concept**. It includes your memories of experiences and accomplishments, your physical traits and distinguishing features, your likes and dislikes, your feelings about yourself, and your experiences communicating with others. It is, in fact, all that you know and believe yourself to be. In this part of the chapter, you'll learn about characteristics of the self-concept and where you get information about who you are.

Characteristics of the Self

Self-concept
The sum total knowledge you have about yourself.

Although everyone's self-concept is unique, some general qualities apply to everyone's self. The following characteristics are core features of everybody's self-concept.

The self is subjective. Your self-concept is inherently subjective; in other words, you are who you think you are. Perhaps not surprisingly, we are often biased in how we think about and evaluate ourselves. For example, you might consider yourself to be a good friend, to have a good sense of humor, or to be a hard worker, but other people may see you differently. Our self-concept reflects how we see ourselves, which may or may not reflect the perceptions of others.

One of our biases is the tendency to interpret new information in ways that are consistent with how we already see ourselves (Swann, 1983). Imagine receiving an exam score that was much higher or lower than usual. Because that grade was not consistent with your view of your abilities, you might conclude that the exam was either especially easy or especially unfair. Conversely, we view experiences that support our self-perceptions as more valid and important. This desire to have our self-concept affirmed can affect our relationships with others. For example, a study of married couples showed that people are most satisfied when their spouse sees them the way they see themselves; on the other hand, being either overrated or underrated by a spouse predicts depression, marital dissatisfaction, and even the likelihood of divorce (Burke & Harrod, 2005).

Another subjective aspect of the self is **self-esteem**, which is a person's overall judgment of his or her own worth and value. Researchers measure self-esteem by asking people how much they agree with statements like these (Rosenberg, 1989):

Self-esteem
An overall judgment of one's self-worth or value.

- On the whole, I am satisfied with myself.
- At times I think I am no good at all.
- I feel that I have a number of good qualities.
- I am able to do things as well as most people.
- I feel I do not have much to be proud of.
- I certainly feel worthless at times.
- I wish I could have more respect for myself.
- I am inclined to feel that I am a failure.

PAUSE & REFLECT

As you reflect on the statements that measure self-esteem, would you say your self-esteem is high, low, or average?

Your self-esteem affects how you communicate. For example, people with low self-esteem tend to rely on covert activities, like asking third parties for information, when they think their romantic relationships are deteriorating (Chory-Assad & Booth-Butterfield, 2001). Likewise, people who believe their self-esteem is threatened are more likely to cope with feeling jealous by covertly manipulating or avoiding their romantic partner (Guerrero & Afifi, 1998). Self-esteem also influences how people communicate at work. In particular, new hires with low self-esteem tend to use indirect strategies, such as surveillance, to gather information about the workplace (Teboul, 1995). These studies show how a low self-esteem can discourage you from communicating directly with others, even when a romantic relationship or new job is at stake.

The self is multifaceted. There are a number of sides to our self-concept that reflect the roles and relationships that we have in different aspects of our lives. Take the example of Janine, who attends college on a rowing scholarship. In her role as a student, Janine's academic goals, abilities, and limitations are primary facets of her self-concept. Out on the water, though, Janine's sense of self emphasizes her strength, her connection to her team, and her commitment to hard work. She is also the child of South American immigrants, an art major, and a sorority sister; each of these roles calls upon a different set of personal qualities or facets of her self. Importantly, people with a complex self-concept tend to experience less depression following stressful life events, perhaps because a negative experience is less likely to undermine all of their different facets of self (Constantino, Wilson, Horowitz, & Pinel, 2006).

The different aspects of your self-concept can be more or less compatible or incompatible with each other. Consider, again, the example of Janine. If Janine's priorities as an athlete interfere with her ability to excel as a student or show commitment to her family, those aspects of her self-concept are incompatible. For example, Janine might skip classes to fit in an additional workout or forego holidays with her family because the team is traveling for competition. On the other hand, Janine's devotion to her team, studies, and family might prompt her to tutor a teammate in exchange for a free ride home to visit her family for a weekend. In this case, the different sides to Janine's self-concept complement each other.

The facets of your self-concept are more likely to be compatible or complementary when they reflect shared core values or beliefs. In Janine's case, her sense of self as an athlete, student, and daughter might be unified by a commitment to perform her best at any task; in turn, Janine can use that over-arching value to guide all of her behavior. When the facets of a self-concept are incompatible, however, a person is more likely to experience depression, loneliness, and low self-esteem (Lutz & Ross, 2003). For example, if Janine's aggressiveness as a competitor conflicts with the respect she is expected to communicate to her parents, she might struggle over how to communicate in a particular situation.

Facets of the self are more or less visible. Although some facets of the self are easily recognized by others, there are other facets that we try to keep private or that we might not even be aware of. The Johari Window is a tool for exploring facets of yourself that are more or less visible (see Figure 3.1). Information about yourself that you are aware of and that is visible to others is referred to as your open self. There are also parts of our self that we don't share with other people. Consider the example of someone who is known as a "tough guy," but who also has a sensitive side. Showing his softer side would diminish the public reputation that he's trying to uphold, so it becomes part of his hidden self – the part of the self that he knows about, but is not visible to others. On the other hand, there are some aspects of the self that other people can see in you that you are unable to see in yourself, which is known as the blind self. For example, teachers may see potential in a student that the student has yet to realize. The final facet of self is the

	Information about yourself that is known to you:	Information about yourself that is not known to you:
Information about you that is known by others:	**OPEN SELF** Information about you that you are aware of and that you share with other people	**BLIND SELF** Information about you that other people are aware of, but you don't realize about yourself
Information about you that is not known by others:	**HIDDEN SELF** Information about you that you are aware of, but that you keep secret from other people	**UNKNOWN SELF** Information about you that neither you nor other people are aware of

FIGURE 3.1 The Johari Window

unknown self, which is the part of your self that is unknown to you and invisible to others. Perhaps you and the people you know never realized how tenacious, motivated, and determined you could be until you were faced with a challenging life situation. The Johari Window helps us to become more aware of the parts of our self we already know and to explore aspects of our self that we have yet to realize.

COMMUNICATION IN ACTION 3.1

Exploring Windows on Yourself

Because who you are is an essential part of how you communicate with others, becoming more self-aware can improve your interpersonal communication experiences. Create your own Johari Window by filling in the form that is available on the **companion website** with the information, attitudes, beliefs, feelings, and behaviors that you see in yourself when you look through each window. When you are done, reflect on how self-knowledge that you are less aware of might be shaping your interpersonal communication experiences.

The self is dynamic. Although the self-concept is multi-faceted, only the facet that is relevant at a particular moment is active or operational. As a result, our sense of self is dynamic – it shifts over time and between situations. The information that dominates a person's sense of self at a particular point in time is called the **working self-concept**. Consider how you might present yourself differently if you were creating a profile for Facebook, versus LinkedIn, versus Match.com. In your Facebook profile, you might emphasize the aspects of yourself as sociable, friendly, witty, and fun. Given the professional nature of your LinkedIn profile, you're more likely to emphasize your intelligence, accomplishments, dependability, and motivation. And in a Match.com profile you would be much more aware of the traits that make you a good mate, such as your compassion for others, your romanticism, or your sex appeal. In a similar fashion, your working self-concept brings forth different facets of self as relevant to your circumstances. Movement between selves is as fluid as changing between online profiles, but when a particular self is active, it dominates that moment.

What we are experiencing in a particular moment – both our internal states and external circumstances – determines which self will be active (Markus & Wurf, 1986). Internal states that cue particular facets of self include the thoughts, goals, motivations, and feelings we have at a particular moment that make a particular aspect of the self more salient. External circumstances, such as the social situation, the physical environment, and external demands can also call forth qualities of the self that resonate with your surroundings. Although certain aspects of our self are spontaneously triggered by different internal and external circumstances, it is also possible to consciously activate a particular facet of self. For example, if you feel anxious about meeting your romantic partner's family, you can deliberately think about your strong family values, your polite demeanor, and other traits they are likely to find appealing. Thus, our self-concept at any particular moment is tailored to our circumstances based on our internal states, external circumstances, and our desired self-image.

Sources of Self-Knowledge

When you recognize the various sources that shape your self-concept, you can become more self-aware and less biased in how you see yourself. Consider, for example, your concept of yourself as a friend. Are you a good friend? Are you fun, caring, supportive, or interesting? How do you know? In the paragraphs that follow, we consider four sources of self-knowledge: your own observations of yourself, your social roles, social comparison, and feedback from others (see Figure 3.2).

Your own observations of yourself. Your firsthand experiences of your thoughts and actions are an important source of your self-concept. In fact, nobody knows better than you whether or not you are truthful, how much effort you put into your schoolwork, how willing you are to volunteer for good causes, and whether or not you are sincere in your relationships with others. Based on your own observations, then, you can support a variety of judgments about yourself. Thus, one way to determine what kind of friend you are is to reflect on how you have seen yourself treat your friends over the course of your life.

You can also learn about yourself by observing your specific actions. A **self-reflexive act** is a behavior that gives you insight into your own state of mind. Rather than thinking about how you generally treat friends, for example, you might think about a particular

---

Working Self-Concept
The information that dominates a person's sense of self at a particular moment.

Self-reflexive Act
A behavior that gives you insight into your own state of mind.

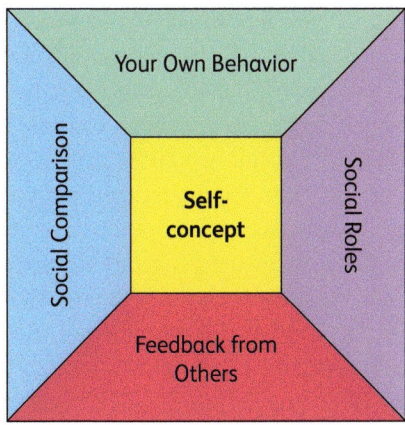

FIGURE 3.2 Sources of self-knowledge

interaction you had with a particular friend. What did you do to mark the friend's last birthday? What did you say when that person asked for help with a class paper? Did you tell the truth or make up an excuse when you didn't want to loan your friend your car? Because the conversations you have reveal your personal qualities, you can reflect on your actions to draw conclusions about yourself.

Your social roles. Another source of your self-concept is the different roles you play in your life. Social roles refer to the positions you hold with respect to other people. Your role as a student is primarily defined by your relationship to a teacher, your role as a child is defined by your relationship to a parent, your role as an employee is defined by your relationship to an employer, and so on. Each of those roles comes with a set of behaviors for performing your character, and enacting different roles allows you to learn different things about yourself.

Consider the self-knowledge you have gained from the different roles you perform. In the role of a student, you have learned the value you place on learning, working hard, and meeting deadlines. If you fill a leadership role at work, you might discover that you are decisive, well-organized, and motivational. And perhaps your relationship with your family has taught you that you are reliable, caring, or independent. One way to recognize how your social roles inform your self-concept is to remember what it was like to anticipate a new role. Before you were a college student, you might have wondered if you could manage the demands of classes, new friends, and a job. Since you had yet to be a college student, your self-concept didn't include the information you needed to answer that question. With a little experience in the role, though, your sense of yourself as a college student develops and may even become a central part of you.

Social Roles
The positions a person holds with respect to other people.

PAUSE & REFLECT

What new things did you discover about yourself when you first became a college student?

Social Comparison
The process of comparing one person's traits and abilities to those of others.

Social comparison. Your self-concept is also the product of **social comparison**, the process of comparing yourself to others to gain insight into your own traits and abilities. On any human quality that varies across people, we look to others to see how we compare. Take the example of a seemingly objective trait like how much you talk. If everybody spoke the same number of words each day, that trait would be as uninformative as noting that someone has two ears or only one head. But because people vary in how much they talk, we develop an impression of ourselves as quiet, average, or talkative. And importantly, our sense of our own talkativeness depends on the people we compare ourselves to. If you come from a family of raucous story tellers, you might think of yourself as just average in talkativeness; on the other hand, if everyone you know is quiet, you could have a much more talkative self-concept.

As you might guess, our comparison points have a lot of influence on our self-concept. Whether you think you are smart, ambitious, generous, kind, or talented all depend on the traits of the people you compare yourself to. And not surprisingly, perhaps, our social comparisons are subject to bias. In general, people prefer to compare themselves to others of the same gender and age (Knobloch-Westerwick & Hastall, 2006). In addition, we tend to compare ourselves to less talented or accomplished people when our self-esteem has been recently threatened (Beauregard & Dunning, 1998). And what if we encounter someone who clearly outranks us on some quality? We exaggerate their accomplishments as extraordinary, amazing, or genius, so that our own less fabulous performance still looks good (Alicke, LoSchiavo, Zerbst, & Zhang, 1997). Although it is clear that the process is far from objective, social comparison provides us insight into ourselves, relative to other people in our lives.

PAUSE & REFLECT

To whom do you compare yourself when you evaluate your own academic ability? Would your self-perceptions change if you picked different people to compare yourself to?

Generalized Other
A mental representation of the combined viewpoints of all other people.

Feedback from others. Finally, other people shape our sense of self by the messages and feedback they communicate to us. The knowledge you gain about yourself can come from specific people, such as when you get information about how attractive you are from the comments that your friends or family make about your appearance. In addition, you come to know about yourself by thinking about how other people, in general, perceive you. In the case of your appearance, your self-perceptions are probably influenced by how attractive you think you are to people, in general. This knowledge isn't based on a specific conversation, but rather on the messages you have received from a variety of people over the course of your life. This point of view is called the **generalized other** because it is a mental composite of other people that you can use to appraise yourself.

Although the feedback provided by others can give us insights into ourselves, this process is also subject to the following biases (Kenny, 1994):

FIGURE 3.3 The Stepmother consulting the Mirror in the film *Snow White and the Huntsman*

- We place a higher value on information from people who are close to us.
- We are more attentive to the perceptions of others when we are experiencing changes in our lives and uncertainty about our selves.
- We overestimate how much different people agree in their perceptions of us.
- We base our self-concept more on what we believe other people think about us, than how they actually perceive us.

Despite these distortions, our self-perceptions are strengthened by the belief that they are shared by others. To continue the earlier example, no matter how attractive you perceive yourself to be, you'll have more confidence in your looks if you believe that other people find you attractive. Thus, the feedback we receive from others has an important impact on our self-concept.

Putting Theory into Practice: Cultivating Qualities You Value

Everyone's self-concept is unique, but we can make some generalizations about how the self operates. With this understanding of the nature and sources of self-knowledge, we can consider strategies for enhancing your self-concept.

Seek out situations that activate important facets of yourself. Keep in mind that only the facets of your self-concept that are relevant to your current internal and external circumstances are operating at any one moment in time. In fact, if you don't draw upon a facet of yourself, that part of you will become a less prominent part of your self-knowledge. In contrast, the working self-concepts that you use most often will come to dominate your sense of self. With this in mind, you can change or enhance your self-concept by seeking out situations where the working self-concept you have is one that you value.

Identify qualities of yourself that you value, but that you don't draw upon very often. Then, try to think of specific situations that would pull that part of you into your working self-concept. When Jen was in high school she was an accomplished actress and competitive debater. When she was in graduate school, she found that the overwhelming amount of time spent on school work and research obscured her sense of self as a dramatic performer. In an effort to seek balance in her life and restore a central part of her self-concept, Jen volunteered to coach a competitive speech and debate team at a local high school. This activity helped Jen to integrate aspects of her self as a performer that had been lost in light of her new role as a scholar.

Behave in ways that reflect who you want to be. One powerful source of information about yourself is your own behavior, so you might want to avoid behaviors that are inconsistent with the person you want to be. One way to take control of your self-concept is to set goals for yourself, and try to behave in ways that support that view of yourself. If you want to see yourself as more honest, moral, caring, or fun, the answer may be as simple as remembering to behave in those ways. Eventually, your patterns of behavior will support the self-concept you want to have.

COMMUNICATION IN ACTION 3.2

Finding Your Ideal Self

One way to enhance your self-concept is to identify the qualities you think you actually have and compare them to qualities that you consider ideal. You can download a form on the **companion website** that will help you reflect on how you typically communicate and how you would ideally communicate in a variety of situations. A discrepancy between the two columns identifies an area where you might change your communication to cultivate a self-concept you value.

Enhance your self-esteem. Recall that self-esteem refers to how you evaluate your self-worth. On any given day, you may encounter situations that make you feel good about yourself and those that make you feel not so good about yourself. Your experiences can have a positive or a negative impact on your self-esteem depending on how you respond to them. Consider the following suggestions for improving your self-esteem and avoiding experiences that threaten it.

■   *Take stock of your strengths and weaknesses*. Make a list of all the things you do well and not so well. When you find yourself feeling down about one of your personal traits, skills, or characteristics, remember all of the positive aspects about yourself and give yourself some credit.
■   *Change self-directed language and labels*. Don't adopt negative labels, like fat, stupid, or lazy, as part of your self-concept. Just as you probably wouldn't tolerate someone else saying such things about you, avoid being so negative about yourself.
■   *Survey your environment*. Consider whether any of your friends, family members, or co-workers makes you feel bad about yourself. Find ways to distance yourself from people who diminish your self-esteem or resolve not to let them have a negative effect on you.
■   *Act confidently*. Even if you don't feel strong, happy, or confident, behave in ways that

make it seem like you do. If you act like a confident and valuable individual, people will begin to respond to you as someone who embodies those traits; in turn, positive reinforcement from others will help you to see yourself as a confident person.

IDENTITY: THE COMMUNICATED SELF

When we communicate with another person, the messages that we create reveal our self-concept and make it visible to others. Imagine how your communication behaviors might change if you had to pretend to be someone else – your best friend, a co-worker, or your parent – for one day of your life. How would this role affect the way you dress and walk, your gestures and expressions, the amount and way that you laugh, what you say, and how you speak? **Identity** is the image of yourself that is embodied in communication. Just as you can think of unique communication behaviors that would allow you to assume the identity of someone else, you have ways of communicating that embody your own self-concept. In this section of the chapter, we will explore the nature of identity and how it is intertwined with interpersonal communication.

Identity
The image of a person that is embodied in communication.

Creating Identity

How do people around you know whether you are assertive, agreeable, shy, or sarcastic? How do they come to know your feelings about topics like sports, animals, or movies? And how do they figure out your political values, your commitment to religion, or your thoughts about having children? Interpersonal communication is a powerful tool that allows us to present ourselves to others; the way we do so, in effect, becomes our identity.

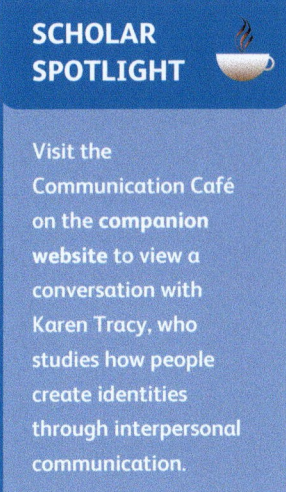

SCHOLAR SPOTLIGHT

Visit the Communication Café on the **companion website** to view a conversation with Karen Tracy, who studies how people create identities through interpersonal communication.

> ### PAUSE & REFLECT
>
> What are some of the communication behaviors someone else would have to adopt if they assumed your identity for a day?

One way that we present ourselves to others is **self-disclosure**, which involves explicitly sharing personal information with another person. When you tell a new acquaintance where you are from, what you are studying in college, and what you do for fun, you are painting a picture of your identity. Likewise, the more private information you share with a friend – your hopes for the future, your concerns about your family, or past behaviors you regret – influence how that friend sees you. If you have a Facebook or Twitter account, every status update and each tweet that you post is a disclosure that provides information about who you are, what you value, how you're feeling, and where you're going. As you'll learn in Chapter 9, self-disclosure is a key part of developing close relationships. More generally, disclosing information about yourself is a direct way in which you represent your identity through interpersonal communication.

Self-disclosure
Explicitly sharing personal information with another person.

We also create our identity more indirectly through the topics we discuss and the qualities we display when we communicate with others. As an example, consider how interactions in a work setting express our traits and values. One study, which involved a close analysis of interactions between co-workers, concluded that people use personal stories to showcase traits or qualities that might otherwise be unexpressed at work (Holmes, 2005). Imagine you had a co-worker who came in every Monday morning with tales of her weekend get-away to go rock climbing, mountain biking, or parasailing. From these stories you might infer that she is an adventurous and athletic risk-taker who enjoys the outdoors and likes to brag about her accomplishments. Similarly, a co-worker who is always telling animated stories about his trouble-maker of a daughter and the schemes he devises to catch her red-handed would convey an image of a family man who has a sense of humor about his daughter's shenanigans and is motivated to stay involved in his daughter's life. Thus, sometimes you come to infer qualities about an individual based on what their stories imply about them, rather than the explicit information they share about themselves.

When you consider how communication behaviors besides self-disclosure reveal your self-concept, you can see that any opportunity to communicate is an opportunity to create your identity. For example, the holiday letters that people send to their friends and relatives paint a picture of accomplishments, positive qualities, and promising futures (Banks, Louie, & Einerson, 2000). In the context of support groups, participants tell stories that invite others to validate their experiences and point of view (Hsieh, 2004). Even when we're not using words, we express our identities through the belongings we display, such as the posters, trophies, photos, and knick knacks that adolescents use to decorate their bedrooms (Brown, Dykers, Steele, & White, 1994).

PAUSE & REFLECT

What do your personal stories, room decorations, Facebook page, and voicemail recording say about you?

Importantly, interpersonal interaction isn't just a source of information about the self, and nor is it simply a portrayal of the self; rather, it is the venue in which identities are created for self and others. Consider how you create your identity when you meet someone new – let's imagine that someone has just moved in next door to you. When you see your new neighbor moving in, you have options for what you might do. You could spy from behind the curtain, offer a smile and wave, take over a note with your phone number, offer to help with the boxes, or order take-out meals to share. What you do in this moment defines who you are in this moment – someone who is a bit shy, friendly but busy, helpful, or outgoing. As you get to know this neighbor, you will also have opportunities to engage in self-disclosure. The details you share about your background, interests, likes and dislikes are the parts of your self-concept made visible as you communicate. In this way, through the self-knowledge that you share with your neighbor and the way that you do so, you create your identity.

COMMUNICATION IN ACTION 3.3

Creating an Online Identity

Online communities like Facebook, LinkedIn, and Twitter have created new outlets for people to express and experiment with their personal identity. Choose three people you know who have a webpage on one of these virtual communities and analyze the content on their page as an expression of their personal identity. How do these three individuals reflect their personal identity through the photos they display, the groups they are affiliated with, and the information they provide? Which aspects of these people's identities are emphasized on their webpage? Is each person's online representation of himself or herself consistent with how he or she expresses their identity in face-to-face communication?

Layers of Identity

Just as your self-knowledge is multi-faceted, your identity has multiple layers. Communication scholar Michael Hecht suggests that a person's identity has four layers or frames (Hecht, 1993; Hecht, Warren, Jung, & Krieger, 2005). In Hecht's view, our identity is like the image that emerges when photographic images are projected on top of each other; each photo makes a unique contribution to the overall picture, and the final image is a composite of all the individual sheets.

The **personal layer of identity** refers to the perceptions you have about yourself that you communicate to others. This layer encompasses your self-concept, because it includes your perceptions of yourself, and it focuses on the self-knowledge that you display to others through communication. This identity is communicated to others not only by what you say, but also through the topics you choose to discuss and the way you talk about them. If you like to cook, for example, you would probably jump right into conversations about cooking and speak with confidence about how to prepare certain dishes; these actions communicate your identity as a good cook even if you don't explicitly claim that you are. When the conversation turns to topics that are less relevant to your personal traits, you would communicate that these skills are not part of your identity by saying less, being less assertive, and perhaps mentioning your lack of expertise. In these ways, the topics you discuss, the way you talk about them, and your specific words reveal information about who you are as a person.

Personal Layer of Identity
The perceptions people have about themselves that they communicate to others.

The **enactment layer of identity** refers to the qualities we reveal in the verbal and nonverbal style of our communication. Are you soft-spoken or loud? Do you tend to be polite or blunt? Do you use a lot of slang or speak more formally? How does your accent or dialect reflect the places you have lived? These features of communication don't involve what you say, but rather how you say it; in other words, your style of communicating reveals to others whether you are introverted, well-mannered, and a Southerner or extroverted, hip, and from the West Coast. In fact, a study of language used in email messages found that women who value their femininity create messages that are longer and more emotionally charged than women for whom femininity is less important (Palomares, 2004). This study shows the subtle ways that a woman's communication behavior enacts her gender identity.

Enactment Layer of Identity
The characteristics of the self that are revealed through a person's verbal and nonverbal style of communication.

FIGURE 3.4 Enacting identity

Source: © Randy Glasbergen / glasbergen.com.

"If I want to impress a woman online, what font should I use? Aristocrat Bold so she'll think I'm rich or Comic Sans so she'll think I'm funny?"

Relational Layer of Identity
Characteristics of the self that are related to relationships with other people.

The **relational layer of identity** includes the various ways in which our personal relationships shape our identities. Our relational partners can either foster or thwart the identities we wish to present. For example, your efforts to present yourself as highly qualified for your job are doomed to fail if your colleagues already think you're incompetent. In addition, your relationships are where you can perform your roles as friend, teammate, spouse, or parent. Conversely, if you aren't involved in a particular type of relationship, you don't have an opportunity to express that identity. Finally, a relationship itself can have an identity. Roommates, couples, fraternity brothers, and best friends are all examples of relationships where the participants share in the relational identity.

Communal Layer of Identity
Characteristics of the self that are related to a person's group memberships.

The final layer, the **communal layer of identity**, captures how people's identities are embedded in their group memberships. Each of us is connected to a variety of groups – cultural groups, ethnic groups, neighborhoods, professional organizations, and/or social clubs. The shared experiences, group history, and the qualities that define the group we belong to become part of our identity. This identity is also embedded in our communication behavior. For example, each branch of the United States military has their own symbolic colors, slogans, songs, or rituals that are representative of significant moments and alliances that define the group's history. Our identity is also shaped by public images of the groups we belong to. Depictions of firefighters as heroes, for example, both honor people in this line of work and burden them with high expectations (Tracy & Scott, 2006).

COMMUNICATION IN ACTION 3.4

Marketing Yourself

Take a moment to write a personal ad about yourself. Although this might be something you would never actually submit to a newspaper or an online dating service, try to create an ad that you think would attract the kind of person you would like to date. Then, analyze your personal ad in terms of the four layers of identity. You can use the form on the **companion website** to guide your analysis. After analyzing your ad, consider how your ad would have been different if you had specifically focused on a single layer of your identity. What differences might there be in the kinds of dating partners attracted by ads that focus on each layer of identity?

INSIDE COMMUNICATION RESEARCH

Studying Communication and Relational Identity

Jordan Soliz and Jake Harwood (2006) studied the role of communication in creating relationships between college students and their grandparents. These scholars noted that the relationships between young adults living on their own and grandparents don't involve strong structural bonds, like sharing a family home; therefore, interpersonal communication might be the main tool through which grandparents and adult grandchildren create a relational identity. In particular, Soliz and Harwood argued that college students can think about their grandparent in two very different ways: as a member of their family or as an elderly person (rather than a family member). The researchers predicted that characteristics of interpersonal communication between grandparents and grandchildren influence whether they create a shared family identity or focus on the age differences that separate them as individuals.

To test their thinking, the researchers surveyed 369 university students about their relationships with their grandparents. The participants were asked to describe the grandparents with whom they had contact in their lives. For each grandparent that was listed, the participants completed a questionnaire about the grandparent and their relationship with him or her. Some of the questions that were asked of participants included whether or not they could turn to their grandparents for advice, how much they or their grandparents would express their feelings to one another, and how much the grandparent related to the grandchild on his/her level.

The study's results showed important links between interpersonal communication experiences and the college students' relational identity. In particular, young adults were more likely to have a grandchild–grandparent family identity when their grandparents disclosed personal information about themselves and when grandparents showed support for the grandchild's interests and feelings. People who were encouraged by their parents to interact with grandparents also had a stronger family identity. In contrast, the study revealed people were more likely to think about their grandparent as an elderly person, rather than a family member, when interpersonal interactions were impersonal, when grandparents or grandchildren patronized or talked down to one another, or when a grandparent suffered from poor health.

This study reveals how interpersonal communication allows some people to create a relational identity that includes their bond with a grandparent. Although grandparents are both family members and older individuals, we come to see them more as one or the other based on our communication experiences. Communication that is more personal, provides social support, and reveals private information about one's self contributes to a bond between grandparents and grandchildren that affects their relational layer of identity.

THINK ABOUT IT

1. This study focused on the grandchildren's perceptions of their family identity. How might the results be similar or different if the researchers had surveyed grandparents instead?
2. This study found that young adults were less likely to have a shared family identity with a grandparent in poor health. In what other ways do the personal characteristics of members of your family (for example, their gender, where they live, or their personality) make it more or less difficult for you to communicate in ways that build a shared relational identity?

Ethnic Identity

The characteristics of self that reflect a person's shared heritage with a particular racial, cultural, national, or tribal group.

We can see the four layers of identity at work in the example of **ethnic identity**, which arises from the perception that you share a heritage with a particular racial, cultural, national, or tribal group. A person's ethnic group is part of the communal layer of identity because it refers to people with whom an individual shares an ethnic identity (Hecht et al., 2005). Ethnicity, in contrast, exists within the personal layer of identity because it focuses on the degree to which membership in an ethnic group is personally important. Our ethnic identity may also be revealed in our style of communication (i.e., the enactment layer) or in the kinds of relationships we want to have (i.e., the relational layer). As summarized in Table 3.1, your ethnic identity spans the four layers of identity.

Because your ethnic identity encompasses the personal, enactment, relational, and communal layers of your identity, it influences many aspects of your life. One survey, for example, found that some African Americans identify their ethnic group as African American, whereas others self-identify as Black; this subtle difference in the communal layer of identity was associated with political values, such that people who self-identified as African American had stronger attitudes about politics (Larkey & Hecht, 1995). That same study also found that a person's ethnic identity affects their satisfaction with interethnic interactions. In particular, European Americans who are strongly attached to their ethnic heritage as German, Irish, Scandinavian, etc., tend to be less satisfied with interethnic interactions; in contrast, African Americans with a strong ethnic identity find communication with other ethnic groups more enjoyable. Ethnic identity has even been linked to drug use among middle-school children. In particular, ethnic pride is associated with less drug use among Mexican Americans and African Americans, but it is associated with more drug use among European Americans (Marsiglia, Kulis, & Hecht, 2001; Miller-Day & Barnett, 2004).

Given the relationships among the layers of ethnic identity, managing diverse ethnic identities can be challenging. What happens when you identify with two different groups? If one ethnic identity is more physically apparent, communication partners are likely to ignore the less visible ethnic identity. A survey of multiracial Japanese European Americans showed that people identify more with the ethnic group that they physically resemble, but they also experience feelings of exclusion from their less obvious ethnic group (Ahnallen, Suyemoto, & Carter, 2006). Another study focused on Israeli adolescents with European mothers and Arab fathers – because their parents were not Israeli,

TABLE 3.1 The layers of ethnic identity

Layers of identity	Ethnic identity
Personal Layer	Ethnicity, or the degree to which membership in the ethnic group is personally important
Enactment Layer	The non-verbal and verbal cues, such as appearance, clothing, or dialect, that reflect ethnic group membership
Relational Layer	The kinds of relationships valued within the ethnic group, and the ways members of the group relate to each other in terms of status or friendship
Communal Layer	The ethnic groups that a person belongs to

FIGURE 3.5 People at Sardar Market at Girdikot, Jodhpur, Rajasthan, Northern India

Source: Photo by Tim Graham/Getty Images.

and there was not a well-formed European-Arab community, these teens were forced to juggle separate European and Arab identities (Abu-Rayya, 2006).

PAUSE & REFLECT

How does your own ethnic group and ethnicity affect your interpersonal communication experiences?

Identity Gaps

Although we have described the layers of identity separately, they are intertwined within interpersonal communication. In other words, our personal, enactment, relational, and communal qualities are all relevant when we interact with other people. As an example, consider how the four layers of identity are connected for members of an Amish community. An Amish person's communal identity includes membership in a cultural group that has distinct social customs, such as refraining from the use of electronics. Those communal norms affect the community members' personal values, such that they embrace a traditional, agricultural life-style. These communal and personal identities shape each person's relational layer of identity by discouraging close relationships with people outside the community and encouraging strong ties with extended family. And the communal, personal, and relational identities dictate people's style of communication, including how they dress, the topics they are comfortable discussing, and to whom they convey respect, authority, or affection. The relationships among the layers of identity are captured by the word **interpenetration**, which refers to how the layers of identity are connected to each other.

    The interpenetrated layers of identity can either complement or contradict one another. When the groups you belong to endorse the relationships you want to have

Interpenetration
A characterization of the layers of identity that captures how they are interconnected or permeate each other.

Identity Gaps

Jung and Hecht (2004a) developed a scale to measure gaps between college students' personal layer of identity and enacted layer of identity, in other words, discrepancies in how people see themselves and present themselves to others. To gain insight into any gaps between the personal and enacted layers of your own identity, visit the **companion website** to complete their measure of identity gaps. As you reflect on items in the scale, can you identify strategies that might help you to reduce the gap between the person you think you really are and the identity you enact for others?

Identity gap

A mismatch in the qualities associated with two or more layers of identity.

FIGURE 3.6 The four interpenetrated layers of identity

and when your communication style is consistent with your self-perceptions, the layers of your identity form a coherent network (Figure 3.6). Sometimes, however, the layers of identity might conflict with one other. Consider the case of Gwen, who moved in with her parents after her divorce so that she could live near her new job. Gwen's personal layer of identity includes her sense of competence and authority as she performs her management duties at work, but her relational layer of identity includes her feelings of failure about her marriage, and feelings of awkwardness about her renewed role as a daughter in her parents' home. When the different layers of identity don't match, an **identity gap** is present (Jung & Hecht, 2004a).

Although some disagreement across layers of your identity is inevitable, large identity gaps can have profound consequences. In one study, Korean Americans living in New York City completed a questionnaire about their experiences of depression and any differences between how they see themselves (the personal layer of identity) and how they communicate with other people (the enactment layer of identity); the results showed that people with bigger identity gaps reported more symptoms of depression (Jung & Hecht, 2004a). Another study found that college students who perceived gaps between their personal and enactment layers of identity were less satisfied with their interpersonal interactions, felt misunderstood by others, and saw their communication experiences as inappropriate and ineffective (Jung & Hecht, 2004b). These studies reveal how experiencing identity gaps can affect how you feel about both yourself and your interactions with others.

Putting Theory into Practice: Being True to Yourself

As we have seen, communication is the tool you use to represent yourself to other people. Because your actions define you as a person, you should take care to communicate in ways that reflect and create an accurate image of who you are.

Communicate with integrity. Communicating with integrity involves being honest and authentic in your interactions with others. Sometimes, it may seem like there are benefits to misrepresenting yourself to others – perhaps exaggerating your qualifications will give you the advantage on the job market, pretending to be confused might encourage a professor's sympathy, or playing hard to get might increase a romantic partner's interest. When you communicate in ways that convey a false identity, though, you can suffer serious consequences. Claiming skills you do not have can get you fired, rather than the training you need; your professor might not mention an internship opportunity to a student who is already overwhelmed; and your dating partner might decide to find someone more interested in a relationship.

As a case in point, Denise recalls a former student who suggested that it was okay to express racist attitudes when it served a purpose; in particular, he said you could avoid jury duty by making prejudiced comments about the defendant's ethnic group. Denise cautioned him against both avoiding his civic duty and failing to recognize the power of an expressed identity. Expressing racism is to create yourself as a racist. Taking advantage of the history of racism in the United States for personal benefit is, in fact, being racist. Giving voice to racist attitudes, even if you claim not to share them, might reinforce someone else's racist opinions. Because the identities you create take on a life of their own, make a point of creating identities you believe in.

Reduce your identity gaps. When the layers of your identity conflict with each other, interpersonal communication can be less satisfying and you might feel worse about yourself. On the other hand, you can improve your well-being if you can reduce your identity gaps. Consider again the example of Gwen, who perceives a gap between her personal layer of identity as a competent office manager and her relational layer of identity as a daughter living with her parents again. Gwen can reduce this gap by bringing the layers of her identity into alignment with the personal qualities that she feels good about. To avoid feeling like a child in her parents' home, she can change her relational layer of identity by paying her parents rent or contributing to the household. She can also make changes in her enactment and communal layers of identity by getting up early, dressing more professionally, and offering to help her parents organize their retirement savings. Making these changes would align her various layers of identity with the personal qualities she values.

Find opportunities to represent multiple identities. Taking steps to reduce identity gaps does not mean that you have to abandon diverse identities that you value. You can be a competent, independent, college student and still enjoy and appreciate the comforts of being a child in your parents' home. In fact, being able to express both aspects of your identity can help you to cope with different life circumstances that might require elements of both identities. Because expressing an identity makes it an active part of who you are, seek out situations that allow you to perform the various identities that matter to you.

Opportunities to express multiple identities may be especially important for people who identify with more than one ethnic or cultural group. American Indians in Oklahoma, for example, have life experiences that intersect with both Indian and Anglo-American cultures. A study that involved interviewing members of this community found that Oklahoma Indians felt more connected with both Anglo and Indian cultures when they had relationships with Whites and non-Indians (Kim, Lujan, & Dixon, 1998). That study also showed that people who identified strongly with both cultures were happier and led more fulfilling lives. These findings suggest that you can improve your own well-being by finding opportunities to express identities that are important to you.

IDENTITIES IN TRANSITION

Our self-concept changes with the different circumstances we experience over the course of our life. As a young child, for example, you may have spent most of your time communicating with siblings and parents; as a result, those relationships figured prominently in your identity. As you progressed through middle school and high school, you might have had more conversations with friends than you did with your parents. In adulthood, college, work, and raising your own family require that you express new identities. In this section of the chapter, we consider two life stages that involve a change in people's self-concept: the transition that takes us from child to adult, and the experience of parents when their adult children move out of the family home.

Emerging Adulthood

Emerging Adulthood

The period spanning ages 18–25, when people in our society are less constrained by their families and not yet burdened by adult responsibilities.

Our self-concept evolves throughout our lives, but the changes we experience are especially striking in the period from adolescence to adulthood (around ages 18 to 25) known as **emerging adulthood**. During this time of life, people in our society are often less constrained by their families and not yet burdened by the responsibilities of adulthood (Arnett, 2000). This relative freedom allows emerging adults to explore a variety of identities before settling on the relationships, jobs, and worldviews that will define their adulthood. This is also a tumultuous phase of life. One study found that college students who believe that they haven't reached adulthood engage in more risky behavior, like illegal drug use or drunk driving, and experience more depression than students who consider themselves to be adults (Nelson & Barry, 2005).

As people develop an adult identity, their relational layer is especially likely to change. For example, young college students identify relationships with parents as an area of their life that changes the most when they enter college, such that they have less contact with their parents, but the quality of their relationship improves (Lefkowitz, 2005). Emerging adults also communicate more honestly with their parents, compared to adolescents in high school (Jensen, Arnett, Feldman, & Cauffman, 2004). As people go through emerging adulthood, their relationships with siblings also improve; despite reduced contact, those relationships are warmer, involve more emotional sharing and less conflict, and are less influenced by sibling rivalries (Scharf, Shulman, & Avigad-Spitz, 2005).

PAUSE & REFLECT

In what ways did your identity change – or how has it been changing – between the ages of 18 and 25?

Importantly, emerging adulthood is also a period when sexual identities become solidified. **Sexual identity** is more than sexual orientation; it refers to how you perceive and express your sexual needs, values, and preferences. Communication experiences are an important part of developing a sexual identity. For example, research shows that adolescent males are especially likely to use weblogs to express and explore a gay or bisexual identity (Huffaker & Calvert, 2005). More generally, teens regularly use online chat rooms to express their sexual identity by referring to sexual activities, using sexual language, or adopting a sexualized screen-name (Subrahmanyam, Smahel, & Greenfield, 2006). Likewise, sexual behavior during this phase of life can affect emerging identities. For example, young women who demonstrate an appetite for sexual contact can be labeled "bad girls," whereas girls who maintain their virginity and refrain from sexual behavior are deemed "good girls" (Ashcraft, 2006). In fact, a significant portion of an adolescent girl's identity is related to whether she has saved her virginity, lost her virginity, and whether or not people know about her sexual status (Fine 1992).

Expressions of a sexual identity and people's responses to those messages have important consequences. For example, talking about sexual identity can help youths solidify perceptions of their self-concept. In particular, a study of lesbian, gay, and bisexual youths found that people who had expressed their sexual identity to another person had more stable identities over a one-year period (Rosario, Schrimshaw, Hunter, & Braun, 2006). Interpersonal interactions about sexual identity can also affect how people feel about themselves. In one study, for example, lesbians kept diaries for two weeks in which they noted if they had any interpersonal communication experiences that devalued their sexual identity; they also recorded how they felt on each day. The results of the study showed that the women tended to feel more depressed and report lower self-esteem on the days when they experienced negative interactions about their sexual identity (Beals & Peplau, 2005). These studies illustrate how interpersonal communication experiences impact both our sexual identity and how we feel about it.

Emerging Adulthood

Emerging adulthood is the label given to the stage of life between around 18 and 25 years of age, but people vary in terms of when they consider themselves an adult. Visit the **companion website** to take a questionnaire that assesses the extent to which a person has met specific criteria for adulthood (Nelson & Barry, 2005). Based on this measure, can you identify ways in which you could express a more mature identity?

Sexual Identity

How a person perceives and expresses sexual needs, values, and preferences.

FIGURE 3.7 Friends hanging out in a park

Source: Getty Images.

The Empty Nest

When you learned to drive a car, your parent stopped being your chauffeur; when you turned 18, your parent stopped being your legal guardian; and when you moved out of your parent's home, your parent stopped being your landlord. As parents see their children transition into adulthood, they must create a new identity that includes a different relationship with their children and a different view of themselves.

One task for the parents of emerging adults is to "let go" of their maturing children, and this process often begins before a child leaves home. In one study, parents of high school seniors were interviewed about their child's upcoming transition to college (Karp, Holmstrom, & Gray, 2004). Parents anticipated their child's departure from the household with mixed emotions, including a sense of profound loss, excitement about their child's future, and happiness at the thought of having more personal freedom. That study also showed the strategies that some families used to make this transition easier. For example, parents and children worked together to decide how far from home the child would move, so that the emerging adult would have sufficient independence but still be close enough to get help and support from the family. In addition, families would often agree to keep the child's bedroom intact, which communicates that the child has a presence in the home. These strategies can help to make the transition to an empty nest more gradual and give parents time to adjust to their new identity.

PAUSE & REFLECT

How did you and your parents address the changes in your lives once you graduated from high school? Did you explicitly take steps to ease that transition by communicating within your family or did your family tend to play it by ear?

Although emptying the nest isn't a universally positive experience, it has several upsides. After the last child moves out, mothers are often happier and experience fewer daily hassles, especially if they don't have a reason to worry about their children (Dennerstein, Dudley, & Guthrie, 2002). Women with an empty nest also perceive their marriages as more equitable than women who still have children living in the home (Feeney, Peterson, & Noller, 1994). In fact, parents tend to be happier with their lives after children move out, provided that they can communicate frequently with their children (White & Edwards, 1990). When you talk with your parents after you have moved out of their home, you give them a chance to perform their parental identity, without burdening them with the tasks they juggled when you were younger.

For parents who don't have other important facets to their identity, the period after children move out can be more difficult. Relative to people with a strong sense of self, people with a less hardy self-concept need to use more coping strategies to deal with the distress they feel when their children leave the home (Crowley, Hayslip, & Hobdy, 2003). Some married couples or domestic partners might also find that they don't want to maintain their relationship once the family structure has changed (Arp, Arp, Stanley,

Markman, & Blumberg, 2000). For some parents, launching children from their home might be taken as a sign of their own progression toward old age (Karp et al., 2004). Although emptying the family nest can be the beginning of an exciting life stage, it can also spark less desirable changes in a person's identity.

REAL WORDS

TRANSITIONING TO THE EMPTY NEST

The following transcript was taken from a study that Jen conducted with Mary Nagy in which they asked married couples who had recently become empty-nesters to talk with one another about how they were adjusting to this new phase of life. Notice how the couple emphasizes both positive and negative aspects of this phase of life.

HUSBAND: Well, I mean, it's definitely become a quieter house, so we have a chance to interact more without being interrupted. That's good for our relationship. Don't you think?

WIFE: Yeah and it's just calmer. There's a lot less things to do during the week. You know, with the kids home, it was a lot, we always were running to activities and we're not doing that now as much.

HUSBAND: Well, we cook together. Right? It seems like whatever we do, we do more together than we did before. Before you would be doing something and I would be doing something separately so that we could accomplish it all in one day. Now it seems like we can accomplish more of it easier. You know because we don't have those interruptions that we used to have.

WIFE: Well, it's also a little stressful though because you kinda feel like you're getting older. We're already where our kids are in college and they've left our house. It's gone a little bit too quickly. I felt like we blinked our eyes and we're in a whole new stage of our life which is a little bit scary.

HUSBAND: That's true. I did wonder how it was going to be prior to it happening, like, what's it going to be like when the kids are out of the house, and, uhh, what do you do with yourself? But I know we're busy. We're still busy. It just seems to be, umm, like we're able to be together more than before.

WIFE: When it's all said and done, I mean, I don't really . . . It doesn't really feel like we should be empty nesters already.

HUSBAND: That's true. Like that we're there! It's one big blur.

Putting Theory into Practice: Supporting Identity Changes

In this section of the chapter, you learned about the changes to identity that occur during emerging adulthood and the pros and cons of emptying the family nest. By understanding the role of interpersonal communication, you can take steps to support both your own unique identity and the changing identities presented to you by others.

Confide in others as your identity changes. The changes we go through during the transition from adolescent to adult can be staggering. We become legally recognized as adults who can join the military, vote on election days, or go to prison. We may be expected to work full time, support ourselves financially, and take care of a family. It can be daunting when the question "What will you be when you grow up?" demands an answer. As you go through this transition, or changes in identity that you may face in the future, keep in mind that communicating with others is a key step is exploring new identities.

Through conversations with your friends, roommates, or co-workers, you might discover that they too are struggling with the new identities they have to adopt as they enter adulthood. Talking about these transitions can help you clarify your thoughts and make you feel less alone during this time. By sharing your feelings and gathering ideas from your peers, you might gain innovative perspectives on how to manage the shift in your identity. Even though you might feel compelled to make decisions about your new identity as an independent adult, consulting your parents, a favorite aunt or uncle, or a respected religious leader can provide valuable insight as to how you should enact your identity as an emerging adult. Maybe your father has some experience and advice that can help you navigate the transition from partier to professional. An older sibling might suggest ways to assert your independence from your parents. Communicating about your changing identity during emerging adulthood can contribute to a smoother transition.

Embrace diverse identities. Take stock of how your actions might constrain the identities that others present to you. For example, do you automatically assume that people you meet are heterosexual? If so, you create a real dilemma for gay, lesbian, bisexual, and trans-gendered people that you encounter. On one hand, your communication partner can let the misperception go uncorrected, but that involves presenting him or herself as heterosexual. As an alternative, your new acquaintance can clarify his or her sexuality, but personal topics like this are often avoided when we meet someone new. Rather than jump to conclusions, give people the opportunity to perform their identity for you. When you do, you can avoid forcing people to correct your mistakes and you can have more fulfilling communication experiences.

It can be hard to see how your own communication practices can marginalize someone else's identity. For example, consider the wedding ceremony as it is often celebrated in the United States. There is a bride and a groom, female and male attendants to support the couple, and a ceremonial tossing of the bouquet and garter to identify the next man and woman who will be married. Would you think that someone who is not heterosexual would feel unwelcome in this setting? Interviews with gay, lesbian, bisexual, and trans-gendered people suggest that the answer is yes (Oswald, 2002). In particular, non-heterosexual identities are marginalized by a ritual in which each person's role is defined by his or her gender, relationship to the bride and groom, and assumed heterosexuality. And as non-heterosexuals meet other guests, they are confronted with the dilemma of either clarifying their sexuality or allowing the error to persist. Even openly gay people attending weddings with their partner can feel frustrated in a context that makes their own sexuality seem out of place.

Support parents as they empty their nest. Interpersonal communication provides you with the tools you need to help your own parents, or other people you know, embrace their new identity as they launch their children into the world. Changes to the family during this stage of life can give rise to new identities, selves, and personal goals that did not previously exist. Everyone will find those changes easier to manage if you talk about them before they occur, discuss how close to each other you will live and how often you will talk, and decide whether you will maintain space for the adult child in the family home.

COMMUNICATION IN ACTION 3.5

Creating Space for Parental Identities

Although you don't need your parents in the same way that you did when you were younger, you can still create opportunities for them to express and enjoy their identity as parents. Visit the **companion website** to complete a table that will help you identify some of the ways your parents were able to express their identity as parents when you were younger and to think of situations that would allow your parents to express those same qualities in different ways now that you are older.

SUMMARY

Every interaction that you have involves the person you believe you are and the image you present to others. As you have seen, the self-concept is not a simple entity. How we see ourselves is inherently subjective, there are many facets to our self-concept, and our self-concept changes based on our present internal and external circumstances. You also learned that interpersonal communication is central to the development of self-knowledge. From a lifetime of experience with our own behavior, we can draw inferences about who we are. In addition, the social roles that we fill create opportunities for us to develop the qualities required by those relationships. We also look to the people around us to determine how we compare. Finally, other people shape our sense of self by the messages and feedback they communicate to us. From the wealth of our interpersonal communication experiences, we come to understand who we are.

Whereas the self-concept refers to the knowledge you have about yourself, identity captures the images that you create for others. Interpersonal communication is a performance of your self; in this sense, communication and identity are inherently connected. Like the self-concept, identity has multiple facets. The image you portray is a blend of the personal traits you communicate, your verbal and nonverbal choices, the relationships you have or would like to have, and the social groups that you belong to. Moreover, the different layers of your identity may or may not complement each other. When they don't, identity gaps can lead to less satisfying communication experiences and decreased well-being.

Throughout our life, our identity continues to develop and change. During emerging adulthood, people experience numerous changes across the layers of their identity as they explore the person they will become as an adult. Another time when identities change a lot is when parents see their adult children move out of the family home. Although both of these transitions can mark an exciting time in our lives, it can be challenging to abandon familiar identities and to develop a new view of yourself. An ability to communicate with others and receive identity support is an important part of making these key life transitions.

Your self and identity are a part of every interpersonal interaction that you have. Although your sense of yourself and the image you project are complex and evolving, you are not a passive observer of yourself. As you learned in this chapter, you can take steps to cultivate qualities you value, stay true to yourself, and support both your own unique identity and the diverse identities that you encounter. Consider the ways that you might use interpersonal communication to confront the ethical issues described below and still help yourself and others develop and display a valued sense of self.

ACTIVITIES FOR EXPLORING COMMUNICATION ETHICS

What Would You/Should You Do?

Imagine that you are at a family reunion, and you've been noticing how your cousin talks to his eight-year-old son. Over the course of the day, your cousin has said a number of hurtful things to the boy. When the child was getting his lunch, his dad said, "If you don't eat more than that, you'll always be scrawny." When the kids were choosing teams for a softball game, your cousin told everyone that this son couldn't hit a pitch if his life depended on it. And when the boy fell off the trampoline and starting crying, his father called him a "cry baby." Given what you know about the effects of messages on a person's self-concept, what would you – or should you – do?

Something to Think About

According to youth-suicide.com (http://www.youth-suicide.com/gay-bisexual/), more than half of male youth suicide attempts involve boys who are gay or bisexual. Based on these statistics, some people have called for counseling services in high schools that provide support to homosexually-oriented youths. Other people, however, have argued that the evidence linking sexual identity to suicide is flawed, and that providing support services will encourage youths toward a homosexual life-style (http://www.leaderu.com/jhs/labarbera.html). What are the ethical issues involved in deciding whether to use school resources to support marginalized identities?

Analyze Communication Ethics Yourself

Television shows often draw upon stereotypes of ethnic groups to develop the drama or shape the plot. For example, the HBO hit, *The Sopranos*, developed an image of Italians that emphasized connections to organized crime. Select a television show that portrays a particular ethnic group, and watch a few episodes. As you do so, take note of how that ethnic group is represented to audiences. Based on your analysis, consider the ethical issues involved in media representations of ethnic identities.

KEY WORDS

communal layer of identity	identity gap	self-esteem
emerging adulthood	interpenetration	self-reflexive act
enactment layer of identity	personal layer of identity	sexual identity
ethnic identity	relational layer of identity	social comparison
generalized other	self-concept	social roles
identity	self-disclosure	working self-concept

LEARNING OBJECTIVES

After reading this chapter, you should be able to:

1. Describe the three stages of perception.
2. Define the dimensions of attribution.
3. Define the fundamental attribution error and the actor-observer effect.
4. Describe the patterns of attributions that occur in satisfying versus dissatisfying relationships.
5. Understand how culture, social group, and personal traits influence perception and attribution.
6. Describe the impact of alcohol consumption on perception and sexual risk-taking.
7. Understand how stereotypes affect perception and interpersonal communication.

PUTTING THEORY INTO PRACTICE

In this chapter, you will learn how to:

1. Direct your attention during interpersonal interactions.
2. Distinguish between facts and inference in your interpretation of a situation.
3. Avoid forming an explanation based only on your own point of view.
4. Focus on behaviors, not personalities.
5. Protect relationships you value by making adaptive attributions.
6. Recognize individual differences in perception and attribution.
7. Recognize when your perception is impaired.
8. Combat the formation of stereotypes.

PERCEPTION AND INTERPERSONAL COMMUNICATION

4

98 STAGES OF PERCEPTION

105 ATTRIBUTION: PERCEIVING AND MISPERCEIVING CAUSES

113 FACTORS THAT AFFECT PERCEPTION

120 SUMMARY

122 ACTIVITIES FOR EXPLORING COMMUNICATION ETHICS

122 KEY WORDS

Source: Photo by Stuart Franklin/Getty Images.

In the 2010 PGA championship, Dustin Johnson finished the 18th hole tied for the lead and poised to compete against two of his fellow golfers in a playoff to determine who would win. PGA officials ruled, however, that he had to take two penalty strokes for grounding his golf club (i.e., letting it touch the ground next to the ball) in what was deemed to be a sand trap. The problem was that the sand trap had been severely trampled by spectators, so he didn't realize that his ball had come to rest within an actual sand trap. From his perspective, the ball was just in a sandy patch of dirt so he didn't think the rules about sand traps would apply. The penalty that he incurred knocked him out of the championship playoff round. In the weeks following the PGA championship, blogs and message boards lit up over the controversy. Supporters of Johnson argued that the golf course was not well maintained, that the spectators had damaged the sand trap beyond recognition, and that there was no way he could have known his ball was in a trap. Other golf enthusiasts argued that the rules of play were very clearly defined by the PGA and that players were warned about some of the odd sand traps on this particular course prior to the tournament, so Johnson should have been more careful about making his shot. Each side saw the controversy from a different point of view and felt that their arguments were justified.

Everyone brings their own unique perspective and viewpoint to their communication experiences. Just as Dustin Johnson and the PGA were at odds over whether that patch of dirt his ball landed in was a sand trap or not, communication partners can reach very different conclusions about why a conversation unfolded as it did. In addition, our personal traits influence both what we take away from interpersonal interactions, and what our communication partners might be assuming about us. At the root of all of these experiences is how we perceive and make sense of events in the world around us.

Cognition refers to the mental processes involved in gaining knowledge and comprehension. In other words, your cognition includes all of the thoughts and ideas that you have in your mind. Because our minds are capable of processing countless thoughts at once, we need a process that helps us to organize all of that information in meaningful and useful ways. **Perception** is the process by which a person filters and interprets information to create a meaningful picture of the world. In the context of interpersonal communication, our perceptions shape how we interpret and react to another person's messages (Figure 4.1). While we cannot remove the filter of perception from our interactions with others, we can become more aware of how that filter operates. And understanding perception will allow you to take steps to improve your interpersonal communication. To that end, this chapter examines the stages of perception, how people perceive – and often misperceive – the causes of behavior, and factors that influence perception.

STAGES OF PERCEPTION

We are bombarded by stimuli of all sorts at all times. Consider all of the information that is available to your senses at this very moment. As you read this page, your eyes focus on the black shapes on white paper, while your peripheral

One person performs a communicative action

The partner perceives and interprets the message

Based on perceptions, the partner reacts

FIGURE 4.1 The role of perception in interpersonal communication

Cognition
The mental processes involved in gaining knowledge and comprehension.

Perception
Filtering and interpreting information to create meaning.

vision conveys images of the table top and the room. Your ears are also gathering information, such as the hum of a furnace, people talking in another room, or traffic noise. Likewise, your nose is helping you keep track of smells that may signal danger, as in the case of a fire, or opportunity, as in the case of freshly baked cookies. Even the nerve endings in your skin are busy telling you whether you are warm or cold, whether your shoes fit comfortably, and how your body feels against your chair. As if this information about your environment weren't enough, you also receive internal stimuli in the form of hunger pangs, emotions, fatigue, etc. As this example makes clear, even sitting quietly trying to read your class assignment exposes you to a vast array of stimuli that need to be processed. The stages of perception refer to the sequence of steps we use to sort through all of the information available at a given moment in order to create a useful understanding of the environment.

> ## PAUSE & REFLECT
>
> Make a list of things that you notice around you at this moment. Then, concentrate on each of your senses – what you see, hear, smell, and feel – one at a time, and make a list of anything new that you perceive. How do the two lists compare?

Selection

The first stage of perception is **selection** or directing attention to a subset of the stimuli available to the senses. In your efforts to read these words, you selectively attend to the marks on the page, and you screen out or ignore the feel of the chair against your body, the noises around you, and thoughts about other tasks you have to do. Selection can be guided through conscious control; for example, you might direct your attention to the conversation at the next table in an effort to eavesdrop. More often, however, the selection of stimuli for further processing happens subconsciously. In other words, our brains

Selection
Directing attention to a subset of sensory information.

automatically screen out a huge quantity of information provided by our senses before we even notice it. Notably, our screening mechanisms aren't haphazard; rather, the selection stage of perception is influenced by several factors, including our point of view, the intensity of stimuli, the personal relevance of information, consistency with expectations, and inconsistency with norms.

Point of view. One basic force that shapes what stimuli we attend to is our point of view or the perspective that we have on a situation. Consider for a moment how your physical perspective on a situation influences what you pay attention to. For example, being on a basketball court during a game, on the sidelines, or high up in the stands directs attention to different facets of the game. In the same way, how close we are to another person, whether we are sitting or standing, and the way our bodies are oriented influence what we notice about interpersonal communication partners. Point of view also includes our psychological orientation toward a situation. Consider how differently a manager and a potential employee might view the same job interview. In fact, the development of expertise at a task involves learning to notice different things about a situation; for example, expert chess players see the patterns on a chess board, rather than the location of individual chess pieces (Anderson, 1985).

The intensity of stimuli. The selection stage of perception is also affected by the intensity of stimuli – how strongly various features stand out in our perceptual field. We typically focus on elements that stand out from the background by virtue of their size, color, movement, or closeness to us. Big, bright, moving things that are nearby are especially likely to block us, blind us, or knock us down; therefore, these stimuli are almost always selected for further processing. You may have noticed that the advertisements that appear in the margins on your favorite websites take advantage of intense stimuli by making their ads very colorful and using animation to draw attention. Similarly, conversational partners who make direct eye contact, lean forward, stand closer, and nod their heads command more attention than less active communicators (Anderson, Guerrero, Buller, & Jorgensen, 1998; Kelley & Gorham, 1988).

Personal relevance. A third factor that influences the selection stage of perception is the personal relevance of information to the perceiver. Research has shown that people automatically attend to information that is relevant to the self, such as their name, even when they have been instructed to ignore it (Bargh, 1982). Likewise, our needs or purposes can influence what we focus on in others. For example, the extent to which people notice attractive features in others is related to whether or not they are already dating someone (Simpson, Gangestad, & Lerma, 1990). In this context, what observers notice depends on whether they are sizing up a potential date for themselves. In more general terms, people attend to information that is relevant to them or their goals in a situation and they are less attentive to information that doesn't apply to them. You have probably become quite skilled at identifying junk mail in your inbox because it is typically from a source who is not a personal friend and contains information that is irrelevant to your circumstances. This cognitive process allows you to delete messages that are not important and focus on the ones that have more relevance to you.

Consistency with expectations. Another force that shapes the selection stage of perception is consistency with expectations; in other words, the degree to which a situation is similar to or different from what we anticipated. Generally speaking, people tend to look for and select information that they expect to be present in a situation. On the first day of class with a professor you've heard good things about, you are primed to look for qualities that have earned that favorable reputation; on the other hand, you'll tend to notice more negative attributes about a class that you've heard is a waste of time. Because we always enter interactions with other people with some assumptions about their behavior, expectations are a powerful force shaping interpersonal perception and communication.

Inconsistency with norms. A final factor shaping selection ensures that we notice the unexpected. Inconsistency with norms is the extent to which events violate our standards for behavior. Norm violations occur when behavior falls outside the range of acceptable behavior; in other words, it is inappropriate given the situation (Levine et al., 2000). To continue the earlier example, imagine how distracted you might be if your professor wore a gorilla costume to class (unless of course, the occasion was Halloween). In fact, when teachers violate classroom norms by being incompetent, offensive, or lazy, students spend more time thinking about interactions with that teacher (Berkos, Allen, Kearney, & Plax, 2001). Not surprisingly, then, atypical information is more likely to be noticed and remembered, at least in the short term (Shapiro & Fox, 2002).

The selection stage of perception is the critical step where we determine what information we will and will not consider. As we have seen, the selection of details selected for further processing is influenced by characteristics of the situation and the perceiver. Thus, from the very moment that your brain selects some information and ignores other details, you have started crafting a perception of reality that is unique to you.

Organization

The second stage of perception is **organization**; during this stage, people sort stimuli to clarify which details are closer or further away, above or below each other, or on the same spatial plane. In other words, people arrange information to create a coherent map of features within a situation. As Figure 4.2 reveals, even a drawing can change form depending on which details we assign to the foreground or background. Within the dynamic world of interpersonal interaction, organization includes efforts to sort events into causes and effects, intentions and accidents, patterns and coincidences, etc. In total, then, the organization stage involves assigning roles and relationships to the information we have selected with the ultimate goal of making sense of it.

How we organize information plays a particularly important role as we form impressions about other people. Think for a moment about all of the information you might gather about someone during a first interaction: you know the person's gender and perhaps his or her ethnicity; you observed your partner's communication style; and you have information that the person shared with you, ranging possibly from name and hometown to career and relationship goals (cf. Wyer, Swan, & Gruenfeld, 1995). As you make sense of this information, you must decide which details are most important or relevant to the person's personality. There are several different theories that describe how people organize information about others into a coherent impression (e.g., Anderson, 1981); the basic point is that the weight you place on different details ultimately affects how you view others.

Organization
The process of arranging information into a coherent pattern.

FIGURE 4.2 "The Image Disappears" (Dali, 1938)

The amount of information we have also influences the impressions we form about our communication partners. In general, email and other computer-mediated exchanges are assumed to provide less social information than face-to-face encounters (Walther, Anderson, & Park, 1994). In these contexts, you can still observe your partner's communication style through their tendency to capitalize (a little or A LOT), punctuate excessively (!!!), or use emoticons (☺); and you also receive the information they choose to communicate to you. At the same time, you don't get a lot of details that are visible in a face-to-face conversation – in fact, you may not even be sure about the other person's gender. The effect of this information shortage is that people form less detailed impressions of an online interaction partner, but the judgments that they do make tend to be more extreme (Hancock & Dunham, 2001). For example, you might be deeply moved by a cancer survivor's courage and optimism after participating in an online support group, but you wouldn't have any idea whether she was athletic, friendly, smart, or even tall or short. Not surprisingly, having fewer pieces of information gives greater weight to the information that is available (Lea & Spears, 1995; Spears & Lea, 1994).

Interpretation

Interpretation

The process of assigning meaning to information.

In the final stage of perception, **interpretation**, we assign meaning to the information that we have selected and organized. To do so, we have to add in details and draw conclusions that aren't actually present in the situation. For an example, look at the image in Figure 4.3. If you don't have any prior information, the image can be pretty hard to figure out. On the other hand, if you know it's a picture of a Dalmation, and you are familiar with what Dalmations look like, you can probably make sense of the image quickly. And notice how once you know what the picture is, it is almost impossible for

FIGURE 4.3 Dalmation on a beach

you to go back to perceiving the image as meaningless. By drawing connections between information in the environment and past experiences or knowledge, we are able to make sense of the stimuli that we encounter.

The interpretation stage of perception also includes making sense of past experiences, and we might reach different conclusions than we did at the time those events occurred. More recent experiences, new information, and how we're feeling in the present can all color how we interpret that past. For example, people recount the history of their close relationships more positively or negatively, depending on their current level of happiness with that partner (Bradbury & Fincham, 1990). In fact, a study which asked dating couples to keep diaries over a three-week period showed that ratings of a partner's physical attractiveness go (or stay) up after positive interactions, but decrease after negative interactions (Albada, Knapp, & Theune, 2002). These examples show how the interpretation stage of perception is an ongoing process through which we form and modify our judgments.

PAUSE & REFLECT

Think about a past romantic relationship or friendship that you are no longer in. How did you describe the day you met that person when your relationship was at its best? How would you describe that day now that the relationship has ended?

Putting Theory into Practice: Paying Attention to Perception

As we reflect on the stages of perception depicted in Figure 4.4, we see how perception is affected by characteristics of the perceiver. Although our perceptions are inherently subjective, we can take steps to be more mindful and careful as we make sense of the world around us.

| **Selection** You notice some elements in the situation, but not others | → | **Organization** You arrange the pieces you noticed into a pattern that makes sense to you | → | **Interpretation** Using your personal knowledge and experience, you decide what the pattern means |

FIGURE 4.4 The stages of perception

Direct your attention during interpersonal interactions. Although attending to every sensory input available to us at a given moment is neither desirable nor feasible, we can consciously focus on details that we might otherwise overlook. Just as you might concentrate to hear a nearby conversation, make a point of noticing details in the situation. Consider the following suggestions for focusing your attention during interaction:

- Before a conversation, take stock of your goals and expectations so that you can look for information that both supports and contradicts your needs or assumptions.
- As you're chatting, look around to see what stands out from your communication partner's point of view.
- Make a point of examining details in the background, rather than just those that stand out or grab your attention initially.

By actively directing your attention during your interpersonal interactions, you'll gain a fuller understanding of your communication experiences.

Distinguish between facts and inference in your interpretations of a situation. Facts are the verifiable details within a situation; inferences involve going beyond the verifiable facts and adding in information that may or may not be true. As you communicate with others, it is important that you recognize that your inferences are your own personal conclusions – they are not facts that everyone accepts. And when you make judgments about a situation, double-check what you've based your conclusions on. Have you reached a judgment after considering facts? Or, is your judgment based on other inferences you have made? The goal is to make inferences that are well grounded in facts, and to recognize the difference between the two.

COMMUNICATION IN ACTION 4.1

Forming Impressions of Others

Find a seat at the library, cafeteria, or coffee shop where you can watch people for a while. Choose someone to observe. Using the form provided on the **companion website**, record your perceptions of this person and reflect on the judgments you make about him or her. This exercise will help you realize all of the judgments you make about people, even when they are total strangers, and reflect on where your perceptions come from.

ATTRIBUTION: PERCEIVING AND MISPERCEIVING CAUSES

One inference that people sometimes make as part of the perception process is a judgment of *why* something happened. **Attributions** are explanations that help us to identify what caused certain events or people's behaviors. A person's desire to understand the causes of events they perceive is particularly great when circumstances are unexpected, negative, or both (Weiner, 1985). For example, while you probably wouldn't feel the need to explain why the driver in the next lane is holding a steady course, you would be more motivated to look for causes when that driver swerves into your lane, and you would be even more focused on causes if you have a collision. Thus, attribution occurs during the interpretation stage of perception when people are prompted to draw inferences about the causes of the circumstances around them. In this section of the chapter, you'll learn about the ways that attributions can vary, common attribution biases, and patterns of attribution in close relationships.

Attributions
Explanations for why something happened.

Dimensions of Attribution

You might explain a communication partner's behavior in many different ways; for example, you might interpret an insult from a friend as a sign that he doesn't like you anymore, she's stressed out from work, he thought you were criticizing him, or it was just a joke. To make sense of the many ways we might explain someone's behavior, it is helpful to think about the basic ways in which attributions can differ. One widely accepted view is that the attributions we make for another person's actions vary in terms of three dimensions (Weiner, 1986). These three dimensions are described in the following paragraphs and illustrated in Table 4.1.

Internal or external? One core question we consider when making attributions is whether a person's behavior is caused by something within the person or something in the situation. **Internal attribution** assumes that personal forces or characteristics of an individual are at the root of his or her behavior, whereas an **external attribution** locates the cause of events in environmental forces that exist outside an individual. To continue the earlier example of the car swerving into your lane, an internal attribution for the driver's erratic behavior is that he has poor driving skills; an external attribution would focus on the squirrel that ran in front of his car.

Internal Attribution
Concluding that behaviors are caused by characteristics of the actor.

External Attribution
Concluding that a person's behaviors are caused by the situation.

PAUSE & REFLECT

Consider your perceptions of people who post comments to blogs, discussion boards, or online news sites. How likely are you to assume that the comments posted reflect the poster's personality? Could there be external forces that prompt someone to post a comment in a public online forum?

TABLE 4.1 The dimensions of attribution

Imagine that you're on your way to the book store to meet up with a new acquaintance, Stephen. As you approach the store, you see Stephen in an argument with another man. Why is Stephen behaving this way? Who or what caused the fight? When we consider the three dimensions of attribution in combination, we can see the many different ways that you might explain Stephen's communication behavior. Notice how the internal, controllable, and stable attribution highlights Stephen's personality as the root of his behavior. In contrast, the external, uncontrollable, and unstable cause places the blame on a mistake by the other guy.

	Internal		External	
	Stable	Unstable	Stable	Unstable
Controllable	Stephen enjoys arguing with strangers	Stephen copes with trouble with his girlfriend by arguing with strangers	The store is a gathering place for protesters – arguments are common	When people get stressed out, they come to this place to blow off steam
Uncontrollable	Stephen has a short temper	Stephen is just the kind of guy some people like to argue with	The other guy often starts arguments with people on the street	The other guy mistook Stephen for the man who stole his girlfriend

Controllable or uncontrollable? We also consider whether an action is controllable or uncontrollable. A behavior is seen as controllable if the person could have acted differently; in fact, control often implies that the person performed the action with the intention of producing certain consequences. Conversely, we sometimes see a person's actions as uncontrollable either because the actor could not have behaved differently or did not mean to produce the consequences. To understand the importance of attributions of control, imagine how differently you would react to a car accident if you thought the other driver actively sought to hit your car rather than simply lost control of his vehicle.

Stable or unstable? A third question is whether the causes of a behavior are ongoing or temporary. Stable causes are those that we expect to persist or to be present into the future; unstable causes are assumed to be either temporary or sporadic. When we attribute a behavior to stable causes, it leaves us feeling more in control because we can anticipate actions and adapt our own behavior accordingly. In contrast, unstable causes leave us unsure when a behavior will or won't occur. For example, if you conclude that driving conditions on a particular stretch of road are always hazardous, you can avoid danger in the future by taking a different route; if you conclude that other drivers will occasionally just drift into your lane, you may suffer quite a bit more anxiety whenever you are driving.

How we explain another person's behavior determines how we communicate with that person. For example, we are less inclined to offer help to someone in need when we judge that person to be responsible for their situation (Weiner, 1995). When we make internal attributions for another person's problems, we are more likely to tell that person to accept responsibility and less likely to convey sympathy and concern (MacGeorge, 2001). Likewise, people are less likely to discuss problems constructively and more likely to use negative problem-solving tactics when they believe a partner's negative behavior is intentional (Bradbury, Beach, Fincham, & Nelson, 1996; Bradbury & Fincham, 1992). As these examples illustrate, our interpersonal communication decisions are closely linked to how we explain other people's behaviors.

Attribution Biases

Although you might think that people seek accurate explanations for things that happen, we are actually quite biased in the attributions we make. **Attribution biases** refer to distortions in the conclusions we reach about the causes of events. There are several types of attribution biases; however, two biases are particularly common and important to interpersonal communication. The **fundamental attribution error** refers to our tendency to link other people's behavior to internal, rather than external, causes. The **actor-observer effect** is the complementary tendency to attribute our own behavior to external, rather than internal, causes. Although there are certainly situations when we deviate from these patterns (see Table 4.2), these two biases typically shape how people make sense of the world.

> **Attribution Biases**
> Distortions in the causal explanations people construct.
>
> **Fundamental Attribution Error**
> Explaining the behaviors of others in terms of internal, rather than external, causes.
>
> **Actor-Observer Effect**
> Explaining one's own behavior in terms of external, rather than internal, causes.

Consider for a moment the many instances of these biases throughout a student's day-to-day experiences. As Zoey commutes to campus, she attributes her own driving errors to external conditions (the weather or animals in the road), but she concludes that another driver's mistakes reflect a lack of skill or intelligence. As she rushes late to class, Zoey reflects on how she was delayed by a talkative teaching assistant; her professor, on the other hand, thinks she wasn't motivated to get to class on time. Likewise, Zoey attributes her low marks on an exam to the vague questions; unfortunately, admission officers at that law school she is applying to are more likely to think her grades reflect qualities like ability or intelligence. Throughout all facets of our interactions with other people, we consistently overestimate the degree to which others are personally responsible for their actions, while we simultaneously downplay our responsibility for our own behaviors.

Why do we make biased attributions? Some of the examples in the previous paragraph might suggest that people are just unfair in their explanations for events. A closer look, however, suggests that these biases are related to characteristics of perception itself. One explanation for both the fundamental attribution error and the actor-observer effect is that we attribute cause to whatever stands out in the situation. When you observe another person's actions, that person is likely to be the most visually intense aspect of the situation. When you are doing something, however, your focus is on the environment rather than yourself. Because actors and observers select different information in the first place, they reach different conclusions about the causes of behaviors.

The fundamental attribution error can also be explained by our need to feel in control of our circumstances. We can generate strategies for dealing with people in the future if we attribute their actions to internal qualities. In contrast, an external attribution leaves us feeling vulnerable to the randomness of life's situations. In other words, we make the

TABLE 4.2 Attribution biases

The fundamental attribution error and the actor-observer effect describe two general biases in how we explain behavior. As you consider the attribution biases described below, notice how the positive or negative impact of behavior and our relationship with the actor can also influence whether we make internal versus external attributions.

Attribution biases	Examples
The Fundamental Attribution Error The tendency to make internal attributions for other people's behavior	Chris didn't pay attention during our conversation because she isn't interested in me
The Actor-Observer Effect The tendency to make external attributions for our own behavior	I didn't pay attention during my conversation with Chris because I was pressed for time
The Self-Serving Bias The tendency to make internal attributions for our successes and external attributions for our failures	I did well in the class debate because I'm a hard-working and intelligent person; I did poorly on the exam because it was tricky
The Defensive Attribution Bias The tendency to make internal attributions for someone's successes and external attributions for that person's failures, if the person is similar to us	Mark is a lot like me – he did well in the debate because he is smart, and he did poorly on the exam because it was tricky
The Hedonic Relevance Effect The tendency to draw inferences about people's personality when their behaviors have negative consequences	Alex was hurt by the feedback he got on his paper; his instructor must be a mean and insensitive person.
The Self-Centered Bias The tendency to conclude that we contribute more to a group task than other group members.	When it comes to keeping things running smoothly, I do more than any of my co-workers

fundamental attribution error because we'd rather be wrong and feel in control, than be right and feel helpless.

In contrast, the actor-observer effect can be explained by our desire to maintain impressions of ourselves that don't change too much over time. Imagine if you had to update your self-concept each time you performed an action: Monday you considered yourself a competent driver, but Tuesday you concluded that you should have your license revoked; an uneventful drive to campus on Wednesday raised your self-esteem again, only to have it plummet after a harrowing lane change late Thursday afternoon. Fortunately, your self-concept provides you with a stable source of information about your internal qualities. Moreover, you maintain your sense of self by attributing daily variations in your behavior to external forces.

FIGURE 4.5 A market. What is your attention drawn to in this store? Do you think it's the same as what the people in the photo are noticing?

Source: Photo by Mary Knox Merrill/The Christian Science Monitor/Getty Images.

The attribution biases reviewed in this section of the chapter once again demonstrate the subjective nature of perception. In our efforts to explain the behaviors of others, we are inevitably influenced by our point of view and our own needs. Not surprisingly, then, different people can reach very different conclusions about why something occurred. When these divergent attributions are followed by communication – watch out! As we act upon our own understanding of a situation, we may very well be contradicting the other person's reality.

Attribution Biases in Close Relationships

Much of what we have learned about perception and attribution so far has focused on interactions with strangers. Perception and attribution are also the tools by which we observe and attach meaning to the actions of the people closest to us. And even in relationships where we know people better, it turns out that biased attributions are the rule rather than the exception. In particular, our attributions for a partner's actions are influenced by how satisfied or dissatisfied we are with the relationship (Bradbury & Fincham, 1990).

As summarized in Table 4.3, people who are satisfied with their close relationships tend to attribute a partner's positive behaviors to internal and stable causes, but explain negative events in terms of external and unstable causes. Why did Denise's spouse remember her birthday and surprise her with concert tickets? He did it because he is thoughtful and loving – both qualities that she sees as part of her spouse and unlikely to change. What if Denise's spouse were to forget her birthday? Because Denise is generally satisfied in her relationship, she would assume that her spouse must be really busy at work these days – a circumstance that doesn't reflect on him personally and (hopefully) is temporary. As you can see, partners in happy relationships are credited for the good things that they do, and excused for their bad behaviors. Attributions that reflect and contribute to a positive view of a relationship are called **adaptive attributions**.

The third column in Table 4.3 reveals the pattern of attributions that dominates when people are dissatisfied with a relationship. In this case, a partner's positive behaviors are attributed to external and unstable causes, while negative behaviors are seen as a

Adaptive Attributions
Explanations that link positive behaviors to internal and stable causes and negative behaviors to external and unstable causes.

TABLE 4.3 Attributions in satisfying and dissatisfying relationships

People who are satisfied or dissatisfied with their relationships reach very different conclusions when their partners behave positively or negatively. Consider the example of Maria and Alan, who are struggling with the demands of two jobs and young children. This table shows the different kinds of attributions Alan might make when Maria either creates problems at home by staying late at work or helps Alan meet a deadline by leaving work early.

The behavior	Adaptive attributions	Maladaptive attributions
Maria stayed late at work and created problems at home	Maria must have had a crisis at work	Maria is self-centered and uncaring
Maria left work early so that Alan could meet a deadline	Maria is a wonderful and loving person	Maria's boss must have canceled her last meeting

reflection of internal and stable qualities. When Jen's parents were facing the dissolution of their marriage, her dad actually did forget her mom's birthday. Her mother attributed his forgetfulness to the fact that he is a thoughtless and insensitive person and she gave up hope of ever getting a birthday present from him again. When he came home one night with a gift certificate for them to have dinner at a nice restaurant, she assumed that he must have gotten it from one of his clients at work and it was about to expire. People who are unhappy with a relationship make **maladaptive attributions** that blame the partner for negative behavior and fail to credit the partner for positive actions.

How we perceive our partner's behavior has enormous consequences for the relationship. On the upside, adaptive attributions can protect happy couples from the occasional problem. Unfortunately, maladaptive attributions seem to lock unhappy couples into a cycle of negativity (Figure 4.6). In fact, three studies that tracked newly-weds over time showed that partners who made maladaptive attributions early in their marriage were less satisfied one to four years later (Fincham & Bradbury, 1987; 1993; Karney & Bradbury, 2000). The attributions we make for other people's behaviors are inevitably subjective and biased – and yet, these explanations have the power to preserve or destroy our relationships.

Maladaptive Attributions
Linking negative behaviors to internal and stable causes and positive behaviors to external and unstable causes.

PAUSE & REFLECT

Think of one couple that you consider happy and one couple you think is unhappy. How can you tell which relationship is happy or unhappy? How would you describe the communication that goes on within each relationship?

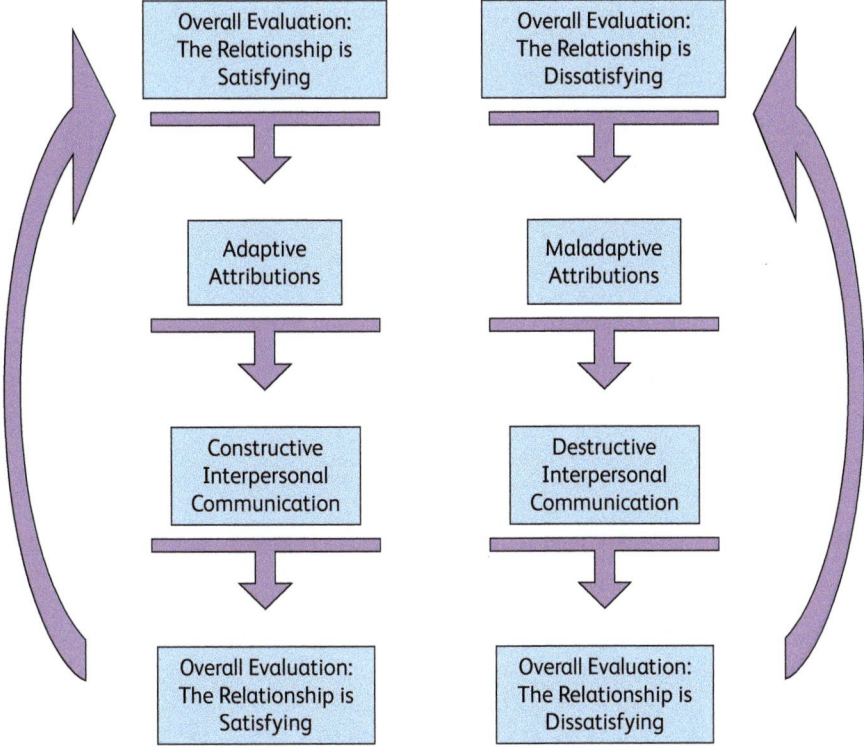

FIGURE 4.6 Cycles of satisfaction and attributions in close relationships

Putting Theory into Practice: Combating Attribution Biases

In this section of the chapter, we have examined how people perceive, and often mis-perceive, the causes of other people's behavior. Our efforts to explain the world around us will never yield flawless results; however, the following strategies can help us limit the impact of attribution biases on our interpersonal communication experiences.

Avoid forming an explanation based only on your point of view. As you seek to understand someone else's actions, think for a moment of how the situation looks to the other person. What must she be focused on? What could be on his mind? How is she likely to be feeling? One way to do this is to imagine yourself as the other person – what would you see, think about, and feel? Another strategy is to ask the other person to share their perspective *before* you draw your conclusions. In fact, just planning to talk to someone about their dissatisfying behaviors appears to be enough to prompt less biased thinking about a conflict (Cloven & Roloff, 1993). Actively adopting the other person's perspective will help you overcome attribution biases and avoid the negative interactions that biases contribute to.

Focus on behaviors, not personalities. When we attribute behavior to someone's traits, we see that person in less flexible terms. The labels we apply to other people create expectations that further direct and limit our perceptions. To avoid these pitfalls, focus your attention on people's behaviors, and don't draw conclusions about what kind of trait that behavior might imply. As you communicate with others, tailor your reactions to the behavior you experienced, and not some judgment about your partner's personality. When you remember to focus on behaviors themselves, you can begin to perceive others without the blinders that labels create.

COMMUNICATION IN ACTION 4.2

Focusing on Behaviors Rather than Traits

This exercise helps you to focus on the specific behaviors that individuals perform rather than relying on broad labels and characterizations that may or may not be accurate. Because labeling individuals constrains our expectations for their behavior, it is important to look for more open-minded and positive ways to characterize another person's behavior. Complete the form on the **companion website** to see how you can change your perceptions to focus more on specific behaviors rather than broad personality traits.

Protect relationships you value by making adaptive attributions. Recall that happy couples tend to make attributions that contribute to their future happiness, and unhappy couples tend to reach conclusions that increase their dissatisfaction. Armed with this knowledge, might you be able to protect relationships you value by actively making adaptive attributions? Research on couples in marital counseling suggests that the answer is yes (Baucom & Lester, 1986; Baucom, Sayers, & Sher, 1990). Although more skillful interpersonal communication is an important contributor to these outcomes (Baucom, Shoham, Mueser, Daiuto, & Stickle, 1998), making more adaptive attributions can help keep your close relationships on the right track. Follow these suggestions for making more adaptive attributions:

- *Look for external causes for behavior*. When your partner has done something that makes you unhappy, consider all of the potential situational explanations for that behavior before jumping to conclusions.
- *Assume that the negative behavior is temporary*. If we believe that our partner's negative behavior is stable and will always occur, it becomes difficult for our partner to overcome that negative attribution. Give your partner the benefit of the doubt and assume that they will behave better in the future.
- *Consider aspects of the situation that were out of the partner's control*. Even when our partner has behaved badly, there might be aspects of the situation that weren't entirely under his or her control. If your partner is late for dinner, she could have controlled when she decided to leave work and the fact that she decided not to call you, but the traffic jam on the way home was really out of her hands. Thus, you might temper your anger with the knowledge that it wasn't entirely her fault.

FACTORS THAT AFFECT PERCEPTION

Previously in this chapter, you learned that perception and attributions are subject to a variety of biases. One reason that biases can emerge is because our perceptions are shaped by our cultural background, social group characteristics, and individual traits. In addition, we can create situations that impair our perception through alcohol consumption or relying on stereotypes to make inferences. In this section, we consider how these factors affect our view of interpersonal communication experiences.

Individual Differences

Various differences between people, such as culture, ethnicity, gender, and personal traits, are influential in the way we perceive the world around us. As a starting point, consider the impact of culture on your perceptions and attributions. Because our culture provides a window through which we make sense of the world around us, cultural differences take root from the very first stage of perception. For example, research has shown that children raised in a European American tradition are encouraged to focus their attention on one thing at a time, whereas children of Mexican or Guatemalan Mayan heritage are taught to attend simultaneously to two competing events (Chavajay & Rogoff, 1999; Correa-Chávez, Rogoff, & Arauz, 2005). In addition, people of Asian cultures are more likely to attend to the surrounding context (for example, the background in a photo or the room in which a conversation occurs), whereas Americans tend to neglect contextual cues (Masuda & Nisbett, 2001). Similarly, Americans pay more attention to *what* is said when they are being evaluated, but Japanese are more attuned to emotional tone or *how* an evaluation is communicated (Ishii, Reyes, & Kitayama, 2003). Not surprisingly, these differences in perception are reflected in attributions. In particular, people from cultures that focus on the accomplishments of individuals are more likely to attribute a person's behavior to internal causes, whereas people from cultures that emphasize the community more than the individual often prefer external attributions (e.g., Hong, Benet-Martinez, Chiu, & Morris, 2003; Peng & Knowles, 2003).

Our membership in different social groups also affects our perception. Consider how men and women differ in their selection, organization, and interpretation of information. In one experiment, participants studied sets of photos of both automobiles and faces, and they were tested one week later to see which photos they could remember; males were better at recognizing automobiles, whereas females were better at recognizing faces (Davies & Robertson, 1993). Another study showed that men and women pay attention to the same features in a map, but then organize that information differently when giving directions (MacFadden, Elias, & Saucier, 2003). In particular, men tend to emphasize distances and direction (i.e., north, south, east, or west), and women more typically mention left/right turns and landmarks. Gender differences are also evident in the attributions people make. When men make a persuasive argument, they tend to attribute their success to their communication ability; women, on the other hand, explain their persuasive ability in terms of how hard they tried (Andrews, 1987). Although we should be careful not to exaggerate differences between men and women (Canary & Hause, 1993), these examples illustrate the variety of ways in which gender can shape perception.

> **PAUSE & REFLECT**
>
> How might men and women's perceptions of communication differ in the work-place? The classroom? The media?

Age is another social category that affects perception. Between the ages of 4 to 7, children begin to see traits as the underlying cause of behavior (Yuill & Pearson, 1998). The tendency to attribute another person's behavior to internal and consistent causes continues to increase through middle childhood (Kalish, 2002) and young adulthood (e.g., Boxer & Tisak, 2003). Continuing across the lifespan, we find that middle-aged adults are less likely than young adults to hold people personally responsible for their actions (Follett & Hess, 2002). In fact, young adults are more likely to make internal attributions for behaviors when they are given time to think about the event, but elderly adults are less likely to make internal attribution when given time to reflect (Chen & Blanchard-Fields, 1997). Over the lifespan, then, internal attributions increase when children begin to understand how traits can motivate behavior, and they decrease as people's lived experiences teach them that actions are often driven by circumstances.

Cognitive Complexity
The extent to which a person tends to notice details and distinctions among features within a situation.

Our individual traits can also influence perception and attribution. One quality on which people differ is **cognitive complexity** – the degree to which they differentiate details within a situation. People who are high in cognitive complexity tend to notice more specific features in their environment. In contrast, a person low in cognitive complexity focuses on the more general picture, rather than the details. In the context of interpersonal interactions, cognitive complexity has been linked to a person's ability to decode nonverbal behavior (Woods, 1996). In addition, people high in cognitive complexity notice a greater variety of traits when sizing up other people, and in turn, they make less extreme judgments about others (Ben-Ari, Kedem, & Levy-Weiner, 1992). A trait that is closely related to cognitive complexity is **attributional complexity**. Attributional complexity refers to people's tendency to explain events in terms of intricate rather than simple causes (Fletcher, Danilovics, Fernandez, Peterson, & Reeder, 1986). People high in attributional complexity try harder to understand complicated causes, and they also reach more accurate conclusions about causes (Fletcher, Rosanowski, Rhodes, & Lange, 1992). In addition, people high in attributional complexity tend to do more perspective-taking and feel more empathy for others (Joireman, 2004).

Attributional Complexity
The extent to which a person tends to explain events in terms of intricate, rather than simple, causes.

Alcohol and Interpersonal Encounters

It is widely known that drinking alcohol can lead to more extreme interpersonal behavior – being more aggressive, taking more risks, flirting more vivaciously, or feeling more forlorn. Although these consequences are generally associated with the chemical effects of alcohol, communication scholars have explored how drunken behavior in interpersonal situations might stem from the effects of alcohol on perception. Myopia, also known as being nearsighted, is a vision problem in which objects near at hand are in focus, but those further away appear blurry. **Alcohol myopia theory** proposes that some of the effects of alcohol occur because drinking makes some aspects of a situation more difficult to see (Steele & Josephs, 1990). In other words, intoxication strikes at the very foundation of interpersonal communication behavior by distorting perceptions of the world around us.

A central assumption of the theory is that alcohol disrupts the normal process by which people balance competing interests. In many situations, people experience some degree of **inhibition conflict**, a condition defined by the presence of both vivid cues that promote a certain response and less vivid cues that inhibit that response. Consider the case of Brian: A friend who wants to gossip about one of Brian's confidential legal cases is a vivid cue encouraging disclosure, but Brian knows the rules against talking about clients in his profession. Normally, people are skilled at balancing vivid cues with less vivid cues and acting appropriately, but alcohol myopia theory suggests that drinking alcohol limits perception to those cues that are most vivid or striking. If Brian is chatting with his friend over happy hour and has already had a few drinks, he is more likely to pay attention to the vivid cues he receives from his talkative friend who wants to gossip and less likely to recall the less vivid cues in that situation that would advise him against disclosing private information about his clients. Blind to more subtle cues within a situation and acting upon only a subset of the relevant information, intoxicated people respond in ways that are often inappropriate and excessive (Steele & Southwick, 1985).

> ## PAUSE & REFLECT
>
> Can you think of a time when you, or someone you know, did something foolish after drinking alcohol? Are there reasons that you or this person don't typically behave that way? Why didn't those reasons matter after consuming alcohol?

Among other things, alcohol's effect on perception can lead to risky sexual behavior. One survey found that intoxication doubled the rate of unprotected casual sex – from 16% to 32% – among men who reported that they typically used a condom (MacDonald, Zanna, & Fong, 1996). In addition, intoxicated women are more likely than sober women to consider a sexual relationship with an attractive, though risky, partner (Murphy, Monahan, & Miller, 1998). In fact, women who have consumed alcohol have greater faith in their ability to detect a partner's HIV status through casual conversation (Monahan, Murphy, & Miller, 1999). And relative to sober persons, intoxicated males and females rate hypothetical episodes involving sexual coercion as more enjoyable and acceptable (Lannutti & Monahan, 2002).

Alcohol Myopia Theory
An explanation for drunken behavior that focuses on the effects of alcohol on perception.

Inhibition Conflict
The simultaneous presence of vivid cues that provoke a response and subtle cues that inhibit that response.

INSIDE COMMUNICATION RESEARCH

Alcohol Myopia and Sexual Risk-taking

Drinking and sexual risk-taking are difficult behaviors to study. Because both activities are somewhat taboo in our culture, people might not provide honest self-reports of their behavior. On the other hand, observing intoxicated people negotiating sexual intimacy would be both difficult and inappropriate. So just how have communication researchers studied alcohol myopia and sexual risk-taking? Jennifer Monahan and Pamela Lanutti's test of alcohol myopia theory shows us how creative methods can shed light on private interpersonal experiences.

These researchers examined the effect of alcohol and self-esteem on women's reactions to flirtatious advances from men (Monahan & Lannutti, 2000). As a first step, Monahan and Lanutti recruited women for the study who met a variety of criteria (for example, they were over the legal drinking age, single, heterosexual, social drinkers, not pregnant, etc.). When these women reported to the research laboratory, they first completed a questionnaire measuring their self-esteem. Then, half were given enough alcohol to produce a .08 blood alcohol level, and half were given a non-alcoholic beverage. Next, each participant had a 10-minute conversation with a man whom they thought was another participant in the study. In actuality, the men were confederates who were instructed to spend five minutes getting to know the participant, and then to begin flirting with the woman. After the interactions, Monahan and Lanutti asked the women to report how anxious the interaction made them feel and whether they thought the man was interested in a relationship. The researchers also examined video-tapes of the interactions to measure how much each woman self-disclosed to the man and how much she flirted in return.

The study revealed several important effects of alcohol among women with low self-esteem. For example, the flirtatious episode produced less anxiety for women with low self-esteem if they were intoxicated. Likewise, women with low self-esteem engaged in more self-disclosure when they were intoxicated. In both cases, alcohol had the effect of making low self-esteem women as comfortable and disclosive as high self-esteem women. Notably, both high and low self-esteem women thought that the man was more interested in a friendship or romantic relationship when they were intoxicated.

THINK ABOUT IT

1. How well do the procedures in this study match what really happens in situations like these? Would you think the study was realistic if you were a participant? What are the strengths and weaknesses of studying alcohol's effects on interpersonal communication in this way?
2. The study found that alcohol makes women with low self-esteem feel and communicate more like women with high self-esteem. How might this create problems for those women in the long run?

Stereotyping

Stereotypes
Over-simplified beliefs about members of a social group.

Stereotyping
Assuming that individuals have certain qualities based on their membership in a social group.

Stereotypes refer to over-simplified beliefs about people who fall into particular social categories. **Stereotyping** occurs when people's stereotypes control their perceptions during an encounter with another person. In other words, stereotyping is automatically assuming that individuals have certain qualities based on their membership in a social group. In turn, stereotyping leads to judgments, behaviors, and interpersonal communication patterns that often perpetuate stereotypes.

Racial and ethnic stereotypes are among the most pervasive sources of distorted perception in our society. Research has shown that people are more likely to judge an African American male as guilty of a hypothetical murder when he has a darker skin tone (Proctor & Snyder, 2000). In fact, pictures of people with physical cues characteristic of an African American heritage are more likely to be judged as showing someone who is unlawful, aggressive, and lazy (Blair, Judd, Sadler, & Jenkins, 2002). Another study showed that people are more likely to mention stereotypical physical features when they describe a photo of an African American who is implicated in a violent crime (Oliver, Jackson, Moses, & Dangerfield, 2004). Whereas stereotypes such as these are partly due to media coverage that over-represents African Americans as lawbreakers (Dixon & Linz, 2000), stereotyping arises from a flawed perception process.

PAUSE & REFLECT

List the traits that you think most people associate with "college students." Do all of those traits apply to you? What traits are important to you, but not on that list? How do stereotypes for college students affect how people communicate with you?

Not surprisingly, stereotypes surface in interpersonal communication. For example, people are more likely to include information that is consistent with stereotypes when they share information with others about someone from another culture (Lyons & Kashima, 2003). In fact, stereotypes have been linked to the very language we choose to convey information about others (Maass, Ceccarelli, & Rudin, 1996; Maass, Salvi, Arcuri, & Semin, 1989). In particular, people prefer generalizations over specific details when describing behavior that is consistent with stereotypes; in contrast, people use specific language when discussing behavior that is inconsistent with a stereotype. For people on the receiving end of these descriptions, the general – and stereotype-consistent – descriptions are more likely than specific details to promote inferences about the person's personality or traits (Wigboldus, Semin, & Spears, 2000). In other words, the language used to describe others cements stereotypical judgments and dilutes details that are inconsistent with stereotypes.

Of course, stereotyping also affects how people communicate with a person they have stereotyped. As one example, researchers have shown how stereotypical judgments of the elderly make intergenerational communication difficult (Barker, Giles, & Harwood, 2004; Ryan, Giles, Bartolucci, & Henwood, 1986). The impact of stereotypes on perception and intergenerational communication is summarized in Figure 4.7. When people have negative stereotypes about the elderly, they will limit communication with an older person, and they will use more patronizing and stylized speech if an interaction can't be avoided. This rather lifeless conversation doesn't offer much for the elderly participant to work with, and he or she ends up making limited and often stereotypical responses. Similarly, people may avoid topics that are complicated or contemporary, based on the stereotypical belief that the elderly lack mental agility. Consequently, their conversations would be fairly simple, mundane, and boring for both. The result is an

SCHOLAR SPOTLIGHT

Visit the Communication Café on the **companion website** to hear Jennifer Monahan talk about her research on alcohol myopia theory, and on perception and communication more generally.

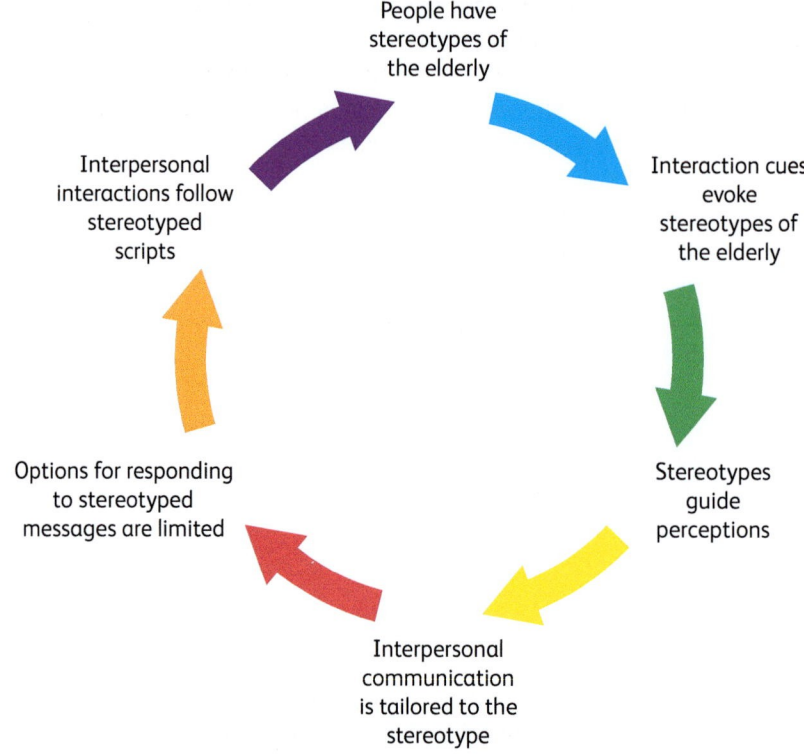

FIGURE 4.7 A general model of stereotypes and intergenerational communication

interaction that both confirms the stereotype and undermines the older person's sense of self. Left unchecked, the cycle of stereotyping and communication contributes to experiences of prejudice and discrimination that divide people in our society.

PAUSE & REFLECT

Consider a positive stereotype you might hold, for example, that Asian Americans are intelligent or that first-born children are ambitious. Can you think of any downsides of being the target of such "positive" stereotypes?

Putting Theory into Practice: Confronting Barriers to Perception

Cultural backgrounds, personality traits, and features of the environment or situation create a constellation of characteristics that come together to shape how we see and explain the world around us. These effects take root during the very first stage of perception and, in turn, contribute to every aspect of our thinking about our experiences. Not surprisingly, all of these features make the perception process vulnerable to errors. Fortunately, you can take steps to confront barriers to perception.

Recognize individual differences in perception and attribution. How often have you found yourself in a conflict with another person because you disagreed about what happened or why? Or you found yourself defending your actions by explaining your point of view? The fact of the matter is that people see and explain events in different ways, so our differences in perceptions and attributions often lead to disagreements with others. When you find yourself arguing with somebody, consider how individual differences in perception might be the reason for your disagreement. By questioning how culture, social group, and personality shape perceptions, you might be able to set aside a conflict to learn about a different point of view. To minimize conflicts stemming from individual differences, ask yourself the following questions:

- How am I different from my partner in ways that might cause me to see this situation differently than he or she does?
- How does my partner's membership in a particular social group shape his or her perceptions of this situation?
- What do we have in common that might allow us to share the same perception of this situation?

Recognize when your perception is impaired. Our ability to perceive the world around us can vary depending on our circumstances. Recognize the conditions that limit your appreciation for nuances, for example, being tired, emotional, or under pressure. Likewise, take stock of how characteristics of the setting, such as a crowded or noisy room, might undermine perception during your interpersonal interactions. In those circumstances, you should be particularly careful about letting your perceptions lead you to easy but flawed conclusions.

Combat the formation of stereotypes. Television is a prolific and widely available source of information about other social groups. And unfortunately, the medium frequently draws stylized, extreme, and hyper-stereotyped portraits of social groups, particularly those constituting minorities in the United States. For example, the television series *Glee* portrays a gay character who loves fashion, enjoys singing and performing, and behaves in a very effeminate manner. Although stereotypes are common fare on television, viewers are not helpless recipients of the messages the media send. In fact, research has shown that young children are more likely to reject gender stereotypes if they watch television with an adult who refutes stereotyped scenes, e.g., "The show is wrong. Lots of girls do things besides paint their nails and put on make-up" (Nathanson, Wilson, McGee, & Sebastian, 2002). Thus, interpersonal communication is a tool we can use to undermine the development of stereotypes from the start.

COMMUNICATION IN ACTION 4.3

Challenging Stereotypes in the Media

Select three television programs or movies that depict a particular social group in stereotyped ways. For example, you might choose *Jersey Shore* for its depiction of Italian Americans, *Sex and the City* for its depiction of single women, *The Nutty Professor* for its depiction of overweight people, or *Barbershop* for its depiction of African Americans. For each program or movie you select, make a list of all the ways the portrayal of that social group is an accurate depiction of that group. Then, make a list of all the ways the portrayal of that social group is based on stereotypes for that group. Is there any overlap between the stereotypes we have about these groups and how they actually behave? What has been the impact of exposure to these stereotypes on your own thinking about those social groups?

SUMMARY

In this chapter, we have examined perception as part of the foundation for interpersonal communication. Perception is a three-stage process by which we select, organize, and interpret information to make sense of our environment. At each step, we impose our own point of view, needs and goals, and experiences to produce our own unique understanding of a situation. Although perception allows us to function in a world saturated with information, we have also seen how this process is inherently subjective.

The interpretation stage of perception sometimes includes our efforts to understand why something happened. The attributions we make for another person's behavior can focus on causes that are internal or external to that person, controllable or uncontrollable, and stable or unstable. Two common attribution biases include the tendencies to attribute other people's behavior to internal causes and our own behavior to external causes. Although the fundamental attribution error and actor-observer effect appear to arise rather innocently from perception processes, they represent a pervasive bias that permeates our interactions with other people. Patterns of attribution in close relationships also revealed that the conclusions we reach about the causes of a partner's behavior are often skewed by our satisfaction with that relationship.

Our perceptions are influenced by personal characteristics, as well as by features of the situation. Our cultural background shapes how we focus our attention, prioritize information, and draw inferences about what we perceive. Characteristics such as gender and age give us life experiences that further influence how we make sense of our environment. People also differ in their tendency to perceive information or causes of events in simple versus complex ways. Thus, the traits and qualities we carry with us into any situation are an inevitable part of our perceptions. Our perceptions are also impaired by alcohol intoxication and stereotyping. Alcohol myopia theory suggests that drunken behavior reflects a breakdown in perception, such that people attend only to the most vivid cues in a situation; importantly, intoxicated people miss the more subtle cues that might inhibit risky behavior. When stereotyping occurs, the source of distorted perceptions is quite different, but process is similar; in this case, pre-existing beliefs about social groups blind perceivers to the unique qualities individuals possess. As these examples demonstrate, impaired perception can have critical consequences.

Perception is the process by which we observe and make sense of other people, and it is at the heart of interpersonal communication experiences. In this chapter, we discovered that these processes are inherently subjective and vulnerable to a variety of biasing forces. At the same time, you do not need to be a victim of your perceptions. By paying attention to perception, combating attribution biases, recognizing individual differences in perception, and confronting barriers to perception, you can become more skillful at interpersonal communication. Now that you know more about perception and attribution, consider the implications of these processes in the following ethical exercises.

ACTIVITIES FOR EXPLORING COMMUNICATION ETHICS

What Would You/Should You Do?

Imagine that you are out for an evening with your friend, Amy, who is pretty shy and hasn't been involved in many romantic relationships. The two of you had a few beers before you went out, walked to a couple of bars, and have ended up at a party. Amy is pretty drunk now, and you notice that a man is hitting on her. She seems to be enjoying the attention, and she is talking a lot for a change. When Amy sees you watching her conversation, she rushes over to you. She is happier and more excited than you've ever seen her as she tells you that this guy is "so great" and "really likes her." Then, she asks if you would mind if you had to go home alone. As a good friend, do you celebrate Amy's joy and hope for the best in this relationship? Or, do you protect Amy from the dangers of alcohol myopia?

Something to Think About

Now that you know about perception and interpersonal communication, you should appreciate that the way we understand the world around us is inherently subjective. Other people have different perceptions, draw different conclusions, and communicate differently than you do. What you've learned implies that you should avoid imposing your interpretations on others. But, is that always the case? When (if ever) is it right to stick to your own perspective and reject another person's point of view? Where is the line between conviction to your values and a lack of perspective-taking?

Analyze Communication Ethics Yourself

Ethical communicators make their values and assumptions clear when they argue for a course of action. To investigate communication ethics in the world around you, examine letters to the editor in the *New York Times* or the "Point/Counterpoint" feature in *USA Today*. What perceptions do the writers use to justify their position? In particular, evaluate the extent to which the writers make clear when their positions are based on fact, inferences, or assumptions. As you do this analysis, think about how these letters might be rewritten to achieve a higher ethical standard.

KEY WORDS

actor-observer effect

adaptive attributions

alcohol myopia theory

attribution biases

attributional complexity

attributions

cognition

cognitive complexity

external attribution

fundamental attribution error

inhibition conflict

internal attribution

interpretation

maladaptive attributions

organization

perception

selection

stereotypes

stereotyping

PART 2 INTERPERSONAL INTERACTION

Visit the Communication Café on the **companion website** to hear Denise and Jen talk about the topics addressed in Part 2 of this book.

When people interact with each other, they do so by creating and responding to messages. In this part of this book, we look at the interactive components of interpersonal communication: language, nonverbal messages, emotions, and listening.

Language is perhaps the most obvious symbol system people use to communicate. Whether we are interacting in person or using some communication technology, our words are a big part of how we create meanings with other people. Although you have spoken at least one language since early in your life, have you thought about how language works? How is it that two (or more) people can use sequences of sounds and silence to accomplish such a powerful thing as communication? In Chapter 5, we examine the nature of language, the ways people use language to communicate, some factors that affect how people use language, and also some problematic uses of language.

Although sometimes less obvious than language, nonverbal behaviors have a major impact on interpersonal communication experiences. As you will discover in Chapter 6, we communicate information to others through a variety of nonverbal cues. Culture and individual characteristics influence nonverbal communication, just as much as they influence the languages that a person speaks. In this chapter, you will also learn about the complexities that can emerge when people weave together verbal and nonverbal messages.

The emotions you experience are also central to the interpersonal communication process. Our emotions can motivate us to communicate with others, we use communication to express emotions, our communication experiences influence how we feel, and how we feel influences how we interpret messages. In Chapter 7, we clarify the nature of emotions, how emotions relate to interpersonal interactions, and some of the ways people differ in their experience of emotions. We also delve into some of the more extreme emotions – hurt, jealousy, and grief – that can be part of our interpersonal communication experiences.

The words, behaviors, and emotions that we use to communicate with others would be meaningless if listening did not occur. Because hearing is one of the five basic human senses, people don't always think about listening as an action that can be performed more or less effectively. In fact, people listen in different ways, encounter several forces that can interfere with listening, and can take active steps to be more engaged listeners. Because interpersonal communication occurs with other people, listening involves making sense of what the interaction means for the relationship between the people involved. These important topics are the focus of Chapter 8.

CHAPTER 5

LANGUAGE AND INTERPERSONAL COMMUNICATION 126

CHAPTER 6

NONVERBAL COMMUNICATION 154

CHAPTER 7

EMOTIONS AND COMMUNICATION 180

CHAPTER 8

LISTENING 206

LEARNING OBJECTIVES

After reading this chapter, you should be able to:

1. Identify the essential characteristics of language.
2. Describe how language rules operate in conversations.
3. Describe differences in how men and women use language.
4. Explain how language changes with power or intimacy in a relationship.
5. Understand how racist, sexist, and heterosexist language marginalizes people in a society.
6. Improve your use of language in interpersonal interactions.

PUTTING THEORY INTO PRACTICE

In this chapter, you will learn how to:

1. Use concrete language.
2. Ask for clarification if a word is ambiguous.
3. Look beyond labels.
4. Attend to connotative meanings.
5. Diagnose topic shifts.
6. Set the stage for conversation.
7. Avoid gender traps.
8. Tailor your language to social contexts.
9. Confront racist language.
10. Develop your gender- and sexuality-neutral repertoire.

LANGUAGE AND INTERPERSONAL COMMUNICATION

5

128 THE NATURE OF VERBAL COMMUNICATION

135 THE RULES OF LANGUAGE

142 FACTORS THAT AFFECT LANGUAGE USE

148 BIASED LANGUAGE

151 SUMMARY

153 ACTIVITIES FOR EXPLORING COMMUNICATION ETHICS

153 KEY WORDS

Source: Photo by Ben Hider/Getty Images.

$3,400

Engineers at IBM have developed a computer named Watson that is capable of understanding and answering questions that are posed in natural language. The ultimate test came for Watson when it was a contestant on *Jeopardy*, competing against the two biggest winners in the game show's history: Ken Jennings and Brad Rutter. *Jeopardy* is a game that requires not only a broad base of knowledge about a variety of topics, but also an ability to untangle sometimes convoluted and backwards statements. Although accessing unlimited amounts of information should be easy for a computer, deciphering the cryptic questions and mastering the art of answering in the form of a question should be more difficult. Despite the inherent challenges of the game, Watson easily beat its competitors, bringing in over $77,000 in winnings compared to Jennings' $24,000 and Rutter's $21,000. Despite its intellectual prowess, Watson was not perfect. In Final *Jeopardy*, the category was U.S. Cities and the clue was "Its largest airport is named for a WWII hero, its second largest for a WWII battle." Watson answered, "What is Toronto," which is not a U.S. city and its main airport was named after the winner of a Nobel Peace Prize, not a WWII hero. (The correct answer is "Chicago.") Although Watson is a great specimen of artificial intelligence, scientists still have a lot of work to do to develop a computer that can replicate the complexity, flexibility, and nuance of verbal communication in interpersonal interactions.

Today's technological world involves a lot of communication between humans and computers, but few computers are as skilled or sophisticated as Watson when trying to match human communication. When you call your bank, your insurance company, or even your university, you might be greeted by a computerized voice that is supposed to help you find information or guide you to the person you need to talk to. It usually becomes obvious very early in the conversation that you are communicating with a non-human interaction partner. These computerized interactions can be frustrating because computers aren't as skilled as humans in their use of language. Our ability to use verbal communication to make a connection with another person – to comfort, amuse, inform, and so on – is what separates us from other animals and, for the moment, from computers.

When our ancestors developed verbal skills, they gained the ability to share ideas, make plans, and reflect upon their relationships. The result was more effective hunting and gathering, improved strategies for protecting the social group, and deeper bonds with others. Of course, verbal messages have also been used to divide and oppress people. Because verbal cues are so central to interpersonal communication, we will examine how they work in some detail. While you may already be a sophisticated speaker of English and perhaps even a second or third language, this chapter can help you become more aware of the effects of your words on others.

THE NATURE OF VERBAL COMMUNICATION

Language encompasses both our vocabulary and our knowledge about when to use particular words, what those words mean, and how we can put words together to create a meaningful message. Some languages, such as American Sign

Language, don't rely on verbal messages, but verbal communication and language share a number of qualities. In particular, verbal communication and language are abstract, arbitrary, culturally determined, and consequential. As we consider each of these qualities, we examine how they make language a powerful but imperfect tool for interpersonal communication.

Language
The words people use to communicate and knowledge about how to use those words to create a meaningful message.

Language Is Abstract

One basic but important feature of language is that it is abstract; this means that words stand for objects, people, ideas, etc., but words are not themselves the things that they represent. This is a simple but powerful point. When you use the word "apple," you do not need to hold a real apple to put an image of one in the mind of your communication partner (see Figure 5.1). In the same way, you can use words to refer to a wide range of objects and concepts which are not physically present, and – as in the case of a concept like "justice" – might not even physically exist. By using language, we create images and ideas in each other's mind.

Although all verbal cues are abstract to some degree, words can be more or less precise. For example, you could send someone to the store to buy some apples, some red apples, or some Macintosh apples. As your language choice becomes more specific, you are more likely to get exactly the kind of apples you want. **Abstract language** refers to words that have very general meanings because they cover a variety of events, objects, or actions. In contrast, **concrete language** includes references to specific events, objects, or actions.

Abstract Language
Words with general meanings that refer to broad categories of object, events, or behavior.

Concrete Language
Words that refer to specific events and behaviors or tangible objects that are available to the senses.

FIGURE 5.1 The relationship between words and ideas

Language allows us to create an image in another person's mind. That image is unlikely to be a perfect match to our own image – how close a match it is will depend on whether communication partners attach the same meaning to verbal cues.

Using concrete language may be especially helpful when you want to avoid miscommunication about sensitive issues. Consider the example of Markesha, who is annoyed with her sister Deirdre for leaving the bathroom a mess. In the transcript presented in Table 5.1, Markesha begins the conversation using abstract language that generally describes her views and doesn't even mention the bathroom specifically. As the conversation continues, Markesha begins to refer to particular events or tangible objects. By the end of the dialog, Markesha is very specific about the circumstances that bother her. Notice how the concrete language Markesha uses at the end of the dialog gives Deirdre a much better idea of what's bothering her sister.

Concrete language helps a communication partner to better understand what the other person is thinking or feeling and to form an appropriate response. In fact, communication scholar Claude Miller and his colleagues (Miller, Lane, Deatrick, Young, & Potts, 2007) found that people pay more attention to persuasive messages that use concrete language (e.g. "sugar causes tooth decay and obesity"), rather than abstract or vague terms (e.g., "sugar is bad for you"). That study also showed that speakers are perceived as more expert and trustworthy when they create messages that are concrete, rather than very abstract. In another study (Douglas & Sutton, 2006), people evaluated speakers as less biased when they described another person using concrete terms (e.g., "Lisa slapped Ann") rather than abstract words (e.g., "Lisa is aggressive").

TABLE 5.1 Talking at high and low levels of abstraction

MARKESHA:	You are such a huge slob, Deirdre! I can't believe you would be so rude.
DEIRDRE:	What are you talking about?
MARKESHA:	It's just so inconsiderate to leave huge messes for me to clean up. I hate it when you do that!
DEIRDRE:	I don't think I left a mess anywhere, and even if I did, you didn't have to clean it up. I never asked you to do that.
MARKESHA:	This morning I went into the bathroom to get ready for work and you had left your dirty stuff on the floor.
DEIRDRE:	I'm sorry, I must have forgotten to pick it up because I was in a hurry. But what's the big deal? All you had to do was throw it in the laundry basket.
MARKESHA:	Well, I was in a hurry too, so it was frustrating to have to deal with your mess before I could get ready myself. Then, I was so mad about it that I couldn't even relax and enjoy my shower.
DEIRDRE:	Oh, I guess I can see your point now.
MARKESHA:	Yeah, maybe some days it wouldn't bother me, but sometimes I'd like to zone out in the morning, and it makes me feel angry and taken for granted when the first thing I encounter is your dirty clothes and wet towel. It makes me feel like you don't respect me. You know what I mean?
DEIRDRE:	Yeah, I do. I'm really sorry. It won't happen again.
MARKESHA:	OK, good. Thanks.

> **PAUSE & REFLECT**
>
> What are some of the different ways you can interpret the phrase "I'm feeling good"? Can you think of ways to make this expression more concrete to fit the different circumstances in which you might use it?

Language Is Arbitrary

Because we understand our native languages so easily and automatically, it might be hard to recognize that language is arbitrary. Language is arbitrary because there is no inherent reason for using a particular word to represent a particular object or idea. As part of your college experience you have to take these things called "classes," but they just as easily could have been called masses, or lasses, or sasses. People in an English-speaking culture assigned the label "classes" to refer to the meetings you have with professors so that we would all have a common way to reference this experience in our speech, but there is nothing about the experience that is inherently linked to the label it was given. As another example, consider the words we have for strong emotions like "anger" and "joy." Although you can readily think of the feelings that those words are linked to, there is nothing about those feelings that necessarily gives rise to those particular terms. In fact, had the labels been reversed, the underlying feelings would remain the same, we would just use a different word to refer to them.

Because there is no fixed connection between words and what they represent, words have ambiguous meanings, which means that people can interpret different meanings for the same word. To make this point in our classes, we ask our students to close their eyes and picture a dog. When students report on the kind of dog they envisioned, answers range from a golden retriever, to a pit bull, or a dachshund, or the mutt their family adopted from a shelter. The word "dog" can be interpreted in many different ways depending on one's own background and experiences. As another example, the word "pain" can refer to an unpleasant physical sensation in one language (English) and a loaf of bread in another (French). Although the word is the same, the way that people interpret that word is different. Research has shown that men and women typically assign different meanings to the word "love." Men are more likely than women to associate the word "love" with romance, passion, and sexual intimacy; women are more likely to include the feelings that exist within friendship in their definition of love (Fehr & Broughton, 2001). Within a workplace, men and women also attach different meanings to flirtatious or sexual remarks. In particular, women rate messages between co-workers that have sexual overtones as more sexually harassing than men do (Solomon & Williams, 1997).

Language Is Related to Culture

Language, like manners, clothing fashions, and traditions, is related to the culture of the people who use it. First of all, characteristics of a language can reveal cultural values and norms. For example, the Korean language emerged within a culture that recognized a strict social hierarchy, so it includes a complex system of honorifics – similar to the English words "ma'am," "sir," or "your honor" – that acknowledge social status. Likewise, the English language emerged within a male-dominated culture, which was reflected for many years in the use of "he" and "man" to refer to men and women in general.

COMMUNICATION IN ACTION 5.1

Exposing Cultural Assumptions about Power

Take some time to create a list of all the titles you can think of that are used to designate a person who holds a position of power. To get you started, identify the different ways that you would complete these sentences, "One person who has power over me is my _____" or "People in charge of _____ are called _____." Try to identify at least 15 terms. Then, review your list to uncover the cultural values embedded within those words. Do the words seem to honor or put down people in power? Do the terms tend to include more masculine or feminine references? What are the cultural assumptions about power that are encoded in the language you use?

Second, language changes with new cultural developments. Consider how language has adapted to changing norms for romance within American culture (Cate & Lloyd, 1992). In the early twentieth century, spending time with a romantic partner was referred to as "courting" because eligible women would be visited in their homes, similar to the way that men who were noble or well behaved were qualified to be present in a royal court. In the 1920s, women enjoyed greater freedom to meet romantic partners outside their home, which required interested parties to set a day and time that they would meet; hence, the term "dating" was used. Greater romantic freedoms in the 1950s and 1960s meant that people might "date" any number of partners, rather than one person at a time. This state of affairs required new terminology to distinguish committed relationships where partners went on dates with each other consistently, otherwise known as "going steady." More recently, eligible singles started to treat relational commitment as something distinct from the pleasure that can be derived from sexual intimacy, so new terms like "hooking up" and "friends with benefits" were needed to distinguish fleeting sexual relationships from those that included an expectation about future involvement. And with the availability of new technologies, some young people have started to refer to potential romantic partners as someone they're "talking to," which reflects the importance of online messaging and texting in their relationship development. These examples show how novel experiences and cultural developments create a need for new language and render old language obsolete.

Finally, language can influence how people perceive the world around them. The

Sapir–Whorf Hypothesis is the idea that the way people think depends on the structure of their language (Whorf, 1956). The hypothesis would argue that if there is no word in your language to represent some object or idea, then you would not be able to understand or comprehend that object or idea. For example, in Indonesian the word *jayus* refers to a joke so poorly told and so unfunny that one cannot help but laugh. The Sapir–Whorf Hypothesis would argue that because there is not an equivalent word for *jayus* in the English language, people who speak English could never understand or think of this sort of social situation. Of course, you have probably had an experience when a cheesy or poorly told joke made you laugh in spite of how bad it was, so does the fact that there is no English word for this situation make it impossible for you to understand? Of course not. Not surprisingly, then, the Sapir–Whorf Hypothesis has fallen out of favor over the decades as people have come to realize that its claims were unfounded. Although the literal interpretation of this claim is now considered overly extreme (Greiffenhagen & Sharrock, 2007), different languages do reflect and create cultural differences in conceptions of reality. This relationship among language, culture, and conceptions of reality is called **linguistic relativity**.

As a concrete test of linguistic relativity, one study compared how information is processed by speakers of English versus Chinese (Zhang & Schmitt, 1998). In the Chinese language, the character for an object includes both a symbol that identifies the specific item and a symbol that identifies what category it falls into; for example, the symbols for river, 河, lake, 湖, stream, 流, and slippery, 滑, all include the same symbol on the left indicating that the word is related to water. In the study, Chinese and English speakers studied a list of words, and then completed tests to see how many of the words they could remember, and they recorded their impressions of the items that the words referred to. Chinese speakers were more likely than English speakers to use category information to help them recall specific words, they perceived more similarities between objects from the same category, and they tended to evaluate items within a category in the same way. This study shows how the language you speak affects how you organize and evaluate your perceptions of the world around you.

Language Is Consequential

When we use language to represent our reality, our words inevitably highlight some aspects of that reality and neglect others. As an example, think about what happens when you try to describe a dream to another person. Some dreams are crazy narratives where the plot jumps around, people pop in or out of the story, the setting for the dream (or even the color of it) might change dramatically, and feelings can be unclear or fleeting. When you try to describe a dream to someone, certain aspects of the dream will be easier to put into words than others. As you do this, the parts of the dream that defy language will recede from your impression of the dream, and the parts you can put into words will become more solid. This tendency for language to resolve – or neglect – nuances in real-life experience is called **totalizing**. Language totalizes reality because words create an incomplete and oversimplified image of real experiences.

When we label individuals or groups, we also create consequences for them. Consider, for example, what happens when teachers attach labels to elementary school

Sapir–Whorf Hypothesis
The assumption that the way people think depends on the structure of their language.

Linguistic Relativity
The assumption that different languages reflect and create cultural differences in conceptions of reality.

Totalizing
Resolving or neglecting details, nuances, or complexity.

children. In one classic study, teachers gave higher grades to a fourth grader's handwritten essay when they were told that the paper was written by a student who was "gifted" (Babad, 1980). Other research shows that teachers are less willing to refer students to a gifted program if they have been labeled with a learning disability or an emotional and behavioral disorder (Bianco, 2005). And children who are tagged as slow learners suffer more emotional and behavioral problems than unlabeled classmates who have similar academic skills (Frey, 2005).

> ## PAUSE & REFLECT
>
> What labels have been given to you in your lifetime? How do you think those labels have affected how people communicate with you?

Reification

Reacting to words as though they are an accurate and complete representation of reality.

Reification occurs when we respond to labels as though they are themselves real. A vivid example of reification comes from interviews that were conducted with women coping with infertility (Steuber & Solomon, 2011). One woman described how her experience with infertility began when she casually mentioned to her doctor that she and her partner hadn't used any kind of birth control for about a year. The doctor told her that she was infertile, and he immediately started to discuss options and prescribe treatments. The woman described how being labeled "infertile" washed over her in the doctor's office and changed her entire view of her life – she was no longer a woman with vague hopes of starting a family, but one with a reproductive disability that would require treatment and might leave her childless. Likewise, the doctor neglected other facets of her experience, never questioned whether the label fit, and focused exclusively on curing her. Although labels can be helpful in diagnosing problems or organizing information, we should be aware of the consequences of allowing those labels to define our reality.

Putting Theory into Practice: Harnessing the Power of Language

In this section, we looked at the characteristics of verbal communication. These qualities reveal language to be a flexible and powerful tool for interpersonal communication, but one that also contributes to miscommunication. It takes effort, then, to harness the power of language.

Use concrete language. Studies show that people will pay more attention to your messages and perceive you as more expert, trustworthy, and unbiased when you use words that are precise and unambiguous. The next time you are in a situation where your communication partner doesn't get your message, consider whether your language is concrete enough. By using words that match the precision of your thoughts, you can communicate more effectively.

COMMUNICATION IN ACTION 5.2

Using Concrete Language

This exercise is designed to help you practice using more concrete language. Complete the form that is available on the **companion website** to transform abstract comments into statements that are more concrete.

Ask for clarification if a word is ambiguous. A humorous example of the effects of ambiguity on understanding comes from a story Jen once heard about a professor of Slavic Studies who was preparing a group of students for a summer studying abroad in Eastern Europe. As the professor reviewed the list of essentials, he informed them that they would be bathing in public showers, and so it was important for them to bring thongs. Only after several raised eyebrows did he think to clarify that he was referring to flip-flops, not underwear. If the students hadn't signaled their misunderstanding, there might have been a far more embarrassing moment overseas.

It is important to ask directly when you need clarification. If your friend makes a request that you don't understand, you might be wise to reply, "What exactly are you asking me to do?" This gets you focused on the concrete behaviors that are at the heart of the request. Another tactic is to use synonyms for key words, to see if you are capturing your communication partner's meanings correctly. For example, if you aren't sure what someone means by "I'm upset," you might ask if he or she is feeling angry, frustrated, or sad. Although it might seem that probing the meaning of words would burden conversation, often it's better than miscommunicating.

Look beyond labels. Although labels help us make sense of our experience, try not to overreact to them. Would you be surprised to learn that many gifted students are also learning disabled in some way? These "doubly exceptional learners" are sometimes hard to identify, because educators can't reconcile the conflicting labels (Brody & Mills, 1997). The important point is to remember that labels don't represent the entire truth, they just summarize part of it.

When you communicate with someone who has been labeled – an athlete, a single-mother, a cancer survivor, a sorority sister – pay attention to the qualities that set this individual apart from the category. The label can help you to identify topics you might talk about, but it surely won't capture everything that is important to know about your communication partner. People are always more complex and interesting than the few words that might describe them.

THE RULES OF LANGUAGE

When you drive a car, you can avoid an accident by obeying the rules about which side of the road to drive on, what to do at a four-way stop, and when to pull over for an emergency vehicle. In the same way, we rely on rules of language to avoid miscommunication. Importantly, we usually don't think consciously about these rules; instead, our knowledge of them automatically shapes how we create and decipher verbal messages. In the following sections, we'll examine the rules for using language to make meaning and for making conversation.

Using Language to Make Meaning

Our use of language is guided by rules that address the structure of words and sentences, the meanings attached to words, and the use of language to accomplish goals (see Figure 5.2). These rules of language both shape the verbal messages we create and how we interpret the messages we receive from others.

At a basic level, **syntactic rules** identify how words and phrases can be structured within a message. Consider how much harder it is to understand a sentence with just two words in the wrong place compared to a sentence with the words in a correct order:

> I put my clothes the washer in dinner after.
> I put my clothes in the washer after dinner.

The order of words can also help us decipher words that have more than one meaning. For example, "the ship sails" and "ship the sails" have the same words, but those words have different meaning depending on where they are placed in the sentence.

We are also influenced by the meanings of words when we use them to craft messages. **Denotative meaning** refers to the literal, public, or conventional definition for the word; for example, "cancer" refers to a category of disease in which mutant cells reproduce and disable a host organism. **Connotative meaning** is the implicit emotional or evaluative tone of a word. If you know someone who died from cancer, that word probably has a special meaning for you and might evoke strong feelings.

Syntactic Rules
Guidelines for structuring words and phrases within a message.

Denotative Meaning
The literal, public, or conventional definition of a word.

Connotative Meaning
The implicit emotional or evaluative interpretation of a word.

PRAGMATIC RULES
Guidelines for performing actions using language

SEMANTIC RULES
Guidelines for using words in phrases based on meanings

SYNTACTIC RULES
Guidelines for structuring words and phrases within a message

FIGURE 5.2 A hierarchy of language rules

PAUSE & REFLECT

What words have an emotional impact on you but may be neutral for another person? Why are those words so meaningful to you?

Semantic rules govern the way you use language based on both denotative and connotative meanings. Of course, we need to use words in a way that is consistent with their meanings; it would be confusing to say you spent the summer "reading bikes" rather than "reading books" or "riding bikes." The connotative meaning of words also influences how we use and understand language, but perhaps in less obvious ways. One study demonstrated the effects of connotative meanings in messages that doctors use to recruit people into studies of experimental medical treatments (Krieger, Parrott, & Nussbaum, 2011). Most messages about medical experiments explain that some people will get the new treatment and some people won't, and that deciding who gets the treatment is random, "like flipping a coin." The study found that older women from rural communities reacted negatively to these messages, which made them think of "gambling" or "playing a game" with their lives. In contrast, explaining that random is "like the sex of a baby" had positive connotations for women with strong family values, and it emphasized to them that either outcome was desirable.

Rules also govern how we use language to accomplish goals. Table 5.2 provides examples of several **speech acts**, which are actions that we perform using language. When we use words to express a compliment, accuse a person of cheating, ask a question, or make a request, we are acting upon our environment; in fact, all of our messages perform some kind of function, even if it is just to provide information. By the very act of speaking, we have changed our circumstances in some way. And some outcomes – such as inaugurating a president or pronouncing a couple legally married – require that someone utter specific words.

Pragmatic rules help us to figure out which speech acts can be performed in specific circumstances. For example, not anyone can inaugurate a president; in the United States, that speech act can only be performed by the Chief Justice of the Supreme Court. Within interpersonal interactions, you cannot always express a compliment, accuse a person of cheating, ask a question, provide information, make a request, etc. For example, before

Semantic Rules
Guidelines for using words in phrases based on meanings.

Speech Acts
Actions that are performed using language.

Pragmatic Rules
Guidelines for performing actions using language.

TABLE 5.2 Examples of speech acts

Propose	Will you marry me?
Compliment	I like how you've decorated your home
Insult	I don't think I've ever seen sloppier work
Hire	Maria, you're perfect for the job – when can you start?
Accuse	I believe that you cheated on the exam
Break up	It's over. I'm leaving you
Apologize	I'm sorry
Vow	I promise to love, honor, and cherish you

you can accuse someone of cheating, there has to be some standard for behavior that can be violated, you have to have some reason to suspect cheating, and you have to have the right to pass judgment.

Pragmatic rules help us identify the messages that are appropriate or inappropriate in a particular situation. For example, before you ask someone for help, you might consider your relationship with that person and whether he or she has the ability to help you. If you make a request that doesn't fit with the circumstances – such as asking your unemployed college acquaintance to pay your tuition bill – your behavior will be inappropriate. Because the speech acts we can perform are linked to qualities of our relationships, different types of relationships involve different types of speech acts. To illustrate this point, communication scholars Daena Goldsmith and Leslie Baxter (1996) asked people to keep a diary of speech acts they experienced over a two-week period and their relationship with the person involved in each interaction. As summarized in Table 5.3, they found that the frequency of small talk, joking, gossip, etc., is affected by the relationship that exists between interaction partners.

Pragmatic rules also help us to interpret the meaning of a message and figure out what speech acts people are performing. Imagine a friend telling you, "I'm moving during finals week." What could this mean? Perhaps the friend is alerting you that she can't socialize during that time or hinting that she'd like to use your car to move. Now, imagine that same message being delivered to your professor. If you mentioned to your professor that you were moving during finals week, he or she might wonder if you are asking to reschedule the exam or explaining why your performance might suffer; however, your professor probably wouldn't think that you were asking to borrow a car. Pragmatic rules help us to eliminate some of the possible meanings of messages, which improves our ability to figure out what people really mean.

TABLE 5.3 Speech acts and types of interpersonal relationships

This table shows the percentage of speech acts that are performed in different relationships. Categories that captured at least 10 % of speech acts within a relationship type are in boldface. Notice how the most common speech acts vary depending on the type of relationship.

Speech act	Acquaintances (%)	Close friends (%)	Parent & child (%)	Romantic partners (%)
Make small talk	**28**	4	3	4
Joke around	**12**	9	8	8
Gossip	8	**27**	8	8
Make plans	8	**12**	**13**	**12**
Catch up	5	**10**	**15**	2
Recap the day	1	5	**10**	**10**
Greet in the morning	0	1	3	**10**
Express love	0	0	2	**14**

Making Conversation

Because verbal communication is abstract and arbitrary, communication partners need to help each other in order to have an effective conversation. The philosopher Paul Grice (1957, 1975) coined the phrase **the cooperative principle** to refer to the assumption that people work together to advance a conversation. In other words, we go into a conversation expecting the other person to make a good faith effort to produce meaningful messages.

The Cooperative Principle
The assumption that people who are talking to each other are working together to advance the conversation.

Grice theorized that there are basic rules, called maxims, that we assume people are following as they cooperate in a conversation. The maxims dictate rules for good behavior in conversations, but more importantly, they identify the assumptions that you can rely on when talking to someone else. The role of these maxims was brought to life in a study of college students engaged in online conversation (Daly, Weber, Vangelisti, Maxwell, & Neel, 1989). The researchers asked the participants to express their thoughts out loud as they communicated. The thoughts that people reported showed that they made inferences about the other person's reasons behind messages and where the conversation was going. Based on these inferences, they would supply additional details, make comments that they thought were pertinent, and try to clarify their statements. The maxims of conversations are assumptions that allow us to make sense of the messages we receive.

PAUSE & REFLECT

Have you ever communicated with someone who didn't seem to share your goal of advancing the conversation? How was their lack of cooperation evident and how did it make you feel?

The **maxim of quantity** specifies that communicators should provide enough information to advance the conversation, and avoid providing either too much or too little information. Imagine that you get a call from a friend; after you say "Hello," the response is a simple "I'm back." Although it's only a two-word phrase, the maxim of quantity lets you assume that your friend is giving you all the information he or she thinks you need. So what can you infer to inform your reply? For one, your friend believes that you know who is calling, otherwise he or she would have stated her name. What else do you know from these two words? Your friend has been away, thinks you know where, and believes you would like to know that he or she is back. Because you can assume that your friend is giving you all the information you need, you are able to draw a lot of meaning from those two words.

Maxim of Quantity
A conversational rule that communicators should provide sufficient information to advance the conversation.

Think about how difficult interpersonal communication would be if we couldn't assume that people speak truthfully? The **maxim of quality** helps us understand even far-fetched utterances, because we can start with the expectation that the speaker means to convey something truthful. Imagine your roommate says, "I'm sorry I didn't clean the kitchen. I've been so stressed by exams I haven't slept for 10 days!" You probably wouldn't

Maxim of Quality
A conversational rule that communicators should make truthful contributions to conversation.

actually believe that it was possible that your roommate has been awake for 240 hours straight, but it isn't hard to find a true interpretation that makes sense (i.e., that she is exhausted and overwhelmed). The maxim of quality also helps us to detect when someone isn't being truthful. We conclude that people are lying when the meanings implied by their messages don't add up (Jacobs, Dwason, & Brashers, 1996). What if your roommate also mentioned the dinner party she threw last night while you were at work? Because being stressed by finals, endless sleepless nights, and throwing a party don't fit together, your friend's story would seem a bit fishy.

Now, let's focus on the **maxim of relevance**, which suggests that communicators should make contributions that are pertinent to the conversation topic. Consider the opening turns in an exchange between Lexi and Scott:

> LEXI: Hey, Scott – what's up? You look upset.
> SCOTT: Oh, I just got a call from my dad. He expects me to drop everything and run over and help him with his taxes, and he got mad when I told him I was busy.
> LEXI: Did I ever tell you about my good friend from high school?

On the surface, Lexi's last comment violates the maxim of relevance, but if we assume that Lexi is following the rules, her high school friend must be relevant in some way. Perhaps the friend takes advantage of Lexi's expertise too, and Lexi is bringing him up to show empathy for Scott. Or, perhaps Lexi's friend is a tax accountant who can help solve the problem. Although we have to get a bit further in the conversation to find out how the high school friend fits in, using the maxim of relevance puts Scott on the lookout for the connection.

Maxim of Relevance

A conversational rule that communicators should make contributions to conversation that are pertinent to the topic.

PAUSE & REFLECT

How do you typically react when someone violates the maxim of relevance – in other words, changes the topic suddenly – during a conversation?

Maxim of Manner

A conversational rule that communicators should strive to be clear, organized, and to the point.

Finally, the **maxim of manner** specifies that we should avoid being vague, wordy, or disorganized; instead, we should craft messages that are as clear and tidy as possible. Consider how confused you might be if someone violated the maxim of manner when giving you directions to a street address, saying: "Turn left at the supermarket, go three blocks, turn right on Main. And oh, back at the supermarket, you'll need to get into the left hand lane as soon as possible, so you don't miss the turn onto 16th Street." Jumping back in the sequence of directions makes it harder for you to organize the information in a meaningful way. Young children are especially likely to violate the maxim of manner because children have trouble imagining what kinds of messages other people will understand (Pellegrini, Brody, & Stoneman, 1987). For example, a child might tell a story that involves enormous detail ("it was black and blue, and kind of spotted; well, the spots were really heart-shaped, but smaller; kind of like a dot") about an experience that her parents don't remember ("that walk we went on") that has no obvious organization ("we walked a long time; before that we had waffles; the butterflies were pretty").

The rules for making conversation highlight why misunderstanding is so common. The maxims of conversation help us make inferences about meaning, but there is still a leap involved in interpreting verbal cues. When someone doesn't give us enough information, says something untrue, shifts the topic suddenly, or is vague, wordy, or disorganized, we have to figure out why. As we sift through various explanations – the topic is sensitive, the person is upset, the speaker is asking us to do something – we may or may not settle on the right implication (Holtgraves, 2002). In other words, the rules of language can help us make conversation, but they can't prevent communication partners from drawing unintended inferences.

FIGURE 5.3 A violation of the maxim of manner

A street sign uses more words than necessary to convey a warning.

Putting Theory into Practice: Reducing Miscommunication

Any tool we might use comes with rules for how to use it, and language is no exception. These rules can help us troubleshoot when verbal communication breaks down.

Attend to connotative meanings. Different words evoke positive or negative feelings and some words evoke stronger emotions than others. Strive to choose words that create the reaction you seek. If your message isn't producing the desired effect, you might ask the person you're trying to reach how they are reacting to your words. In the same way, be attentive to the words that cause you to react with strong emotions. Being aware of words that trigger strong reactions within you can help you to avoid overreacting to someone else's message.

COMMUNICATION IN ACTION 5.3

Exploring the Meanings of "Help"

In this exercise you will explore how subtle changes in a message can promote different connotative meanings, especially when you consider the source of the message and your relationship with that person. Visit the **companion website** to test your skills at deciphering connotative meanings in messages.

Diagnose topic shifts. Have you ever been in a conversation where your interaction partner seemed to change the topic suddenly? It can seem like the person isn't listening or has a different agenda. The maxim of relevance suggests, however, that even a seemingly unrelated comment is probably connected to your utterance in some way. Rather than being miffed at the topic change, try to find out why your partner responded in that way. You might ask, "Is that related to what I just said?" or express confusion by saying, "I'm not sure how that connects to what I was talking about." If this was a blatant topic shift, at least your partner knows you noticed. And if it wasn't, you give your partner a chance to clarify his or her intentions.

Of course, topic shifts are a natural part of conversation, and they don't always violate the maxim of relevance. Communication scholar Galina Bolden (2006) examined recorded conversations to identify how people verbally signal a topic change. She found that people use the word "so" (e.g., "so, how are you?" or "so, I hear it's your birthday") to signal a shift to a new topic or a topic that was previously set aside. Bolden also observed that people use "oh" to introduce new information that has just been noticed or remembered, and it suggests some degree of urgency. For example, "Oh, that reminds me. . ." indicates that your partner intends to talk about something new and it is pressing enough to discard the topic at hand. Verbal cues like these illustrate how we use language to change topics without violating the maxim of relevance.

Set the stage for conversation. We sometimes have difficulty being organized, clear, and precise, because we don't know what our communication partner already knows about a topic. Consider what happens in a conversation between co-workers Dwayne and Lydia when Lydia mistakenly assumes that Dwayne has heard about an upcoming meeting. When Lydia opens with, "Are you ready for Friday?" Dwayne has no idea what she's talking about. Lydia might continue making references to the Friday meeting, until Dwayne says, "Wait, I didn't know about this meeting." At that point, Lydia might start over, "About 6 months ago, there was an awful mix-up in shipping; it was a huge mess." Now Dwayne might have to interrupt this recounting of events, "I know about all that, but what's going on this Friday?" Lydia's story has to start again, this time describing the agenda and focus of the meeting.

You can avoid disorderly conversations by taking a little time to set the stage. In other words, before launching into a conversation on a topic, find out what the other person already knows. "Did you hear about . . .?" "When was the last time you talked to . . .?" and "How much do you know about . . .?" are simple questions that can help you and a conversational partner figure out where you need to elaborate, where you can gloss some details, and where to start your discussion so that you can have an coherent interaction.

FACTORS THAT AFFECT LANGUAGE USE

Thus far, you have learned about the general features and rules of language use. Now, we consider variations in how people use language based on gender, power, and intimacy.

Gender

Gender differences in speech emerge in childhood, between 5 and 7 years old, and these distinctions only grow stronger with age (Leaper, 1991). Girls are more likely than boys to express agreement, acknowledge what another person has said, and soften their speech to avoid asserting dominance (Leaper, 1994). Boys tend to be more coercive, controlling, demanding, and confrontational than girls (Leaper, 1994; Maccoby, 1990). These childhood differences lay the foundation for several gender differences in language that are present in adulthood.

One difference between men and women's speech is the tendency for women to make more hesitant or qualified claims (e.g., Bradac, Mulac, & Thompson, 1995; Lakoff,

SCHOLAR SPOTLIGHT

Visit the Communication Café on the **companion website** to view a conversation with Steven Wilson, who has conducted a wide variety of studies of language use in interpersonal interactions.

1973). In particular, women are more likely than men to insert hedges, qualifiers, or tag questions into their messages. Compare the following variations on the claim "That's a good idea."

- Hedge: "That's *sort of* a good idea."
- Qualifier: "*I'm not really sure*, but that *seems* like a good idea."
- Tag question: "That's a good idea, *isn't it*?"

When women use hedges, qualifiers, and tag questions, they appear unsure of themselves, and they invite disagreement from others.

Women also tend to use more emotional terms and more passive verb forms, whereas men are more factual and to the point in their word choice. Communication scholar Anthony Mulac has studied the linguistic styles of men and women for over 30 years. In one of his classic studies, 20 men and 20 women described the same landscape photograph to a researcher (Mulac & Lundell, 1986). Men's speech focused on facts, such as the number of objects present and their location, whereas women were more likely to describe their feelings when looking at the landscape (see also Mulac, Bradac, & Gibbons, 2001). Men also used more short, declarative, and judgmental sentences; women used longer and more detailed sentences, more adverbs, and less concrete verb forms. Differences have also been found in how men and women communicate in television interviews – women use plain language and discuss their feelings, but men are more likely to use jargon and depersonalize the conversation (Brownlow, Rosamond & Parker, 2003).

Men and women also communicate differently online. In a study that examined messages posted by students in an introductory psychology class, women posted more tentative claims and expressed agreement with other students, whereas men made more assertions and expressed more disagreement with others (Guiller & Durndell, 2006). Men talking to men in chat rooms also use more figures of speech and slang than women chatting with women (Hussey & Katz, 2006). These gender differences are even more

"When you say 'It's all good' what you really mean is 'I don't care'."

FIGURE 5.4 What you really mean

Source: © William Haefeli/The New Yorker Collection/www.cartoonbank.com.

pronounced when people are discussing gendered topics, like sports or fashion, rather than gender-neutral topics (Thomson, 2006).

PAUSE & REFLECT

Do you think you can tell whether someone is male or female based on an online posting? If so, what cues do you use to figure out someone's gender?

You might be wondering how people react to gender differences in the use of language. The gender-linked language effect refers to the impact of men's and women's speech patterns on people's perceptions of speakers. Remember the differences Anthony Mulac found in how men and women describe a landscape photo? When other people read those descriptions, they rated women's descriptions of the landscape higher in aesthetic quality and more intellectual, but they found men's descriptions to be more dynamic (Mulac et al., 2001). People also have different perceptions of speeches given by men and women (e.g., Mulac & Lundell, 1982). Specifically, messages with feminine characteristics are seen as less persuasive, authoritative, and appealing (Carli, 1990; Gibbons, Busch, & Bradac, 1991).

Power and Intimacy

Language use also varies according to the relationship that exists between conversational partners. Consider how your own speech changes as you talk to different people over the course of your day. How would your greetings change if you were speaking to an acquaintance in class, one of your professors, a good friend, your parents, or someone who works for you? Chances are, you have a lot of different ways of saying hello, and the way you talk depends on the power dynamics and degree of intimacy in your relationship with the other person.

Politeness theory is a perspective on language use that highlights how relationship qualities affect communication (Brown & Levinson, 1987). Specifically, the theory focuses on how we perform speech acts that might have a negative effect on a partner – criticizing a person, asking for a favor, or interrupting a conversation. When the other person has more power, we try to minimize the negative impact of our words. In addition, we have less freedom to impose on people with whom we have a more distant relationship. When we need to soften the impact of an intrusive speech act, we use polite messages like the ones summarized in Table 5.4.

In the workplace, employees depend on a manager for work assignments, performance evaluations, and promotions. How do these power differences affect language? In one study, college students imagined that they were new employees at a company meeting where someone had taken their seat and moved their belongings (Morand, 2000). When the "seat-stealer" had higher status, the students used more polite messages to request their seat and possessions (Morand, 1996a). Power also affects how people

TABLE 5.4 Verbal cues that increase politeness

Indirectness	Are you going to be using your car this weekend?
Hedging	I was kind of wondering if you would mind helping me
Conditional language	If you were going by the coffee shop, could you get me a muffin?
Minimized consequences	I need a little of your time
Apologies	I'm so sorry to bother you, but can I borrow your phone?
Past tense (which decreases urgency)	I had been planning to ask you about a loan

address each other within an organization. Managers are free to call employees by their first names, and employees tend to use their boss's formal title (Morand, 1996b). In fact, subordinates sometimes avoid using any name for their supervisor, because a first name is too informal and a formal title is too stiff (Morand, 2005).

INSIDE COMMUNICATION RESEARCH

Evaluations of High and Low Power Speech

Characteristics of a person's language use can be influential in the impressions that listeners form about a speaker. Powerless language is marked by hedges, hesitations, tag questions, and intensifiers (as in "that was a *really* good idea"). Which of the elements of powerless speech have the biggest impact on perceptions of a speaker? Communication researchers Lawrence Hosman and Susan Siltanen (2006) predicted that hedges and tag questions would contribute to the most negative evaluations.

To test their predictions, the researchers took a sample of high-power speech from a criminal trial transcript. They created three low-power speech samples by adding hedges, intensifiers, or tag questions to the same excerpt. Study participants were asked to read one of the four passages and rate the speaker's competence, control of self, and control of other.

The results of this study partially confirmed the researchers' hypothesis. In particular, speakers in the version of the transcript that included hedges were perceived as being the least competent and having the least control over self and others. In contrast, speakers who used intensifiers were rated as having significantly more control over self and others than the speakers who used hedges or tag questions. In fact, the speakers who used intensifiers were seen as more in control than the speakers in the original version of the transcript.

THINK ABOUT IT

1. This study asked participants to evaluate transcripts from a criminal trial that had been modified by the researchers, rather than spoken messages within an interpersonal interaction. What are some the limitations of using court transcripts to support claims about interpersonal communication?
2. The results of this study showed that speakers who use hedges were evaluated most negatively. Given evidence that women are more likely to use hedges in interpersonal interactions (Bradac et al., 1995), do you think their language use could place women at a disadvantage in the workplace?

Idiom

A term, phrase, or reference that has a special meaning known only to members of a social group.

In intimate relationships, our use of language is more informal. One linguistic feature that surfaces in close relationships is the **idiom**, which refers to a term or phrase that has a special meaning known only to members of a social group. Denise recalls an idiom that emerged within a group of graduate students who had, at one time or another, met her dog Tupelo. As a bloodhound, Tupelo had an ample supply of saliva, which she could send flying across the room with the toss of her head. One student coined the term "Tupeloed" to describe being slobbered on by the dog, and the rest of the students quickly adopted her language. Over time, "Tupeloed" became an idiom to describe any unfortunate mess – if a student came back from lunch and said he or she had been "Tupeloed," everyone knew that a spill had occurred. In this way, idioms arise from shared experiences, are adopted by members of the social group, and become part of the linguistic code used by group insiders.

Not surprisingly, idioms commonly arise in friendships and romantic relationships. One study asked college undergraduates to describe the idioms that were used in a close same-sex friendship (Bell & Healey, 1992). The researchers found that friends with more solidarity used more idioms to identify each other, reference activities or objects, express affection, and confront each other. Closeness in a friendship also allows partners to use and understand ironic insults, compliments, humor, and teasing (Pexman & Zvaigzne, 2004). Likewise, romantic partners who report more love and commitment have more idioms to express affection, initiate sexual encounters, and refer to sexual matters (Bell, Buerkel-Rothfuss, & Gore, 1987).

PAUSE & REFLECT

What are some of the nicknames, inside jokes, and terms that have a special meaning within your close relationships? Where did these idioms come from?

Intimacy is even reflected by the pronouns that people use to refer to themselves and their partner (Agnew, Van Lange, Rusbult, & Langston, 1998). In one study, dating partners talked for 10 minutes while being videotaped (Knobloch & Solomon, 2003). Partners who were more intimate and interdependent tended to use more pluralistic pronouns like "we" and "us," and partners who were less close used more singular pronouns like "you" and "I." This study shows how the intimacy of a relationship affects language use in subtle ways.

Putting Theory into Practice: Fine-tuning Your Language

Studies that have analyzed people's language use over time show that our verbal behavior does not change significantly (Pennebaker, Mehl, & Niederhoffer, 2003). Nonetheless, we are not trapped into gendered speech patterns, and we can take steps to tailor our language to the interpersonal communication situations that we find ourselves in.

FIGURE 5.5 Friends can use language to reinforce their bond

Source: Getty Images.

Avoid gender traps. A long-standing explanation for gendered speech patterns is that women use more hesitant language because they have held a less powerful position in society than men (Lakoff, 1973). Although this explanation may have been more valid 40 years ago, we need to be sure that our language reflects the more equal positions men and women hold nowadays. More to the point, you can avoid using stereotypically male speech (e.g., making assertions of fact, passing judgment, being impersonal) or stereotypically female language (e.g., using tentative language, focusing on feelings, or being personal). Instead, choose words that are assertive or tentative, fact- or emotion-focused, and personal or impersonal to fit the context.

COMMUNICATION IN ACTION 5.4

Analyze Your Speech Patterns

Use a recording device, such as a digital recorder or even your cell phone, to record one of your naturally occurring conversations. Then, listen closely to the words and phrases you used in that interaction. Take note of how often you assert a fact, insert a hedge or qualifier, ask a tag question, reference your feelings, and issue a command. As you reflect on the results of your analysis, can you think of ways in which you can make your language less gendered? If you are a man, are there times when you assert information as a fact, when it is really an impression or guess? If you are a woman, do you find that you soften assertions you believe are true by hedging or qualifying your words?

Tailor your language to social contexts. When you are in a subordinate position, consider whether your language communicates an appreciation of status differences. You needn't refrain from expressing opinions or asserting yourself; however, you should strive for politeness. Try to be less forceful with your requests, apologize for imposing, and use appropriately formal terms of address. If you are in a position of authority, keep in mind that you can confuse people by using indirect and tentative language to speak your mind. A supervisor who issues directions too politely leaves subordinates wondering whether they have received an instruction, a suggestion, or friendly advice (Markham, 1996).

In a similar fashion, adjust the familiarity of your language to the level of intimacy you share with a communication partner. When you use nicknames, special greetings, and idioms, you convey solidarity with a friend or family member. These terms can foster a sense of closeness and make intimacy tangible. At the same time, avoid overly familiar language with people you're not close to. When you adopt terms of endearment, special words or phrases, and inside jokes that belong to others, you run the risk of violating relationship boundaries.

BIASED LANGUAGE

A hammer can be used to put things together or smash things to pieces. In the same way, language can be used to promote well-being, build relationships, and foster communities, or it can be used to undermine someone, weaken an interpersonal bond, or divide people. In this section of the chapter, we consider some forms of language that contribute to problematic communication experiences.

Racist Language

Racist language includes words and utterances that undermine a person's ethnic group. By doing so, these verbal messages dehumanize their targets and render people vulnerable to both discrimination and acts of violence. Consider the racist propaganda that Nazis used to justify the extermination of Jews, the origins and usage of racial slurs in American culture, and messages of hatred produced by Al Qaeda to intimidate citizens of the Western world.

Sometimes racist messages are obvious. For example, when Michael Richards, who played Kramer in the hit comedy *Seinfeld*, was heckled during a stand-up comedy act, he responded by hurling racial slurs at an audience member. French TV personality, Pascal Sevran, similarly found himself in hot water for making explicit slurs against black people on his television program. But racism often surfaces in more subtle linguistic forms. One study found that people attempt to justify racist attitudes by drawing on personal experiences or news stories about the people they're denigrating, and by using disclaimers such as "I'm not racist, but . . ." (Verkuyten, de Jong, & Masson, 1994). These denials do not change the fact that giving voice to words that belittle a racial group constitutes racism.

How can you talk about race while avoiding racist language? Two researchers who were involved in an interracial relationship in South Africa – where interracial sexual relations were a crime until 1985 – conducted a study of the language people used when raising issues of race in their presence (Barnes, Palmary, & Durrheim, 2001). The couple recorded conversations with friends, family members, colleagues, and strangers. When analyzing these conversations, the couple noticed several linguistic devices that people used to discuss matters of race. Humor was the most common strategy for bringing the topic of race into a conversation, because it inhibits angry responses from listeners and reduces the tension associated with racial discourse. They also found that people referenced personal experiences to ground their racial perceptions in some external reality. People also waited for the couple to raise the topic of race, thereby giving them permission to discuss the topic. Although tensions may make it difficult to discuss race openly, taking care with your language can help you avoid racist talk while still discussing racial issues.

> ### PAUSE & REFLECT
>
> Have you ever been involved in or the target of a racist conversation? If so, how did the person making the racist comment justify or hide the racism?

Sexist Language

Sexist language includes words or expressions that differentiate between the sexes or exclude and trivialize either gender (Parks & Roberton, 1998). Consider words in the English language that reflect men's historically dominant position in society. For example, the United States Declaration of Independence states that "all men are created equal" and that the laws set forth in the declaration are for the benefit of all "mankind." Until recently, writers typically used "he" as the pronoun of choice to refer to both men and women. And more than one political reporter has noted the fact that American society lacks a term to label the male spouse of a female president (Anthony, 2007). In 2009, the European Union banned members of the European Parliament from using the terms Miss and Mrs to refer to women because they felt it was sexist to refer to a woman's marital status when a similar language structure did not exist for men. This means that Madame and Mademoiselle, Frau and Fraulein, and Senora and Senorita were also banned. Instead, women are simply to be called by their name. Figure 5.6 identifies just a few of the professional titles that are linked to the sex of the person in that position, as well as some gender-neutral alternatives.

Although the women's movement made people aware of how language can marginalize women, sexist language lingers along with sexist attitudes. For example, people who endorse sexist beliefs are more likely to use the pronoun "he" to describe a business executive or professor (Swim, Mallett, & Stangor, 2004). Sexist men are also more likely to use the terms "girl" or "lady," rather than the more neutral word "woman" (Cralley & Ruscher, 2005). Men also continue to be more likely than women to use gender-exclusive language in their writing and speech (Rubin, Greene, & Schneider, 1994). But men can also be marginalized by sexist language. Consider the implications that are derived from "Mommy and Me" swim lessons at your local YMCA or "maternity leave" that is offered to new mothers but less frequently to new fathers. Such labels create expectations about which parent should be the primary caretaker and create barriers for fathers who might want to play a more active role in their child's life.

Sexist language may seem harmless, but it is related to some significant social consequences. For one, people who endorse gender biased language also have more negative attitudes toward women (Parks & Roberton, 2004). The exchange of sexist jokes by men is also one way that men exclude women from conversations and reject femininity

HOW DO YOU RATE? 5.1

Attitudes Toward Sexist/Nonsexist Language

As communicators, we are often unaware of the sexist implications of our language. Visit the **companion website** to complete a scale to assess your attitudes toward sexist language. Once you determine whether your attitude toward sexist language is positive, negative, or neutral, consider how this attitude is reflected in your communication behavior.

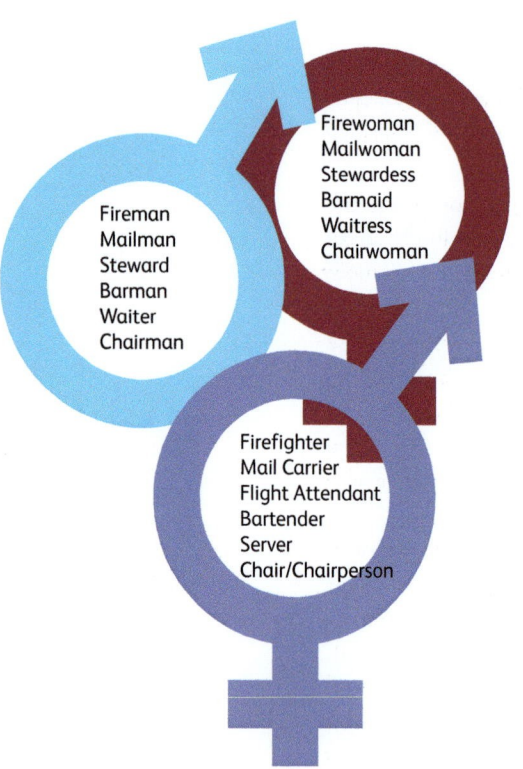

FIGURE 5.6 Sex-specific job titles

(Lyman, 1987). Moreover, men who enjoy sexist humor tend to engage in more sexual harassment, have more hostile views of women, and are more aggressive with romantic partners (Pryor, Giedd, & Williams, 1995; Ryan & Kanjorski, 1998).

Heterosexist Language

Language can also marginalize gay, lesbian, bisexual, and transgendered people. Heterosexist language is language that assumes heterosexuality is superior to other sexual orientations. In the most explicit form, heterosexist language includes derogatory comments, insults, jokes, or threats about the sexual practices of someone who is not heterosexual. Heterosexist language also surfaces in more subtle ways, such as references to romantic partners that assume a heterosexual relationship or medical forms that exclude "domestic partner" as an option for next of kin.

Using heterosexist language isn't just insensitive – it can also damage the development of professional and personal relationships. In one study, lesbian and gay volunteers read a transcript in which a counselor's language was edited to have either a heterosexist bias or no bias (Dorland & Fischer, 2001). In the heterosexist version, the counselor assumed the female client's partner was male and that the client would participate in heterosexual traditions like marriage. Perhaps not surprisingly, readers of the transcript rated the heterosexist counselor as less credible, less helpful, and less likely to encourage openness than the unbiased counselor.

Specific terms in the English language also perpetuate heterosexism. Consider some of the labels used to identify different sexual orientations. If "heterosexual" is equivalent to "straight," does that imply that other sexualities are somehow crooked? If homosexual men are "gay" does that mean that they are frivolous, superficial, and incapable of being serious? In contrast, Native Americans called people who weren't heterosexual "two-spirited," which implied an ability to see both male and female perspectives. Consistent with the positive connotations of this label, two-spirited people were considered especially wise, and they held an honored place in the society (Jacobs, Thomas, & Lang, 1997).

Sometimes heterosexist language is used because of the way our language is constructed, with no intention of marginalizing alternative sexualities. Other times people use derogatory sexual terms as an insult. Homophobic verbal abuse is an increasing problem, particularly among high school students (Kitzinger, 1996). Name-calling is the most prominent form of homophobic abuse (Nayak & Kelly, 1996), but it is not directed exclusively at homosexual individuals. The term "gay" is used to refer to anything or anyone deemed unmasculine or uncool (Armstrong, 1997). In one study, British teens were able to identify more than 600 insulting words and phrases that included an offensive reference to a person's sexuality (Thurlow, 2001).

Putting Theory into Practice: Using Inclusive Language

Racist, sexist, and heterosexist language is clearly damaging to interpersonal relationships and people's sense of self-worth. Given these significant consequences, we should all take steps to avoid and eliminate racist, sexist, and heterosexist language.

Confront racist language. Even if you don't produce racist messages, you contribute to racism when you allow others to use racist language. It can be challenging to speak up when someone is using language in a hurtful way, but you contribute to a more inclusive society when you confront racist language.

What can you do to stifle racist remarks? People who receive racist comments use polite corrections, witty repartee, and strong put-downs to quiet someone who is making racist remarks (Guerin, 2003). A simple comment, such as "I find that kind of language unacceptable" can go a long way toward decreasing expressions of racism. And if you are concerned that confronting a racist speaker will escalate a situation, you can vote with your feet and leave the situation.

Develop your gender- and sexuality-neutral repertoire. You may not even be aware of all the ways your language reflects gender and sexuality biases, but increasing your consciousness of these language patterns can help you to make more inclusive linguistic choices. Eliminating sexist language involves replacing terms that indicate gender with genderless equivalents – *chairperson* rather than *chairman*, *fire fighter* rather than *fireman*, *flight attendant* rather than *stewardess*, etc. Likewise, you can combat heterosexist language by integrating gender-neutral terms like *partner*, *spouse*, or *significant other* into your speech. This use of language might seem awkward at first, but with time it will become second nature. And people who encounter heterosexism throughout their lives will be grateful to find someone who doesn't assume that their romantic relationships involve a person of the opposite sex.

One particular problem that people sometimes struggle with is avoiding the use of masculine pronouns to refer to both men and women. Students often argue that using "he" or "his" is less cumbersome than writing "he or she" or "his or her." As an alternative, you can rephrase a sentence to use a gender-neutral plural pronoun. The sentence "A doctor should be polite to *his* patients" excludes the possibility of female doctors, but "Doctors should be polite to *their* patients" makes the same point without the gender bias. In the same way, you can replace masculine terms to refer to humans with gender-inclusive alternatives. Instead of saying "*Man* cannot live without water," you could say "*One* cannot live without water" or "*People* cannot live without water." Avoiding sexist language isn't all that difficult, but it may take conscious effort; the pay-off is more effective interpersonal communication.

SUMMARY

Language has four core characteristics: it is abstract, arbitrary, culturally determined, and consequential. Because language is abstract, our conversations can transcend the physical world, and we can communicate about ideas, hopes, and dreams. At the same time, language is arbitrary, and it can be ambiguous; although language enables the richness of human interaction, it also introduces the potential for miscommunication. Our language is also inherently tied to our culture – in fact, language both reflects the values of a cultural group and affects how users of that verbal code process their experiences. Language can have especially profound consequences when we allow the words we use to overshadow the nuances and complexity of reality.

When we use language to communicate interpersonally, we are guided by some basic and important rules. Semantic, syntactic, and pragmatic rules inform how we structure words and utterances, use words based on their denotative and connotative meaning, and accomplish speech acts. Researchers have also identified rules or maxims that make it possible for us to make sense of verbal messages. The maxims of conversation specify that we should provide enough information (but not too much), speak truthfully, make relevant contributions to a conversation, and avoid being terse, wordy, or disorganized.

Although general features and rules of language apply in all situations, people vary in how they use language. Gender differences in language use have shown up in women's tendency to use hedges, hesitations, and tag questions more often than men. People choose more formal language and polite phrasing when dealing with those who have greater status or power. In close relationships, informal language includes the use of nick-names, idioms, and private jokes. People even represent their intimacy through verbal cues, such as the pronouns "we" and "us."

Language also has destructive powers. Racist, sexist, and heterosexist language share the quality of marginalizing people within a society. In addition, words and phrases that implicitly privilege being White, male, or heterosexual create barriers for other ethnic groups, women, or homosexual individuals in our society. Language at its worst can undermine people's ability to contribute to their community.

Although you have been using language all of your life, you can still take steps to improve how you use verbal messages when you communicate with others. By attending to your use of language, you can harness the power of words, reduce miscommunication, reinforce the relationships that you have with interaction partners, and ensure that your verbal messages promote effective interpersonal communication. Developing your lan-guage skills may take effort and practice at first, but these communication strategies will eventually become a habitual part of more effective interpersonal interactions. Armed with the knowledge you have gained in this chapter, you are ready to consider ethical issues like those highlighted in the following exercises.

ACTIVITIES FOR EXPLORING COMMUNICATION ETHICS

What Would You/Should You Do?

Imagine that you are out with a group of friends and someone tells a joke in which they use derogatory language to refer to a particular ethnic group. No one of that ethnicity is represented in your social group, but you still recognize the power of language to marginalize certain groups of people. All of your friends are enjoying a hearty laugh at the joke. You don't want to appear as though you have no sense of humor, but you also don't want to promote such derogatory references among your peer group. What would you – should you – do in this situation?

Something to Think About

In the year 2000, a Census Bureau report indicated that 1 in 5 Americans spoke a language other than English in their home. The number of people who speak a foreign language at home more than doubled between 1990 and 2000. Of those who reported that they speak a foreign language at home, only 55 % indicated that they also spoke English "very well." California, New Mexico, and Texas lead the country in the number of non-English-speaking households, with residents in Laredo, Texas, reporting that 9 in 10 households spoke a foreign language. What are the implications of living in a community in which people don't use the same language to express themselves? Should the United States require all citizens to speak the same language? How might such a decision further marginalize or better integrate different social groups?

Analyze Communication Ethics Yourself

Visit a local clinic and pick up an assortment of pamphlets that provide information about a variety of health topics. Review the pamphlets for evidence of racist, sexist, and heterosexist language. For example, do the pamphlets clarify whether the health information provided applies equally to people of different races, or does it assume that readers are White? Does the text use "he" or "him" to refer to men and women, or is the language more gender-neutral? And are care-givers automatically assumed to be women, while men are assumed to have employment outside the home? Do the topics covered and the language that is used to refer to relationships assume that readers are heterosexual? As you reflect on the results of your analysis, consider whether people of various races, genders, and sexualities would find the health information equally helpful.

KEY WORDS

abstract language	linguistic relativity	Sapir–Whorf hypothesis
concrete language	maxim of manner	semantic rules
connotative meaning	maxim of quality	speech acts
cooperative principle	maxim of quantity	syntactic rules
denotative meaning	maxim of relevance	totalizing
idiom	pragmatic rules	
language	reification	

LEARNING OBJECTIVES

After reading this chapter, you should be able to:

1. Identify the channels and characteristics of nonverbal communication.
2. Explain the functions of nonverbal messages.
3. Describe similarities and differences in nonverbal behavior across cultures and genders.
4. Describe how verbal and nonverbal messages work together.
5. Describe the ways that nonverbal cues can reveal deception.

PUTTING THEORY INTO PRACTICE

In this chapter, you will learn how to:

1. Monitor nonverbal behavior more thoroughly.
2. Question your assumptions about the meaning of nonverbal behavior.
3. Make sure nonverbal cues reflect the nature of the relationship.
4. Use nonverbal cues to improve the flow of your conversations.
5. Educate yourself about nonverbal differences when you visit other cultures.
6. Be sensitive to gender differences when communicating with the opposite sex.
7. Rely on uncommon cues to detect deception.
8. Recognize the limitations of nonverbal messages.

NONVERBAL
COMMUNICATION

6

156 WHAT IS NONVERBAL COMMUNICATION?

162 THE FUNCTIONS OF NONVERBAL MESSAGES

169 INDIVIDUAL DIFFERENCES

172 COMBINING VERBAL AND NONVERBAL CUES

178 SUMMARY

179 ACTIVITIES FOR EXPLORING COMMUNICATION ETHICS

179 KEY WORDS

Source: Photo Researchers.

The Sociable Machines Project at MIT has developed a robot called Kismet that is designed to interact with humans and to mimic human emotion and appearance. The robot simulates human emotion through various facial expressions, vocalizations, and movement. Kismet is able to make facial expressions through movements of ears, eyebrows, eyelids, lips, jaw, and head, just like a human. Kismet can also move and orient its eyes like a human, which allows it to control the direction of its gaze, to simulate human visual behaviors, and to focus on important items in its perceptual field. Thus, Kismet can regulate interaction by paying attention to when an interaction partner looks away as they start speaking and when they look back as they finish. When Kismet sees a person, but senses that they are too far away to converse normally, he is programmed to summon them closer. If a person gets too close to the robot, he will jump back and look startled, just as you might do if someone invaded your personal space.

A lthough the verbal messages you construct during interaction are important, your unspoken behaviors and actions are equally, if not more, vital to the communication process. Your facial expressions, posture, and vocal tones help to facilitate turn-taking during interaction, show emotion, and reveal your affection for others. The robot Kismet is able to have intelligent social interactions with humans because he has been programmed to identify and interpret nonverbal cues in a human's face, posture, and voice, as well as to mimic nonverbal expressions in his response. Similarly, you have been "hard-wired" to communicate nonverbally with others, such that you can send and interpret nonverbal messages with ease.

From the moment you wake in the morning to the minute your head hits the pillow at night, you engage in actions and behaviors that have the potential to communicate meaning to others. **Nonverbal behaviors** are human actions that have the potential to form meaningful messages. Nonverbal behaviors become nonverbal communication if they stimulate meaning in the mind of a receiver. Thus, **nonverbal communication** is defined as the process of one person creating meaning in the mind of another person through nonverbal behaviors. Communication scholars have argued that only 35% of the meaning humans derive from interaction comes from words (e.g., Birdwhistell, 1970), which means that as much as 65% of meaning comes from nonverbal behaviors. Some scholars have argued that nonverbal behavior constitutes an even greater portion of our communication, with as much as 90% being nonverbal. These statistics are difficult to test, but no one can deny the pervasive influence of nonverbal communication in shaping interaction. In this chapter, we will examine the characteristics of nonverbal communication, the functions that are served by nonverbal behaviors, and the individual differences that create challenges to nonverbal communication. In the final section of the chapter, we will consider the ways in which verbal and nonverbal messages work together by examining how interpersonal communication is used to deceive others and negotiate sexual intimacy.

WHAT IS NONVERBAL COMMUNICATION?

Have you ever been in a situation where you were able to exchange meaningful messages with an interaction partner without speaking a word? Imagine, for example, attending a boring party with a friend. Your friend catches your eye from across the room, she rolls her eyes and tilts her head in the direction of the door, you smile and nod and head for the closet to get your coats. Without speaking a word, your friend was able to convey her desire to leave and you were able to agree to her request. This example shows how nonverbal cues can provide a very efficient way to communicate with others.

Channels

When people communicate with one another, they send messages back and forth through a channel. A **channel** is the medium through which information is conveyed during interaction. When you communicate nonverbally, you send information through a variety of channels on your body or in your environment. Channels for nonverbal communication include facial expressions, eye contact, body movement, gestures, touch, and physical appearance. In addition, you share or gather meaning from the physical environment, from the time you devote to interaction, and from smells. Table 6.1 summarizes the channels through which nonverbal communication occurs and gives examples of what might be conveyed through each channel.

SCHOLAR SPOTLIGHT

Visit the Communication Café on the **companion website** to view a conversation with Judee Burgoon, a leading researcher on nonverbal communication.

Nonverbal Behaviors
Human actions that have the potential to form meaningful messages.

Nonverbal Communication
The process of creating meaning in the minds of others through nonverbal behaviors.

Channel
Medium through which information is conveyed.

PAUSE & REFLECT

Make a list of the nonverbal behaviors you noticed during your last conversation. Are there particular channels that you tend to pay attention to? How many channels identified in Table 6.1 were left off your list?

TABLE 6.1 The channels of nonverbal behavior

Channels	Behaviors	Examples
Kinesics	Movement of the body: includes gestures, orientation of the body during conversation, posture	When you arrive late to a party by yourself, a friend waves and motions for you to come over by her. The people she's talking to turn toward you to greet you.
Facial expressions	Movement of the facial muscles: primarily for the communication of various emotions	Your friends throw you a surprise party for your birthday. When you walk in, your eyes open wide, your eyebrows raise, and your mouth drops open, revealing your surprise.
Eye behavior	Movement of the eyes: includes looking, gazing, eye contact, and pupil dilation	When studying in the library, the person at the next table keeps looking in your direction. You have made eye contact a number of times, which

TABLE 6.1 continued

Channels	Behaviors	Examples
		prompts you to say good-bye as you leave.
Haptics	Touching behavior: includes shaking hands, hugging, kissing, patting on the back, tickling, or holding someone; as well as touching your own body, such as rubbing your eyes to show that you're tired	Your friend is very sad over the death of her dog. In an effort to comfort her, you put your arm around her, rub her back, and then give her a hug.
Paralinguistics	Characteristics of the voice: includes volume, tone, rate of speech, pitch, intensity, vocal attributes, laughter, and silence	You pick up the telephone and recognize your best friend's voice on the other end. She is speaking softly and there is a quiver in her voice, prompting you to ask "What's wrong?"
Physical appearance	Visible features of the body: includes body shape and size, hair style, gender, ethnicity, clothing, accessories, beauty and attractiveness	Students who attend private high schools are often required to wear a school uniform. This uniform ensures that students will appear "clean cut" and identifies the students as belonging to that institution.
Proxemics	Use of physical space: includes arrangements of objects in physical space, markers of personal territory, and a need for personal space	You are riding in an elevator when another passenger enters, so you move to the far left corner and the other passenger stands in the far right corner to preserve your physical space. Another rider enters and stands near the front of the elevator.
Chronemics	Orientation toward time: a desire to do one thing at a time versus a preference to engage in many activities at once; use of time to communicate cultural values and beliefs, power, intimacy	You arrive early to an interview for a job you really want. The interviewer still isn't back from lunch, but you wait patiently because she has power over you in this situation, and culture dictates that you should wait for more powerful people.
Olfaction	Scents and odors: includes body odor, pheromones, colognes and perfumes, cleanliness, and smells in the environment	Your newest love interest has agreed to come over for dinner. To prepare for the date, you bake cookies to make your house smell good, apply perfume or cologne to your body, and light a scented candle.

Notice how each channel described in Table 6.1 is capable of sending a variety of messages. Consider, for example, the category of eye behavior. When you make eye contact with another person, you could be trying to get that person's attention, showing that you're listening to what he or she has to say, flirting with a stranger, sharing an intimate moment with a romantic partner, or exerting dominance over a subordinate. The fact that such a subtle behavior like eye contact could have so many potent meanings speaks to the power of nonverbal behavior for communicating with others. On the other hand, this example reveals the complexity of creating and interpreting nonverbal messages.

Characteristics

As you saw in the previous chapter, words have no physical connection to the object they represent. Nonverbal communication, on the other hand, is an analogic code system. **Analogic codes** bear a direct, physical resemblance to the object or idea that they represent. Consider the difference between using language versus nonverbal behaviors to communicate sadness. Using language, you might communicate sadness by speaking the words, "I feel sad." People who know how these words are defined will get your message, but the words themselves do not resemble the feeling of sadness. Using nonverbal behavior, you might communicate sadness through downcast eyes, a pouting mouth, crying, and a slumped body posture. These behaviors reveal the lack of physical strength and depression that a sad person typically experiences. Even in online contexts where nonverbal channels are limited, people often substitute emoticons like a sad face (☹) in place of a verbal articulation of their feelings. In the sections that follow, we highlight some of the characteristics of analogic codes that define nonverbal communication.

Analogic Codes
Symbols that bear a physical resemblance to the thing they represent.

Potential for universal meaning. Because analogic codes are more likely to resemble the object or idea that they refer to, they are often more easily recognized across cultures and contexts. When symbols mean the same thing to people, regardless of cultural differences, they have universal meaning. If you have ever traveled in a country where you are unfamiliar with the language, you know all too well the communicative value of nonverbal behavior. You might point at a location on a map in order to get directions; you might mimic swimming motions to ask someone directions to the beach; or you might rub your stomach in order to find a restaurant. When you and a communication partner do not share the same meaning for digital codes, your nonverbal behaviors become especially important for interpersonal communication.

Nonverbal expressions of emotion, in particular, are widely recognized in all cultures (Scherer & Wallbott, 1994). The similarity of emotional cues across cultures makes sense if you think about how an ability to express and understand feelings may have contributed to the evolution of humans. Recognizing fear on the faces of others alerted people to the dangers of an approaching predator. Being able to show love and attraction enabled people to mate and produce offspring. Because the ability to express and read certain emotions evolved with the human species, expressions of emotion are similar in all cultures on the globe.

Variable Intensity
Nonverbal behaviors can show a lot or a little of the idea that they represent.

Variable intensity. Nonverbal behaviors range in terms of the strength with which they are transmitted; this quality is known as **variable intensity**. For example, the strength

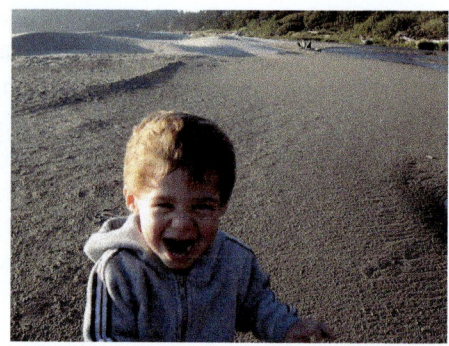

FIGURE 6.1 Denise's son Quincy showing moderate happiness

FIGURE 6.2 Quincy showing intense happiness

of your touch can fluctuate from light tickling to a tight squeeze; the smell of your cologne might vary from weak to strong; and the duration of your eye contact might constitute a fleeting glance or a long stare. Variations in nonverbal behavior are especially apparent in expressions of emotion. For example, nonverbal behaviors that convey fear – wide eyes, a contracted facial expression, and a tense body – can express a range of meanings from "a little afraid" to "scared to death." Variations in intensity are easy to see when you consider the nonverbal channel involving the voice. The volume of your voice can range from a whisper to a shout; your rate of speech can vary from very slow to very fast; and the pitch of your voice can fluctuate from very high to very low. Through these variations, you can express a range of meanings.

Simultaneous transmission. People can send multiple signals through different channels at the same time. Consider the example of a father who is angry with his son. The content of his verbal message might be, "I can't believe you did that, I am very angry right now." His words only express one feeling: anger. His nonverbal behavior, on the other hand, can communicate many details about his anger, as well as other feelings, all at once. The husband might simultaneously speak at a loud volume to show just how angry he is, fold his arms across his chest to show defensiveness, shake his head in disbelief, maintain very intense eye contact with his wife to show dominance, and sigh heavily to show his disappointment. Unlike words, nonverbal behaviors allow you to communicate many messages at once (see Figure 6.3).

Spontaneous transmission. Most of the time, you don't have to think about how to communicate nonverbally with others. For example, if you were feeling nervous, you might unconsciously tap your foot, fidget with your hands, and speak faster at a higher pitch. Sometimes you choose nonverbal behaviors carefully to convey a specific meaning (for example, when you make a peace sign with your hand), but nonverbal communication typically requires little thought or planning. You can send signals through nonverbal channels without consciously constructing the message. Even when you know what you want to communicate, you may not be aware of your nonverbal signals. People can communicate more or less liking for a partner by changing their posture, gesturing, gazing, smiling, and nodding; however, 75% of individuals cannot accurately report an awareness of the nonverbal behaviors they use to convey increased or decreased liking for their partner (Palmer & Simmons, 1995).

DIGITAL SYMBOL SYSTEM

WORDS

ANALOGICAL SYMBOL SYSTEM

FACIAL EXPRESSION

EYE CONTACT

KINETICS

HAPTICS

PROXEMICS

FIGURE 6.3 Communication symbol systems

PAUSE & REFLECT

How can you tell when someone likes you? Have you ever thought that someone liked you, but it turned out that they didn't? What led you to misinterpret their behavior?

Automatic processing. Just as you don't have to think very carefully about how to send nonverbal messages, you can comprehend and respond to nonverbal messages without conscious awareness. Automatic processing refers to the ability to interpret nonverbal messages without consciously thinking about the meaning behind the behavior. Have you ever taken a single look at a friend and known that they were upset? Or, have you ever had an interaction with someone who made you feel uncomfortable, but not known why? Perhaps it was his or her close proximity during conversation, shifty eyes, or inappropriate touching that made this interaction awkward, even though you couldn't put your finger on it while you were talking. You might be so quick to make judgments about other people, or to draw inferences about their feelings or relationship to you, that you don't even realize what those conclusions are based on.

Putting Theory into Practice: Being Aware of Nonverbal Cues

Nonverbal communication is a complex web of behaviors that work together to convey information. Although nonverbal cues are processed automatically, it is possible to increase your awareness of nonverbal messages.

Monitor nonverbal behavior through several channels. Remember that you have a number of different channels that can send information to an interaction partner. Try to become more aware of how you and your partner are using those channels to communicate. Are you engaging all of your nonverbal channels to send messages to others? Is each of your partner's nonverbal channels communicating the same information, or are different channels sending conflicting messages? Your communication will be improved if you use all of your channels during interaction to communicate one clear message. Make a point of consciously noticing at least five different channels for nonverbal communication every time you interact with other people. Over time, you'll find it easier to attend to more channels during your conversations. And when you take advantage of all of the nonverbal cues available to you, you'll have a more complete understanding of your interpersonal interactions.

Question your assumptions. Because you can send and process nonverbal cues spontaneously and automatically, you might have to guard against false assumptions and snap judgments. Consider how crying can be an indication of sadness, but also a sign of happiness, frustration, anger, or hurt. Interpreting nonverbal messages correctly might require you to question your initial reactions and consider the context for the interaction.

COMMUNICATION IN ACTION 6.1

Witnessing Nonverbal Behavior in Context

This exercise asks you to compare the meaning of various nonverbal behaviors depending on the context and the relationship in which they are enacted. Use the form on the **companion website** to take notes as you observe people interacting from each of the categories listed. How did the nonverbal behaviors differ from one category of relationship to another? Did behaviors that occurred in each interaction (for example, touch) mean the same things? Were there ways in which the meaning behind the nonverbal behaviors were the same, regardless of the relational context?

THE FUNCTIONS OF NONVERBAL MESSAGES

Nonverbal communication accomplishes a variety of social tasks, such as revealing your feelings, showing people that you like them, conveying respect to a superior, and managing the flow of conversation. Your nonverbal channels play an important role in communicating each of these different messages. In this section, we focus on the ways that the different nonverbal channels combine to serve a variety of functions during interaction.

Communicating Emotion

One primary function of nonverbal messages is to let other people know what we're feeling. Sometimes it's hard to verbalize emotions to others and nonverbal expressions come more easily. For example, finding the words to describe feelings of anger can be challenging, but your tense body, scowling face, and loud voice automatically display your underlying emotions.

PAUSE & REFLECT

Have you had a feeling that you couldn't fully express through words? How did the emotion reveal itself through your body? How does your voice change when you're feeling happy, frightened, angry, or sad?

The face is an especially powerful channel for revealing emotions. People express emotions through three regions of the face: the mouth, the eyes, and the forehead. For example, in the lower part of the face, a smile corresponds with happiness, a frown indicates sadness, and a wide open mouth reveals surprise. The eyes also distinguish between different emotions, for example, they open wide in fear and glare in anger. When you study the forehead, you'll see that the eyebrows raise up during surprise, furrow during anger, and droop during sadness. Interestingly, people can recognize emotions when shown only one region of the face, and many facial expressions of emotion – happiness, sadness, fear, anger, disgust, surprise, contempt, shame, shyness, and guilt – are universally recognized (Ekman & Friesen, 1975; Izard, 1977).

COMMUNICATION IN ACTION 6.2

Forming Facial Expressions of Emotion

This exercise will make you more aware of the nuances in your facial expressions of emotion. Sit in front of a mirror and form a facial expression for each of the emotions listed in the table on the **companion website**. For each emotion, write down the characteristics that you see in each of the three areas of the face. Which emotion was easiest or hardest for you to express? What region of the face reveals the most information about the underlying emotion?

The voice is another channel that reveals emotions. In fact, vocal cues sometimes convey emotions better than facial expressions (Planalp, 1998). When your best friend calls on the phone, you can tell whether he or she is having a good day or a bad day in the first 30 seconds of the conversation just by the tone in his or her voice. A slower, quieter, and lower pitched voice communicates depression (Segrin, 1998), while a higher pitch and more varied inflection communicates joy (Scherer & Wallbott, 1994). Because the voice is more difficult to control than facial expressions, it can be a more reliable indicator of a person's feelings.

Although much of nonverbal behavior is natural and automatic, some of it is also a learned response to social situations. **Simulation** occurs when you display emotions that you are not actually feeling. For example, you might smile for a photograph even though you aren't feeling particularly happy. **Intensification** occurs when your display of a particular emotion is stronger than you are actually experiencing. When someone gives you a gift, you might display stronger happiness than you are actually feeling to ensure that they know you are grateful. **Deintensification** refers to the tendency to downplay particularly strong emotions. For example, you might be elated over the A you received on your midterm, but you might act only mildly pleased so that your friend who got a D doesn't feel badly. Finally, **masking** occurs when people show an entirely different emotion from the one that they are truly feeling. An Oscar nominee for best supporting actress might clap and smile when one of the competitors wins the award, but she probably feels disappointed and maybe a little jealous.

Communicating Liking

How do you behave when you like someone? How can you tell when someone really likes you? You may determine whether a person likes you or not by focusing on the immediacy of their nonverbal behavior. **Immediacy** is the degree of physically or psychologically perceived warmth and involvement between people. In general, people are more well liked when they show more immediate nonverbal behaviors, because they seem friendly, supportive, and kind. In this section, you'll learn about some of the nonverbal behaviors that contribute to perceptions of immediacy.

Eye contact is central to expressions of liking. During conversation, people often judge how interested or involved a partner is based on the amount of eye contact that he or she displays. People rate partners who make a lot of eye contact as more intimate, more attracted to one another, and more trusting than partners who make less eye contact (Burgoon, Buller, Hale, and deTurck, 1984). Likewise, your own eye contact reveals your feelings for a partner. For example, communication partners who are in love are more likely to gaze at one another (Andersen, 1985).

Touch is another nonverbal behavior that reveals liking and intimacy in a relationship. Touch is a strong communicator of immediacy, because it brings people together, both physically and psychologically. People who engage in more touch are generally perceived as more self-confident and warm (Andersen & Sull, 1985; Jones & Brown, 1996). Touch also reveals the amount of intimacy in a relationship. In fact, a study which examined couples waiting in line at the movies found that partners who were seriously dating engaged in twice as much touch as partners who were either casually dating or married (Guerrero & Andersen, 1991).

Simulation
Displaying emotions that are not actually felt.

Intensification
Displaying emotions that are stronger than the felt emotion.

Deintensification
Downplaying particularly strong emotions.

Masking
Displaying a different emotion from the one that is truly felt.

Immediacy
The degree of physically or psychologically perceived closeness.

PAUSE & REFLECT

Can you think of a situation when you were uncomfortable with a touch that you received from someone? What were the circumstances that made this touch problematic?

Body movements can also contribute to perceptions of immediacy and liking. A study by Susanne Jones and Laura Guerrero (2001) asked participants to have a conversation with another person about a personal problem and then rate how supportive their partner was during the interaction. The study showed that people who showed more smiling, nodding, gesturing, relaxed posture, and a direct body orientation were perceived as more supportive than people who demonstrated fewer of these behaviors. These findings demonstrate the impact of body movements on perceptions of immediacy, supportiveness, and liking.

Communicating Power and Status

In the United States, people are socialized to recognize differences in power and status. Power refers to a person's ability to influence and control the actions of others. People can gain power based on their status, which is their social position within a given community or culture. In other words, status refers to a person's position in the social or professional hierarchy, and power refers to the degree of influence that person derives

HOW DO YOU RATE? 6.1

Nonverbal Immediacy

Visit the **companion website** to complete a scale that measures people's tendency to display nonverbal immediacy. As you reflect on your nonverbal immediacy score, think about how your interaction partner may have perceived you during the interaction. Do you think your partner felt liked or disliked by you? What can you do to be perceived as more immediate in your future interactions?

FIGURE 6.4 Showing disinterest

Source: www.CartoonStock.com.

from their position. In general, powerful people tend to make a good first impression. Even before any words are spoken, a person's physical appearance communicates volumes about his or her power and status. Research indicates that people who have a polished business appearance receive more promotions and get salary offers that are 8–28% higher than individuals with a less professional look (Bixler & Nix-Rice, 1997). In addition, people who are physically attractive are seen as having more power and higher status than others. This phenomenon is known as the **halo effect**, or the tendency to attribute positive personality traits to attractive people.

Your voice also reveals a great deal about your status and power. People with more power tend to have vocal qualities associated with assuredness, confidence, maturity, animation, and extroversion. Compare, for example, the different degrees of authority associated with the low-pitched, sultry voice of James Earl Jones (the voice of Darth Vader) versus the high-pitched, squeaky voice of Mickey Mouse. People perceive speakers who are louder overall and who change their volume throughout an utterance as more dominant (Tusing & Dillard, 2000). Thus, a variety of vocal cues can reveal power and status in interpersonal interactions.

High power people also command more physical space. In the business world, people who have the most status within an organization are typically given the most spacious and private offices. In addition, people with higher status adopt more relaxed postures, whereas people with less power are more tensed. High status people will likely lean back in their chair and adopt an open posture with their arms and legs, but a low status person is more likely to lean forward and slouch a bit during interaction. In general, these behaviors allow the high status person to stretch their bodies, whereas the low status person is confined to a smaller space.

Regulating Conversation

Interpersonal communication is like a carefully choreographed dance that requires the coordination of behaviors between two individuals. People can send and respond to cues that guide them in initiating a conversation, taking turns speaking, and signaling the desire to end it. Consider all of the ways you signal that you are ready and willing to communicate with another person. You might initiate interaction by making eye contact with another person. For example, heterosexual women initiate eye contact with potential male suitors in an effort to invite the male to engage in interaction with them (Moore, 1985). You could also initiate interaction by moving closer to others and sometimes touching them to get their attention. The use of nonverbal behaviors to control the start of conversations was clearly revealed in a study of interactions between doctors and patients during British medical consultations – that study found that doctors orient their bodies away from patients until they are ready to hear the patient's physical ailments and then turn toward patients when it is okay for them to speak (Robinson, 1998).

Once a conversation is underway, the intricate dance of turn taking begins (see Figure 6.5). Duncan and Fiske's (1979) model of turn-taking behavior outlines the behaviors that people enact depending on their goal during the interaction. When you want to speak during a conversation, you might nod your head several times in rapid succession and/or start making sounds. **Back-channel communication** refers to

Halo Effect
The tendency for physically attractive people to be perceived as having other positive characteristics.

Back-channel Communication
Non-language utterances that show understanding or involvement and help to move an interaction along.

TAKING THE FLOOR
- Nod several times in succession
- Use back-channel communication
- Interrupt at a higher volume

KEEPING THE FLOOR
- Speak more loudly
- Gesture more vigorously
- Avoid eye contact

AVOIDING THE FLOOR
- Nod head
- Use back-channel communication
- Avoid eye contact

YIELDING THE FLOOR
- Establish eye contact
- Relax gestures
- Increase or decrease vocal pitch

FIGURE 6.5 Nonverbal cues for regulating conversation

non-language utterances like "mm-hmm" and "uh-huh." When you make back-channel sounds while a person is still speaking, it shows that you understand your partner and either encourages them to continue or signals that he or she can stop talking. When you are speaking and you don't want someone to interrupt, you might talk more loudly and gesture more vigorously. When you are finished making a point and want your partner to speak, you establish eye contact, relax your gestures, and increase or decrease the pitch of your voice at the end of your sentence. And what if your partner stops talking, and you have nothing to say? You can try to avoid talking by nodding your head or using back-channel communication instead. In combination, these nonverbal behaviors help to move the interaction along and manage turn taking between partners during the conversation.

PAUSE & REFLECT

What do you do when you are talking on the telephone to help regulate the interaction? Are there ways in which this process is more or less challenging than face-to-face communication?

Finally, a number of nonverbal behaviors mark the end of a conversation. As partners draw near the end of their interaction, they partially turn away from one another. They tend to move farther from each other, nod more, and reduce eye contact as they reveal their desires to end the conversation. Partners also tend to start talking over one another at the end of conversations. The last moment in an interaction often involves some sort of touch, such as a pat on the upper arm, a handshake, a hug, or a kiss. In these ways, you use nonverbal behaviors to bring your conversations with others to an end.

Putting Theory into Practice: Managing Relationships and Interaction

As you have seen, your nonverbal behaviors serve critical functions within interpersonal interactions. In this section, we discuss how you might harness the power of nonverbal communication to improve your relationships and interactions with others.

Make sure nonverbal cues reflect the nature of a relationship. Using words to express how much you like a person can be difficult or uncomfortable, but nonverbal behaviors are a clear and easy way to show others that you like them. Make an effort to enact nonverbal behaviors that let other people know that you care about them; your actions will make those relationships more rewarding and secure. In particular, smiling and nodding during conversations with friends shows them that you enjoy their company. Hugging a family member demonstrates your support during difficult times. Kissing a romantic partner for the first time can be an important turning point in the relationship (Baxter & Bullis, 1986). Even when you have a hard time expressing your feelings in words, nonverbal cues can still communicate how you feel.

Similarly, skillful communicators are clear about power dynamics so that messages can be exchanged more effectively. Denise used to get puzzled when some students refused her offer to call her by her first name; eventually, however, she realized that those individuals were more comfortable communicating with her when their status differences were clear. When you are the one with more status, remember that you are expected to set the emotional tone for the interaction, to act with dignity or authority, to signal the beginning and end of the conversation, and to accept messages that convey respect. When the nature of your power relations are clear, you and your partner can focus your attention on other aspects of your interaction.

Use nonverbal cues to improve the flow of your conversations. Look for cues from your interaction partner to know when it is appropriate to speak. If your partner is gesturing actively and looking away from you, recognize that he wants to keep talking. When you simply must break in, don't just interrupt your partner; instead, use head nods and back-channel sounds to signal your eagerness to contribute. When you have the speaking floor, be sure that you are responsive when your partner uses those same signs to let you know she has something to say. And you can avoid catching your partner off-guard by giving cues that you are about to stop talking; making eye contact with your partner, relaxing your gestures, and changing your pitch are signals that invite your partner to get ready to speak. When you regulate interactions using these nonverbal behaviors, your communication will be more efficient, effective, and enjoyable.

COMMUNICATION IN ACTION 6.3

Charting the Course of Interaction

In this exercise, you'll learn to recognize the nonverbal cues that serve to regulate interaction. Observe two people engaged in conversation and pay attention to the nonverbal behaviors they use to regulate their interaction. Complete the table on the **companion website** with the different behaviors you notice as people initiate conversation, begin or end a speaking turn, interrupt a partner, or end the interaction.

INDIVIDUAL DIFFERENCES

Generally, people are more similar than different in the ways that they communicate nonverbally. Many of the behaviors you enact to display your emotions, manage relationships, and facilitate interactions are similar across cultures. Likewise, males and females have many of the same goals for interaction, and they are able to communicate with one another with relatively few misunderstandings. Nevertheless, differences do exist in nonverbal behavior across cultures and between genders.

Differences across Cultures

Famous actors from around the globe have portrayed characters from cultures different from their own. Renee Zellweger played the British spinster Bridget Jones. Mike Meyers adopted a Scottish accent for the voice of Shrek. British actor Hugh Laurie plays a cranky American doctor in the TV drama *House*. What nonverbal behaviors do these actors have to use in order to perform their cross-cultural roles convincingly? Nonverbal markers of cultural identity are so deeply ingrained that you rarely even recognize the symbols and behaviors that display your culture. Only when you are given the opportunity to interact with people from other cultures do you begin to realize how you take your nonverbal codes for granted.

One of the most recognizable and problematic differences between cultures involves the use of gestures called emblems. **Emblems** are gestures that have a direct verbal translation, such as the peace sign, waving hello or goodbye, the OK symbol, or extending your middle finger. These gestures have very specific meanings in American culture, but they are often interpreted differently in other cultures around the world. For example, the OK sign indicates understanding or implies that everything is good in the United States, but the same gesture in Brazil is an insult similar to raising your middle finger. In France, the OK sign means zero, and in Japan it is the symbol for money. These differences create countless opportunities for misunderstanding when people from different cultures communicate.

Emblems
Gestures that have a direct verbal translation.

Another prominent difference between cultures is how people think about and use time. A **monochronic time orientation** reflects a desire to do one thing at a time. Countries that adopt a monochronic orientation toward time include Britain, Germany, Finland, Norway, Sweden, Canada and the United States. In these countries, people keep rigid schedules and they view time as a commodity that can be spent, saved, or wasted. In contrast, a **polychronic time orientation** disregards artificial schedules and stresses informality. Many Latin American and Arab cultures adopt a polychronic time orientation, where people are comfortable scheduling many activities at once and don't adhere to a rigid schedule. Likewise, "island time" refers to the relaxed view of time common in many tropical locations.

Monochronic Time Orientation
A cultural trait that reflects a desire to do one thing at a time.

Polychronic Time Orientation
A cultural trait that stresses informality and reflects little regard for artificial schedules.

PAUSE & REFLECT

Do you tend to be punctual or more relaxed about your time commitments? How is your personal preference rewarded or punished in your culture?

Each culture also has a different idea about what is attractive in terms of clothing, body shape, ornamentation, and artifacts (Burgoon, Buller, & Woodall, 1996). In Western cultures like the United States, perceptions of beauty have become heavily influenced by media representations of thin, full-lipped, large-breasted female supermodels and muscular, broad-chested, male athletes. These images are not the gold standard of beauty in other cultures. One of Jen's friends was traveling in India when she noticed two male shopkeepers looking her up and down and commenting to one another as she shopped. She assumed that they were talking about how beautiful she was, but her translator told her that they were actually disgusted by how thin she was. The thin ideal that is valued in the United States is far from universal. Some media outlets have started to recognize the need to provide more diverse images of beauty and are more inclusive in their advertising. In the United States, Dove started using more "regular-sized" models in their advertising. In Germany, *Brigitte* magazine went so far as to ban professional models from appearing in the publication and replaced them with images of "real-life" women.

Differences between Males and Females

Have you noticed any differences in the ways that men and women communicate nonverbally? Although men and women sometimes enact different nonverbal behaviors, most researchers agree that the sexes are more similar than different in their communication patterns (Andersen, 1998; Kunkel & Burleson, 1998). Although men and women do not have radically different communication behaviors, there are some subtle differences.

Evolution accounts for some of the variation in nonverbal behavior between males and females. For example, males and females evolved with different body structures and appearances in order to facilitate mating and carry out traditional gender roles. Furthermore, women tend to be more expressive in the face and tend to reveal their emotions, especially positive emotions, more frequently than men (Brody & Hall, 1993; Coates & Feldman, 1996). Men, on the other hand, are more likely than women to display anger (Coates & Feldman, 1996). These differences probably evolved because of the roles males and females played in ancient societies. An ability to express frequent and positive emotions would have helped women provide nurturing to infants, whereas anger might have helped men ward off predators. Thus, some of the differences in the nonverbal behaviors of men and women likely served important evolutionary functions.

> ## PAUSE & REFLECT
>
> Consider the ways that parents interact with their babies. How do mothers and fathers differ in their nonverbal behaviors? In what ways are their nonverbal behaviors similar?

An alternative explanation for gender differences in nonverbal communication is related to the ways that men and women are socialized into their respective gender roles. From a very young age, girls learn how to behave as women by watching their mothers, and boys learn how to behave as men by watching their fathers. Research has shown that infants can imitate some facial expressions and gestures within the first few days of life (Meltzoff & Moore, 1983). In addition, parents display different behaviors for their sons than for daughters. Mothers tend to be more expressive and show more positive emotions with their daughters than with their sons (Fogel, Toda, & Kawai, 1988). In turn, girls are more skilled than boys at recognizing facial expressions of emotion (McClure, 2000), and women tend to be more emotionally expressive than men (Brody & Hall, 1993). As these adults become models for their own children, they hand down gender differences in emotional expression to the next generation.

One final explanation for gender differences in nonverbal behavior is that gendered behaviors are reinforced. In general, young girls are rewarded for performing traditionally "female" behaviors, and young boys are rewarded for performing traditionally "male" behaviors. For a specific example, consider how males and females might come to prefer different degrees of closeness during interaction. As infants, girls tend to be cradled and held more close to the body, whereas boys are more often playfully tossed into the air or allowed to lie independently in a crib or on a blanket. As boys and girls start to grow up, the toys, games, and activities that girls tend to enjoy (e.g., dolls, playing house) require less space than the games that boys like to play (e.g., trucks, cops and robbers). Thus, from a very early age, boys are conditioned to want and need more physical space, and girls are socialized to want and need less space. Not surprisingly, then, women interact at closer distances and have been found to face their interaction partner more directly than men (Guerrero, 1997). In contrast, men require and are given more physical space both during interactions and for their daily activities.

Putting Theory into Practice: Embracing Individual Differences

Although nonverbal communication is more similar than different across cultures and genders, increasing your awareness of individual differences in nonverbal behavior can lead to more effective communication.

Educate yourself about nonverbal differences when you visit other cultures. When you plan foreign travel, learn some key nonverbal emblems along with handy phrases. The Communication in Action 6.4 exercise can get you started. And when you are at home, cultivate tolerance toward those who are struggling with the nonverbal codes of

American culture. Deal patiently with errors in cross-cultural interactions and try to explain the behaviors that are appropriate in your culture.

COMMUNICATION IN ACTION 6.4

Nonverbal Meaning across Cultures

Do some research about a culture that you have always been interested in learning more about, or a culture that you plan to visit one day. For this activity, you might find some fascinating differences if you focus on a culture that is very different from the United States, like African, Middle Eastern, or Asian cultures. Use search engines on the Internet to find answers to the following questions: What are the meaningful nonverbal gestures and emblems in this culture? What is considered appropriate styles of dress for men and women? What is proper etiquette during meal time? How are power and status denoted in the culture? When you have identified meaningful cultural practices, compare that culture's behaviors to those in the United States. How are they similar and how are they different?

Be sensitive to gender differences when communicating with the opposite sex. Even though men and women are mostly similar in their nonverbal behaviors, you'll communicate more effectively if you are sensitive to the potential for gender differences. In particular, men might try to be more expressive with their nonverbal cues in order to match the expressiveness of their female interaction partners. In addition, women would be wise to remember that men still experience strong emotions, even if their nonverbal cues of emotion are not as strong as women's. Understanding the small differences in the ways males and females communicate nonverbally will make a big difference in how you understand nonverbal messages.

COMBINING VERBAL AND NONVERBAL CUES

Complementing
When nonverbal cues enhance ideas that are being spoken.

Accenting
When nonverbal cues add emphasis to a word or phrase.

Substituting
When nonverbal cues replace a word that conveys the same meaning.

Contradicting
When nonverbal cues are in contrast to the words that are spoken.

Verbal and nonverbal messages weave a complex web of understanding during the communication process. Table 6.2 summarizes four of the ways that verbal and nonverbal messages combine during interaction. Nonverbal behaviors can **complement** language, meaning that they enhance or help to illustrate the ideas that are being spoken. Nonverbal behaviors can also **accent** verbal messages by adding emphasis to particular words or phrases. Nonverbal behaviors sometimes **substitute** verbal messages, by replacing a word that conveys the same meaning. Finally, nonverbal behaviors can **contradict** verbal messages when nonverbal cues are in contrast to the words that are spoken.

In combination, verbal and nonverbal cues can either clarify or confuse the intended meaning of the message. When verbal and nonverbal messages are consistent, there are fewer opportunities for miscommunication. At other times, discrepancies between verbal and nonverbal cues create challenges to communication. Consider the examples of deceptive communication and negotiations of sexual intimacy. In the first case, we'll see that the effort required to craft untrue messages is often revealed by nonverbal cues.

TABLE 6.2 Combinations of verbal and nonverbal messages

Function	Definition	Example
Complementing	When nonverbal messages enhance or help to illustrate the ideas that are being spoken	You might hug and kiss a romantic partner while speaking the words "I love you"
Accenting	When nonverbal behaviors add emphasis to particular words and phrases	When professors want to make sure that students understand an idea, they might pause after a sentence to indicate that this was an important thought
Substituting	When nonverbal behaviors replace a word that conveys the same meaning	If someone asked you how you did on your midterm exam, you might make the "OK" symbol with your hand instead of saying "I did fine"
Contradicting	When nonverbal behaviors are in contrast to the words that are spoken	A person might say "I'm all right," but his or her tear-stained face and quivering voice would send a different message

When sexual involvement is being negotiated, an ambiguous mix of verbal and nonverbal cues can have more dire consequences.

The Signs of Deception

Everybody lies. One study revealed that 91% of Americans lie regularly (Patterson & Kim, 1991), and another reported that people tell as many as 46 lies during the course of a week (DePaulo, Kashy, Kirkendol, Wyer, & Epstein, 1996). You can probably remember a time when you tried to deceive someone. What was your lie about? Was it a big lie, or a little white lie? Did you get away with it, or did you get caught? **Deception** is defined as intentional and strategic behavior designed to promote a false belief or conclusion within another person. In this section, we describe the ways in which verbal and nonverbal cues combine to reveal deceit, and we discuss some of the nonverbal cues that are markers of deception.

> **Deception**
> Intentional and strategic behavior designed to promote a false belief within another person.

Patterns of behavior that reveal deception. People unconsciously signal that they are lying through inconsistencies in their nonverbal behavior. If you have ever caught someone in a lie, you might have noticed that statements made later in the conversation contradicted statements made at the beginning, or perhaps his or her gestures seemed to contradict the words being spoken. The person may have acted calm and aloof, but at the same time kept tapping his or her foot, fidgeting with a button or piece of jewelry, and speaking with a higher pitch. Examinations of people's perceptions of courtroom testimony reveal that stereotypically deceptive behaviors don't necessarily trigger suspicion, but inconsistent nonverbal behaviors are frequently interpreted as deceptive regardless of the specific actions that are performed (Henningsen, Cruz, & Morr, 2000).

Research has also shown that familiarity with a person's typical nonverbal behaviors makes it easier to identify discrepancies and detect deception. In particular, people are better able to tell whether a partner is telling the truth or lying when they have previous experience with that person's truthful behavior (Feeley, deTurck, & Young, 1995). In close relationships, people have the benefit of increased knowledge about a person's normal behavior, which should make it easier to detect inconsistencies. On the other hand, people tend to believe that the people they care about are usually truthful, so they aren't always on the lookout for deception (Levine & McCornack, 1992).

Specific cues that reveal deception. Supposedly, liars can't look you in the eye, they fidget nervously, or they might smile when not speaking the truth. In fact, because these traits are generally seen as revealing a lie, many people become skilled at controlling these behaviors. The result, then, is that cues to deception arise in channels that are more difficult for people to control. **Nonverbal leakage** occurs when a deceiver subconsciously reveals their deception through uncontrollable nonverbal behaviors. For example, a liar may not have shifty eyes, but the eyes can signal whether a person is lying or telling the truth. The pupils may dilate during deception, which is an impossible behavior to control (DePaulo, Stone, & Lassiter, 1985). Research also shows that deception corresponds with increased blinking of the eyes (DePaulo et al., 1985).

Nonverbal leakage

When a deceiver subconsciously reveals their deception through uncontrollable nonverbal behaviors.

PAUSE & REFLECT

Is there a person in your life whom you can always peg as honest or dishonest? How does their behavior change when they lie? What cues do you rely on to tell if they are lying or telling the truth?

The voice is another nonverbal channel that is difficult to control and, therefore, it provides a cue to deception. One of the most consistent findings is that deceivers display a higher rate of speech errors, such as stutters, mispronunciations, and other disfluencies (Burgoon et al., 1996; Vrij & Winkel, 1991). In addition, research indicates that deception is associated with higher vocal pitch (see Burgoon et al., 1996) and a shorter duration of speaking turns (Vrij & Winkel, 1991).

Finally, there are two types of facial expressions that indicate potential deception. Some scholars argue that smiles are used to mask the emotions people feel when they are lying (Ekman, 1988); these smiles are usually lopsided and more strongly portrayed on the right side of the face. A second and especially telling sign of deception is the presence of **micro-momentary facial expressions** – fleeting and virtually unobservable expressions of underlying emotion. In the case of deception, there is often a micro-momentary expression of distress in which the eyebrows rise up, creating a cluster of wrinkles in the center of the forehead. For example, when former President Bill Clinton gave testimony denying his alleged affair with Monica Lewinsky, videos of the testimony played in slow motion revealed micro-momentary signals of distress (Figure 6.6). The research described in Inside Communication Research shows how hard it can be to detect deception with all the nonverbal cues you have to keep track of in an interaction.

Micro-momentary Facial Expressions

Brief unobservable expressions of underlying emotion.

FIGURE 6.6 President Bill Clinton denies having affair with former White House intern Monica Lewinsky.

Source: Photo by Diana Walker//Time Life Pictures/Getty Images.

INSIDE COMMUNICATION RESEARCH

Detecting Deceit

Communication scholar Judee Burgoon has conducted numerous studies examining deception cues and deception detection. In one study, she examined how accurate people were in detecting deceit when their assumptions about the interaction were biased (Burgoon, Blair, & Strom, 2008). Burgoon and her colleagues argued that people use mental shortcuts when judging people's truthfulness that lead to biases, such that people tend to overestimate a speaker's truthfulness, tend to rely heavily on visual cues, tend to link a credible demeanor to truthfulness, and tend to judge unusual behavior as deceptive. The researchers predicted that these biases would contribute to inaccurate assessments of people's truth or deception.

Participants in the study were asked to determine whether a suspect being interviewed about a theft was being truthful or deceptive about the crime. Some of the participants watched a video of the interview, some listened to an audio tape of the interview, and some read a transcript of the interview. Afterward, the participants were asked to rate the suspect in terms of the information provided, their behavior, their personal demeanor, and their truthfulness.

The results of the study revealed that participants who watched the video and could see the suspect's nonverbal cues judged the suspect as providing more complete, honest, and clear information, being more involved in the interaction, and appearing more credible compared to the participants who only heard or read the interview. In fact, when people had access to the nonverbal cues, they tended to judge the deceiver as more credible than the truth-teller. Thus, the researchers found that people had the most biases when they were presented with both audio and visual information. The people who were most accurate at detecting the deceiver were the ones who listened to an audio tape of the interview without visual cues.

THINK ABOUT IT

1. Why do you think people were less skilled at detecting deception when they had access to all audio and visual cues? How can you be more aware of your biases in this situation?
2. How do the results of this study inform your thinking about how best to detect deception in your own life? What circumstances can you control to better detect deception?

Negotiating Sexual Intimacy

When it comes to talking about sex, people prefer to let their actions speak for themselves. Research has shown that people do not communicate very openly before engaging in sex, and they rely primarily on nonverbal cues to consent to acts of sexual intimacy (Edgar & Fitzpatrick, 1993; Moore, 1985; Perper & Weis, 1987). In fact, one study showed that both women and men often use non-resistance – letting their partner undress them, not stopping their partner from kissing or touching them, and not saying no – to signal sexual consent (Hickman & Muehlenhard, 1999). In another study, participants reported that fondling male genitals communicated sexual consent as clearly as a verbal statement of agreement (Byers, 1980).

Although people might rely on nonverbal cues to consent to sexual activity, they recognize the benefits of more direct communication about sexual intimacy (Greer & Buss, 1994). Men view sexual initiation strategies as most effective when they include a direct request for sex and verbalize desire for sexual contact, followed by increasing sexual and nonsexual contact and behaving seductively. Women also rate verbalizing desire for sexual contact as the most effective way to negotiate sexual intimacy, followed by implying commitment, acting nice, and increasing attention in one's target. These results show that despite the prevalence of nonverbal cues for negotiating sexual intimacy, both men and women prefer more directness.

When you are interested (or not interested) in pursuing sex with a partner, it is important that your verbal and nonverbal cues are sending the same message. Even when you think you're being clear about your sexual desires, other people can misinterpret your behavioral cues. Men tend to interpret the behaviors of females as more seductive, promiscuous, and flirtatious than women do (Shotland & Craig, 1988). As a result, men are more likely than women to perceive friendly behaviors as signs of sexual interest. Thus, women need to establish clear boundaries for sexual involvement and men need to accept those boundaries. In general, though, men and women should both work hard to send clear messages when it comes to sexual intimacy.

PAUSE & REFLECT

Have you ever had a sexual experience that made you feel bad afterward? How was that experience different from sexual encounters that made you feel good afterward?

When people rely only on nonverbal behaviors to communicate their consent to sexual intimacy, they experience more negative reactions following sexual activity. One study revealed that when people were not direct in their communication about a first sexual encounter with a partner, they experienced more anger, fear, and sadness, had more negative thoughts about the encounter, and believed that the experience was bad for their relationship (Theiss & Solomon, 2007). In contrast, people who communicate openly about sexual intimacy tend to be more satisfied with both their sexual encounters and their relationships (Byers & Demmons, 1999; Cupach & Comstock, 1990). Thus, sexual episodes can have negative repercussions when people rely only on nonverbal messages to negotiate intimacy, but they can have positive outcomes when people combine signs of sexual interest with a clear verbal statement of sexual consent.

Putting Theory into Practice: Combining Verbal and Nonverbal Cues

When you consider verbal and nonverbal messages in combination, you can see opportunities for both greater clarity and greater complexity in your interpersonal interactions. Now that you have seen two examples of how verbal and nonverbal messages combine to create meanings, consider the following strategies for becoming a more skillful communicator.

Rely on uncommon cues to detect deception. A lack of eye contact and fidgeting are commonly thought to be cues to deception, but because many liars can control these behaviors, they are actually poor predictors of deception. To figure out if someone might by lying to you, look for signs of deception that are out of that person's conscious control. In particular, try to tell if they are blinking more than usual, pay attention to vocal cues like an unusual pitch and either a faster or slower speaking rate, and look for brief displays of anxiety in facial expressions. In addition, look for inconsistencies in your partner's behaviors over the course of the conversation, contradictions between the verbal and nonverbal messages, and deviations from your partner's typical communication style. Both behaviors that are hard to control and inconsistent patterns of communication can reveal when a person is lying to you.

Recognize the limitations of nonverbal messages. Although there is no guarantee that your verbal messages will be understood, there are times when nonverbal messages are just too ambiguous. When people miscommunicate about sexual intentions, the result can range from unwanted sexual contact to sexual assault or rape. Rather than run this risk, use clear verbal and nonverbal messages to convey the level of sexual activity that you are comfortable with.

COMMUNICATION IN ACTION 6.5

Creating a Sexual Script

One way to have more effective conversations about sexual intimacy with a potential partner is to anticipate what you might say when you find yourself in that situation. Use the form on the **companion website** to help you formulate a script for negotiating sexual intimacy and to reflect on the nonverbal behaviors that might complement your verbal messages. Does your script include a clear request for sexual contact, a direct statement of consent, a discussion of risks, and the precautions you might take to prevent those risks?

SUMMARY

Nonverbal messages are an important part of the interpersonal communication process. Nearly every part of the human body and many features of the environment can be channels for communicating information to others. In addition, nonverbal communication is an analogic symbol system, which means that most nonverbal behavior is spontaneous, automatic, and universal. When you learn about the nature of nonverbal messages, you can see that they are very pervasive and powerful tools for communication.

Nonverbal messages have four important functions. First, nonverbal behaviors are essential for expressing emotion. Nonverbal cues are also important to show people that you like them and to figure out when others are attracted to you. Another function of nonverbal communication is that it reveals your power and social status. Finally, nonverbal behavior helps you to regulate your interactions with others. Clearly, nonverbal behaviors accomplish critical functions in your interpersonal interactions.

Individual differences influence nonverbal behavior. Although different cultures and different sexes are more similar than different, there are several important distinctions. For example, people from different cultures use gestures in unique ways, have different orientations toward time, and place value on different physical characteristics. Gender differences in nonverbal communication arise from men and women's unique physical qualities, the ways in which emotional expressiveness is modeled for boys and girls, and how boys and girls are encouraged to adopt different orientations toward space.

Verbal and nonverbal cues work in combination. Nonverbal messages can complement, accent, replace, or contradict verbal messages. Inconsistencies between verbal and nonverbal behaviors are one of the signs that a communication partner might be deceptive. When negotiating sexual intimacy, nonverbal messages sometimes replace verbal messages, but there are consequences for relying too heavily on nonverbal messages during these interactions.

In Chapter 5, you witnessed the power of language and the versatility of verbal messages for creating shared meanings between people. In this chapter, the equal – if not greater – impact of nonverbal messages was examined. By drawing upon multiple channels and the unique qualities of analogic codes, nonverbal cues are unparalleled in their ability to communicate feelings, affection, perceptions of power, and participation in a conversation. By recognizing individual differences in nonverbal expression and the complexity of weaving together verbal and nonverbal messages, you can draw upon nonverbal messages to improve your interpersonal communication experiences.

ACTIVITIES FOR EXPLORING COMMUNICATION ETHICS

What Would You/Should You Do?

You're out with some friends and you notice a man and a woman having a heated discussion near the bathroom. They are shouting at one another, pointing fingers in one another's faces, and making facial expressions showing anger and disgust. Eventually, the woman starts hitting the man with her purse. He grabs the woman's wrists to restrain her, but she starts kicking him and trying to get free from his grasp. What should you do when other people's nonverbal behaviors are dangerous to others and to themselves?

Something to Think About

In some cases, people mask their emotions by displaying different emotional cues from what they are really feeling inside. For example, people who are telling a lie might try to look calm, even though they are feeling very anxious. Some people might flirt by smiling, moving closer to their target, and even touching the other person, even though they may not be interested in pursuing a romantic connection with the person. When people play poker, they try to hide their excitement when they are dealt a good hand, and they try to appear confident when they don't have any good cards. To what extent is it ethical to hide your true feelings? When would concealing your true emotion have a negative impact on the people around you?

Analyze Communication Ethics Yourself

In work or institutional settings, power and status are revealed and reinforced by the allocation of physical space, the openness of personal territory to others, standards for dress or appearance, personal artifacts that people can or cannot display, etc. One context where nonverbal markers of status play an important role is the United States prison system. Think about representations of prison culture that you have seen in the media. How are inmates and prison guards different in the ways they are allowed to dress, the personal artifacts they are allowed to carry, the way they schedule their days, and the amount of space they are given. Consider the function of these cues within the institution of prisons, as well as the impact of these messages on inmates. Based on your analysis, what are the ethical issues at stake when nonverbal communication is used to constrain people's freedoms?

KEY WORDS

accenting	emblems	nonverbal communication
analogic codes	halo effect	nonverbal leakage
back-channel communication	immediacy	polychronic time orientation
channel	intensification	simulation
complementing	masking	substituting
contradicting	micro-momentary facial expression	variable intensity
deception	monochronic time orientation	
deintensification	nonverbal behavior	

LEARNING OBJECTIVES

After reading this chapter, you should be able to:

1. Recognize types of emotions.
2. Understand how people experience emotion.
3. Identify components of emotions.
4. Describe the role of emotions in interpersonal communication.
5. Understand how messages are involved in intensely painful emotions.

PUTTING THEORY INTO PRACTICE

In this chapter, you will learn how to:

1. Seek out specific labels to describe feelings.
2. Address all of the components of emotions when you express or respond to feelings.
3. Locate the cause of emotions within people's appraisals.
4. Express emotions verbally rather than just showing them nonverbally.
5. Consider other people's goals when you respond to their emotions.
6. Consider context when you express your feelings to others.
7. Use the social context to understand the emotions expressed by others.
8. Buffer yourself and others from the consequences of dark emotions.

EMOTIONS AND COMMUNICATION

7

182 WHAT ARE EMOTIONS?

190 FEELINGS AND COMMUNICATION

193 FACTORS THAT AFFECT EMOTIONS AND COMMUNICATION

198 THE DARK SIDE OF EMOTIONS IN CLOSE RELATIONSHIPS

203 SUMMARY

205 ACTIVITIES FOR EXPLORING COMMUNICATION ETHICS

205 KEY WORDS

Souce: Photo by Ezra Shaw/ Getty Images.

Winning or losing the World Series can be an emotional experience for baseball players and their fans. When the St. Louis Cardinals beat the Texas Rangers in the seventh game of the World Series in 2011, the emotion of their come-from-behind victory was written all over their faces. The players rushed the field shouting and cheering, fans were seen in the stands hugging and laughing, and media footage showed people watching in bars and restaurants all over St. Louis who were exuberant with joy. Conversely, the disappointment among the Texas Rangers players and fans was palpable. The players retreated to their dugout hanging their heads, the media focused on a child in the stands who was crying, and fans generally were dumbfounded at the loss. During major sporting events like the World Series, players and fans experience a wide range of emotions.

St. Louis fans felt pride and joy in their team's success, and Texas fans felt disappointment and frustration upon losing the final game in the series. In your own life, you feel emotion in response to your own triumphs and hardships, and you experience emotions when good or bad things happen to people you care about. For example, you might feel grief at the funeral of a loved one, joy at your best friend's wedding, frustration when your team loses the World Series, and pride when you accept your college diploma. **Moods** are pervasive or lasting feelings that range from bad to good, and **emotions** are more fleeting feelings that arise in particular situations. Emotions are especially relevant to interpersonal communication, because interactions evoke feelings and your feelings shape how you communicate. In this chapter, we examine the nature of emotions, look at how feelings are at work when we communicate with others, and consider how the communication situation shapes the way we express our feelings. Finally, we explore the painful emotions that sometimes arise in our interactions with friends, family, and romantic partners.

WHAT ARE EMOTIONS?

Consider all of the different emotions you might have over the course of a typical day. When you wake up, you might feel content with a good night's sleep, eager to face the day, or perhaps fearful about a midterm exam. As you make your way to work or campus, you could become frustrated by a traffic jam, worried about being late, or pleased when you run into a friend. After a class, you might be happy with high marks on an assignment, or disappointed by a low grade. And as you communicate with others, you might find yourself angered by an insult, grateful for a compliment, hurt by a careless remark, or embarrassed when you say the wrong thing. These examples show how your everyday experiences are rich with emotions. In this section of the chapter, we will take a closer look at types of emotions, the causes of emotions, and distinct facets of emotional experiences.

Vader assesses what mood he is in today.

FIGURE 7.1 Vader assesses his mood

Source: www.CartoonStock.com.

Moods
Feelings that are lasting or ongoing.

Emotions
Short-term feelings that are linked to specific situations.

PAUSE & REFLECT

Reflect on your life and identify one experience that was especially important to you. How did that experience make you feel? How important were your feelings as a part of that experience?

Types of Emotions

The different emotions that you feel allow you to relate to your circumstances in nuanced ways. And when you recognize different emotions in yourself and in others, you gain a more complete understanding of your interpersonal communication experiences. To help you appreciate the variety of emotions you experience, the following paragraphs examine three frameworks for distinguishing the emotions people experience.

One way to distinguish emotions is to focus on how positive or negative they are and how intensely the emotion is felt (Yik, Russell, & Barrett, 1999). In Figure 7.2, the horizontal dimension distinguishes between pleasant and unpleasant emotional experiences. Pleasant emotions include happiness, joy, and contentment, whereas unpleasant emotions include anger, sadness, and fear. The vertical dimension contrasts emotions that involve a high or low degree of arousal. As examples, consider the difference between annoyance and anger or contentment and happiness. This way of thinking about emotions emphasizes how emotions are generally more or less positive and more or less strong.

Another way to understand emotions is to identify the different types of feelings people have. **Basic emotions** include common and universal feelings like happiness,

Basic Emotions
Common or primary feelings that are experienced universally.

FIGURE 7.2 Dimensions of feelings

Source: Adapted from Clore & Schnall (2005).

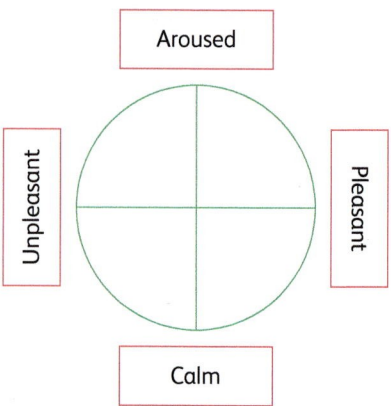

surprise, sadness, fear, and anger. Each of these primary or "pure" emotions can take various forms (see Figure 7.3). For example, fear includes the feelings evoked by a poisonous snake, a horror film, a roller coaster, or a job interview (Russell & Barrett, 1999). Furthermore, basic emotions can come together to create blended emotions. As one example, consider the feelings involved in jealousy: fear that your love interest will leave you, anger at the interloper, and maybe just a dash of sadness that your relationship isn't as strong as you hoped it was (Sharpsteen, 1991). This perspective helps you to

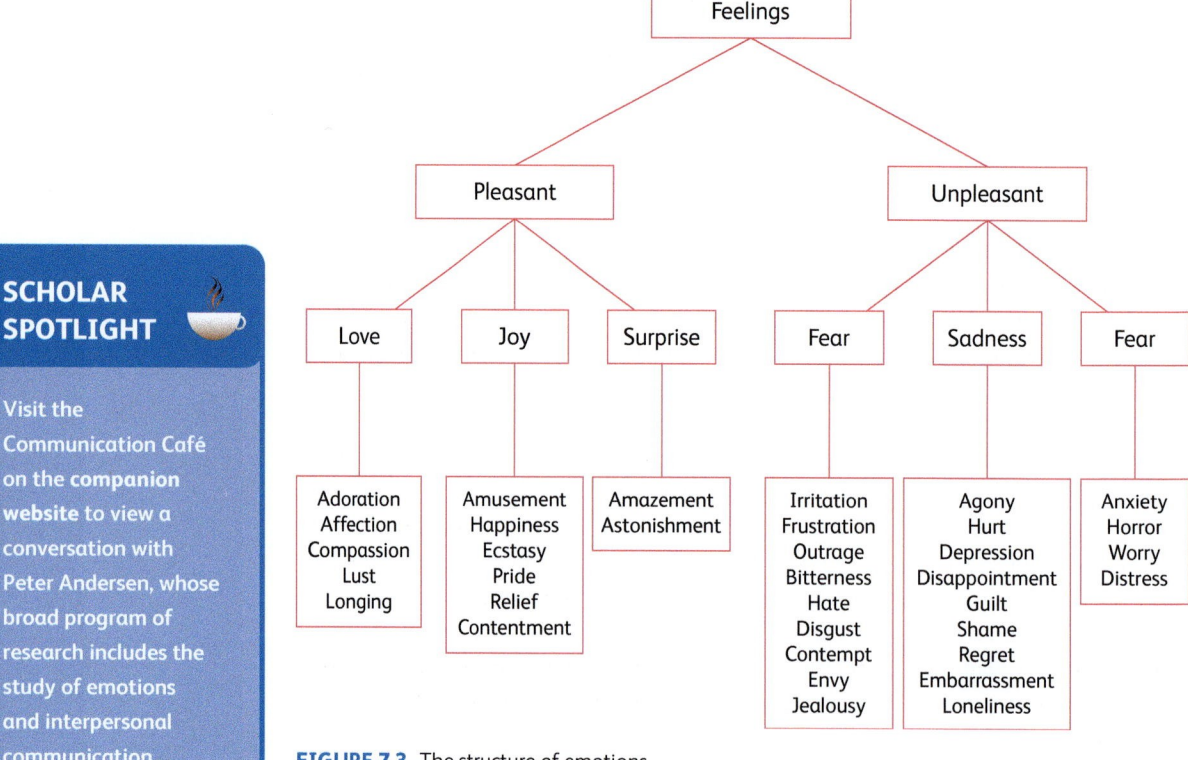

SCHOLAR SPOTLIGHT

Visit the Communication Café on the **companion website** to view a conversation with Peter Andersen, whose broad program of research includes the study of emotions and interpersonal communication.

FIGURE 7.3 The structure of emotions

Source: Shaver, Schwartz, Kirson, & O'Connor (1987).

TABLE 7.1 The social emotions

Affectionate emotions	Self-conscious emotions	Melancholic emotions	Hostile emotions
Love	Embarrassment	Sadness	Anger
Passion	Shame	Depression	Hate
Warmth	Guilt	Grief	Jealousy
Joy	Pride	Loneliness	Envy
			Hurt

understand the most common emotions you experience, as well as how those emotions are related to more precise or more complex feelings.

Some emotions are specifically tied to your relationships or communication with other people (Guerrero & Andersen, 2000). These **social emotions** take four distinct forms (see Table 7.1). Affectionate emotions create attachment and closeness with other people. Self-conscious emotions arise from a focus on how the self is perceived by others. Melancholic emotions occur when interpersonal experiences aren't fulfilling or have changed for the worse. Hostile emotions emerge from feelings of injury or threat in the context of interpersonal relationships. Although some of these emotions can occur outside of interpersonal experience, social contexts dramatically intensify these feelings. For example, imagine how differently you would feel if you tripped in the front of an empty classroom versus one that was filled with other students.

Social Emotions

Feelings that occur in interpersonal communication or relationships.

Causes of Emotions

Where do your emotions come from? The starting point is your perceptions of your circumstances. More specifically, **appraisals** are perceptions of whether you are getting what you want in a situation and whether conditions are favorable or unfavorable to your goals. For example, if your goal is to get your friend to loan you her car, you would take stock of barriers to that goal (the fact the she appears ready to drive to the store) or cues that suggest you might succeed (she is busy studying for an exam). You also make more specific appraisals concerning, for example, how hard you will have to work achieve your goals under the circumstances, how much you can control the situation, or how certain you are about what will happen (Dillard & Seo, in press). Thus, appraisals capture a variety of judgments you make about your circumstances.

Appraisals

Evaluations of how favorable a situation is to the goals that you have.

Appraisal theories of emotion claim that different appraisals of the environment elicit different emotional responses (e.g., Roseman & Smith, 2001). Generally speaking, when you believe that the situation will enable you to achieve your goals, you experience positive emotions, and when you think that the situation will interfere with your goals, you experience negative emotions. Within this general framework, specific emotions are distinguished by the particular appraisals that you make (Planalp, 1999; Scherer, Schorr, & Johnstone, 2001; see Table 7.2).

The link between appraisals and emotions are particularly relevant in the context of close relationships. Consider how you might feel if you saw your romantic partner

Appraisal Theories of Emotion

A collection of theories that link evaluations of a situation to emotional experiences.

TABLE 7.2 Appraisals and their corresponding emotions

Appraisal of the situation or event	Emotion
An injustice is interfering with a desired and obtainable goal	Anger
Something of value has been lost and can't be recovered	Sadness
The situation allows a desired goal to be met	Happiness
An unpleasant outcome is possible, but not certain	Fear
I have behaved in a way that violates my moral ideals	Shame
I have behaved in a way that makes me look inept to others	Embarrassment

flirting with someone else, or if your romantic partner wanted to have a talk about the future of your relationship. These types of events can increase your doubts and uncertainty about a relationship, which affects your emotional reactions to the event. In particular, people who perceive that they will have to work to resolve the situation tend to feel more anger, sadness, fear, and jealousy; people who believe they need to pay attention to the situation feel more sadness and fear; and people who see the situation as predictable are happier (Knobloch, 2005). Thus, appraisals of a situation are closely linked to the emotions we experience during interpersonal interactions.

PAUSE & REFLECT

Think of the last time that you knew something wasn't going to work out the way you wanted. What was the reason for that outcome? Did you feel mostly anger, sadness, grief, or anxiety? What role did other people play in your emotional experience?

Components of Emotions

The feelings that are set in motion by your appraisals have four distinct parts. Consider the example of Wendy, who is waiting for an important job interview. As you think about how Wendy is feeling, you can probably identify multiple facets of her emotional experiences.

Perhaps the most obvious component of emotions is your **self-perceptions of emotion**; in other words, your own awareness of how you feel. For example, Wendy will probably recognize if she is feeling nervous rather than confident about the interview. Because your perceptions of your emotions reflect how you label and interpret your feelings, they are an essential part of your experiences. In fact, people who have experienced traumatic events, like fighting in a war, develop a better understanding of their complex

Self-perceptions of Emotion
People's own awareness of how they feel.

feelings once they are able to put those emotions into words (Pennebaker, 1997). Thus, self-perceptions of your emotions allow you to define your feelings for yourself and others.

Anyone who has experienced intense anger, fear, or elation knows that emotions also have a physiological component. As Wendy awaits her interview, no doubt her heart is beating a bit faster, her skin temperature rises a bit, and she may even be queasy. Even variations on positive emotions, such as different types of love, correspond with distinct physiological reactions within your body (Shiota, Neufeld, Yeung, Moser, & Perea, 2011). The **physiology of emotion** refers to the physical changes that occur within body systems when you experience feelings. Within the cardiovascular system, heart rate, blood flow to different parts of the body, and oxygen or adrenaline levels in the blood vary with different emotions. Likewise, the respiratory system may speed up or slow down depending on experiences of sadness, anger, fear, etc. In a very real sense, emotions are physical experiences.

The physical changes during emotion are often visible to others. **Nonverbal markers of emotion** are changes in appearance that coincide with the experience of emotion. Nonverbal displays can be unconscious reflections of the physiological changes emotions produce, for example, the increase in blood flow to the face caused by embarrassment is visible as blushing. You can also consciously display or exaggerate nonverbal markers of emotion in an effort to communicate feelings to other people. In fact, people are likely to feel an emotion more strongly when they intentionally display that feeling (Matsumoto, 1987). Thus, while Wendy's feelings of apprehension might be revealed by her crossed arms, her wide eyes, and her rigid posture, she might feel more at ease if she can relax her body and smile at the secretary. In these ways, nonverbal markers of emotion are the visible features that both reflect and affect your feelings.

Wendy's emotions fuel her behavior during the interview – her anxiety prompts her to pay attention to the interviewer's every word, and her confidence leads her to share information freely. The behaviors that emotions compel us to perform are called **action tendencies**. In fact, the physiological component of emotions makes the body ready to perform behaviors appropriate for particular feelings. For example, think of the last time that you felt really angry. Your heart was pounding, you were probably quite alert, and your muscles were tense. These changes poised you to do battle with the source of your anger. Alternatively, remember the last time that you felt sad. Your slow heart and respiratory rate were better suited to pulling the covers over your head. The behaviors promoted by emotions depend on the characteristics of the specific situation, but Table 7.3 summarizes some general action tendencies that have been associated with various emotions (Oatley, 1992). Because these links have been found across different cultural groups (Matsumoto, 2001), action tendencies are assumed to be a basic part of the experience of emotions.

From your perceptions of a situation to the actions you take, your feelings allow you to interface with the world around you. Appraisals focus on discrepancies between what you desire and what is present in a situation. These appraisals elicit specific emotions. Emotions, in turn, involve physiological changes to the body that allow you to perform certain actions. Those actions, quite conveniently, are often the very behaviors that can close the gap between your actual and preferred circumstances. In this sense, emotions are part of a finely tuned system that promotes fitting responses to the communication situations in which you find yourself.

The Physiology of Emotion
Physical changes that occur in conjunction with feelings.

Nonverbal Markers of Emotion
Changes in appearance that occur when a person experiences affect.

Action Tendencies
The behaviors that emotions compel us to perform.

TABLE 7.3 Emotional action tendencies

Emotion	Action	Purpose	Example
Anger	Attack	Conquer a barrier to obtaining a desired outcome	The anger Mark feels when his co-workers haven't done their share gives him the energy he needs to finish the project alone
Sadness	Retreat	Provide time to adjust to a loss	Sarah's sadness at the break-up of her romantic relationship slows her down so that she can revise her future plans
Happiness	Approach	Take advantage of favorable circumstances	T.J.'s happiness at finding the printer he needs on sale helps him decide to make the investment
Fear	Fight or flight	Eliminate a threat by either conquering it or out-running it	Lacey's fear when the exam study guide was handed out motivates her to devote extra study time
Shame	Make amends	Restore one's sense of oneself as moral	Brian's shame over losing his temper with his daughter compels him to apologize
Embarrassment	Escape	Get away from people who witnessed the incompetence	Rachel's embarrassment over her poor class presentation prompts her to cut class the following week.

> **PAUSE & REFLECT**
>
> Think of the last situation that made you feel anxious. How was your increased vigilance an advantage or disadvantage as you coped with that situation?

Putting Theory into Practice: Recognizing and Communicating Emotions

Emotions arise out of your perceptions of your circumstances, and your feelings involve several components that work in concert. This knowledge can help you to more clearly identify and describe both your own emotional experiences and the emotions of people around you.

Seek out specific labels to describe feelings. Rather than describe how you are feeling in general, try to use the wealth of emotion labels to capture your precise emotions. Instead of "angry," are you really frustrated, merely annoyed, exasperated, or raging mad? Similarly, encourage your communication partners to identify their specific feelings. For example, if your friend says that he is sad, probe those feelings to clarify whether he is gloomy, depressed, hurt, or heartbroken. By seeking out specific labels to describe feelings, you will help other people to understand your own emotions and you can respond more effectively to other people's feelings. You can practice this skill by completing Communication in Action 7.1 exercise.

COMMUNICATION IN ACTION 7.1

Charting Your Emotions

This exercise is intended to help you understand your emotional experiences in greater detail. Using the form you download from the **companion website**, keep a diary of your emotions over the course of one full day. By logging your emotions every hour, and noting details about the situations surrounding your emotional experiences, you'll gain insight into the circumstances that evoke emotions and how you tend to describe those emotions.

Address all of the components of emotions when you express or respond to feelings. You can use your knowledge about the different parts of an emotional experience to both express and respond to feelings more effectively. Beyond your self-perceptions of emotion ("I'm frightened"), you might describe your physiological state ("my heart is pounding") or how your emotions make you want to act ("I feel like hiding out in my room"). These descriptions can help others empathize with what you are feeling and appreciate its full effect on you. Likewise, keep in mind the multiple facets of emotions when other people share their feelings with you. The Communication in Action 7.2 activity will help you identify the physiological and behavioral aspects of your emotions.

COMMUNICATION IN ACTION 7.2

Beyond Self-perceptions of Emotion

This exercise will help you think about the physical changes you experience when you have different emotions. Visit the **companion website** for the instructions and to download a form for this activity.

Locate the cause of emotions within people's appraisals. In the heat of the moment, you might find yourself pointing an emotional finger at others: "*You* make me angry." "*You* hurt my feelings." "*You* are bringing me down." But remember, emotions arise from *your* appraisals of how a situation fits with *your* goals. In other words, the feelings you experience are the result of perceptions and objectives that exist within you. As you make sense of your feelings and communicate them to others, acknowledge that your own perceptions and goals are at the root of your emotions. Similarly, encourage other people to own their own emotions by helping them to identify the goals and appraisals that are fueling their feelings. The following questions might help you sort out your appraisals of your emotions:

- What is your goal in this situation?
- What is preventing you from reaching your goal?
- Why are you upset about the barriers preventing you from reaching your goal?
- How can you eliminate the barriers to your goal?
- How can you change how you are reacting to your unmet goals?

FEELINGS AND COMMUNICATION

Emotions and interpersonal communication go hand-in-hand. The strongest emotions you experience – for example, love, hate, or shame – occur within social situations. Even emotions that you experience by yourself, such as grief and loneliness, are connected to relationships with others. In this section, we examine how feelings shape and reflect interpersonal communication.

Feelings Cause Communication

Most emotions can be addressed by using communication to confront, avoid, embrace, or repair the situation that provoked your feelings. The anger you feel when someone interferes with your goals might compel you to raise your voice and argue. Likewise, you can relive situations that made you happy by telling your friends about those experiences. Research shows that feeling lonely or disconnected causes people to engage others through social media, such as Facebook (Sheldon, Abad, & Hinsch, 2011). In the workplace, feeling guilty often motivates people to work harder and, in turn, feel greater commitment to their job (Flynn & Schaumberg, 2012). In ways such as these, the emotions you experience underlie many of your communication experiences.

Emotions also explain why people react to a particular situation in different ways. For example, people who feel sympathy for a friend in distress use communication to solve the problem or to make their friend feel better, whereas people who feel angry will try to make the friend take responsibility for the problem (MacGeorge, 2001). Similarly, when people feel angry about an unexpected event in a dating relationship, they are more likely to confront their partner, but when they feel sad, they prefer to avoid communication (Knobloch, 2005). As these examples illustrate, your communication goals and behaviors reflect the action tendencies of specific emotions (Burleson & Planalp, 2000; Dillard & Seo, in press).

Communication Describes Feelings

Some of the most intimate interpersonal interactions involve messages about emotions and feelings themselves. You might unconsciously reveal your emotions through physical displays, such as teary eyes or slumped shoulders, and you also deliberately communicate your feelings to others. Research shows that most people describe their emotions to at least one other person (Rimé, Mesquita, Philippot, & Boca, 1991). Indeed, many people use emoticons in email, instant, or text messages to convey feelings to communication partners (Carter, 2003). Discussing emotions can also be a prominent part of coping with negative life events, such as losing a job (Buzzanell & Turner, 2003). Both consciously and unconsciously, our verbal and nonverbal behaviors convey our emotions to others.

Communication Affects Feelings

From the warmth you experience after a jovial exchange with a friend to the elation of hearing "I love you" from that someone special, the messages you receive from others have tremendous emotional potential. Not surprisingly, people sometimes tap that potential to shape the emotions of people around them. People sometimes craft messages to make others feel embarrassed (Bradford & Petronio, 1998), guilty (Chang, 2011; Vangelisti, Daly, & Rudnick, 1991), or jealous (Goodboy & Bolkan, 2011). You can also use communication to make people feel better. For example, when Jen's grandfather was dying of lung disease, she didn't dwell on medical tests and gloomy topics when she went to visit him. Instead, she tried to entertain him with stories about graduate school and debates about politics. You can also cheer people up by helping them to change the appraisals that are at the root of bad feelings (Burleson & Goldsmith, 1998). For example, when Denise's friend lost her job, Denise tried to persuade her to view the situation not as a loss, but as an opportunity to start her own business or perhaps go back to school. In these ways, producing or changing emotions might be the driving force behind interpersonal communication.

> **PAUSE & REFLECT**
>
> Recall a time when you actively tried to influence someone's emotions. What emotion were you focused on and what messages did you use?

Feelings Shape Interpretations of Messages

Your feelings also influence how you interpret messages from others. At a general level, moods influence how people perceive a situation, and people in a bad mood react more critically when they are asked to do something (Forgas, 1995, 1998). You also tend to

HOW DO YOU RATE? 7.1

Messages that Evoke Guilt

Visit the **companion website** to complete a scale that measures your likelihood to use or be affected by guilt-inducing messages. As you reflect on your scores, do you think you use guilt to manipulate others more than you should? Do you need to be on your guard against other people's efforts to use guilt to influence you?

focus on information that is relevant to your specific emotions. For example, people who are afraid of the consequences of drunk driving are more likely to seek information on how to protect themselves (Nabi, 2003). Similarly, people who feel positively toward a presidential candidate tend to notice the strengths of that candidate's performance in a political debate (Hullett, Louden, & Mitra, 2003).

Research by James Dillard and Eugenia Peck (2000) shows how messages can cause emotions that, in turn, shape how people respond to the messages. Dillard and Peck studied public service announcements (PSAs), which encourage viewers to buckle their seatbelts, stop smoking, avoid recreational drugs, practice safer sex, or stop littering. These televised messages evoke a variety of emotions, including surprise, fear, anger, sadness, happiness, and contentment. Dillard and Peck found that the emotional responses viewers had to the PSA predicted their subsequent attitudes about the advice given in the message. For example, people who felt fear in response to a PSA were more likely to be persuaded by the message, but people who felt anger tended to reject the advice offered in the PSA. In a similar fashion, your feelings and your interpretations of messages are intertwined within interpersonal interactions.

Putting Theory into Practice: Expressing and Responding to Emotions

Emotions are woven into the fabric of interpersonal interactions. Once you embrace feelings as an inevitable part of communicating with others, you can take steps to improve both how you express your emotions and how you respond to the feelings expressed to you by others.

If you're going to show your emotions, you might as well express them. Oftentimes, people leave it to their nonverbal cues to convey emotions to others. In other words, instead of expressing your joy, you simply act happy; instead of apologizing, you act remorseful; or instead of explaining your anger, you act mad. Of course, there are occasions when you might want to downplay your emotions (such as when you've just received an awful birthday present from your romantic partner). When you want to share your emotions, you'll be more effective if you can find a way to verbalize your feelings. Use the Communication in Action 7.3 exercise to help you put your emotions into words.

COMMUNICATION IN ACTION 7.3

Verbal Expressions of Emotion

This exercise involves using the form on the **companion website** to think of a time when a friend, romantic partner, sibling, parent, or co-worker did something that upset you, and to reflect on how you can put those emotions into words.

Consider other people's goals when you respond to their emotions. When people express their feelings to you, think about what's driving those messages and tailor your responses to those goals. When a friend shares his fears with you, he may want you either to protect him from harm or to reassure him that he is safe. If you are on the receiving end of someone's anger, explore whether she wants you to understand her feelings, to help her achieve a goal, or to get out of her way. By recognizing the action tendencies that accompany emotions, you can more effectively help your friends recover from embarrassment, relieve a parent of guilt, cheer up a sad co-worker, and prolong a child's joy. When you find yourself on the receiving end of someone's emotional expression, use the following questions to guide your response:

- Why is this person telling me about this event?
- Am I the cause of this emotion or am I supposed to help this person resolve the emotion?
- What might I have done to contribute to this emotion?
- How is this emotion relevant to the context of this interaction?
- What is this person trying to accomplish by expressing this emotion?
- What can I do to help this person achieve his or her goal?

FACTORS THAT AFFECT EMOTIONS AND COMMUNICATION

The links between emotions and communication depend on the cultural context, characteristics of the people involved, and their interpersonal relationship. By understanding how these factors shape how feelings are expressed, you can improve your ability to decipher other people's emotional messages. In turn, you will be able to respond more effectively to the emotions that communication partners express to you.

Cultural Norms

Some aspects of emotional experiences are shared across cultures – these include the automatic or unconscious parts of emotion such as physiological changes, facial displays, and action tendencies. Moreover, basic emotions such as happiness, sadness, anger, fear, and surprise are experienced by people of all cultures. However, when it comes to how people consciously act upon their emotions, culture plays a major role. A culture's **display rules** tell its members when, where, and how emotions should be expressed. Consider, for example, how people of different religions grieve the death of a loved one. Within Judaism, a death is followed by seven days of intensive mourning, during which mirrors are covered, men do not shave, and family members wear a black ribbon. In contrast, Buddhism sees death as part of the normal order of the universe, and only a one-hour period of prayer or meditation is typical.

In a similar fashion, culture dictates how people express everyday emotions like happiness, anger, jealousy, pride, etc. In general, culture shapes people's willingness to rely on others for emotional support (Ryan, La Guardia, Solky-Butzel, Chirkov, & Kim, 2005). For example, compared to the United States, people from Costa Rica are more comfortable

Display Rules

Cultural prescriptions about when, where, and how emotions should be expressed.

expressing positive emotions to either family or non-family members, but they are generally less comfortable expressing negative emotions (Stephan, Stephan, & de Vargas, 1996). Another study concluded that Japanese culture discourages the display of both strong negative emotions and positive emotions, compared to North American cultures (Safdar et al., 2009). In the context of romantic relationships, European Americans report feeling and expressing emotions more intensely than Japanese Americans do (Aune & Aune, 1996). As these examples illustrate, culture influences whether, to whom, and how intensely emotions are communicated.

PAUSE & REFLECT

In what ways do your experiences and expressions of happiness, pride, anger, and sadness reflect your cultural background?

Culture can also set different standards for emotional expression based on a person's age. In American society, we tolerate extreme expressions of anger, frustration, sadness, and joy from children in their "terrible twos" (Figure 7.4) – can you imagine a middle-aged adult expressing raw emotions in the same way? Relative to older adults, adolescents and young adults experience more negative emotions when they have interpersonal problems (Birditt & Fingerman, 2003). Moreover, elderly people exert more emotional control than younger adults (Thomsen, Mehlsen, Viidik, Sommerlund, & Zachariae, 2005). Although older adults are sometimes overcome by their emotions, people generally expect mature individuals to manage their emotions and express their feelings responsibly. Complete the Communication in Action 7.4 activity to test your assumptions about emotions and aging.

Biological sex has been linked to the experience and expression of emotions in ways that both span and reflect cultural norms. In general, studies of people from different nations and age groups suggest that women experience emotions more frequently and

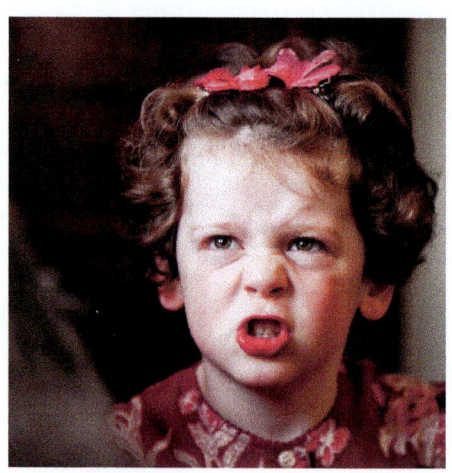

FIGURE 7.4 A defiant toddler

Source: Getty Images.

COMMUNICATION IN ACTION 7.4

Expressing Emotions across the Lifespan

To shed light on how people in different age groups express their emotions, download and complete the form on the **companion website**.

intensely than men do (Brebner, 2003; Thomsen et al., 2005). A study of people from Japan, Canada, and the United States found similar sex differences across these cultures, such that men tended to express powerful emotions like anger more than women, while women were more likely than men to express sadness, fear, and happiness (Safdar et al., 2009). Within American society, display rules also tend to discourage men from disclosing their emotions (Burleson, Holmstrom, & Gilstrap, 2004). Accordingly, research conducted in the United States shows that women are more willing than men to rely on others for emotional support (Ryan et al., 2005). In addition, American women notice more distinctions and nuances in feelings than men do (Barrett, Lane, Sechrest, & Schwartz, 2000). Thus, these findings highlight how culture shapes how men and women express and make sense of emotional messages.

PAUSE & REFLECT

Under what conditions would you consider it "normal" for a woman to cry? Under what conditions would you consider it "normal" for a man to cry? How do you explain any differences in your lists?

Emotional Intelligence

Within any cultural group, you'll find that some people are more tuned into emotional messages than others. **Emotional intelligence** refers to people's ability to understand and manage their own feelings, as well as the moods and emotions of others. Because feelings are complex, emotional intelligence requires self-awareness, self-control, motivation, empathy, and social skill (Singh, 2004). More specifically, emotional intelligence includes being able to recognize emotional nuances, to put emotional information to use, to understand how emotions work, and to either promote or suppress emotional experiences in one's self and in others (Goleman, 2006). Thus, an emotionally intelligent person is insightful, articulate, and in control when it comes to affective experiences; someone who is agreeable, likeable, and respected by others; and someone who engages in positive social experiences, rather than personally or interpersonally destructive behaviors (Mayer, Salovey, & Caruso, 2004). The How Do You Rate? 7.2 exercise can help

Emotional Intelligence
The ability to understand and manage one's own feelings, as well as the moods and emotions of others.

**HOW DO
YOU RATE?** 7.2

Willingness to Rely on Others for Emotional Support

Do you tend to "go it alone," or do you turn to others in times of need? Complete the scale on the **companion website** to assess how much you turn to others when you are experiencing strong emotions. Ryan et al. (2005) found that the average score for emotional reliance on friends among participants in their study was 4.36. How do you compare? If you repeat this test, thinking about a family member or co-worker instead of a friend, how different would your scores be?

you to learn about one facet of emotional intelligence: an ability to rely on others for emotional support.

Research has connected emotional intelligence to several important outcomes. For example, people who are higher in emotional intelligence report having a better quality of life, in general (Singh, 2004). Emotional intelligence has also been linked to both leadership ability and a person's performance as a member of a problem-solving team (George, 2000; Jordan & Troth, 2004). In contrast, a lack of emotional intelligence is associated with a variety of negative outcomes, including drug and alcohol abuse, deviant behavior, and poor relationships with friends (Brackett, Mayer, & Warner, 2004). Moreover, romantic couples in which both partners are low in emotional intelligence are more superficial, less supportive, and more prone to conflict than couples where at least one partner is emotionally intelligent (Brackett, Warner, & Bosco, 2005). When viewed in this light, emotional intelligence is revealed as a consequential aspect of people's personality.

The Relationship Context

Another factor that shapes the expression of emotions is the nature of the relationship between partners. Close relationship partners have many opportunities to help or hinder each other's goals in ways that evoke emotions (Berscheid & Ammazzalorso, 2004). Research has shown that having a romantic partner who fulfills your needs increases your day-to-day experience of positive emotions (Le & Agnew, 2001). Conversely, people experience more intense negative emotions when a romantic partner, rather than a friend, dismisses their concerns (Fehr & Harasymchuk, 2005). Moreover, people's disagreeable behaviors in relationships make their partner feel worse the more often they occur (Cunningham, Shamblen, Barbee, & Ault, 2005). In these ways, our closest relationships are also the most emotionally volatile.

Communicating emotions leaves you vulnerable to the other person's response; therefore, you are more likely to express your emotions to relationship partners you trust. Not surprisingly, then, people are generally more willing to express emotions to partners in personal, rather than business, relationships (Clark & Finkel, 2005). In addition, college students in the United States report that they rely on their best friends for emotional support more than anyone else (Ryan et al., 2005, studies 1 and 2). Within romantic associations, both the expression of jealousy and the perceived appropriateness of expressing jealously increase with the length of the relationship (Aune, Buller, & Aune, 1996; Aune & Comstock, 1997). As these examples illustrate, the nature and duration of a relationship influence how much the partners disclose their feelings.

PAUSE & REFLECT

How do you express strong emotions like anger or love with different people, such as your parents, grandparents, friends, siblings, or a romantic partner?

One notable exception to the tendency for people to express emotions in close, rather than nonintimate, relationships is the practice of sharing emotions in online venues. For some people, visiting chatrooms, using Twitter, or blogging gives them a place to describe their feelings to an often large number of friends, acquaintances, and even strangers. If you have a Facebook account, take a quick look at the newsfeed coming in from your array of friends. On any given day, you might find a diversity of emotions running through your friendship network. Perhaps one friend expresses disappointment that her favorite NFL team lost (while another friend's spirits are lifted by the opposing team's victory). Or, maybe you have friends who use Facebook to comment on their frustration with their job, their children, their parents, or their neighbor's noisy dog. While it's true that many people prefer to discuss their emotions with close friends and relationship partners, the Internet also allows us to share our feelings with a much broader audience.

Putting Theory into Practice: Developing Emotional Intelligence

Within the boundaries set by culture, people's personal traits and skills influence how they communicate emotions, and the relationship between communicators shapes emotional messages. Armed with an understanding of how context shapes emotional messages, you can increase your emotional intelligence.

Consider context when you express your feelings to others. Although some aspects of your emotional experiences are automatic, emotional intelligence involves tailoring emotional messages to fit the situation. Here are strategies for incorporating context into your communication of emotions:

- If you are communicating with someone from a culture other than your own, keep in mind that your communication partner may have different rules for expressing emotions.
- Ask yourself in what ways your age, gender, or other characteristics might influence how others perceive your emotional messages.
- If you have especially strong or complex feelings to work through, seek out a friend who has the emotional intelligence to appreciate and respond to your emotions.
- Consider the extent to which your relationship with a communication partner allows you to share your feelings openly.

If you adapt your emotional messages to the situation, your communication partner will be more likely to understand your feelings and respond in the ways you had hoped.

Use the social context to understand the emotions expressed by others. Many people can recognize the emotions conveyed by a smile, a glare, or a trembling lip. Being able to understand the intensity or complexity of the feelings behind these displays, however, can be considerably more challenging. As you make sense of other people's emotional messages, think about how the context might be shaping their messages. In particular, consider these issues:

- How might your communication partner's cultural display rules require or prohibit the expression of particular emotions?

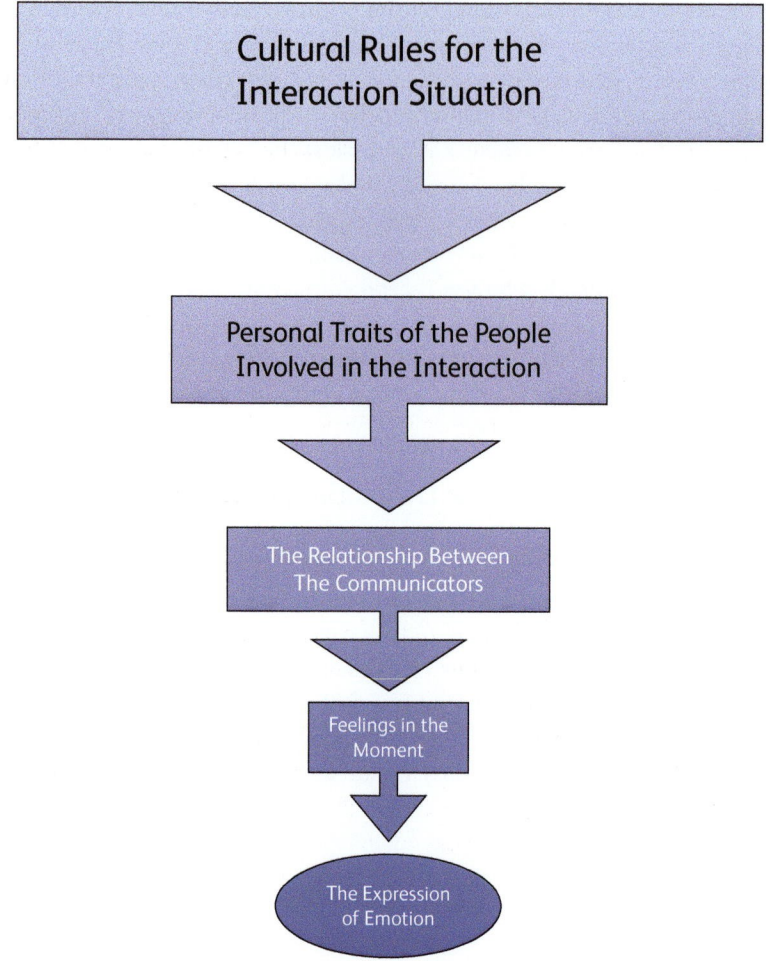

FIGURE 7.5 The hierarchy of influences on expressions of emotion

- How skilled is your communication partner when it comes to expressing feelings – is this someone you can read like a book, or a person who typically sends ambiguous emotional messages?
- Is your relationship prompting a partner to hide their emotions from you or express their feelings at full strength?

Paying attention to cultural norms, your partner's emotional intelligence, and the kind of relationship you have can help you determine whether your communication partners are considerably more angry, sad, frightened, or happy then they appear.

THE DARK SIDE OF EMOTIONS IN CLOSE RELATIONSHIPS

Throughout this chapter, you have seen how feelings are an inevitable part of interpersonal communication. In this final section, we turn our attention to the intensely negative emotions that can arise within our closest relationships. The **dark side of interpersonal communication** includes those aspects of interaction that relate to socially inappropriate goals, harmful behaviors, or painful experiences (for example, deception, violations, and abuse; Cupach & Spitzberg, 2007). To highlight how people use interpersonal communication to both cause and relieve painful emotions, consider hurt, grief, and jealousy.

Dark Side of Interpersonal Communication
Aspects of interaction that involve socially inappropriate goals, harmful behaviors, or painful experiences.

Hurt, Grief, and Jealousy

The intimacy that makes close relationships so special can also leave people vulnerable to the hurtful actions of their partners. **Hurt** is considered a blended emotion that includes sadness, fear, and sometimes anger (Feeney, 2005; Vangelisti, Young, Carpenter-Theune, & Alexander, 2005). It is a uniquely social emotion, in that it arises from the injury produced by another person's words or actions (Vangelisti & Sprague, 1998). More specifically, you feel hurt when someone communicates that they don't appreciate you, they don't value the relationship as much as they used to, or they don't feel they need to be supportive, faithful, open, and trustworthy (Feeney, 2005; Leary, 2001; Mills, Nazar, & Farrell, 2002). The form of a hurtful message also influences the pain it causes (Vangelisti, 1994). Compare two hurtful messages that Olivia might receive from her father, Alan. If Alan says, "I think you're making a mess of your life," Olivia might be hurt, but she can also argue the point. If Alan says, "I never loved you as much as your brother," she is left without a rebuttal. These examples show both how interpersonal communication can be hurtful, and how some messages do more harm than others.

Hurt
A blended emotion that includes sadness, fear, and sometimes anger.

In the case of hurt, interpersonal communication creates negative feelings – for other emotions, interpersonal communication might be your only option for relieving your pain. **Grief** is a state of extreme sadness that includes feelings of despair, panic, guilt, and anger (Golish & Powell, 2003; Hogan, Greenfield, & Schmidt, 2001). Grief arises from the loss of something that was deeply valued, that you expected to enjoy into the future, and that is irreplaceable. Consider, for example, how grief might be associated with events such as a romantic break-up, a loved one's cancer diagnosis, the loss of a job, or a death in the family. In cases such as these, grief is made worse when the loss is sudden, untimely, preventable, or violent (Stewart, 1999).

Grief
An extreme state of sadness that includes feelings of despair, panic, guilt, and anger.

FIGURE 7.6 Nias, Indonesia, March 30, 2005: A woman waits as rescuers search for the bodies of her missing family during rescue operations following an earthquake.

Source: Photo by Daniel Berehulak/Getty Images.

Although grief involves a sense of hopelessness, interpersonal communication does provide some relief. For example, research has shown that talking about an infant's death allows parents to reconstruct their fractured identity (Hastings, 2000), and it decreases the experience of both grief and melancholy thoughts (Kamm & Vandenberg, 2001; Lepore, Silver, Wortman, & Wayment, 1996). Even the specific language used to discuss a terminal illness or to communicate with the grief-stricken can help to control intense feelings and show concern and support (Adamolekun, 1999; Frey, Adelman, & Query, 1996). In fact, one of the most helpful things you can do to comfort someone who is grieving is simply to express your willingness to listen (Range, Walston, & Pollard, 1992). Although nothing can recover the losses that lead to grief, interpersonal communication can be a key part of a person's emotional recovery. The study that is described in the Inside Communication Research box focuses on the links between interpersonal communication and grief.

INSIDE COMMUNICATION RESEARCH

Communication and Grief

Given the tragic and personal nature of events that cause grief, studying how communication influences the recovery process is no simple task. People might be reluctant to talk to researchers about their losses. Even when people want to participate in studies of grief, their feelings might be too overwhelming or complex for them to describe easily. How, then, do scholars study interpersonal communication and grief? One example is provided by Tamara Golish and Kimberly Powell, who examined how grief and joy are intertwined when parents experience the premature birth of a child (Golish & Powell, 2003).

Golish and Powell began by posting an announcement on list-serves for parents of premature babies that asked for volunteers to participate in a study of the impact of premature births on family communication. People who responded were emailed a questionnaire, which they completed and sent back to the researchers. This questionnaire took the form of open-ended questions that encouraged participants to tell the story of the childbirth and their reactions to it.

Golish and Powell then conducted a qualitative/interpretive analysis of responses to the questionnaire. This method required both researchers to read and re-read the questionnaire responses in search of themes or issues. After reaching consensus about the themes that were present, the researchers read the questionnaires a final time to note how frequently each issue was mentioned.

The researchers concluded that the premature birth of a baby creates a crisis stemming from an ambiguous loss. On one hand, participants described their shock, sadness, and anger about both their infant's medical condition and the loss of a full-term pregnancy; at the same time, these parents were celebrating the birth of their child. Communication also served many functions for the participants. Parents used communication to educate both themselves and their family members about premature births. In addition, communication from others was a source of support, reassurance, and community. Couples also used communication to develop a sense of solidarity and to stay connected with each other's experience of the crisis. Finally, parents coped with the situation by focusing their talk on the present, rather than mourning the past or worrying about the future. These results provide a nuanced portrayal of the crisis created when the celebration of birth is mixed with grief.

TALK ABOUT IT

1. What biases do you think might be present in a study such as this? Are you confident that Golish and Powell's interpretation of the themes represents the parents' stories accurately? What are the strengths and weaknesses of studying strong emotions and interpersonal communication in this way?
2. This study found that communication with family members was challenging because people were caught between celebrating the birth of the child and grieving the conditions of the birth. Now that you understand the complexity of the emotions involved in this situation, can you generate some messages that would be particularly comforting to parents coping with a premature birth?

Jealousy is yet another emotion that arises from perceptions of vulnerability and loss – in this case, feelings result from the perception that a valued relationship is threatened by a partner's competing interests (White & Mullen, 1989). Jealousy includes feelings of passion, fear, envy, hostility, irritation, guilt, sadness, and even love (Guerrero & Andersen, 1998; Guerrero, Trost, & Yoshimura, 2005). How do people cope with such varied and intense emotions? As summarized in Table 7.4, people can use interpersonal communication to pursue a variety of goals when they feel jealous. Table 7.4 also reveals that the responses to jealousy include options as diverse as denying feelings, confronting the rival, accusing the partner of infidelity, or showcasing one's strengths as a partner.

Jealousy
An emotion that arises from perceptions that a valued relationship is threatened by a partner's competing interests.

How people respond when they are jealous is influenced by the emotions they feel most strongly. For example, hostility promotes more violent reactions to jealousy, but fear leads people to try to regain their partner's affections (Guerrero et al., 2005). Although it isn't always easy to control negative reactions when your relationship is threatened, research has shown that communicating constructively and sharing feelings can heal the relationship (Andersen, Eloy, Guerrero, & Spitzberg, 1995). The process linking the emotions of jealousy to relationship outcomes is depicted in Figure 7.7. As you review that model, note how short-lived feelings of jealousy can lead to communication decisions that have a long-term impact on a romantic relationship.

TABLE 7.4 Communication goals and strategies for responding to jealousy

Goals for communication about jealousy

Maintain the relationship: *We have to find a way to get through this together.*

Recover from the loss of self-esteem: *I'm going to show that it's her loss!*

Reduce uncertainty about the situation and/or relationship: *I need to know what's going on.*

Reassess the nature of the relationship: *This changes how I feel about her.*

Retaliate against the partner or rival: *I'm getting even, no matter what!*

Responses to jealousy

Physically distance yourself from the partner: *I need to get away for awhile.*

TABLE 7.4 continued

Psychologically distance yourself from the partner: *I'm not going to think or talk about this.*

Engage in covert surveillance to gather more information: *I wonder what is going on?*

Display negative affect by crying or acting upset: *I'm upset with you.*

Confront and accuse the partner: *I think you have been unfaithful.*

Communicate or behave violently: *You're not getting away with this!*

Manipulate your partner's feelings: *As if I haven't had lot of offers better than you.*

Contact and confront the rival: *How dare you?*

Discuss the situation with your partner to gather information: *Tell me what happened.*

Be especially nice, so your partner will prefer you: *I'd like to take you out to a special dinner.*

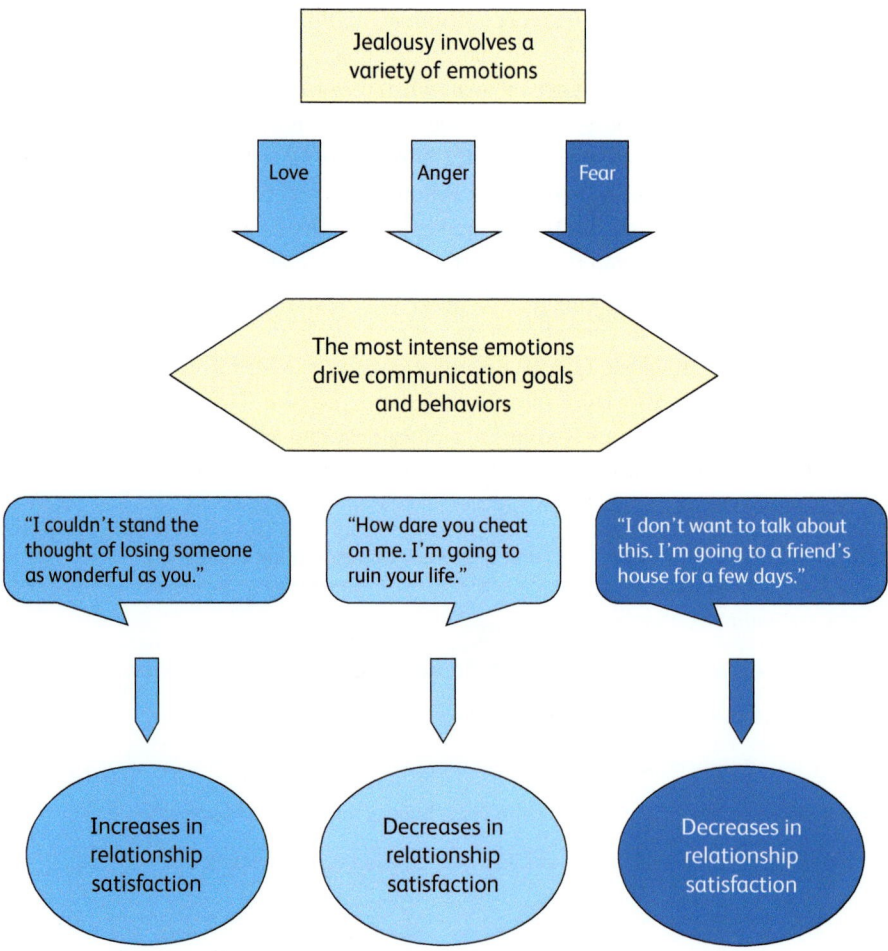

FIGURE 7.7 The impact of jealous emotions

PAUSE & REFLECT

Have you ever felt jealousy? What caused your feelings? What specific emotions did you feel, and what did you do? In the end, did your relationship become closer or more distant because of the experience?

Putting Theory into Practice: Keeping Emotional Consequences in Check

As interpersonal communication is intertwined with the experience, management, and resolution of some of the darkest emotions, use your communication skills to limit the effect of these feelings within relationships you value.

Buffer yourself and others from the consequences of dark emotions. When we experience intense emotions, we might find ourselves responding in extreme ways. To keep your negative emotions from wreaking havoc on relationships you value, learn to recognize when you are in the throes of these intense and dark emotions. At those times, be especially cautious about going where your feelings would take you. Might it be worth it to gather more information about your partner's hurtful comment before ending the relationship? Might talking with someone help you recover from your terrible loss? Might those feelings of jealousy point you to issues in your relationship that you can address and improve? Attention to the dark side of interpersonal communication reminds us that hurt, loss, and infidelity are as much a part of interpersonal relationships as love and joy; however, we needn't be hostage to these feelings.

SUMMARY

This chapter focused on feelings as a part of interpersonal interaction. As a foundation for this discussion, we began by clarifying the nature of emotions. You saw that emotions can range from positive to negative and involve more or less arousal, they can be pure or blended forms of several basic emotions, and they can be distinguished by the social functions that they serve. You also learned that emotions arise from people's appraisals of their environment, and that the experience of emotion involves self-perceptions, physical reactions, nonverbal markers, and action tendencies. In short, the experience of emotion is a complex phenomenon.

Our examination of the relationship between emotions and interpersonal communication revealed four distinct links. Because emotions involve action tendencies, they can motivate communication to address the conditions that produced our feelings. In addition, you might use communication to describe your feelings to others. You also employ communication to influence how other people feel – perhaps to cheer them up, make them feel guilty, or evoke feelings of love. Finally, your own feelings frame how you interpret the messages you receive from others. In these ways, emotions permeate both the creation and perception of interpersonal communication.

The expression of emotion during interpersonal interactions is also shaped by culture, the traits of the people involved, and the relationship that exists between the parties. Cultural display rules specify which emotions you should express, as well as when and to whom you can express your feelings. Emotional intelligence – the ability to perceive and manage feelings – helps you to communicate your feelings more carefully and to respond to other people's emotions more skillfully. And within the constraints and opportunities created by the cultural context and your personal skills, your relationship with another person influences whether and how you express feelings. In particular, close interpersonal relationships are a place where some of our most negative emotions are created and soothed.

ACTIVITIES FOR EXPLORING COMMUNICATION ETHICS

What Would You/Should You Do?

You're out running errands with your father, and things haven't been going well. Your day started off with a dead battery in your car, which made you late for your father's doctor's appointment. The doctor ordered some tests, and so that appointment went over time too. Now you have to pick up your mother at work, and neither of you have had lunch. You decide to zip through a drive-through window. As your father is ordering, the server keeps interrupting him – "Do you want cheese on that?" "Do you want fries?" etc. These interruptions put your father over the edge. He starts to be rude and insulting to the person taking his order. You know that he's just frustrated by the day, and you feel bad for the person on the receiving end of his tirade. What should you do when you see someone taking out his or her bad feelings on an innocent bystander?

Something to Think About

When people have strong opinions about something, they are often influenced by both beliefs and emotions. Consider a public issue that you feel strongly about: Should abortion be legal? Should the United States withdraw troops stationed in the Middle East? Should the death penalty be eliminated? Take a moment to consider how much your position stems from facts or arguments that you believe, and how much your position is fueled by your feelings about that issue. To what extent is it ethical for people to let emotions influence their positions on important issues?

Analyze Communication Ethics Yourself

Emotions are an inevitable part of public policy debates. Ethical participants in these discussions own their emotions, and they don't manipulate other people's feelings in order to win. Locate the text or a video of a speech that addresses a controversial public issue – for example, whether creationism should be taught in public schools, whether social security should be changed, or an issue important in your own community. As you examine this speech, note the speaker's use of emotion. Does the speaker reveal his or her own feelings about the issue? Does the speaker try to evoke emotions in the audience? Based on your analysis, has the speaker incorporated emotion into his or her speech in an ethical manner?

KEY WORDS

action tendencies

appraisal theory of emotions

appraisals

basic emotions

dark side of interpersonal
   communication

display rules

emotional intelligence

emotions

grief

hurt

jealousy

moods

nonverbal markers of emotion

physiology of emotion

self-perception of emotion

social emotions

LISTENING

208 WHAT IS LISTENING?

219 ACTIVE LISTENING

226 LISTENING FOR RELATIONAL MEANINGS

231 SUMMARY

233 ACTIVITIES FOR EXPLORING COMMUNICATION ETHICS

233 KEY WORDS

In 2007, Kleenex launched a new line of television advertisements that they called the "Let It Out" Tour. The advertisements featured a blue couch placed on a busy city street where people would sit down with an interviewer to chat. The interviewer asked passers-by to share personal stories of triumph and pain from the comfort of the blue couch while he listened. The individuals laughed and cried into Kleenex tissues while telling the interviewer about their experiences. The interviewer listened intently to each participant, leaning in toward them, nodding his head to show understanding, laughing at their funny stories, and even crying when appropriate. Many of the participants told the interviewer how good it felt just to get something off their chest. The relief that these participants described is due to the fact that the interviewer was such a good listener. Feeling like we're understood and showing others that we care about what they have to say are important components of the interpersonal communication process.

The "Let It Out" Tour commercials highlight the importance of listening during interpersonal interactions. Listening can be a rewarding, informative, and enlightening part of the interpersonal communication process. In fact, one estimate suggests that college students spend more than half of their time communicating engaged in listening (Emanuel et al., 2008). And people enjoy and appreciate being listened to. Have you ever felt relieved after venting to a friend about some frustrating circumstances? Even if that person doesn't have much to say in response, having the opportunity to express your thoughts and feelings to someone who listens attentively can be a rewarding experience. Listening can also be an important tool because it allows you to gather information and deepen your knowledge and understanding. You can pick up on an important detail in a lecture or see a relationship in a new light based on how you interpret another person's message. Attentive listening helps us understand complex information and improve the nature of our interpersonal relationships. In this chapter, we examine the process of listening, strategies for active listening, and how people listen for information about their relationships. Learning about these topics can help you enjoy the benefits of being a good listener.

PAUSE & REFLECT

Do you know anybody you consider to be an especially good listener? What does that person do when you are engaged in a conversation?

WHAT IS LISTENING?

Have you ever been asked, "Are you listening to me?" The difference between simply being present and being engaged in an interaction highlights the distinction between hearing and listening. **Hearing** is one of your five senses that gives you the ability to perceive sound by detecting vibrations in your ear. During an interaction, you might be able to hear the other person talking, but if your mind is elsewhere you're not actually listening to that person's message. According to the International Listening Association (1996; http://www.listen.org/), **listening** is "the process of receiving, constructing meaning from and responding to spoken and/or nonverbal messages." Listening requires more effort than simply relying on your sense of hearing, and you probably engage in the listening process to a greater or lesser degree in different interactions. For example, you might occasionally space out during a class lecture while you are thinking about the errands you need to run after class. Or maybe during a recent conversation with your mother you paid only perfunctory attention to her criticisms of your best friend. In this section, we'll discuss features of the listening process, different ways that people can listen, barriers to effective listening, and forms of nonlistening.

The Listening Process

The process of listening unfolds through several phases that repeat over the course of a conversation (see Figure 8.1). This process begins when you pay attention to a communication partner's message, and it ends when you respond to that message. Communication scholar Brant Burleson (2011) clarified that the listening process involves both mindful activities where you are consciously engaged, and also mindless activities that unfold automatically during a conversation. Let's look more closely at the different behaviors and goals that characterize each stage of the listening process.

Hearing
The ability to perceive sound by detecting vibrations in your ear.

Listening
The process of receiving, constructing meaning from and responding to spoken and/or nonverbal messages.

RESPONDING: Forming a reply to the message

ATTENDING: The process of noticing specific cues provided by a communication partner

The Listening Process

INTERPRETING: Attaching meaning to cues provided by a communication partner

EVALUATING: The process of critically analyzing information to determine how truthful, authentic, or believable you judge the message to be

REMEMBERING: Recalling information that has been shared with you

FIGURE 8.1 The listening process

Attending

The process of noticing specific cues provided by an interaction partner.

Attending. The first stage of the listening process is **attending** – the process of noticing specific cues provided by a communication partner. This stage of listening resembles the selection stage of the perception process, as described in Chapter 4 on perception. Selection involves noticing only a subset of the stimuli that are available to your senses at any given moment. Similarly, during the attending phase of the listening process, you select among the various cues available from your conversation partner. Just as effective perception requires that you sort out important details from all the other stimuli around you, effective listening means that you focus on cues that are particularly relevant to understanding a conversation. For example, Jen recalls going on a job interview that involved going out for dinner at a busy and loud restaurant. During that part of the interview, she had to filter out the noise from surrounding tables to focus on what her companions were saying. She could also minimize her attention to her colleagues' side comments about enticing menu options, but she had to pay full attention to the questions they asked about her qualifications and abilities. As this example illustrates, the first stage of the listening process allows you to identify the details that are most relevant to the interaction and tune out other information that could interfere with your efforts to listen.

Interpreting

Attaching meaning to cues you have noticed in interaction.

Interpreting. During the next stage of the listening process, **interpreting**, you attach meaning to the cues that you have noticed. In other words, the interpreting phase involves your efforts to understand the cues you have received. As summarized in Table 8.1 and described below, there are several strategies people can use to achieve understanding during conversation:

■ *Try to determine the organization of the message so that it's easier to identify the speaker's main points.* Some people make their point up front and use the rest of the interaction to support their cause, others lead up to their point more tentatively and finally get to what they want to say at the end of the interaction. By examining the organization of a message, you can identify main points more effectively and interpret periphery comments in context.

TABLE 8.1 Strategies for interpreting messages

Determine Organization	Is the main point made up front or at the end?
	Does supportive information come before or after the point?
Attend to Nonverbal Cues	Do nonverbal cues match the verbal cues?
	What additional information is conveyed nonverbally?
Paraphrase	Can you put your partner's ideas into your own words?
	Does your interpretation of the situation overlook anything that the partner emphasized?
Question	What information do you need to make sense of the conversation?
	Are you making assumptions that need to be clarified?

- *Rely on both verbal and nonverbal cues to decipher a message.* Although people often think of listening as focusing primarily on the verbal component of a message, nonverbal cues can help you understand an interaction. Someone might tell you verbally that they agree with you, but their lack of eye contact and skeptical facial expressions might send a different message, so effective listening might require attention to both verbal and nonverbal messages.

- *Increase understanding by silently paraphrasing what you think your partner is trying to say.* Paraphrasing involves putting your partner's statement into your own words, which can help you to determine if you understand the message the way it was intended.

- *Ask questions.* If you aren't sure about the meaning of a particular message, it is important to seek more information. Asking for clarification will ensure that you understand what your partner means and that you're not making inaccurate assumptions to help you fill in missing information.

Paraphrasing
Putting your partner's statement into your own words.

Remembering. The remembering stage of the listening process involves recalling and retaining the information that has been shared with you. During the course of a conversation you need to remember what has been previously stated so that you don't repeat yourself or ask questions that have already been answered. Remembering what happens in an interaction also has some long-term implications for professional and relational success. For your classes, you probably take notes to record specific points, and you study for an exam by reading your notes several times to help you remember the information. Retaining content you learn in class or at your job can help you get a good grade or earn a promotion. In social contexts, remembering information that interpersonal communication partners share with you is also very important. You show your interaction partners that you are a competent communicator by recalling information they have shared with you. Remembering messages and important details can also tell people that you care about them. In fact, relationships become closer as partners remember and build upon the interactions they've had with each other.

Remembering
Recalling and retaining the information that has been shared with you.

> ## PAUSE & REFLECT
>
> How do you feel when you discover that a friend, co-worker, or family member forgot personal information that you communicated?

Evaluating. The next stage of the listening process is evaluating – the process of critically analyzing information to determine how truthful, authentic, or believable you judge it to be. Have you ever heard a friend tell a story and thought that it sounded a bit far-fetched? Have you ever caught someone in a lie and then looked for inconsistencies in their other messages? Have you ever been persuaded to make a purchase based on a salesperson's arguments? You make judgments like these during the evaluating stage of the listening process. When you evaluate messages effectively, you carefully examine the information you have received so that your conclusions are based on accurate facts or

Evaluating
The process of critically analyzing information to determine how truthful, authentic, or believable you judge it to be.

Responding

Forming a reply to a message.

plausible arguments. When you encounter inconsistencies or unbelievable information, you can seek additional information to help you make sense of the interaction by focusing on nonverbal cues and asking questions to get to the bottom of the problem.

Responding. The final stage of the listening process is **responding**, which involves forming a reply to the message. During an interpersonal interaction, your partner expects you to respond to show that you have been listening and that you understand the message. You might respond throughout the interaction with various nonverbal cues. For example, you can show that you're listening and that you understand by nodding your head in agreement, matching your partner's emotional expressions, or maintaining eye contact. People can also show they are listening by using back-channel communication; as you learned in Chapter 6, back-channel communication includes short utterances, such as "um-hmm," "I know," and "absolutely," that signal attention and encourage a speaker to continue. When used as part of listening, back-channel responses help support the communication going on in the main channel (Bavelas, Coates, & Johnson, 2000).

Your partner will likely expect you to also respond with a more substantive comment at some point as well. One type of verbal response is to acknowledge and confirm what was said, such as when you repeat back your supervisor's instructions for a task at work. Another type of verbal response might demonstrate an understanding of your partner's feelings. For example, if your friend tells you that he failed an exam, you might respond by saying "That's too bad, you must be really disappointed." Verbal responses can also reflect socially and relationally appropriate messages, like relating what your partner said about a previous relationship experience that you've shared. You have an array of verbal and nonverbal choices when responding to an interaction partner, but appropriate reactions will show your partner that you've been listening.

PAUSE & REFLECT

What kinds of verbal and nonverbal cues tell you someone is listening to you? How can you tell someone is listening when you are communicating by phone or even text-based communication technologies?

You exchange many messages with a partner over the course of a conversation; therefore, the cycle shown in Figure 8.1 occurs over and over again as you attend to new messages, seek to understand, retain, and evaluate them, and respond both verbally and nonverbally. In this way, listening is an ongoing part of interpersonal communication.

Ways of Listening

People can approach the process of listening in a variety of ways. In some cases, different ways of listening reflect the requirements of different interpersonal communication situations. For example, when you are in a staff meeting at work, you might listen for feedback on your performance and for information about specific tasks you are expected to perform. People also tend to privilege certain types of listening, no matter what the situation. For example, you might know someone who always seems to find fault, correct, or criticize people. By understanding different types of listening, as well as more persistent listening styles, you can adapt your communication to fit both the situation you are in and the person you are talking to.

Types of listening. As a starting point, let's consider the different types of listening summarized in Table 8.2. **Discriminatory listening** involves distinguishing between different words, sounds, and meanings, which can be helpful when you are trying to make sure that you understand the details in a message correctly. For example, when you strain to listen through a poor cell phone connection to distinguish certain words and phrases, you're engaged in discriminatory listening. Other times, you might find yourself engaged in **appreciative listening**, which is listening purely for enjoyment, for example, at a poetry reading or a concert. **Comprehensive listening** focuses on receiving and remembering messages, so it can be useful for organizing details, such as when you are meeting someone for the first time or receiving complicated instructions. A situation calls for **evaluative listening** when you need to judge whether a message is accurate, honest, and complete. You might engage in evaluative listening when you're trying to determine if a salesperson is being truthful about a product and giving you a good deal. Finally, **active-empathic listening** involves focusing on another person's feelings to understand what they must be going through. Typically you would engage in empathic

Discriminatory Listening
Listening to distinguish between different words, sounds, and meanings.

Appreciative Listening
Listening to derive pleasure and enjoyment.

Comprehensive Listening
Listening to receive and remember new information.

Evaluative Listening
Listening to judge the accuracy, honesty, and completeness of a message.

Active-empathic Listening
Listening to comfort and help others.

TABLE 8.2 Types of listening

Listening type	Definition	Example
Discriminatory listening	Listening to distinguish between different words, sounds, and meanings	Listening to determine if your friend wants to meet at 5:15 or 5:50, the directions to the place where you will meet, and whether or not this is a romantic date
Appreciative listening	Listening to derive pleasure and enjoyment	Listening to your grandfather tell a funny story that he shares at every family reunion
Comprehensive listening	Listening to receive and remember new information	Listening to a new romantic partner describe his or her ideal birthday, so that you can plan the perfect celebration
Evaluative listening	Listening to judge the accuracy, honesty, and completeness of a message	Listening to determine if your employee's explanation for an error is truthful and thorough
Active-empathic listening	Listening to comfort and help others	Listening to your best friend describe a recent break-up to show that you care, and also to figure out how you can best help your friend

FIGURE 8.2 Listening to a story

Source: Getty Images.

listening when you are called upon to provide comfort, support, and help (Gearhart & Bodie, 2011). These different types of listening accomplish different goals, so they are useful in different types of situations.

Listening styles. Do you prefer to listen to facts and statistics or personal stories and examples? Do you like to linger and reflect on the content of a message, or would you prefer speakers to be direct and to the point? Although different situations might call for specific listening strategies, like whether you are listening for information or listening for pleasure, most people tend to have a preference for listening in the same way across a variety of different situations. A **listening style** is similar to a personality trait in that it is an approach to listening that a person uses in many different situations.

There are four general listening styles (see Figure 8.3). People with an action-centered listening style see listening as a means to an end; they prefer messages to be highly organized, concise, and error-free, so that they can figure out what is meant and move ahead. People with a content-centered listening style also tend to focus on the facts and details of the message, but they value accurate and clear messages that allow them to comprehend and evaluate information. A time-centered listening style characterizes an impatient listener; people with this style are unconcerned with the details of someone's message, and they prefer speakers who get to the point quickly. A final listening style reflects concern with other people's feelings or emotions; individuals with a people-centered listening style tend to seek out common interests with others, and they are particularly responsive to the emotional experiences of others. You can complete the How Do You Rate? 8.1 exercise to gain insight into your own listening style.

Specific personality characteristics have been linked to a person's listening style. In particular, people who are very outgoing tend to have a people-centered listening style, which is consistent with their sociable personalities (Weaver, Watson, & Barker, 1996). People who are typically nervous and anxious are more likely to adopt action-centered or time-centered listening styles (Villaume & Bodie, 2007). These listening styles minimize the need for interaction, which tends to make anxious individuals uncomfortable. People who are very self-centered and verbally aggressive are less likely to adopt people-centered or content-centered listening styles because they prefer not to spend too much time dwelling on other people's experiences or feelings (Worthington, 2005). In contrast, people who enjoying thinking and analyzing topics tend to use a content-centered listening style (Worthington, 2008).

Listening Style

The way a person tends to listen in any situation.

FIGURE 8.3 Styles of listening

PAUSE & REFLECT

How does your preferred listening style relate to your own personality or your approach to interpersonal communication?

Listening styles have also been linked to biological sex. One research study showed that women are more likely to report a people-centered listening style, whereas men are more likely to have a content-centered listening style (Sargent & Weaver, 2003). This sex difference also showed up in people's descriptions of their peers' listening styles. Specifically, both men and women perceived women as people-centered listeners and men as content-centered listeners. Although it is not clear from this study how men and women actually listen in particular conversations, it does show that people have different beliefs about how men and women typically listen.

Across the different interpersonal communication situations you encounter, you'll find yourself engaging in different types of listening, and you may also have a particular approach to listening that you prefer to use. Different types and styles of listening follow the same general process, but they differ in how each step of listening is performed. If you are engaging in evaluative listening, you might attend more to inconsistencies in a message, whereas empathic listening would focus you on the person's feelings and emotions. Appreciative listening might lead you to retain the warm feelings evoked by an interaction, but comprehensive listening emphasizes recall for specific instructions or detailed pieces of information. And you might show that you appreciate your uncle's funny story by laughing, but empathic listening demands a response that is appropriate, sensitive, and comforting. Whether driven by the situation or your own preferred listening style, different ways of listening involve attending to different parts of a message, seeking different kinds of understanding and retention, using different standards for evaluating, and having different goals for responding.

Barriers to Effective Listening

Although listening is an important part of interpersonal communication, people tend not to be very good at it. In fact, one study concluded that people are able to recall only about 10% of what was said during a conversation they had just five minutes earlier (Stafford & Daly, 1984). People also retain less and less of the information from a conversation as time passes (Stafford, Burggraf, & Sharkey, 1987). If we consider the many barriers to effective listening, perhaps we shouldn't be surprised that people tend to be poor listeners.

Noise. One obstacle you confront when listening to a communication partner is noise in the environment around you. Have you ever tried to have a conversation with someone in a crowded restaurant? Have you ever struggled to hear a professor's lecture over a loud air conditioner or the whispers of other students sitting near you? Perhaps static on the phone line made it difficult to make out what the person on the other end of the line was saying. Chances are good that loud chatter, rumbling undercurrents, and ambient noises in your environment make it difficult to concentrate on the messages that are sent your way.

Features of the message. Features of the message being communicated can also serve as obstacles to effective listening. Denise remembers a student who described his frustration after talking to a salesperson about buying a car. One factor that made listening such a challenge for him in that interaction was the complexity of the message. He didn't have the same expertise that the salesperson did about how a car worked or about how to take out a loan. Consequently, he was confused by some of the words the salesperson used, and he had difficulty understanding parts of the conversation. Another feature of this message that was an obstacle to listening was that the message was overloaded: There was so much information, from learning about mechanical and aesthetic aspects of the vehicle to considering how to get the best interest rate on a loan, that the listener could not take everything in, and effective listening was compromised.

Thoughts and feelings. Barriers to listening also come from thoughts or feelings within a listener. In particular:

- Effective listening is more difficult if you are preoccupied. When your mind is filled with your own thoughts, ideas, or concerns, you can't listen to someone else's messages.
- If you get wrapped up in the anger, sadness, frustration, or joy that a message evokes, you may tune out important details in the rest of the conversation.
- Listening is compromised when you prejudge a message. If you believe that you already know what the other person is going to say and how you are going to respond to it, you may not feel a need to listen carefully.

When you are distracted, emotionally reactive, or judgmental, your internal thoughts and feelings drown out the information your communication partner presents.

PAUSE & REFLECT

Reflect on a recent conversation that you had. Besides the conversation itself, what other kinds of things did you think about? How did these other thoughts affect your conversation?

Lack of effort. One prominent obstacle to listening is a simple lack of effort. When people don't pay attention, don't ask questions, or don't try to empathize during a conversation, they don't listen well. A related problem occurs when you don't adapt your listening style to the situation at hand and, as a result, you listen in a way that misses the point. Consider what might happen if you used a people-centered listening style during a meeting with an academic advisor – you might come away from the conversation with an appreciation for the advisor's warmth and kindness, but will you get all the details you need about graduation requirements? And what if you use a time-centered listening style when your friend needs to talk about a bad break-up? Your

TABLE 8.3 Forms of nonlistening

Form	Definition
Pseudolistening	Pretending to listen when you're not
Monopolizing	Focusing communication on yourself instead of listening
Selective listening	Focusing only on specific parts of the message that are relevant to you
Defensive listening	Perceiving personal attacks in messages that are not criticism
Ambushing	Listening to gain information that will allow you to attack the speaker
Literal listening	Listening only for content and ignoring cues about the relationship

impatience may end up leaving your friend feeling even worse. When you don't bother to listen well or adapt your ways of listening to the specific situation, you can miss important parts of a message and have less-than-positive listening outcomes.

Nonlistening. Nonlistening is a complete breakdown of the listening process, because it involves enacting behaviors that make it look like you are listening when you really are not. Table 8.3 describes some common forms of nonlistening. In its simplest form, nonlistening can involve pretending to listen, perhaps by maintaining eye contact and nodding – even though your mind is on something else entirely. Another form of nonlistening occurs when you spend a conversation talking only about yourself. Nonlistening also includes attending to only a part of a message, taking messages too personally, focusing on finding flaws in the messages, or interpreting messages too literally. When you engage in any of these activities, you are not processing the messages that your interaction partner is sending.

Surprisingly, you are most likely to engage in nonlistening when you are communicating with someone you know especially well. With a stranger, you are on the lookout for information that will help you learn about your partner, and you may work extra hard to decipher messages and figure out how to respond appropriately. In contrast, if your communication partner is a family member or someone you've known a long time, you might believe you already know what he or she has to say. As a result, you might tune out, stop listening, and start thinking ahead to your response. When you do this, you are engaging in nonlistening. Married partners are especially vulnerable to problems of nonlistening. Studies show that spouses don't spend much time thinking about their partner's perspective, and that they have an especially hard time listening during conflicts (Sillars, Roberts, Leonard, & Dun, 2000). Also, people often believe that their spouse agrees with them far more often than they actually do (Sillars, Folwell, Hill, Maki, Hurst, & Casano, 1994). In other words, spouses don't always listen to each other very well, and they often don't realize that their conclusions are flawed.

Nonlistening
Enacting behaviors that make it look like you are listening, although you are not really doing so.

PAUSE & REFLECT

Do you have a relationship so close that you can predict what your partner will say and perhaps even finish her or his sentences? If so, does relying on your expectations in this way ever lead to miscommunication between you?

Putting Theory into Practice: Using Appropriate Listening Strategies

Although listening is a complex and sometimes challenging process, there are ways that you can improve your listening skills and become a more effective communicator.

Complete the listening process. Listening isn't a single event – it is a process that is completed only if you work through all of the steps. Complete the Communication in Action 8.1 exercise to find out which stages of the listening process you perform well, and which you might need to improve.

COMMUNICATION IN ACTION 8.1

Uncovering Listening Strengths and Weaknesses

Complete the form on the **companion website** to help you think about how well you listen during your interpersonal interactions.

Tailor your way of listening to the situation. Although people tend to have particular styles of listening, different situations call for different types of listening. You can be a more effective listener if you look for cues that will help you to adjust your listening style. As you talk to a communication partner, think about your goal in the conversation. In addition, try to figure out your partner's goal. If you have an idea about your own and the other person's goals for the situation, you can enact the type of listening appropriate to the situation. Try the Communication in Action 8.2 exercise to build these skills.

Prepare yourself to listen. You can enhance your communication experiences by overcoming obstacles to listening. To do so, eliminate as many distractions as possible so you can focus your attention on the listening process. When preparing yourself to be an effective listener, strive for the following goals:

■ *Eliminate any physical impediments to listening*. Turn off the television, turn down the radio, or shut down the computer – eliminate anything that might distract you as you listen.

COMMUNICATION IN ACTION 8.2

Identifying Listening Goals

Complete the form on the **companion website** by identifying the most suitable listening style for each situation and the behaviors that would be most effective in helping you accomplish the listening goals of the interaction. If you can remember this exercise the next time you are faced with a listening goal, you will be better equipped to adapt your listening style to the situation.

- *Prepare yourself mentally to listen.* Set aside your own stressors and thoughts so that you won't be preoccupied with your own issues during conversation.
- *Transition completely from speaker to listener.* Don't spend your time listening trying to think of what you will say next. When you're a speaker you can speak, when you're a listener you should listen.
- *Hear your partner out completely before you react.* It's easy to get defensive or reactive if your partner says something that offends you or hurts your feelings, but if you react immediately you might not hear everything that your partner has to say.
- *Don't jump to conclusions.* It can be hard not to jump to conclusions when you know a person very well. Guard against nonlistening by focusing on what's new or unique about your partner's message and continue to test your assumptions against reality.

Overcoming barriers to effective listening is an ongoing process, and you'll never be completely successful. Nonetheless, making an active effort to prepare yourself to listen can help you minimize the obstacles you encounter when you communicate with another person.

ACTIVE LISTENING

Do you know people who are particularly good listeners? What do they do during an interaction to let you know that they are paying close attention? Do you know people who are especially poor listeners? Why do these people consistently fail to lend an ear? You have probably had enough interpersonal communication experiences to know that certain people are better listeners than others. For instance, individuals who are detail-oriented tend to be skilled at remembering information that was shared during interaction (Neuliep & Hazelton, 1987). Likewise, people who have good interpersonal skills recall conversations more accurately than people who are anxious during interpersonal interactions (Miller, deWinstanley, & Carey, 1996). Everyone, however, can improve their listening outcomes by being more active listeners (Cegala, 1984). **Active listening** involves engaging in the exchange of ideas and taking steps to better understand your partner. In this section, we examine two techniques you can use to become a more active listener: asking questions and being empathic. We also consider the ways in which active listening can distort what you take away from a conversation.

Active Listening
Engaging in the exchange of ideas and taking steps to better understand you partner.

Asking Questions

One way to be an active listener is to ask questions. Asking questions can help to clarify information that you don't understand. Appropriate and well-timed questions also show your interaction partner that you're paying attention. Notice the use of questions in the Real Words transcript, which was drawn from a study of married couples (Priem, Soloman, & Steuber, 2009). Kevin asks a lot of questions, which encourage Sara to expand on her thoughts. His questions are challenging at times – such as when he asks, "Did that ever stop you before?" – but the overall effect is to bring more information into the conversation. By the end, they realize that Sara doesn't just want a new hobby, she wants to find something that she and Kevin can enjoy together, and when Kevin understands that goal, he agrees to work on it with her. In this section, we consider some of the ways that asking questions can improve your listening outcomes.

REAL WORDS

SARA: I wanna do something else beside work and exercise . . . I need something else to do.
KEVIN: Like what?
SARA: I don't know. You don't like me being involved in theatre but I'd love to go down and try out.
KEVIN: Well, why didn't you?
SARA: Because you don't like that.
KEVIN: Did that stop you before?
SARA: No, but you don't like it. Do you?
KEVIN: I've never stopped you. If that's something you wanted to do, then why didn't you do it?
SARA: I guess I gotta feel my way around, figure out what's going on. But that'd be fun.
KEVIN: Well, what else is stopping you?
SARA: Would you like to work in theatre? You wouldn't like it. You wouldn't do it. See, I'd like to do something you'd like to do, too. But . . . like with a private church that has a choir.
KEVIN: Well, let's try to work on that.

Educational settings are one context where asking questions can lead to better listening and understanding. Children who ask questions when messages are ambiguous tend to understand information more accurately and learn more effectively than children who simply rely on the existing information about a message (Patterson, Massad, & Cosgrove, 1978). Similarly, students who learn to ask themselves questions during a lecture – such as "I wonder how that relates to what we discussed yesterday?" – show improved understanding and retention of information (King, 1991). These studies indicate that asking questions can improve listening and learning.

PAUSE & REFLECT

Do you tend to ask questions in your classes or when talking to people? Why or why not?

The right kind of questions can also improve communication for both partners in an interaction. For example, a physician's communication behavior affects how patients communicate during an appointment. One study investigated the types of questions physicians use at the end of an appointment and revealed two different strategies that produce very different results (Robinson, 2001). One strategy is the "topic-closing sequence" in which the physician seeks confirmation that the patient will comply with instructions by saying "Okay?" or "All right?" These questions steer the patient toward agreeing, rather than inviting further discussion. Another strategy is the "final concerns sequence" in which the doctor solicits any final questions or problems from the patient. Robinson found that when physicians said "Anything else?" to elicit final concerns, patients felt obligated to say no. When physicians asked "What other concerns do you have?" the patients felt more comfortable raising additional issues. This study shows that the way doctors phrase their final questions influences whether patients will raise additional concerns. Learn more about communication between physicians and patients by reading Inside Communication Research.

INSIDE COMMUNICATION RESEARCH

Physician and Patient Listening

When patients visit their physicians, they may wish to discuss many different conditions or symptoms, including medical problems, requests for information, and requests for prescriptions or referrals. Whether or not they get the opportunity to discuss all of these issues depends a great deal on the types of questions the physician uses to start the visit, which can ultimately affect the patient's health and his or her satisfaction with the physician. John Heritage and Jeffrey Robinson (2006), who study interactions between physicians and patients, conducted a study to explore the types of questions physicians use during visits and the effect they have on patient satisfaction.

Robinson and Heritage suggested that there are two types of questions that physicians might use to start a visit with a patient. The first type of question is an open-ended general inquiry, such as "What can I do for you today?" or "Tell me what's going on." Open-ended questions make the patient the authority on his or her own health condition and tend to encourage longer descriptions that include more distinct symptoms. The second type of question is a closed-ended request for confirmation, such as "I understand you're having some leg problems?" or "Sore throat, huh?" Confirmation questions reveal that the physician has prior knowledge of the patient's condition and they tend to encourage simple yes or no answers.

In the study, the researchers video-taped visits that 28 physicians had with 142 patients and used conversation analysis to evaluate the kinds of questions that the doctors asked to start the visit. The conversation analysis method involves close scrutiny of naturally occurring conversation to identify and describe the norms and rules of interpersonal interaction. Later, they surveyed the patients about their satisfaction with the visit. Patients reported that physicians who used open-ended questions were better listeners and fostered more positive relational communication. This was especially true for patients who had a long-term relationship with their doctor. Physicians who used confirmation questions were rated as poor listeners by the patients, who perceived that the physicians did not engage in positive relational communication.

This study shows that the way doctors phrase their initial inquiries into a patient's condition influences how the patient evaluates the physician. Specifically, the results show that physicians are perceived as better listeners when they ask questions that encourage patients to talk more. More generally, Robinson and Heritage's study highlights how questioning is an important part of listening, because questions shape the kind of information you might get from a communication partner.

THINK ABOUT IT

1. What practical advice can you offer to physicians and patients about how to improve information exchange and listening during medical appointments?
2. How do these patterns of communication compare to interactions you have had in medical settings? What other kinds of interactions might these findings be relevant to?

Expressing Empathy

Empathy

The ability to vicariously experience another person's situation or feelings.

Another way to be a more active listener is to convey an attitude of empathy to your communication partner. **Empathy**, which is the ability to understand and vicariously experience another person's situation or feelings, can dramatically change your reaction to another person. For example, people listened to a woman in distress on a radio broadcast and were asked either to remain objective, to imagine how the woman must feel, or to imagine how they would feel in that situation (Batson, Early, & Salvarani, 1997). When listeners remained objective, they experienced relatively little empathy.

Selective Hearing For Men

FIGURE 8.4 Men and listening

Source: www.CartoonStock.com.

FIGURE 8.5 A nurse listening to people in a hospital waiting room

Source: iStockPhoto.

They were more motivated to help when they imagined how the woman felt, and they actually felt distressed themselves when they imagined how they would feel in the woman's situation. Being empathic can increase your involvement in a conversation and help you engage in active listening.

Of course, your efforts to experience a communication partner's thoughts and feelings are not always successful. **Empathic accuracy** refers to the ability to accurately infer the content of another person's thoughts and feelings. Empathic accuracy depends, to an extent, on how actively you listen. For example, attending to verbal information, and to a lesser extent to nonverbal cues, increases empathic accuracy during interpersonal interactions (Hall & Schmid Mast, 2007). Women may have greater empathic accuracy than men, in part because women tend to be more motivated to experience empathy than men (Graham & Ickes, 1997; Ickes, Gesn, & Graham, 2000). When you pay attention to verbal and nonverbal cues and you try to empathize, you can understand a communication partner's thoughts and feelings more accurately.

Empathic Accuracy
An ability to accurately infer the content of another person's thoughts and feelings.

Although empathic accuracy can improve your listening outcomes, it does not always improve your relationships – that depends on what a conversation is about. For example, in conversations about a nonthreatening relationship issue, empathic accuracy leads spouses to feel closer to each other after the interaction. When the topic was threatening to the relationship, however, empathic accuracy leads spouses to feel less close (Simpson, Orina, & Ickes, 2003). So the relationship benefits of being an empathic and active listener might be limited to conversations that aren't about touchy topics.

Transcendence

We often think about listening as something one person does when another person has the speaking floor. In fact, listening is a much more interactive process, wherein communication partners give their attention to each other to start the listening process described previously. Communication scholars John Greene and Lauren Herbers (2011) suggest that sometimes people engage in "listening in the extreme." In other words, communicators become completely engrossed in an interaction.

SCHOLAR SPOTLIGHT

Visit the Communication Café on the **companion website** to view a conversation with John Greene, an expert on the production of interpersonal message who has written about the experience of transcendence in interpersonal communication.

Transcendance
A state of listening characterized by intense, mutual engagement in an interaction.

Greene and Herbers (2011) defined **transcendence** as a state of listening characterized by intense engagement in an interaction. In particular, four factors are considered part of transcendence:

- Transcendence is characterized by a strong sense of mutuality, in that both partners perceive the other to be fully engaged in the interaction.
- This mutuality fosters a sense of connection or shared responsibility for the meanings created within the interaction.
- The level of mutual engagement and connection promotes creativity and insight, as the ideas that any one individual might have are embellished and emboldened by the connection with another person.
- Together the partners in an interaction discover new ways of thinking and being.

Biased Listening

Active listening has benefits, but there are some pitfalls to be aware of. Namely, we use active listening in some types of situations more than others, and that can lead to biases. Active listening can also lead you to distort messages from other people. You'll learn about some of the biases that accompany active listening in this section.

People tend to engage in active listening in some situations more than others. Consider the following research findings (Samp & Humphreys, 2007):

- People recall information more accurately when they interact with a friend than with a stranger.
- People remember more about disagreements than conversations where both partners agreed.
- When partners disagree, they recall negative information more accurately than positive information, especially in conversations with friends.

What do these findings mean? Active listening may be more likely or easier when you encounter disagreeable messages in close relationships. If you don't offset this trend with equal attention to positive messages, your active listening might lead you to think more negatively than you should about relationships you value.

> ### PAUSE & REFLECT
>
> Think back to the last time that you and a partner disagreed about what was said during a conversation. To what extent do you think your different memories were due to nonlistening versus active, but biased, listening?

Efforts to listen actively can also distort information. What might you do if someone you cared about was sending you messages that you didn't want to hear? Sometimes people go to extra effort to interpret threatening information in benign or nonthreatening ways. For example, if you had to imagine how your romantic partner might feel about another highly attractive individual, what would you think? Studies suggest that people who are extremely close and people who are insecure about their relationship are the least accurate in predicting how their partner would feel about that highly attractive alternative (Simpson, Ickes, & Blackstone, 1995). Specifically, they underestimated how much their partner would be attracted to the person to minimize the threat. Similarly, if your romantic partner starts hinting that they want to break up or they don't see a future, you might look for alternative ways to interpret their messages that fit with your own goals and expectations for the relationship.

In general, active listening helps you understand a communication partner. Asking questions and being empathic allow you to get more information from a partner than you might if you listened more passively. Sometimes, though, being an active listener serves as a defense mechanism. If a friend is being disagreeable, you might be especially attentive. On the other hand, people sometimes take steps to avoid messages that they'd rather not hear.

Putting Theory into Practice: Attending to Detail

In this section of the chapter, you learned about some extra effort you might make to be a more active listener, as well as how active listening sometimes goes too far. By embracing effective strategies for active listening and avoiding the pitfalls, you can get the most out of your interpersonal interactions.

Use questions strategically. You can enjoy many benefits as a listener when you ask questions. At the same time, you need to be strategic and judicious in your questioning strategy. How, then, do you find a balance between actively asking questions and overdoing it? Here are some strategies you can put to work in your own interactions.

- *Follow-up on ambiguities.* Ask questions that focus on specific phrases that are unclear to you, such as "What did you mean when you said 'you're interested' in this project?" or "Does 'later this week' mean Wednesday, Thursday, or Friday?" When you limit your questions to parts of the message that are unclear to you, you let your partner stay on track while you address any sources of misunderstanding.
- *Question yourself.* If interrupting a communication partner with your questions would be inappropriate – perhaps because of status differences or the emotional tone of the topic – you can still keep track of where you need more information. Ask yourself questions while you listen, such as "I wonder why he feels that way?" or "Is this task a priority for my work team?" Keeping track of these questions can pinpoint important issues so that you can follow up on them at a more appropriate time.
- *Ask open-ended questions.* If you want to get more information out of a communication partner, avoid questions that allow for a yes or no answer. Instead, use open-ended questions that let your partner take control of the conversation, leave a lot of room for answers, and allow for longer and more informative replies. For example, rather than, "Is this assignment due this week?" you might ask, "What's

the timeline for this project?" Or, rather than "Have you made up your mind?" you could ask "What's the process for your decision making?" Open-ended questions can yield more complete information.

■ *Avoid conversation closers.* Some questions suggest to communication partners that you're ready to be done with a conversation, so avoid these when your real goal is active listening. "Is that all?" "Anything else?" and "Are we done here?" all suggest an eagerness to wrap up. In contrast, "Can you tell me more about this?" "What else can you tell me?" and "What other information should I have?" leave the door open to lengthier replies.

Empathize within limits. Connecting with another person's emotions can be a powerful way to appreciate that person's message. At the same time, you don't want to become overly emotional as you listen to a partner. If you do, your own emotions might drown out how your communication partner is feeling, making it harder for you to communicate effectively. The Communication in Action 8.3 exercise can help you focus on other people's emotions, rather than your own.

COMMUNICATION IN ACTION 8.3

Developing Empathic Accuracy

Pair up with another student to hone your empathy skills. To begin, identify a few topics that the two of you will discuss – perhaps what you are doing after graduation, how you feel about your hometown, or what you did on the last break from classes. Then, each of you should privately identify feelings about those topics that you will communicate – your fear or excitement about the future, your longing or distaste for home, your happiness or disappointment with your last vacation. Next, discuss those topics while each of you tries to figure out the other person's feelings. When you are done, check how close your perceptions were to the feelings your partner had during your conversation. If you take advantage of opportunities to practice and assess your ability to empathize, you can heighten your sensitivity to other people's feelings.

LISTENING FOR RELATIONAL MEANINGS

In Chapter 1, you were introduced to the idea that messages carry both content and relational meanings. In other words, messages provide information based on what the words and nonverbal cues mean, and they also provide information about the relationship between you and your communication partner. Understanding listening in the context of interpersonal communication includes considering the ways in which people make sense of the relational meanings that are exchanged during an interaction (Edwards, 2011). In this section of the chapter, we consider how people listen for the relational meanings present in a message.

Relational Messages

As defined in Chapter 1, relational messages are verbal and nonverbal expressions that indicate how two people feel about each other or their relationship. Sometimes relational meanings are clear from the content of an utterance, such as when a partner says "I love you" or "I never want to see you again!" Even when relational messages are not so clear, listening can help you figure out how much a communication partner likes you, who has more power in your relationship, whether you can trust each other, and many other important things. When you listen for relational messages, you can learn a lot about the relationship you actually have, as well as about the type of relationship that your partner wants.

Table 8.4 identifies eight distinct relationship topics that can be more or less present in any conversation (Burgoon & Hale, 1987). In fact, research shows that different relational messages are present to greater or lesser degrees in different kinds of conversations (Hale, Lundy, & Mongeau, 1989). As you might expect, relational messages that

TABLE 8.4 Relational message topics

Topic	Examples of verbal messages
Dominance vs. Submission	"Just do what I tell you to do and don't ask any questions."
	"Whatever you want for dinner is fine with me."
Composure	"You're so easy to talk to – I feel so comfortable around you."
	"Let's just hang out; we can relax."
Similarity & Depth	"I played rugby in college too. We should form a team together."
	"We seem to have a lot in common! What other kinds of things do you like to do for fun?"
Formality vs. Informality	"Excuse me, sir? Could I please ask you a question?"
	"Hey, what's up?"
Equality	"It would be great to work together on that project."
	"Let's split the workload – we both know what we're doing."
Closeness & Affection	"You have the most beautiful blue eyes!"
	"I know you've had a long day, so I'll give you a back rub after I finish making you dinner."
Task vs. Social Orientation	"I'd really rather just focus on studying for our exam."
	"This job can wait – tell me about your weekend."
Receptivity & Trust	"I've never told anyone this before, but I know you won't tell anybody so I'm willing to share it with you."
	"I'm here for you if you need me."

Relational Framing
Using either affiliation or dominance as a framework to interpret messages about a relationship.

express closeness and affection, similarity and depth, receptivity and trust, composure, and equality are all common in relationships that people perceived as intimate. In addition, people communicate the least amount of dominance when talking to their best friend, and the greatest amount of dominance in conversations with a co-worker. Relational messages also shape the consequences of hurtful interactions. In particular, dating partners perceive interactions that involve criticism as less hurtful if partners communicate affiliation and informality at the same time (Priem, McLaren, & Solomon, 2010). The How Do You Rate 8.2 exercise can help you to evaluate the relational messages that occur in your own interpersonal interactions.

> ## PAUSE & REFLECT
>
> How might each of these dimensions of relational communication be expressed through nonverbal behavior rather than verbal expressions? How might they be expressed in online communication?

Framing Relational Messages

Paying attention to all of the different relational messages can be difficult, in part because there are so many of them. One way that people keep track of them all is through specific ways of listening (Dillard, Solomon, & Samp, 1996). Listening for relational messages begins with identifying whether the interaction is generally about how much the partners like each other or how much power each of them has. This process is called **relational framing**, because a listener uses either liking *or* power as a framework for making sense of a conversation. If a conversation is about liking, messages are seen as communicating how close, friendly, or positively partners feel toward each other. If a conversation is about power, messages are interpreted as signs of dominance, expressions of status, or submission to a partner's control.

Although you might consciously choose how to frame a conversation, this step in the process often happens automatically. Which frame you use depends on several factors (see Figure 8.6). Most specifically, the content of utterances themselves can clarify whether interactions are about power ("If you don't follow my rules, I'll fire you") or liking ("I'm so glad that I have a friend like you at work"). At a higher level of abstraction, the type of interaction can focus attention on issues of power (e.g., a performance review) or affiliation (e.g., a birthday greeting). If partners have a history of interactions that focus on either power or liking, that pattern would direct attention within a particular exchange. Likewise, some people have a general tendency to focus on status rather than friendship. At the most general level, social and cultural norms direct attention to power or liking cues within an interaction (Solomon & McLaren, 2008).

The Cultural or Social Context:
The Relational Messages Expected to Occur in the Particular Situation

The Person's History:
Individual Tendencies to Look for Particular Messages

The Relationship History:
The Relational Messages Observed in the Past

Goals of the Social Episode:
What the Interaction is About

Utterances:
The Meaning of Words Spoken

FIGURE 8.6 Factors that affect relational framing

PAUSE & REFLECT

What cues tell you whether a conversation is about how much you and a partner like each other, rather than how much power or status you each have?

Not surprisingly, the frame you use to listen for relational messages shapes how you interpret cues in the conversation. When people view an interaction in terms of friendship, they interpret verbal and nonverbal cues as signs of liking or disliking. When people view an interaction in terms of power, they interpret messages as signs of dominance or submission (Dillard, Solomon, & Palmer, 1999). For example, think about how your perceptions of an interaction with a potential romantic partner might differ from your perceptions of an interaction with a condescending supervisor at work. In these types of interactions, your crush and your boss might enact similar behaviors that are perceived very differently based on the way you frame the interaction. In either interaction your partner might have leaned toward you, maintained steady eye contact, and touched you. If you were interacting with a potential romantic partner, these behaviors were probably perceived as signs that your partner liked you. In the interaction with your supervisor, you would probably interpret these behaviors as signs that your partner was trying to exert dominance and control. In other words, your interpretation of a partner's involvement in an interaction depends on the frame you use to make sense of those cues.

Putting Theory into Practice: Making Sense of Relational Messages

Your communication partners don't often tell you directly how they feel about you or what kind of relationship you have with them. Instead, you figure out your relationships with other people by listening for relational messages. Although this can be challenging, you can take steps to draw more correct inferences about relationships from your interpersonal interactions.

Read between the lines. One of the challenges you face when making inferences about your relationships is that you often have limited or indirect information. Your romantic interest might not come right out and tell you that he or she is attracted to you. Your professor may not explicitly clarify whether you should use her formal title or her first name. The Communication in Action 8.4 exercise highlights clues you can use to decipher relational messages.

COMMUNICATION IN ACTION 8.4

Interpreting Relational Meaning

Complete the form on the **companion website** as you think about a recent conversation where the relational meaning was unclear. Doing so may help you decipher interpersonal encounters more effectively in the future.

Don't read too much into messages. Understanding relational messages can help you be a more effective communicator, but avoid the pitfalls that come from obsessing over hidden meanings. Rather than drawing conclusions that aren't supported, base your interpretations of relational messages on the cues you have. If you can't reach firm conclusions, that's okay – it's better than reaching faulty ones.

This lesson was brought home for Miranda, a character on *Sex and the City*, when she had to come to terms with a dating partner who didn't seem to like her. As Miranda's female friends generated several elaborate explanations for her date's behavior, a male character, Berger, bluntly told her, "He's just not that into you." Although Miranda was shocked by Berger's honesty, she was also empowered by the simplicity of this insight. When she tried to share this newfound wisdom with other women, Miranda found that not everyone was receptive. For her, however, accepting relational messages at face value was far better than searching for messages that aren't there. Although it can be difficult to accept the truth, making convoluted inferences only complicates your interactions and relationships with other people.

SUMMARY

Listening is a crucial part of interpersonal communication. Listening is an active process of taking in messages from a communication partner – it involves attending to messages, interpreting them, retaining meanings, evaluating information, and crafting a response. People use different types of listening, depending on whether a situation requires them to discriminate details in a message, appreciate the listening experience, comprehend information, evaluate facts or argument, or express empathy with a partner's feelings. People may also have a general preference for action-centered, content-centered, time-centered, or people-centered listening. Thus, listening is an active process that can unfold in a variety of ways within a particular conversation.

Given how involved listening can be, we shouldn't be surprised that there are many barriers to effective listening. Those obstacles include noise in the environment around you, message complexity and information overload, and your own state of mind. When your own mind is overactive – because you're preoccupied with other thoughts, wrapped up in your emotional reaction to an interaction, or prejudging a partner's messages – you can have trouble focusing on the information being communicated to you. Your state of mind can also interfere with listening when you don't put out the effort to listen or to adapt your listening style to the specific interaction. Nonlistening is an especially problematic form of communication, because you don't receive and process messages sent your way, but you give off signals that can make your partner think you are listening.

Active listening involves performing actions that improve listening outcomes. When you ask questions of a communication partner, you can convey your interest in the conversation, address points of confusion, and encourage your partner to provide more information. In educational and medical settings, an ability to ask the right kinds of questions can be the difference between learning and not learning or between getting a diagnosis right or wrong. Trying to empathize with a communication partner's feelings can also help you to understand where he or she is coming from during a conversation. When you try hard to listen for another person's feelings, the meanings you take away from an interaction can be more accurate and complete, and you might even experience a state of "transcendence." Although being an active listener can help you communicate more effectively, keep in mind that the extra effort needed can lead to biased or distorted interpretations of a conversation.

In addition to the content information we listen for when we engage in interpersonal communication, we gain insights into our relationship with an interaction partner. People attend to a variety of relational messages, including messages conveying dominance versus submission, composure, similarity and depth, formality versus informality, equality, closeness and affection, task versus social orientation, and receptivity and trust. Moreover, people organize all these relational messages by framing their interactions in terms of liking and friendship or dominance and power. These general frameworks help people make sense of the specific relational messages that they receive during a conversation.

Interpersonal communication fails without effective listening. Being a conscientious listener can help you and your interaction partner get more out of a conversation. Attentive listening also communicates sincerity, interest, and competence to a partner. When you ask questions strategically and use empathy appropriately, you enrich and expand your understanding of messages. And when you are attentive to relational messages, you gain insight into how interpersonal communication can shape your current and future relationship with an interaction partner.

ACTIVITIES FOR EXPLORING COMMUNICATION ETHICS

What Would You/Should You Do?

Your friend comes to you to complain about an interaction she recently had with her boyfriend, who informed her that he can no longer be her date at her cousin's wedding due to obligations at work. It's clear from her description of the situation that she believes her partner deliberately scheduled work for that weekend to avoid being with her and that he doesn't feel badly about letting her down. You already spoke to your friend's boyfriend earlier in the day, at which time he expressed disappointment over not being able to attend the wedding but sensed that his girlfriend understood and wasn't upset by the situation. Based on what you've heard from both individuals, you have concluded that they are misunderstanding how one another feels because they aren't listening effectively to what their partner is saying. What would you or should you do in this situation to help your friends better understand one another?

Something to Think About

When Hillary Clinton campaigned to become a New York Senator, she went on a "listening tour" of communities in upstate New York. Ostensibly, the goal of her visits was to listen to people so she could understand their concerns. Of course, Clinton was also campaigning for votes, trying to overcome the fact that she had never been a resident of the state, and hoping to improve her political reputation. Can listening be authentic and sincere when the person doing the listening is also trying to advance his or her personal goals?

Analyze Communication Ethics Yourself

Visit any discussion board devoted to a social issue; for example, you might visit a website for breast cancer survivors, political conservatives, people hoping to adopt a child, global warming, or anything of that sort. At that site, follow one of the discussion board strings to see how contributors to that discussion respond to each other. Look closely at follow-up messages, and evaluate whether each responder is respecting the ideas presented earlier. Based on your analysis, what do you think are the ethical issues that apply when people "listen" and respond to each other in online venues?

KEY WORDS

active listening	empathy	paraphrasing
active-empathic listening	evaluating	relational framing
appreciative listening	evaluative listening	remembering
attending	hearing	responding
comprehensive listening	listening	transcendence
discriminatory listening	listening style	understanding
empathic accuracy	nonlistening	

PART 3 INTERPERSONAL RELATING

Visit the Communication Café on the **companion website** to hear Denise and Jen talk about the topics addressed in Part 3 of this book.

Perhaps one of the most powerful outcomes we produce through interpersonal communication are the creation, negotiation, maintenance, and dissolution of interpersonal relationships. As you learned in Chapter 8, all of our interpersonal communication conveys information about our relationship with an interaction partner. In this unit, we focus on the personal relationships that emerge from repeated engagement in interpersonal communication over time. Your friendships, romantic relationships, and family relationships are associations that may have a lasting influence on your identity and your well-being. We'll explore how interpersonal communication is the foundation for those relationships.

All of the relationships you have, with the exception of some family bonds, began as an interaction between strangers. Interpersonal communication is a reflection of the changes that occur as people become familiar with each other and form sometimes lasting ties. Interpersonal communication is also a tool we use to move our relationships to more or less close levels of engagement. Chapter 9 traces the path of developing and dissolving relationships, and sheds light on the role of interpersonal communication within these associations.

Humans are also capable of forming intimate bonds, whether between friends or romantic partners. Intimacy is a complex phenomenon, capturing feelings of excitement that can characterize a new love, companionship between long-term friends, and many things in between. Although often very rewarding, intimate relationships can also be fraught with tension. Chapter 10 delves into the intricacies of intimate relationships and showcases interpersonal communication at the heart of these bonds.

Chapter 11 turns attention to family relationships. Families take many forms in contemporary society, and interpersonal communication is essential to all of them. Families can also be a challenging context for interpersonal communication as members navigate multiple family roles and numerous family rules. Adding to this complexity is the way that families change as their members change. In this chapter, then, you'll learn about how interpersonal communication contributes to family life across the lifespan.

x
CHAPTER 9

DEVELOPING AND ENDING RELATIONSHIPS

236

CHAPTER 10

INTIMACY AND INTERPERSONAL COMMUNICATION

264

CHAPTER 11

COMMUNICATION IN FAMILIES

292

LEARNING OBJECTIVES

After reading this chapter, you should be able to:

1. Understand how people cope with uncertainty in initial interactions.
2. Understand how people promote positive outcomes in new relationships.
3. Describe four issues that underlie the escalation of relationships.
4. Describe four issues that underlie the dissolution of relationships.
5. Recognize the behaviors that constitute obsessive relational intrusion and stalking.
6. Strengthen your ability to develop or to end relationships gracefully.

PUTTING THEORY INTO PRACTICE

In this chapter, you will learn how to:

1. Make your self-disclosure appropriate and interesting.
2. Make the most of small talk.
3. Balance breadth and depth in your self-disclosure.
4. Talk about your uncertainty.
5. Give interdependence time and effort.
6. Weigh the pros and cons of decreasing intimacy.
7. Manage face threats when ending close relationships.
8. Clarify and respect relationship boundaries.

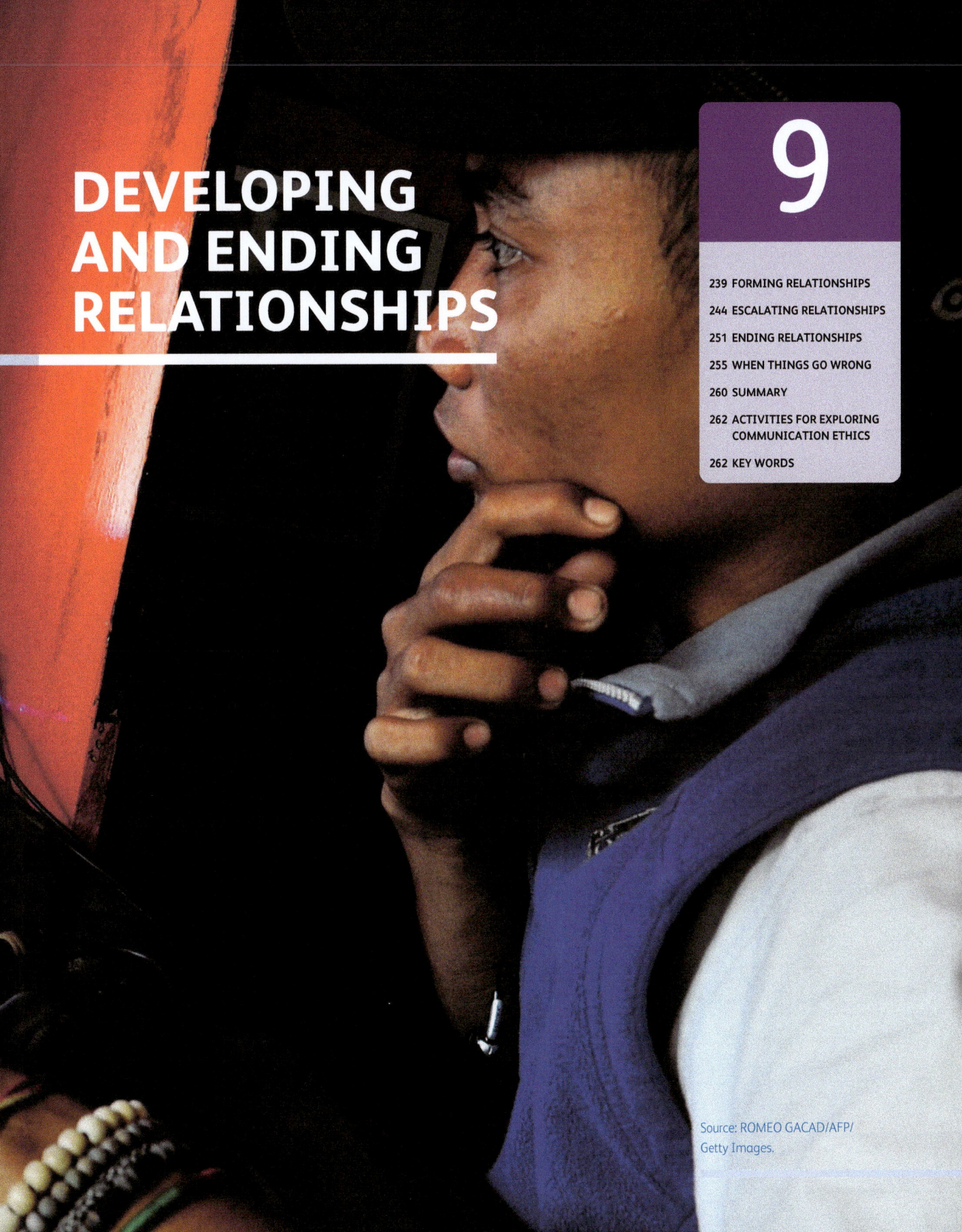

DEVELOPING AND ENDING RELATIONSHIPS

9

239 FORMING RELATIONSHIPS

244 ESCALATING RELATIONSHIPS

251 ENDING RELATIONSHIPS

255 WHEN THINGS GO WRONG

260 SUMMARY

262 ACTIVITIES FOR EXPLORING COMMUNICATION ETHICS

262 KEY WORDS

Source: ROMEO GACAD/AFP/ Getty Images.

"Friend request accepted!" If you have a Facebook account, you're probably pleased when you receive this message. The explosion of online communities like Facebook, LinkedIn, and Twitter has created numerous relationship opportunities for subscribers. These websites enable users to connect with old friends and network with new friends. In fact, relationships sometimes develop more quickly when people communicate online rather than face-to-face (Hian, Chuan, Trevor, & Detenber, 2004). Unfortunately, the relative ease and anonymity of these online relationships can sometimes make it difficult to maintain appropriate boundaries. Because individuals sometimes share private information about themselves in this context, like their email address, phone number, and relationship status, people can easily get information about an acquaintance that might not be readily shared in a face-to-face interaction. Many students admit to "Facebook stalking" when they want to find out information about a potential crush or track the relationship status of a previous romantic partner, and many students consider this to be a normal and even acceptable by-product of belonging to online social networks.

I nterpersonal communication plays a central role in the development, escalation, and dissolution of close relationships. If you have had experience with any of the social networking websites mentioned in the opening vignette, you know that in some cases beginning or ending a friendship or romantic relationship can be as simple as the click of a mouse. Although developing relationships offline might require a bit more effort, both contexts for relationship development involve decisions about revealing or concealing information about yourself and gathering information about others.

What happens in a relationship that moves people from acquaintances to intimate partners? When people are asked to identify important turning points in their friendships, they mention events like discovering shared interests, disclosing private information, spending time with mutual friends, taking a trip together, and living together (Johnson, Wittenberg, & Haigh, 2004; Johnson, Wittenberg, Villagran, Mazur, & Villagran, 2003). In romantic relationships, people point to the first big fight (Siegert & Stamp, 1994), saying "I love you" (Metts, 2004), meeting a partner's family and friends (Baxter & Bullis, 1986), and the first sexual experience (Theiss & Solomon, 2007) as markers of developing intimacy. As illustrated in Figure 9.1, some relationships move through these turning points quickly, others run into roadblocks along the way, and some take time to develop intimate bonds.

PAUSE & REFLECT

Consider a friendship or romantic relationship you've developed in the past few years. Can you identify specific events that changed your relationship?

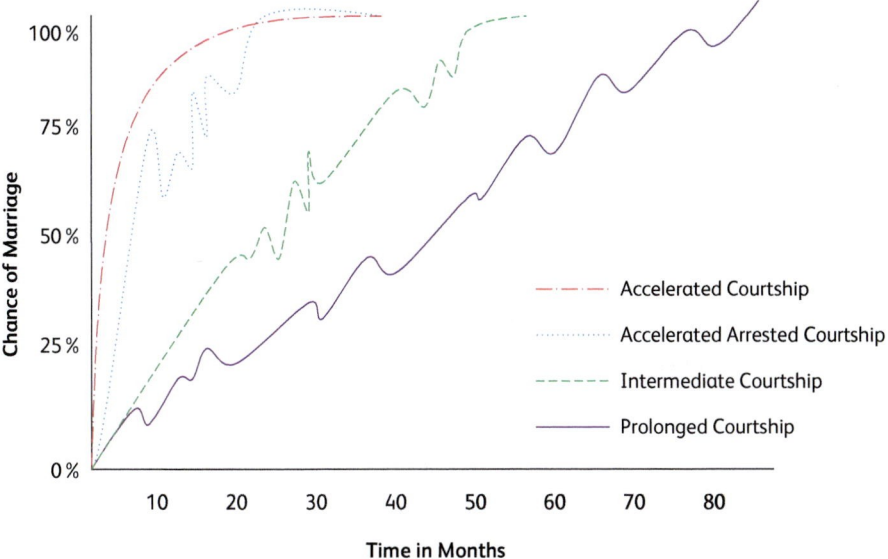

FIGURE 9.1 Four trajectories of courtship

Catherine Surra (1985) identified four pathways to commitment. Some people have an accelerated courtship in which they move quickly toward a committed relationship and never look back, while others start on a fast track to intimacy but encounter turbulence just before making that commitment. Some relationships have a slow, steady, prolonged courtship, whereas others move steadily but more quickly toward mutual commitment.

Another way of thinking about relationship development focuses on a series of stages that partners move through as relationships develop (Knapp, 1984). Movement through stages can be fast or slow, but all couples experience these phases as they develop or dissolve a relationship (see Figure 9.2). In fact, college students who describe important events in romantic relationships tend to organize their expectations around these developmental stages (Honeycutt, Cantrill, & Allen, 1992; Honeycutt, Cantrill, & Greene, 1989). You can gain insight into the role of communication in friendships and romantic relationships by focusing on the goals and messages that characterize the formation, escalation, and dissolution of intimacy.

FORMING RELATIONSHIPS

Over the course of a day, you might find yourself talking to any number of people you are meeting for the first time. You might chat with someone while you wait in line at a coffee shop, you might share a table with someone new at the library, you might exchange messages with someone in an online chat room, or you might meet the friend of a friend at a club. Although many of the interactions that you have go no further than that single conversation, all of your close relationships – excluding family – began with a conversation between strangers. What sets some relationships on the path to closeness, while others are quickly forgotten? Where you go from those initial interactions depends on your ability to accomplish two basic tasks: figuring out how

FIGURE 9.2 Knapp's model of relationship development and dissolution. This model of relationship development shows the steps people go through as they develop or dissolve a relationship. Couples can increase or decrease intimacy by going up the development side or down the dissolution side from whichever level they are on.

to communicate with the other person and discovering opportunities for positive experiences.

Coping with Uncertainty

One of the primary challenges to communicating with strangers is that you know so little about them. Shall you talk about your favorite professional football team? What if he doesn't like sports? Perhaps you should ask about her major – but maybe she isn't a student. Without knowing about the other person's cultural background, you can't even be sure that your tendency to make eye contact, gesture, and lean forward while you talk won't be perceived as invasive and rude. Uncertainty, a lack of information about a conversational partner, undermines your ability to communicate. In particular, uncertainty makes it difficult to set goals for the conversation, to plan a course of action, and to enact verbal and nonverbal messages (Berger, 1997). Thus, your initial interactions with other people are typically focused on gathering information that will help you communicate – a process called **uncertainty reduction** (Berger & Calabrese, 1975).

In the formative stages of relationship development, you reduce your uncertainty about each other by exchanging information. **Self-disclosure** is the general term that refers to telling another person about your characteristics, experiences, feelings, attitudes or beliefs. Within initial interactions, your self-disclosures focus on public information, such as name, age, and hometown (Greene, Derlega, & Mathews, 2006). Although this

Uncertainty
A lack of information about a conversational partner.

Uncertainty Reduction
The process of gathering information about an interaction partner.

Self-disclosure
Telling another person about your characteristics, experiences, feelings, attitudes, or beliefs.

information might seem superficial, it allows you to orient yourself with respect to your communication partner. For example, when Jen's sister took a trip with a diverse group of college students to repair a community damaged by Hurricane Katrina, one of the first questions she asked in initial interactions was what school a person attended; based on the answer, she could discuss anything that was revealed by the name and location of the college. In general, then, gathering public information about another person can help you and a partner find topics to talk about.

In addition to discovering topics to discuss, you need to determine what style of communication you should use. Should you be open and direct, or would your partner find less explicit messages to be more appropriate? How much detail should you go into on the topics you discuss? Is humor or sarcasm okay, or does your partner expect you to be more serious? To cope with uncertainty about how to communicate in initial interactions, people follow a **norm of reciprocity** in which they match their own

Norm of Reciprocity
The tendency to match our own disclosures to those made by our partner.

REAL WORDS

AN INITIAL INTERACTION

As you review this script from a typical initial interaction, notice how the partners match the topic, expansiveness, and tone of each other's self-disclosures. How would the information being shared help you communicate with either Julia or Rob?

JULIA: Hi. My name's Julia.
ROB: Hey, I'm Rob. I have a sister named Julia.
JULIA: Really? That's cool. So then you'll never forget it!
ROB: Yeah.
JULIA: Is she your only sister?
ROB: No, I have four older sisters. I'm the baby in the family and the only boy. What about you?
JULIA: Just one older brother.
ROB: So you're the baby too.
JULIA: Yeah. It's the best. Well, at least for me, I got kind of spoiled.
ROB: Do you still live at home with your parents?
JULIA: No, my family is back in Philadelphia. I came out here for school.
ROB: Oh . . . what are you studying?
JULIA: Psychology. My dad wanted me to get a business degree, but . . . I don't know . . . I just couldn't really get into it.
ROB: Too boring?
JULIA: Yeah, I guess. Are you in school? Or . . . um . . . what do you do?
ROB: I just graduated. Trying to find a job.
JULIA: Doing what?
ROB: Well, I had a boring business degree . . . so. . .
JULIA: Oh no! How embarrassing! I'm sorry. It wasn't really *that* boring.

disclosures to those made by their partner. The transcript presented in the Real Words feature shows how the norm of reciprocity helps us to navigate initial interactions. Notice how the self-disclosures are not dominated by one person or the other; instead, each person takes turns sharing a detail, and that detail is matched by the other person.

In reciprocating disclosures, partners attend to three issues. First, they typically address the same topic that was raised by the other person: Julia tells Rob her name and he tells her his name; Rob says he has four sisters and Julia reveals she has one brother. Second, they tend to match the length or expansiveness of the other person's message. Rob elaborates on being the baby in the family and Julia goes on to describe the merits of being a youngest sibling, but it would be unusual if Julia responded by going into great detail about her relationship with each person in her family. Finally, they match qualities of their messages – for example, use of explicit language, humor, or politeness – to qualities of their partner's speech. Julia and Rob both become more casual in their speech as the conversation evolves. Although the norm of reciprocity might make initial interactions a bit scripted, it structures conversations when you otherwise lack information about how to communicate with a person. The result is a more fluid interaction that can advance your relationship to the next level.

PAUSE & REFLECT

How do you feel when a conversation with a new acquaintance doesn't follow the norm of reciprocity? Is this more or less noticeable in face-to-face or online interactions?

Exploring Possibilities

Predicted outcome value

The rewards a person expects to get from a future relationship with a new acquaintance.

As you reduce uncertainty in the formative stage of relationships, you are also trying to discover and promote positive outcomes. The **predicted outcome value** of an interaction or a relationship refers to the rewards you expect to get from a future relationship with a new acquaintance. When predicted outcome value is high, people tend to talk more, ask more questions, and use nonverbal behaviors that communicate liking and encourage disclosures (Sunnafrank, 1988; 1990). A survey of members of an online dating service found that people make more honest, frequent, and intentional self-disclosures to online partners when they want to continue that relationship face-to-face (Gibbs, Ellison, & Heino, 2006). In fact, the predicted outcome value based on conversations at the beginning of a semester influences how close classmates become by the ninth week of the semester (Sunnafrank & Ramirez, 2004). Because predicted outcome value has powerful effects on interpersonal communication and relationship development, people spend initial interactions trying to assess and maximize future rewards.

In an effort to predict the value of a relationship, you expand your conversations with new acquaintances beyond generic, public self-disclosures by engaging in small talk. Although the specific content of small talk isn't very important to interaction partners, participating in the conversation builds rapport (Coupland, 2003). Small talk also allows partners to cover a lot of topics in search of commonalities that can foster a relationship. As you engage in small talk, two rules keep the conversation moving in a positive direction. First, limit your self-disclosures to positive, rather than negative, information. Remember, your interaction partner is trying to decide if he or she wants a relationship with you, so you want to keep your less desirable traits under wraps for a while. Second, follow broadly held social norms. Eventually, your quirky traits might be endearing; however, at this point in your relationship, you should avoid behaviors that might suggest you're abnormal. When you keep the content of your disclosures positive and show that you aren't too unusual, you increase the likelihood that someone will be willing to have a relationship with you.

As part of the relationship development process, then, it's important to weigh the risks and rewards associated with self-disclosures. Do you know this person well enough to trust him or her with your deeply personal information? Will your disclosure have the desired effect on the relationship? One study asked college students to explain their reasons for sharing or not sharing a piece of positive information about themselves (Derlega, Anderson, Winstead, & Greene, 2011). Some of the reasons for sharing the information included: (a) feeling close to the partner (e.g., "We have a really good relationship, I can tell her anything"), (b) similarity of experiences and interests (e.g., "He has been in the same situation, so he could easily relate"), and (c) building closeness (e.g., "It would help him get to know me better"). Some of the reasons for withholding the information included: (a) wanting to avoid a negative reaction (e.g., "I didn't want our relationship to become weird"), (b) not feeling close enough to share the information (e.g., "I don't have enough rapport with him"), (c) lacking enough similarity for a partner to understand (e.g., "I don't think he would be able to relate to my experience"), and (d) wanting to maintain privacy (e.g., "There are just some things that are too personal to share"). These results reveal the thought processes behind people's disclosure decisions, as well as the potential risks and rewards that can arise from sharing personal information with a relationship partner.

PAUSE & REFLECT

During an initial interaction, either face-to-face or online, what personal information or traits might you withhold to improve your partner's impression of you?

Putting Theory into Practice: Starting Out on the Right Track

Your experiences during the formative stage of relationship development determine which relationships will grow into friendships and romances, and which will end as brief and forgettable encounters. By developing skills to reduce uncertainty and promote positive outcomes, you can open the door to interpersonal relationship opportunities.

Toe the line as you self-disclose. Initial interactions require you to package your unique and interesting qualities in familiar scripts for self-disclosure, but just because you're following norms for initial interactions, doesn't mean that you can't make these conversations interesting. Here are some guidelines for making your self-disclosure appropriate and interesting:

- Exchange public information, no matter how ordinary it might seem, to help a new acquaintance to locate you within a diverse society ("I went to Springfield High School, here in town" or "My parents came to the US from India, and I was born here").
- Reciprocate conversational behaviors to work with a partner in setting the course, the pace, and the tone of the interaction – in other words, if your partner comments on the weather, say what you think about it; if your partner brings up her favorite sports, comment on your interest in sports or something else you enjoy.
- Spice up your introductions by focusing on qualities that aren't private or personal, but that set you apart from others (Are you from an especially large family? Do you have an uncommon pet? Is there anything unique about your hometown?)
- Portray yourself truthfully – making exaggerated or misleading disclosures doesn't allow your partner to reduce uncertainty, it doesn't help your partner predict the value of a relationship with you, and it can undermine a relationship once your true qualities are revealed.

You can promote relationship development by following the script for initial interactions, helping your partner communicate with you, and showing that you're not someone ordinary.

Make the most of small talk. Small talk has a big job to do: it's your tool for ferreting out common ground on which you can build a relationship. Given that important task, be sure to take advantage of opportunities for small talk.

COMMUNICATION IN ACTION 9.1

Making the Most of Small Talk

Complete this exercise using the form on the **companion website** to help yourself prepare for your next conversation where small talk is called for.

ESCALATING RELATIONSHIPS

When your formative experiences are promising, you escalate relationships through continued interpersonal communication. Although relationships develop and change in many different ways, four general issues underlie the escalation of any friendship or romance: (a) people need to develop a sense of connection and intimacy; (b) they need to resolve questions and doubts about the relationship; (c) they need to learn how to coordinate their behaviors; and (d) they need to figure out how to balance the rewards and costs they each experience. In this section of the chapter, we explore the communication strategies that contribute to relationship escalation.

Creating a Connection

You create a connection with other people by spending time with them and sharing information with them. **Social penetration theory** is a description of relationship escalation that focuses on how communication allows partners to probe each other's self-concepts (Altman & Taylor, 1973). As illustrated in Figure 9.3, this theory highlights how our personalities are organized into layers within segments representing different domains or aspects of our lives. Public information is at the outermost layer of each segment, and internal layers contain increasingly more personal information; the innermost layer is where you keep your most private attitudes, beliefs, and fears. Establishing

Social Penetration Theory
A model that focuses on how communication allows partners to probe each other's self-concepts.

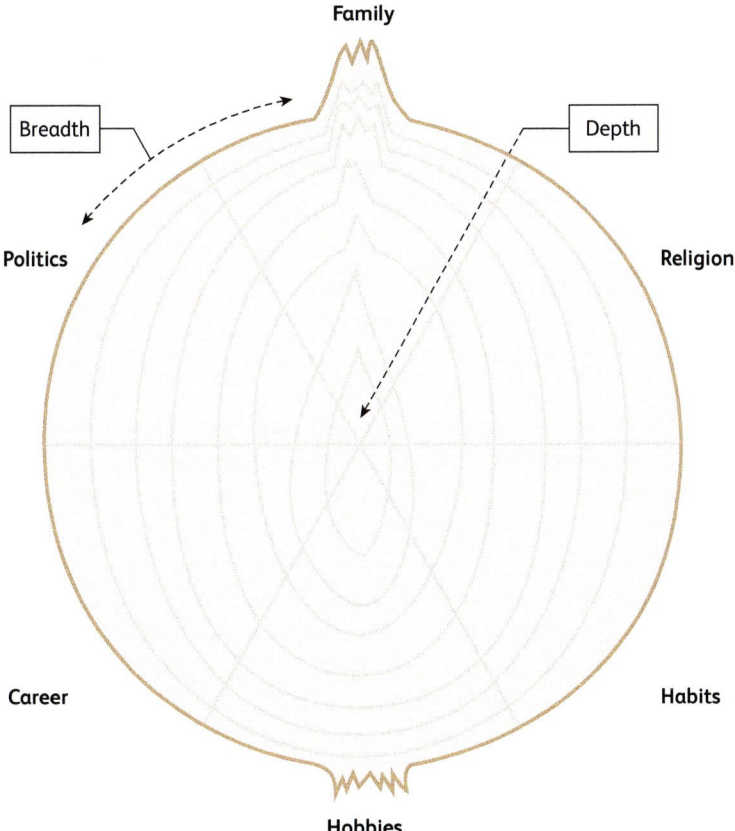

FIGURE 9.3 Social penetration theory. Social penetration theory suggests that our personalities are multi-layered like the layers of an onion. The wedges in the onion below represent the different topics that we might disclose about to an interaction partner. In all segments, the outer layers of the circle contain public information that is easy to reveal to others, whereas the innermost circle represents our most private values and beliefs. Relationships escalate as self-disclosure increases in both breadth – the variety of topics – and depth, the extent to which the information reveal is personal or private.

Depth
The extent to which shared information is personal or private.

Breadth
The variety of topics that we share with a partner.

a relationship involves increasing both **depth**, how personal or private information is, and **breadth**, the variety of life's segments you share with a partner. When you increase the depth and breadth of shared knowledge by self-disclosing to another person, you promote the development of intimacy in that relationship.

Recall that self-disclosure in the formative stages of relationship development is guided by the norm of reciprocity, such that the information offered by one person is immediately matched by the partner. In escalating relationships, this "tit-for-tat" pattern of exchange is replaced by responses to disclosures that convey understanding and validation (Greene et al., 2006). Consider the example of Terry and Allyson, who are escalating their new relationship. When Terry shares news of her promotion at work, Allyson can respond in one of two general ways: she can describe her own recent success at work, or she can show excitement for Terry's news. Although a matching disclosure might make sense if Terry and Allyson are still getting to know each other, it doesn't do much to celebrate Terry's good news. In contrast, Allyson can prolong Terry's celebration by keeping the focus on the promotion.

PAUSE & REFLECT

Do you know anyone who typically responds to your news or problems by talking about their own experiences? How does that response make you feel?

Another change that occurs as relationships escalate involves the appearance of negative self-disclosures. As the depth of your disclosures increases, you move beyond positive, public information, and you begin to offer up more problematic details. For example, you might show your friend that you have a bit of a temper, tell your partner about a past indiscretion, or reveal that you hold an unpopular opinion. When you share less flattering details about yourself, you show partners that you trust them with sensitive information. In fact, one study found that people were rated as more attractive when they disclosed negative as opposed to positive information because a willingness to disclose negative information reveals vulnerability and trustworthiness (Ellingson & Galassi, 1995). And if a partner accepts and validates your less desirable qualities, the effect is to build an even greater sense of trust. Thus, changes in self-disclosure, and the opportunities for responsiveness that they create, are an essential part of building a personal connection within emerging relationships.

Resolving Doubts

Relational Uncertainty
The lack of knowledge people have about their relationships.

As discussed previously in this chapter, initial interactions involve considerable uncertainty about a new acquaintance, and the formation of a relationship requires gathering information that allows you to communicate. When an acquaintance becomes something more special, questions about the relationship itself start to occupy you. **Relational uncertainty** refers generally to the lack of knowledge people have about their relationships (Knobloch & Solomon, 1999; 2002), and it includes three kinds of doubts. Specifically, self uncertainty involves your questions about your own involvement in a relationship, partner uncertainty refers to doubts that you have about your partner's commitment to the relationship, and relationship uncertainty includes your doubts about the very nature of the relationship. Although the three sources of relational uncertainty focus on distinct issues, they each reflect unknowns that can block relationship escalation.

What can you do to address relational uncertainty and escalate a promising relationship? Ironically, being uncertain about a relationship often leads people to be more indirect in their communication with a partner (Knobloch & Carpenter-Theune, 2004; Theiss & Solomon, 2006). In fact, one study found that college students diagnose whether their friendships have romantic potential by using a variety of **secret tests**, covert activities designed to reveal information about a partner's involvement in a relationship (Baxter & Wilmot, 1984). For example, a person might flirt with a third party to see if a partner cares enough to get jealous. Or, one partner might impose a separation – perhaps by not calling – to see how long it takes for the other person to initiate contact. A person might also update their Facebook status to "In a Relationship" to see if their partner will agree with their definition of the relationship and update his or her status as well. Although secret tests can answer questions about the relationship, you should be cautious about using them in relationships you value; not everyone appreciates being the target of a covert investigation.

HOW DO YOU RATE? 9.1

Relational Uncertainty

Visit the **companion website** to complete an adapted version of Leanne Knobloch and Denise Solomon's (1999) relational uncertainty scale. How does your level of uncertainty in a relationship influence the way you behave in that relationship?

Secret Tests
Covert actions designed to reveal information about a partner's involvement in a relationship.

PAUSE & REFLECT

How would you react if you knew someone was testing you to see how involved you were in that relationship?

An alternative to secret tests is **relationship talk**, communicating with your partner about your relationship. Relationship talk can be risky because it might reveal that one partner wants the relationship more than the other, but it can also help people resolve doubts that are blocking relationship development. In one study, partners in developing romantic relationships were asked to discuss positive, negative, or surprising events, and report their perceptions of the relationship talk (Knobloch, Solomon, & Theiss, 2006). The results showed that relationship talk was more likely to improve the quality of the relationship during the early stages of a relationship than in later stages of a relationship when partners were already highly intimate. Despite the risks, then, relationship talk offers a way to address uncertainties that may be holding relationships back.

Relationship Talk
Communication with a partner about your relationship with him or her.

Coordinating Behavior

As partners escalate a relationship, they also begin to coordinate and integrate their day-to-day activities. Consider the numerous ways that Audrey relies on her relationships

SCHOLAR SPOTLIGHT

Visit the Communication Café on the **companion website** to view a conversation with Leanne Knobloch, a leading scholar on relational uncertainty in the field of interpersonal communication.

Interdependence
A state that exists when relationship partners rely on each other to accomplish their goals.

Relational Turbulence Model
A perspective highlighting the difficulties that emerge when people try to establish interdependence with each other.

over the course of her day: She walks dogs with her best friend Diane in the morning, she borrows her roommate's sweater when she gets dressed, she sits next to her buddy Sean in class, she gets a ride home from campus with her brother Blake, and she makes plans for the weekend with her boyfriend Daniel. In similar ways, Audrey's friends, family, and romantic partner depend on her to dog sit occasionally, do laundry for the household, share lecture notes, chip in with gas money, and make the weekend more fun. **Interdependence** exists when partners can count on each other to accomplish their everyday goals.

Finding ways to integrate new people into your daily routine can be challenging. The **relational turbulence model** highlights how establishing interdependence can be a source of difficulty within developing relationships (Solomon & Knobloch, 2001, 2004). According to the model, people move beyond the formative stage of relationship development by allowing a partner to influence or affect their day-to-day experiences; for example, you might start carpooling to campus with your new friend, arrange a study date to get ready for midterms, or reschedule your daily workout so your partner can join you. When you revise your activities to include your partner, your routine will initially suffer – you end up late to campus because your friend isn't a morning person, your studying suffers because the two of you can't stay focused, and you find it easier to blow off exercise late in the day. Thus, the relational turbulence model suggests that an unavoidable part of relationship escalation is the fact that a partner might create interference or barriers to your personal goals. Keep in mind that interference occurs because you are involving a partner in routines that he or she doesn't fully understand. If you talk with your partner about your goals, you might find even better ways of achieving them that include your partner. And when partners coordinate their behaviors so that they help each other achieve everyday goals, they become interdependent and, therefore, more intimate.

PAUSE & REFLECT

What goals do your relationship partners help you meet?

Striving for Equity

Social Exchange
The voluntary transfer of personal resources from one partner to another.

As partners escalate a relationship, they get benefits from each other and they give up things they value for each other. **Social exchange** is the voluntary transfer of personal resources from one partner to another (Thibaut & Kelley, 1959). When a partner provides you with a benefit, such as giving you a ride home, lending you class notes, or making your leisure time more fun, you have experienced a reward. And when you give up something for a partner – the fuel and time it takes to provide that ride home, the convenience of keeping your class notes with you, or the fun you might have with a different person – you have experienced a cost. Just like a good shopper, you prefer to receive as many rewards as possible, while incurring the fewest costs. The challenge in escalating relationships, then, is to find a way to exchange resources in ways that both partners see as profitable and fair.

Social exchange in ongoing relationships is guided by **the rule of distributive justice**, which dictates that each partner's rewards should be proportional to his or her costs. When partners achieve a balance between the costs and rewards they each experience, they have achieved equity. Perhaps not surprisingly, equity fosters intimacy and satisfaction in close relationships (e.g., Buunk & VanYperen, 1991). Unfortunately, equity can also be hard to achieve. In economic exchanges, you know the exact price of something, and you might even be able to get a refund if you're dissatisfied with the product; in social exchanges, the value of rewards and costs is much harder to determine, and therefore, harder to balance.

> **The Rule of Distributive Justice**
> A guideline dictating that each partner's rewards should be proportional to his or her costs.

Consider the end-of-season dinner Denise hosted for the rest of her volleyball team while in college. What would be reasonable "payment" for that meal? Although you could tally up the cost of the food and add wages for Denise's time, that cold calculation probably wouldn't capture the value of the meal. The fact that Denise gave the team a place to gather, cooked foods they all enjoy, and helped them end the season in style all add value to the meal. Denise's efforts to clean the house before the party and the dirty kitchen afterward might also figure into her costs. As this example shows, equity is hard to achieve because you can't clearly establish the value of the rewards and costs you experience through social exchange. Part of learning about a new relationship partner is finding out what he or she enjoys and dislikes. If you and your partner can balance your gains and losses, you'll develop an equitable foundation for a long-term relationship.

Putting Theory into Practice: Navigating the Road to Intimacy

You may know from experience just how challenging it can be to establish close friendships or romantic relationships. Interpersonal communication is a tool for overcoming these challenges and establishing an intimate bond with another person. The following tips should also help you navigate the challenges associated with escalating a close relationship.

Balance breadth and depth in your self-disclosure. When escalating a relationship, keep in mind that both breadth and depth of self-disclosure contribute to building a sense of connection. You can avoid relationships that are superficial or unidimensional by balancing your disclosures in terms of both breadth and depth.

COMMUNICATION IN ACTION 9.2

Mapping Your Self-disclosures

Consider a relationship you are involved in that is more than an acquaintanceship, but still has room to grow, and map out the aspects of your life that you have and have not shared with this partner. To do this, complete the form on the **companion website** to create a picture like the one in Figure 9.3.

Talk about your uncertainty. If you are having questions about a relationship, seeking answers from a partner can be intimidating – you may not be sure what you want, maybe you can't predict how your partner will respond, and you might not even know if such a conversation is allowed in this relationship. When your doubts are left unaddressed, however, you create even more uncertainty. Because relationship talk is risky, you need to take steps to promote a positive interaction:

■ Make conversations about the relationship a regularly scheduled event. Plan a monthly date with a romantic partner or a regular get together with a friend where you talk about how things are going.

■ When you are engaged in relationship talk, be sure to address your partner's questions, as well as your own. If you only ask your partner to provide information, he or she might wonder why you are asking.

■ Begin the discussion by explaining your own thoughts and feelings about your relationship. By providing information that addresses your partner's uncertainty, you can encourage him or her to do the same for you.

Although you need to use caution, talking about your relationship gives you opportunities to clarify what's going on and to check that you and your partner are on the same page.

Give interdependence time and effort. The process of developing a relationship necessarily involves interference from partners, so try to be patient and take constructive action when you become frustrated at the ways a new friend or romantic partner disrupts your day.

■ Expect and forgive some degree of annoyance – in fact, celebrate it as a sign of growing intimacy.

■ When you find yourself experiencing interference from a partner, talk about what goal you are trying to achieve, and how your partner can help.

■ Make equity a priority by paying attention to times when you are giving more than you're getting, and making sure that you offer rewards on par with your partner's costs.

COMMUNICATION IN ACTION 9.3

Creating a Relationship Balance Sheet

Using the form on the **companion website**, make a list of all of the rewards you gain from a particular relationship, as well as all of the costs that you incur by being in that relationship. Reflecting on these lists can help you think of ways you could make your relationship more rewarding, less costly, and more equitable.

ENDING RELATIONSHIPS

Inevitably, some friendships and romantic relationships come to an end. One study of high school students found that more than 25% had experienced the break-up of a romantic relationship in the past year (Monroe, Rohde, Seeley, & Lewinsohn, 1999). Among college students, fewer than 50% of committed romantic relationships are likely to last more than three years (Kirkpatrick & Davis, 1994; Sprecher, 2001). In another study of adults aged 55 to 84, 68% of participants had a friendship that was fading away and 25% had recently ended a friendship (Adams & Blieszner, 1998). Thus, ending relationships is common throughout our lives.

Relationship dissolution refers to the process by which previously developed relationships become less close. As you saw in Figure 9.2, ending a relationship involves using communication to undo the bonds created during the development of intimacy. Within this general framework, a break-up can be one-sided or mutual, it can be accomplished directly or indirectly, it can be gradual or sudden, and it may or may not involve attempts at reconciliation (Baxter, 1984). In this section, we consider the challenges people confront as they travel the often uncomfortable path from closeness to dissolution.

Relationship Dissolution
The process by which previously developed relationships become less close.

Making a Decision

Relationship dissolution often begins when one person loses interest in a partner or the relationship, gets involved in other activities, or becomes attracted to other people (Battaglia, Richard, Datteri, & Lord, 1998). What causes your feelings for a friend or dating partner to fade away? In friendships, the most common reason for relationship dissolution is a lack of shared interests and activities (Urberg, Degirmenciouglu, & Tolson, 1998). For romantic partners, break-ups can be sparked when one person feels there isn't enough independence, similarity, support, shared time, equality, or romance in the relationship (Baxter, 1986). In some cases, you might even become annoyed by the unique qualities that you initially found attractive in your partner (Felmlee, 1998), such as when your partner's refreshing silliness becomes tiresome immaturity. Thus, people can become less enthralled with a friendship or romantic relationship for a variety of reasons.

PAUSE & REFLECT

Have you ever had to end a friendship or romantic relationship? What reasons did you have for terminating that relationship?

External events can also create or reveal fractures in a relationship. For example, a study of first-year university students found that more than half of the best friendships people had in high school had become less close when they entered college (Oswald & Clark, 2003). Friendships can also be disrupted when one partner starts dating someone seriously or gets married (Rose & Serafica, 1986). One classic study that followed romantic relationships between college students over the course of two years showed that break-ups were more likely to occur at the beginning or end of a semester (Hill, Rubin, & Peplau, 1976). In fact, Valentine's Day, with its focus on celebrating romance, can prompt less committed partners to end a relationship (Morse & Neuberg, 2004). As these examples illustrate, circumstances outside a relationship can set partners on the road to dissolution.

The Investment Model
A theory about commitment to relationships.

The deterioration of a relationship often leads one or both partners to evaluate the pros and cons of a break-up. The **investment model**, presented in Figure 9.4, predicts that you are likely to stay in a relationship when you receive more rewards than costs, you lack alternatives to the relationship, and you have invested a lot of time, energy, or resources in the relationship (Rusbult & Buunk, 1993). Conversely, you are more likely to end a relationship when you conclude that it isn't rewarding, you have better alternatives, or you don't have much to lose. The investment model highlights how deciding to decrease intimacy can be difficult, especially when we gain specific rewards from a partner or we have invested a lot in a relationship (Roloff, Soule, & Carey, 2001; Rusbult & Martz, 1995). Because there are often downsides to both staying together and breaking up, a critical part of relationship dissolution is figuring out whether you or your partner wants to exit the relationship.

Managing Face Threats

Face Threats
Experiences that can make either partner feel constrained or disliked.

A key concern guiding your communication during relationship dissolution is preventing or managing **face threats** – experiences that can make either partner feel constrained or disliked. If you think your partner wants out of your relationship, you may want to respect those wishes, show that you still value him or her, and yet retain your pride. And if you're the one initiating a break-up, you might worry about forcing your partner into a bad situation, making your partner feel inadequate, appearing insensitive, or later regretting that you ended the relationship (Kunkel, Wilson, Olufowote, & Robson, 2003). Thus, relationship dissolution is a complicated balancing act between protecting your partner and protecting yourself from face threats.

One strategy for decreasing threats to your own face is to use covert strategies to determine whether a partner wants less out of the relationship. Just as people might use secret tests to diagnose relationship escalation, they sometimes test the limits to determine whether a previously close relationship is on the decline (Chory-Assad & Booth-Butterfield, 2001). People worried about the dissolution of a relationship pay more attention to how dominating or friendly a partner is during conflicts (Hubbard, 2001). In fact, partners on their way to a break-up are especially motivated to uncover negative

| Commitment | = | Satisfaction (Rewards – Costs) | – | Availability of Attractive Alternatives | + | Resources Invested in Relationship |

FIGURE 9.4 The investment model

information about their relationship (Ickes, Dugosh, Simpson, & Wilson, 2003). Thus, doubts about the future of a relationship can prompt us to be more vigilant in our covert efforts to understand a partner's agenda.

When you are the one initiating relationship dissolution, you can manage face threats by using indirect strategies for withdrawing from the relationship. People often end relationships by limiting self-disclosure (Baxter, 1979), avoiding a partner and sensitive topics (Baxter & Philpott, 1982), or cycling through periods of withdrawal and reconciliation (Baxter, 1984). Although indirect communication can help you to minimize face threats while you are ending relationships, it has some downsides. When people disengage from a romantic relationship by simply neglecting it, their friendships with those former dating partners are strained (Busboom, Collins, Givertz, & Levin, 2002). Dating partners also have a better chance of becoming friends if they refrain from indirect strategies to end the relationship (Metts, Cupach, & Bejlovec, 1989). As you're going through a break-up, keep in mind that indirect communication can soften the blow, but avoiding the issue completely can cause misunderstandings and bad feelings.

Reasserting Independence

Because relationships develop as partners share themselves with each other and mesh their everyday routines, relationship dissolution requires people to re-establish their independence. When you developed a friendship, perhaps you discovered new interests or hobbies, you altered or deepened certain beliefs, or you came to rely on your partner to facilitate important goals. Ending that relationship, then, requires that you find ways to refocus or sustain those pastimes, beliefs, and goals without your friend. Not surprisingly, when people adopt new interests or develop values because of a relationship partner, they feel diminished or lost as that relationship ends (Lewandowski, Aron, Bassis, & Kunak, 2006). Thus, the process of breaking up involves recovering a sense of yourself that is not tied to that relationship.

You can reassert your own identity both in the activities you engage in and the way you talk about yourself and your relationship. As you withdraw from one relationship, for example, you might spend more time with other members of your social network (Emmers & Hart, 1996). Some people even develop avoidance rituals or routines that allow them to limit contact with a relationship partner. For example, a person might stop calling a partner, ignore the partner when they are together, or limit time with the partner by changing schedules or taking on other commitments (Emmers & Hart, 1996). By engaging in activities alone or with other people, you can develop hobbies, beliefs, and goals that don't involve a relationship partner.

PAUSE & REFLECT

Have you ever taken steps to avoid contact with a relationship partner? If so, what were some of the strategies you used and what did they accomplish?

Your language also changes in subtle ways that reflect emerging independence. When people are in long-term, stable relationships, like a satisfying marriage, they tend to use collective pronouns, such as "we" or "us," that signal their interdependence (Sillars, Shellen, McIntosh, & Pomegranate, 1997). In the same way, partners who are committed to their dating relationship link their identities through collective pronouns, whereas less committed partners use "I" and "you" to refer to each other (Agnew, VanLange, Rusbult, & Langston, 1998). In fact, when dating partners experience interference from each other, they use fewer collective pronouns when they have a conversation (Knobloch & Solomon, 2003). In these ways, you use language to shift your sense of self from a state of "we-ness" to a state of "me-ness."

Coming to Terms

Regardless of whether you or your partner initiates a break-up, dissolving a friendship or romantic relationship can be stressful (Koenig Kellas & Manusov, 2003). The metaphors people use to describe relationship dissolution convey images of descent ("the relationship started going downhill"), desolation ("there is a hole in my heart where he/she used to be"), and injury or death ("I was torn to shreds") (Owen, 1993). People going through a break-up also experience plenty of negative emotions and volatile swings between feeling good and feeling bad (Sbarra, 2006). In fact, high school students who have experienced the end of a romantic relationship in the past year have a greater risk of developing a major depressive disorder for the first time (Monroe et al., 1999). Thus, the end of a close relationship can be a stressful and significant event with which people have to come to terms.

Grave-Dressing

Using communication to finalize the dissolution of a relationship.

The communication behaviors that people use to finalize a relationship are called **grave-dressing** (Duck, 1982) – the creation of stories about the relationship and its demise that help the partners make sense of what happened (Cupach & Metts, 1986). People feel better about a break-up when the accounts they create include a clear sequence of events (Koenig Kellas & Manusov, 2003). Individuals also feel better about ending a relationship when they focus on how the situation, rather than their own flaws, contributed to the break-up (Tashiro & Frazier, 2003), or how their partner is not really as wonderful as they once believed (Geher et al., 2005).

Despite the finality of the term "grave-dressing," you should avoid thinking about the end of a relationship as a specific event that completely severs all contact between former partners. Typically, relationship dissolution is a gradual process through which you realize that you want less intimacy, you signal decreased closeness through your communication, and you start to do more things without your partner. And although you may eventually have to come to terms with the end of the relationship, you might give the relationship another chance, postpone calling it quits, or find a new way to relate to your partner. In fact, sometimes romantic partners who split up go on to become friends (Wilmot, Carbaugh, & Baxter, 1985). Thus, coming to terms with relationship dissolution is about coping with the changes in your circumstances and understanding how you will (or will not) communicate with your partner in the future.

Putting Theory into Practice: Exiting Gracefully

Ending a friendship or romantic relationship is far from simple, especially when that relationship was once close. Although effective communication strategies will not eliminate the sting of a break-up, you can take steps to promote a more graceful ending to a once close relationship.

Weigh the pros and cons. When you begin to feel less engaged by a friendship or romantic relationship, take some time to reflect on the pros and cons of decreasing intimacy. Within close relationships, it can sometimes be difficult to notice all the ways that a partner provides us with resources and helps us to achieve our goals. Think about what you get out of this relationship, including tangible rewards, assistance, and companionship. Are you really going to be better off with a less close relationship? You might also consider the possibility that external changes in your situation – a new class schedule, a change of career goals, pressures at home – might be making this relationship less enjoyable at the moment. If you can sort out how much value you get out of the relationship and how much your disinterest might be caused by external forces, you can avoid later regretting that you ended the relationship.

Manage face threats. Perhaps the greatest challenge to ending relationships gracefully is managing the threats to both you and your partner. If you are sure that you want to end a relationship, be direct, respectful, and kind in your communication with your partner. When you emphasize what you valued about your partner and the relationship, you can ease the transition to less intimate involvement (Metts et al., 1989). And remember that both you and your partner will come to terms with the break-up more quickly if you can understand what happened to end it and where you want to go in the future.

COMMUNICATION IN ACTION 9.4

Identifying Strategies for Ending Relationships

Song-writer Paul Simon claimed that there are 50 ways to leave your lover, but some strategies are certainly better than others. Ask 10 people to identify the best and worst way that someone has ended a friendship or romantic relationship with them. The form on the **companion website** can help you organize this information. As you reflect on the information you gathered, can you recommend some do's and don'ts for ending relationships?

WHEN THINGS GO WRONG

With so many challenges to overcome in the formation, escalation, and dissolution of relationships, you shouldn't be surprised that things sometimes go awry. One of the hardest parts of negotiating relationship development is establishing the ground rules for interaction. Sometimes, one partner refuses to respect the boundaries the other person sets. At other times, relationship partners jointly decide to push the limits. In this section, we consider some of the situations that can arise when people cross the line in developing relationships.

Unrequited Love and Stalking

Obsessive Relational Intrusion
Repeated and unwanted pursuit that constitutes an invasion of privacy.

Stalking
Malicious and repeated harassment of another person that threatens his or her safety.

Sometimes people are attracted to potential partners who do not share their interest in developing a relationship. Moreover, barriers to a relationship sometimes motivate would-be lovers to pursue the object of their affection even more vigorously. **Obsessive relational intrusion** is the repeated and unwanted pursuit that constitutes an invasion of privacy. The behaviors that characterize obsessive relational intrusion can range from mildly intrusive behaviors – like being pestered for a date, receiving unwanted gifts, and being the target of seemingly endless phone calls – to property damage, verbal threats, or physical assaults (Cupach & Spitzberg, 1998). In the extreme, these obsessive behaviors comprise **stalking**, which is malicious and repeated harassment of another person that threatens his or her safety.

New technologies have made it easier to keep tabs on someone with whom a romantic relationship is desired. In one study of college students in the Midwestern United States, 40.8% of participants reported that they had been the victim of cyberstalking, but only 4.9% reported that they had ever been the perpetrator of online stalking (Reyns, Henson, & Fisher, 2012). The large difference between these two statistics suggests that either a small minority of individuals are responsible for instigating the vast majority of stalking, or more likely, people are unaware of the ways their behavior might be inappropriate or unwilling to admit to their own intrusive behaviors. One study identified the obsessive relational intrusion tactics that people might employ on Facebook (Chaulk & Jones, 2011), including: (a) using information on Facebook to make contact (e.g., using

FIGURE 9.5
Playing hard to get

Source: © Barbara Smaller/The New Yorker Collection/www.cartoon bank.com.

"He's playing very hard to get—he's got a restraining order."

a person's status update to know where he/she will be at a certain time); (b) monitoring a person's conversations and actions; (c) making contact with others in a person's social network; (d) making overly affectionate expressions of liking on Facebook (e.g., sending virtual gifts or writing affectionate messages on their wall); and (e) sending a person unwanted invitations to join groups or events. The study also found that females were more likely than males to engage in these types of cyber-intrusions and that they were most prominent among individuals of college age. When you consider these various forms of online relational intrusion, it's easy to see how some of the behaviors you might perform innocently to keep track of someone you are interested in could be interpreted as something more sinister.

Stalking and obsessive relational intrusion can be difficult to study, because the victims don't always come forward and the perpetrators are unlikely to discuss their behaviors with researchers. One question that researchers have studied concerns the personality traits that characterize individuals who are prone to stalking behavior. Researchers asked victims of stalking to identify the personality characteristics they perceived in their unwanted pursuer and compared those traits to the personality characteristics that non-victimized individuals perceived in their "normal" romantic partner (Spitzberg & Veksler, 2007). Unwanted pursuers were perceived as less socially competent, more emotional and dramatic in their behavior and speech, and more borderline obsessive-compulsive than partners who had not engaged in unwanted pursuit. Individuals who had been the target of unwanted pursuit also reported that they felt more victimized when their partner possessed high levels of these personality characteristics.

A 1998 CNN report suggested that 20% of all stalking cases in the United States involve celebrities, but the majority of victims are acquainted with their stalker (Spitzberg, 2002). In fact, people who become obsessive in the pursuit of a partner are often trying to develop a romantic relationship that they think will be filled with happiness (Cupach, Spitzberg, & Carson, 2000). Of course, a relationship that is grossly one-sided has a limited future, especially when one person's expressions of affection become aggressive. Because stalking situations persist for almost two years, on average, it is important that one or both parties seek help breaking this potentially dangerous connection.

Friends-with-Benefits

A relatively new phenomenon, especially on college campuses, is the **friends-with-benefits** relationship – an association in which friends engage in sexual activity, but do not define their relationship as romantic. Studies of friends-with-benefits suggest that between 50–60% of college students have experience of this type of relationship (Afifi & Faulkner, 2000; Mongeau, Ramirez, & Vorrell, 2003). What makes this relationship appealing? One survey of college students suggested that people pursue friends-with-benefits relationships to increase sexual opportunities, avoid commitment, simplify romance, experience an emotional connection, or experiment with that type of relationship (Hughes, Morrison, & Asada, 2005). Thus, friends-with-benefits receive the rewards of friendship and the rewards of a sexual relationship, but they don't incur any of the responsibilities and commitment that are implied by a romantic relationship.

Friends-with-Benefits
A friendship in which partners engage in sexual activity but do not define the relationship as romantic.

FIGURE 9.6 Mila Kunis and Justin Timberlake negotiating their relationship in the movie *Friends With Benefits*

PAUSE & REFLECT

Have you ever known someone who was involved in a friends-with-benefits relationship? What did you see as the challenges in this relationship?

Friends-with-benefits relationships are unique because they violate the social norms and expectations for both friendships and sexual relationships. Accordingly, partners must develop a unique set of rules to maintain relationships of this sort. As summarized in Table 9.1, the rules that college students follow within a friends-with-benefits relationship cover many aspects of intimacy, including emotional closeness, communication, sex, friendship, commitment, and privacy (Hughes et al., 2005). The complexity of these rules highlights just how difficult it can be to maintain relationships that cross familiar boundaries.

TABLE 9.1 Rules for relating between "friends with benefits"

Emotional rules	Partners should not fall in love
	Partners should not get hurt or jealous about other relationships
Communication rules	Partners should be honest with one another
	Partners should adhere to appropriate conversation topics
	Partners should limit the frequency of contact
Sex rules	Partners should only engage in agreed upon sexual behaviors
	Partners should take appropriate safe-sex precautions
Friendship rules	Partners should place higher importance on the friendship than on the sexual relationship

TABLE 9.1 continued

| Permanence rules | Partners agree that the sexual aspect of the relationship is temporary |
| Secrecy rules | Partners agree that other people in their social network should not find out about the sexual aspect of the friendship |

INSIDE COMMUNICATION RESEARCH

Negotiating Friends-with-Benefits Relationships

People enter into friends-with-benefits relationships for a variety of reasons, but maintaining this type of relationship can be a difficult task. Partners are likely to face a number of questions about the nature of their association, and they will need to find a way to resolve their uncertainties. Communication scholars Melissa Bisson and Timothy Levine (2009) conducted study to identify the questions that arise in friends-with-benefits relationships, as well as the communication strategies that partners use to resolve those questions and negotiate a satisfying relationship.

The researchers surveyed 90 undergraduate students who had been or were currently involved in a friends-with-benefits relationship. Almost half (48.9 %) of the participants indicated that they had questions about their friends-with-benefits relationship. Most of the questions that arose in friends-with-benefits relationships had to do with uncertainty about the nature of the relationship. Participants reported uncertainty about how to label their relationship, how to maintain the relationship, the future of the relationship, their feelings about the relationship, and whether or not they would be able to stay friends after the sexual aspect of their relationship ended.

The researchers also asked participants how they negotiated or talked about these uncertainties with their partner. The overwhelming majority of respondents indicated that they never initiated a talk with their partner about these issues, but a few said that they used humor to initiate the talk and even fewer said they negotiated the rules of their relationship at the time of their first sexual encounter. When asked about the content of their talk, the relatively few participants who did communicate with their partner indicated that they discussed their expectations for the relationship, the effect that sex would have on the relationship, the justifiable reasons for engaging in a sexual relationship, and confirmation that the friend was agreeable to having sex. The researchers also asked the participants how they negotiated the ground-rules for their friends-with-benefits relationship. The vast majority of participants (77.3 %) indicated that they had never negotiated the rules of their relationship with their partner. For those who did negotiate some rules for their relationship, most said that the rules were mutually agreed upon through conversation.

THINK ABOUT IT

1. What are the implications of not discussing a complicated relationship like friends-with-benefits? What are the risks? Are there any benefits?
2. How might the various uncertainties in friends-with-benefits relationships contribute to the lack of communication between partners?

Putting Theory into Practice: Staying on Course

In this section, we have addressed some of the darker and more complicated aspects of friendships and romantic relationships. These issues may arise from unclear relationship boundaries, but their results can range from frustrating to downright frightening. In this section, we consider how you can keep your friendships and romantic relationships on track.

Clarify and respect relationship boundaries. Relationship development is necessarily collaborative; in other words, it is something that you coordinate with your partner. You can't have a more intimate relationship than your partner is willing to have with you. And you and a partner both need to understand the challenges that come with blurring the line between friendship and romance. By identifying and maintaining boundaries that you and a partner establish together, you can avoid problems in your friendships and romantic relationships. To make sure that you and a partner are on the same page, spend some time thinking about how you each see the relationship. What are your goals for the relationship? What kind of activities do you enjoy sharing with your partner, and what behaviors do you want to keep out of the relationship? Are there any actions, such as cheating or lying, that would be a serious problem for you? After you answer these questions, consider how your partner might feel about these issues. If your relationship allows it, you might even talk with your partner about your answers. If you and your partner have similar views, you can be more confident that you can respect important boundaries for the relationship. And if you and your partner disagree on these issues, you'll know where you need to bring your views of the relationship into better alignment.

SUMMARY

One of the most important goals we accomplish through interpersonal communication is managing the rise and fall of friendships and romantic relationships. From the moment you first meet someone, interpersonal communication allows you to gather information and promote positive outcomes. And by remembering basic rules for communication, like following the norm of reciprocity and engaging in small talk, you can get a new relationship off to a good start.

When a relationship seems promising, you turn to communication to transform your acquaintance into a friend or dating partner. By sharing personal information about a variety of topics, you create a sense of connection with another person. You can also use communication to help you resolve questions that emerge as your relationship grows closer, coordinate your behavior in mutually satisfying ways, and make sure that your experience of rewards and costs is equitable. In these ways, your ability to use interpersonal communication effectively is central for building close friendships and romances.

Of course, not all relationships last forever; in fact, you will experience the dissolution of friendship and romantic relationships throughout your life. Relationships end in many ways and for many reasons, but break-ups might be easier if you keep in mind the features that they have in common. Once a decision to decrease intimacy is made, partners must manage face threats as they detect or communicate a desire for less involvement. In addition, partners need to re-establish their lives and self-concepts separate from the relationship. And if decreases in intimacy result in the end of a relationship, people can create accounts that may help them come to terms with the break-up.

Coordinating the development of a friendship or dating relationship requires that you work with a partner to establish your level of involvement and the boundaries for acceptable and unacceptable behavior. Most of the time, people are pretty good at creating relationships in which the partners are equally involved, and both parties understand and follow the rules. When this balancing act goes awry, though, one-sided love affairs and relationships that cross the line between friendship and romance can emerge.

The voluntary relationships that you form with friends and romantic partners can be some of the most rewarding bonds you experience. These relationships don't emerge automatically; rather, they are the result of specific communication behaviors that are skillfully enacted. Although the relationships you have had throughout your life have given you lots of experience with the processes described in this chapter, you can also take steps to improve your communication in interpersonal relationships. By applying some of the knowledge you gained in this chapter, you can foster promising relationships, deepen bonds that are important to you, soften the consequences of a break-up, and keep your relationships on track.

ACTIVITIES FOR EXPLORING COMMUNICATION ETHICS

What Would You/Should You Do?

Imagine that you are in a friendship or romantic relationship with someone who is more invested or committed to the relationship than you are. Because your partner likes you so much, he or she provides you with lots of rewards and incurs a lot of costs on your behalf. For example, maybe you find that you're eating at your friend's house a lot, your friend runs errands for you and drives you around, and you get a lot of compliments and support from this person. Your partner also doesn't seem to demand much from you; you don't pay for food or fuel, you leave your partner hanging at the last moment if something better comes up, and you aren't really all that interested in his or her problems. If you find yourself benefiting from an inequitable relationship, what would you – or should you – do?

Something to Think About

The description of relationship dissolution offered in this chapter highlighted the need to tread lightly when ending a relationship. At the same time, you shouldn't just avoid a partner, neglect the relationship, or secretly manipulate the other person into breaking up with you. Because communicating directly about a relationship in decline can be perceived as either too blunt or incredibly kind, you need to find a balance between avoidance and openness. What are the ethical issues involved in deciding how direct to be about your desire to end a previously close relationship?

Analyze Communication Ethics Yourself

Recent years have seen a dramatic increase in opportunities to meet people online. In places like Match.com, people can provide a description of themselves designed to attract potential friends or suitors. Just as we would expect in a face-to-face interaction, people seeking a relationship partner online are motivated to portray themselves in a positive light. When you don't have the information provided by face-to-face contact, though, these self-portraits can be misleading. Explore some of the online sites devoted to matchmaking, and examine the strategies people use to present themselves. What strategies do you find more or less ethical when people portray themselves in cyberspace?

KEY WORDS

breadth

depth

face threats

friends-with-benefits

grave-dressing

interdependence

investment model

norm of reciprocity

obsessive relational intrusion

predicted outcome value

relational turbulence model

relational uncertainty

relationship dissolution

relationship talk

rule of distributive justice

secret tests

self-disclosure

social exchange

social penetration theory

stalking

uncertainty

uncertainty reduction

INTIMACY AND INTERPERSONAL COMMUNICATION

10

266 THE NATURE OF INTIMACY

272 COMMUNICATION IN INTIMATE RELATIONSHIPS

277 INDIVIDUAL DIFFERENCES IN INTIMACY

284 EXTREMES OF INTIMACY

288 SUMMARY

290 ACTIVITIES FOR EXPLORING COMMUNICATION ETHICS

290 KEY WORDS

On the NBC reality series, *The Bachelor*, 25 women compete for the love and affection of one desirable bachelor. Although the interactions the Bachelor has with the contestants at the beginning of the show are carefully staged, their interactions become more intimate as he narrows his focus to just a few of the women. In fact, the Bachelor typically shares physical intimacy with multiple women on the show and each season ends with participants expressing feelings of true love. When the Bachelor makes a final decision about which relationship he'll continue off-screen, the last two women shed tears of heartache or joy. Ultimately, the Bachelor and the winner are separated for several months while the show airs so that the final outcome of the show isn't ruined when people see them together. Being forced into a long-distance relationship so soon after the relationship began typically spells disaster for the couple. After sixteen seasons, none of the couples have stayed together for long after the end of the show, which reveals how challenging it can be to maintain intimacy in a close relationship.

The primary quality that defines close relationships is **intimacy** – a connection between two people that includes psychological, emotional, and behavioral bonds. Because of these ties, intimate relationships provide us with companionship, entertainment, and support. When the Bachelor chooses which women to keep on the show, he typically says he's looking for someone with whom he has a connection, can have fun, and can imagine a future. At the same time, the complexities of intimacy can be a source of frustration and stress. The Bachelor often has to struggle with jealousy among the women and most of the resulting relationships fail shortly after the show ends. Although the carefully engineered circumstances on the Bachelor make this situation unique, you will probably also struggle with jealousy and failed relationships in your lifetime. Learning about communication in intimate relationships can help you to understand the important experiences you have with close friends and romantic partners. To that end, this chapter examines the nature of intimacy, how you can use communication to maintain intimate relationships, how people differ in their approaches to intimacy, and how intimacy is sometimes taken to extremes.

THE NATURE OF INTIMACY

The bonds of intimacy can be present in your relationships with friends, romantic partners, siblings, parents, mentors, and even pets. Thus, intimacy can take a variety of forms. This section of the chapter reveals the complex nature of intimacy by examining the components of intimate relationships and the various ways that people experience love.

Components of Intimacy

Intimacy isn't any one quality; rather, it is a bond that exists when a number of qualities are present in a relationship. Consider the example of Jacob, who identifies his best friend Mark and his girlfriend Suzanne as his most intimate relationships. With Mark, Jacob enjoys talking about sports and politics, just hanging out and listening to music, and

TABLE 10.1 The components of intimacy

Feeling	Definition
Closeness	A feeling of union between two people that emerges when people spend time together and influence one another's actions and beliefs
Openness	Our willingness to reveal private information about ourselves to a relationship partner through self-disclosure
Trust	The feeling that a relationship partner will keep us safe and protect us from harm
Affection	The positive feelings that we have for another person that we communicate through our actions with that person
Mutuality	When both partners in a relationship acknowledge and value the bond that exists between them

Intimacy
A connection between two people that includes psychological, emotional, and behavioral bonds.

knowing that Mark will always be there for him in a pinch. With Suzanne, Jacob knows there are some things he can't discuss and he sometimes worries about the future, but they share a deep affection for each other. As this example illustrates, intimacy involves several different components that can be more or less present in a relationship. Table 10.1 and the following paragraphs describe some of the features that contribute to intimacy in close relationships.

The core of intimacy is closeness. As Figure 10.1 illustrates, closeness reflects the degree to which your own identity overlaps with another person's identity (Aron & Aron, 1986). Closeness arises when people spend a lot of time together, do a variety of things together, and influence each other's actions and beliefs (Berscheid, Snyder, & Omoto, 2004). Closeness is also revealed in communication between friends and romantic partners. For example, nonverbal behaviors that reduce physical distance, such as a direct body orientation, eye contact, and touching, are more frequent within intimate relationships (Guerrero, 1997; Guerrero & Andersen, 1994). People also communicate closeness through language; for example, saying "we," "us," and "our" signals a closer union than saying "you and I" or "yours and mine" (Agnew, Van Lange, Rusbult, & Langston, 1998). Thus, closeness represents the bond that is at the core of intimacy.

A second component of intimacy is openness, which also requires a degree of trust. When friends and romantic partners share personal information about their values and beliefs, their relationship becomes increasingly intimate. As a result, your intimate partners often know all sorts of details about you, including your most embarrassing moment, your goals in life, or your insecurities. Intimate partners get to know many private details about you, and feeling comfortable sharing ourselves with relationship partners requires trust. When you trust a partner, you have confidence that he or she will not hurt you and that the information you share won't be revealed to others. Not surprisingly, then, trust increases communication about personal topics (Greene, Derlega, & Mathews, 2006; Wheeless, 1978). The more you trust a relationship partner, the more comfortable you will be sharing information with them, and the more information and experiences you share with a person, the more intimate your relationship will become.

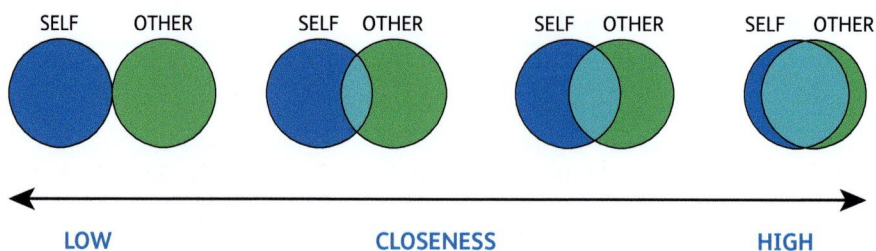

FIGURE 10.1 Aron and Aron's inclusion of other in self

Another aspect of intimacy – affection – captures the positive feelings you have for another person that you communicate through your actions (Pendell, 2002). Affectionate behaviors include hugging, kissing, holding hands, caressing a partner, making prolonged eye contact, and sitting or standing close to a partner (Lee & Guerrero, 2001). Verbally, people communicate affection for romantic partners in the same way that parents show affection for their children: they use pet names, simple sentence structures, a higher pitch, and a softer tone (Bombar & Littig, 1996; Floyd & Ray, 2003; Zebrowitz, Brownlow, & Olson, 1992). Thus, affection involves the messages you use to reveal your positive feelings for relationship partners.

The final component of intimacy is mutuality, which means that both partners in the relationship acknowledge and value the bond between them. Children tend to prefer friendships with peers who reciprocate their same level of intimacy and openness (Rotenberg & Mann, 1986). Adults also tend to be attracted to people who demonstrate liking and attraction (Sprecher, 1998). In fact, when relationships aren't mutual – one person values the relationship more than the other – the differences between partners limit the intimacy that they share. Jen has a friend who briefly dated a man who had developed much stronger feelings for her than she had for him. Not wanting to give her partner false hope, she consistently prevented the relationship from becoming too intimate by limiting her disclosures and dodging any suggestion of increased commitment. Thus, in order for relationships to become truly intimate, both partners must feel a mutual sense of closeness, openness, trust, and affection.

Different Styles of Loving

The intimacy you share with relationship partners is sometimes experienced as love or especially strong or deep feelings of affection. Within this general definition, love is as varied as the camaraderie of siblings, the protection a parent offers a child, the passion of star-crossed lovers, and the devotion of lifelong partners (Fehr, 1994). People feel love for both friends and romantic partners, but those experiences are unique in important ways. In addition, you have different experiences of love with different friends or within different romantic relationships. To shed light on the mysteries of love, this section examines the kinds of love you might experience in close relationships.

One view of love suggests that it is made up of three components: intimacy, passion, and commitment (Sternberg, 1986). As discussed previously, intimacy captures feelings of closeness and affection. The second ingredient is passion, which is the arousal that you experience when you are attracted to another person. Finally, commitment involves the decision to maintain a relationship over time. According to this model, **complete** or **consummate love** exists when intimacy, passion, and commitment are all present in a relationship. As illustrated in Figure 10.2, you can also experience different types of love

Complete/Consummate Love
When relationships are characterized by intimacy, passion, and commitment.

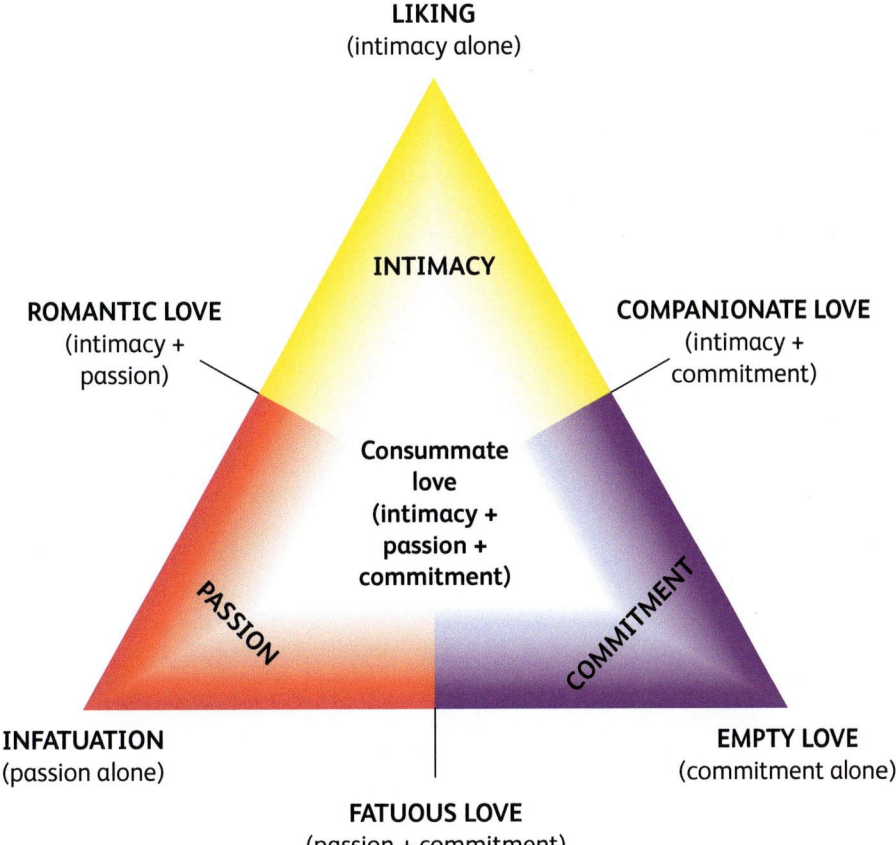

FIGURE 10.2 Sternberg's triangular theory of love

in which only one or two of the components are present. Thinking about love as a mixture of intimacy, passion, and commitment can help you to appreciate its complexity and understand love's many different forms.

An alternative perspective on love emphasizes the different ways that people experience and express their feelings for intimate partners (Hendrick & Hendrick, 1990). In this model, love is assumed to take three primary forms: **eros**, which is an erotic love preoccupied by beauty and sexuality; **ludus**, which portrays love as a game that is entertaining and exciting; and **storge**, which is a peaceful, friendship-based love that develops gradually over time. As shown in Figure 10.3, combinations of eros, ludus, and storge create three additional love styles. Mania blends the passion of eros with the games of ludus, resulting in a dramatic love that involves both elation and depression. Pragma combines the strategies of ludus with storge's focus on friendship to create the love that emerges when someone meets your criteria for a good partner. And when the passion of eros meets the companionship of storge, a compassionate and selfless love called agape is produced.

Love styles have been shown to have important consequences in romantic relationships. For example, approaches to love shape conflict behaviors, such that erotic and agapic lovers are more collaborative, and ludic lovers tend to avoid communication or withdraw during conflicts (Richardson, Hammock, Lubben, & Mickeler, 1989). In addition, the ludus love style is associated with the least satisfaction in romantic relationships

Eros
Love characterized by beauty and sexuality.

Ludus
Love characterized as a game that is entertaining and exciting.

Storge
Love characterized as peaceful and grounded in friendship.

HOW DO YOU RATE? 10.1

What's Your Love Style?

Visit the **companion website** to complete a scale designed to help you identify your primary love style (Hendrick & Hendrick, 1990). In what ways is your love style a strength in terms of engaging in romantic relationships? In what ways is it a weakness?

FIGURE 10.3 Hendrick and Hendrick's love styles

(Meeks, Hendrick, & Hendrick, 1998). People who have other-focused love styles, like eros and agape, rate their romantic relationships as more rewarding, more satisfying, and more committed (Morrow, Clark, & Brock, 1995). Thus, a person's love style can have a profound impact on intimacy.

PAUSE & REFLECT

Have you ever been in love? If so, would you describe your partner's love style and similar or different from your own? How did that similarity or difference affect your relationship?

Putting Theory into Practice: Promoting Well-Rounded Relationships

In this section of the chapter, you learned about both components of intimacy and the various ways in which people experience love in intimate relationships. Although every intimate relationship you will have in your life will be unique, consider the following strategies for promoting more intimate bonds in those relationships.

Address different facets of intimacy. The five components of intimacy – closeness, openness, trust, affection, and mutuality – highlight the various ways in which we might experience intimacy in a close relationship. In the same way, the love triangle might point you to qualities that dominate a close relationship, as well as those facets of love that might be missing. By taking inventory of intimacy in your close relationships, you can identify areas that might merit more attention.

COMMUNICATION IN ACTION 10.1

Filling Gaps in Intimate Relationships

Complete the form on the **companion website** to help you evaluate whether the components of intimacy are over-developed or under-developed in a close relationship that you value.

Expand your repertoire for love. If you are able to identify a particular style that characterizes your love relationships, try to think about how you can develop other approaches to love. By communicating across love styles, you can break out of your current mold and broaden your experience of love within an intimate relationship. Here are some ways you can experiment with other love styles:

■ If your relationship lacks passion (eros), tell your partner what you find physically and sexually appealing about him or her to remind each other that passion is important.

- If your relationship lacks friendship (storge), ask your partner to share experiences that you enjoy or must do, but that don't have romantic meaning for you, like running errands.
- If your relationship lacks fun (ludus), plan a surprise event for your partner or make a game out of a routine event. For example, you might each plan half of a romantic date night.

COMMUNICATION IN INTIMATE RELATIONSHIPS

Intimate relationships are dynamic and constantly changing. Perhaps your best friend or romantic partner needs some extra support from you today in order to meet an important deadline. Maybe you've grown bored with your relationship and you need to restore the excitement you once had. Or perhaps a brewing conflict is threatening the future of your relationship. Within intimate relationships, interpersonal communication helps you to give and receive help, revitalize your routine, and manage tensions. In this section, we explore the ways in which communication can be used to maintain intimacy and manage relational tensions.

Maintaining Intimacy

Between the ebbs and flows of relationship development described in the previous chapter, you maintain intimacy in relationships you value. In general, **relational maintenance** refers to the actions people take to keep their relationship in a desired state (Dindia & Canary, 1993). **Strategic maintenance** includes behaviors that are intentionally performed with the goal of sustaining the relationship (Dainton & Stafford, 1993). For example, people might have conversations about the relationship, help their partner complete a task, compliment a partner, or offer an apology to ensure that the relationship continues. In contrast, **routine maintenance** refers to less intentional actions that, nonetheless, help to keep a relationship going (Dainton & Stafford, 1993). These behaviors might be enacted as part of your daily routine, like making dinner, taking out the garbage, and chatting about your day (Stafford, Dainton, & Haas, 2000). Both strategic and routine behaviors play an important role in maintaining close relationships.

People maintain their relationships using a variety of communication strategies, such as providing assurances of one's love and commitment, being open, being positive, sharing tasks, enjoying social networks, giving advice, and managing conflict (Stafford & Canary, 1991; Stafford et al., 2000). People who regularly employ maintenance strategies tend to report more liking for their partner, more commitment to the relationship, and more shared control over the relationship (Canary, Stafford, & Semic, 2002). In addition, the use of maintenance behaviors increases relational satisfaction (Dainton & Aylor, 2002). In particular, providing assurances, such as saying "I will always love you" or "I would be lost without you," is a maintenance strategy that tends to be most strongly associated with liking, commitment, satisfaction, and the mutuality of control (Stafford et al., 2000). Gay and lesbian couples are more likely than heterosexual couples to pursue an equitable division of household tasks, which is a relational maintenance

Relational Maintenance
The actions people take to keep their relationship in a desired state.

Strategic Maintenance
Behaviors that are intentionally performed with the goal of maintaining the relationship.

Routine Maintenance
Behaviors that are performed unintentionally but that help to keep a relationship functioning.

SCHOLAR SPOTLIGHT

Visit the Communication Café on the **companion website** to view a conversation with Jennifer Samp, a communication scholar who studies a wide range of issues related to intimacy and interpersonal communication.

strategy that increases satisfaction (Kurdek, 2006). As these findings indicate, enacting relational maintenance strategies can positively influence people's perceptions of their close relationships.

INSIDE COMMUNICATION RESEARCH

Maintaining Military Relationships

Even during the mundane routines of everyday life, maintaining a romantic relationship requires hard work and effort. When couples face unexpected and challenging circumstances in their relationship, they must employ even more varied and unique strategies to maintain closeness and intimacy. One context in which romantic partners may be highly vigilant about their efforts at relational maintenance is when military couples are separated during deployment. To better understand how military couples maintain their relationship when one partner is deployed, Andy Merolla (2010) interviewed 33 wives of deployed U.S. service members about the strategies they used to maintain their relationship. The results of his study revealed that relational maintenance is both uniquely challenging and uniquely rewarding during deployment.

During the interviews, the 33 military wives were asked how they maintain feelings of connection with their spouse who was deployed. The interviews were then evaluated to identify similar themes across all of the women's experiences. The first way that military wives maintain closeness with their partners during deployment is through intrapersonal strategies, or behaviors they can do when they are alone to feel more connected. Examples of intra-personal strategies include prayer, journaling, remembering happy times together, and thinking about the future. The second strategy used to maintain military relationships was mediated interaction between partners. For example, the wives reported using phone calls, video messages, letters, and webcams to connect with their deployed husband. The final way that wives maintained a sense of connection with their spouse was through social networks. In other words, they relied on support from their family, peers, and community to strengthen their relationship.

The interviewees also reported a number of internal and external factors that influenced their relational maintenance. In terms of external factors, the couples were often constrained in terms of when they could communicate and for how long. In terms of internal factors, many couples restrained themselves in terms of what topics to discuss. They didn't want to share information that might cause distress or worry and they avoided topics that might lead to disagreement or conflict. This study shows how challenging circumstances in relationships can alter the ways in which people attempt to maintain their closeness, but also that partners are able to adapt their behaviors in response to life events.

THINK ABOUT IT

1. In what ways might a couple's relational maintenance strategies differ if they were separated by circumstances other than deployment, such as a job or school? How might the risks of deployment create unique conditions for relational maintenance?
2. In this study, Merolla only interviewed the wives of deployed military personnel. Do you think the results would have been different if he had interviewed the deployed service member instead? Why or why not?

Coping with Tension

Your efforts to maintain intimacy are complicated by tensions that naturally arise within close relationships. **Relational dialectics theory** is a perspective that emphasizes the trade-offs and conflicting desires that create tension within close relationships (Baxter & Montgomery, 1996). In general, a dialectic is a conflict between two opposing, but also unified, ideas or forces. For example, liberalism and conservatism are two political perspectives that exist in opposition to each other, but that also gain meaning and strength by existing in contrast to each other. In the context of a close relationship, a **relational dialectic** refers to opposition between alternative ways of being intimate. These tensions can be internal, meaning that opposing views of intimacy exist within the relationship, or external, in which the tension is between the relationship as a unit and people outside the relationship. Just as opposing political views are preferred at different times by different people, different relationship ideals might be preferred by one partner more than the other, or might be more or less desirable at different times. As summarized in Table 10.2 and the paragraphs that follow, relational dialectics theory highlights three core tensions that can surface as both internal and external dialectics.

One basic source of tension in close relationships arises from the trade-offs between being open and maintaining privacy. As an internal dialectic, this tension creates a struggle between disclosing information to a partner and keeping silent on some issues. Although you may want to share personal details in order to develop your bond, revealing or withholding too much information could threaten the relationship. As an external dialectic, this tension surfaces in the sometimes difficult decision to share news of a relationship with other people. Revealing information about a relationship to outsiders allows them to support your bond, but it also invites them to criticize or interfere with your relationship. In fact, people report the greatest amount of interference from their social network when they are escalating a romantic relationship from casual to serious involvement (Knobloch & Donovan-Kicken, 2006). Thus, revealing and concealing your relationship both have advantages and disadvantages.

HOW DO YOU RATE? 10.2

Strategies for Maintaining Intimate Relationships

To evaluate the extent to which you use the various relational maintenance strategies in your own relationship, visit the **companion website** to complete Daniel Canary and Laura Stafford's (1992) relational maintenance scale. As you reflect on your score, is the amount of relationship maintenance you do a good match for your level of commitment or satisfaction in this relationship?

TABLE 10.2 Internal and external relational dialectics

Core issues	Internal One partner vs. The other partner	External Both partners vs. Others
Openness vs. Privacy	Share everything with a partner vs. Keep some matters to yourself	Reveal your relationship to others vs. Conceal your relationship from others
Novelty vs. Predictability	Maintain mystery and intrigue vs. Know what is going to happen	Have a special and unique relationship vs. Avoid a weird and unusual relationship
Autonomy vs. Connection	Be an independent person vs. Maintain a close, interdependent bond	Spend time together away from others vs. Spend time together with others

PAUSE & REFLECT

How do you manage the tension between revealing and concealing information when you communicate using social media? Do you tend to reveal more information, because of the physical separation, or less information?

Another core tension stems from your desire to have both novelty and predictability in close relationships. If you feel bored when a relationship is predictable but uneasy when there are too many surprises, you may have difficulty finding the right blend of routine and mystery. You might also struggle with how novel or predictable you would like your relationship to appear to outsiders. You probably don't want to have an "ordinary" or "typical" relationship, and prefer that your relationship was considered "special." At the same time, other people might question your relationship if it's too unusual – for example, if you became close more rapidly than normal, if you have unusual rules about how often you see each other, or if you allow behaviors that are typically off-limits. Whether this tension is internal or external, it captures your need for certainty in a relationship, as well as that "spark" that makes it interesting and unique.

Finally, you can experience internal and external dialectics caused by wanting to have both independence and autonomy while maintaining an intimate connection. Internal tension, about autonomy and connection may be especially prevalent within more intimate romantic relationships (Baxter, 1988). When you and a partner have integrated your activities, goals, and values, you may begin to feel like your own identity is getting lost; but if you assert your independence, you might make the relationship less close. Research on homosexual dating couples reveals that lesbian couples tend to favor connection and are quick to merge their lives together, whereas gay males are more likely to foster autonomy in their romantic associations (Gray & Isensee, 1996). As an external tension, the autonomy and connection dialectic reflects the struggle for a couple to interact with the social network and still have time to be alone together. If the couple spends too much time together, they lose touch with the group and the others might resent their relationship. But if they never get to be alone together, they lose their special connection. The tension, then, is between cementing a relationship and being constrained by it.

Dialectical contradictions are an ongoing tension in relationships, but partners are not necessarily helpless against these influential forces. Table 10.3 summarizes eight coping strategies people might use in the face of relational dialectics (Baxter & Montgomery, 1996). Although some strategies, like denial and disorientation, might seem dysfunctional because they do not acknowledge both sides of a dialectic, they can provide a break when tensions are overwhelming. Other strategies, including spiraling alteration and segmentation, allow partners to pursue different sides of tension at different times or in different aspects of the relationship. Partners might also find a way to embrace both sides of a dialectic through strategies that balance or integrate competing forces. And through strategies such as recalibration and reaffirmation, partners might come to accept dialectical tensions as either complementary or at least inevitable.

TABLE 10.3 Strategies for coping with dialectical tensions

Coping strategy	Example
DENIAL: Selecting one pole of a dialectical tension and ignoring the other	You give up your own autonomy and put all your energy into achieving an intimate connection with your partner.
DISORIENTATION: Retreating into feelings of helplessness and limited dialogue	You withdraw from the relationships to avoid the stress created by the dialectical tension.
SPIRALING ALTERATION: Cycling between the different sides of a dialectical tension at different times	You and your partner spend Friday evenings and Saturdays with each other, but Saturday nights you each go out with your own friends.
SEGMENTATION: Pursing different sides of a dialectical tensions in different aspects of a relationship	You and your partner decide to share information about your feelings and goals for the relationship, but you keep the issues that upset you at work or school to yourself.
BALANCE: Acknowledging the legitimacy of both sides of a dialectical tension and seeking a compromise	You and your partner recognize the importance of spending time alone as a couple and together with your group of friends; you talk openly about making time for both.
INTEGRATION: Finding ways to respond to both sides of a dialectical tension simultaneously	You and your partner agree upon a regularly scheduled date night, but you take turns planning unique and special dates to share together.
RECALIBRATION: Reframing a situation so that the two sides of a dialectical tension no longer seem to be in conflict	You and your partner focus on how pursing your independent interests and goals allows you to have a more interesting and desirable connection.
REAFFIRMATION: Accepting that dialectical tensions will always be part of the relationship	You and your partner appreciate tensions as natural and even rewarding byproducts of being in love and sharing an intimate relationship.

Putting Theory into Practice: Maintaining Intimate Relationships

Keeping your intimate relationships running smoothly is not an easy task. Not unlike a car, your relationships need to be given fuel, have regular tune-ups, and occasionally get major service or repairs.

Make strategic relational maintenance part of your routine. Recall that routine maintenance refers to activities you do with or for your partner as a matter of course; although they aren't intentionally designed to keep you and your partner close, they have that effect. Strategic maintenance is more purposeful action that has the goal of keeping your relationship in a desired state. When you make strategic maintenance a part of your routine, you can prevent problems from emerging in the first place.

COMMUNICATION IN ACTION 10.2

Making Relational Maintenance Part of the Routine

Visit the **companion website** to complete a form that will help you reflect on the ways you can make relational maintenance a more strategic component of your relationship.

Develop skills for coping with dialectical tensions. Although clear guidelines for responding to dialectical tensions are not possible, you can improve your coping potential by having several strategies at your disposal. If you have several ways that you can cope with these tensions, you increase the likelihood that you'll find one that works when you need it.

COMMUNICATION IN ACTION 10.3

Coping with Relational Dialectics

Think of your most recent experience with a dialectical tension in either a friendship or romantic relationship. Then, note which of the eight strategies for coping with relational dialectics (see Table 10.3) you used in that situation. Using the form on the **companion website**, generate some additional steps that you can take to address that relational dialectic in the future.

INDIVIDUAL DIFFERENCES IN INTIMACY

One challenge to intimate relationships is that they involve two people who might have quite different approaches to close relationships. For example, people have different ways of thinking about intimacy, depending on the experiences they had as young children. Likewise, men and women sometimes have distinct ways of relating in social situations. Our age and experience also cause us to view relationships in different ways. In this section, we discuss some of the personal characteristics that shape how people communicate within intimate relationships.

FIGURE 10.4 Mother playing with young child

Source: iStockPhoto.

Attachment Style

A general orientation toward close relationships that reflects how people see themselves in relation to others.

Secure Attachment

A bond characterized by comfort with closeness and an ability to trust or be trusted by others.

Insecure Attachment

A bond characterized by a lack of confidence in close relationships.

Attachment Styles

One personal trait that is especially relevant to romantic relationships is **attachment style** – a general orientation toward close relationships that reflects how people see themselves in relation to others. **Secure attachment** is characterized by comfort with closeness and an ability to trust or be trusted by others. In contrast, **insecure attachment** is characterized by less confidence in relationships. Moreover, an attachment style formed in early childhood is assumed to influence how people approach their romantic relationships as adults (Hazan & Shaver, 1987).

Attachment styles develop based on the bond between parents and children. As summarized in Table 10.4, four adult attachment styles can be distinguished by the views of self and others that emerge from childhood experiences (Bartholomew, 1990). People with a secure attachment style have a positive view of both themselves and others, which allows them to feel equally comfortable with intimacy and autonomy. A preoccupied attachment style combines a positive view of others with relatively low self-esteem; people with this style desire closeness with others, but worry that their partners don't really want the relationship. Because a dismissing attachment style couples a positive view of the self with a negative view of others, people with this style tend to distrust others, deny the need for closeness in their lives, and are comfortable with independence. Finally, people with a fearful attachment style have a negative view of both self and others that causes them to get anxious when people get too close to them.

Because an attachment style reflects a person's way of thinking about intimate bonds, it affects a wide variety of experiences in romantic relationships. For example, people with a secure, rather than insecure, attachment style describe their romantic relationships as lasting longer, being more satisfying, and involving more intimacy, commitment, and

TABLE 10.4 Adult attachment styles defined by positive and negative views of self and others

		View of Self	
		Positive	*Negative*
View of Others	*Positive*	**SECURE** People with this style are comfortable being close to others; they feel that they can trust and be trusted by others	**PREOCCUPIED** People with this style want to be close to others, but doubt whether other people really care about them
	Negative	**DISMISSING** People with this style believe that other people are unreliable or untrustworthy; accordingly, they avoid relationships and deny the need for closeness	**FEARFUL** People with this style trust neither themselves nor others; as a result, being close to other people makes them feel uncomfortable and anxious

trust (Collins & Read, 1990; Feeney & Noller, 1991). Securely attached people also tend to use more prosocial maintenance strategies, such as providing assurances and being romantic, than people with insecure attachment styles (Simon & Baxter, 1993). The benefits of a secure attachment style have also been observed in friendships, where the partners of securely attached people report greater relationship satisfaction, more prosocial maintenance behaviors, and more compromising conflict behavior than the friends of people with other attachment styles (Bippus & Rollin, 2003). Although this work suggests that secure attachment styles promote happy relationships, the more general point is that people bring different views of intimacy to their relationships.

PAUSE & REFLECT

How does your attachment style affect how you communicate with close relationship partners?

Sex Differences and Intimacy

When we talk about personal relationships in our classes, students often report frustration over the way an opposite sex partner handles aspects of their relationship. They wonder, "Why doesn't he open up to me more?" "Why does she always want to talk about the same things over and over again?" "Why won't he do things to show me that he loves me." Or, "I told her that I love her, what more does she want?" Although carefully conducted research concludes that the differences between males and females are often exaggerated (Canary & Hause, 1993), there do seem to be some important differences that emerge in the context of intimate relationships.

One distinction between males and females is how they tend to enact intimacy in close, same-sex friendships. In general, female friendships feature mutual self-disclosure, whereas male friendships typically involve the enjoyment of shared activities (Fehr, 2004; Floyd, 1997). This claim doesn't mean that males don't sometimes share their thoughts and feelings, and that females don't engage in adventures together. But not unlike the portrayal of female friendship in the series *Sex and the City*, women are more likely than men to pass their time together discussing their relationships, their personal failings and goals, and how they feel about anything from their shoe size to their values. Although male friendships can be very close and very important to the partners, they are more likely than female friendships to involve shared activities like participating in sports together, going places together, or talking about matters – politics, sports, or work – that are more public issues.

There are also sex differences in how males and females approach heterosexual romantic relationships. Although many sex differences are exaggerated, some important distinctions between males and females may stem from the unique roles they play in heterosexual mating and reproduction (Buss, 1995). For example, because females are the ones who must bear children and can have fewer offspring than males, they may select

FIGURE 10.5 Two women chatting over coffee

Source: iStockPhoto.

mates more carefully (Kenrick, Trost, & Sundie, 2004) and work harder at maintaining a good relationship (Dainton & Stafford, 1993). In addition, males tend to be drawn to females who are physically attractive, and females tend to be attracted to males who have resources and are willing to make a commitment (Buss & Reeve, 2003). For these reasons, males tend to become more distressed when romantic rivals have more resources, and females tend to become more distressed when romantic rivals are more physically attractive. In addition, males are more likely to become angry when a partner withholds sex and is moody or self-absorbed, and females are more likely to become angry when a partner is inconsiderate, condescending, or inattentive.

When it comes to explaining differences between men and women in close relationships, biological sex may be less relevant than **gender orientation**, the extent to which a person identifies with feminine and/or masculine characteristics. When masculinity and femininity are seen as separate dimensions of personality, we can recognize the four different gender orientations that are identified in Table 10.5. Gender orientation is a good predictor of how hard people work on maintaining a relationship; in particular, femininity is associated with more routine openness, advice giving, nurturing, and conflict management; whereas masculinity corresponds with the strategic use of

Gender Orientation

The extent to which a person identifies with feminine and/or masculine characteristics.

TABLE 10.5 Four gender orientations

		Femininity	
		High	*Low*
Masculinity	*High*	**ANDROGYNS** People who integrate contents of both masculine and feminine gender orientations into their identity	**MASCULINES** People who identify primarily with typically masculine traits, characteristics, and feelings
	Low	**FEMININES** People who identify primarily with typically feminine traits, characteristics, and feelings	**UNDIFFERENTIATED** People who do not identify with any of the thoughts, characteristics, or feelings that are ascribed to either gender orientation

openness and shared tasks (Aylor & Dainton, 2004; Lamke, Sollie, Durbin, & Fitzpatrick, 1994). Research has also found that people with androgynous gender orientations are more likely to maintain satisfying relationships than individuals who are predominantly masculine or feminine (Ickes, 1985).

Friendship across the Lifespan

Although friendships are important from childhood through old age, changes across the lifespan give rise to different ways of experiencing intimacy. Expectations for friendship

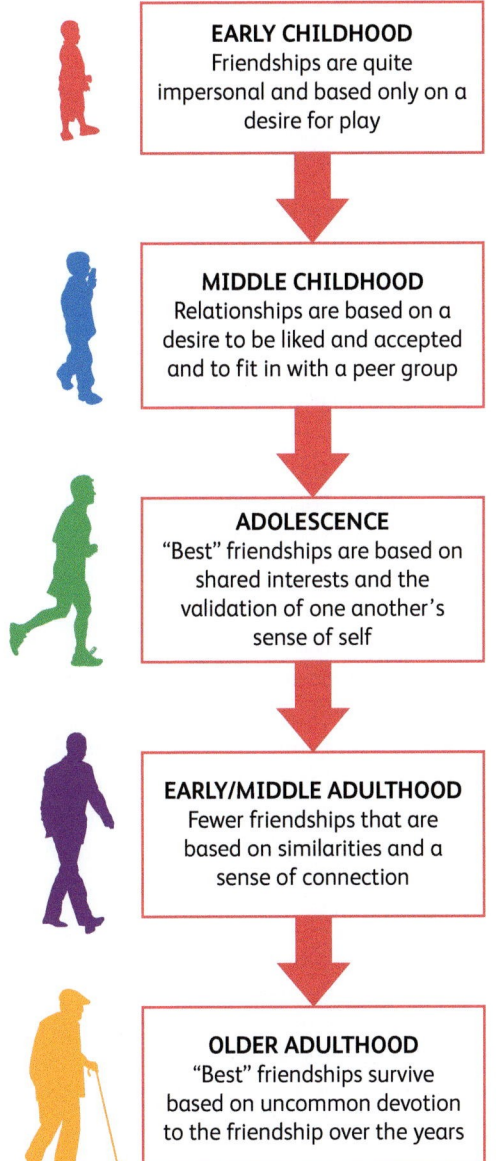

EARLY CHILDHOOD
Friendships are quite impersonal and based only on a desire for play

MIDDLE CHILDHOOD
Relationships are based on a desire to be liked and accepted and to fit in with a peer group

ADOLESCENCE
"Best" friendships are based on shared interests and the validation of one another's sense of self

EARLY/MIDDLE ADULTHOOD
Fewer friendships that are based on similarities and a sense of connection

OLDER ADULTHOOD
"Best" friendships survive based on uncommon devotion to the friendship over the years

FIGURE 10.6 Qualities of friendship across the lifespan

are remarkably stable in light of the huge changes people go through as they age (Rawlins, 2004). At the same time, the meanings you attach to intimacy evolve throughout your life. Figure 10.6 shows the lifespan changes in views of friendship that are described in this section.

From childhood to adolescence. A close look at the friendships that children form with their peers shows important changes from early childhood through adolescence. For young children, the foundation of friendship is play (Haslett & Samter, 1997). In fact, the friendships of children are quite impersonal, especially in comparison to relationships formed later in life. Denise recalls a young girl asking her son, then age 5, if he wanted to be friends; his blunt "no" was shocking to Denise, but the little girl took it in stride. "I guess he doesn't want to do anything," she said calmly. The challenge for young children is coordinating activities, but feelings and conflict are largely (and fortunately!) irrelevant.

PAUSE & REFLECT

What memories do you have of your earliest childhood friend? How did you and your friend spend your time together?

In middle childhood, friendships are about fitting in and being accepted. Being a good friend at this age involves following the rules for play, providing tangible help, and being a skillful communicator (Samter, 2003). In particular, children who can communicate emotions appropriately, have fluent conversations, use humor to make interactions fun, and manage conflicts have distinct advantages over children who can't control their emotions, have speech difficulties, are less playful, and can't resolve disputes. Thus, middle childhood sees the emergence of a view of intimacy that is closely tied to interpersonal communication.

In adolescence, children face desires for both individuality and close bonds with people outside their family; as a result, adolescent friends must find a balance between independence and closeness (Rawlins, 1989; Shulman & Knafo, 1997). The solution appears to be the formation of "best" friendships with people who share values, have similar interests, and validate the teen's emerging sense of self. To these ends, friendships at this age revolve around self-disclosure, problem-solving, and feeling understood (Samter, 2003). A five-year longitudinal study also showed that adolescents are more likely to work at resolving conflicts with a friend, rather than withdrawing or reacting in anger (von Salisch & Vogelgesang, 2005). In total, then, the years from early to late childhood see friendship changing from an impersonal focus on shared activities to a deeply personal focus on a shared identity.

From younger to older adulthood. People have the most friends in late adolescence (and in college, if they attend), and then the size of friendship networks begins to shrink (Dainton, Zelley, & Langan, 2003). In fact, adulthood sees decreases in both the number of friends people have and the amount of time they spend with friends (Noller, Feeney, & Petersen, 2001). These trends may reflect a greater focus on the spousal and parental roles people may fill as adults. In addition, adults juggle demands on their time created by work, home-making, and taking care of aging parents. Like the relationships formed in late adolescence, adult friendships are defined by similarities and a sense of connection; but at this stage of life, day-to-day demands limit the energy people can devote to their friends.

In older adulthood, views of friendship are transformed once again. The elderly tend to be more discriminating about who counts as a best friend, and they reserve that title for someone who has demonstrated uncommon devotion to the relationship (Patterson, Bettini, & Nussbaum, 1993). Geographical separation has less of an impact on the friendships of older adults, relative to relationships earlier in life (Nussbaum, Hummert, Williams, & Harwood, 1996); however, older adults benefit from having local friends who give them opportunities to socialize (Bitzan & Kruzich, 1990; Gupta & Korte, 1994). Especially for residents of nursing homes, having a friend can be a crucial to feeling satisfied with life (Nussbaum, 1991).

One particular challenge for elderly friends is finding a balance between maintaining independence and providing help (Rawlins, 2004). The friends of older adults provide a confidant, a companion, and someone to chat with who is outside the family network (Samter, 2003). The feelings of independence fostered by friendship, however, can be undermined when older adults have to rely on those friends for more tangible assistance, like transportation and medical advice. In fact, older adults feel lonely when they have to rely on their friends too much or when their friends are overly dependent on them (Rook, 1987). After a lifetime forging friendships grounded in similarity and mutuality, older adults may find it difficult to adopt passing time and providing help – those qualities that define childhood friendships – as the basis for their intimate relationships.

Putting Theory into Practice: Embracing Individual Differences

This section of the chapter has explored just a few of the ways that people can differ in their experience of intimacy. Armed with this knowledge, you can embrace individual differences in relationships.

Avoid "attachment-centrism." Keep in mind that your attachment style is only one of the ways in which people might view close relationships. By respecting the relationship beliefs of others, you might find ways to relate to other people on their own terms.

COMMUNICATION IN ACTION 10.4

Assessing the Pros and Cons of Attachment Styles

Review the four attachment styles summarized in Table 10.4. For each style, use the form on the **companion website** try to identify two strengths or benefits enjoyed by people with that attachment style, and two challenges those individuals must face.

Keep sex and age differences in perspective. Although sex and age differences in approaches to intimacy are worth noting, it's also important that you don't exaggerate their effects. One of the mistakes we make in life is assuming that men and women are locked into male and female ways of communicating. Or that young people can't experience mature relationships and that the elderly can't be enthralled by a romantic fling. You can enrich your experience of intimacy in your relationships by being open to the variety of ways in which you can experience close bonds with others. Begin by thinking about how your approach to close relationships might be limiting your options. As you reflect on your close relationships, try to identify the qualities – shared activities, a sense of belonging, feeling understood, or tangible help – you have used to define your intimate relationships. After identifying your priorities for intimacy, take note of the aspects of intimacy that you tend to neglect. By incorporating those qualities into your close relationships, you might have more complete and fulfilling experiences.

EXTREMES OF INTIMACY

As we have seen thus far in this chapter, intimacy includes a variety of components, it can present certain challenges, and people can experience it in different ways. You can also gain an understanding of communication in intimate relationships by considering what happens when intimacy is taken to an extreme – when intimacy is overwhelmingly positive or shattered by infidelity. In this section, we explore the realms of romantic infatuation and betrayal.

Romantic Infatuation

Perhaps one of the strongest and most wonderful emotions you can experience in a relationship is romantic love. When in the throes of romantic love, each day can seem brighter, each problem solvable, and the future unlimited. In the extreme, though, romantic love is not unlike a mental illness; when people are "madly" in love, they might obsess about a partner, feel depressed if separated from a lover, and become emotionally dependent on a partner (Tallis, 2005). People who are intensely in love even show unique patterns of brain activity when they look at pictures of their beloved (Aron et al., 2005), and they have heightened levels of oxytocin, a euphoria-inducing hormone, when they are discussing their affection for a beloved partner (Gonzaga, Turner, Keltner, Campos, & Altemus, 2006). Because intense romantic love is experienced by people of all cultures (Jankowiak & Fischer, 1992), you should be aware of the pros and cons of these strong feelings.

What is romantic love? Romantic love is embodied in four beliefs: love will find a way, one true love exists, relationship perfection is possible, and people can fall in love at first sight (Sprecher & Metts, 1989; Figure 10.7). People who endorse these beliefs generally report more love, satisfaction, and commitment in their romantic relationship (Sprecher & Metts, 1999). People are also happier when they idealize a partner and believe that a partner idealizes them (Murray, Holmes, & Griffin, 1996). College students who believe that true love can overcome obstacles also feel that love is more important

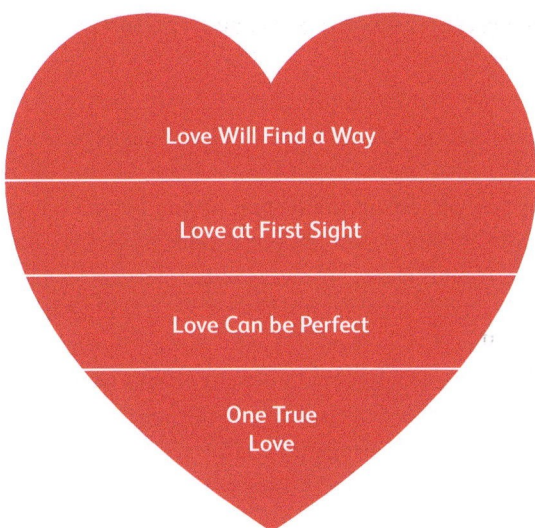

FIGURE 10.7 Romantic beliefs

than sexual intimacy, love should come before sex, sex is an expression of love, and sexual intimacy decreases with the length of a love relationship (Hendrick & Hendrick, 2002). Moreover, people who believe that they are destined to love their partner are also more likely to avoid conflict (Knee, 1998) or give in on conflict issues (Franiuk, Cohen, & Pomerantz, 2002). Thus, believing in and experiencing romantic love can have several benefits for relationship partners.

> ### PAUSE & REFLECT
>
> Have you ever been "head over heels" in love? If so, what impact did your feelings have on your communication with your beloved partner?

Being in love, however, is not without some downsides. If you endorse the notion of one true love, but don't think you're dating him or her, you'll probably be less satisfied with that relationship (Franiuk et al., 2002). Moreover, you may lose your ability to see your partner's faults when you are under love's spell. When people are infatuated, they tend to disregard relationship warning signs, such as evidence that the other person has different values (McLanahan, Gold, Lenney, Ryckman, & Kulberg, 1990; Thompson, Gold, & Ryckman, 2003). People who are in love even overestimate how in love they think other couples are (Aloni & Berneirni, 2004). Thus, infatuation or a belief in romantic ideals may represent a rather immature form of love, more commonly endorsed by young adults in their late teens (Knox, Schacht, & Zusman, 1999; Noller, 1996).

Romantic Betrayal

Sexual Infidelity
Having physical intimacy with someone other than a committed romantic partner.

Emotional Infidelity
Devoting time, attention, and feelings to someone other than a committed romantic partner.

Whereas romantic love highlights the euphoria you can feel in close relationships, romantic betrayal focuses on one of the most devastating experiences that can occur. In the context of a close relationship, infidelity involves violating the obligation to forego intimacy with other people. **Sexual infidelity** is having physical closeness with someone outside the primary relationship, and **emotional infidelity** is devoting time, attention, and feelings to someone other than the relationship partner. Both types of infidelity violate expectations for monogamy in committed romantic relationships, but they evoke different reactions. In particular, sexual infidelity causes partners to become angry and blame the "cheater," whereas emotional infidelity causes victims to feel hurt (Green & Sabini, 2006). Men also find it more difficult than women to forgive a partner for sexual infidelity (Shackelford, Buss, & Bennett, 2002).

Precise estimates of the frequency of infidelity are hard to obtain; however, one study found that 65% of college students reported being intimately involved with someone else while in a committed dating relationship (Shackelford, LeBlanc, & Drass, 2000). What influences whether a person is unfaithful to a dating partner? Perhaps not surprisingly, people are less likely to cheat on a partner they are committed to or find sexually desirable (Drigotas, Safstrom, & Gentilita, 1999; Regan, 2000). Conversely, people are more susceptible to infidelity when a current relationship doesn't fulfill their needs (Lewandowski & Ackerman, 2006). Certain kinds of people may also be more likely to cheat than others. In particular, people who are generally promiscuous, impulsive, and have a dismissive or fearful attachment style are more likely to engage in sexual infidelity (Feldman & Cauffman, 1999; McAlister, Pachana, & Jackson, 2005).

Reactions to infidelity can range from ending the relationship to forgiving the cheater – just how people respond to infidelity is influenced by the circumstances of the betrayal, its discovery, and how partners make sense of it. For example, people find infidelity involving someone new to be less upsetting and more forgivable than being unfaithful with a former partner (Cann & Baucom, 2004). Infidelity also has a less negative impact on the relationship when people hear about the affair directly from their partner, as opposed to catching their partner in the act or hearing about it from other people (Afifi, Falato, & Weiner, 2001). And ultimately, whether relationships can survive betrayal depends on whether the victims of an unfaithful partner can manage to forgive the transgression (Hall & Fincham, 2006).

PAUSE & REFLECT

What would you do if a partner was unfaithful to you? Would you react differently to sexual versus emotional infidelity?

An unfaithful person can also shape the consequences of infidelity through his or her communication with the partner. Confessing an affair can elicit more forgiveness than waiting until a partner discovers the infidelity or forces the truth to come out (Afifi

FIGURE 10.8 Timing

Source: www.cartoonstock.com.

et al., 2001), but communicating about infidelity is a complicated matter. One study asked college students to describe what they would say to a romantic partner if they committed a hypothetical act of sexual infidelity (Mongeau & Schulz, 1997). The results of that study showed that people are more likely to offer an explanation and to be honest about an affair when they are sure a partner already knows about it. When people want to maintain their relationship, they also offer more concessions and excuses, rather than justifying their behavior. The study also highlighted the dilemma created when people aren't sure whether a partner knows about an affair. Under those circumstances, unfaithful partners tend to hold back an admission of guilt, while they offer more excuses for their behavior; by doing so, they can clarify why an affair might have happened, without providing too much information that the partner doesn't already have.

Putting Theory into Practice: Keeping Your Head When Falling In Love

When you're in the throes of intense love, you might be compelled to do anything for your partner, forgive his or her offenses, and take risks to be with that partner. And if you experience a partner's infidelity, you might also be moved to extreme behavior – perhaps ending a relationship you value or maintaining it despite the violation. The common thread that runs through experiences of infatuation or infidelity is the need to keep your wits about you when communicating with your partner.

Stay grounded when you're head over heels. Intense romantic love is a physical condition; your body and brain chemistry experience real changes when you are infatuated with a romantic partner. This intense experience can create a lifelong bond between partners, but the euphoria of being in love can make you blind to trouble spots in your relationship. You can avoid overlooking problems when you're in love by taking steps to maintain a realistic point of view:

- Ask your friends to point out potential issues that may present challenges in the future.
- Take short breaks from the relationship so that you can catch your breath and reassess the situation.
- Avoid doing anything that you would find unacceptable if you weren't intoxicated by your feelings.

By reminding your friends and yourself that infatuation needs supervision, you can make sure that your feelings of love don't lead you astray.

Take charge of infidelity. Infidelity is one of the worst betrayals a person can commit or experience. At the same time, infidelity isn't uncommon in romantic relationships. Are there ways that communication can help you weather the storm created by unfaithful behavior? Although perhaps nothing can prepare you for the consequences of violating a partner's trust or having that trust violated, there are strategies that might help you control the course of infidelity:

- If you are being unfaithful to your partner because you lack commitment to the relationship, you need to find a more appropriate way to dissolve that bond.
- If you are being unfaithful, but you are committed to maintaining that primary relationship, you need to end your affair and address your betrayal.
- Keep in mind that your partner will take the news of your infidelity better if he or she hears it from you first.
- Be prepared to take responsibility for your actions and be aware that your partner is largely in control over his or her forgiveness and the future of your relationship.
- If you find yourself on the receiving end of a confession of infidelity, it is important that you know your own boundaries for what you can and cannot accept in a relationship and that you take time to decide what you want to happen in that relationship.
- Keep in mind that infidelity isn't uncommon.

Whether you feel that the betrayal can never be overcome or you value the relationship enough to try again, your communication choices can control what direction you go in the future.

SUMMARY

This chapter opened by exploring the nature of intimacy in close friendships and romantic relationships. Rather than being a single entity, intimacy is a blend of closeness, openness, trust, affection, and mutuality. The love you might feel for a relationship partner can also vary depending on the amount of intimacy, passion, or commitment that is present. In fact, people can experience love in different ways, depending on their focus on sexuality, game-playing, or friendship.

Once you achieve close bonds with a friend or romantic partner, communication becomes a tool for maintaining intimacy. Relational maintenance behaviors include a variety of activities – providing assurances, being open, being positive, sharing tasks, enjoying social networks, giving advice, and managing conflicts – that help you to keep a relationship going. Although you might perform these behaviors strategically with the goal of maintaining intimacy, they also occur as part of routine communication in close relationships. Communication and relational maintenance can be especially important when you are confronted with tensions arising from relational dialectics. Whether your problems stem from internal or external dialectics focused on the trade-offs between openness and privacy, novelty and predictability, or autonomy and connection, you can use communication to manage the pushes and pulls we feel in intimate relationships.

Communication in close relationships is further complicated by the fact that people bring distinct views of intimacy to their friendships and romances. Because a person's attachment style is a view of intimacy based on early childhood experiences, it may be an especially strong influence on adult romantic relationships. Likewise, men and women may be predisposed to view certain aspects of friendships and romantic relationships in distinct ways. As you age, you also go through changes or have experiences that shape how you view friendship. As you form friendships and romantic relationships throughout your life, you will undoubtedly encounter many different views of intimacy.

Another way to think about how intimacy varies is to reflect on the extreme experiences created by infatuation and infidelity. Intimacy can be a life-changing, positive experience when you find yourself in the throes of intense, romantic love. You should also bear in mind that love can, in fact, blind you to your partner's flaws and relational fault lines. And intimacy can be a life-changing, devastating experience when you engage in or discover sexual or emotional infidelity. Keeping in mind the frequency, causes, and outcomes of infidelity might help you to keep these betrayals from undermining intimate relationships that you value.

Intimate friendships and romantic relationships are the context for some of your most important interpersonal communication experiences. From the ways in which you experience and express intimacy to the behaviors that you use to maintain intimate bonds, communication is at the core of your closest relationships. When you recognize the enormous task that communication performs within intimate relationships, and the complexities introduced by individual differences and intimate extremes, you might wonder if there is any way to communicate more effectively with intimate partners. As we have seen in this chapter, you can take an active role and develop communication skills that will help you to foster and enjoy intimate relationships.

ACTIVITIES FOR EXPLORING COMMUNICATION ETHICS

What Would You/Should You Do?

In this chapter, you learned that mutuality is an important part of intimacy; in other words, intimacy involves partners who share interest in and responsibility for their relationship. What would you do if you had a friend who was investing a lot more in a romantic relationship than his or her partner? Perhaps your friend is doing all of the routine and strategic maintenance, or perhaps you know that your friend's partner has been spending time with other people. What would you, or should you, do when someone you care about is being taken advantage of by another relationship partner?

Something to Think About

Among the more compelling and popular explanations for sex differences in communication is that men and women developed different approaches to social relationships through the process of evolution and natural selection. More specifically, because men and women play distinct roles in reproduction and child bearing, they have distinct priorities and strategies when it comes to sexual relationships. Although scholars working from these assumptions would argue that there is a lot of evidence to support them (see Buss & Reeve, 2003), it's important to remember the by-products of evolution were shaped by the conditions experienced by long-ago ancestors. What are the ethical limits of using evolution to explain human behavior in the present?

Analyze Communication Ethics Yourself

Ageism in American society ranges from job discrimination to people's tendency to communicate with older adults as though they are children. One form of ageism is assuming that the elderly have outgrown the need for non-familial friendships and romantic relationships. This bias can have serious consequences within nursing homes, where institutional structures can determine whether or not residents have an opportunity to enjoy social relationships. Visit a nursing home in your community and observe the opportunities for socializing provided by that institution. Are residents treated like adults who have social needs? Can you identify any practices that encourage or discourage friendships and romantic relationships? As you reflect on your observations, consider the ethical responsibilities created when an institution is in control of people's communication opportunities.

KEY WORDS

attachment style

attachment theory

complete/consummate love

emotional infidelity

eros

gender orientation

insecure attachment

intimacy

ludus

relational dialectic

relational dialectics theory

relational maintenance

routine maintenance

secure attachment

sexual infidelity

storge

strategic maintenance

After reading this chapter, you should be able to:

1. Explain the functions that are served by the family.
2. Identify the different parts of a family system.
3. Understand why family members keep and reveal secrets.
4. Describe the communication patterns that occur within different types of couples.
5. Understand the communication challenges that emerge across the family lifespan.
6. Strengthen your ability to promote family well-being through interpersonal communication.

PUTTING THEORY INTO PRACTICE

In this chapter, you will learn how to:

1. Expand your family to meet your needs.
2. Address the challenges of blending families.
3. Communicate protection and affection.
4. Respect the boundaries of your family system.
5. Practice safe secrets.
6. Anticipate changes over the family lifespan.
7. Keep the lines of communication open.

COMMUNICATION IN FAMILIES

11

294 WHAT IS A FAMILY?

299 COMMUNICATION IN FAMILY SYSTEMS

305 THE FAMILY LIFESPAN

315 SUMMARY

317 ACTIVITIES FOR EXPLORING COMMUNICATION ETHICS

317 KEY WORDS

Source: Photo by James Devaney/WireImage.

Angelina Jolie and Brad Pitt have been the target of much public scrutiny about their relationship and their children. Both Angelina and Brad have been married previously, but in their relationship together they have chosen not to enter this legally binding commitment and share somewhat of a nontraditional relationship. They are also the parents to six children. Before meeting Brad, Angelina adopted her son, Maddox, from Cambodia and her daughter, Zahara, from Ethiopia. After Brad and Angelina got together, Brad became the adoptive father of Maddox and Zahara and the couple adopted their third son, Pax, from Vietnam. Brad and Angelina are also the biological parents to three children: their daughter Shiloh and their twins Knox and Viviene. Although the diversity of the "Brangelina" clan is somewhat unique, Brad and Angelina's decisions about their family mirror some of the trends that have been observed in the modern American family, such as an increased number of step-families, blended families, and non-married parents. Not surprisingly, these diverse family situations confront unique communication challenges.

Throughout people's lives, family remains one of the stable touchstones that they can turn to for comfort or help. At the same time, family life can sometimes be distressing, frustrating, or hurtful. Brad Pitt and Angelina Jolie have created a loving and open family for themselves and their children, but consider the challenges that their family might face. They may struggle to keep their family matters private from the media. The children might enjoy having many siblings to play with, but they might also have to compete for the attention of their parents. And not unlike non-celebrity families, divorce and the formation of a family with adopted and biological children can strain relationships between family members. In this chapter, we examine the rewards and challenges of interpersonal communication within families so that you can promote the well-being of these critical relationships.

WHAT IS A FAMILY?

Ideas about what constitutes the typical American family have changed significantly over the last half century, and family dynamics have changed with them. We see these changing images of family reflected in TV sit-coms and dramas. Consider the 1960s hit, *Leave It to Beaver*, which focused on a nuclear family made up of a working father, stay-at-home mother, and two sons. The 1970s brought *The Brady Bunch*, which told the story of a blended family formed by the marriage of formerly single parents. In the eight-year run of *The Cosby Show* in the 1980s, the Huxtables nuclear family (now with a working mother) evolved into an extended family complete with grandparents, adult children, and step-grandchildren. More recently, *Modern Family* depicts the life of a complex extended family, with the divorced patriarch of the family married to a much younger woman who has a child from a previous relationship, his gay son who has adopted a daughter from Vietnam with his partner, and his daughter who is married with three children. In this section, we look at the facts behind these images as we explore the dynamics of contemporary family life.

The Changing Face of Families

Sociologists analyzing U.S. census data have detailed the changing face of families (Mather & Lavery, 2010). Compared to previous generations, today's adults typically wait longer to marry and might never marry. In the 1960s, more than 80% of adults aged 25–34 were married, but in 2010 only 45% of adults in the same age group reported that they were married. Among the total population over the age of 18, only 52% of adults were married in 2010, which is the lowest percentage of married individuals since the U.S. started collecting data on marriage rates 100 years ago. A number of reasons account for the decline in marriage in recent years, including rising divorce rates, an increase in women's educational attainment and participation in the work force, and a rise in cohabitation as an alternative or precursor to marriage. Between 2009 and 2010 alone, there was a 13% increase in the number of opposite sex couples who were cohabiting, with 7.5 million cohabiting couples, and a 30% increase in the number of same-sex partners who were cohabiting, up to 620,000 couples (Kreider, 2010). Divorce is also on the rise with about 40% of marriages eventually terminating (Hurley, 2005). These statistics remind us that many people remain single, live with a partner, or form a domestic partnership rather than get legally married.

Decreases in marriages and the frequency of divorce have contributed to changes in family structure. As of 2010, 16% of white children, 27% of Hispanic children, and 52% of African American children lived in a single-parent household (Mather, 2010). And when people marry or remarry after they have children, they also face the task of combining their pre-existing households within a stepfamily. Interviews with members of stepfamilies reveal important challenges (Golish, 2003). For example, children often feel caught between their parents and they struggle to negotiate the roles of the non-custodial parent and the step-parent. In addition, members of stepfamilies often compete over resources, have trouble managing different conflict styles, and struggle to develop a sense of solidarity. On a more positive note, stepfamilies are more aware of their struggles, so they are sometimes better at solving problems.

PAUSE & REFLECT

Did you grow up living with two parents, a single parent, grandparents, or a stepfamily? How did that experience influence your view of "family"?

Other U.S. population statistics suggest several alternatives to the family made up of a mother, a father, and their biological children. In vitro fertilization, artificial insemination, or surrogate mothering allow people to have offspring who may or may not be genetically related to them. Adoption is another common way to expand a family – approximately 120,000 children are adopted each year, and 2–4% of American families include an adopted child (U.S. Department of Health and Human Services, 2004). Within the gay community, one-third of lesbian households and one-fifth of gay male households have children (U.S. Census Bureau of Household and Family Statistics,

FIGURE 11.1 Non-traditional family

Source: iStockPhoto.

2000). And the 2002 U.S. Current Population Survey reported that 3.7 million children were living in households managed by a grandparent (Goodman & Silverstein, 2006). Clearly, families can develop and expand in a variety of different ways.

As the characteristics of families have changed over the years, the definitions of marriage and family have expanded to include different kinds of family relationships. Researchers suggest that a family could include any of the following relationships: (a) people who are connected legally, genetically, or because they live together; (b) a group that fills certain needs for its members; or (c) a group that is united by a shared identity, history, and future (Fitzpatrick & Wamboldt, 1990). In general, then, a **family** is a network of people who create a sense of home, share a collective identity, experience a common history, and envision a similar future.

Family

A network of people who create a sense of home, share a collective identity, experience a common history, and envision a similar future.

Functions of the Family

Although families can take many different forms, families of any sort perform a few core functions for their members. For some people, a family provides a network of safety or support that isn't always available from friends. Even people who don't have close relationships with family members gain important social and interpersonal knowledge from their family interactions. In this section, we explore the functions that are served by family relationships.

One of the most basic functions of family is the promise of protection. From birth through childhood, your family members protect you and fulfill your most basic needs for food, shelter, clothing, and warmth. Even after childhood, families may offer support; for example, college students who live in dorms or rentals during the school year might return to their family's home during the summer months. Likewise, some college graduates will live at home until they get a job and can afford to move out on their own. And later in life, family members might find themselves living together again for financial or health reasons.

Family Socialization

The process by which parents teach their children behaviors that are appropriate, expected, moral, or polite.

In addition to the tangible resources that you receive, your family also plays an important role in your socialization as a human being. **Family socialization** is the process by which parents teach their children behaviors that are appropriate, expected, moral, or polite. Through socialization, parents help their children become competent, socially skilled, and emotionally aware (Van Egeren & Barratt, 2002). Consider the example of Jen's aunt, who has two young sons and an infant daughter. Although there are plenty of second-hand boys' clothes in the house, Jen's aunt dresses her daughter in feminine outfits to communicate her gender to other people. She also encourages her boys to say "please" and "thank you" when making requests, rewards the children for sharing with each other, and issues "time outs" when the kids start fighting. And although the oldest son gets his own money through a weekly allowance, he is expected to set some of it aside for charity. Through these efforts, Jen's aunt reinforces gender norms, teaches her children how to be polite and get along with others, and promotes financial responsibility and compassion. As this example suggests, a family provides a context in which we learn social roles and appropriate behaviors.

Beyond teaching children behaviors that are valued and appropriate, the family also educates its members about the traditions and beliefs of the culture in which they live. This process is known as **transmission** – the teaching of cultural practices from one generation to the next. Whereas socialization teaches children how to behave as a well-mannered person in general, transmission teaches family members how to belong to a particular social group with unique cultural practices. For example, parents tell children stories and teach them songs that help them to learn about the history of their country, the beliefs of their religion, or the trials and triumphs of their ethnic group. Likewise, families might display the American flag or religious icons in their home as a reminder of the values that are important to them. And on dates that mark important events within the culture, families have parties, attend religious services, or participate in community celebrations. Through this range of activities, children learn to accept and cherish the same cultural beliefs that are meaningful to their parents.

Transmission
The teaching of cultural practices from one generation to the next.

PAUSE & REFLECT

What are some of the cultural practices you learned from your family? How did your family teach you these practices?

A fourth function served by family is the promise of emotional support and comfort. Being able to turn to your family can be particularly important during difficult times. In fact, one study showed that patients receiving radiation treatment for cancer coped more effectively when they received emotional support from their family (Gotcher, 1993). Kory Floyd, a communication scholar who specializes in family relationships, has paid particular attention to expressions of affection between fathers, sons, and brothers. In general, he has found that today's fathers are more affectionate with their sons than fathers used to be (Morman & Floyd, 2002). Moreover, expressions of affection can improve the father–son relationship (Floyd & Morman, 1998) and the bond between brothers (Floyd, 1997). On the other hand, surveys of fathers and sons have found that heterosexual men tend to receive more affection from their fathers than gay men do, which could contribute to less close family relationships (Floyd, Sargent, & Di Corcia,

2004). In this program of research, Floyd shows how the strength of family ties is influenced by whether members fulfill the promise of support and comfort.

Putting Theory into Practice: Strengthening Family Bonds

Although the characteristics of families have changed considerably in the past few decades, these relationships remain vital to your health and happiness. With an understanding of the functions of family, you can enhance your interpersonal communication experiences.

Expand your family to meet your needs. Although families might be expected to perform the functions previously described, many families fall short of these goals. When families face financial hardships or can't perform their functions because of health, mental, or emotional limitations, its members might not receive the support that they need. What might you do if your family has trouble taking care of you? Remember that family is more than parents and their offspring. A family can include other relatives, as well as unrelated people with whom you have a relationship. Many young adults who are separated from their families to attend college or start a new job will assemble a group of friends to celebrate major holidays, organize birthday parties, or coordinate a ride to the airport. By reaching beyond your nuclear family, you might discover a lot of other people who can perform family functions.

Address the challenges of blending families. People face a number of challenges within blended families. Talking within the family about the difficulties you are facing can help improve the family environment. When families come together, it's important to clarify the role that stepparents should have with the children, strategies for addressing conflict, and the family traditions that you want to preserve. In addition, think about the strengths and weaknesses that each primary family brings to the table and consider strategies that capitalize on each family's strengths and minimize their weaknesses. Perhaps one primary family is really good at addressing conflict and can help the members of their stepfamily adopt better strategies. Maybe one primary family isn't very good at expressing love and affection and could learn how to be better by adopting some of their stepfamily's behaviors. By adopting each family's strengths and discussing how to avoid each family's weaknesses, your blended family can forge the foundation for more effective communication.

Communicate protection and affection. Because protection and emotional support are basic human needs, you can strengthen family bonds by communicating to people that you're there for them. Perhaps you could remind a sibling that he or she can move in with you if they ever need to. Or, you could tell your parents that you'll help them out when they get older. When you protect members of your family from life's hardships, you strengthen family ties and ensure that someone will be there for you when you need help. Expressing affection for family members might even make you feel better yourself. Adults who express more affection to other people have lower levels of stress hormones over the course of their workday (Floyd, 2006), and writing affectionate notes can actually reduce cholesterol levels over time (Floyd, Mikkelson, Hesse, & Pauley, 2007). Thus, expressing affection to family members can both strengthen those relationships and promote your own well-being.

COMMUNICATION IN ACTION 11.1

Expressing Affection

Select a member of your family with whom you would like to share an affectionate message. Then, sit down to write a card or an email to this person explaining all of the reasons you love and care about him or her. Try to be as specific as possible when constructing your message to identify and explain all of the traits that you appreciate about your family member. When you're finished, you might even send the affectionate letter. Whether or not you decide to send the letter, you'll still receive all of the positive benefits to your health and your relationship by expressing your affection.

COMMUNICATION IN FAMILY SYSTEMS

Systems theory is a general perspective that emphasizes how different objects work together to form a larger entity. The human body, for example, is made up of several systems, including the digestive system, the respiratory system, and the neurological system. Each of these systems has several organs, which work together to process food, deliver oxygen to our cells, and send information to and from our brain. There are many other examples of systems in nature, ranging from molecular systems to solar systems. Humans also create systems, such as transportation systems, school systems, or systems of government. In this section, we'll examine the family as a system, as well as the role of communication within family systems.

Systems Theory
A general perspective that emphasizes how different objects work together to form a larger entity.

The Family System

Generally defined, a **system** is a bounded set of objects that interrelate with one another to form a whole. As illustrated by the family system in Figure 11.2, all systems have four core qualities. First, systems are made up of distinct objects – the organs in the digestive system, planets in a solar system, or the members of a family. Second, the objects within a system have specific characteristics, as in the case of family members who have different roles or are different ages. Third, the parts of a system are related to each other in different ways; particular members of a family have special relationships with each other. Finally, a system is bounded, which means that the combined parts create a whole and recognizable entity.

System
A bounded set of objects that interrelate with one another to form a whole.

The family system is made up of several smaller **subsystems**, which are relationships among only a few members of the larger system. For example, a marriage or domestic partnership might be a system that is subsumed within a family. Other subsystems that occur within families might include the relationship between a parent and child, the bonds between siblings, or the ties between divorced parents. Although family members might form their own subsystems, they do not operate in isolation. Rather, the actions, decisions, and communication behaviors within each subsystem both shape and are shaped by the larger system as a whole.

Subsystems
Relationships that are formed between just a few members of the larger system.

PAUSE & REFLECT

What subsystems do you belong to in your family? Do you communicate differently within the different subsystems you belong to?

Enmeshed Systems
Families that prioritize closeness among members rather than rigid boundaries between members or subsystems.

Disengaged System
Families with rigid boundaries that promote the independence of members or subsystems.

Open Families
Families that encourage experiences outside of the family and integrate those experiences into family life.

Closed Families
Families that discourage participation in activities and relationships outside the family.

Figure 11.2: shows how families create different kinds of boundaries between members or subsystems, as well as between the family and outside elements. Within **enmeshed systems**, family members have very little privacy or independence, and they communicate about a wide range of topics. In contrast, **disengaged systems** have rigid internal boundaries, such that family members don't exchange much information, affection, or support. Families can also establish open or closed boundaries between the system and the outside world. In **open families**, members interact freely with outsiders, and they are encouraged to share social experiences with the family. Conversely, members of **closed families** are discouraged from participating in activities and relationships outside their home. The core difference among these family systems is how much members communicate with each other and people outside the family.

FIGURE 11.2 A family system. This depiction of a family illustrates the components of a system:

OBJECTS: The six family members.

CHARACTERISTICS OF OBJECTS: The members of the family vary in terms of their size, age, and gender. Family members also bring other characteristics to the family, such as compassion, sense of humor, or supportiveness.

RELATIONSHIPS: As you can see in the figure, some members of the family have closer relationships than others. The parents are close to each other by virtue of their marriage, the parents have a closer relationship with the infant than some of the other children due to the reliance of infants on their parents to meet needs, and the younger sisters appear to have a closer relationship to each other by virtue of their similar age and gender than do to their older brother.

BOUNDARY: The entire system is bounded because it is recognized as a single family entity.

Managing Communication Boundaries

Managing system boundaries involves controlling who has access to your private information and who does not (Petronio, 2002; Petronio, 2010). Consider all of the private information that members of your family might know about you. Did they witness your most embarrassing moment? Do they remember how scared you were at your first horror film? Do they know how long you sucked your thumb, how you failed your first driving test, and about your first love? Even in less close families, family members have considerable knowledge about each other.

How do family members maintain each other's privacy and create system boundaries? Families establish privacy rules or guidelines for who owns information and whether information is shared with others (Petronio, 2002; Petronio, 2010). Some privacy rules govern the exchange of information between individuals or subsystems within a family. For example, you and your siblings might have a shared understanding that limits what you tell your parents about each other, or perhaps you've refused your parents' friend requests on Facebook so that they can't monitor the information you share online. Privacy rules also let family members know what to tell non-family members. A

SCHOLAR SPOTLIGHT

Visit the Communication Café on the **companion website** to view a conversation with Sandra Petronio, a pioneer in the study of communication boundaries and privacy management in families.

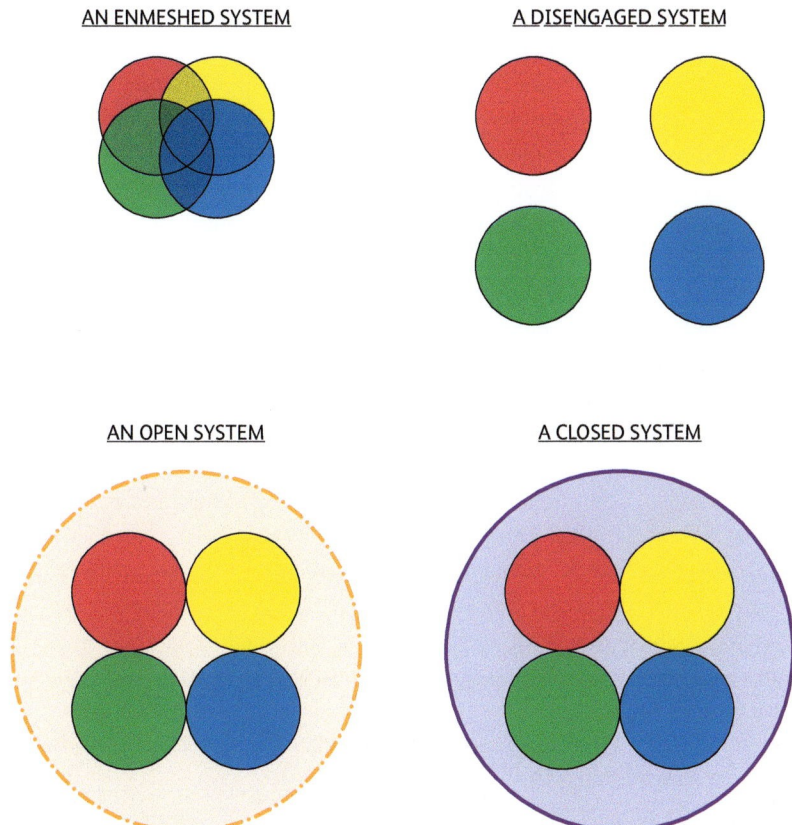

FIGURE 11.3 Variations on the family system

family with an alcoholic member, for example, might agree to keep that information from outsiders.

Of course, members of a family don't always follow or agree about privacy rules. When privacy rules are broken or contradictory, conflicts can result. Consider what might happen if Kyleigh knew that her sister was slipping out after midnight to get high and break into the town pool with friends. Although the privacy rules between the sisters might require Kyleigh to keep that information from their parents, another family rule might require her to alert a parent when her sister is in danger. Because families are complex social systems, conflict is inevitable. Communication is the system's way of creating, crossing, and repairing boundaries.

Family Secrets

When a family's privacy rules create rigid boundaries that discourage communication about particular topics, family secrets can develop. In general, **family secrets** are the events or information that family members hide from one another or from outsiders. Family secrets can be shared among all family members and withheld from outsiders, shared among some family members but not others, or kept by an individual from the rest of the family (Vangelisti, 1994). For example, family members might collectively try to hide another member's drinking problem from non-family members, a couple that became parents through an unplanned pregnancy might not tell their daughter that she was an "accident," or a homosexual teenager might refrain from sharing this information with other family members until he or she feels ready. Whether family secrets are shared by everyone, just a few family members, or only one person, they are a common aspect of family relationships that constitute a unique communication challenge.

Secrets can serve important functions within families (Vangelisti, 1994). By sharing secret information, you build a sense of closeness and trust between family members. Similarly, having insider information can strengthen your identity as a member of the family – you must be a part of the group if you're in on the secret. Family secrets also protect the family structure, perhaps by hiding conditions like alcoholism or abuse that might cause outsiders to interfere. Finally, secrets protect family members from social disapproval or embarrassment; when you keep undesirable information under wraps, you can maintain your family's public image.

Within families, you might also keep secrets because you are afraid of negative consequences. Consider what might happen if a family member revealed an important secret to an outsider. If the person who revealed the information has a lot of power within the family, the rest of the family may tolerate the betrayal. But if the person who reveals the secret doesn't have power, he or she might be punished by more powerful family members. Not surprisingly, then, research has shown family members are more likely to conceal their secrets from outsiders when they perceive other family members to have more power than they do (Afifi & Olson, 2005), or when they fear negative consequences for revealing a secret (Afifi, Olson, & Armstrong, 2005).

Although you may often have good reasons for keeping a family secret, there are times when you might want or need to tell someone else. Table 11.1 summarizes ten different criteria that people consider when deciding whether or not to reveal a secret

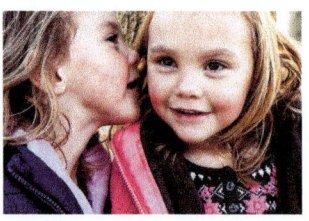

FIGURE 11.4 Sisters sharing a secret

Source: iStockPhoto.

(Vangelisti, Caughlin, & Timmerman, 2001). These criteria suggest that you are more likely to share a secret when the conversation is already intimate. In addition, you might disclose a secret when exposure is imminent or it becomes dangerous to maintain the secret. On the other hand, a person might keep a secret forever if the relationship or the urgency of the information doesn't require revelation.

> ### PAUSE & REFLECT
>
> What are some of the conditions that would prompt you to reveal a family secret to someone outside your family?

As the example of Suzanna in Table 11.1 might suggest, keeping a family secret can be a burden. Perhaps not surprisingly, people who report family secrets are also less satisfied with their families (Vangelisti & Caughlin, 1997). Conversely, a study of college students found that they are more satisfied in their families when they perceive that there are few secrets being kept within the family (Caughlin, Golish, Olson, Sargent, Cook, & Petronio, 2000). Even though keeping secrets might help families to bond, it seems that family members are happiest when they have fewer details that they have to keep under wraps.

Putting Theory into Practice: Improving System Operations

In a system of planets and a sun, the heavenly bodies have orbits that allow them to move both independently and in concert with each other. In the same way, members of a family develop norms that allow the system to function. When you view families as similar to other kinds of systems, you can identify specific strategies for improving system operations.

Respect system boundaries. The boundaries that define a system are as important as the parts of the system themselves. Members of a family are likely to form unique bonds and relationships with one another and managing these subsystems in the family are vital to the well-being of the larger family system. For example, it is important that siblings develop special bonds with one another, which may involve sharing secrets or helping one another escape punishment. Siblings need to respect the boundaries around their shared information in order to maintain one another's trust, and parents need to recognize that sometimes their children may share secrets with one another that they won't share with mom or dad. Similarly, couples may develop rules for how they share information with one another that are different from their rules for keeping their children in the loop. Along these lines, children of divorce often suffer when their parents neglect the boundaries between parent and child and disclose too many details about the break-up of the marriage (Afifi, McManus, Hutchinson, & Baker, 2007). Within your own family system, then, you can improve communication by respecting system boundaries and not interfering in subsystems to which you don't belong.

TABLE 11.1 Criteria for revealing family secrets

Consider the example of Suzanna, who keeps a secret about her brother's serious drug problem. When Suzanna becomes close to Aubrey, she wonders if she should share this information. Here's how Suzanna might weigh criteria as she decides whether to reveal her secret.

The conversation is intimate
Suzanna and Aubrey were talking late one night about a variety of private topics. Suzanna wonders if this would be a good time to mention her brother.

The secret is about to be exposed
Suzanna just got a text message indicating that her brother was stopping by in an hour. Suzanna wonders if she should tell Aubrey her secret before Aubrey figures it out herself.

Revealing the secret is urgent
Suzanna's brother has overdosed, and Suzanna needs Aubrey to take her to meet him in the emergency room.

The other person is likely to be accepting of the secret
In their family communication class today, Aubrey talked about how family members shouldn't be blamed for the actions of individual members. Suzanna begins to think that Aubrey won't think less of her if she knows the secret.

Sharing the secret is appropriate given the conversation
Suzanna and Aubrey were chatting about their families, when Aubrey asked Suzanna point blank why she never says much about her brother. Suzanna wonders if it's better to answer the question, rather than to try to change the topic.

The relationship can survive the secret
Suzanna and Aubrey just finished a grueling week of finals, and they celebrated with a nice dinner out. When Aubrey says that she thinks they will always be friends, Suzanna wonders if it's time to share her secret.

There is an important reason to share the secret
Suzanna's brother asked Aubrey to loan him money, and Aubrey is eager to help out her new friend's brother. Suzanna wonders if she should tell Aubrey her secret before Aubrey makes a big mistake.

Revealing the secret is allowed
Suzanna's parents recently said that they all should stop protecting her older brother by keeping his condition secret. Suzanna considers telling Aubrey, now that she has the family's permission.

The person is a member of the family
Suzanna and Aubrey discover they are second cousins on their mothers' side. Because Aubrey is family, Suzanna wonders if it is okay to tell her about her brother.

Practice safe secrets. Although family secrets can be an important part of maintaining boundaries around your family system, keeping secrets can burden family members. You should carefully consider the family secrets that you ask others to keep and that you agree to respect.

COMMUNICATION IN ACTION 11.2

Mapping Boundaries Within Families

You can respect boundaries within your family more effectively if you are aware of where those boundaries exist. Complete the form on the **companion website** to help you better understand the subsystems that exist within your family.

COMMUNICATION IN ACTION 11.3

Evaluate Your Family Secrets

Using the form on the **companion website**, make a list of the secrets that exist within your family and the pros and cons of keeping that information from others. This exercise can help you make more informed decisions about the secrets you keep within your family.

THE FAMILY LIFESPAN

When families are formed, partners (and any children they may have) face the challenge of creating a shared bond. If partners choose to raise children, their addition to the family system creates new challenges. And families continue to evolve in important ways as children move out of the home and parents age. Importantly, the lifespan of a family involves more than just the structural changes that occur as people join or leave the family circle. People also experience changes in who they are and how they define family. In the first few years as a couple, for example, partners come to have traits that more closely resemble the qualities their partner prefers (Ruvolo & Ruvolo, 2000). Over time, people also redefine their "family" as the one they have created, rather than the one that raised them (Brennan & Wamboldt, 1990). In this section of the chapter, we explore the communication issues that arise over the lifespan of the family.

The Early Years

The first few years of marriage or domestic partnership are sometimes called the "honeymoon stage," because people assume that newlyweds experience more passion and less conflict than other couples. To an extent, this characterization of the early years of family life is true. Young couples report more frequent sexual contact than more established couples (Call, Sprecher, & Schwartz, 1995). They are also highly committed to each other and are optimistic about their future together (Veroff, Douvan, Orbuch, & Acitelli, 1998).

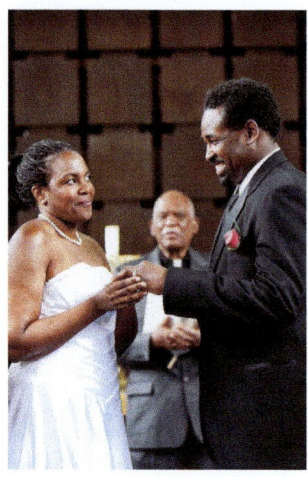

FIGURE 11.5
A wedding celebration

Source: Getty Images.

Traditional Marriage
A union characterized by a clear division of labor, companionship, and cooperation.

Independent Marriage
A union characterized by an emphasis on quality time together, individuality, and frequent negotiation of household tasks.

In fact, newlyweds tend to describe their partner in extremely positive terms, sometimes viewing their partners more positively than the partners even see themselves (Murray, Holmes, & Griffin, 1996).

PAUSE & REFLECT

Do you know any recently married couples? If so, how is their communication different from couples you know who have been married for many years?

As they form a family, couples must also work out the norms for their relationship. After more than a decade of research on married couples, Mary Anne Fitzpatrick (1988) detailed the communication patterns that develop within marriages. Fitzpatrick's insights shed light on fundamental differences in couple relationships. In her view, each of us develops assumptions about relationships based on our family experiences and the images we see in our society. In turn, these assumptions affect how people behave in their own relationships and how they interpret their partner's behavior. When the beliefs that we hold as individuals are combined with a partner's view of the couple bond, one of four distinct types of relationships is created.

One type of relationship is called the **traditional marriage**. Importantly, this label doesn't mean that these relationships are necessarily structured around traditional roles, such as a working husband and stay-at-home wife; instead, this term highlights the value that partners place on filling specific roles in the relationship, being companions, and cooperating for the good of the household. Historically, traditional couples have divided up responsibilities so that one partner earns wages and the other takes care of the home, but even households where both partners work outside the home can develop distinct family roles. For example, one partner might do all the yard work, handle finances, and cook for the household, while the other partner takes care of the car and does all of the cleaning and laundry. Because traditional partners have such specialized roles, they are very interdependent; in other words, they rely on each other to perform their different jobs. Generally speaking, then, the traditional couple functions like a well-oiled machine where each member has a distinct role, but the system is well-coordinated.

A very different type of relationship develops when partners have less clearly divided roles, place less value on companionship, and put their own interests ahead of the household. In the **independent marriage**, partners emphasize spending quality time together, but they also put their individual attitudes, goals, and desires ahead of obligations to the household. Of course, partners in both traditional and independent relationships have jobs, hobbies, and friends outside their home; but whereas the traditional partner will see his or her family role as a priority, the independent partner believes that the relationship shouldn't constrain personal activities. In fact, partners in an independent marriage schedule their activities with little input from each other, create private spaces in the home that are off limits to the other person, and might even have different last names. How do independent couples coordinate their household activities? Whereas the traditional couple is all about cooperation, independent couples negotiate who will do what on a daily basis. To a traditional partner, all that negotiation would be tiresome, but independent couples thrive on a relationship that encourages and supports their individuality.

When couples have clearly divided roles like a traditional couple, but don't prioritize companionship, a **separate marriage** develops. More specifically, partners in a separate relationship organize their household around a clear division of tasks, but they resemble independent partners in that they value their individual freedom. Separate partners perform their household tasks out of a sense of duty, rather than a desire to contribute to a companionate relationship, and they seek fulfilling experiences outside their couple relationship. Although this arrangement leaves separate couples psychologically and emotionally distant from each other, these relationships can be very strong and satisfying for partners. In particular, separate couples share a strong sense of commitment to their relationship and they gain pleasure from its stability; for day-to-day fun, however, these partners enjoy interests that do not involve each other.

Separate Marriage
A union characterized by a clear division of labor, psychological and emotional distance, and a strong commitment to the relationship.

PAUSE & REFLECT

Do you know anybody in a traditional, independent, or separate marriage? If so, how does that couple communicate when they have free time together?

If partners have different expectations for marriage, a **mixed marriage** is the result. A mixed couple can reflect any combination of partners with traditional, independent, or separate orientations; their common feature is that partners disagree about fundamental aspects of their relationship. Should responsibilities be clearly divided or renegotiated regularly? Should partners spend a lot of time together, only quality time together, or avoid contact with each other? How much priority should be given to household responsibilities, careers and personal hobbies, or external relationships? Because partners in a mixed relationship have such different expectations, they have to work especially hard to develop shared goals, norms, and assumptions.

Mixed Marriage
A union in which the partners differ in their preferences for a traditional, independent, or separate relationship.

As you might expect, the type of marriage a couple has influences how partners talk to each other. As summarized in Table 11.2, traditional couples place a premium on spending time together and expressing love and affection; although it might be hard to believe, these activities simply aren't priorities for the other couple types. More specifically, traditional partners share their thoughts and feelings with each other, turn to each for support, and cooperate when conflicts arise. Independent couples, on the other hand, constantly negotiate their household roles and personal goals. To do so, these couples engage in a lot of self-disclosure; however, they also support themselves – rather than each other – and they are more combative during conflicts than partners in other types of couples. The separate relationship involves the least amount of communication: partners don't disclose much to each other, they avoid conflict, and they rely on other family members and friends for support. Finally, although communication within mixed marriages depends on the specific combination of partners, these couples generally experience more uncertainty and conflict about relationship norms.

TABLE 11.2   Communication in different types of marriage

	Traditional	Independent	Separate	Mixed
Division of labor	Responsibilities follow traditional gender roles	Responsibilities are negotiated to maintain equity	Responsibilities follow traditional gender roles	Responsibilities assigned to each spouse are unclear
Relational priorities	Coordinate behavior and share time, love, and affection	Respect individual goals and interests, spend quality time together	Maintain the stability of the marriage as an institution	Develop an understanding of each other's different views
Approach to support	Rely on each other in good times and bad	Rely on themselves in good times and bad	Rely on other family members and friends for everything	Rely on themselves or seek help from other family members or friends
Approach to conflict	Cooperate and compromise over issues that are important to the marriage	Aggressively confront issues that threaten individual needs and goals	Avoid conflicts if at all possible	Experience serial conflicts about the goals and norms for the relationship

Students are often surprised to learn that there are alternatives to a close, affectionate couple relationship that partners can still find satisfying. What is important to keep in mind is that traditional, independent, and separate relationships are fulfilling to the extent that they match the goals, expectations, and values people bring to the relationship. For someone who seeks the companionship, affection, and teamwork of a traditional relationship, the independent and separate relationships would be a disappointment. But for a person who values his or her independence, doesn't like being constrained by family routines, and enjoys the romantic sparks of quality time with a partner, the traditional relationship would be stifling. And although partners in a separate relationship don't have either the affection or the romance of the other couple types, they enjoy an especially high level of certainty in the stability of their family arrangement. Whatever norms develop within the couple relationship, discovering how to relate to each other is an important task for couples in the early years of family life.

The Transition to Parenthood

Whether it occurs early in the couple relationship or after several years, the transition to parenthood is a tumultuous phase in the family life cycle. In fact, families start to change even as couples decide whether to have children, take steps to promote a healthy pregnancy or pursue adoption, and anticipate the birth of a child. During pregnancy, many couples report stronger feelings of togetherness as they prepare for parenthood (Feeney, Hohaus, Noller, & Alexander, 2001). Wives also report that their spouse takes better care of them during pregnancy, perhaps by doing household chores or pampering them (McHale & Huston, 1985), and this is especially true for women in traditional marriages (Fitzpatrick, Vangelisti, & Firman, 1994). Not unlike the honeymoon phase of marriage, anticipating the birth of a child is a time of closeness and affectionate communication between partners.

> ## PAUSE & REFLECT
>
> Do you have or expect to have children? How do you think having children changes how couples communicate with each other during the early years of marriage?

Although looking forward to parenthood brings couples closer, the actual arrival of the baby can create stress and a lot of extra work. Prior to becoming parents, wives report an average of 3.9 chores per day and husbands report an average of 1.9 chores per day; after becoming parents, wives increase to 42 chores per day and husbands increase to 8.3 chores per day (Huston & Holmes, 2004). Mothers are likely to do more than 80% of routine child care tasks, such as changing diapers, feeding, soothing, dressing the child, and managing the child's sleep schedule. Although some partners might share the load more equally and same-sex parents might distribute chores differently, having children clearly changes a couple's routine and can create a sense of inequity between partners.

Interviews with couples who have newly become parents reveal a variety of challenges that new parents must negotiate (Stamp, 1994). One prominent difficulty that new parents face is trying to balance free time and shared time. Not surprisingly, parents report that their freedoms become constrained by a baby who doesn't have a predictable schedule. Parents also feel like they compete with each other for free time – when one partner does something on his or her own, the other is forced to babysit. A partner's individual activities, such as exercising, also cut into shared time as a couple. This study found that couples struggle to talk about these concerns in a way that is open, but nonthreatening. Because becoming parents disrupts opportunities for both time together as a couple and time alone, communication about these issues is a delicate matter.

Another communication challenge concerns people's efforts to assume their identity as parents (Stamp & Banski, 1992). In particular, parents might help or hinder each other as they try to develop their parental roles. As an example, Denise has an especially vivid memory of a bath that her spouse gave their first son when he was a week old. As much as Denise and her spouse both wanted him to assume his role as "father," she was irrationally afraid that he would drown the baby. Certainly, a "good mom" would express her concerns, but doing so would undermine the father's confidence. So Denise paced in the hallway, trembled with fear, and suppressed the urge to "save her baby." By allowing her spouse to complete the bath without interruption, Denise helped him to establish

FIGURE 11.6
A couple contemplating parenthood

Source: © Randy Glasbergen/ glasbergen.com.

"Let's try getting up every night at 2:00 AM to feed the cat. If we enjoy doing that, then we can talk about having a baby."

his efficacy as a father; at the same time, leaving her baby in what felt like a dangerous situation meant that she violated her image of a good mother. Parenthood provides many such opportunities to help or hinder each other's identity as a parent.

Raising a Family

After children are brought into a family, parents are faced with the challenge of raising those children into mature adults and instituting norms and rules for behavior within the family. Consider your own family for a moment. Does everyone have an equal say in family decisions? Are you encouraged to speak your mind, even if you disagree with the rest of the family? How might your family respond if one member criticized a parent's behavior or opinion? How did the communication rules in your family influence how you communicate in your adulthood? When parents and children share a household, the family develops norms for communication that influence who says what, to whom, and in what manner (Koerner & Fitzpatrick, 2004).

One difference among families is the value that members place on conversation with each other. **Conversation orientation** refers to the extent to which a family encourages communication about a wide variety of topics. In families with a high conversation orientation, communication is frequent, spontaneous, and unrestrained. In these families, members share their individual thoughts, feelings, and actions with other members of the family, and everyone is encouraged to share their opinion when family decisions are being made. Parents who foster a high conversation orientation believe that communication is the main means for socializing children, as well as the key to an enjoyable family life. Conversely, when conversation orientation is low, family members are discouraged from communicating openly with each other, parents do not seek out their children's point of view, and siblings are less inclined to share their thoughts and feelings with each other. Parents with a low conversation orientation don't see a connection between disclosure of thoughts and feelings and a child's education and socialization.

A second quality that distinguishes family communication patterns is a family's **conformity orientation**, the importance the family places on members having similar attitudes, beliefs, and values. Families with a high conformity orientation believe that family members should share the same beliefs and attitudes, most often those that are

Conversation Orientation
The extent to which a family encourages communication about a wide variety of topics.

Conformity Orientation
The extent to which the family encourages members to have similar attitudes, beliefs, and values.

PAUSE & REFLECT

How might your family's communication pattern affect how you communicate with non-family members?

---

endorsed by the parents. Accordingly, children are expected to show obedience to their parents and older adults during conversations. In contrast, families with a low conformity orientation are comfortable when members have conflicting viewpoints and even tolerate different positions on core values related to topics like religion or politics. In the low conformity orientation family, these differences don't threaten the family structure, and they might even contribute to the family's well-being.

Because families can be high or low on conversation orientation and high or low on conformity orientation, four distinct family types can be identified (Koerner & Fitzpatrick, 2004). As summarized in Figure 11.7, a family that is low in conversation orientation and high in conformity orientation is a **protective family**. Within protective families, members do not communicate freely, they discourage differences of opinion, and children are expected to accept authority. Interestingly, family communication patterns are related to whether the parents have a traditional, independent, separate, or mixed couple type (Fitzpatrick & Ritchie, 1994). Protective family norms are likely to

Protective Family

Families whose members do not communicate freely, discourage differences, and respect authority.

HIGH CONFORMITY ORIENTATION	
PROTECTIVE FAMILY Emphasis on obedience to parental authority. Little concern for open communication among family members. Parents make all of the decisions for the family and feel little need to explain these decisions to the children.	**CONSENSUAL FAMILY** Pressure to agree and preserve family hierarchy. Desire for open communication and exploring new ideas. Parents make decisions, but also listen to their children and try to explain the reasoning behind those decisions.
LAISSEZ-FAIRE FAMILY All family members are allowed to make their own decisions. Family members rarely communicate about their decisions or other topics. Parents allow their children to make their own decisions, and they have little interest in communicating with the children about those decisions.	**PLURALISTIC FAMILY** All family members are involved equally in decision making. Value open and unconstrained communication. Children are allowed to participate equally in family decision making because opinions are based on merit rather than family status.
LOW CONFORMITY ORIENTATION	

(Left axis: LOW CONVERSATION ORIENTATION; Right axis: HIGH CONVERSATION ORIENTATION)

FIGURE 11.7 Types of families

develop when parents have a separate relationship. Just as separate couples attend to their household duties and keep their distance from each other, the protective family places high value on following the rules, but not on communicating with each other.

A **consensual family** is also defined by a high conformity orientation, but these families value open communication as a way of reaching a shared position. Perhaps not surprisingly, consensual families are most likely to be headed by parents who fit a traditional couple type (Fitzpatrick & Ritchie, 1994). As in the traditional relationship, consensual family members use communication to coordinate activities around a united family front. In fact, a study that compared family types and teacher's perceptions of children found that boys from consensual families become more self-restrained as they age (Fitzpatrick, Marshall, Leutwiler, & Krcmar, 1996). A survey of college students also revealed that consensual families are especially likely to value and perform family rituals (Baxter & Clark, 1996). Thus, across the lifespan of raising children, a consensual environment fosters involvement in and conformity with the family.

Some families value open communication, but don't require members to have the same attitudes, beliefs, or values. Does this description remind you of one of the couple types described earlier in this chapter? Independent partners, who value individuality in their relationship, tend to create a **pluralistic family** where different opinions are expressed, tolerated, and even welcomed (Fitzpatrick & Ritchie, 1994). Members of a pluralistic family don't feel compelled to hide or resolve their differences; instead, they express their thoughts, debate their positions, and are happy to agree to disagree. In fact, pluralistic family members are more likely than members of other types of families to have conflicts with each other and to seek help from each other when they have personal problems (Koerner & Fitzpatrick, 1997). And whereas the study of school children described previously found boys from consensual families becoming more self-restrained over the years, boys from pluralistic families tend to be less self-restrained and withdrawn as they age (Fitzpatrick et al., 1996). In this way, pluralistic families encourage their members to express their individuality and embrace their differences.

A fourth family type, the **laissez-faire family**, is created when both conversation orientation and conformity orientation are low. Members of the laissez-faire family have relatively little contact with each other, and there is no expectation that family members will have a shared point of view. In fact, members of a laissez-faire family tend to develop stronger ties with people outside the family. As a result, research shows that members of laissez-faire families are unlikely to engage in conflict and they don't turn to each other for support (Koerner & Fitzpatrick, 1997). Which couple type is most likely to promote a laissez-faire family environment? According to the study by Fitzpatrick and Ritchie (1994) described previously, the laissez-faire family tends to emerge from mixed couples where parents have different visions of their relationship. Perhaps because the parents have difficulty working out the norms for their own relationship, they aren't able to set a clear course for the family.

The Mature Family

As children grow and parents age, the family changes in significant ways. A major turning point occurs as children move out of the family home and parents retire from the

---

Consensual Family

Families whose members use open communication to coordinate activities around a united family front.

Pluralistic Family

Families whose members are encouraged to express individuality and embrace differences.

Laissez-faire Family

Families in which members have little contact with one another and aren't expected to share a similar point of view.

HOW DO YOU RATE? 11.2

Family Communication Patterns

Visit the **companion website** and complete the Revised Family Communication Pattern Instrument (Ritchie & Fitzpatrick, 1990) to learn about the type of family communication patterns present in your own family. How does your family communication style influence the way you manage conflict? How does it influence the way you provide support?

FIGURE 11.8
An older married couple

Source: Getty Images.

workforce. For some couples, this can be a time of renewed relational bliss – they might travel, rediscover shared hobbies, and perhaps enjoy their grandchildren. In fact, sharing activities and time together can help people at this stage of life become more satisfied with their relationship (Vinick & Ekerdt, 1990). At the same time, these dramatic changes in relationships can disrupt a well-run family system. Perhaps not surprisingly, then, partners have more conflicts about daily tasks and household responsibilities following retirement (Harper, Schaalje, & Sandberg, 2000).

Health concerns are one issue in later life that can affect the couple relationship. Older individuals might find physical activities to be difficult, experience vision and hearing problems that disrupt communication, and find themselves more susceptible to illness (Dickson, Christian, & Remmo, 2004). And when one partner's health deteriorates, the other might find him or herself in the role of caretaker. The shift from spouse or partner to caretaker is a difficult one for many people. Older persons who become caretakers for their ailing partner sometimes experience depression, physical illness, and isolation (Gagnon, Hersen, Kabacoff, & Van Hasselt, 1999). Moreover, caretakers who are less satisfied with their life tend to communicate in a more patronizing fashion, which causes care-receivers to experience more negative emotions (Edwards & Noller, 1998). Perhaps not surprisingly, then, health problems are often cited as a prominent reason for a decline in relationship satisfaction (e.g., Booth & Johnson, 1994).

INSIDE COMMUNICATION RESEARCH

Couples Coping with Alzheimer's Disease

Caring for an aging partner is an inevitable part of long-term relationships; however, some disabilities are more challenging than others. When people experience memory loss and dementia, they lose the ability to communicate with relationship partners. To explore how people cope with partners under these conditions, Leslie Baxter, Dawn Braithwaite, Tamara Golish, and Loreen Olson (2002) conducted a study of women whose husbands had Alzheimer's disease. Specifically, the researchers wondered about the challenges the wives experienced, as well as the communication strategies they used to manage those difficulties.

The researchers conducted interviews with 21 elderly women, who were married to men living in a nursing home. All of the husbands suffered from Alzheimer's disease or other dementia-related diseases, and only two of the husbands were able to sustain a conversation. In the interviews, the wives described their feelings of closeness with their husband, changes in their relationship over time, communication experiences, important rituals in their lives, and relationships with family and friends. The researchers then examined transcripts of the interviews to identify experiences that the women had in common with each other.

The results of the study revealed that the women grappled with several tensions. First, the wives felt obligated to continue a relationship with a husband who was physically present, but mentally or emotionally absent. Second, women doubted their interactions with their husband – when wives received a message from their husband, they weren't sure if he had been lucid for a brief moment, or if their mind was playing tricks on them. Third, the women questioned what topics to discuss with their husbands and what topics to avoid. Finally, the wives experienced a longing for their past relationship, but they had to cope with the realities of the present.

The study also identified communication strategies that the women used to cope with the tensions they experienced. One strategy was to use nonverbal communication, like handholding or hugging, to make up for the lack of meaningful verbal messages. Second, the wives worked especially hard to find meaning in the cues they received from their husband, which enabled them to create an emotional presence in their spouse. Third, the women turned to nursing home staff to provide information that would allow them to feel close to their husbands. Finally, some women coped by limiting contact with their spouse, which alleviated stress but also made them guilty about neglecting their spouse.

THINK ABOUT IT

1. This study focused on the communication challenges and strategies that women face when their spouse has Alzheimer's disease. How might the results of this study differ if the researchers had examined other types of ailments that the elderly confront, such as heart disease or cancer?

2. What is the role of intention in interpersonal communication? These results suggest that wives searched for meaning in their husbands' behavior, which may or may not have reflected his actual thoughts or feelings. Are there any risks or rewards in interpreting meaning from a partner where no meaning was intended?

In mature families, parents also need to redefine their relationship with their children. One way that the parent–child relationship shifts is that children gain expertise over their parents on contemporary topics and new technology. Many of our students, for example, say that they taught their parents how to set up an email account or use the text-messaging feature on their cell phones. Although these students report frustration with their aging parents' lack of competency in using new technology or their violations of social norms for use, parents who must rely on their children's expertise in these matters are probably equally discouraged by the situation. Because parents have always had the expertise necessary to function in their daily lives and to oversee the lives of their children, it can be a frustrating change of events when adult children surpass their parents with knowledge or expertise that the aging parents don't have.

Another important shift occurs if adult children are called upon to take care of a parent. How do parents and children handle this role reversal? Adult children often use humor to relieve some of the tension that arises when they care for their elderly parents

> ## PAUSE & REFLECT
>
> What are some of the ways that you take care of older members of your family?

(Bethea, Travis, & Pecchioni, 2000). People might create humorous stories that help them feel better about daily hassles, safety concerns, and their parents' declining health. Adult children also become more assertive in making decisions for their older parents. In one study, for example, mothers and their adult children were asked to role-play an interaction where they made a decision together about the mother's finances (Cicirelli, 2006). That study found that children dominate the decision by talking more, introducing more ideas, and getting what they want; but mothers often regret the resulting decision. These patterns reflect a reversal of the family's roles over time.

Putting Theory into Practice: Coping with Family Changes

When you enter into a long-term relationship with a romantic partner and create a family, the only certainty is that your relationship will evolve. Although you can't predict the specific experiences that you will encounter, you can take steps to cope with the changes you will face.

Anticipate changes over the family lifespan. Transitions in families can be challenging because people have to adapt to new routines, find new ways of meeting goals, and adjust to the addition or departure of family members. One reason people get caught off-guard by family transitions is that they do not consider the subtle ways their life will change. Consider a study that explored the problems people encounter when they give medication to an ailing family member (Travis, Bethea, & Winn, 2000). Would you have guessed that scheduling medications and dealing with an uncooperative patient were the most frequent problems? Even positive changes in a family, like the marriage of a sibling or the birth of a grandchild, transform the roles that individuals must perform in the family. A sibling who was once a best friend must now take a back seat to the new spouse. New grandparents must give their children enough room to figure out their own parenting style. As you look toward the changes that will inevitably confront your family, try to keep in mind that even basic parts of your routine will need your attention.

Keep the lines of communication open. As families change through marriage, children, divorce, remarriage, stepchildren, aging, and retirement, family members will have different responsibilities, different relationships, and different roles. By reintroducing ourselves to each other, family members can forge relationships that fit with their new situation.

SUMMARY

Families include both the voluntary bonds you form as adults and the relationships you are born or adopted into. These relationships have changed a lot in the last half a century

COMMUNICATION IN ACTION 11.4

Renewing Family Relationships

Focus on the most recent transition that you and your family have gone through. Maybe it was when you moved out of your family home to go to college, when you and your spouse changed schedules so you could go back to school, or when you got a new job. Then, write a letter to a member of your family in which you describe how you have changed because of this transition. You might address the same details that you would include in a letter to a new acquaintance, for example, mention your hobbies, your goals, and the things that you worry about. Even if you don't send this letter, it may help you to see how the changes in your life might be affecting your family relationships.

– fewer people marry, people commonly divorce and remarry, children can be conceived in a doctor's office or adopted from faraway lands, and non-parents frequently participate in child-rearing. Despite the many forms that family can take, any family can help its members meet basic needs, teach children what it means to be human or a member of a culture, and provide its members with affection and support.

Families can be viewed as systems that are made up of different people who have distinct qualities and relationships, but who exist together as part of the family entity. Over time, family systems develop internal and external boundaries that create sub-systems and influence how much family members interact with non-family members. By developing privacy rules, families can coordinate and regulate the disclosure of information both within and outside the family. Over the course of life, family members might collect experiences that they keep hidden from others. Family secrets can serve several functions for members, but having lots of secrets to keep can make family life less satisfying.

Of course, numerous changes occur over the family lifespan. The early years of family life can be challenging because partners in a marriage or domestic partnership have to coordinate both their behaviors and their views of the relationship. The transition to parenthood introduces new challenges, especially because it constrains both individual freedoms and shared time; partners might also interfere with each other's efforts to develop a confident identity as a parent. In families focused on the task of raising children, norms for communication promote the development of protective, consensual, pluralistic, or laissez-faire families. These family communication patterns both structure interaction among family member and shape the communication behaviors that children develop. For families still together in old age, retirement, illness, and adult children require further shifts in family roles and communication behavior.

Family relationships are perhaps the most important relationships you will have in your life. Families perform important functions for their members, they develop their own systems of communication, and they evolve over the course of our life. To promote the well-being of these critical relationships, use interpersonal communication to strengthen family bonds, fine-tune family systems, and cope with the ways your family will change in your lifetime.

ACTIVITIES FOR EXPLORING COMMUNICATION ETHICS

What Would You/Should You Do?

Imagine that you have a friend who confides in you that her stepbrother sexually assaulted her. She says that she hasn't shared this private information with anyone else, but she felt that she needed to tell someone and she knew that she would be able to trust you. She makes you promise that you won't tell anyone, because she's worried about how her mother and stepfather might react if they knew. On the one hand, you don't want to violate your friend's trust by revealing this private information against her will. On the other hand, the sexual assault is a crime and should be reported to the authorities. What would you – should you – do in this situation?

Something to Think About

When married couples have children and their marriage subsequently ends in divorce, 90% of the time the biological mother is granted primary custody of the children. The fathers are sometimes granted visitation rights and are usually expected to pay the mother child support to assist with the expenses associated with raising the children. Every year, 30–50% of fathers fail to pay the child support that is owed to their ex-wives to care for their children. What are the ethical issues at stake as divorced parents negotiate their family obligations?

Analyze Communication Ethics Yourself

The website www.youdebate.com/DEBATES/gay_adoption.htm sponsors a public debate over whether or not gay and lesbian couples should be able to adopt children. The website presents several of the facts about gay adoption and allows people to post arguments for or against gay adoption. Read the facts on this page about gay adoption and some of the pro and con arguments that people have posted on this topic. What is your opinion on this issue? What arguments would you make in favor of or against gay and lesbian adoptions?

KEY WORDS

closed families	family secrets	protective families
conformity orientation	family socialization	separate marriage
consensual families	independent marriage	subsystems
conversation orientation	laissez-faire families	system
disengaged systems	mixed marriage	systems theory
enmeshed systems	open families	traditional marriage
family	pluralistic families	transmission

PART 4 STRATEGIC INTERPERSONAL COMMUNICATION

Visit the Communication Café on the **companion website** to hear Denise and Jen talk about the topics addressed in Part 4 of this book.

You would have an incomplete picture of interpersonal communication if we neglected to consider some of the powerful outcomes you can achieve in your interactions with other people. There are numerous tasks you can perform through communication, but we focus this part of the book on three that are especially important to your personal and relational well-being: influencing others, resolving conflicts, and communicating support and comfort.

Chapter 12 takes up the topic of interpersonal influence. Think for a moment about how much you rely on other people to hold attitudes or engage in behaviors that make your life better. When you seek approval from another person, when you encourage them to help you (or stop hindering you), and whenever you call upon others to adjust their actions to accommodate your priorities, you engage in an attempt to influence. This chapter breaks down this complex process by elaborating on the goals that we pursue through interpersonal communication, the messages we use to influence others, and the strategies we employ to be effective in both ordinary and difficult situations.

The focus of Chapter 13 is interpersonal conflict. Disagreements and arguments are inevitable when humans come into contact. Despite being quite common, conflicts are often emotionally and mentally taxing events because they have the potential to damage our relationships and create personal distress. In this chapter, we clarify what conflict is, and the many different forms it comes in. In addition, you'll learn about strategies for addressing conflicts through interpersonal communication. When you can understand the complexity of conflict and how communication is part of conflict dynamics, you increase your ability to take control of the conflicts that will confront you in your life.

We end this book with one of most compassionate outcomes you can achieve through interpersonal communication: providing comfort and support to others. The messages we use to make someone feel better, to help them tackle a problem, or to communicate our availability to help are some of the most powerful tools in our communication tool box. Receiving support can have a positive effect on the immediate situation, as well as the individual's personal health and well-being. Giving and receiving comfort is also a cornerstone of strong interpersonal relationships. Your ability to provide and receive comfort and support can make a lasting difference in your life and the lives of people you care about, which is why we believe that it is a fitting capstone to your exploration of interpersonal communication.

CHAPTER 12

INTERPERSONAL INFLUENCE 320

CHAPTER 13

INTERPERSONAL CONFLICT 346

CHAPTER 14

COMMUNICATING COMFORT AND SUPPORT 376

LEARNING OBJECTIVES

After reading this chapter, you should be able to:

1. Identify types of interpersonal influence goals.
2. Describe three strategies for managing multiple interpersonal influence goals.
3. Identify three dimensions on which influence messages can vary.
4. Recognize patterns of communication that occur in influence interactions.
5. Recognize obstacles to interpersonal influence.
6. Describe how intimacy and power shape the influence messages that people use.

PUTTING THEORY INTO PRACTICE

In this chapter, you will learn how to:

1. Identify goals for interpersonal communication.
2. Attend to your secondary goals.
3. Weigh options for managing multiple goals.
4. Remember that messages matter.
5. Plan for interpersonal influence interactions.
6. Respect people's right to refuse.
7. Enable upward influence.
8. Avoid strategic ambiguity.

INTERPERSONAL INFLUENCE

12

322 GOALS

328 INFLUENCE MESSAGES

334 INTERPERSONAL INFLUENCE IN ACTION

343 SUMMARY

345 ACTIVITIES FOR EXPLORING COMMUNICATION ETHICS

345 KEY WORDS

Source: Getty Images/© David Sacks.

In one episode of NBC's hit sitcom *The Office*, Michael Scott learned that his branch had a budget surplus and was informed that the extra money needed to be spent by the end of the day or they would lose the money altogether. When the employees found out about the surplus they immediately started lobbying for different ways to spend the money. Some people wanted a new copy machine and another group wanted more comfortable chairs for the office. The people who wanted a new copy machine tried to persuade Michael to spend the extra money on this item by demonstrating how the copy machine was flawed and taking him out for lunch where they tried to win his favor by telling jokes and being friendly. The receptionist, Pam, tried to convince Michael to spend the money on new office chairs by providing evidence that they spend more time in their chairs each day than making copies and by flirting with him. When he consulted the CFO about what to do, Michael learned that as the branch manager he would get a bonus if they didn't spend the money. Unable to make a decision, Michael delegates the decision making to the employees. Since more people wanted the chairs, they all agreed that it would be better to have new chairs than to give the money to Michael as a bonus.

■ ■ ■ ■ ■

Situations like the one on *The Office* are a common part of life. Perhaps you've recently had a conversation where someone was trying to influence a decision you were making – maybe about who to vote for, what to do with your free time, or what to do after you graduate. Or perhaps you have tried to influence someone yourself – to cover your shift at work, to lend you money, or to hire you for your dream job. **Interpersonal influence** refers to the use of communication to change another person's beliefs, attitudes, or actions. This chapter explores the goals and messages that characterize interpersonal influence interactions so that you can be more successful when you find yourself in these kinds of interactions.

GOALS

In general, **goals** are end-states or outcomes that a person seeks to achieve or maintain. Your goals exist within your mind – they include the knowledge, expectations, and desires that motivate your behavior. You may be very aware of a goal before an interaction – such as when you plan to ask a family member to loan you money. Even when you aren't thinking about your goals, however, they are probably affecting your communication behavior. For example, during a conversation with your mother about money, you would probably behave differently, based on whether you were trying to secure a loan, get her to repay money she borrowed, or convince her that you are responsible with money. Because goals always influence interpersonal interactions, learning about them can help you be a more effective communicator.

Types of Influence Goals

Interpersonal influence goals are desired outcomes you can achieve only if you convince another person to cooperate with you. Table 12.1 lists the most common interpersonal influence goals (Dillard, Anderson, & Knobloch, 2002). Notice how achieving each of the goals involves another person. For example, you can't give advice unless someone is there to receive it. And as Table 12.1 shows, whether you achieve your interpersonal influence goals depends on your ability to use communication to change another person's thoughts or behaviors.

Do different influence goals require different types of interpersonal communication? Research suggests that the answer is yes. American and Japanese students report that they would persist longer and apply more pressure when enforcing an obligation, compared to asking a favor (Cai & Wilson, 2000). When crafting messages, you also have to consider that people on the receiving end may react differently to different kinds of goals. For example, being the target of advice makes people feel more surprised, angry, sad, and guilty than being asked for help (Dillard, Kinney, & Cruz, 1996).

> ### PAUSE & REFLECT
>
> How do you feel when someone tries to influence you? Are there types of messages that you especially dislike?

The goals described here aren't the only concerns that you have when you seek to influence another person. For example, when you try to affect another person's thoughts and actions, you might wonder if the other person will think less of you, if you'll damage your relationship, or if you can maintain your composure during the interaction. These concerns aren't your driving goal in the conversation, but they affect how you communicate with the other person. As shown in Figure 12.1, the interpersonal influence goal that motivates communication is the **primary goal**, and the other considerations that arise during interpersonal influence interactions are **secondary goals** (Dillard, Segrin, & Harden, 1989).

Interpersonal Influence Goals
Desired end-states or outcomes that can only be achieved if another person engages in cooperative activity.

SCHOLAR SPOTLIGHT

Visit the **Communication Café** on the **companion website** to view a conversation with James Dillard, who conducted ground-breaking research on interpersonal influence goals.

Interpersonal Influence
The use of communication to change another person's beliefs, attitudes, or actions.

Goals
End-states or outcomes that a person seeks to achieve or maintain.

Primary Goal
The influence goal that motivates the interaction.

Secondary Goals
Considerations other than the primary goal that arise during interpersonal influence interactions and shape communication strategies.

TABLE 12.1 Influence goals

Type of goal	Example
Gain assistance	Can I borrow your class notes?
Give advice	I think you should quit smoking.
Share activity	Let's do something tonight.
Change orientation	Here's why you're wrong about gun control.
Change relationship	We should agree not to date other people.
Obtain permission	Hey, Dad, can I use the car?
Enforce rights and obligations	You promised to take out the trash. So, how about it?

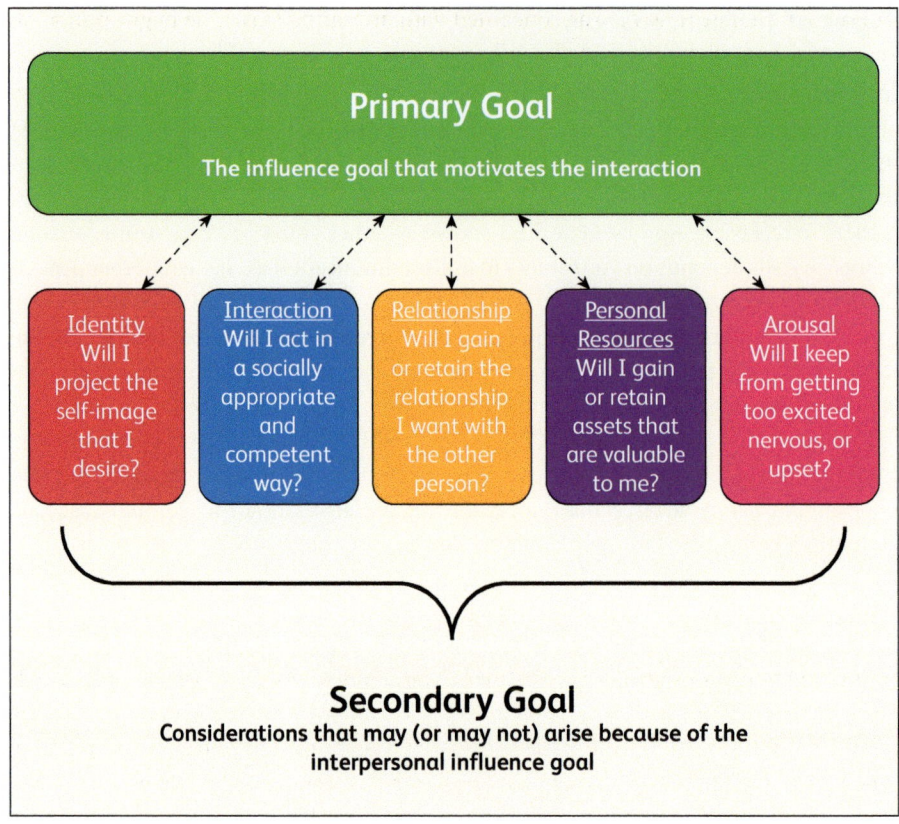

FIGURE 12.1 Primary and secondary goals for interpersonal influence

Let's consider the example of Davis who asks Kelly to study with him for a midterm exam. Davis's primary goal might be to get help, share an activity with Kelly, change their relationship, or (if it was part of an earlier deal) enforce Kelly's obligation to help him out. No matter what the primary goal is, Davis will no doubt have secondary goals as well.

- *Identity goals* concern the image you want to project. In Davis's case, he may want Kelly to think he's smart.
- *Interaction goals* focus on managing the conversation. Perhaps Davis is concerned about stammering when he asks Kelly to study with him.
- *Relationship goals* address your association with your communication partner. For example, Davis might want to show his respect for Kelly as he makes this request.
- *Personal resource goals* involve maximizing your assets and minimizing costs. If Davis is hoping that studying with Kelly will involve her making dinner for him, he's attending to personal resource goals.
- *Arousal goals* refer to managing your emotions. In Davis's case, he might want the conversation with Kelly to leave them both feeling happy, rather than disappointed.

You might think that secondary goals are less important to interpersonal communication – they are, after all, "secondary." Actually, secondary goals have a major impact on the messages that you use to pursue your primary influence goal. Consider again the example of Davis and Kelly. If Davis was concerned with appearing smart, he might phrase his request as more of an offer to help Kelly prepare for the exam. If he wanted to manage their relationship, he might state how much he admires the comments she makes in class. Although your primary goal determines what your conversation is about, your secondary goals determine the specific messages that are exchanged during an influence interaction (Dillard, 2008).

> ### PAUSE & REFLECT
>
> Can you remember a time when you had to influence a more powerful individual like a professor or work supervisor? If so, what secondary goals were salient to you in that situation?

Managing Multiple Goals

Influence interactions always involve managing multiple goals, in part because people always have both primary and secondary goals. How do you pursue your influence goal, while also attending to one or more secondary goals? These challenges are even greater when your goals are incompatible with each other, a condition known as **goal strain**. For example, your desire to appear strong and independent may be at odds with your desire to maintain a high-quality relationship with a close friend. Or, perhaps your goal of influencing a close friend to lose weight conflicts with presenting yourself as likable and nonjudgmental. Because goal strain can complicate your efforts to influence other people, let's consider some options for managing multiple goals (see Table 12.2).

   Prioritize. If you find yourself struggling to achieve multiple goals, you might decide which goal is most important to you. Although focusing on a single goal means you won't get everything you want, at least you will attend to your top priority. Keep in mind that the most important goal might not be your primary influence goal. People tend to rate the secondary goals of maintaining the relationship, accepting fault for a problem, and being likable as important goals when discussing a problem with a close friend or romantic partner, even if those aren't their primary goals for the conversation (Samp & Solomon, 1998; Schrader & Dillard, 1998). If you decide to focus on only one of multiple goals, make sure you address the one that matters to you most.

> ### PAUSE & REFLECT
>
> Can you think of a time when you had two goals that were incompatible with each other? If so, did you abandon one of the goals, or did you try to accomplish both?

HOW DO YOU RATE? 12.1

The Intensity of Secondary Goals

In any conversation, some goals are going to be more prominent and influential than others. To evaluate the intensity of various goals in one of your recent conversations, complete the measure of goal intensity on the **companion website**. Did the outcome of the conversation adequately address your secondary goals? How might the interaction have gone differently if you had a different secondary goal?

Goal Strain

The existence of two or more goals for interpersonal influence that are incompatible with each other.

TABLE 12.2   Options for managing multiple goals

Strategy	Definition	Example
Choose one goal	Pursue the single, most important goal, and abandon all the rest	Davis decides that appearing smart is most important to him, so he only hints indirectly that he'd like a study partner
Sequence goals	Pursue goals one at a time, over the course of an interaction	Davis begins by complimenting Kelly, so she'll know he respects her, and then focuses on showing her that he's smart
Integrate goals	Focus on a general concern that is common to all of your goals	Davis focuses on having a fun interaction with Kelly, because that is likely to let her know he respects her, protect his identity, and net him a study partner all at the same time

Pursue goals in sequence. Another option is to try to pursue goals sequentially, or one after another. Think about how you might persuade a neighbor to keep his dog from barking outside every evening. Your goal is to get your neighbor to keep the dog inside so you can study in peace, but you might also be concerned with having a good relationship with your neighbor and not coming across as a jerk. You could start by pointing out the constant barking, the neighborhood rules, and your need to study – after you make headway on this goal, you might offer to help your neighbor rake his leaves or tell some jokes. On the other hand, you might start by being friendly and helpful, and then mention the barking dog when your neighbor is feeling especially friendly toward you. Whichever course you follow, sequencing goals involves focusing your attention on one goal at a time, but trying to get to everything that matters to you.

Pursue all goals simultaneously. Although it is somewhat more challenging, you might pursue several goals at the same time. To do this, you need to find some ways in which your goals are compatible with each other. Let's return to the example of the barking dog next door. How might you stop the noise, maintain neighborly relations, and be a nice person? One option might be to offer to keep the dog at your house when your neighbor is working the swing shift. As this example shows, accomplishing all your goals at once can take some creativity, and it isn't always possible. But if you can find underlying ways in which multiple goals are compatible with each other, you can address more than one goal at the same time.

Putting Theory into Practice: Thinking Strategically

You probably have conversations in which you try to influence other people several times over the course of your day. Being conscious of your goals and sorting through your priorities can help you to be effective in achieving them.

Identify goals for interpersonal communication. Make a point of recognizing when an influence goal is part of your communication experiences. Then, try to figure out what the exact goal is, and whether it's you or the other person who is trying to do the influencing. Jen remembers an exchange she had with a student about the format of a midterm exam. The student sent her an email that included reasons why he thought the proposed format was flawed, and Jen responded giving reasons in favor of the exam format. When Jen and the student had a chance to talk face-to-face, she asked him what his goal was: to change her approach to exams, to give her advice about testing, or something else. Once the student realized that his real goal was to get permission to take an alternative form of the exam, they had a productive conversation. If you identify your goals for an interaction, you can focus your messages and be more effective.

COMMUNICATION IN ACTION 12.1

Identifying Influence Goals

Keep a diary of your interpersonal interactions over the course of an entire day. After you talk to someone, jot down whom you talked to, what you discussed, any influence goals that you had, and any influence goals the other person seemed to have. At the end of the day, use the form on the **companion website** to tally the various goals you attended to. As you reflect on your conversations, think about how being more aware of these goals help you communicate more effectively.

Attend to your secondary goals. Your secondary goals in an influence situation can be more important than your primary goals, because secondary goals represent concerns and priorities that constrain your options for pursuing a primary goal. Given this, be sure to take stock of your secondary goals as you prepare to pursue a primary goal. Suppose your primary goal is to get permission to use a friend's laptop to give a class presentation. If you ignore your secondary goals, you might just say, "Hey, can I borrow your laptop to give my class presentation?" This message might work, but it doesn't protect your secondary concerns. If you're worried about seeming rude or demanding, you would be wise to be more polite. If you don't want to damage your relationship, you might preface this request by saying, "I don't want to put any pressure on you, and I want you to feel comfortable saying no to me." When you face influence situations in your own life, identify your secondary goals and try to craft messages that take those concerns into consideration.

Weigh options for managing multiple goals. If your goals are incompatible – in other words, achieving one goal puts another goal in jeopardy – follow these steps:

1. Identify your most important goal.
2. Consider whether it would be possible to achieve your most important goal after you address a different goal. If so, you can sequence your goals in ways that don't undermine your first priority.
3. Consider whether it would be possible to achieve your less important goals after you address your top priority. If so, you can sequence your goals in ways that achieve your most important goal, as well as perhaps some others.

4. If pursuing any particular goal, in any order, puts the others at jeopardy, focus your communication efforts on the goal that is most important to you.

INFLUENCE MESSAGES

Now that you have learned about influence goals, let's focus on the messages people use to achieve those goals. In this section of the chapter, we examine characteristics of influence messages, patterns that emerge within influence interactions, and sequences of messages that are especially effective.

Characteristics

Compliance-seeking Messages
Utterances that are designed to get a person to agree with a request.

Compliance-seeking messages are utterances designed to get somebody to agree with a request. Table 12.3 lists 16 specific message strategies you might use to influence a communication partner. Notice how some involve being nice or focusing on positive outcomes, whereas others are pretty negative. In addition, some message types make the request quite clear, but others don't. We can organize influence messages like these along three main dimensions: explicitness, dominance, and amount of argument (Dillard, Wilson, Tusing, & Kinney, 1997).

TABLE 12.3 Compliance gaining messages

Type of message	Example
Pre-giving	I bought you a present, but first you need to clean the apartment.
Liking	I think you're great. Would you clean the apartment?
Promise	I'll make your favorite dinner if you clean the apartment.
Threat	If you don't clean the apartment, I'm going to be mad.
Aversive simulation	I'm going to be mad at you until you clean the apartment.
Positive expertise	If you clean the apartment, your friends will want to spend more time with you.
Negative expertise	Nobody will want to spend time with you if you don't clean the apartment.
Positive self-feelings	You'll feel good about yourself if you clean the apartment.
Negative self-feelings	You'll feel bad about yourself if you don't clean the apartment.
Positive altercasting	Respectable people keep their apartments clean.
Positive esteem	People will look up to you if you clean the apartment.
Moral appeal	It's a sin to keep this apartment so messy when some people don't even have a place to live.
Altruism	For my sake, will you clean the apartment?
Debt	I took care of everything when you had exams; now I need you to clean the apartment for me.
Negative altercasting	Only a slob would refuse to clean the apartment.
Negative esteem	People will be disappointed in you if you don't clean the apartment.

PAUSE & REFLECT

Which of the tactics in Table 12.3 are you more or less likely to use to influence another person? Which messages do you think are especially effective when somebody seeks to influence you?

Explicitness is the degree to which a message clearly reveals a speaker's intentions. For example, "I want us to date each other exclusively" is an explicit statement – it clearly expresses the speaker's desire to change the relationship. In contrast, an inexplicit or implicit version of the same message is "I can't imagine wanting to spend time with anyone but you."

Dominance is the extent to which a speaker expresses power through the form and content of an influence message. Dominance can be conveyed through assertive language ("You *must* do this") or nonverbal cues, such as direct eye contact, vivid gestures, or a forward body lean (Burgoon, Dunbar, & Segrin, 2002). The dominance of an influence message might reflect the speaker's perception that he or she controls the message target. A mother who says "Take the trash out tonight" clearly communicates her assumed authority over her son. Alternatively, a speaker might craft a dominant message to take control. For example, someone might say, "I'm going to run today's meeting." In either case, dominant influence messages seek compliance by dictating what the message receiver will do.

The amount of **argument** in an influence message refers to whether it includes reasons for compliance. For example, "Can I turn my paper in late?" is a request that is low in argument because it doesn't explain why the request should be granted. In contrast, "I've been diagnosed with mono and I can't attend class for two weeks, so can I turn my paper in late?" is high in argument. The argument dimension captures only the extent to which reasons are given in a message, not their quality. Thus, the following message would be considered as being high in argument: "I forgot to check the syllabus, I overslept this morning, and then I discovered that my printer is out of toner, so can I turn my paper in late?" Most instructors, however, wouldn't consider these especially good reasons for granting the request.

As you might expect, the degree of explicitness, dominance, and argument in an influence message affects how people react to the message. Consider the different forms a date request might take. How would you respond to a purely dominant message ("You're coming with me on Friday") compared to one that is worded as an explicit request ("Would you like to see a movie on Friday?") or that offers you some reasons to agree ("There's a great film showing; we'll have fun")? Here are some findings from research on this topic (Dillard et al., 1996; Dillard et al., 1997):

- People perceive explicit requests for help from a friend ("Please help me clean out my garage on Saturday") as creating an obstacle for them, which in turn makes them feel less happy and more angry, sad, and guilty.
- People perceive dominant messages ("You have to help me") as negative and illegitimate, which makes them feel surprised and angry.

Explicitness
The degree to which a message clearly reveals the speaker's intentions.

Dominance
The extent to which a speaker expresses power through the form and content of an influence message.

Argument
The degree to which reasons are given for complying with a request.

HOW DO YOU RATE? 12.2

Perceptions of Influence Messages

Messages with varying degrees of explicitness or dominance are likely to be perceived in different ways by a receiver and may produce diverse outcomes. Visit the **companion website** to evaluate the explicitness of various influence messages and rate your perceptions of those messages. How would you respond to influence attempts with varying degrees of explicitness or dominance?

■ People perceive requests that are explicit and provide arguments as more polite ("You have to help me because I let you store your stuff in the garage"), whereas they judge dominant messages negatively ("You're showing up at noon on Saturday").

In other words, the characteristics of your influence messages shape how people respond to you.

Communication Patterns

The messages that we use to influence other people don't stand alone – they occur within conversations. For this reason, the success of an influence attempt depends on how communication partners interact with each other. In this part of the chapter, we'll examine some of the patterns that unfold during interactions when one person is trying to influence the other.

Try, try again. One common sequence captures what happens when a person fails in an initial attempt to influence someone – for example, the message target refuses a request for help. What happens when someone turns you down? The most common reaction to a refusal is to try again, usually with more force. People tend to become less concerned with being nice to partners who turn them down (Hample & Dallinger, 1998). As a result, influence messages tend to become more aggressive in the face of resistance.

PAUSE & REFLECT

How did you feel the last time someone turned down a request that you made? What did you say in response?

Oscillate. People also tend to cycle between explicit influence attempts and segments of talk where the influence goal isn't mentioned. In medical settings, for example, doctors respond to resistance from a patient by dropping the topic for a while, but returning to it later in the conversation (Bylund, 2000). Parents also mix different types of strategies within messages that they use to influence their children; for example, they might include a direct request, promise a reward, and slip in a threat (Wilson, Cameron, & Whipple, 1997). The Real Words transcript that follows shows how talk about a request unfolds during a naturally occurring compliance-seeking conversation between sisters Pat and Mary. Notice how Pat initiates the request, backs off when Mary resists, and chats about Mary's schedule instead. Then Pat resumes the influence attempt later in the conversation.

Influence first, explain later. Influence interactions tend to unfold in one of two general ways (Sanders & Fitch, 2001). Consider how you might ask an academic advisor to waive a requirement. One option is to open with a fairly explicit request and then offer reasons to comply and address barriers you encounter as the conversation unfolds.

REAL WORDS

AN INTERPERSONAL INFLUENCE INTERACTION

PAT: Hey Mary, are you using the . . . the Prelude tomorrow? The car.

MARY: Yeah.

PAt: You're going to school then?

MARY: I gotta go to school, and then I have a meeting, and then I gotta go skating. So I need the car.

PAT: What time is your . . . what time is your school at?

MARY: I leave at . . .

PAT: Well listen, I need to borrow the car tomorrow and since there's only one car here . . .

MARY: Pat!

PAT: So tell me more about your day.

MARY: I have a meeting with that club I joined . . . I told you? . . . I don't know what to expect.

PAT: I'm sure you'll be glad you joined; it sounds like it could help you find a job after graduation . . . How is skating going?

MARY: I like it, but it's a hassle too. I either carry my gear or come home to get it. My day's busy enough . . .

PAT: Okay, why don't I . . . why don't you wake me up in the morning, and I'll take you to school. Around 7:45?

MARY: Pat!

PAT: I'll borrow the car, and take you out to lunch if you want . . . Then I'll pick you up at 3:00.

MARY: Hmmm. . .

PAT: Is that okay?

MARY: Yeah, that'd be okay.

Adapted from: Sanders & Fitch (2001)

For example, you might start by saying, "I know I haven't taken that prerequisite yet, but I'm hoping that you'll let me declare my major anyway." If the advisor argues against you, perhaps by explaining the reason for the rule, you would then offer rebuttals ("I'm taking that course during summer, and I can't enroll for the fall classes that I need unless I'm a major"). One advantage of this approach is that you make your request clear from the start, and you can focus on arguments that target the specific objections the advisor raises.

Investigate first, influence later. Another route involves trying to identify and counter sources of resistance before you make your request clear. This approach involves a little investigative work – for example, you might begin by asking, "Do you ever let anyone declare the major before they take this course?" or "How do summer school courses figure in when I'm registering for fall classes?" Once you figure out what barriers exist, you can make your explicit request. Hopefully, by that point, you've managed to locate the reasons why the advisor would say no and, as a result, avoid them.

> **PAUSE & REFLECT**
>
> Do you tend to lead off with your requests, or do you identify potential barriers first?

Short Influence Messages

Although most interpersonal influence interactions involve the give-and-take described in the previous section, sometimes you might have to make a request quickly. Perhaps you are talking to a stranger, and there isn't really any other reason for the conversation except your influence goal. For example, if you need to borrow a cell phone from a stranger to place an important call, you wouldn't work up to your request by making small talk. Even when the target of your influence message is not a stranger, time limits or a power difference might force you to keep your message very short.

Even in these circumstances, you can sequence parts of your influence messages to increase your effectiveness (Dillard et al., 2002). Several effective influence strategies require only one or two speaking turns (see Figure 12.2). Sometimes people wonder if these strategies are ethical, because they seem like tricks designed to manipulate other people. If you use these techniques, you need to make sure that the information you give is sound, you are respecting your communication partner, and your actions align with your values. The success of these strategies shows how simple adjustments to your communication strategies can significantly improve your chances of achieving an influence goal.

Putting Theory into Practice: Crafting Effective Influence Messages

Crafting influence messages involves adapting your communication behavior to increase the likelihood that you'll meet your goals. By being thoughtful about the messages you use to influence other people, you can improve your chance of success.

Remember that messages matter. Keep in mind that your messages have important effects on communication partners. In particular:

- Dominant influence messages tend to evoke negative reactions. Your partner may reject your request, or you may get what you want but damage your image or your relationship with the message target.
- Explicit messages create challenges for message targets, because these direct messages force a partner to respond. When explicit messages put pressure on a partner, a negative response is more likely.
- When explicit messages are accompanied by reasons or argument, message targets respond more positively. In the best-case scenario, then, you make your influence goals clear, offer good reasons, and avoid being too bossy.

ONE SPEAKING TURN	
That's-Not-All	Offer reward for complying with a request, and at the very last moment in the speaking turn, add something extra to the reward.
If you let me borrow your notes from the class that I missed, I'll share my study guide with you . . . and I'll proofread your final paper for you.	
Even-A-Penny	Emphasize that even a small contribution can be important.
I was wondering if I could borrow your notes from the class that I missed; even just looking at them for a few minutes would be a huge help.	

TWO SPEAKING TURNS	
Pregiving	Use the first speaking turn to offer a gift. Use the second speaking turn to make the request.
Let me help you with all your books! . . . Hey, could I borrow your notes from the class that I missed?	
Relational Obligations	Use the first speaking turn to identify a relationship shared with the message target. Use the second speaking turn to make the request.
Hey, I ride the No. 8 bus to campus just like you do! . . . Do you think I could borrow your notes from the class that I missed?	
Door-in-the-Face	Use the first speaking turn to make a large request that is likely to be rejected. Use the second speaking turn to make a smaller request.
Do you think I could borrow all of your notes for the whole semester? . . . How about just the ones from the class that I missed.	
Foot-in-the-Door	Use the first speaking turn to make a small request that is likely to be granted. Use the second speaking turn to make a larger request.
Do you have an extra pen that I could use? . . . Hey, do you think I could borrow your notes from the class that I missed?	
Foot-in-the-Mouth	Use the first speaking turn to find out how the message target is feeling. Use the second speaking turn to make the request.
How are you doing today? . . . That's great — hey, do you think I could borrow your notes from the class that I missed?	

FIGURE 12.2 Strategies for short influence interactions

What does this mean in practice? Instead of saying to a co-worker, "You have to cover my shift," or even "Will you please cover my shift?" try something like "Can you possibly cover my shift on Friday evening? My parents are coming to visit and I need to pick them up. I'd be happy to cover for you one day next week in exchange."

Plan for interpersonal influence interactions. Advance planning can greatly improve your communication effectiveness. Think about what you might do if your first request is rejected, and form a back-up plan. Also, decide in advance whether to chat for a bit first or to lead off with your request: if information you might gather would help you form a more effective influence message, you might want to ask some questions at the beginning of the conversation. Even when you have only a few speaking turns to influence a communication partner, advance planning can pay off.

COMMUNICATION IN ACTION 12.2

Creating Interpersonal Influence Messages

Imagine that you are waiting to have a short meeting with a professor about adding her class to your schedule for next semester. You know that the class is full, but you've heard great things about it and it's relevant to the kind of job you're hoping to get. Your primary goal is to register for the class, but you'd also like the professor to think you're capable and to get your relationship off to a good start. Write out what you would say to the professor. Then, show this message to three other people and ask them if they would be influenced by it. After getting their feedback, think about whether changing the order of your messages or adjusting the degree of dominance, explicitness, and argument might make the message better. Planning like this can help you be more successful when you pursue interpersonal influence goals.

INTERPERSONAL INFLUENCE IN ACTION

Interpersonal influence interactions unfold as partners exchange messages and they occur within relationships. In this section of the chapter, you'll learn about how you can overcome obstacles to achieving your influence goals, how relationship characteristics shape your communication options, and how to deal with high-stakes influence interactions.

Overcoming Obstacles

Interpersonal influence communication sometimes resembles a tug-of-war: one party tries to exert influence and the other party tries to resist it. Your partner's resistance can be more or less successful, depending on the strength of your strategy. Likewise, how influential you are depends on how you react to resistance. And by understanding the strategies that people use to refuse a request, you can arm yourself with the tools necessary to resist unwanted influence. In general, you can become a more effective communicator if you understand how to resist influence and how to overcome resistance when you influence others.

PAUSE & REFLECT

Think of a recent episode when your communication partner rejected your influence attempt. What reason, if any, were you given for the refusal?

Let's start by considering the reasons that people refuse a request. Table 12.4 summarizes six obstacles to interpersonal influence (Ifert & Roloff, 1998). People draw upon

TABLE 12.4 Obstacles to interpersonal influence

Obstacle	Definition	Example
Lack of possession	The message target doesn't possess the resources needed to comply	I can't support your candidate for the school board because I'm not eligible to vote in this state
Imposition	Complying with the influence attempt would impinge on the message target's prior plans	I can't loan you my car because I need it to take my mother to an appointment
No incentive	The speaker doesn't perceive a reason to comply with the influence attempt	I'm not going to change my eating habits; my diet is fine for a person my age
Recalcitrance	The speaker doesn't want to comply with the influence attempt	I don't want to date you exclusively
Postponement	The speaker puts off complying with the influence attempt until some unspecified time in the future	I'll clean up the apartment when I'm not so busy with my classes
Violation	The message target sees the influence attempt as inappropriate or something the message source is responsible for	You shouldn't ask me to proofread your paper – you should take care of that for yourself

knowledge of these obstacles both when they create influence messages and when they refuse influence attempts. First, consider how you craft an influence message. You might just blurt out your request and see what happens. As a more strategic alternative, however, you could tailor your request to neutralize the obstacles that you anticipate. Consider how you might go about asking a classmate to lend you a book. If you think that your classmate might refuse because it would be an imposition, you can word your request to minimize the burden ("I'll return it right away"). If you think that your classmate isn't motivated to help you, you could offer an incentive along with your request ("I'll lend you my lecture notes in exchange"). Figure 12.3 identifies some strategies that you can use to address obstacles to requests.

When you are the target of an unwanted influence attempt, you can use these obstacles as reasons for refusing. In any given situation, you could say, "I don't want to help," "I can't help," or "You don't deserve my help." As you might expect, your choice of words has consequences. If you say you don't want to, you might damage your relationship with your communication partner: this kind of refusal might communicate that you don't value your partner (Ifert & Roloff, 1994). How you refuse a request can also determine whether your communication partner gives up or keeps asking. In particular, people are more persistent in their efforts to influence a message target who is unwilling to comply rather than unable to (Ifert & Roloff, 1996). By saying that you

If You Think a Message Target will Say No Because …	You Can Neutralize that Obstacle By …
The request is too big; What an imposition! I could never go along with that!	Specify the Limits of the Request: "Can I use your computer? I just need about an hour to edit and print this paper. It won't take long."
I don't possess the resources that are needed to comply. I have to say no because I'm not in a position to go along with the request.	Confirm Required Resources First: "Are you doing anything Sunday Afternoon? … Great, it sounds like you are free to help me move."
I don't feel like it, and I don't see any reason to say yes.	Offer an Inducement or a Threat: "If you let me borrow your car to go home this weekend, I'll do your laundry for the rest of the month."
The request is really inappropriate – you have no business asking for something like that. There's no way I'll go along with that.	Explain or Apologize in Advance: "I'm sorry to ask this. I know it's my fault that I'm in this mess. Can I please take the exam late?"
I don't have any obligation to help you.	Make Your Relationship Salient: "It's so nice to have someone from my hometown in class. Hey, do you think I could borrow your notes?"
It's not a good time to comply with the request; I'll just put it off.	Make the Request Open-ended: "Working every Saturday gets old. Do you think you could swap schedules with me some time?"

FIGURE 12.3 Tailoring requests to neutralize obstacles

can't comply with a request, you can put an end to an influence attempt without damaging your relationship.

People also adapt their refusals based on whether the request is time sensitive. To explore this process, Gaylen Paulson and Michael Roloff (1997) asked college students to write out what they might say to turn down a request for a date. The study included a variety of different kinds of date requests, and the results showed that date refusals differ depending on whether the request specified a time for the date. In particular, if a request specifies a time ("Do you want to get together on Sunday afternoon?"), a temporary obstacle is sufficient ("I'd love to, but I have a study group then"). If a request is open-ended ("Would you be interested in getting together sometime?"), the refusal must be lasting ("I'm sorry, but I'm dating someone else").

People vary in their ability to anticipate and overcome obstacles to interpersonal influence. In children aged from 4–9, girls are more accurate than boys at predicting the difficulty of influencing a friend or parent, and boys and girls in the first or second

FIGURE 12.4 Overcoming obstacles in an influence interaction

Source: www.CartoonStock.com.

grades are better at anticipating specific obstacles to requests than preschool children (Marshall & Levy, 1998). Among adults, people who have more control over their own communication behavior are more persistent when confronted with a message target who is unable or unwilling to comply (Ifert & Roloff, 1997). In general, then, the development of communication competence can improve people's chances in an influence interaction.

PAUSE & REFLECT

Do you sometimes find yourself doing something that is disagreeable to you because you couldn't fend off an influence attempt? What kinds of obstacles could you use to avoid this problem?

Relationship Characteristics and Influence Messages

Because intimacy and power affect obstacles to interpersonal influence, they affect the messages people use to influence a communication partner. **Politeness theory** is a set of assumptions about how intimacy and power are related to the use of more or less polite influence messages (Brown & Levison, 1987). Politeness theory suggests that we all have **face**, which is the public image of ourselves we put out into the world. There are two types of face: **positive face** refers to our desire to be well-liked and admired by others, and **negative face** refers to our desire to be autonomous and unconstrained. Given that we all have these desires, any request for compliance has the potential to violate one or both types of face; we call this a **face-threatening act**. When you attempt to influence people, you threaten their negative face because you are asking them to do what you want rather than respecting their desire for autonomy and to do what they want to do. In addition, your influence attempts can create a threat to your own positive face because people may not like you as much if you make too many demands. Politeness theory suggests that we use a variety of strategies when we attempt to influence others to limit the amount of face threats in our requests. Specifically, politeness theory suggests that we alter the directness of our requests in an effort to preserve face.

The extent to which you alter your directness may depend on the size of the request and degree of intimacy or power in your relationship. Figure 12.5 shows the factors that

Politeness Theory
A set of assumptions about how intimacy and power are related to the use of more or less polite influence messages.

Face
The public image of ourselves that we put out into the world.

Positive Face
The desire to be well-liked and admired by others.

Negative Face
The desire to be autonomous and unconstrained.

Face-threatening Act
A request for compliance that violates one's positive or negative face.

shape how polite an influence message needs to be. For example, consider two requests you might receive from your brother: he'd like to tag along with you and your friends on Saturday night and he'd like to move in with you for a few months. He'll have to word the second request more politely than the first, because it's a much bigger imposition and a much larger threat to your negative face. If you and your brother have a close relationship, he can phrase both requests more casually, because it's less of an imposition to hang out with – and even live with – a brother you like. Similarly, if your brother has a lot of power in the relationship, maybe because he has a well-paying job or he's well-liked within your family, both the imposition of these requests and the need to word them politely goes down.

Intimacy and influence messages. People in close relationships can use influence messages that are direct and to the point. Does this mean that you are less polite or even rude to your close friends, romantic partner, and family members? In one sense, yes, because you don't always say "please," "if you could," or "I'm sorry to trouble you." At the same time, your close relationship partners are less likely to consider your direct messages as rude (Dillard et al., 1997). In fact, people consider it less polite when close friends *aren't* direct: when your best friend beats around the bush and makes you work to unearth the point of an influence message, you are likely to become irritated (Dillard et al., 1997).

Although intimacy frees you up to use explicit influence messages, it may also allow you to use less explicit messages. Consider the messages you might use to try to get someone to stop smoking around you. In a nonintimate relationship, you face some challenges: you don't know whether your influence attempt will annoy the message target, and you don't want to look bad to the people around you. These concerns might prompt you to be indirect in your approach. Unfortunately, an indirect message, such as "My asthma is acting up today," might not be recognized as an influence message. So, you're forced to be a little more explicit: "If it wouldn't be too much trouble, could you please put out your cigarette?" In a close relationship, you're on firmer ground with the message target, which leaves you free to be more direct: "Hey, put out your cigarette –

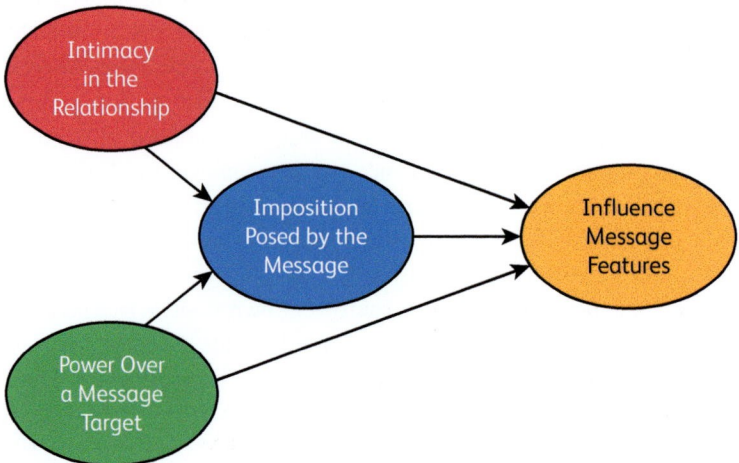

FIGURE 12.5 Factors that shape influence messages

the smoke is bothering me." And if you and your partner really know each other well, an indirect message, such as "I need air" or even just coughing, might make your point.

When you communicate using computer-mediated channels, such as in online discussion boards or via email, the intimacy of these interactions also shape influence messages. One study showed that when communication online is based on membership is some group, such as Dallas Cowboys fans or alumni of your high school, the absence of feelings of intimacy is associated with more obvious influence messages (Postmes, Spears, Lee, and Novak, 2005). In contrast, that study found that a lack of intimacy leads to less obvious influence messages when online relationships aren't predetermined. Using computer-mediated options for influencing other people can also affect your chances of success. In particular, research shows that women are less persuaded by online influence messages then men are, in part because online channels are less intimate venues for communication (Guadagno & Cialdini, 2002).

Power and influence messages. Power affects influence messages in much the same way that intimacy does: powerful people have the freedom to be more direct in their influence attempts, and they can get away with being more indirect. For example, your supervisor at work has a lot of influence over you. She can make a request directly, such as "Clean up the staff lounge today," and you probably wouldn't find that request rude or inappropriate. Or, she might make that request indirectly, saying "The staff lounge is sure a mess," and you could reasonably see that statement as a request. Can you imagine using either message to influence your boss? The direct message might get you fired, and the indirect message might be seen as volunteering to clean up. It is unlikely that either message would prompt your supervisor to start cleaning up.

There are five common sources of power. The first type of power is **coercive power**, which refers to one's ability to use threats and punishment to achieve their desired outcomes. In contrast, **reward power** involves the use of incentives to gain compliance toward a desired goal. **Legitimate power** is gained by individuals on the basis of their position or title. Next, people gain **referent power** when others look up to them with admiration, acceptance, and approval. Finally, **expert power** is accrued by people who have high amounts of information, knowledge, and expertise. Your boss has legitimate power on the basis of his or her position in the company, expert power based on the fact that he or she has more information than you about the operations of your company,

Coercive Power
The ability to use threats and punishment to gain compliance.

Reward Power
The ability to use incentives to gain compliance.

Legitimate Power
The degree of power gained by one's position or title.

Referent Power
The extent to which individuals are well-liked and admired.

Expert Power
The extent to which individuals have information, knowledge, and expertise on a given topic.

FIGURE 12.6 Kandahar, Afghanistan, June 20, 2008: British paratrooper from 3rd Battalion the Parachute Regiment Sgt. Berry Seakins, 37, from Southend, England, gives orders while on patrol

Source: Photo by Marco Di Lauro/Getty Images.

reward power based on his or her ability to give you a raise or a promotion, coercive power given that he or she may fire you for unsatisfactory performance, and potentially referent power to the extent that you like him or her. Thus, your boss does not need to be concerned about being polite or making a strong argument in order to convince you to do your job. Given that your boss has high power, he or she can be more explicit and dominant in telling you what to do at work.

Upward Influence

Seeking compliance from a communication partner who has more power.

When you lack power, you need to be careful about how you make a request. Upward influence – seeking compliance from people with more power – is an important skill for people within organizations (Waldron, 1999). In fact, a person's use of upward influence strategies has been linked to better wages and more favorable performance evaluations (Wayne, Liden, Graf, & Ferris, 1997). How can you go about influencing people who have power, without offending them or being seen as inappropriate? Two message strategies are most likely to be used by people influencing someone with more power (Yukl, Falbe, & Youn, 1993). In particular, people with less power sometimes build coalitions with other workers. For example, if all of the employees band together to ask the boss for more vacation days, they can pool their limited power as individuals and exert more influence. The second effective strategy is an appeal to friendship and loyalty. By appealing to your personal relationship with your manager ("How is your mom feeling? Did I mention that I need the afternoon off to help my mother move?"), you might set power differences aside and achieve your influence goal.

High Stakes Episodes

High Stakes Episodes

Interpersonal influence interactions that involve a lot of secondary goals.

Interactions that involve a lot of secondary goals are **high stakes episodes** (Schrader & Dillard, 1998). Two influence situations where the stakes are high are initiating a romantic relationship and gaining assistance from somebody in power. People who have these primary goals are often also concerned about having a smooth interaction, managing their relationship with the other person, retaining their personal resources, and keeping their anxiety under control. In this section of the chapter, we'll take a close look at one particular high stakes influence situation – asking someone out on a date.

Making a bid for more intimacy or shared time with another person can be risky. In fact, initiating or intensifying a romantic relationship can be threatening in three different ways (Kunkel, Wilson, Olufowote, & Robson, 2003):

- You run the risk of making the target of your romantic interest feel forced to go out with you. If you've ever been asked out by someone and found it hard to say no, you know what this pressure feels like.
- A bid to increase intimacy could damage the relationship. If you ask a partner to spend a special day together – perhaps your birthday or Valentine's Day – and you are rejected, you might find it hard to continue the relationship.
- You can damage your image by seeming either presumptuous or desperate.

In crafting a date request message, you need to be attentive to all of these concerns, as well as your primary goal of getting your partner to spend time with you. As you learned previously, the degree of intimacy in your relationship shapes the message strategies you might use. In a study that Denise conducted, she asked people to call a person they had dated at least once before and request a date (Solomon, 1997). The study showed that people ask for dates more explicitly in nonintimate relationships (where they have to be clear to be understood) and in very intimate relationships (where a date request isn't as threatening). When people were somewhat close, yet unsure about their relationship, they gravitated toward more indirect date requests. In particular, some people would chat for a bit before bringing up the date request, and they would only hint about going out together. The study described in the Inside Communication Research box shows how relationship characteristics other than intimacy can affect date requests.

INSIDE COMMUNICATION RESEARCH

Date Requests

Communication scholar Leanne Knobloch studies the role of relational uncertainty in shaping close personal relationships. *Relational uncertainty* refers to the degree of confidence that people have in their perceptions of a relationship – and when people doubt their views of a relationship, communication can become complicated. Knobloch (2006) conducted a study to examine how relational uncertainty affected people's communication strategies when making requests for a date. She concluded that date requests were a unique context for examining communicative influence strategies, because persuading others to spend time with us is one of our primary influence goals, but date request messages can be challenging to craft effectively.

College undergraduates who were involved in romantic relationships at varying stages of development participated in the study. Individual participants completed a questionnaire about their relationship and the amount of relational uncertainty they felt. Then participants were asked to imagine that they were calling their romantic partner but that he or she was unable to take their call, so they were forced to leave a message on the partner's answering machine. Participants dialed one number if their partner was male and a different number if their partner was female, so that a male or female voice would greet them saying, "Hi. It's me. Please leave a message." The participants were asked to leave a message with the goal of making plans to spend time together. After making their date request, the participants filled out another questionnaire assessing their perceptions of the effectiveness of their message. A team of research assistants then coded each message to evaluate how smooth it was, how friendly, the degree to which it focused on the relationship, and how explicitly the date request was worded.

The results of the study revealed that individuals who were experiencing relational uncertainty produced date request messages that were less fluent, less friendly, less focused on the relationship, and less explicit than individuals who felt relatively certain about their relationship. Moreover, participants who were uncertain about their relationship believed that their date request was more ineffective than did individuals who were certain about their relationship. These findings suggest that when people lack confidence in their perceptions of a relationship, their attempts to influence a romantic partner to spend time with them tend to be ineffective.

THINK ABOUT IT

1. How might relational uncertainty affect people's efforts to influence relationship partners in other situations, such as requesting sexual intimacy or suggesting an exclusive relationship?
2. To what extent did the method used in this study produce realistic date request messages? Can you think of any ways to make this laboratory study more realistic?

What can you take away from this closer look at date requests? First, if you find it hard to ask people out, don't judge yourself harshly – this is challenging for a lot of people. Second, you might make the task easier by focusing more on the relationship and less on the date request. Try to build closeness and reduce uncertainty by chatting, exploring common interests, and expressing your liking for the other person through your verbal and nonverbal behaviors. Third, you can reduce the threats that go along with a date request by leaving your partner a lot of room to say no. One easy way to do this is to make your request time-specific ("Do you want to catch the 7:30 movie?") – if your partner doesn't want to go out with you, the person can just say that he or she can't make it. If you ask a person to go out with you "anytime, ever," you may force that partner to say "no, never," which can be awkward for both of you.

PAUSE & REFLECT

Have you ever felt foolish after you made a request that was refused? How might you reword your influence message to avoid future refusals?

Putting Theory into Practice: Ethical Influence

In this part of the chapter, you learned how to anticipate and neutralize obstacles to compliance, employ strategies for exerting upward influence, and avoid some of the risks that go along with intensifying a romantic relationship. As you put what you have learned into practice, be sure that your skillful communication is also ethical interpersonal influence. Let's look more closely at what that means.

Respect obstacles. Thinking ahead and crafting influence messages that sidestep some of the common obstacles to compliance can help you to achieve your influence goals. Keep in mind, though, that ethical communicators don't use their words to trap interaction partners. Practicing ethical influence involves balancing your own desire to achieve your influence goals against your partner's right to refuse. If a person rejects your influence attempt, you have two key issues to consider:

■ Are you trying to advance your own goals at someone else's expense? Or are you trying to promote the well-being of the relationship or your community?
■ Does your partner have specific barriers, such as a scheduling conflict or a lack of resources, that you might be able to negotiate around? Or would persisting subject your partner to discomfort or embarrassment?

Your answers can help you decide whether it's ethical to continue. For example, trying to persuade someone to chair a committee because you know she is the best person for the job is ethical. Trying to persuade her because you don't want to do it yourself is not.

Enable upward influence. You can also promote more ethical communication by allowing people who have less power than you to exert interpersonal influence.

Organizations are moving away from the strict power hierarchies that were common in the past. As a member of the workforce, you'll probably find yourself working in teams with people who have more or less power than you. You can be a more effective communicator by using some of the influence strategies described in this chapter, and by creating channels for people with less power than you to achieve their influence goals.

COMMUNICATION IN ACTION 12.3

Inviting Upward Influence

People who find themselves in powerful positions can create opportunities for individuals with less power to exert interpersonal influence and achieve their goals. Complete the form on the **companion website** to identify strategies for encouraging upward influence.

Avoid strategic ambiguity. Sometimes communicators are intentionally ambiguous when they pursue an influence goal. You might casually mention to your roommate that you have done a lot of dishes lately. If your roommate asks if you want her to help out more, you could deny that you were making a request. Ambiguous messages create a dilemma for receivers, because they can't tell if the influence attempt was real or imagined.

You'll be a more ethical communicator if you take ownership of your attempts to influence other people. When you have an influence goal, make your agenda clear and allow your partner to accept or reject your influence attempt. Of course, you'll use more or less explicit messages depending on how intimate your relationship is or how much power you have. In any case, try to avoid making influence messages that are unnecessarily vague and do not deny your underlying influence goals. If you treat your communication partner with respect, you may find that he or she is more willing to grant your requests.

SUMMARY

Interpersonal influence occurs anytime you or a communication partner use messages to affect each other's attitudes, beliefs, and actions. In this chapter, you learned about some of the most common interpersonal influence goals we pursue when we communicate with others. In addition to your primary goal for an interaction, keep in mind that you have secondary goals – such as preserving your self-image or maintaining a relationship – that shape your communication options. By recognizing your influence goals and keeping both primary and secondary concerns in mind, you may be more effective at managing the multiple influence goals you may have within an interpersonal interaction.

The messages you use to pursue interpersonal influence goals vary in important ways. You can craft influence messages that make your goal more or less explicit, communicate more or less dominance over your partner, and provide more or fewer arguments to support your case. Conversations in which influence messages unfold may also take different forms, ranging from interactions that start right off with the influence message to those in which a communicator gradually brings up an influence goal. Even very short influence interactions, which might have only a few speaking turns, can be sequenced in ways that increase your likelihood of success.

When you put interpersonal influence messages to work for you, keep in mind the obstacles you may encounter, characteristics of your relationship with a partner, and challenges you may face in a high stakes episode. A communication partner might reject your influence attempt for a variety of reasons – if you take these obstacles into account when crafting your message, you might just be able to neutralize and overcome them. Intimacy in a relationship and having power with respect to a partner also gives you more options for communicating influence; in particular, you can be both more explicit and more indirect when you influence a close relationship partner or someone you have power over. And remember that high stakes influence situations are those where your primary goal goes hand-in-hand with several secondary concerns. Crafting effective messages in situations like these might require you to weigh your affection for a communication partner, your certainty about the relationship, and how to minimize the risks that you may encounter.

ACTIVITIES FOR EXPLORING COMMUNICATION ETHICS

What Would You/Should You Do?

You have noticed that your supervisor at work often uses his power to influence less powerful workers to do things that aren't part of their job description. He regularly asks one of your co-workers to give him a ride home after work. You're also pretty sure that he's tried to date a couple of the interns who have worked in the office. Because the supervisor has the power to punish these people, you see them reluctantly agree to his requests. You realize that he is misusing his power, but addressing his misuse of power could jeopardize your job. What would you or should you do?

Something to Think About

In the 2008 presidential election, both political parties made a concerted effort to register college students to vote, especially in swing states like Pennsylvania and Ohio. From people with clipboards on the street to announcements in classrooms, college students were bombarded with influence messages. Computer-mediated solicitations also encouraged voters who were already registered to make sure that their friends and family were signed up. Voting is a civic duty, but it is also a choice. What are the ethical considerations involved in using such an aggressive and multi-pronged strategy for influencing new voters to register?

Analyze Communication Ethics Yourself

One of President Obama's first acts in office was to initiate the closing of the prison camps at Guantanamo Bay. One factor underlying this action was concern about the tactics allegedly being used to get information from known terrorists and prisoners. Many human rights organizations have objected to the use of torture to obtain information from prisoners. The Council on Foreign Relations has published the following website on the use of torture and interrogation techniques: http://www.cfr.org/publication/9209/. How does the information contained on this webpage shape your opinion about the use of torture as an influence strategy to obtain information?

KEY WORDS

argument

coercive power

compliance-seeking messages

dominance

expert power

explicitness

face

face-threatening act

goal strain

goals

high stakes episodes

interpersonal influence

interpersonal influence goals

legitimate power

negative face

politeness theory

positive face

primary goal

referent power

reward power

secondary goals

upward influence

LEARNING OBJECTIVES

After reading this chapter, you should be able to:

1. Describe different forms, levels, and components of interpersonal conflict.
2. Identify four goals that are relevant in conflict situations.
3. Describe three conflict strategies and five styles of conflict management.
4. Understand how biased attributions can escalate conflict.
5. Describe the effects of interpersonal power on conflict avoidance.
6. Describe the patterns of interpersonal communication that occur during conflict interactions.

PUTTING THEORY INTO PRACTICE

In this chapter, you will learn how to:

1. Diagnose your conflicts.
2. Focus on behaviors, rather than traits.
3. Unravel conflicts one component at a time.
4. Plan for multiple goals.
5. Match your strategies to your goals.
6. Branch out from your conflict style.
7. Question your attribution for conflict.
8. Keep your power in check.
9. De-escalate, rather than escalate, conflict.

INTERPERSONAL CONFLICT

13

348 WHAT IS CONFLICT?

354 MANAGING CONFLICT

364 CONFLICT DYNAMICS

372 SUMMARY

374 ACTIVITIES FOR EXPLORING
COMMUNICATION ETHICS

375 KEY WORDS

Source: Getty Images/Cultural
Howard Kingsnorth.

Conflicts are a common part of everyone's life, but tempers really flare when people who live together are also competing against each other. The reality television series *America's Next Top Model* documents the lives of women who share living quarters while they vie for a modeling contract and the approval of the show's creator, Tyra Banks. Since the show first aired, every group of models has had its share of disagreements, arguments, conflicts, and fights. During cycle 5, models Bre and Nicole clashed over food. Bre, convinced that Nicole had stolen her granola bars, was caught on video in the middle of the night pouring Nicole's energy drink down the sink. When confronted the next day, Bre denied any wrongdoing, refused to talk to anyone, and talked trash about another model, Kim, who tried to intervene. In return, Bre found herself in the hot seat for elimination at the end of the episode. In the end, Bre wasn't eliminated, but she received a stern reprimand from Tyra. Conflicts like this one highlight the challenges that can arise between friends, roommates, and co-workers, as well as some of the strategies that people use to address their complaints.

C an you remember a particularly intense conflict with a close friend, roommate, co-worker, or family member? What caused the conflict? How did you resolve it? The example from *America's Next Top Model* suggests that interpersonal conflict is inevitable when people live together. Bre and Nicole expressed their disagreements through acts of vengeance, yelling, and ignoring each other, but there are constructive ways of handling conflict as well. In this chapter, we examine the characteristics of interpersonal conflict, the communication behaviors you can use to manage conflict, and conflict dynamics that unfold in interpersonal relationships.

WHAT IS CONFLICT?

When you think of the word "conflict," what thoughts and feelings come to mind? People characterize conflicts in many different ways: conflicts can be playful or serious, they can escalate into shouting matches or involve the silent treatment, and they can be ongoing or a sudden blow-up (Baxter, Wilmot, Simmons, & Swartz, 1993). Although interpersonal conflicts can be painful, they also offer an opportunity to improve your relationships. You will be better able to realize the advantages of interpersonal conflict if you understand the nature of conflict.

Conflict Takes Many Forms

Interpersonal conflicts can be challenging because they can take a variety of forms. An important step in improving your conflict communication, then, is learning to recognize the type of conflict you are experiencing. As shown in Figure 13.1, conflict experiences vary along two dimensions (see Cupach & Canary, 2000). A first dimension distinguishes between conflicts that are tied to specific experiences and those that span several different experiences. For example,

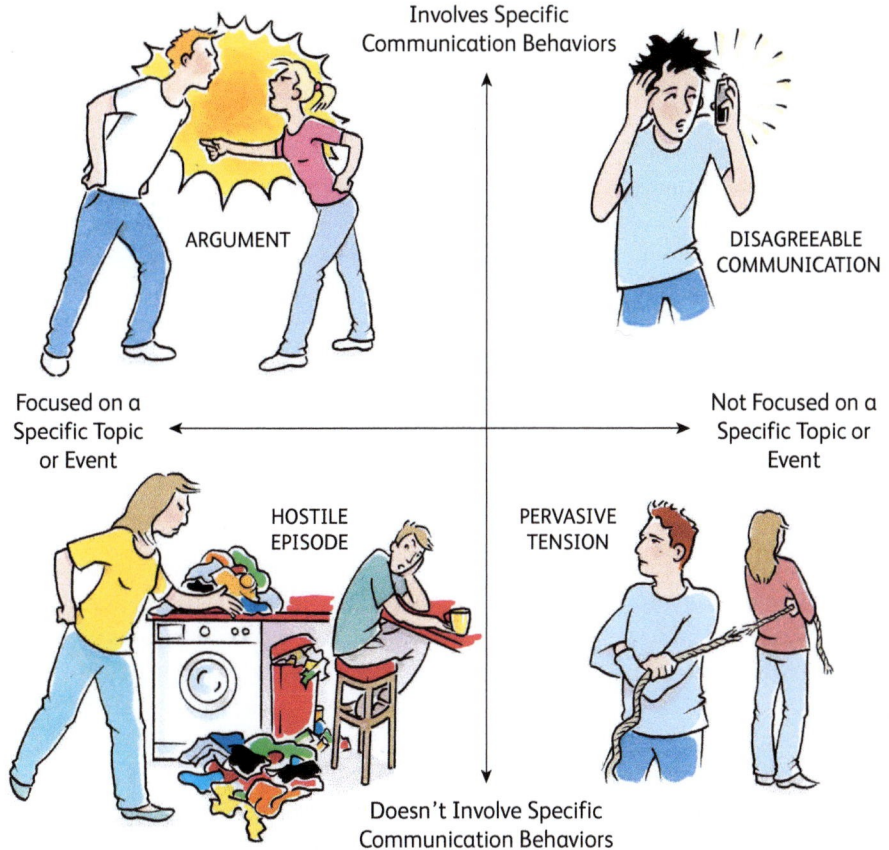

FIGURE 13.1 Forms of interpersonal conflict

you might have a conflict with your neighbors because their dog barks when they are away from home, or you might generally dislike your neighbors and feel annoyed by most of their actions. The second dimension contrasts conflicts that involve specific communication behaviors, such as when you confront your neighbor about the noisy dog, and conflicts that affect all communication behaviors between the parties, such as when you tend to be rude to your neighbors because you dislike them. These two dimensions of conflict result in four distinct forms of conflict: argument, disagreeable communication, hostile episode, or pervasive tension.

When you communicate explicitly with another person about a particular disagreeable situation, you are having a conflict in the form of an **argument**. An argument is an especially concrete type of conflict because it is clearly about a specific issue, event, or circumstance. And your communication behavior during an argument clearly reveals the reason for the conflict. In other words, your words and behaviors during the conversation focus specifically on a singular source of dissatisfaction. An argument is perhaps the most clear-cut type of conflict.

Disagreeable communication involves communication behaviors that are similar to an argument, but the communication isn't about any specific problem or issue. Disagreeable communication occurs when partners contradict each other, insult each

Argument
An explicit conversation with another person about a particular disagreement.

Disagreeable Communication
Using specific behaviors, such as contradicting, insulting, and yelling, during a conversation.

other, and raise their voices, but there's no particular issue up for debate. Ray Romano's parents on the sitcom *Everybody Loves Raymond* are a good example of this kind of conflict. Ray's parents, Frank and Marie Barone, frequently complain about each other, treat each other rudely, and bicker. But when their son Ray finally decided to help them end their marriage, the Barones were shocked that he thought they weren't happy. Disagreeable communication seems to express disagreement, although no issue or topic of disagreement may actually exist.

At the other extreme, you might experience a conflict in which there is a clear underlying problem, but you don't communicate about that issue directly. This form of conflict is called a **hostile episode**, because one person is filled with hostility or resentment toward another person for a period of time (Cupach & Canary, 2000). In an ongoing relationship, day-to-day annoyances can make one person feel frustrated with the other person. Does your sibling keep misplacing your cell phone? Does your co-worker point out your mistakes in front of the boss? When you become dissatisfied and irritated by someone's behavior, you might experience the feelings of hostility that make up this form of conflict.

A fourth form of conflict, **pervasive tension**, consists of friction that is present every time people communicate with each other. This form of conflict does not involve specific communication behaviors, and it is not about a particular event or topic. Instead, every interaction that occurs between conflict parties is characterized by discomfort and misunderstanding. Even a simple conversation can be difficult, as you struggle to coordinate speaking turns, introduce new topics, and bring the interaction to an end. Pervasive tension undermines all communication between partners, so it is especially threatening to the future of a relationship. In fact, the presence of criticism, contempt, defensiveness, and withdrawal in conflict interactions between newlyweds is predictive of divorce later in their marriage (Gottman, 1994).

Hostile Episode

A period of negative feelings or resentment toward another person.

Pervasive Tension

A friction that is present when people communicate with each other.

PAUSE & REFLECT

Which form of conflict do you experience most often: arguments, disagreement communication, hostile episodes, or pervasive tension?

Conflict Exists at Multiple Levels

As you have seen, there are several different types of conflict. In addition, a single conflict can be seen in many different ways. Consider the example of a conflict that exists between André and his good friend Luke, who both work as servers in a restaurant. Lately, Luke has been asking André to cover for him when he's late and then taking over some of André's tables to make up for the tips that he missed. When André becomes frustrated with his friend, he could think about the conflict in several different ways: as a problematic behavior, as a violation of relationship roles, or as an example of an undesirable trait of Luke's. As summarized in Table 3.1, André might perceive this conflict in terms

TABLE 13.1 Levels of conflict

Level	Definition	Example
Problematic behavior	The conflict stems from specific actions performed by the other person	André is irritated by Luke's habit of coming to work late and then taking his tables
Relationship roles	The conflict stems from the other person's violations of expectations or norms for the relationship	André is irritated because Luke is violating André's standards for friendship by taking advantage of him
Undesirable traits	The conflict stems from the other person's problematic personality or enduring qualities	André is irritated because Luke is self-centered and doesn't think about his co-workers' needs

of the specific actions that he finds annoying, a violation of his expectations for friendship, or as a sign that Luke is a bad person. As this example illustrates, even a relatively straightforward conflict might be defined in a variety of ways.

Although you might emphasize any of the three levels in your view of a conflict, you are least likely to focus on specific behaviors. In a study of college students' journal entries about conflict, 24% of the entries focused on a partner's behaviors, 38% addressed violations of norms, and 37% emphasized the conflict partner's personal traits (Allen & Berkos, 2005/2006). Does the level at which you define your conflicts matter? The answer is yes. Research shows that people are more aggressive toward relationship partners when they attribute conflicts to that person's personality (O'Leary, Smith Slep, & O'Leary, 2007; Smith Slep & O'Leary, 2007). These findings are especially noteworthy because people often link conflicts to undesirable traits.

Components of Conflict

Because there are many forms and levels of conflict, figuring out what is going on in any particular situation can be difficult. It might help you to keep in mind that conflicts are made up of three properties: disagreement, interference, and negative emotion (Barki & Hartwick, 2004).

Disagreement is the perception that parties have different opinions, values, goals, priorities, or beliefs. On its own, disagreement isn't a conflict. Two people might be fans of different baseball teams and disagree about which team is best. Likewise, members of a family might have different political values, vote for different presidential candidates, and disagree about the importance of voting. Although these disagreements might contribute to interpersonal or family conflicts, the differences of opinion in themselves are not conflicts. Interpersonal conflicts emerge only when disagreement is combined with the other two components.

A second component, interference, refers to the perception that one person's interests, goals, or outcomes are being negatively affected by another person. You probably

FIGURE 13.2 Lost love or a scheduling conflict?

Source: © Peter C. Vey/The New Yorker Collection/www. cartoonbank.com.

"I'd like to dedicate this next song to all those who thought they'd loved and lost only to find out years later that it was just some sort of scheduling conflict."

encounter interference in a variety of ways as you go through your day. Did your friend show up late to a study session? Did your boss give someone else the extra shift you were hoping to work? When the other components of conflict aren't present, these experiences are just the inevitable disruptions that occur in an ordinary day. When combined with the other conflict components, troubles coordinating your life with a partner can be at the root of relationship problems.

Negative emotion is the component of conflict that includes all the bad feelings – anger, frustration, tension, hostility, jealousy – associated with another person. Conflicts typically involve two types of negative emotions: hard emotions, such as anger or aggravation, and soft emotions, including sadness and hurt (Sanford, 2007). Of course, you can also experience negative feelings about somebody when you aren't having a conflict. For example, you might feel guilty that you haven't spent more time with your family, disappointed that your romantic partner didn't win a scholarship, or sad about a parent's failing health. As these examples illustrate, negative emotions are not themselves experiences of conflict.

Figure 13.3 shows how the three components of conflict combine to create interpersonal conflict. As discussed previously, you might experience each of these components of conflict by itself; that experience might be intense, but it isn't conflict. You might also

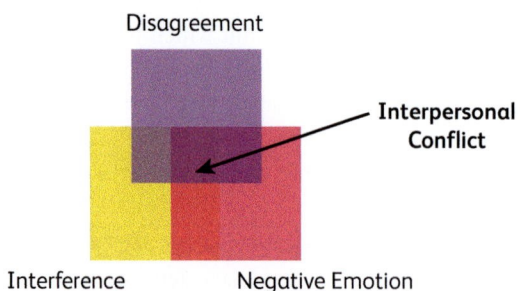

FIGURE 13.3 Components of interpersonal conflict

experience situations in which only two of the components are present. For example, two athletes competing for a starting position on a team probably disagree about who should be in the starting line-up, and each takes steps to interfere with the other's goal of starting (for example, by striving to improve her own skills). As long as the situation isn't tainted by bad feelings, the situation is better described as a rivalry, rather than a conflict. Interpersonal conflict, then, arises in situations where disagreement, interference, and negative emotion are all present. More specifically, **interpersonal conflict** exists when two people recognize that they hold different opinions, beliefs, or values; they see those points of disagreement as sources of interference in their lives; and the situation evokes negative emotions.

Interpersonal Conflict
A situation in which people disagree with each other, interfere in each other's lives, and experience negative emotions.

> ## PAUSE & REFLECT
>
> Based on your experiences, which component of conflict do you think is the most important?

Putting Theory into Practice: Understanding Your Conflicts

Conflicts can take a variety of forms, you can perceive them in different ways, and they involve a combination of disagreement, interference, and negative emotion. This knowledge can help you to make sense of the conflicts that occur in your own life.

Diagnose your conflicts. Diagnosing your conflicts can help you communicate about them more effectively. Jen recalls how two of her friends in college saw their relationship deteriorate once they became roommates. One woman was bothered by the fact that her roommate left dirty dishes in the sink, always had her boyfriend spend the night, and frequently bragged about her good grades. The other woman was bothered that her roommate wouldn't make time for them to hang out together and resented the fact that the roommate had taken the larger bedroom but didn't pay a higher portion of the rent. As the situation escalated to include a lot of pervasive tension, it was hard to remember what caused the conflict, which in turn made communicating about it very difficult. You can avoid falling into a similar situation if you figure out what your conflict is really about.

> ## COMMUNICATION IN ACTION 13.1
>
>
> ### Diagnosing Your Conflicts
>
> This exercise will help you diagnose the level and form of a recent conflict. Complete the form on the **companion website** to diagnose a recent conflict. Keep this exercise in mind when you are confronted with a new conflict, so that you can communicate with a better understanding of your situation.

Focus on behaviors, rather than traits. Conflicts can be easier to talk about when you link them to specific behaviors, rather than to a person's traits. Consider how you might confront a friend who was late for an appointment with you – again. If you focus on your friend's traits, you might find yourself saying something that attacks your friend's identity ("You're such a slacker – you're always late"). This approach would probably prompt your friend to defend himself; after all, his only other option is to accept this negative quality as true. In contrast, consider what might happen if you focus on the behavior itself ("You tend to be about 10 minutes late every time we agree to meet, and it bothers me.") A statement like this focuses squarely on the specific behaviors that are causing the conflict, and it lets your friend know how you react. In response, your friend might explain his behaviors, agree to change them, or apologize. Although a focus on behaviors won't always prevent an argument, you open the door to better conflict outcomes when you avoid attacking the other person's personality.

Unravel conflicts one component at a time. Because interpersonal conflict is a blend of disagreement, interference, and negative emotion, you can improve a difficult situation by targeting these components one at a time. Removing just one component from the equation can make the situation more manageable.

- To undo a disagreement, identify deeper values that you and a conflict partner have in common. For example, even if you and members of your family disagree about which candidate to vote for, you can appreciate that you share a strong sense of civic duty.
- Restructure your activities to keep a disagreement and negative emotions from interfering with your own goals. If you and a friend have heated arguments about the rival football teams that you support, find other shared interests and don't spend your weekends together watching the games.
- Manage negative emotions by enjoying the predictable, humorous, or positive aspects of a situation. In a recurrent and upsetting conflict, you might marvel at the consistency of the problem, make a joke about the situation, or keep in mind how your relationship compares favorably to others.

By finding points of agreement, reducing opportunities for interference, or managing your negative feelings, you can transform an interpersonal conflict.

MANAGING CONFLICT

One of the most difficult communication tasks we all face is managing interpersonal conflicts so that we achieve our goals for the interaction. In this part of the chapter, you will learn about the different goals you might have during conflicts, the communication strategies you can use to manage conflict, and the reasons you might prefer some strategies over others.

Conflict Goals

In Chapter 12, goals were defined as end-states or outcomes toward which a person strives. **Conflict goals** refer to the outcomes a person hopes to achieve at the end of the dispute. The goals that people have when they experience interpersonal conflicts are summarized in Table 13.2 and discussed in the following paragraphs.

Perhaps the most obvious conflict goal is to obtain certain resources or benefits. This conflict goal is called the **instrumental goal**, and it refers to the specific or tangible reasons for a conflict. A person's instrumental goal can involve just about any kind of resource – two siblings might battle over space on the couch or the largest piece of pizza; an employee and a supervisor might disagree about wages, hours, or health benefits. Instrumental goals are objective and measurable resources that people hope to retain or gain through conflict.

Another type of conflict goal, the **relational goal**, concerns the type of relationship people want to have with a partner once the conflict is ended. For example, you may want your parents to respect your independence and allow you to make your own decisions. Even if you don't have a particular relational goal in mind during a conflict, your relationship can be affected by the conflict. For example, the first big fight between partners in a dating relationship can reveal insurmountable differences and lead to a break-up or it can leave partners feeling closer to each other (Siegert & Stamp, 1994). In general, then, your relational goal includes your desire to decrease, maintain, or increase intimacy – or other relationship qualities – after a conflict.

Conflict Goals
The outcomes a person hopes to achieve at the end of a dispute.

Instrumental Goal
The tangible outcomes or resources people hope to achieve through conflict.

Relational Goal
The type of relationship people want to have with a partner once the conflict is ended.

TABLE 13.2 Types of conflict goals

Goal	Definition	Example
Instrumental	Specific or tangible resources or benefits a person hopes to gain or retain	In a conflict with a parent, a son wants permission to go camping with friends
Relational	The type of relationship a person wants to have with a partner at the end of the conflict	In a conflict with an employee, a manager wants to gain the employee's trust and respect
Identity: Self	The self-image that a person wants to project or protect during a conflict	In a conflict with a doctor, a patient wants to demonstrate intelligence, expertise, and an ability to make treatment decisions
Identity: Other	The self-image that a person wants the partner to have at the end of the conflict	In a conflict with a student, an instructor wants to promote the student's confidence and self-esteem
Process	The steps or rules for conflict management that a person wants to follow	In a conflict within an online support group, a person wants to discourage flaming and other inappropriate remarks

FIGURE 13.4 Madison, WI, February 16, 2010: Teacher Cyndi Ehrhart (L) and Anne McClure (R) join protesters marching at the State Capitol building in Madison, Wisconsin. Protesters were demonstrating against Wisconsin Gov. Scott Walker's proposal to eliminate collective bargaining rights for many state workers

Source: Photo by Mark Hirsch/Getty Images.

Self-Identity Goal

How a person hopes to be perceived by other people after the conflict.

Other-Identity Goal

How a person hopes a conflict partner will be perceived after the conflict.

Process Goal

How a person prefers to communicate about conflict.

You might have goals for how you see yourself or for how your partner sees him or herself. The **self-identity goal** in a conflict situation refers to how a person hopes to be perceived by other people after the conflict. If you have ever worried that someone might think you were mean or weak after a conflict, these worries reflected your self-identity goal in that situation. You may also have an **other-identity goal** during conflict: a goal for how the other person perceives him or herself after the experience. For example, you might want a partner to recognize her flaws, or you might want to protect a conflict partner's self-esteem.

The **process goal** highlights your preferred way to manage conflict. Process goals surface in your beliefs about how people should behave during conflict. For example, people in dating relationships typically expect partners to behave affectionately and not try to have everything their own way during conflicts (Ebesu Hubbard, 2001). In business relationships, people believe that success and conflict resolution require trust or refraining from opportunistic behavior (Edelenbos & Klijn, 2007). Groups that communicate only online tend to have more conflicts during the early stages of group development about process and relationships than groups that communicate face-to-face (Hobman, Bordia, Irmer, & Chang, 2002). You may not always be aware of your process goals during a conflict, but they reflect important standards for how to behave.

PAUSE & REFLECT

What behaviors would violate your rules about how people should behave during conflict?

In all likelihood, you strive for more than one of these goals in any given conflict. Evidence to this point comes from a study in which people described their goals as they reviewed a video in which they discussed a conflict with a dating partner (Keck & Samp, 2007). This study showed that most people have mixed goals at any given moment, but instrumental goals tend to be the most prominent. Second, people typically reported different goals at different points during the interaction. These findings suggest that people juggle a variety of goals when communicating about conflict, and those goals can change over the course of a conversation.

COMMUNICATION IN ACTION 13.2

Recognizing Your Conflict Goals

Keep a journal each day for two weeks in which you record any conflicts that you experience. After each journal entry, note whether you were concerned about instrumental, relational, self- or other-identity, or process goals during that conversation. Do you notice any patterns in your priorities when you experience conflict? Do your conflict goals depend on your relationship with each conflict partner?

Conflict Strategies

Chances are you pursue your conflict goals by using a variety of verbal and nonverbal communication techniques. Perhaps you show anger through facial expressions or tone of voice, your verbal messages might criticize a partner or express good will, or you might change the topic. Your **conflict strategy** is your overall plan for how you will communicate about a conflict.

> **Conflict Strategy**
> An overall plan for how you will communicate about a conflict.

One option for managing conflict is to approach the situation as a competition and the other person as your opponent. This approach, called a **distributive conflict strategy**, involves actively confronting a person with the goal of destroying his or her position. Distributive conflict often includes criticism, expressing anger, justifying your own point of view, and denying the other person's claims. A distributive conflict strategy is considered a "win–lose" approach, because you try to win the battle by defeating your opponent. People tend to use a distributive conflict strategy when they are focused on instrumental and self-identity goals (Keck & Samp, 2007). Distributive communication behaviors are also common when people have feelings of hostility, irritation, or anger (Guerrero, Trost, & Yoshimura, 2005; Knobloch, 2005). In addition, people are more likely to use distributive strategies in work-group conflicts that occur online versus face-to-face (Zornoza, Ripoll, & Peiro, 2002).

> **Distributive Conflict Strategy**
> An approach that involves competing with a conflict partner to obtain personal goals and to undermine the partner's outcomes.

In contrast, an **integrative conflict strategy** is a cooperative approach to resolving conflict. This strategy, which is also known as a "win–win" approach, emphasizes working with the other person to find a mutually satisfying solution. Doing so requires asking questions ("What are you feeling?" "What's important to you?"), as well as providing honest answers, so that each person's point of view is understood. When using an integrative conflict strategy, you strive to understand and respect the other person's perspective, not to discredit that person. Perhaps not surprisingly, integrative behaviors are more likely when dating relationships are intimate, rather than casual (Knobloch, 2005), and when people are concerned about supporting a partner's identity (Keck &

> **Integrative Conflict Strategy**
> Cooperating with a conflict partner to identify a mutually satisfying solution.

Avoidant Conflict Strategy

Limiting communication with a conflict partner about a problematic situation.

Samp, 2007). In addition, working groups employ more positive conflict strategies when they communicate face-to-face rather than online (Zornoza et al., 2002).

A third option is to use an **avoidant conflict strategy**. Conflict avoidance can be considered a "lose–lose" approach to conflict, because you don't care if either partner wins. Instead, conflict avoidance involves attempts to limit communication about a conflict with the person involved. People avoid conflict by withholding complaints, suppressing arguments, and declaring controversial topics off-limits (Roloff & Ifert, 2000). To suppress arguments, people pretend to agree with the other person, minimize the problem, or even walk out on a conversation. Avoidance is a risky strategy, because it does not solve the problem, but it can be useful in some situations (see Table 13.3). Conflict avoidance is neither inherently good nor bad – like any conflict strategy, its effectiveness depends on your goals and circumstances.

PAUSE & REFLECT

Which conflict strategy did you use in your last major conflict? Did that approach help you achieve your goals for that conflict?

Conflict Styles

Conflict Styles

Trait-like tendencies to think about problems in particular ways and to respond to problems with particular behaviors.

Because individuals tend to manage all of their conflicts in more or less the same way, some researchers believe that a person's approach to interpersonal conflict is a personality trait. **Conflict styles** are trait-like tendencies to think about problems in particular ways and to respond to problems with particular behaviors. In other words, your conflict style captures the goals that you typically have and the conflict strategies that you typically use.

Conflict styles vary on two dimensions: how much people tend to their own goals, and how much people attend to the goals of others (see Figure 13.5). Some people pursue their own goals eagerly and assertively, while others care less about getting what they want for themselves (vertical axis). Similarly, some people focus on making sure the other person is satisfied, whereas others don't worry about their conflict partner's outcomes (horizontal axis). Based on these two dimensions, there are five primary conflict styles (Rahim, 1983).

Dominating

A conflict style that involves confronting problems, competing with a partner, and trying to win.

People with a **dominating** conflict style tend to confront problems for personal gain. This conflict style is also called "competing" because people with this orientation try to get as much as they can for themselves at a conflict partner's expense. For people with a dominating conflict style, winning is a priority and conflict is exhilarating, whereas losing represents weakness and a loss of status. Dominators have great faith that their position is right, so they feel justified in confronting – and correcting – other people. For these reasons, people with a competing style tend to use a distributive conflict strategy; they bolster their own position and attack the other person's arguments, even if it means distorting the truth. For someone with a dominating conflict style, conflict is a battle in which only one party can be victorious.

TABLE 13.3 When to use conflict avoidance

Conflict avoidance is not an effective way of resolving the cause of a conflict, but it can reduce arguing and avoid damage to a relationship in some circumstances. Here are some guidelines for using an avoidant conflict strategy effectively.

Conflict avoidance requires substantial tolerance

If you decide to avoid communication that might resolve a conflict, you need to be able to agree to disagree and to put up with circumstances that might annoy you. If you can't put up with a situation without being bothered, conflict avoidance isn't the best choice for you.

Conflict avoidance requires other coping strategies

If you decide to let a problem persist, you need to find something positive to balance your negative feelings. Strategies like thinking about how a relationship is better than your alternatives or having fun together can make it easier for you to put up with the conflict you're avoiding.

Conflict avoidance should be used selectively

Reserve your use of conflict avoidance for situations that are relatively minor, have few practical consequences, and don't involve values that are important to you. If a situation has a big impact on your life, disrupts your activities in significant ways, or involves values that you hold dear, conflict avoidance may not be a good long-term strategy.

Conflict avoidance requires other communication skills

Conflict avoidance doesn't mean you totally avoid a controversial topic. When the issue comes up, you will have to respond with verbal and nonverbal messages. Make sure you have the ability to deflect conversations gracefully, and use positive communication behaviors to keep the unresolved problem from souring other aspects of your relationship.

Conflict avoidance requires perspective-taking and individual problem solving

If you decide to avoid conflict, you close yourself off to opportunities to learn about your partner's point of view and to work with that person on a solution. To compensate, you need to be especially skilled at thinking about the other person's perspective on the conflict. You also need to be able to work out a solution to the problem on your own.

Adapted from Roloff & Ifert (2000).

People who try to satisfy both their own goals and their partner's have an **integrating** conflict style. This style is also called "collaborating" because people work with a conflict partner to find the best possible solution for both parties. Moreover, integrators try to find the underlying cause of a conflict so that they can identify a long-term solution. People with this style encourage open and honest disclosures from everyone involved; they try to understand the situation fully and address the problem to everyone's benefit.

Some people are content to let problems slide, because they are focused on the well-being of the other person and their relationship. This **obliging** conflict style, also known as "accommodating," involves prioritizing the other party's goals. Obligers tend to believe

Integrating
A conflict style that involves collaborating with a partner to find a solution that is satisfying to everyone.

Obliging
A conflict style that involves accommodating or giving in to a conflict partner's needs and desires.

FIGURE 13.5 Conflict styles

that disagreement communicates a lack of closeness or affection and runs the risk of hurting or offending the other person. Given this viewpoint, people with this style try to smooth over differences, downplay conflicts, and focus on positive aspects of their relationships. In general, the obliging style involves a low commitment to the person's own conflict goals and a high commitment to helping the other person get what he or she wants.

People with an **avoiding** conflict style pay limited attention either to their own or their partner's goals. People with this style tend to dislike discussing conflict because they think that such a conversation is unpleasant, useless, or even dangerous. The prospect of talking about a conflict can even make people with this conflict style feel physically ill! Given these views and reactions, avoiders protect themselves by physically withdrawing from conversations about conflicts, keeping their complaints to themselves, or pretending to agree with the other person.

In the middle of the grid is **compromising**. People with this style tend to believe that conflicts escalate because each partner wants too much. Accordingly, they keep conflicts in check by trying to find a balance between their own priorities and the other party's goals. Compromisers are comfortable talking about conflicts, but they don't like to see arguments get out of control or go on too long. Their goal is to find the middle ground where both parties get some of what they want. Although compromising might seem like a way to please everyone, it is dissatisfying to people who have other conflict styles. In particular, dominators would be frustrated with a less-than-total victory, integrators would feel that they hadn't found the very best solution, obligers would worry that the other person was unhappy, and avoiders would dislike being forced to address the conflict. A compromiser's ability to address a problem, split the difference, and then let it go is a unique conflict style, not a merging of the other four styles.

Avoiding
A conflict style that involves trying to limit communication about a conflict situation.

Compromising
A conflict style that involves finding a middle ground where both parties get some of what they want.

PAUSE & REFLECT

Which conflict style do you think it would be hardest for you to learn? Can you think of times when that conflict style would be useful to know?

HOW DO YOU RATE? 13.1

Conflict Styles

Visit the **companion website** to complete Rahim's Organizational Conflict Management Inventory (Rahim, 1983), which will reveal your personal conflict style. What outcomes does your conflict style generally produce during interpersonal conflict?

As you might expect, your style during a conflict interaction affects how your partner perceives you. These effects were documented in a study in which business school students role-played a conflict about an organizational downsizing (Gross & Guerrero, 2000). The study showed that people who characterized their partner's behavior as integrating and compromising also rated that partner as more effective in the negotiation. In contrast, partners who showed an avoiding conflict style were rated as less effective. Compromising partners were also seen as more appropriate or relationally sensitive, whereas people with a dominating conflict style were seen as less appropriate. These findings suggest that your conflict partner may view you as more or less competent, based on your conflict style.

Culture, Gender, and Conflict Management

Although conflict styles are similar to personality traits, they are also related to a person's culture and gender. One study examined 36 different investigations that tested for culture and gender differences in conflict styles (Holt & DeVore, 2005). Combining the results across the set the studies revealed some interesting conclusions. The study found that people from individualistic cultures are more likely to have a dominating conflict style, whereas people from collectivistic cultures are more likely to have avoiding, compromising, and integrating conflict styles. In addition, within individualistic cultures, females are more likely to have a compromising conflict style and males are more likely to have a dominating conflict style.

Let's focus on the two conclusions that highlight cultural differences in conflict management. When people from the United States, which is generally an individualistic culture, engage in conflict, they may be comfortable expressing demands, criticizing each other, and arguing assertively. Those behaviors would be considered inappropriate or out of line in a collectivist culture, such as China, where people expect conflicts to be handled more delicately and cooperatively. What might happen when people with such different cultural norms have a disagreement? The individualist comes off as rude and aggressive, while the collectivist seems weak or disinterested in solving the problem. Both parties might be doing what they consider to be best, but they are quite possibly offending each other.

Gender differences in conflict management within individualistic cultures create the same problem we saw for conflict between two cultures: A man's dominating style might be offensive to a woman who prefers compromising, and a woman's compromising approach might be seen as selling out by a man who prefers to engage conflict fully. These norms also affect how men and women are perceived when they break from the cultural

FIGURE 13.6 Muscat, Oman, October 19, 2011. Omani Minister Responsible for Foreign Affairs Yussef bin Alawi bin Abdullah meets with US Secretary of State Hillary Clinton. According to officials, Clinton visited Oman for talks with Sultan Qaboos on rising tensions with Iran over its alleged plot to kill a Saudi envoy, according to officials

Source: MOHAMMED MAHJOUB/AFP/Getty Images.

script. How would you react to a woman versus a man who was using a dominating style? And what if you interacted with a woman versus a man who was compromising? Because gender-based expectations affect how people evaluate men and women, people who don't follow the norms for their gender can be judged negatively. In these ways, gendered norms for conflict management both shape and constrain how men and women handle conflicts.

PAUSE & REFLECT

Is your conflict style similar to or different from the ways that people in your culture or of your gender tend to manage conflict?

Putting Theory into Practice: Expanding Your Options

Managing conflicts is one of the most difficult communication challenges you face. Fortunately, you can improve your conflict skills by focusing on your goals, adapting your conflict strategies to fit particular situations, and keeping your conflict style in mind.

Plan for multiple goals. Chances are you'll have a mix of instrumental, relational, identity, and process goals in any conflict. If you focus only on the most noticeable or strongest goal, you might end up losing something else that also matters to you. On the other hand, keeping all of your goals in mind can help you find positive solutions even when conflicts are serious. A good example comes from a woman who rented part of her house to Denise many years ago. This woman had been dating a man for several years, and they got married when her daughters moved out of the house. Just six months later, the moving van was back and a divorce was in the works. Apparently, the new husband's young children were an unexpected source of stress. Was this the end of the relationship? Surprisingly, no. The newly divorced couple continued to date from their separate homes, and several years later – when his children were older – they remarried. By focusing on the specific source of the conflict, and keeping their other goals in mind, this couple managed to resolve a serious disagreement while maintaining a relationship that they clearly valued.

Match your strategies to your goals. Once you have a clear idea of your goals for a conflict, choose conflict strategies that match those objectives. Table 13.4 shows how different conflict strategies might match up with particular conflict goals. In the table, an arrow pointing up means that the conflict strategy promotes the goal, while an arrow point down means that a strategy can make a goal more difficult to achieve. As you think about all of your goals for a conflict, try to use the strategy that maximizes the outcomes that you care about.

Branch out from your conflict style. You aren't locked into your conflict style – any person can enact all of the different conflict styles. Rather than being trapped by your own particular approach, work to develop your repertoire of responses to conflict.

TABLE 13.4 Conflict goals and strategies

		Conflict goals			
	Instrumental	Relational	Other-Identity	Self-Identity	Process
Distributive	↑ You can improve your chances of winning	↓ You can damage your relationship	↓ You might hurt the other person	You can seem strong and confident, but also mean or unreasonable	You stick to your beliefs, but could violate standards for fairness
Integrative	↑ You can improve your chances of winning	↑ You can improve your relationship	↑ You show that you value the other person	↑ You appear reasonable and cooperative	↑ You express your beliefs and listen to others
Avoidant	↓ You decrease your chance of winning	You can avoid damaging the relationship, but you also miss the opportunity to improve it	You can avoid harming the other person, but you also miss the opportunity to express your appreciation	You can appear uncommitted to important issues, but you might seem easy going	↑ You prevent an unpleasant interaction from occurring

(Left margin label: **CONFLICT STRATEGIES**)

COMMUNICATION IN ACTION 13.3

Building Your Conflict Toolkit

This exercise helps you role-play various conflict situations using each of the different conflict styles. Complete the activity on the **companion website** to reflect on how you would manage each of the conflict scenarios using different strategies.

CONFLICT DYNAMICS

Our discussion of conflict styles highlighted the general approach a person might take when managing a conflict. Communication about conflict is also affected by your perceptions of the particular situation, how much power you have with respect to your conflict partner, and the messages you get from your partner about the conflict. Because these factors often make a conflict situation worse, understanding them can help you manage conflicts more effectively.

Attribution and Escalation

As described in Chapter 4, attributions are the explanations you create for why something happened. In the context of interpersonal conflict, attributions are the judgments you make about who is responsible for the disagreement. Do you remember the two key attributions biases discussed in Chapter 4 – the fundamental attribution error and the actor-observer effect? These biases describe our tendency to explain other people's actions in terms of internal causes (the fundamental attribution error), and our own behavior in terms of external causes (the actor-observer effect). In other words, you might think your grouchy roommate is an ill-tempered person, but your own grouchiness is because you didn't get enough sleep last night. In a conflict situation, people are even more likely to show these biases.

Attribution biases were clearly documented in a study that asked married partners to describe the same conflict (Shütz, 1999). That study showed that each spouse tends to see the other person as the source of the conflict, and each attributes his or her own behavior to good intentions, circumstances, or stress (see Figure 13.7). People also described themselves as trying to solve problems much more often than partners. As a result of these biases, two partners in a conflict can end up with very different accounts of the same dispute.

What effect do these attributions have on a conflict? When people blame the other person for the conflict, they tend to use a distributive conflict strategy (O'Leary et al., 2007; Smith Slep & O'Leary, 2007). After all, if the other party is undeniably wrong, why wouldn't you point out his or her errors and misconceptions. And if you are innocent of any wrongdoing, why wouldn't you demand what you rightfully deserve without

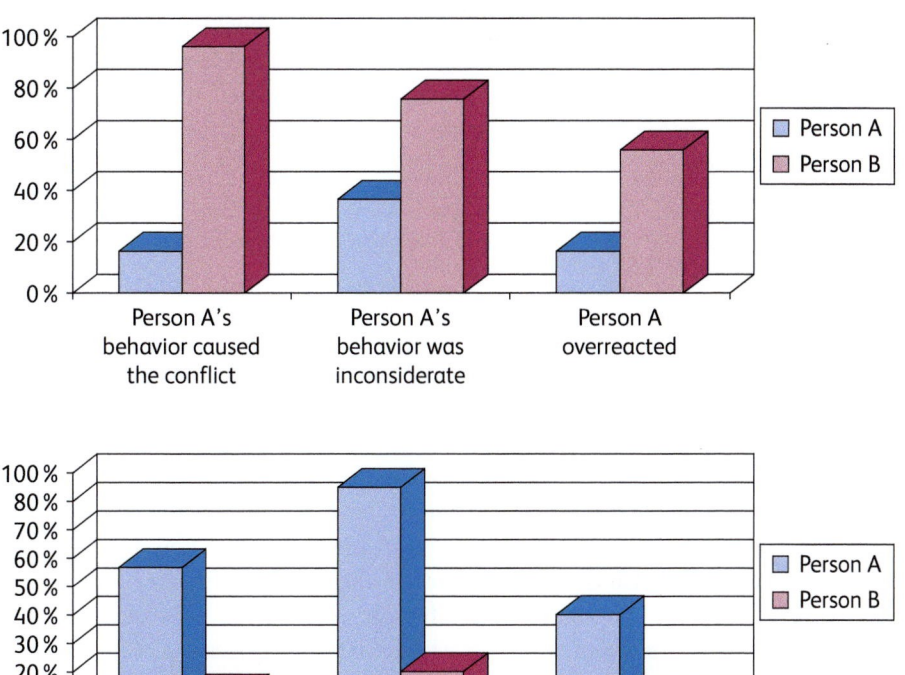

FIGURE 13.7 Biased accounts of interpersonal conflicts. These graphs are based on the results of a study that examined the stories that married partners told about the same conflict. The numbers reflect the percentage of stories that contained each element. Notice how people are unlikely to say that they caused the conflict, were inconsiderate, or overreacted, but they often describe their partner in those roles. Likewise, people describe their own good intentions, justify their actions based on the circumstances, and report trying to solve the problem much more than they give similar credit to their partner.

PAUSE & REFLECT

Can you recall a time when you and a conflict partner had very different perceptions of your disagreement? Looking back, to what extent were attribution biases fueling that conflict?

---

compromising? Unfortunately, if each person thinks that the other person is at fault, parties can become locked in an escalating conflict.

If conflicts escalate when people blame each other, what happens when they overcome these biases? The evidence on this point is very clear: empathizing with conflict partners promotes constructive problem solving and reduces competitive conflict behavior (de Wied, Branje, & Meeus, 2006). In fact, people who take another person's perspective are less likely to be dominating and more likely to prefer either integrating or compromising to manage their conflicts (Corcoran & Malinckrodt, 2000). Having concern for another person's goals also promotes constructive problem solving, compromising, and more agreeable communication (Janssen & van de Vliert, 1996). Although attribution biases are common in conflict situations, overcoming them can change the course of your interpersonal conflicts.

The Chilling Effect of Power

Interpersonal power. The ability to affect both one's own outcomes and another person's behaviors, attitudes, and outcomes – is another force that shapes how conflicts unfold. Within interpersonal relationships, power comes in two primary forms: dependence power and punitive power. When one person is willing and able to end a relationship, he or she gains dependence power over a partner who is committed to that union. A dependent person might worry that a partner will end the relationship and therefore the dependent person relinquishes control to that partner. Punitive power refers to the influence people gain when they are perceived as likely to lose their temper or behave aggressively. Because people want to avoid this type of punishing behavior, they yield to a potentially aggressive partner. People who possess interpersonal power are free to choose what they want to talk about, how topics are discussed, and how conflicts are resolved.

In the context of an ongoing relationship, power exerts a chilling effect on complaints, such that people keep their feelings to themselves to avoid provoking their partner. In dating relationships, people withhold the most irritations from partners who are perceived to be uncommitted to the relationship and to have good dating alternatives (Roloff & Cloven, 1990). Likewise, children keep secrets from parents, in part, because they depend on their parents for so many things (Afifi & Olson, 2005). When people have experienced aggression within their family, they are more likely to conceal secrets from members of their family, and they consider themselves less able to communicate about sensitive topics (Afifi, Olson, & Armstrong, 2005).

SCHOLAR SPOTLIGHT

Visit the Communication Café on the companion website to view a conversation with Michael Roloff, a leading scholar who has studied power, conflict, and conflict avoidance.

Interpersonal Power
The ability to affect both one's own outcomes and another person's behaviors, attitudes, and outcomes.

Dependence Power
The influence one person has when he or she is willing and able to end a relationship with a partner who is committed to that union.

Punitive Power
The influence people gain when they are perceived as likely to lose their temper or behave aggressively.

PAUSE & REFLECT

What kind of power does each member of your family have? How does power affect the way family members communicate with each other?

Why does power tend to suppress conflict communication? In one study of conflict avoidance in the workplace, university employees gave a number of reasons why they don't voice complaints (Barsky & Wood, 2005):

- Avoidance is the norm in the organization.
- The benefits of complaining are not worth the costs.
- Complaints might not be kept confidential.

- People are resigned to the situation.
- The people in charge are indecisive.
- The problem will resolve itself with time.

In addition, people perceive potential problems as less serious when their partners have either dependence or punitive power over them (Solomon & Samp, 1998). In other words, power has two different effects: it can directly inhibit complaining, and it can lead people to perceive a situation in ways that encourage them to avoid conflict.

The chilling effect of power can create a vicious cycle in a relationship (see Figure 13.8). If we begin at the left side of Figure 13.8, we see that a person who perceives a partner to be powerful is more likely to avoid conflict. When complaints are not expressed, the partner's problematic actions go unchecked. As a result, that partner enjoys greater freedom to behave as he or she pleases and to set the terms of the relationship. He or she can also invest energy in other relationships, and that partner might get away with more aggressive behavior. Until something happens to correct the power imbalance, the powerless partner will have less and less effect on the course and conduct of the relationships.

Communication Patterns

Conflict interactions frequently begin when one person voices a complaint. If the partner responds positively, the issue might be resolved then and there. In contrast, conflicts escalate when a partner rejects the complaint and the person who complained ignores the rebuttal or becomes sarcastic (Dersley & Wootton, 2000). In this section, you'll learn about three patterns of conflict behavior: demand/withdraw, reciprocity, and forgiveness. Understanding these patterns can help you recognize when your interpersonal communication is fanning the flames of conflict or leading you to resolution.

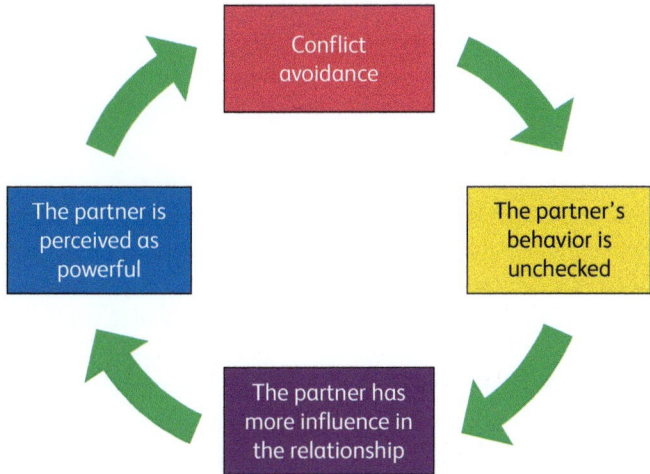

FIGURE 13.8 The cycle of power and avoidance

Demand/withdraw communication. A common conflict communication pattern is demand/withdraw. The sequence begins when one partner demands something from the other, for example, "You need to take the garbage out more often!" The demand may be for change in behavior, agreement with a position, or even just attention during the discussion. In response, the partner withdraws from the conversation by not answering or not paying attention. The withdrawal prompts the demander to become more assertive, and the persistent demands prompt the withdrawer to become more withdrawn. Perhaps not surprisingly, married couples who engage in demand/withdraw communication are less satisfied with their relationship than couples who do not (Caughlin & Huston, 2002). Similarly, demand/withdraw communication between parents and adolescent children has been linked to dissatisfaction with the relationship and even with drug abuse by both parents and children (Caughlin & Malis, 2004a, 2004b). Thus, demand/withdraw communication is typically a destructive pattern in an ongoing relationship.

PAUSE & REFLECT

Have you ever been involved in a demand/withdraw interaction in an ongoing relationship? How did that communication experience affect that relationship?

INSIDE COMMUNICATION RESEARCH

The Consequences of Demand/Withdraw

Serial arguments occur when individuals consistently engage in arguments or disagreements about the same recurring topic. Rachel Malis and Michael Roloff (2006) examined the outcomes of the demand/withdraw pattern in serial arguments. These scholars suggested that demand/withdraw communication can lead to a variety of stress-related outcomes for both the person who demands and the person who withdraws. If so, demand/withdraw communication during serial arguments could have a cumulative detrimental impact on people's health over time. For this reason, Malis and Roloff examined how the demand/withdraw pattern is related to stress and stress-related problems in serial arguments.

The researchers asked individuals to complete questionnaires about their conflicts in a current or former romantic relationship. First, respondents described a serial argument: how often the argument occurred, who initiated it, the perceived resolvability of the conflict, and the extent to which the respondent tried to avoid the conflict. Then, the participants described their demand/withdraw patterns during these arguments. Finally, the participants answered questions about their well-being in terms of stress, emotional distress, and physical symptoms of stress.

The results confirmed that the demand/withdraw pattern can have negative consequences. Individuals who consistently initiate conflicts with a partner who withdraws from the argument tend to report intrusive thoughts and feelings about the event, attempts to avoid thinking about the event, physiological arousal, and health issues

– like headaches or fatigue – that disrupt their daily routines. Individuals who withdraw from arguments experience even more stress than their demanding partner, but they do not tend to have as many stress-related ailments.

THINK ABOUT IT

1. This study focused on the detrimental psychological and physiological effects of the demand/withdraw pattern. What long-term consequences might result from use of this pattern in serial conflicts?
2. Since the stress-related effects are more severe for the individuals who initiate the demand/withdraw pattern, how would you recommend they go about resolving their conflicts with a partner who withdraws from arguments

How can you avoid the pitfalls of demand/withdraw communication? Check out the conversation in the Real Words box. As this cohabiting couple discusses money problems, Angie accepts the complaint against her. Even when she explains herself, she does so in a way that expresses agreement with the problem Daryl raises. In return, Daryl is willing to acknowledge that the problem only happens once in a while. By avoiding demand/withdraw communication, the couple fosters agreement about the situation, rather than discord.

REAL WORDS

AVOIDING DEMAND/WITHDRAW IN A CONFLICT DISCUSSION

This transcript comes from a study where romantic couples were asked to identify and discuss sources of irritation in their relationship.

DARYL: Spending money . . . like a crazy lady.
ANGIE: Sometimes . . . I know. I, I, I agree with that.
DARYL: Like whenever, spending money, significant amounts of money uncontrollably.
ANGIE: Not uncontrollably. Just spontaneously.
DARYL: Spontaneously.
ANGIE: It's not uncontrollably.
DARYL: It is. It only happens once in a while though.
ANGIE: Yeah. I mean this weekend I hadda go buy a new outfit for the wedding. But we spent seventy bucks on a shirt and tie for you the other week. You know, it's okay for me to spend seventy bucks on a whole new outfit, shoes and all. I mean, yeah, it was more money than we have right now, but . . . I do know what you're talking about though. Like an $800 bed on the spur of the moment.
DARYL: And on the car. I thought you jumped on that too fast. I didn't even get to look at it before you were like, "Yeah, I wanna buy it." You already bought it before I even saw it.

ANGIE: Well, I thought we'd agreed that it wasn't gonna be ours, and then afterwards we'd agreed that it was, and now I regret that because the car's too small for you. Way too small. Hell, it's almost too small for me.

Reciprocity. Another pattern that can escalate conflict is reciprocity, which involves matching a partner's behavior. Reciprocity occurs whenever you respond to a partner's behavior with an action that conveys a similar message. Here are some destructive patterns that can emerge from reciprocity during conflict discussions:

■ *Complaint/Counter-complaint*. One person's complaint about a partner prompts the partner to complain in turn. For example, "You never do the dishes" begets "You never walk the dog."
■ *Proposal/Counter-proposal*. One person's recommended outcome prompts the other person to recommend a different outcome. For example, "We should save money by eating out less" begets "We should save money by carpooling."
■ *Attack/Counter-attack*. One person's insult prompts the other person to respond with an insult. For example, "I've never really liked you" begets "I think you're boring."

As you might expect, this kind of reciprocity can intensify a conflict. In fact, partners in abusive marriages often reciprocate each other's verbally aggressive communication (Burman, Margolin, & John, 1993; Sabourin, Infante, & Rudd, 1993). In the business world, conflicts escalate when negotiators reciprocate argumentative messages (Brett, Shapiro, & Lytle, 1998).

Forgiveness. One more conflict dynamic merits mention. Forgiveness is the communication process by which partners transcend the disagreement, interference, and negative emotions that define a conflict. As shown in Table 13.5, forgiveness can take five different forms (Waldron & Kelley, 2005). Forgiveness is explicit when a person says, "I forgive you." Forgiveness also occurs through discussion when partners use verbal messages to identify and accept a shared understanding of the situation. Sometimes, forgiveness is expressed nonverbally by cues such as eye contact, facial expressions, and head nods. When people tie resolution of the conflict to a requirement, such as a promise to behave better in the future, they have granted conditional forgiveness. People might also forgive through minimization, which means that the conflict partners have characterized the problem as trivial or unimportant. Research shows that explicit forgiveness and nonverbal forgiveness tend to strengthen relationships, but conditional forgiveness is associated with the deterioration of intimacy (Waldron & Kelley, 2005).

Putting Theory into Practice: Promoting Healthy Conflicts

Attribution biases, the chilling effect of power, and typical communication patterns can complicate efforts to communicate effectively and resolve conflicts. Now that you

TABLE 13.5 Forms of forgiveness

Form	Definition	Messages
Explicit forgiveness	Performing a speech act that clearly conveys closure to the conflict	I forgive you
Forgiveness through discussion	Reviewing the reasons for the conflict and the beliefs and values involved, and reaching a mutually acceptable definition of what happened	I can understand what you were thinking when you did what you did. I was thinking about it differently. I can see that we didn't see the event the same way
Nonverbal forgiveness	Using behavioral cues to communicate solidarity after the conflict	Eye contact, gentle touching, head nods
Conditional forgiveness	Specifying that acceptance of the situation is contingent on certain requirements	If you'll promise never to do something like this again, I'll forgive you
Forgiveness through minimization	Communicating that the issue is trivial or unimportant	It's no big deal really. It's nothing to worry about

know about these common dynamics, you can take steps to overcome them in your own life.

Question your attributions for conflict. To help overcome attribution biases, think about how both your partner's behavior and your own actions might be contributing to the conflict. Then, focus on what you can control – your own behavior – as you look for ways to change the conflict dynamics. For example, if you and a roommate battle over access to the shower in the morning, maybe you can reduce the tension by changing your routine. Similarly, consider the ways in which the situation is constraining options and alternatives for you and your partner. Are your conflict behaviors shaped by the fact that you're under a lot of pressure at work, low on cash, or worried by a family crisis? How might factors like those be contributing to your partner's behavior in this conflict? If you can think about how the context is intensifying your conflict, you might identify strategies for changing your circumstances so that you both have more choices. Finally, look for and appreciate your partner's efforts to resolve the conflict, and help your partner recognize your own efforts on that front. Even when those attempts at resolution fail, knowing that you are both doing your best can create good will between you.

Keep your power in check. If you have power in a relationship you may be creating an environment in which your partner can't speak freely. It's important to remember that you might be doing things that annoy your partner that you aren't even aware of. Keep track of how power dynamics might be leading you to avoid serious conflicts, but also when your own power advantage is silencing someone else.

COMMUNICATION IN ACTION 13.4

Knowing Your Own Strength

This exercise will help you to reflect on the amount of power you have in your relationships and how you wield your power during conflict. Complete the form on the **companion website** to reflect on how you typically handle conflicts in relationships where you have different levels of power. How does your power affect your communication behavior during conflicts with each partner?

De-escalate, rather than escalate, conflict. What can you do to break the demand/withdraw or reciprocal cycles that escalate conflict? Table 13.6 lists some specific communication moves you can use to keep a conflict from getting out of control.

TABLE 13.6 Alternatives to conflict escalation

When your partner . . .	You can escalate conflict by . . .	Or you can de-escalate conflict by . . .
Demands *You have to clean up after yourself*	Withdrawing *Leave me alone!*	Engaging *Let's talk about it. What would you like me to do differently?*
Complains about you *You are so uptight — can't you just relax?*	Counter-complaining *Well, you're just plain lazy!*	Asking for details *What exactly am I doing that bothers you?*
Proposes a solution *We could get take-out Chinese.*	Making a counter-proposal *We could go to that new restaurant downtown.*	Considering the proposal *Chinese is always good, especially if we want to eat at home.*
Attacks you *I can't believe I'm dating someone as awful as you.*	Lodging a counter-attack *You're no prize either!*	Acknowledging feelings *You must be feeling pretty bad right now; I can see you're upset.*

SUMMARY

Learning to manage conflicts is an important part of interpersonal communication, but conflict communication isn't a straightforward process. Conflicts may take several different forms, including arguments, disagreeable communication, periods of hostility, and pervasive tension. You may experience conflict because of another person's behaviors, because a person violated relationship rules or norms, or because you perceive a personality flaw in another person. At their core, however, all conflicts essentially boil down to disagreements, involve interference in your goals and activities, and are accompanied by negative feelings.

As you prepare to communicate about a conflict, keep in mind that there are a variety of goals, strategies, and styles that may surface in your interaction. Within any particular conflict, you may have instrumental objectives that you want to achieve, alongside relationship qualities that you hope to promote or maintain, preferences for how you and your partner enact your identities, and rules of conduct that you hope to follow. As you weigh these goals, you might draw upon distributive, integrative, or avoidant conflict strategies. Remember, too, that some people tend to manage all of their conflicts using a particular conflict style. Whether someone engages in dominating, integrating, obliging, avoiding, or compromising could have as much to do with their personal preferences as with the particulars of the conflict at hand.

Once you are in a conversation about a conflict, be prepared for a number of dynamics that might unfold. Remember that attribution biases are especially common in conflict situations. In all likelihood, your partner's perceptions about the conflict are very different from yours, and these differences often cause conflicts to escalate. Interpersonal power also affects how forcefully people communicate during conflict; in fact, a person's power can prevent a partner from even voicing concerns or complaints. Your conflict discussions are also subject to dynamics that unfold from one speaking turn to the next. Demand/withdraw communication and reciprocating negative messages can be especially harmful in the context of ongoing relationships. On the other hand, forgiveness can be a powerful tool for moving beyond conflict.

Despite their complexity, you can communicate effectively when conflicts surface in relationships that you care about. Take time to figure out what kind of conflict you are having. In addition, focus on behaviors, rather than a partner's undesirable personality, and try to address the components of the conflict one at a time. Consider all of your conflict goals, and tailor your conflict strategies to those goals. Although your conflict style might be familiar to you, be sure that the style you generally prefer is a good match for the particular conflict you face. Once you are engaged in a conflict discussion, work to overcome the ill effects of attribution biases, power, and escalatory patterns of communication. With effort, you can use your communication skills to manage your conflicts and promote the well-being of your interpersonal relationships.

ACTIVITIES FOR EXPLORING COMMUNICATION ETHICS

What Would You/Should You Do?

Imagine that you have started a new job. After only a few weeks, you realize that your supervisor regularly comes to work late, spends her time in the office playing computer games, and consistently passes her responsibilities on to you. The situation isn't fair, and you're doing more work than you planned on when you took the job. You never have any downtime to rest or eat lunch, and you're required to work significantly more hours than you expected. Although you are frustrated with the situation, you also recognize that your supervisor has the power to fire you or to withhold desirable resources, such as bonuses, vacation time, or salary increases. What would you or should you do in this situation?

Something to Think About

Consider an especially messy conflict that a student in Denise's class shared a few years ago. Caitlyn had been in a serious car accident over winter break, and she couldn't return to campus for spring semester. She couldn't take care of business, such as paying bills, because she was in a coma. Caitlyn's roommates were very supportive throughout her recovery, but months later they told her she owed them hundreds of dollars for her share of the rent. Caitlyn was shocked by the request (as well as unable to pay it), and her roommates were equally shocked that she expected a free ride. With each side seeing the situation so differently, their conversations over the phone were typically heated. Each side accused the other of dishonesty and inappropriate behavior, and finally Caitlyn stopped answering their phone calls or returning their text messages. Eventually lawyers were called in, and the case went to court. What kind of communication behaviors do you think escalated this conflict, and what messages could have made the conflict less extreme?

Analyze Communication Ethics Yourself

Conflicts are continually unfolding all around you in your community. Perhaps there is a contentious issue dividing your local school board, a controversy about campus expansion, or a disagreement between a big landlord and your city government. Identify a conflict going on in your community and gather together newspaper articles and public relations about it. As you review the information in these accounts, look for attribution biases, expressions of power, and the types of language that tend to escalate conflict. Based on your analysis, what ethical standards were and were not met as the parties involved communicated about the conflict?

KEY WORDS

argument	disagreeable communication	interpersonal power
avoidant conflict strategy	distributive conflict strategy	obliging
avoiding	dominating	other-identity goal
compromising	hostile episode	pervasive tension
conflict goals	instrumental goal	process goal
conflict strategy	integrating	punitive power
conflict styles	integrative conflict strategy	relational goal
dependence power	interpersonal conflict	self-identity goal

LEARNING OBJECTIVES

After reading this chapter, you should be able to:

1. Describe the nonverbal behaviors that communicate support.
2. Identify characteristics of supportive verbal messages and different strategies for providing comfort.
3. Describe gender differences in support and comforting.
4. Understand how personal qualities affect the ways people communicate support.
5. Recognize some of the most effective ways to support cancer survivors and people grieving the death of a loved one.
6. Improve your ability to provide support to others.

PUTTING THEORY INTO PRACTICE

In this chapter, you will learn how to:

1. Communicate nonverbal immediacy.
2. Focus on feelings.
3. Help the speaker clarify thoughts, feelings, and ideas.
4. Practice perspective-taking.
5. Appreciate, but don't exaggerate, gender differences.
6. Practice cultural sensitivity.
7. Attend to the complexity of the situation.
8. Focus on what you can do to make life easier.
9. Don't overreach if you can't find the words.

COMMUNICATING COMFORT AND SUPPORT

14

378 PROVIDING COMFORT

389 INDIVIDUAL DIFFERENCES IN COMFORTING BEHAVIOR

394 COMFORT WHEN IT COUNTS

398 SUMMARY

400 ACTIVITIES FOR EXPLORING COMMUNICATION ETHICS

400 KEY WORDS

People who are struggling with sorrow or stress often turn to friends and family for support. New technologies have made it easier for people to join online communities for the support that they seek. At fertilityforums.com, couples who are struggling with infertility come together to express their anguish and provide support for others. One woman posted to the message board to say that she was upset because her husband's brother shared the news that he and his wife were expecting a baby girl. She said, "It just hurts so bad because we lost our twins and we don't get to experience that happiness right now . . . I just have been a mess and figured I always feel better after coming here and getting the great support." The responses to this post were indeed supportive: "vent away," "I know what it's like to be in your shoes," "we've all been there," "keep your chin up," and "your day will come." Channels for interpersonal communication like this message board help people meet an ancient and universal need for comfort and support.

H ow would you respond if a friend told you about an upsetting situation, such as a fight with a romantic partner, a tense climate at work, or a medical problem? The responses to the posting on the fertility forum contain all of the hallmarks of effective comforting and supportive behavior: they acknowledge the poster's feelings, they show understanding of what the poster is going through, and they offer encouragement. Producing these kinds of messages is challenging, so you might struggle to find the right words or actions when someone needs your support. You might also find it hard to get support from others when you are upset. What are the benefits of meeting these challenges? When you comfort a friend, family member, or romantic partner, you promote that person's emotional, mental, and physical well-being. And when you talk about your own feelings of distress, you may leave the conversation feeling empowered to address your problems or at peace with a difficult situation. In this chapter, you'll learn about supportive communication, ways that people differ in their comforting communication, and contexts in which support is especially important.

PAUSE & REFLECT

Think about the last experience you had that left you feeling upset, frustrated, or anxious. How did you communicate with others about that experience, and how did those communication experiences affect your feelings about that event?

PROVIDING COMFORT

What can you say to make a person feel better about a bad situation? What can you do to comfort someone and show that you care? Messages of support and comfort can take a variety of forms. A hug or a sympathetic facial expression goes a long way. A thoughtful comment or attentive conversation can bring comfort. And through computer-mediated communication, people seek and provide support in forms as varied as text messages, comments on Facebook newsfeeds, and engagement with online support groups (High & Solomon, in press). In this section, we examine nonverbal and verbal messages that provide support, and we identify some communication behaviors that can make a bad situation worse.

Nonverbal Support Messages

When you want to comfort another person, nonverbal behaviors can be as helpful as carefully chosen words. Many people automatically produce supportive nonverbal messages in response to a distressing situation. For example, you might find yourself mirroring the facial expressions of a communication partner as you empathize with his emotions, or you might automatically reach out to touch a friend who is upset. You can also communicate support through **nonverbal immediacy**, which is the involvement and warmth suggested by behaviors like being physically close, leaning forward, having an expressive face, looking a person in the eyes, and touching.

Nonverbal Immediacy
The involvement and warmth a person communicates through physical closeness, leaning forward, facial expressions, eye contact, and touching.

Several communication studies show the benefits of nonverbal immediacy in supportive conversations (e.g., Jones & Burleson, 2003; Jones & Guerrero, 2001; Jones & Wirtz, 2006). In these studies, participants discussed something upsetting with someone who seemed to be another participant, but who was actually a confederate of the researchers. Sometimes confederates showed a high level of nonverbal immediacy by leaning forward, moving closer to the participant, orienting their body to face the other person, increasing eye contact, and using warm vocal tones. Other times the confederate showed very little nonverbal immediacy by leaning back in their chair, increasing physical distance, turning their body away from the participant, reducing eye contact, refraining from animated facial expressions, and generally appearing bored or tired. Which type of behaviors do you think produced the most comfort? Participants felt better about their circumstances and rated the confederate as more helpful and skilled at providing comfort when the confederate displayed high levels of nonverbal immediacy.

PAUSE & REFLECT

How does it make you feel when someone appears to be bored, uninterested, and uncaring when you're talking about a distressing situation?

One interpersonal communication skill that enhances a person's ability to provide nonverbal support strategies is the experience of **empathy** – the ability to feel a vicarious emotional response that mirrors the emotional experiences of others. When you empathize with another human being, you actually share his or her emotional experiences. In fact, when people observe emotions, their brains show patterns of activation revealing that they themselves are experiencing an emotional response (see Figure 14.1).

Empathy
The ability to feel a vicarious emotional response that mirrors the emotional experiences of others.

FIGURE 14.1 Brain activation and empathy: The top row shows three different views of brain activation as participants look at videos of people happy to see a familiar face. The bottom row shows, from left to right, activation in part of the brain that registers emotion as participants saw videos of people who were happy to see a familiar face, witnessing an unpleasant situation, and looking at an unusual image. In this image brighter colors indicate stronger brain activation.

Source: Powers et al. (2007) Used with permission..

In other words, when your friend is happy, elated, or joyful, you might share in her enthusiasm and pleasant emotions. If your friend is sad, distressed, or dismayed, you might take on similar negative emotions. When you experience the same negative emotions as your partner, you are likely to mirror that person's facial expressions and body postures. And because matching a partner's nonverbal behaviors indicates warmth and involvement, empathy is an important skill in the provision of nonverbal social support.

Verbal Support Messages

Like nonverbal messages, verbal messages communicate more or less warmth, interest, or responsiveness to an interaction partner. Verbal messages can also provide specific content that addresses different aspects of a difficult situation. In this section, we consider the tone, content, and orientation of the verbal messages you might use to provide comfort or support.

Person-centered messages. Supportive messages are characterized by **person-centeredness**, which means that they validate, recognize, or acknowledge the recipient's feelings and experiences. Table 14.1 categorizes verbal support messages based on how person-centered they are (Burleson, 1994). Comforting messages that are highly person-centered explicitly recognize and legitimize the recipient's feelings, help the recipient

Person-centeredness
A quality of messages that validate, recognize, or acknowledge the recipient's feelings and experiences.

TABLE 14.1 Examples of high, medium, and low person-centered messages

High person-centered messages	I can imagine this is a really hard time for you I'm really concerned about you and how you must be feeling right now I know you were really hoping for a different outcome and I'm sorry things didn't turn out the way you expected them to Whenever you feel like talking about it I'm here to listen to you
Moderately person-centered messages	Most things happen for a reason, even if you can't see it at the time Maybe it's for the best Let's go to the movies to take your mind off things for a while I was in a similar situation once and everything worked out just fine
Low person-centered messages	I don't know why you're so upset. This really isn't that big of a deal You shouldn't take things so personally all the time. Don't let this get you down Just get on with your life and keep yourself busy You know, you're probably partially to blame for this situation. Have you thought about that?

describe feelings, promote efforts to explain those feelings, and help the recipient see upsetting experiences in new ways. Moderately person-centered messages demonstrate an implicit recognition of the other's feelings by expressing sympathy and distracting attention from the situation. Messages that are not person-centered deny, criticize, or challenge the recipient's feelings.

Do some of the responses in Table 14.1 seem better to you than others? People rate highly person-centered messages as the most sensitive and effective means of providing emotional support, and they see low person-centered messages as the least comforting (Jones & Burleson, 1997; Jones & Guerrero, 2001; Samter, Burleson, & Murphy, 1987). Highly person-centered messages are effective because they focus on the emotions, perspectives, and needs of the distressed individual. By being attentive to your communication partners, you give them the time and attention necessary to address and resolve their problems.

Take a look at the transcript in the Real Words box. This conversation came from a study Denise conducted in which married partners discussed sources of distress that they were experiencing (Priem, Solomon, & Steuber, 2009). Notice how the conversation begins with the wife describing her concerns about her mother-in-law, while her husband tends to neglect those concerns. As the conversation develops, though, the wife's guilt about not doing enough comes through, and her husband responds by validating both her feelings and her actions. Notice how his messages become more person-centered as the conversation progresses.

REAL WORDS

VERBAL MESSAGES OF SUPPORT

KRISTA: What's stressful to me is the demands of aging and elderly parents and relatives and that sort of thing that people that need things from us and we're not uh, we're not located close enough.

CALEB: Yeah, but we can offer just so much help in that way. I don't know how much help we can be to my mother. We've talked about this already.

KRISTA: I guess I think that we need to continue to follow up with her. She's not real good about getting in touch with us or letting us know when she's having issues come up. It's usually that we'll call her and then she'll say, out of the blue, "Oh, I keep getting these bills from the hospital" or "This Medicare hasn't settled with this provider yet" or

CALEB: Usually when we call she has something of that sort.

KRISTA: Right. But it seems like she doesn't call us and ask so I'm wondering where she is getting . . . I suppose it's possible that she's taking care of these things on her own but unlikely given what we know about her. She was so reliant on your father.

CALEB: I wouldn't say that . . . So. So I, see, I'm making an assumption that, okay, well, these things are going to work out because she's going to have to address them.

KRISTA: My concern is what will happen if she becomes ill or unable to care for herself, what choices and decision we'll have to make then.

CALEB: Well, my sister will go down there and make all the decisions . . . which I guess is another stressor.

KRISTA: Maybe she has the time, I just don't know if she has the expertise. And she might decide that it was too expensive or too whatever, too difficult to have someone come in.

CALEB: So what would we do then?

KRISTA: One of us would go down, I think, and help make a joint decision. And I guess it should probably be you. But I, I worry about . . . I didn't have a lot of fun when you were down there when your dad died, in the winter with the blizzards and the sub-zero temperatures, trying to keep my life together, and having a number of people point out that I really should have been there. I'm not sure what I was supposed to do with our minor child that goes to school. The stress comes from just not being real sure what my role is in these, you know, situations.

CALEB: Well, I've – I didn't criticize you and I thought you made the right choice. Do you feel guilty about it? I mean, that's, that's part of it, right?

KRISTA: Sure. I should have been there.

CALEB: Well, I can imagine feeling that way, but you made the right choice.

Topics of support messages. The topics we discuss when communicating with someone in distress also vary considerably. Suppose you learned that a close friend was having serious marital problems. Would you give advice, listen attentively while your friend complained about the marriage, give him or her the number of a good divorce lawyer, offer your couch as a place to sleep, or remind your friend about all of his or her great qualities as a person? These are all supportive messages, even though they address different topics. **Informational support** involves giving advice or pointing out facts that

Informational Support

Messages that give advice or point out helpful facts.

TABLE 14.2 Examples of support messages

Mononucleosis or "mono" is a common illness among students on a college campus, and the impact of being sick can be stressful to people juggling school, work, and extra-curricular activities. Here are some support messages you might use to comfort someone coping with this illness.

Message	Example
Informational	It's a virus, so there isn't much you can do to cure it. Just be sure to get a lot of sleep and fluids. Pain relievers can help too, and sucking on hard candy can make your throat feel better.
Emotional	It must be so hard to fall behind in your classes and to feel like there's nothing you can do. It's okay to be upset about that. You aren't alone in this, and you can tell me how you are feeling.
Network	A friend of mine had mono last semester. I'm going to have him call you to tell you how he got through it.
Tangible	There's a lot I can do to help – go to the store for you, talk to your professors, walk your dog – you just name it.
Esteem	Everyone knows what a good student you are. Once you are feeling better, I know you'll catch up in your classes in no time.

can help a person cope. **Emotional support** messages focus on how a person is feeling and try to make that person feel better. When people offer **network support**, they try to link someone in distress to others who can help. **Tangible support** means providing practical aid – such as driving someone to the emergency room. Finally, **esteem support** involves pointing out positive personal qualities to build people up so they can better handle difficulties. Table 14.2 gives examples of these types of support messages.

All of these types of support can help a person in distress, but not every type of support helps every person and every situation (Xu & Burleson, 2001). Getting advice from someone who does not have any experience with your problem can be annoying (Feng & MacGeorge, 2006). Being asked to focus on your feelings can seem like a waste of time when you need practical help. Network support can introduce you to someone helpful, but it can also feel like your friend handed you off to a stranger. Tangible support can be insulting when you are able to meet your needs on your own. And esteem support can seem insincere when you think you are the source of your own troubles. As the cartoon in Figure 14.2 illustrates, support that doesn't match your needs isn't helpful.

Emotional Support
Verbal messages that focus on how a person is feeling and attempt to make that person feel better.

Network Support
Messages that link someone in distress to others who can help.

Tangible Support
Practical aid that addresses the source of a person's distress.

Esteem Support
Messages that point out positive personal qualities.

PAUSE & REFLECT

What type of support strategy would you prefer to receive if you were coping with the break-up of a romantic relationship, getting turned down for a summer internship, or a grandparent's death? How would you feel if you received one of the other types of support instead?

Perspective-taking
The ability to understand a situation from someone else's point of view.

Solace
A support strategy that combines approach-based and emotion-focused messages to elicit positive emotions and foster intimacy.

Solve
A support strategy that combines approach-based and task-focused messages to find solutions to the problem.

FIGURE 14.2
When the type of support doesn't match the situation

Source: www.cartoonstock.com

How can you figure out what sort of support to provide to someone? Take time to figure out what your interaction partner might be looking for. We call this kind of effort **perspective taking** – the ability to understand a situation from someone else's point of view. Skilled communicators notice how others are feeling and responding to messages, and they know how to adapt their communication to produce the desired effect. Jen recalls how an old friend used to comfort her during times of distress by saying, "Well, it is what it is." Although he probably found comfort in the philosophical notion that we should accept what we cannot change, he failed to recognize Jen's perspective. Because she likes to feel like she controls and understands a situation, Jen finds messages that provide advice ("Here are some ideas for solving the problem") or insight ("I wonder how much this happens to other people in your situation") more comforting. The survey in the How Do You Rate? 14.1 box can help you to understand your own preferences for support, which is a starting point for recognizing the unique support preferences of others.

Supportive communication strategies. We've seen that one way to categorize support messages is by the topic they focus on. Another way to think about verbal support is to focus on supportive communication strategies: whether people communicate about a problem, and whether they focus on feelings or solutions. In Figure 14.3, the horizontal axis shows how directly a person addresses a problem (whether the person talks about the problem explicitly and in detail or avoids talking about it). The vertical axis in Figure 14.3 differentiates between problem-focused versus emotion-focused strategies. People who are problem-focused strive to eliminate the problem that is creating distress. People who focus on emotions try to make the person in distress feel better. These two dimensions, considered together, give rise to four support strategies (Barbee & Cunningham, 1995):

- *Solace*: Approach-based and emotion-focused responses to elicit positive feelings and foster intimacy: "I know you've been very sad lately, and I want you to know that I'm here for you if you ever want to talk about how you're feeling."
- *Solve*: Approach-based and task-focused responses to find a solution to the distressing situation: "I really want to help you fix this situation. What can I do to help?"

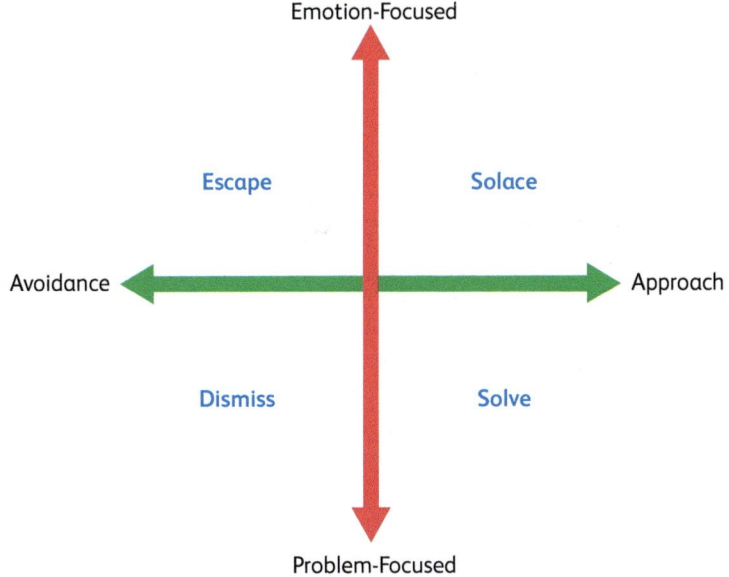

FIGURE 14.3 A typology of supportive communication strategies

- *Escape*: Avoidance-based and emotion-focused responses: "This is too depressing to even think about, let's go do something fun."
- *Dismiss*: Avoidance-based and task-focused responses: "You're making way too much out of this problem; just deal with it."

PAUSE & REFLECT

When comforting others, do you like to talk about the problem, or do you try to distract from the problem? Do you try to fix the problem or talk about the emotions that underlie it?

Escape
A support strategy that combines avoidance-based and emotion-focused messages to discourage the experience and expression of negative emotion.

Dismiss
A support strategy that combines avoidance-based and task-focused messages to minimize the significance of the problem.

Some of these strategies are more sensitive and effective than others. People perceive solace strategies and, to a lesser degree, solve strategies as functional and effective in comforting situations. People tend to rate escape and dismiss strategies as particularly unhelpful (Barbee & Cunningham, 1995). In other words, helpers are rated positively when they attempt to provide comfort, whereas people who try to sidestep the issue and dodge conversations about distressing events are perceived as insensitive and ineffective.

Ineffective Support Messages

Now that we've seen what makes a support message effective, let's take a look at some messages that are ineffective. Table 14.3 shows common mistakes people make when they try to comfort another person.

Putting yourself first. One of the most common mistakes we make when attempting to comfort others is to offer messages that we would find supportive, without considering whether that approach works for the person in distress. For example, if you find venting a waste of time and only turn to others for solutions, you might find it difficult to be a good listener to a friend who needs to talk about a troubling situation. Effective support requires you to overcome the tendency to do what works for you and put your partner's needs first.

Minimizing or maximizing. Providing effective support also involves finding a balance between failing to react enough and over-reacting. In a study that asked people with multiple sclerosis to rate the helpfulness of different support messages, two approaches were perceived as particularly unhelpful (Lehman & Hemphill, 1990). Minimizing messages challenge or undermine the seriousness of the problem (see Figure 14.3). Someone who tries to comfort you in this way might say, "It's not that big of a deal, you have nothing to worry about, this is nothing to get upset over." Maximizing messages overstate the seriousness of the problem and express excessive protection for the recipient. Someone who tries to comfort you by maximizing the situation might say, "This is terrible, you're never going to recover from this, your whole life will be ruined!" Whereas minimizing messages tell people that you don't take their problems seriously, maximizing messages can produce greater distress instead of comfort.

Cold comfort. One of the most ineffective responses to another person's troubles is cold comfort, or limited consolation, sympathy, or encouragement in response to serious distress. Denise still remembers vividly the response she got from a co-worker when her beloved 18-year-old cat was dying of cancer: "I had a cat that died once. Don't worry, you'll like the next cat too." Cold comfort usually involves superficial empathy ("oh, that's too bad"), minimizing messages ("things could be worse"), and oversimplified solutions ("just don't worry about it").

Cold Comfort

Messages that provide limited consolation, sympathy, or encouragement in response to serious distress.

TABLE 14.3 Ineffective support messages

Support message	Example
Putting yourself first	Well, when *my* mom died it was really helpful for people to take me out so that I could forget about it for a while. Let's go to the movies – that should make you feel better.
Minimizing	This isn't that big of a deal. If you really think about it, things could definitely be worse.
Maximizing	I can't believe this is happening to you! You must feel totally helpless. I don't know how you can carry on after this!
Cold comfort	Oh, well, that's really too bad. But I'm sure everything will be fine.

INSIDE COMMUNICATION RESEARCH

Gendered Perceptions of Poor Comforting

What are the consequences of providing insensitive support? The answer depends on whether you are male or female. A team of communication researchers, Amanda Holmstrom, Brant Burleson, and Susanne Jones (2005), studied how people perceive males and females who provide insensitive emotional support. The results of two experiments showed that females are especially harsh in their evaluations of other females who provide cold comfort.

In the first experiment, college students completed questionnaires that asked them to evaluate a transcript of one person providing comfort to someone in distress. Research participants were told that they were reading about a conversation between two males or two females, and different versions of the transcript presented either low, moderate, or high person-centered messages. For example, the low person-centered version included messages telling the person in distress that there were more important things to think about, and the high person-centered version encouraged the distressed person to talk about their feelings. In the second experiment, the research participants were instructed to discuss an upsetting event with another student, who was actually a confederate in the study. The confederate was trained to respond with either low, moderate, or high person-centered messages. In both experiments, participants rated how much they liked the supportive partner and how effective or supportive they found those messages.

Not surprisingly, both studies showed that the low person-centered messages were seen as less supportive than the high person-centered support. Evaluations of the people who provided insensitive support, however, depended on the sex of the sender and the receiver. In particular, males in the study rated both male and female providers of poor support as equally unlikeable. On the other hand, females in the study rated females who provided insensitive support as significantly less likeable than males who provided insensitive support. In fact, the lowest ratings of liking, supportiveness, and effectiveness were given by females who read about or experienced females giving low person-centered messages.

THINK ABOUT IT

1. Why do you think females are especially judgmental when they encounter another female who is providing low quality support?
2. This study reports two experiments that each used different methods. What do you see as the pros and cons of the two ways of presenting support messages to the research participants?

Putting Theory into Practice: Expanding Your Comforting Toolkit

When you try to comfort someone in distress, remember that you have a number of effective supportive messages you can try, as well as some messages that you should avoid.

Communicate nonverbal immediacy. When you are with someone who is feeling low, show that you care by staying physically close and making direct eye contact. Stand or sit near your communication partner, lean forward rather than away, orient your body so you are directly facing the other person, and look your partner in the eyes. If it's appropriate for your relationship, you might also place your hand gently on his or her hand, arm, or back. If you close the distance between you and your partner in these ways, you are literally "being there" for that person in times of need.

COMMUNICATION IN ACTION 14.1

Becoming More Nonverbally Immediate

Practice communicating nonverbal immediacy in some low-risk situations, such as a conversation with a sales clerk, bus driver, or receptionist in an office. In these interactions, turn your body directly toward the person, lean in, make direct eye contact, and display a friendly and expressive face. Notice how people respond when you are more nonverbally immediate. This exercise helps you practice nonverbal immediacy so that you are prepared to help when someone you care about needs you to show concern.

Focus on feelings. People in distress generally find messages that encourage them to talk about their problems and focus on their feelings to be most helpful. Two important lessons follow from this point:

- *Don't avoid conversations about another person's problems* – Talking to a distressed person is helpful even if you aren't quite sure what to say. If you can't talk at the time that a problem is mentioned, set a time and place when you will be able to listen and provide support. Your friends will appreciate the effort that you're making to help them.
- *Explicitly acknowledge how the other person is feeling* – People who are distressed want to be able to vent their frustrations and to feel understood and appreciated, so encourage them to reflect on how the situation makes them feel. Try to avoid relating the other person's experience to a similar situation that you've been through, and do your best to focus the interaction on the other person's feelings and perceptions.

Help the speaker clarify thoughts, feelings, and ideas. Sometimes the key to truly understanding what people are going through is to help them express what happened and how it made them feel. Have you ever felt down or depressed but you couldn't put your finger on what was bothering you? Imagine how helpful it would have been to have someone help you pinpoint the source of your distress by asking questions, paraphrasing what you said, or trying different perspectives on for size. Here are some strategies for helping someone clarify his or her emotions, with examples focused on coping with the end of a romantic relationship:

- *Repeat what the other person says*: "So, you're upset about the break-up, and you're feeling betrayed." Sometimes hearing our own words repeated back to us helps us to identify perceptions and feelings.
- *Paraphrase what you think the person means*: "When I hear you talk about the break-up, it's sounds like you're upset you didn't get a chance to make it work." When

you translate another person's message into your own words you add a level of interpretation that might help the person see the situation differently.

- *Share your perceptions of the situation*: "I wonder if you feel cheated, because you weren't told that things were getting so bad until it was too late." Just as perspective taking can help you be supportive, sharing your perceptions can help a distressed individual see the situation from a different point of view.
- *Ask purposeful questions*: "How did you feel when you found out? Why do you think you reacted that way?" When you help people tap into their underlying emotions and motivations, you can really get to the heart of the matter.
- *Avoid agreeing or disagreeing*: "This is a messy situation, and there's a lot going on here." Fully agreeing with everything a distressed person says can prevent further reflection, and firmly disagreeing can make the person too defensive to talk or reflect.

Practice perspective-taking. The key to providing effective emotional support is understanding what kinds of messages the other person would find comforting. Perspective-taking allows you to tailor your support messages to another person's underlying experience.

COMMUNICATION IN ACTION 14.2

Seeing Through Someone Else's Eyes

This exercise will help you engage in perspective-taking. Visit an online message board or support group for a distressing situation that you have no experience with. You might try fertilityforums.com for couples struggling with infertility, cancercompass.com for people and their families who are fighting cancer, or addictionrecovery guide.com for individuals coping with drug and alcohol addiction. Read and reflect on five posts, and complete the form on the **companion website**.

INDIVIDUAL DIFFERENCES IN COMFORTING BEHAVIOR

Our personal characteristics influence the kinds of support messages that we produce and the types of comforting strategies that we find most satisfying. In this section, we explore three characteristics that influence people's ability to seek and provide comfort: sex, cognitive complexity, and culture.

PAUSE & REFLECT

Whom do you typically turn to when you need support? What characteristics make that person a reliable source for comfort?

Sex Differences

When you are upset and need to talk to someone, are you most likely to turn to a woman or a man for comfort and support? Studies show that males and females are both similar and different when it comes to communicating comfort and support. In this section, we'll briefly review the effects of sex on supportive communication.

In general, males and females prefer to receive the same type of support, and they evaluate different support messages in similar ways. Both males and females perceive person-centered messages as sensitive, effective, and helpful (Jones & Guerrero, 2001, Jones & Burleson, 2003). In addition, both males and females rate senders of support messages as likable and popular when they use person-centered messages (Burleson, Delia, & Applegate, 1992; Samter et al., 1987). When you try to comfort someone, whether it's a male or a female, try to use messages that acknowledge and validate feelings ("You must be going through a hard time"), rather than messages that disregard the other person ("I think you should just calm down").

Although males and females prefer the same types of support messages, they do tend to produce different types of messages when they are acting as comforters. Females are more willing than males to offer support when requested to do so, and they are more likely to offer support without being asked (Trobst, Collins, & Embree, 1994). Females are also more confident in their ability to provide skilled and effective social support and comfort (Clark, 1993). Females tend to place greater value on support messages that effectively address and manage the distressed person's emotions (Burleson, Kunkel, Samter, & Werking, 1996), so it's not surprising that females also tend to produce more highly person-centered messages than males (Burleson, 1982; Hale, Tighe, & Mongeau, 1997). In short, females are more likely than males to provide the kind of support that both males and females find comforting.

Cognitive Complexity

Creating person-centered messages requires knowing a lot about other people, as well as how to respond to issues that come up during an interaction (Burleson & Samter,

FIGURE 14.4 Woman comforting her husband

Source: iStockPhoto.

1985). Some people have an easier time with this task than others do. **Cognitive complexity** is an individual trait that refers to the level of sophistication in people's perceptions of the world around them (Delia, 1987). Individuals who are high in cognitive complexity tend to notice more details and to see how those details are related to each other. In contrast, people who are low in cognitive complexity tend to view their environment in simpler and less nuanced ways. Cognitive complexity helps people perceive specific qualities in an interaction partner, as well as how those qualities fit together. And when someone needs help, cognitive complexity influences how well you understand the situation.

Cognitive complexity is often measured by looking at the words that people use to describe someone (e.g., Burleson, 1982). Let's consider the example of Jamar, a student at a large university in the Midwestern United States. Jamar is an engineering major and will participate in an internship for a major corporation next summer. He keeps himself busy on campus as the treasurer for his fraternity and he plays trombone in the university marching band. Jamar goes on dates with lots of different women, but he is currently single. What traits would you use to describe Jamar? The first column in Table 14.4 shows a typical description that might be produced by someone high in cognitive complexity, and the second column shows how someone low in cognitive complexity might describe Jamar.

People who think about other people in more sophisticated ways can produce more person-centered messages. High cognitive complexity corresponds with higher person-centeredness in support messages (Applegate, Burleson, & Delia, 1992; Burleson, 1984; Samter & Burleson, 1984). Females tend to have somewhat higher levels of cognitive complexity than males (Burleson & Denton, 1992), which may explain why females tend to produce more sensitive and person-centered support messages than males (Samter, 2002). Cognitively complex people also tend to appreciate support messages that are

Cognitive Complexity
The extent to which people perceive details in the world around them, as well as how those details are related to each other.

TABLE 14.4 Examples of descriptions reflecting high and low cognitive complexity

High cognitive complexity	Low cognitive complexity
Intelligent	Smart
Motivated	Popular
Hard working	Hard working
Privileged	Outgoing
Intellectual	Involved
Professional	
Leader	
Well-organized	
Active	
Involved	
Popular	
Promiscuous	
Well-liked	
Friendly	
Outgoing	

sophisticated and sensitive (Samter, Burleson, & Basden-Murphy, 1989). Thus, cognitive complexity is a personal quality that shapes both the comforting messages people produce and the support that they prefer to receive from others.

Culture

Culture has a pervasive effect on interpersonal communication and comforting interactions are no exception. Because cultural values shape the way people experience and express emotion, the way we communicate about feelings of distress is closely tied to our culture. One especially relevant dimension of culture is the extent to which the community emphasizes the individual or the group. As we discussed in Chapter 2, individualist cultures – such as the United States, in general – value personal goals and encourage independence. In contrast, collectivist cultures, like China, value group goals and emphasize group membership. These differences influence many aspects of support and comforting communication, including the kinds of events people find distressing and how people communicate about distress.

In individualist cultures, distress centers on events that block individual needs, goals, and desires (Mesquita, 2001). For example, personal failure contributes to more frustration and disappointment for European-Americans than for Chinese citizens (Mortenson, 2006). In contrast, people from collectivist cultures tend to experience distress over situations that have negative social consequences or disrupt the well-being of the group (Mesquita, 2001). In fact, individuals from collectivist cultures try to protect their friends and family from their personal problems; for example, they might hide emotions like fear and sadness to avoid burdening others (Mortenson, 2006).

People from both individualist and collectivist cultures prefer messages that are emotionally sensitive to the distressed person (Burleson & Mortenson, 2003). Beyond this preference, however, the cultural groups are quite different in their preferences for supportive communication. People in individualist cultures prefer support messages that help them work through and discuss their feelings (Burleson & Mortenson, 2003). Accordingly, European-Americans are more likely than Chinese to communicate directly with people about their problems and to seek social support when in distress (Mortenson, 2006). In contrast, Chinese people prefer comforters who distract them from their problems or offer solutions that will eliminate them (Mortenson, 2006). These types of supportive messages allow members of a collectivist culture to minimize the disruption within the community that their personal troubles might create (Mortenson, M. Liu, Burleson, Y. Liu, 2006). It's no surprise, then, that Chinese immigrants turn to computer-mediated social support as an efficient means of gaining support in their new community (Chen & Choi, 2011).

PAUSE & REFLECT

What would you say or do to comfort someone from an individualist culture, such as the United States? What if you were trying to comfort someone from a collectivist culture, such as China – how would you change your behavior?

Putting Theory into Practice: Overcoming Obstacles to Support

This section of the chapter highlighted people's different preferences and abilities when it comes to seeking and providing support. Consider the following suggestions for adapting supportive messages so that these differences don't become obstacles.

Appreciate, but don't exaggerate, sex differences. You learned in this section that males and females, in general, have some similarities and some differences when it comes to supportive communication. Although some sex differences exist, it's important not to exaggerate them. Being able to give and receive support is an important skill, and both males and females can master it. When you recognize and respond to differences between people, you are on your way to providing person-centered support. The exercise in Communication in Action 14.3 can help you to understand how a person's sex affects your supportive communication.

COMMUNICATION IN ACTION 14.3

Overcoming Sex Bias in Comforting Messages

This exercise will help you think about how to tailor support messages to males and females. Complete the form on the **companion website** thinking about how to provide comfort to a male or a female in various situations. How different are the messages? As you reflect on the messages you created, think about whether you are overcoming obstacles or creating them when you adapt your comforting messages to your partner's sex.

Practice cultural sensitivity. Keep in mind that people from individualist and collectivist cultures may feel differently about emotional distress and emotional support. If you ever find yourself in a situation where you are called upon to comfort someone from a different culture, begin by learning about your communication partner's cultural values. Let's take the example of Shen Ming, a Chinese woman studying in the United States, and her European-American neighbor, Rachel. Rachel discovers that Shen Ming is upset by news from home that her father is ill. If Rachel considers Shen Ming's culture preferences, she might invite Shen Ming over to watch TV or help her make plans to visit home. By doing so, she focuses on solving the problem rather than on Shen Ming's feelings about it. The Communication in Action 14.4 exercise can help you think about how culture affects everyone's experience of distress and support.

Complexity helps. No matter what your own level of cognitive complexity might be, it helps to attend carefully to the specifics of a partner's stressful situation, use empathy and perspective-taking to understand the other person's point of view, and avoid overly general responses to problems. Here are two suggestions to help you provide more complex comfort:

- *Read between the lines*. Consider what the person *isn't* saying that might still be true about the situation. For example, when someone describes a situation as frustrating,

COMMUNICATION IN ACTION 14.4

Appreciating Culturally Diverse Comforting Needs

In this exercise, you will reflect on how people from different cultures might experience distress and create support messages that are culturally appropriate. Complete the form on the **companion website** by thinking about five experiences you've had giving comfort to someone else and how the situation would have been different if that person was from another culture.

think about the other emotions that tend to accompany feelings of frustration, such as anger, embarrassment, or helplessness, and try to address those as well.

■ *Say it another way.* Consider multiple ways to communicate comfort and support and you'll increase the chance that you'll say something helpful. For example, if your best friend's father dies, a simple "I'm sorry for your loss" might help. When you communicate support in a variety of ways, with messages like "I'm sorry for your loss," "He must have been very special because you are so wonderful," and "I'm here for you during this difficult time," you are more likely to offer the words that can help a person feel better.

COMFORT WHEN IT COUNTS

What can you say to comfort someone who has just been diagnosed with cancer? How can you help someone who is mourning the death of a loved one? These are times when your actions and words are most important. In fact, people who receive support from friends and family have stronger immunological responses, which can help them fight illness (Uchino, 2006). In this section, you will learn to provide the best support you can in situations when comfort really counts.

PAUSE & REFLECT

Have you experienced a serious stressor – a major illness, the death of a loved one, or a personal tragedy? If not, do you know someone who has? In your experience, what messages provide support in those extreme circumstances?

Coping with Cancer

A diagnosis of cancer can cause severe emotional trauma to the patient and his or her family. People feel vulnerability, loss of control, and uncertainty about their future

FIGURE 14.5 A family receiving news from a doctor

Source: iStockPhoto.

(Sammarco, 2001). Two different coping processes allow people to deal with both the practical and emotional sides of serious illness. **Problem-focused coping** emphasizes controlling the illness and making sense of complex medical information. **Emotion-focused coping** emphasizes controlling negative reactions to the illness and managing emotional distress. To cope with illness at both levels, patients must interact with a social network that includes family, friends, doctors, nurses, and other health-care professionals.

Three types of support discussed previously in this chapter are especially beneficial to cancer patients: emotional support, informational support, and tangible support (Arora, Rutten, Gustafson, Moser, & Hawkins, 2007). Providing emotional support might involve telling the patient how much you care about him and reminding him that you'll always be there for him. Providing informational support might involve helping to locate and interpret medical information. Tangible support might include watching the person's kids for a weekend, cleaning the house, running an errand, or providing transportation to radiation treatments. One study of adolescents coping with cancer revealed that they receive a tremendous amount of informational and emotional support through online support groups (Elwell, Grogan, & Coulson, 2010). Among the topics that adolescents discussed in their online forum were concerns about cancer treatments, losing friends, and struggling in school. The informational and emotional support that the adolescents received from their peers online was an important tool for coping with their illness. In general, participating in online support groups to cope with illness contributes to increased social support, decreased depression, increased quality of life, and increased self-efficacy to manage one's health condition (Rains & Young, 2009).

People with cancer often do not get the support they want and need. One study examined online support groups and discussion boards established for breast cancer survivors to identify sources of distress (Weber & Solomon, 2008). Many women described the difficulties they had in getting support from others and their feelings of isolation. For example, one woman wrote, "People that I thought were once friends . . . stopped phoning and even when I would meet them . . . they shunned me . . . They acted as though I was not there" (p. 554). Another lamented, "I don't think anyone really knows what we go through unless they walk in our shoes" (p. 554). Perhaps people who

Problem-focused Coping
Addressing a difficult situation by focusing on understanding and resolving it.

Emotion-focused Coping
Addressing a difficult situation by focusing on controlling the negative feelings and distress that it generates.

are cancer-free want to distance themselves from the illness or have difficulty understanding what a cancer patient is going through. And although friends and family are often supportive immediately after a diagnosis of cancer, all forms of support decrease significantly just five months after the initial diagnosis (Arora et al., 2007).

Your own emotions about a friend or loved one's diagnosis may actually prevent you from offering support. For example, women with breast cancer say that it can be challenging to tell people about their diagnosis because of the strong reactions others have to their news (Weber & Solomon, 2008). The cancer patient's goal may be to disclose her diagnosis and get comfort from someone close to her, but as soon as she mentions cancer, she may find herself comforting her loved one! What can you do to break this dynamic? Find ways to cope with your own reactions to someone's illness that don't further burden the cancer survivor, such as talking to someone who doesn't know the patient. In addition, provide tangible support by offering to tell other friends and family the news, so that those people can come to terms with their own feelings without relying on the patient.

HOW DO YOU RATE? 14.2

Support for Bereavement

Visit the **companion website** to complete a survey designed to measure your reactions to various types of support messages designed to comfort someone after the loss of a loved one.

Bereavement

The death of a loved one is a universal experience that is often shared with others. Family members, friends, and acquaintances of the deceased collectively grieve the loss, so understanding how to provide comfort in this context is an important social skill. Grief management strategies are types of emotional support designed to cope with extreme depression arising from extraordinary events. Unlike day-to-day disappointments, the loss of a loved one often produces intense emotions that call for carefully constructed support messages.

Finding the right words to comfort someone who is coping with the death of a loved one can be difficult. As you might expect, some messages are more effective than others. In one study, bereaved adults indicated that only 20% of people's responses to their grief were perceived as helpful (Davidowitz & Myrick, 1984). The responses that bereaved individuals rate as most supportive include offers to be there for the person, providing opportunities to vent feelings, complimenting the deceased, and expressions of concern for the bereaved (Hogan & DeSantis, 1994; Lehman, Ellard, & Wortman, 1986; Marwit & Carusa, 1998). The least helpful messages are those that minimize the significance of the loss, diminish the feelings of the bereaved, tell the bereaved what to do, and give unsolicited advice. Complete the How Do You Rate? 14.2 survey to explore your own reactions to support messages in these situations.

PAUSE & REFLECT

Have you ever grieved the loss of someone you loved? What kinds of things did people say to you that were most helpful or unhelpful?

What makes some grief management messages more effective and helpful than others? Messages that are high in person-centeredness tend to be perceived as the most supportive and comforting (Rack, Burleson, Brodie, Holmstrom, & Servaty-Seib, 2008; Servaty-Seib & Burleson, 2007). Characteristics of the individual and the context also influence the types of support messages that are perceived as most effective. For example, people who are optimistic about getting the support they need evaluate specific support messages as more helpful than individuals who are pessimistic about getting support (Kaul & Lakey, 2003; Servaty-Seib & Burleson, 2007). The context also affects how people respond to supportive messages during bereavement (Servaty-Seib & Burleson, 2007). For example, bereaved individuals who were extremely close to the deceased in life tend to feel more comforted by messages that express concern and positive regard for the deceased. In addition, philosophical perspectives on death and the provision of advice are perceived as more helpful shortly after the death occurred, but less helpful after some time has passed.

Putting Theory into Practice: Providing Support in Times of Need

Even though it is hard for you to know what to say or do for a person who is facing serious illness or bereavement, think about how much harder it is for the person who is going through it. In this section, we suggest some actions you can take to provide even a small amount of comfort during these difficult times.

Focus on what you can do to make life easier. Remember that tangible support is often just as important as emotional support. Are you a good cook? Make a couple of dinners that would keep well in the freezer for an easy weeknight meal or bake a batch of cookies that they can turn to for comfort. Do you have a car? Offer to go to the grocery store, shopping mall, or pharmacy, or offer to pick up the kids from school. Are you skilled at working outdoors? Perhaps you could mow their lawn, tend to their garden, or shovel their driveway in the winter. When people are struggling to cope with circumstances that are larger than life, day-to-day tasks can seem impossible to keep up with.

COMMUNICATION IN ACTION 14.5

Different Types of Support

This exercise is designed to get you thinking about the different types of support you can offer someone in need. Think of someone you know who might be going through a life-changing event, even something positive like the birth of a first child. Using the form on the **companion website**, identify three things that you could do to provide each type of social support for this person.

Don't overreach. Remember that during a traumatic event, it's difficult to find verbal messages that will provide comfort. When there is literally nothing you can say to fix the situation, problem-focused support strategies might be unhelpful and insensitive. Attempting to offer emotion-focused support is also tricky in this context, because you may not fully understand the scope of the emotional trauma and you could accidentally respond in an inappropriate way. In these situations, it's often best to keep your support efforts simple. A hug, a promise to be there, an offer to help with some tangible task are all modest but helpful ways to provide support. In addition, stay in touch and keep expressing your concern through both nonverbal immediacy and verbal messages. When people are facing major life stressors, the coping process is a lengthy one; by checking in and providing support over the long haul, you can make an enormous difference.

SUMMARY

In this final chapter, we have turned our attention to one of the most wonderful tasks we accomplish through interpersonal communication: providing comfort and support. Through the messages we send to other people, we can make them feel better about bad news, give them strength to manage a difficult situation, or remind them that they are valued and cared for. Moreover, giving the gift of a comforting message isn't expensive or difficult. By simply displaying nonverbal immediacy, by making direct eye contact, showing sympathetic facial expressions, leaning forward, and facing a person, we communicate concern for a partner. Through verbal communication, you can attend to a variety of topics and use different communication strategies to provide comfort. By practicing these communication skills, and avoiding especially ineffective support messages, you can go a long way to improving the lives of people you care about.

As you offer messages of support to other people – or seek comfort from someone else – keep in mind that people experience distress differently and prefer different kinds of support. Although males and females both appreciate comforting messages that are person-centered, females are more likely than males to offer emotional support using person-centered messages. Remember, also, that some people might be better at providing support because they perceive interpersonal communication in more complex and nuanced ways. Culture is another factor that affects both the kinds of events people consider distressing, and what they consider supportive when they are in need.

When you tune in to opportunities to provide comfort and support, you'll discover many everyday situations when your nonverbal and verbal messages can make a difference. You may also find yourself in a position to provide support to somebody who really needs it. When people in your life experience a serious illness or the death of a loved one, interpersonal communication is a tool you can use to soften the blow. Although you can't undo a diagnosis or take away a person's grief, you can go a long way toward letting someone know that you care about them and you are there for them. By providing a variety of forms of support – from nonverbal immediacy to practical aid – you can help another person cope with what might otherwise be devastating circumstances.

The ability to use messages to comfort others is one of the most important interpersonal communication skills you can develop. Even though personal qualities like sex, cognitive complexity, and culture might predispose you to provide support in particular ways, you can take steps to expand your comforting toolkit, overcome obstacles to providing support, and provide support when it really matters. Like the other communication skills you learned about in this textbook, you can improve your ability to communicate comfort and support. When you do, you will understand how interpersonal communication can truly change people's lives for the better.

ACTIVITIES FOR EXPLORING COMMUNICATION ETHICS

What Would You/Should You Do?

One of your friends has been acting depressed, so you decide to address whatever issue is making her feel sad and try to make her feel better. When you approach your friend, she tells you about a variety of circumstances that are making her sad. She seems hopeless and apathetic and implies that she has been considering suicide. What would you or should you do?

Something to Think About

In some situations, the source of a person's distress is invisible to outsiders. For example, infertility affects 1 out of 6 couples in the United States, but you'll never know who is experiencing it unless they tell you. In fact, an infertile couple might look to you like a husband and wife who are putting their jobs first or planning for a lifetime free from the hassles of children. Supportive communication is more than just offering the right response to sad news – it also involves creating a space where people don't feel pressured to divulge private information or stigmatized for conditions beyond their control. Instead of the usual questions that many childless couples encounter ("So when are you planning to have a baby?"), how might you communicate in ways that are less hurtful and more supportive?

Analyzing Communication Ethics Yourself

One of the challenges to ethical support is providing messages that help people, while simultaneously respecting their rights to cope with their problems the way that they see fit. Ethical communication also makes clear the values that support a course of action and avoids simple directive statements. Monitor an advice column, website, or televised talk show for a period of time to observe the advice messages that are given. To what extent do advice-givers make clear the values and evidence that support their recommendations? Do the messages tend to respect the person's autonomy, or do they dictate a particular response? Based on your analysis, what might these sources of advice do to provide their service in more ethical ways?

KEY WORDS

cognitive complexity

cold comfort

dismiss

emotion-focused coping

emotional support

empathy

escape

esteem support

informational support

network support

nonverbal immediacy

person-centeredness

perspective taking

problem focused coping

solace

solve

tangible support

Bibliography

1 WHAT IS INTERPERSONAL COMMUNICATION?

Afifi, T. D. (2003). "Feeling caught" in stepfamilies: Managing boundary turbulence through appropriate communication privacy rules. *Journal of Social and Personal Relationships, 20,* 729–755.

Afifi, W. A., & Burgoon, J. K. (1998). "We never talk about that": A comparison of cross-sex friendships and dating relationships on uncertainty and topic avoidance. *Personal Relationships, 5,* 255–272.

Arnett, R. C., Harden Fritz, J. M., & Bell, L. M. (2009). *Communication ethics literacy.* Thousand Oaks, CA: Sage.

Baxter, L. A., & Wilmot, W. W. (1985). Taboo topics in close relationships. *Journal of Social and Personal Relationships, 2,* 253–269.

Caplan, S. E. (2005). A social skill account of problematic Internet use. *Journal of Communication, 55,* 721–736.

Cegala, D. J., McGee, D. S., & McNeilis, K. S. (1996). Components of patients' and doctors' perceptions of communication competence during a primary care medical interview. *Health Communication, 8,* 1–27.

Collier, M. J. (1996). Communication competence problematics in ethnic friendships. *Communication Monographs, 63,* 314–336.

Fairhurst, G. T., & Putnam, L. (2004). Organizations as discursive constructions. *Communication Theory, 14,* 5–26.

Floyd, K. (2006). Human affection exchange: XII. Affectionate communication is associated with diurnal variation in salivary free cortisol. *Western Journal of Communication, 70,* 47–63.

Floyd, K., Mikkelson, A. C., Hesse, C., & Pauley, P. M (2007). Affectionate writing reduces total cholesterol. *Human Communication Research, 33,* 119–142.

Floyd, K., Mikkelson, A. C., Tafoya, M. A., Farinelli, L., La Valley, A. G., Judd, J., Haynes, M. T., Davis, K. L., & Wilson, J. (2007). Human affection exchange: XIII. Affectionate communication accelerates neuroendocrine stress recovery. *Health Communication, 22,* 123–132.

Golish, T. D., & Caughlin, J. P. (2002). "I'd rather not talk about it": Adolescents' and young adults' use of topic avoidance in stepfamilies. *Journal of Applied Communication Research, 30,* 78–106.

Gray, J., & Laidlaw, H. (2004). Improving the measurement of communication satisfaction. *Management Communication Quarterly, 17,* 425–448.

Haslett, B. B., & Samter, W. (Eds.). (1997). *Children communicating: The first 5 years.* Mahwah, NJ: Lawrence Erlbaum.

Holladay, S. J., & Seipke, H. L. (2007). Communication between grandparents and grandchildren in geographically separated relationships. *Communication Studies, 58,* 281–297.

Johnson, P., Lindsey, A. E., & Zakahi, W. R. (2001). Anglo Americans, Hispanic Americans, Chilean, Mexican and Spanish perceptions of competent communication in initial interaction. *Communication Research Reports, 18,* 36–43.

Larkey, L. K., & Hecht, M. L. (1995). A comparative study of African American and European American ethnic identity. *International Journal of Intercultural Relations*, *19*, 483–504.

Nussbaum, J. F., Pecchioni, L. L., Baringer, D. K., & Kundrat, A. L. (2002). Lifespan communication. In W. B. Gudykunst (Ed.), *Communication Yearbook 26* (pp. 366–389). Mahwah, NJ: Lawrence Erlbaum.

Priem, J. S., McLaren, R. M., & Solomon, D. H. (2010). Relational messages, perceptions of hurt, and biological stress reactions to a disconfirming interaction. *Communication Research*, *37*, 48–72.

Miller, K. I., Considine, J., & Garner, J. (2007). "Let me tell you about my job": Exploring the terrain of emotion in the workplace. *Management Communication Quarterly*, *20*, 231–260.

Solomon, D. H. (2006). A relational framing perspective on perceptions of social-sexual communication at work. In R. M. Dailey & B. A. LePoire (Eds.) *Applied interpersonal communication matters: Family, health, and community relations* (pp. 271–298). New York: Peter Lang.

Spitzberg, B. H. (2003). Methods of interpersonal skill assessment. In J. O. Greene & B. R. Burleson (Eds.) *Handbook of communication and social interaction skills* (pp. 93–134). Mahwah, NJ: Lawrence Erlbaum.

Spitzberg, B. H. (2006). Preliminary development of a model and measure of computer-mediated communication (CMC) competence. *Journal of Computer-Mediated Communication*, *11*, 629–666.

Spitzberg, B. H., & Cupach, W. R. (2002). Interpersonal skills. In M. L. Knapp & J. A. Daly (Eds). *Handbook of interpersonal communication* (3rd ed., pp. 564–611). Thousand Oaks, CA: Sage.

Wilson, S. R., & Sabee, C. M. (2003). Explicating communicative competence as a theoretical term. In J. O. Greene & B. R. Burleson (Eds.), *Handbook of communication and social interaction skills* (pp. 3–50). Mahwah, NJ: Lawrence Erlbaum.

Xu, Y., & Burleson, B. R. (2001). Effects of sex, culture, and support types on perceptions of spousal social support: An assessment of the "support gap" hypothesis in early marriage. *Human Communication Research*, *27*, 535–566.

2 CULTURE AND INTERPERSONAL COMMUNICATION

Baumeister, R. F., Zhang, L., & Vohs, K. D. (2004). Gossip as cultural learning. *Review of General Psychology*, *8*, 111–121.

Baxter, L. A. (1987). Symbols of relationship identity in relationship cultures. *Journal of Social and Personal Relationships*, *4*, 261–280.

Baxter, L. A., & Clark, C. L. (1996). Perceptions of family communication patterns and the enactment of family rituals. *Western Journal of Communication*, *60*, 254–268.

Baxter, L. A., & Goldsmith, D. (1990). Cultural terms for communication events among some American high school adolescents. *Western Journal of Speech Communication*, *54*, 377–394.

Bell, R. A., & Healey, J. G. (1992). Idiomatic communication and interpersonal solidarity in friends' relational cultures. *Human Communication Research*, *18*, 307–335.

Braithwaite, D. O. (1995). Ritualized embarrassment at "coed" wedding and baby showers. *Communication Reports*, *8*, 145–157.

Braithwaite, D. O., Baxter, L. A., & Harper, A. M. (1998). The role of rituals in the management of the dialectical tension of "old" and "new" in blended families. *Communication Studies*, *49*, 101–120.

Bruess, C. J. S., & Pearson, J. C. (1997). Interpersonal rituals in marriage and adult friendship. *Communication Monographs*, *64*, 25–46.

Bullis, C. (1993). Organizational socialization research: Enabling, constraining, and shifting perspectives. *Communication Monographs*, *60*, 10–17.

Cassell, J., & Tversky, D. (2005). The language of online intercultural community formation. *Journal of Computer-Mediated Communication*, *10*, article 2. Available at: http://jcmc.indiana.edu/vol10/issue2/cassell.html.

Cherlin, A. J. (2004). The deinstitutionalization of American marriage. *Journal of Marriage and the Family, 66,* 848–861.

Christian, A. (2005). Contesting the myth of the "wicked stepmother": Narrative analysis of an online stepfamily support group. *Western Journal of Communication, 69,* 27–47.

DeTurk, S. (2001). Intercultural empathy: Myth, competency, or possibility for alliance building. *Communication Education, 50,* 374–384.

Dickinson, G., Ott, B. L., & Aoki, E. (2005). Memory and myth at the Buffalo Bill museum. *Western Journal of Communication, 69,* 85–108.

Dindia, K., & Canary, D. J. (2006). *Sex differences and similarities in communication.* Mahwah, NJ: Erlbaum.

Dougherty, D. S. (2001). Sexual harassment as [dys]functional process: A feminist standpoint analysis. *Journal of Applied Communication Research, 29,* 372–402.

Duranti, A. (1997). Universal and culture-specific properties of greetings. *Journal of Linguistic Anthropology, 7,* 63–97.

Duranti, A. (2006). The social ontology of intentions. *Discourse Studies, 8,* 31–40.

Fitch, K. L. (1998). *Speaking relationally: Culture, communication, and interpersonal connection.* New York: Guilford Press.

Gallois, C. (2003). Reconciliation through communication in intercultural encounters: Potential or peril. *Journal of Communication, 53,* 5–15.

Gallois, C., & Callan, V. J. (1985). The influence of ethnocentrism and ethnic label on the appreciation of disparagement jokes. *International Journal of Psychology, 20,* 63–76.

Gallois, C., Ogay, T., & Giles, H. (2005). Communication accommodation theory: A look back and a look ahead. In W. B. Gudykunst (Ed.), *Theorizing about intercultural communication* (pp. 121–148). Thousand Oaks, CA: Sage.

Giles, H., Mulac, A., Bradac, J. J., & Johnson, P. (1987). Speech accommodation theory: The first decade and beyond. In M. L. McLaughlin (Ed.), *Communication Yearbook 10* (pp. 13–48). Beverly Hills, CA: Sage.

Gudykunst, W. B. (1993). Toward a theory of effective interpersonal and intergroup communication: An anxiety/uncertainty management perspective. In R. L. Wiseman, & J. Koester (Eds.), *Intercultural communication competence* (pp. 33–71). Newbury Park, CA: Sage.

Gudykunst, W. B. (2005). An anxiety/uncertainty management (AUM) theory of effective communication. In W. B. Gudykunst (Ed.), *Theorizing about intercultural communication* (pp. 281–322). Thousand Oaks, CA: Sage.

Gudykunst, W. B., & Nishida, T. (2001). Anxiety, uncertainty, and perceived effectiveness of communication across relationships and cultures. *International Journal of Intercultural Relations, 25,* 55–71.

Gudykunst, W. B., & Shapiro, R. (1996). Communication in everyday interpersonal and intergroup encounters. *International Journal of Intercultural Relations, 20,* 19–45.

Hallstein, D. L. O. (2000). Where standpoint stands now: An introduction and commentary. *Women's Studies in Communication, 23,* 1–15.

Harkins, D. A., & Ray, S. (2004). An exploratory study of mother–child storytelling in east India and northeast United States. *Narrative Inquiry, 14,* 347–367.

Harwood, J. (2000). Communicative predictors of solidarity in the grandparent–grandchild relationship. *Journal of Social and Personal Relationships, 17,* 743–766.

Harwood, J., & Giles, H. (1992). "Don't make me laugh": Age representations in a humorous context. *Discourse & Society, 3,* 403–436.

Hofstede, G. (2001). *Culture's consequences: Comparing values, behaviors, institutions, and organizations across nations* (2nd ed.). Thousand Oaks, CA: Sage.

Hornsey, M., & Gallois, C. (1998). The impact of interpersonal and intergroup communication accommodation on perceptions of Chinese students in Australia. *Journal of Language and Social Psychology, 17,* 323–347.

Hylmö, A. (2006). Telecommuting and the contestability of choice. *Management Communication Quarterly, 19,* 541–569.

Hopper, R., & Chen, C. (1996). Languages, cultures, relationships: Telephone openings in Taiwan. *Research on Language and Social Interaction, 29*, 291–313.

Katriel, T. (1999). Rethinking the terms of social interaction. *Research on Language and Social Interaction, 32*, 95–101.

Kellas, J. K. (2005). Family ties: Communicating identity through jointly told family stories. *Communication Monographs, 72*, 365–389.

Leaper, C., Anderson, K. J., & Sanders, P. (1998). Moderators of gender effects on parents' talk to their children: A meta-analysis. *Developmental Psychology, 34*, 3–27.

Lee, C. M., & Gudykunst, W. B. (2001). Attraction in initial interethnic interactions. *International Journal of Intercultural Relations, 25*, 373–387.

Lin, M. C., & Harwood, J. (2003). Accommodation predictors of grandparent–grandchild relational solidarity in Taiwan. *Journal of Social and Personal Relationships, 20*, 537–563.

Martin, C. L., Fabes, R. A., Evans, S. M., & Wyman, H. (1999). Social cognition on the playground: Children's beliefs about playing with girls versus boys and their relation to sex segregated play. *Journal of Social and Personal Relationships, 16*, 751–771.

Martin, D. M. (2004). Humor in middle management: Women negotiating the paradoxes of organizational life. *Journal of Applied Communication Research, 32*, 147–170.

McCabe, M. P., & Hardman, L. (2005). Attitudes and perceptions of workers to sexual harassment. *Journal of Social Psychology, 145*, 719–740.

McKenna, K. Y. A., & Bargh, J. A. (1998). Coming out in the age of the Internet: Identity "demarginalization" through virtual group participation. *Journal of Personality and Social Psychology, 75*, 681–694.

Mongeau, P. A., & Carey, C, M. (1996). Who's wooing whom II: An experimental investigation of date initiation and expectancy violation. *Western Journal of Communication, 60*, 195–213.

Mongeau, P. A., Hale, J. L., Johnson, K. L., & Hillis, J. D. (1993). Who's wooing whom: An investigation of female initiated dating. In P. J. Kalbfleisch (Ed.), *Interpersonal communication: Evolving interpersonal relationships* (pp. 51–68). Hillsdale, NJ: Lawrence Erlbaum.

Murphy, B. O., & Zorn, T. (1996). Gendered interaction in professional relationships. In J. T. Wood (Ed.), *Gendered relationships* (pp. 213–232). Mountain View, CA: Mayfield.

Myers, K. K. (2005). A burning desire: Assimilation into a fire department. *Management Communication Quarterly, 18*, 344–384.

Neuliep, J. W., Hintz, S. M., & McCroskey, J. C. (2005). The influence of ethnocentrism in organizational contexts: Perceptions of interviewee and managerial attractiveness, credibility, and effectiveness. *Communication Quarterly, 53*, 41–56.

Neuliep, J. W., & McCroskey, J. C. (1997). The development of intercultural and interethnic communication apprehension scales. *Communication Research Reports, 14*, 145–156.

Pená, J., & Hancock, J. T. (2006). Analysis of socioemotional and task communication in online multiplayer video games. *Communication Research, 33*, 92–109.

Phillipsen, G. (1997). A theory of speech codes. In G. Phillipsen & T. L. Albrecht (Eds.), *Developing communication theories* (pp. 119–156). Albany: SUNY Press.

Phillipsen, G., Coutu, L. M., & Covarrubias, P. (2005). Speech codes theory: Restatement, revisions, and response to criticisms. In W. B. Gudykunst (Ed.), *Theorizing about intercultural communication* (pp. 55–68). Thousand Oaks, CA: Sage.

Propp, K. M. (1995). An experimental examination of biological sex as a status cue in decision-making groups and its influence on information use. *Small Group Research, 26*, 451–474.

Rawlins, W. K. (1993). Communication in cross-sex friendships. In L. P. Arliss & D. J. Borisoff (Eds.), *Women and men communicating* (pp. 51–70). New York: Harcourt Brace.

Rodgers, S., & Chen, Q. (2005). Internet community group participation: Psychosocial benefits for women with breast cancer. *Journal of Computer-Mediated Communication, 10*, article 5. Available at: http://jcmc.indiana.edu/vol10/issue4/rodgers.html.

Rodino-Colocino, M. (2006). Laboring under the digital divide. *New Media & Society, 8*, 487–511.

Rose, S., & Frieze, I. H. (1993). Young singles' contemporary dating scripts. *Sex Roles, 28*, 499–509.

Ross, K. A. (1999). Can diversity and community coexist in higher education?: The case of heritage college. *American Behavioral Scientist, 42*, 1024–1040.

Ruud, G. (2000). The symphony: Organizational discourse and the symbolic tensions between artistic and business ideologies. *Journal of Applied Communication Research, 28,* 117–143.

Sigman, S. J. (1991). Handling the discontinuous aspects of continuous social relationships: Toward research on the persistence of social forms. *Communication Theory, 1,* 106–127.

Silva, V. T. (2005). In the beginning was the gene: The hegemony of genetic thinking in contemporary culture. *Communication Theory, 15,* 100–123.

Solomon, D. H. (2006). A relational framing perspective on perceptions of social-sexual communication at work. In R. M. Dailey, & B. A. LePoire (Eds.), *Applied interpersonal communication matters: Family, health, and community relations.* New York: Peter Lang.

Stafford, L., Kline, S. L., & Dimmick, J. (1999). Home e-mail: Relational maintenance and gratification opportunities. *Journal of Broadcasting & Electronic Media, 43,* 659–669.

Stapleton, K. (2003). Gender and swearing: A community practice. *Women and Language, 26,* 22–33.

Stephan, W., & Stephan, C. (1985). Intergroup anxiety. *Journal of Social Issues, 41,* 157–166.

Tannen, D. (1991). *You just don't understand: Women and men in conversation.* New York: HarperCollins.

Ting-Toomey, S., Yee-Jung, K. K., Shapiro, R. B., Garcia, W., Wright, T. J., & Oetzel, J. G. (2000). Ethnic/cultural identity salience and conflict styles in four US ethnic groups. *International Journal of Intercultural Relations, 24,* 47–81.

Vrooman, S. S. (2002). The art of invective. *New Media & Society, 4,* 51–70.

Williams, A., & Giles, H. (1996). Intergenerational conversations: Young adults' retrospective accounts. *Human Communication Research, 23,* 220–250.

3 IDENTITY AND INTERPERSONAL COMMUNICATION

Abu-Rayya, H. M. (2006). Ethnic self-identification and psychological well-being among adolescents with European mothers and Arab fathers in Israel. *International Journal of Intercultural Relations, 30,* 545–556.

Ahnallen, J. M., Suyemoto, K. L., & Carter, A. S. (2006). Relationship between physical appearance, sense of belonging and exclusion, and racial/ethnic self-identification among multiracial Japanese European Americans. *Cultural Diversity and Ethnic Minority Psychology, 12,* 673–686.

Alicke, M. D., LoSchiavo, R. M., Zerbst, J., & Zhang, S. (1997). The person who outperforms me is a genius: Maintaining perceived competence in upward social comparison. *Journal of Personality and Social Psychology, 73,* 781–789.

Arnett, J. J. (2000). Emerging adulthood. *American Psychologist, 55,* 469–480.

Arp, D. H., Arp, C. S., Stanley, S. M., Markman, H. J., & Blumberg, S. L. (2000). *Fighting your empty nest marriage: Reinventing your relationship when the kids leave home.* San Francisco, CA: Jossey Bass.

Ashcraft, C. (2006). Ready or not . . .?: Teen sexuality and the troubling discourse of readiness. *Anthropology and Education Quarterly, 37,* 328–346.

Banks, S. P., Louie, E., & Einerson, M. (2000). Constructing personal identities in holiday letters. *Journal of Social and Personal Relationships, 17,* 299–327.

Beals, K. P., & Peplau, L. A. (2005). Identity support, identity devaluation, and well-being among lesbians. *Psychology of Women Quarterly, 29,* 140–148.

Beauregard, K. S., & Dunning, D. (1998). Turning up the contrast: Self-enhancement motives prompt egocentric contrast effects in social judgments. *Journal of Personality and Social Psychology, 74,* 606–621.

Brown, J. D., Dykers, C. R., Steele, J. R., & White, A. B. (1994). Teenage room culture: Where media and identities intersect. *Communication Research, 21,* 813–827.

Burke, P. J., & Harrod, M. M. (2005). Too much of a good thing? *Social Psychology Quarterly, 68,* 359–374.

Chory-Assad, R. M., & Booth-Butterfield, M. (2001). Secret test use and self-esteem in deteriorating relationships. *Communication Research Reports*, *18*, 147–157.

Constantino, M. J., Wilson, K. R., & Horowitz, L. M. (2006). The direct and stress-buffering effects of self-organization on psychological adjustment. *Journal of Social and Clinical Pscyhology*, *25*, 333–360.

Constantino, M. J., Wilson, K. R., Horowitz, L. M., & Pinel, E. C. (2006). Measures of self-organization and their association with psychological adjustment. *Journal of Social and Clinical Psychology*, *25*, 333–360.

Crowley, B. J., Hayslip, B., & Hobdy, J. (2003). Psychological hardiness and adjustment to life events in adulthood. *Journal of Adult Development*, *10*, 237–248.

Dennerstein, L., Dudley, E., & Guthrie, J. (2002). Empty nest or revolving door? A prospective study of women's quality of life in midlife during the phase of children leaving and re-entering the home. *Psychological Medicine*, *32*, 545–550.

Feeney, J., Peterson, C., & Noller, P. (1994). Equity and marital satisfaction over the family life cycle. *Personal Relationships*, *1*, 83–99.

Fine, M. (1992). Sexuality, schooling, and adolescent females: The missing discourse of desire. In M. Fine (Ed.), *Disruptive voices: The possibilities of feminist research* (pp. 31–60). Ann Arbor, MI: Michigan State University Press.

Guerrero, L. K., & Afifi, W. A. (1998). Communicative responses to jealousy as a function of self-esteem and relationship maintenance goals: A test of Bryson's dual motivation model. *Communication Reports*, *11*, 111–122.

Hecht, M. L. (1993). 2002 – A research odyssey: towards the development of a communication theory of identity. *Communication Monographs*, *60*, 76–82.

Hecht, M. L., Warren, J. R., Jung, E., & Krieger, J. L. (2005). The communication theory of identity: Development, theoretical perspective, and future directions. In W. B. Gudykunst (Eds.), *Theorizing about intercultural communication* (pp. 257–278). Thousand Oaks, CA: Sage.

Holmes, J. (2005). Story-telling at work: A complex discursive resource for integrating personal, professional and social identities. *Discourse Studies*, *7*, 671–700.

Hsieh, E. (2004). Stories in action and the dialogic management of identities: Storytelling in transplant support group meetings. *Research on Language and Social Interaction*, *37*, 39–70.

Huffaker, D. A., & Calvert, S. L. (2005). Gender, identity, and language use in teenage blogs. *Journal of Computer-Mediated Communication*, *10*, article 1. Available at: http://jcmc.indiana.edu/vol10/issue2/huffaker.html.

Jensen, L. A., Arnett, J. J., Feldman, S. S., & Cauffman, E. (2004). The right to do wrong: Lying to parents among adolescents and emerging adults. *Journal of Youth and Adolescence*, *33*, 101–112.

Jung, E., & Hecht, M. L. (2004a). Elaborating the communication theory of identity: Identity gaps and communication outcomes. *Communication Studies*, *52*, 265–283.

Jung, E., & Hecht, M. L. (2004b). Korean Americans' identity gaps in interethnic interaction and levels of depression. Unpublished manuscript.

Karp, J. A., Holmstrom, L. L., & Gray, P. S. (2004). Of roots and wings: Letting go of the college-bound child. *Symbolic Interaction*, *27*, 357–382.

Kenny, D. A. (1994). *Interpersonal perception: A social relations analysis.* New York: Guilford Press.

Kim, Y. K, Lujan, P., & Dixon, L. D. (1998). "I can walk both ways": Identity integration of American Indians in Oklahoma. *Human Communication Research*, *25*, 252–274.

Knobloch-Westerwick, S., & Hastall, M. R. (2006). Social comparisons with news personae: Selective exposure to news portrayals of same-sex and same-age characters. *Communication Research*, *33*, 262–284.

Larkey, L. K., & Hecht, M. L. (1995). A comparative study of African American and European American ethnic identity. *International Journal of Intercultural Relations*, *19*, 483–504.

Lefkowitz, E. S. (2005). "Things have gotten better": Developmental changes among emerging adults after the transition to university. *Journal of Adolescent Research*, *20*, 40–63.

Lutz, C. J., & Ross, S. R. (2003). Elaboration versus fragmentation: Distinguishing between self-complexity and self-concept differentiation. *Journal of Social and Clinical Psychology*, *22*, 537–559.

Markus, H., & Wurf, E. (1986). The dynamic self-concept: A social psychological perspective. *American Review of Psychology, 38*, 299–337.

Marsiglia, F. F., Kulis, S., & Hecht, M. L. (2001). Ethnic labels and ethnic identity as predictors of drug use and drug exposure among middle school students in the Southwest. *Journal of Research on Adolescence, 11*, 21–48.

Miller-Day, M., & Barnett, J., M. (2004). "I'm not a druggie": Adolescents' ethnicity and (erroneous) beliefs about drug use norms. *Health Communication, 16*, 207–228.

Nelson, L. J., & Barry, C. M. (2005). Distinguishing features of emerging adulthood: The role of self-classification as an adult. *Journal of Adolescent Research, 20*, 242–262.

Oswald, R. F. (2002). Who am I in relation to them? Gay, lesbian, and queer people leave the city to attend rural family weddings. *Journal of Family Issues, 23*, 323–348.

Palomares, N. A. (2004). Gender schematicity, gender identity salience, and gender-linked language use. *Human Communication Research, 30*, 556–588.

Rosario, M., Schrimshaw, E. W., Hunter, J., & Braun, L. (2006). Sexual identity development among lesbian, gay, and bisexual youths: Consistency and change over time. *Journal of Sex Research, 43*, 46–58.

Rosenberg, M. (1989). *Society and the adolescent self-image* (Revised ed.). Middletown, CT: Wesleyan University Press.

Scharf, M., Shulman, S, & Avigad-Spitz, L. (2005). Sibling relationships in emerging adulthood and in adolescence. *Journal of Adolescent Research, 20*, 64–90.

Soliz, J., & Harwood, J. (2006). Shared family identity, age salience, and intergroup contact: Investigation of the grandparent–grandchild relationship. *Communication Monographs, 73*, 87–107.

Subrahmanyam, K., Smahel, D., & Greenfield, P. (2006). Connecting developmental constructions to the Internet: Identity presentation and sexual exploration in online teen chat rooms. *Developmental Psychology, 42*, 395–406.

Swann, W. B., Jr. (1983). Self-verification: Bringing social reality into harmony with the self. In J. Suls, & A. G. Greenwald (Eds.), *Psychological perspectives on the self* (Vol. 2, pp. 33–66). Hillsdale, NJ: Erlbaum.

Teboul, J. B. (1995). Determinants of new-hire information seeking during organizational encounter. *Western Journal of Communication, 59*, 305–329.

Tracy, S. J., & Scott, C. (2006). Sexuality, masculinity, and taint management among firefighters and correctional officers: Getting down and dirty with "America's Heroes" and the "Scum of Law Enforcement." *Management Communication Quarterly, 20*, 6–38.

White, L., & Edwards, J. N. (1990). Emptying the new and parental well-being: An analysis of National Panel Data. *American Sociological Review, 55*, 235–242.

4 PERCEPTION AND INTERPERSONAL COMMUNICATION

Albada, K. F., Knapp, M. L., & Theune, K. E. (2002). Interaction appearance theory: Changing perceptions of physical attractiveness through social interaction. *Communication Theory, 12*, 8–40.

Anderson, J. R. (1985). Development of expertise. In J. R. Anderson, *Cognitive psychology and its implications* (2nd ed., pp. 232–260). New York: Freeman and Co.

Anderson, N. H. (1981). *Foundations of information integration theory*. New York: Academic Press.

Anderson, P. A., Guerrero, L. K., Buller, D. B., & Jorgensen, P. F. (1998). An empirical comparison of three theories of nonverbal immediacy exchange. *Human Communication Research, 24*, 501–535.

Andrews, P. H. (1987). Gender differences in persuasive communication and attribution and failure. *Human Communication Research, 13*, 372–385.

Bargh, J. A. (1982). Attention and automaticity in the processing of self-relevant information. *Journal of Personality and Social Psychology, 43*, 425–436.

Barker, V., Giles, H., & Harwood, J. (2004). Inter- and intragroup perspectives on inter-generational communication. In J. F. Nussbaum, & J. Coupland (Eds.), *Handbook of communication and aging research* (2nd ed., pp. 139–165). Mahwah, NJ: Lawrence Erlbaum.

Baucom, D. H., & Lester, G. W. (1986). The usefulness of cognitive restructuring as an adjunct to behavioral marital theory. *Behavior Therapy, 17*, 385–403.

Baucom, D. H., Sayers, S. L., & Sher, T. G. (1990). Supplementing behavioral marital therapy with cognitive restructuring and emotional expressiveness training: An outcome investigation. *Journal of Consulting and Clinical Psychololgy, 58*, 636–645.

Baucom, D. H., Shoham, V., Mueser, K., Daiuto, A. D., Stickle, T. R. (1998). Empirically supported couple and family interventions for marital distress and adult mental heath problems. *Journal of Consulting and Clinical Psychology, 66*, 53–88.

Ben-Ari, R., Kedem, P., & Levy-Weiner, N. (1992). Cognitive complexity and intergroup perception and evaluation. *Personality and Individual Differences, 13*, 1291–1298.

Berkos, K. M., Allen, T. H., Kearney, P., & Plax, T. G. (2001). When norms are violated: Imagined interactions as processing and coping mechanisms. *Communication Monographs, 68*, 289–300.

Blair, I. V., Judd, C. M., Sadler, M. S., & Jenkins, C. (2002). The role of Afrocentric features in person perception: Judging by features and categories. *Journal of Personality and Social Psychology, 83*, 5–25.

Boxer, P., & Tisak, M. (2003). Adolescents' attributions about aggression: An initial investigation. *Journal of Adolescence, 26*, 559–573.

Bradbury, T. N., Beach, S. R. H., Fincham, F. D., & Nelson, G. M. (1996). Attributions and behavior in functional and dysfunctional marriages. *Journal of Consulting and Clinical Psychology, 64*, 569–576.

Bradbury, T. N., & Fincham, F. D. (1990). Attributions in marriage: Review and critique. *Psychological Review, 107*, 3–33.

Bradbury, T. N., & Fincham, F. D. (1992). Attributions and behavior in marital interaction. *Journal of Personality and Social Psychology, 63*, 613–628.

Canary, D. J., & Hause, K. S. (1993). Is there any reason to research sex differences in communication? *Communication Quarterly, 41*, 129–144.

Chavajay, P., & Rogoff, B. (1999). Cultural variation in management of attention by children and their caregivers. *Developmental Psychology, 35*, 1079–1090.

Chen, Y., & Blanchard-Fields, F. (1997). Age differences in stages of attributional processing. *Psychology and Aging, 12*, 694–703.

Cloven, D. H., & Roloff, M. E. (1993). Sense-making activities and interpersonal conflict, II: The effects of communicative intentions on internal dialogue. *Western Journal of Communication, 57*, 309–329.

Correa-Chávez, M., Rogoff, B., & Arauz, R. M. (2005). Cultural patterns in attending to two events at once. *Child Development, 78*, 664–678.

Davies, G., & Robertson, N. (1993). Recognition memory for automobiles: A developmental study. *Bulletin of the Psychonomic Society, 31*,103–106.

Davis, M. H. (1980). A multidimensional approach to individual differences in empathy. *JSAS Catalog of Selected Documents in Psychology, 10*, 85–105.

Dixon, T. L., & Linz, D. (2000). Overrepresentation and underrepresentation of African Americans and Latinos as lawbreakers on television news. *Journal of Communication, 50*, 131–154.

Fincham, F. D., & Bradbury, T. N. (1987). The impact of attributions in marriage: A longitudinal analysis. *Journal of Personality and Social Psychology, 53*, 510–517.

Fincham, F. D., & Bradbury, T. N. (1993). Marital satisfaction, depression, and attributions: A longitudinal analysis. *Journal of Personality and Social Psychology, 64*, 442–452.

Fletcher, G. J. O., Danilovics, P., Fernandez, G., Peterson, D., & Reeder, G. D. (1986). Attributional complexity: An individual differences measure. *Journal of Personality and Social Psychology, 51*, 875–884.

Fletcher, G. J. O., Rosanowski, J., Rhodes, G., & Lange, C. (1992). Accuracy and speed of causal processing: Experts versus novices in social judgment. *Journal of Experimental Social Psychology, 28*, 320–338.

Follett, K., & Hess, T. M. (2002). Aging, cognitive complexity, and the fundamental attribution error. *Journal of Gerontology: Series B: Psychological Sciences and Social Sciences, 57B*, 312–323.

Hancock, J. R., & Dunham, P. J. (2001). Impression formation in computer-mediated communication revisited. *Communication Research, 28*, 325–347.

Hong, Y., Benet-Martinez, V., Chiu, C., & Morris, M. W. (2003). Boundaries of cultural influence: Construct activation as a mechanism for cultural differences in social perception. *Journal of Cross-Cultural Psychology, 34*, 453–64.

Ishii, K., Reyes, J. A., & Kitayama, S. (2003). Spontaneous attention to word content versus emotional tone: Differences among three cultures. *Psychological Science, 14*, 39–46.

Joireman, J. (2004). Relationships between attributional complexity and empathy. *Individual Differences Research, 2*, 197–202.

Kalish, C. W. (2002). Children's predictions of consistency in people's actions. *Cognition, 84*, 237–265.

Karney, B. R., & Bradbury, T. N. (2000). Attributions in marriage: State or trait? A growth curve analysis. *Journal of Personality and Social Psychology, 78*, 295–309.

Kelley, D., H., & Gorham, J. (1988). The effects of immediacy on recall of information. *Communication Education, 37*, 198–207.

Lannutti, P. J., & Monahan, J. L. (2002). When the frame paints the picture: Alcohol consumption, relational framing, and sexual communication. *Communication Research, 29* (4), 390–421.

Lea, M., & Spears, F. (1995). Love at first byte? Building personal relationships over computer networks. In J. T. Wood, & S. Duck (Eds.), *Understudied relationships: Off the beaten track* (pp. 197–233). Thousand Oaks, CA: Sage.

Levine, T. R., Anders, L. N., Banas, J., Baum, K. L., Endo, K., Hu, A. D. S., & Wong, N. C. H. (2000). Norms, expectations, and deception: A norm violation model of veracity judgments. *Communication Monographs, 67*, 123–137.

Lyons, A., & Kashima, Y. (2003). How are stereotypes maintained through communication? The influence of stereotype sharedness. *Journal of Personality and Social Psychology, 85*, 989–1005.

Maass, A., Ceccarelli, R., & Rudin, S. (1996). Linguistic intergroup bias: Evidence for in-group-protective motivation. *Journal of Personality and Social Psychology, 71*, 512–526.

Maass, A., Salvi, D., Arcuri, L., & Semin, G. (1989). Language use in intergroup contexts: The linguistic intergroup bias. *Journal of Personality and Social Psychology, 57*, 981–993.

MacDonald, T. K., Zanna, M. P., & Fong, G. T. (1996). Why common sense goes out the window: Effects of alcohol on intention to use condoms. *Personality and Social Psychology Bulletin, 22*, 763–775.

MacFadden, A., Elias, L, & Saucier, D. (2003). Males and females scan maps similarly, but give directions differently. *Brain and Cognition, 53*, 297–300.

MacGeorge, E. L. (2001). Support providers' interaction goals: The influence of attributions and emotions. *Communication Monographs, 68*, 72–97.

Masuda, T., & Nisbett, R. E. (2001). Attending holistically versus analytically: Comparing the context sensitivity of Japanese and Americans. *Journal of Personality and Social Psychology, 81*, 922–934.

Monahan, J. L., & Lannutti, P. J. (2000). Alcohol as social lubricant: Alcohol myopia theory, social self-esteem, and social interaction. *Human Communication Research, 26* (2), 175–202.

Monahan, J. L., Murphy, S. T., & Miller, L. C. (1999). When women imbibe: Alcohol and the illusory control of HIV risk. *Psychology of Women Quarterly, 23*, 643–651.

Murphy, S. T., Monahan, J. L., & Miller, L. C. (1998). Inference under the influence: The impact of alcohol and inhibition conflict on women's sexual decision making. *Personality and Social Psychology Bulletin, 24*, 517–528.

Nathanson, A. I., Wilson, B. J., McGee, J., & Sebastian, M. (2002). Counteracting the effects of stereotypes on television via active mediation. *Journal of Communication, 52*, 922–937.

Oliver, M. B., Jackson II, R. L., Moses, N. N., & Dangerfield, C. L. (2004). The face of crime: Viewers' memory of race-related facial features of individuals pictured in the news. *Journal of Communication, 54*, 88–104.

Peng, K., & Knowles, E. D. (2003). Culture, education, and the attribution of physical causality. *Personality and Social Psychology Bulletin, 29*, 1272–1284.

Proctor, D. C. B., & Snyder, L. B. (2000, August). Do skin tones matter when judging the guilt of accused African Americans pictured in news crime stories? Paper presented at the annual conference of the Association for Education in Journalism and Mass Communication, Phoenix, AZ.

Ryan, E. B., Giles, H., Bartolucci, G., & Henwood, K. (1986). Psycholinguistic and social psychological components of communication by and with the elderly. *Language and Communication, 6*, 1–24.

Shapiro, M. A., & Fox, J. R. (2002). The role of typical and atypical events in story memory. *Human Communication Research, 28*, 109–135.

Simpson, J. A., Gangestad, S. W., & Lerma, M. (1990). Perception of physical attractiveness: Mechanisms involved in the maintenance of romantic relationships. *Journal of Personality and Social Psychology, 59*, 1192–1201.

Spears, R., & Lea, M. (1994). Panacea or panopticon? The hidden power in computer-mediated communication. *Communication Research, 21*, 427–459.

Steele, C. M., & Josephs, R. A. (1990). Alcohol myopia: Its prized and dangerous effects. *American Psychologist, 45*, 921–933.

Steele, C. M., & Southwick, L. (1985). Alcohol and social behavior I: The psychology of drunken excess. *Journal of Personality and Social Psychology, 48*, 18–34.

Walther, J. B., Anderson, J. R., & Park, D. (1994). Interpersonal effects in computer-mediated interaction: A meta-analysis of social and anti-social communication. *Communication Research, 21*, 460–487.

Weiner, B. (1985). "Spontaneous" causal thinking. *Psychological Bulletin, 97*, 74–84.

Weiner, B. (1986). *An attributional theory of motivation and emotion.* New York: Springer-Verlag.

Weiner, B. (1995). *Judgments of responsibility: A foundation for a theory of social conduct.* New York: Guilford Press.

Wigboldus, D. H. J., Semin, G. R., & Spears, R. (2000). How do we communicate stereotypes? Linguistic bases and inferential consequences. *Journal of Personality and Social Psychology, 78*, 5–18.

Woods, E. (1996). Associations of nonverbal decoding ability with indices of person-centered communicative ability. *Communication Reports, 9*, 13–22.

Wyer, R. S., Swan, S., & Gruenfeld, D. H. (1995). Impression formation in informal conversations. *Social Cognition, 13*, 243–272.

Yuill, N., & Pearson, A. (1998). The development of bases for trait attribution: Children's understanding of traits as causal mechanisms based on desires. *Developmental Psychology, 34*, 574–586.

5 LANGUAGE AND INTERPERSONAL COMMUNICATION

Agnew, C. R., Van Lange, P. A. M., Rusbult, C. E., & Langston, C. A. (1998). Cognitive interdependence: Commitment and the mental representation of close relationships. *Journal of Personality and Social Psychology, 74*, 939–954.

Anthony, C. S. (2007, May 28). And you do what, exactly? *Daily Edition Newsweek*, available at: http://www.msnbc.msn.com/id/3032542/site/newsweek/.

Armstrong, J. D. (1997). Homophobic slang as coercive discourse among college students. In A. Livia, & K. Hall (Eds.), *Queerly phrased: Language, gender, and sexuality.* New York: Oxford University Press.

Babad, E. (1980). Expectancy bias in scoring as a function of ability and ethnic labels. *Psychological Reports, 46*, 625–626.

Barnes, B., Palmary, I., & Durrheim, K. (2001). The denial of racism: The role of humor, personal experience, and self-censorship. *Journal of Language and Social Psychology, 20*, 321–338.

Bell, R. A., Buerkel-Rothfuss, N. L., & Gore, K. E. (1987). "Did you bring the yarmulke for the Cabbage Patch Kid?" The idiomatic communication of young lovers. *Human Communication Research*, *14*, 47–67.

Bell, R. A., & Healey, J. G. (1992). Idiomatic communication and solidarity in friends' relational cultures. *Human Communication Research*, *18*, 3070–335.

Bianco, M. (2005). The effects of disability labels on special education and general education teachers' referrals for gifted programs. *Learning Disability Quarterly*, *28*, 285–293.

Bolden, G. B. (2006). Little words that matter: Discourse markers "so" and "oh" and the doing of other-attentiveness in social interaction. *Journal of Communication*, *56*, 661–688.

Bradac, J. J., Mulac, A., & Thompson, S. A. (1995). Men's and women's use of intensifiers and hedges in problem-solving interactions: Molar and molecular analyses. *Research on Language and Social Interaction*, *28*, 93–116.

Brody, L. E., & Mills, C. J. (1997). Gifted children with learning disabilities: A review of the issues. *Journal of Learning Disabilities*, *30*, 282–296.

Brown, P., & Levinson, S. C. (1987). *Politeness: Some universals in language usage*. Cambridge: Cambridge University Press.

Brownlow, S., Rosamond, J. A., & Parker, J. A. (2003). Gender-linked linguistic behavior in television interviews. *Sex Roles*, *49*, 121–132.

Carli, L. L. (1990). Gender, language, and influence. *Journal of Personality and Social Psychology*, *59*, 941–951.

Cate, R. M., & Lloyd, S. A. (1992). *Courtship*. Newbury Park, CA: Sage.

Cralley, E. L., & Ruscher, J. B. (2005). Lady, girl, female, or woman: Sexism and cognitive busyness predict use of gender-biased nouns. *Journal of Language and Social Psychology*, *24*, 300–314.

Daly, J. A., Weber, D. J., Vangelisti, A. L., Maxwell, M., & Neel, H. (1989). Concurrent cognitions during conversations: Protocol analysis as a means of exploring conversations. *Discourse Processes*, *12*, 227–244.

Dorland, J. M., & Fischer, A. R. (2001). Gay, lesbian, and bisexual individuals' perceptions: An analogue study. *The Counseling Psychologist*, *29*, 532–547.

Douglas, K. M., & Sutton, R. M. (2006). When what you say about others says something about you: Language abstraction and inferences about describers' attitudes and goals. *Journal of Experimental Social Psychology*, *42*, 500–508.

Fehr, B., & Broughton, R. (2001). Gender and personality differences in conceptions of love: An interpersonal theory analysis. *Personal Relationships*, *8*, 115–136.

Frey, N. (2005). Retention, social promotion, and academic redshirting: What do we know and need to know? *Remedial and Special Education*, *26*, 332–346.

Gibbons, P., Busch, J., & Bradac, J. J. (1991). Powerful versus powerless language: Consequences for persuasion, impression formation, and cognitive response. *Journal of Language and Social Psychology*, *10*, 115–133.

Goldsmith, D. J., & Baxter, L A. (1996). Constituting relationships in talk: A taxonomy of speech events in social and personal relationships. *Human Communication Research*, *23*, 87–114.

Greiffenhagen, C., & Sharrock, W. (2007). Linguistic relativism: Logic, grammar, and arithmetic in cultural comparison. *Language & Communication*, *27*, 81–107.

Grice, H. P. (1957). Meaning. *The Philosophical Review*, *66*, 377–388.

Grice, H. P. (1975). Logic and conversation. In P. Cole, & J. L. Morgan (Eds.), *Syntax and semantics 3: Speech acts* (pp. 41–58). New York: Academic Press.

Guerin, B. (2003). Combating prejudice and racism: New interventions from a functional analysis of racist language. *Journal of Community and Applied Social Psychology*, *13*, 29–45.

Guiller, J., & Durndell, A. (2006). "I totally agree with you": Gender interactions in educational online discussion groups. *Journal of Computer Assisted Learning*, *22*, 368–381.

Holtgraves, T. (2002). Comprehending speaker meaning. In W. B. Gudykunst (Ed.), *Communication Yearbook 26* (pp. 2–35). Mahwah, NJ: Lawrence Erlbaum.

Hosman, L. A., & Siltanen, S. A. (2006). Powerful and powerless language forms: Their consequences for impression formation, attributions of control of self and control of others, cognitive responses, and message memory. *Journal of Language and Social Psychology*, *25*, 33–46.

Hussey, K. A., & Katz, A. N. (2006). Metaphor production in online conversation: Gender and friendship status. *Discourse Processes*, *42*, 75–98.

Jacobs, S., Dwason, E. J., & Brashers, D. (1996) Information manipulation theory: A replication and assessment. *Communication Monographs*, *63*, 70–82.

Jacobs, S., Thomas, W., & Lang, S. (1997). *Two-spirit people: Native American gender, sexuality, and spirituality*. Urbana, IL: University of Illinois Press.

Kitzinger, C. (1996). Speaking of oppression: Psychology, politics, and the language of power. In E. D. Rothblum, & L. A. Bond (Eds.), *Preventing heterosexism and homophobia* (pp. 3–19). Thousand Oaks, CA: Sage.

Knobloch, L. K., & Solomon, D. H. (2003). Manifestations of relationship conceptualizations in conversation. *Human Communication Research*, *29*, 482–515.

Krieger, J. L., Parrott, R. L., & Nussbaum, J. F. (2011). Metaphor use and health literacy: A pilot study of strategies to explain randomization in cancer clinical trials. *Journal of Health Communication*, *16*, 3–16.

Lakoff, R. (1973). Language and women's place. *Language in Society*, *2*, 45–80.

Leaper, C. (1991). Influence and involvement in children's discourse: Age, gender, & partner effects. *Child Development*, *62*, 797–811.

Leaper, C. (1994). Exploring the consequences of gender segregation on social relationships. In C. Leaper (Ed.), *Childhood gender segregation: Causes and consequences* (pp. 67–86). San Francisco: Jossey-Bass.

Lyman, P. (1987). The fraternal bond as a joking relationship: A case study of the role of sexist jokes in male group bonding. In M. S. Kimmel (Ed.), *Changing men: New directions in research on men and masculinity* (pp. 148–163). Thousand Oaks, CA: Sage.

Maccoby, E. E. (1990). Gender and relationships: A developmental account. *American Psychologist*, *45*, 513–520.

Markham, A. (1996). Designing discourse: A critical analysis of strategic ambiguity and workplace control. *Communication Studies*, *9*, 389–421.

Miller, C. H., Lane, L. T., Deatrick, L. M., Young, A. M., & Potts, K. A. (2007). Psychological reactance and promotional health messages. *Human Communication Research*, *33*, 219–240.

Morand, D. A. (1996a). Dominance, deference, and egalitarianism in organizational interaction: A sociolinguistic analysis of power and politeness. *Organization Science*, *7*, 545–556.

Morand, D. A. (1996b). What's in a name? An exploration of the social dynamics of forms of address in organizations. *Management Communication Quarterly*, *9*, 422–451.

Morand, D. A. (2000). Language and power: An empirical analysis of linguistic strategies used in superior–subordinate communication. *Journal of Organizational Behavior*, *21*, 235–248.

Morand, D. A. (2005). Black holes in social space: The occurrence and effects of name-avoidance in organizations. *Journal of Applied Social Psychology*, *35*, 320–334.

Mulac, A., Bradac, J. J., & Gibbons, P. (2001). Empirical support for the gender-as-culture hypothesis: An intercultural analysis of male/female language differences. *Human Communication Research*, *27*, 121–152.

Mulac, A., & Lundell, T. L. (1982). An empirical test of the gender-linked language effect in a public speaking setting. *Language and Speech*, *25*, 243–256.

Mulac, A., & Lundell, T. L. (1986). Linguistic contributors to the gender-linked language effect. *Journal of Language and Social Psychology*, *5*, 81–101.

Nayak, A., & Kelly, M. J. (1996). Playing it straight: Masculinities, homophobias and schooling. *Journal of Gender Studies*, *5*, 211–230.

Parks, J. B., & Roberton, M. A. (1998). Contemporary arguments against non-sexist language: Blaubergs (1980) revisited. *Sex Roles*, *39*, 445–461.

Parks, J. B., & Roberton, M. A. (2000). Development and validation of an instrument to measure attitudes toward sexist/nonsexist language. *Sex Roles*, *42*, 415–438.

Parks, J. B., & Roberton, M. A. (2004). Attitudes toward women mediate the gender effect on attitudes toward sexist language. *Psychology of Women Quarterly*, *28*, 233–239.

Pellegrini, A. D., Brody, G. H., & Stoneman, Z. (1987). Children's conversational competence with their parents. *Discourse Processes*, *10*, 93–106.

Pennebaker, J. W., Mehl, M. R., & Niederhoffer, K. G. (2003). Psychological aspects of natural language use: Our words, our selves. *Annual Review of Psychology, 54*, 547–577.

Pexman, P. M., & Zvaigzne, M. T. (2004). Does irony go better with friends? *Metaphor and Symbol, 19*, 143–163.

Pilling, M., & Davies, I. R. L. (2004). Linguistic relativism and colour cognition. *British Journal of Psychology, 95*, 429–455.

Pryor, J. B., Giedd, J. L., & Williams, K. B. (1995). A social psychological model for predicting sexual harassment. *Journal of Social Issues, 51*, 69–84.

Rubin, D. L., Greene, K., & Schneider, D. (1994). Adopting gender-inclusive language reforms: Diachronic and synchronic variation. *Journal of Language and Social Psychology, 13*, 91–114.

Ryan, K. M., & Kanjorski, J. (1998). The enjoyment of sexist humor, rape attitudes, and relationship aggression in college students. *Sex Roles, 38*, 743–756.

Saygin, A. P., & Cicekli, I. (2002). Pragmatics in human-computer conversations. *Journal of Pragmatics, 34*, 227–258.

Solomon, D. H., & Williams, M. L. M. (1997). Perceptions of social-sexual communication at work: The effects of message, situation, and observer characteristics on judgments of sexual harassment. *Journal of Applied Communication Research, 25*, 196–216.

Steuber, K. R., & Solomon, D. H. (2011). Managing information within social networks during infertility. In M. Miller-Day (Ed.), *Family communication, connections, and health transitions* (pp. 297–322). New York: Peter Lang.

Swim, J. K., Mallett, R., & Stangor, C. (2004). Understanding subtle sexism: Detection and use of sexist language. *Sex Roles, 51*, 117–128.

Thomson, R. (2006). The effect of topic discussion on gendered language in computer-mediated communication discussion. *Journal of Language and Social Psychology, 25*, 167–178.

Thurlow, C. (2001). Naming the "outsider within": Homophobic pejoratives and the verbal abuse of lesbian, gay, and bisexual high-school pupils. *Journal of Adolescence, 24*, 25–38.

Verkuyten, M., de Jong, W., & Masson, K. (1994). Racial discourse, attitude, and rhetorical maneuvers: Race talk in the Netherlands. *Journal of Language and Social Psychology, 3*, 278–298.

Whorf, B. L. (1956). *Language, thought, and reality: Selected readings.* Cambridge, MA: Technology Press of Massachusetts Institute of Technology.

Zhang, S., & Schmitt, B. (1998). Language-dependent classification: The mental representation of classifiers in cognition, memory, and ad evaluations. *Journal of Experimental Psychology: Applied, 4*, 375–385.

6 NONVERBAL COMMUNICATION

Andersen, P. A. (1985). Nonverbal immediacy in interpersonal communication. In A. W. Siegman & S. Feldstein (Eds.), *Multichannel integrations of nonverbal behavior* (pp. 1–36). Hillsdale, NJ: Erlbaum.

Andersen, P. A. (1998). Researching sex differences within sex similarities: The evolutionary consequences of reproductive differences. In D. J. Canary & K. Dindia (Eds.), *Sex differences and similarities in communication* (pp. 83–100). Mahwah, NJ: Erlbaum.

Andersen, P. A., & Sull, K. K. (1985). Out of touch, out of reach: Tactile predispositions as predictors of interpersonal distance. *The Western Journal of Speech Communication, 49*, 57–72.

Baxter, L. A., & Bullis, C. (1986). Turning points in developing romantic relationships. *Human Communication Research, 12*, 469–493.

Birdwhistell, R. L. (1970). *Kinesics and context.* Philadelphia: University of Pennsylvania Press.

Bixler, S., & Nix-Rice. (1997). *The new professional image.* Holbrook, MA: Adams Media Corporation.

Brody, L. R., & Hall, J. A. (1993). Gender and emotion. In M. Lewis & J. M. Haviland (Eds.), *Handbook of emotions* (pp. 447–460). New York: Guilford Press.

Burgoon, J. K., Blair, J. P., & Strom, R. E. (2008). Cognitive biases and nonverbal cue availability in detecting deception. *Human Communication Research, 34,* 572–599.

Burgoon, J. K., Buller, D. B., Hale, J. L., & deTurck, M. A. (1984). Relational messages associated with nonverbal behaviors. *Human Communication Research, 10,* 351–378.

Burgoon, J. K., Buller, D. B., & Woodall, W. G. (1996). *Nonverbal communication: The unspoken dialogue.* New York: McGraw-Hill.

Byers, E. S. (1980). Female communication of consent and nonconsent to sexual intercourse. *New Brunswick Psychology, 5,* 12–18.

Byers, E. S., & Demmons, S. (1999). Sexual satisfaction and sexual self-disclosure within dating relationships. *Journal of Sex Research, 36,* 180–189.

Coates, E. J., & Feldman, R. S. (1996). Gender differences in nonverbal correlates of social status. *Personality and Social Psychology Bulletin, 22,* 1014–1022.

Cupach, W. R., & Comstock, J. (1990). Satisfaction with sexual communication in marriage: Links to sexual satisfaction and dyadic adjustment. *Journal of Social and Personal Relationships, 7,* 179–186.

DePaulo, B. M., Kashy, D. A., Kirkendol, S. E., Wyer, S. M., & Epstein, J. A. (1996). Lying in everyday life. *Journal of Personality and Social Psychology, 70,* 979–995.

DePaulo, B. M., Stone, J. I., & Lassiter, G. D. (1985). Deceiving and detecting deceit. In B. Schlenker (Ed.), *The self and social life* (pp. 323–370). New York: McGraw-Hill.

Duncan, S., & Fiske, D. W. (1979). Dynamic patterning in conversation, *American Scientist, 67,* 90–98.

Edgar, T., & Fitzpatrick, M. A. (1993). Expectations for sexual interaction: A cognitive test of the sequencing of sexual communication behaviors. *Health Communication, 5,* 239–261.

Ekman, P. (1988). Lying and nonverbal behavior: Theoretical issues and new findings. *Journal of Nonverbal Behavior, 12,* 163–175.

Ekman, P., & Friesen, W. V. (1975). *Unmasking the face: A field guide to recognizing emotions from facial clues.* Englewood Cliffs, NJ: Prentice-Hall.

Feeley, T. H., deTurck, M. A., & Young, M. J. (1995). Baseline familiarity in lie detection. *Communication Research Reports, 12,* 160–169.

Fogel, A., Toda, S., & Kawai, M. (1988). Mother–infant face-to-face interaction in Japan and the United States: A laboratory comparison using 3-month-old infants. *Developmental Psychology, 24,* 398–406.

Greer, A. E., & Buss, D. M. (1994). Tactics for promoting sexual encounters. *Journal of Sex Research, 31,* 185–201.

Guerrero, L. K. (1997). Nonverbal involvement across interactions with same-sex friends, opposite sex friends, and romantic partners: Consistency or change? *Journal of Social and Personal Relationships, 14,* 31–59.

Guerrero, L. K., & Andersen, P. A. (1991). The waxing and waning of relational intimacy: Touch as a function of relational stage, gender, and touch avoidance. *Journal of Social and Personal Relationships, 8,* 147–165.

Henningsen, D. D., Cruz, M. G., & Morr, M. C. (2000). Pattern violations and perceptions of deception. *Communication Reports, 13,* 1–9.

Hickman, S. E., & Muehlenhard, C. L. (1999). "By the semi-mystical appearance of a condom": How young women and men communicate sexual consent in heterosexual situations. *Journal of Sex Research, 36,* 258–272.

Izard, C. E. (1977). *Human emotions.* New York: Plenum.

Jones, S. E., & Brown, B. C. (1996). Touch attitudes and touch behaviors: Recollections of early childhood touch and social self-confidence. *Journal of Nonverbal Behavior, 20,* 147–163.

Jones, S. M., & Guerrero, L. K. (2001). The effects of nonverbal immediacy and verbal person centeredness in the emotional support process. *Human Communication Research, 27,* 567–596.

Kunkel, A. W., & Burleson, B. R. (1998). Social support and the emotional lives of men and women: An assessment of the different cultures perspective. In D. J. Canary & K. Dindia (Eds.), *Sex differences and similarities in communication: Critical essays and empirical investigations of sex and gender in interaction* (pp. 101–125). Mahwah, NJ: Lawrence Erlbaum Associates.

Levine, T. R., & McCornack, S. A. (1992). Linking love and lies: A formal test of the McCornack and Parks model of deception detection. *Journal of Social and Personal Relationships*, *9*, 143–154.

McClure, E. B. (2000). A meta-analytic review of sex differences in facial expression processing and their development in infants, children, and adolescents. *Psychological Bulletin*, *126*, 424–253.

Meltzoff, A. N., & Moore, M. K. (1983). Newborn infants imitate adult facial gestures. *Child Development*, *54*, 702–709.

Moore, M. M. (1985). Nonverbal courtship patterns in women: Context and consequences. *Ethnology and Sociobiology*, *6*, 237–247.

Neuliep, J. W. (1997). A cross-cultural comparison of teacher immediacy in American and Japanese college classrooms. *Communication Research*, *24*, 431–451.

Palmer, M. T., & Simmons, K. B. (1995). Communicating intentions through nonverbal behaviors: Conscious and nonconscious encoding of liking. *Human Communication Research*, *22*, 128–160.

Patterson, J., & Peter, K. (1991). *The day America told the truth*. New York: Penguin Books.

Perper, T., & Weis, D. L. (1987). Proceptive and rejective strategies of U.S. and Canadian college women. *Journal of Sex Research*, *23*, 455–480.

Planalp, S. (1998). Communicating emotion in everyday life: Cues, channels, and processes. In P. A. Andersen & L. K. Guerrero (Eds.), *Handbook of communication and emotion: Research, theory, applications, and contexts* (pp. 29–48). San Diego, CA: Academic Press.

Richmond, V. P., Gorham, J., & McCroskey, J. C. (1987). The relationship between selected immediacy behaviors and cognitive learning. In M. McLaughlin (Ed.), *Communication Yearbook 10* (pp. 574–590). Newbury Park, CA: Sage.

Robinson, J. D. (1998). Getting down to business: Talk, gaze, and body orientation during openings of doctor–patient consultations. *Human Communication Research*, *25*, 97–123.

Scherer, K. R., & Wallbott, H. G. (1994). Evidence for universality and cultural variation of differential emotion response patterning. *Journal of Personality and Social Psychology*, *66*, 310–328.

Segrin, C. (1998). Interpersonal communication problems associated with depression and loneliness. In P. A. Andersen & L. K. Guerrero (Eds.), *Handbook of communication and emotion: Research, theory, applications, and contexts* (pp. 216–242). San Diego, CA: Academic Press.

Shotland, R. L., & Craig, J. M. (1988). Can men and women differentiate between friendly and sexually interested behavior? *Social Psychology Quarterly*, *51*, 66–73.

Theiss, J. A., & Solomon, D. H. (2007). Communication and the emotional, cognitive, and relational consequences of first sexual encounters in heterosexual dyads. *Communication Quarterly*, *55*, 179–206.

Tusing, K. J., & Dillard, J. P. (2000). The sounds of dominance: Vocal precursors of perceived dominance during interpersonal influence. *Human Communication Research*, *26*, 148–171.

Van Swol, L. M. (2003). The effects of nonverbal mirroring on perceived persuasiveness, agreement with an imitator, and reciprocity in a group discussion. *Communication Research*, *30*, 461–480.

Vrij, A., Akehurst, L., Soukara, S. Bull, R. (2004). Detecting deceit via analyses of verbal and nonverbal behavior in children and adults. *Human Communication Research*, *30*, 8–41.

Vrij, A., & Winkel, F. W. (1991). Cultural patterns in Dutch and Surinam nonverbal behavior: An analysis of simulated police citizen encounters. *Journal of Nonverbal Behavior*, *15*, 169–184.

7 EMOTIONS AND COMMUNICATION

Adamolekun, K. (1999). Bereavement salutations among the Yorubas of western Nigeria. *Omega: Journal of Death & Dying*, *39*, 277–285.

Andersen, P. A., Eloy, S. V., Guerrero, L. K., Spitzberg, B. H. (1995). Romantic jealousy and relational satisfaction: A look at the impact of jealousy experience and expression. *Communication Reports*, *8*, 77–85.

Aune, K. S., & Aune, R. K. (1996). Cultural differences in the self-reported experience and expression of emotions in relationships. *Journal of Cross-Cultural Psychology, 27*, 67–81.

Aune, K. S., Buller, D. B., & Aune, R. K. (1996). Display rule development in romantic relationships: Emotion management and perceived appropriateness of emotions across relationship stages. *Human Communication Research, 23*, 115–145.

Aune, K. S., & Comstock, J. (1997). Effect of relationship length on the experience, expression, and perceived appropriateness of jealousy. *Journal of Social Psychology, 137*, 23–31.

Barrett, L. F., Lane, R. D., Sechrest, L., & Schwartz, G. E. (2000). Sex differences in emotional awareness. *Personality and Social Psychology Bulletin, 26*, 1027–1035.

Berscheid, E., & Ammazzalorso, H. (2004). Emotional experience in close relationships. In M. B. Brewer & M. Hewstone (Eds.), *Emotion and motivation* (pp. 47–69). Malden, MA: Blackwell Publishers.

Birditt, K. S., & Fingerman, K. L. (2003). Age and gender differences in adults' descriptions of emotional reactions to interpersonal problems. *Journals of Gerontology: Series B: Psychological Sciences & Social Sciences, 58B*, P237–P245.

Brackett, M. A., Mayer, J. D., & Warner, R. M. (2004). Emotional intelligence and its relation to everyday behaviour. *Personality and Individual Differences, 36*, 1387–1402.

Brackett, M. A., Warner, R. M., & Bosco, J. S. (2005). Emotional intelligence and relationship quality among couples. *Personal Relationships, 12*, 197–212.

Bradford, L., & Petronio, S. (1998). Strategic embarrassment: The culprit of emotion. In P. A. Andersen, & L. K. Guerrero (Eds.), *Handbook of communication and emotion: Research, theory, applications, and contexts* (pp. 99–121). New York: Academic Press.

Brebner, J. (2003). Gender and emotions. *Personality and Individual Differences, 34*, 387–394.

Burleson, B. R., & Goldsmith, D. J. (1998). How the comforting process works: Alleviating emotional distress through conversationally induced reappraisals. In P. A. Andersen, & L. K. Guerrero (Eds.), *Handbook of communication and emotion: Research, theory, applications, and contexts* (pp. 245–280). New York: Academic Press.

Burleson, B. R., Holmstrom, A. J., & Gilstrap, C. M. (2005). "Guys can't say that to guys": From experiments assessing the normative motivation account for deficiencies in the emotional support provided by men. *Communication Monographs, 72*, 468–501.

Burleson, B. R., & Planalp, S. (2000). Producing emotion(al) messages. *Communication Theory, 10*, 221–250.

Buzzanell, P. M., & Turner, L. H. (2003). Emotion work revealed by job loss discourse: Backgrounding-foregrounding of feelings, construction of normalcy, and (re)instituting of traditional masculinities. *Journal of Applied Communication Research, 31*, 27–57.

Cappella, J. N. (1993). The facial feedback hypothesis in human interaction: Review and speculation. *Journal of Language and Social Interaction, 12*, 13–29.

Carter, K. A. (2003). Type me how you feel: Quasi-nonverbal cues in computer-mediated communication. *A Review of General Semantics, 60*, 29–39.

Chang, C. (2011). Guilt appeals in cause-related marketing. *International Journal of Advertising, 30*, 587–616.

Clark, M. S., & Finkel, E. J. (2005). Willingness to express emotion: The impact of relationship type, communal orientation, and their interaction. *Personal Relationships, 12*, 169–180.

Clore, G. L., & Schnall, S. (2005). The influence of affect on attitude. In D. Albarracín, B. T. Johnson, & M. P. Zanna (Eds.), *The handbook of attitudes* (pp. 437–489). Mahwah, NJ: Lawrence Erlbaum.

Cunningham, M. R., Shamblen, S. R., Barbee, A P., & Ault, L. K. (2005). Social allergies in romantic relationships: Behavioral repetition, emotional sensitization, and dissatisfaction in dating couples. *Personal Relationships, 12*, 273–296.

Cupach, W. R., & Spitzberg, B. H. (2007). *The dark side of interpersonal communication* (2nd ed.). Hillsdale, NJ: Lawrence Erlbaum.

Daly, M., & Wilson, M. (1988). *Homicide*. New York: Aldine.

Dillard, J. P., & Peck, E. (2000). Affect and persuasion: Emotional responses to public service announcements. *Communication Research, 27*, 461–495.

Dillard, J. P., & Seo, K. (in press). Persuasion and affect. In J. P. Dillard & L. Shen (Eds.), *The persuasion handbook*. Thousand Oaks, CA: Sage.

Feeney, J. A. (2005). Hurt feelings in couples' relationships: Exploring the role of attachment and perceptions of personal injury. *Personal Relationships, 12*, 253–272.

Fehr, B., & Harasymchuk, C. (2005). The experience of emotion in close relationships: Toward an integration of the emotion-in-relationships and interpersonal script models. *Personal Relationships, 12*, 181–196.

Flynn, F. J., & Schaumberg, R. L. (2012). When feeling bad leads to feeling good: Guilt-proneness and affective organizational commitment. *Journal of Applied Psychology, 97*, 124–133.

Forgas, J. P. (1995). Mood and judgment: The affect infusion model (AIM). *Psychological Bulletin, 117*, 39–66.

Forgas, J. P. (1998). Asking nicely? The effects of mood on responding to more or less polite requests. *Personality and Social Psychology Bulletin, 24*, 173–185.

Frey, L. R., Adelman, R. B., & Query, J. L., Jr. (1996). Communication practices in the social construction of health in an AIDS residence. *Journal of Health Psychology, 1*, 383–397.

George, J. M. (2000). Emotions and leadership: The role of emotional intelligence. *Human Relations, 53*, 1027–1055.

Goleman, D. (2006). *Emotional intelligence: 10th anniversary edition*. New York: Bantam.

Golish, T. D., & Powell, K. A. (2003). "Ambiguous loss": Managing the dialectics of grief associated with premature birth. *Journal of Social and Personal Relationships, 20*, 309–334.

Goodboy, A. K., & Bolkan, S. (2011). Attachment and the use of negative relational maintenance behaviors in romantic relationships. *Communication Research Reports, 28*, 327–336.

Guerrero, L. K., & Andersen, P. A. (1998). The dark side of jealousy and envy: Desire, delusion, desperation, and destructive communication. In B. H. Spitzberg & W. R. Cupach (Eds.), *The dark side of close relationships* (pp. 33–70). Mahwah, NJ: Lawrence Erlbaum.

Guerrero, L. K., & Andersen, P. A. (2000). Emotion in close relationships. In C. Hendrick & S. S. Hendrick (Eds.), *Close relationships: A sourcebook* (pp. 171–183). Thousand Oaks, CA: Sage.

Guerrero, L. K., Trost, M. R., & Yoshimura, S. M. (2005). Romantic jealousy: Emotions and communicative responses. *Personal Relationships, 12*, 233–252.

Hastings, S. O. (2000). Self-disclosure and identity management by bereaved parents. *Communication Studies, 51*, 352–371.

Hogan, N. S., Greenfield, D. B., & Schmidt, L. A. (2001). Development and validation of the Hogan grief reaction checklist. *Death Studies, 25*, 1–32.

Hullett, C. R., Louden, A. D., & Mitra, A. (2003). Emotion and political cognition: A test of bipolar, two-dimensional, and discrete models of emotion in predicting involvement and learning. *Communication Monographs, 70*, 250–263.

Jordan, P. J., & Troth, A. C. (2004). Managing emotions during team problem solving: Emotional intelligence and conflict resolution. *Human Performance, 17*, 195–218.

Kamm, S., & Vandenberg, B. (2001). Grief communication, grief reactions and marital satisfaction in bereaved parents. *Death Studies, 25*, 569–582.

Knobloch, L. K. (2005). Evaluating a contextual model of responses to relational uncertainty increasing events. *Human Communication Research, 31*, 60–101.

Le, B., & Agnew, C. R. (2001). Need fulfillment and emotional experience in interdependent romantic relationships. *Journal of Social and Personal Relationships, 18*, 423–440.

Leary, M. R. (2001). Toward a conceptualization of interpersonal rejection. In M. R. Leary (Ed.), *Interpersonal rejection* (pp. 3–20). New York: Oxford University Press.

Lepore, S. J., Silver, R. C., Wortman, C. B., & Wayment, H. A. (1996). Social constraints, intrusive thoughts, and depressive symptoms among bereaved mothers. *Journal of Personality and Social Psychology, 70*, 271–282.

MacGeorge, E. L. (2001). Support providers' interaction goals: The influence of attributions and emotions. *Communication Monographs, 68*, 72–97.

Matsumoto, D. (1987). The role of facial response in the experience of emotion: More methodological problems and a meta-analysis. *Journal of Personality and Social Psychology, 52*, 769–774.

Matsumoto, D. (2001). Culture and emotion. In D. Matsumoto (Ed.), *The handbook of culture and psychology*. New York: Oxford University Press.

Mayer, J. D., Salovey, P., & Caruso, D. R. (2004). A further consideration of the issues of emotional intelligence. *Psychological Inquiry, 15,* 249–255.

Mills, R. S. L., Nazar, J., & Farrell, H. M. (2002). Child and parent perceptions of hurtful messages. *Journal of Social and Personal Relationships, 19,* 731–754.

Nabi, R. L. (2003). Exploring the framing effects of emotion: Do discrete emotions differentially influence information accessibility, information seeking, and policy preference? *Communication Research, 30,* 224–247.

Oatley, K. (1992). *Best laid schemes: The psychology of emotions.* Cambridge: Cambridge University Press.

Pennebaker, J. W. (1997). *Opening up: The healing power of expressing emotions.* New York: Guilford Press.

Planalp, S. (1999). *Communicating emotion: Social, moral, and cultural processes.* New York: Cambridge.

Range, L. M., Walston, A. S., & Pollard, P. M. (1992). Helpful and unhelpful comments after suicide, homicide, accident, or natural death. *Omega: Journal of Death & Dying, 25,* 25–31.

Rimé, B., Mesquita, B., Philippot, P., & Boca, S. (1991). Beyond the emotional event: Six studies of the social sharing of emotion. *Cognition and Emotion, 5,* 435–465.

Roseman, I. J., & Smith, C. A. (2001). Appraisal theory: Overview, assumptions, varieties, controversies. In K. R. Scherer, A. Schorr, & T. Johnstone (Eds.), *Appraisal processes in emotion: Theory, methods, research* (pp. 3–19). New York: Oxford University Press.

Russell, J., & Barrett, L. (1999). Core affect, prototypical emotional episodes, and other things called emotion: Dissecting the elephant. *Journal of Personality and Social Psychology, 76,* 805–819.

Ryan, R. M., La Guardia, J. G., Solky-Butzel, J., Chirkov, V., & Kim, Y. (2005). On the interpersonal regulation of emotions: Emotional reliance across gender, relationships, and cultures. *Personal Relationships, 12,* 145–163.

Safdar, S., Friedlmeier, W., Matsumoto, D., Yoo, S. H., Kwantes, C. T., Kakai, H., & Shigemasu, E. (2009). Variations of emotional display rules within and across cultures: A comparison between Canada, USA, and Japan. *Canadian Journal of Behavioural Science, 41,* 1–10.

Scherer, K. R., Schorr, A., & Johnstone, T. (Eds.). (2001). *Appraisal processes in emotion: Theory, methods, research.* New York: Oxford University Press.

Scherer, K. R., & Wallbott, H. G. (1994). Evidence for universality and cultural variation of differential emotion response patterning. *Journal of Personality and Social Psychology, 66,* 310–328.

Sharpsteen, D. J. (1991). The organization of jealousy knowledge: Romantic jealousy as a blended emotion. In P. Salovey (Ed.), *The psychology of jealousy and envy* (pp. 31–51). New York: Guilford Press.

Sheldon, K. M., Abad, N., & Hinsch, C. (2011). A two-process view of Facebook use and related-ness need-satisfaction: Disconnection drives use, and connection rewards it. *Journal of Personality and Social Psychology, 100,* 766–775.

Shiota, M. N., Neufeld, S. L., Yeung, W. H., Moser, S. E., & Perea, E. F. (2011). Feeling good: Autonomic nervous system responding in five positive emotions. *Emotion, 11,* 1368–1378.

Singh, S. (2004). Development of a measure of emotional intelligence. *Psychological Studies, 49,* 136–141.

Stephan, W. G., Stephan, C. W., & de Vargas, M. C. (1996). Emotional expression in Costa Rica and the United States. *Journal of Cross-Cultural Psychology, 27,* 147–160.

Stewart, A. E. (1999). Complicated bereavement and posttraumatic stress disorder following car crashes: Recommendations for death notification practice. *Death Studies, 23,* 289–321.

Thomsen, D. K., Mehlsen, M. Y., Viidik, A., Sommerlund, B., & Zachariae, R. (2005). Age and gender differences in negative affect: Is there a role for emotion regulation? *Personality and Individual Differences, 38,* 1935–1946.

Vangelisti, A. L. (1994). Messages that hurt. In W. R. Cupach & B. H. Spitzberg (Eds.), *The dark side of interpersonal communication* (pp. 53–82). Hillsdale, NJ: Lawrence Erlbaum.

Vangelisti, A. L., Daly, J. A., & Rudnick, J. R. (1991). Making people feel guilty in conversations: Techniques and correlates. *Human Communication Research, 18,* 3–39.

Vangelisti, A. L., & Sprague, R. J. (1998). Guilt and hurt: Similarities, distinctions, and conversational strategies. In P. A. Andersen & L. K. Guerrero (Eds.), *Handbook of communication and emotion: Research, theory, applications, and contexts* (pp. 123–154). New York: Academic Press.

Vangelisti, A. L., Young, S. L., Carpenter-Theune, K. E., & Alexander, A. L. (2005). Why does it hurt? The perceived causes of hurt feelings. *Communication Research, 32,* 443–477.

White, G. L., & Mullen, P. E. (1989). *Jealousy: Theory, research, and clinical strategies.* New York: Guilford Press.

Yik, M. S. M., Russell, J. A., & Barrett, L. F. (1999). Structure of self-reported current affect: Integration and beyond. *Journal of Personality and Social Psychology, 77,* 600–619.

8 LISTENING

Batson, C. D., Early, S., & Salvarani, G. (1997). Perspective taking: Imagining how another feels versus imagining how you would feel. *Personality and Social Psychology Bulletin, 23,* 751–758.

Bavelas, J. B., Coates, L., & Johnson, T. (2000). Listeners as co-narrators. *Journal of Personality and Social Psychology, 79,* 941–952.

Burgoon, J. K., & Hale, J. L. (1987). Validation and measurement of the fundamental themes of relational communication. *Communication Monographs, 54,* 23–47.

Burleson, B. (2011). A constructivist approach to listening. *International Journal of Listening, 25,* 27–46.

Cegala, D. J. (1984). Affective and cognitive manifestations of interaction involvement during unstructured and competitive interactions. *Communication Monographs, 51,* 320–338.

Dillard, J. P., Solomon, D. H., & Palmer, M. T. (1999). Structuring the concept of relational communication. *Communication Monographs, 66,* 49–65.

Dillard, J. P., Solomon, D. H., & Samp, J. A. (1996). Framing social reality: Of relevance of relational judgments. *Communication Research, 23,* 702–723.

Edwards, R. (2011). Listening and message interpretation. *International Journal of Listening, 25,* 47–65.

Emanuel, R., Adams, J., Baker, K., Daufin, E. K., Ellington, C., Fitts, E., Himel, J., Holladay, L., & Okeowo, D. (2008). How college students spent their time communicating. *International Journal of Listening, 22,* 13–28.

Gearhart, C. C., & Bodie, G. D. (2011). Active-empathic listening as a general social skill: Evidence from bivariate and canonical correlations. *Communication Reports, 24,* 86–98.

Graham, T., & Ickes, W. (1997). When women's intuition isn't greater than men's. In W. J. Ickes (Ed.), *Empathic accuracy* (pp. 117–143). New York: Guilford Press.

Greene, J. O., & Herbers, L. E. (2011). Conditions of interpersonal transcendence. *International Journal of Listening, 25,* 66–84.

Hale, J. L., Lundy, J. C., Mongeau, P. A. (1989). Perceived relational intimacy and relational message content. *Communication Research Reports, 6,* 94–99.

Hall, J., & Schmid Mast, M. (2007). Sources of accuracy in the empathic accuracy paradigm. *Emotion, 7,* 438–446.

Heritage, J., & Robinson, J. D. (2006). The structure of patients' presenting concerns: Physicians' opening questions. *Health Communication, 19,* 89–102.

Ickes, W., Gesn, P. R., & Graham, T. (2000). Gender differences in empathic accuracy: Differential ability or differential motivation? *Personal Relationships, 7,* 95–109.

International Listening Association (1996). Retrieved from http://www.listen.org/ March 24, 2011.

King, A. (1991). Improving lecture comprehension: Effects of a metacognitive strategy. *Applied Cognitive Psychology, 5,* 331–346.

Miller, J. B., deWinstanley, P., & Carey, P. (1996). Memory for conversation. *Memory, 4,* 615–631.

Neuliep, J. W., & Hazelton, V. (1987). Enhanced conversational recall and reduced conversational interferences as a function of cognitive complexity. *Human Communication Research*, *13*, 211–224.

Patterson, C. J., Massad, C. M., & Cosgrove, J. M. (1978). Children's referential communication: Components of plans for effective listening. *Developmental Psychology*, *14*, 401–406.

Priem, J. S., McLaren, R. M., & Solomon, D. H. (2010). Relational messages, perceptions of hurt, and biological stress reactions to a disconfirming interaction. *Communication Research*, *37*, 48–72.

Priem, J. S., Solomon, D. H., & Steuber, K. R. (2009). Accuracy and bias in perceptions of emotionally supportive communication in marriage. *Personal Relationships*, *16*, 531–552.

Robinson, J. D. (2001). Closing medical encounters: Two physician practices and their implications for the expression of patients' unstated concerns. *Social Science and Medicine*, *53*, 639–656.

Samp, J. A., & Humphreys, L. R. (2007). "I said what?" Partner familiarity, resistance, and the accuracy of conversational recall. *Communication Monographs*, *74*, 561–581.

Sargent, S. L., & Weaver, J. B. (2003). Listening styles: Sex differences in perceptions of self and others. *International Journal of Listening*, *17*, 5–18.

Schneider, B. A., Daneman, M., Murphy, D. R., & Kwong See, S. (2000). Listening to discourse in distracting settings: The effects of aging. *Psychology and Aging*, *15*, 110–125.

Sillars, A. L., Folwell, A. L., Hill, K. C., Maki, B. K., Hurst, A. P., & Casano, R. A. (1994). Marital communication and the persistence of misunderstanding. *Journal of Social and Personal Relationships*, *11*, 611–617.

Sillars, A. L., Roberts, L. J., Leonard, K. E., & Dun, T. (2000). Cognition during marital conflict: The relationship of thought and talk. *Journal of Social and Personal Relationships*, *17*, 479–502.

Simpson, J. A., Ickes, W., & Blackstone, T. (1995). When the head protects the heart: Empathic accuracy in dating relationships. *Journal of Personality and Social Psychology*, *69*, 629–641.

Simpson, J. A., Orina, M. M., & Ickes, W. (2003). When accuracy hurts, and when it helps: A test of the empathic accuracy model in marital interactions. *Journal of Personality and Social Psychology*, *85*, 881–893.

Solomon, D. H., & McLaren, R. M. (2008). Relational framing theory: Drawing inferences about relationships from interpersonal interactions. In L. A. Baxter & D. O. Braithwaite (Eds.), *Engaging theories in interpersonal communication* (pp. 103–115). Los Angeles: Sage.

Stafford, L., Burggraf, C. S., & Sharkey, W. F. (1987). Conversational memory: The effects of time, recall, mode, and memory expectancies on remembrances of natural conversations. *Human Communication Research*, *14*, 203–229.

Stafford, L., & Daly, J. A. (1984). Conversational memory: The effects of recall mode and memory expectancies on remembrances of natural conversations. *Human Communication Research*, *10*, 379–402.

Villaume, W. A., & Bodie, G. D. (2007). Discovering the listener within us: The impact of trait-like personality variables and communicator styles on preferences for listening style. *International Journal of Listening*, *21*, 102–123.

Watson, K. W., Barker, L. L., & Weaver, J. B. (1995). The Listening Styles Profile (LSP-16): Development and validation of an instrument to assess four listening styles. *International Journal of Listening*, *9*, 1–13.

Weaver, J. B., Watson, K. W., & Barker, L. L. (1996). Individual differences in listening styles: Do you hear what I hear? *Personality and Individual Differences*, *20*, 381–387.

Worthington, D. L. (2005). Exploring the relationship between listening style preference and verbal aggressiveness. *International Journal of Listening*, *19*, 3–11.

Worthington, D. L. (2008). Exploring the relationship between listening styles and need for cognition. *International Journal of Listening*, *22*, 46–58.

9 DEVELOPING AND ENDING RELATIONSHIPS

Adams, R. G., & Blieszner, R. (1998). Structural predictors of problematic friendship in later life. *Personal Relationships, 5*, 439–447.

Afifi, W. A., & Faulkner, S. L. (2000). On being "just friends": The frequency and impact of sexual activity in cross-sex friendships. *Journal of Social and Personal Relationships, 17*, 205–222.

Agnew, C. R., VanLange, P. A. M., Rusbult, C. E., & Langston, C. A. (1998). Cognitive interdependence: Commitment and the mental representation of close relationships. *Journal of Personality and Social Psychology, 74*, 939–954.

Altman, I., & Taylor, D. A. (1973). *Social penetration: The development of interpersonal relationships.* New York: Holt, Rinehart, & Winston.

Battaglia, D. M., Richard, F. D., Datteri, D. L., & Lord, C. G. (1998). Breaking up is (relatively) easy to do: A script for the dissolution of close relationships. *Journal of Social and Personal Relationships, 15*, 829–845.

Baxter, L. A. (1979). Self-disclosure as a relationship disengagement strategy: An exploratory investigation. *Human Communication Research, 5*, 215–222.

Baxter, L. A. (1984). Trajectories of relationship disengagement. *Journal of Social and Personal Relationships, 1*, 29–48.

Baxter, L. A. (1986). Gender differences in the heterosexual relationship rules embedded in breakup accounts. *Journal of Social and Personal Relationships, 3*, 289–306.

Baxter, L. A., & Bullis, C. (1986). Turning points in developing romantic relationships. *Human Communication Research, 12*, 469–493.

Baxter, L. A., & Philpott, J. (1982). Attribution-based strategies for initiating and terminating relationships. *Communication Quarterly, 30*, 217–224.

Baxter, L. A., & Wilmot, W. W. (1984). "Secret tests": Social strategies for acquiring information about the state of the relationship. *Human Communication Research, 11*, 171–201.

Berger, C. R. (1997). *Planning strategic interaction: Attaining goals through communicative action.* Mahwah, NJ: Lawrence Erlbaum.

Berger, C. R., & Bradac, J. J. (1982). *Language and social knowledge: Uncertainty in interpersonal relationships.* London: Edward Arnold.

Berger, C. R., & Calabrese, R. J. (1975). Some explorations in initial interaction and beyond: Toward a developmental theory of interpersonal communication. *Human Communication Research, 1*, 99–112.

Bisson, M. A., & Levine, T. R. (2009). Negotiating a friends with benefits relationship. *Archives of Sexual Behavior, 38*, 66–73.

Busboom, A. L., Collins, D. M., Givertz, M. D., & Levin, L. A. (2002). Can we still be friends? Resources and barriers to friendship quality after romantic relationship dissolution. *Personal Relationships, 9*, 215–223.

Buunk, B. P., & Van Yperen, N. W. (1991). Referential comparisons, relational comparisons, and exchange orientation: Their relation to marital satisfaction. *Personality and Social Psychology Bulletin, 17*, 709–717.

Chaulk, K., & Jones, T. (2011). Online obsessive relational intrusion: Further concerns about Facebook. *Journal of Family Violence, 26*, 245–254.

Chory-Assad, R. M., & Booth-Butterfield, M. (2001). Secret test use and self-esteem in deteriorating relationships. *Communication Research Reports, 18*, 147–157.

Coupland, J. (2003). Small talk: Social functions. *Research on Language and Social Interaction, 36*, 1–6.

Cupach, W. R., & Metts, S. (1986). Accounts of relational termination: A comparison of marital and nonmarital relationships. *Communication Monographs, 53*, 311–334.

Cupach, W. R., & Spitzberg, B. H. (1998). Obsessional relational intrusion and stalking. In W. R. Cupach and B. H. Spitzberg (Eds.), *The dark side of close relationships* (pp. 233–264). Mahwah, NJ: Lawrence Erlbaum.

Cupach, W. R., Spitzberg, B. H., & Carson, C. L. (2000). Toward a theory of obsessive relational intrusion and stalking. In K. Dindia & S. Duck (Eds.), *Communication and personal relationships* (pp. 131–146). New York: John Wiley and Sons.

Derlega, V. J., Anderson, S., Winstead, B. A., & Greene, K. (2011). Positive disclosure among college students: What do they talk about, to whom, and why? *Journal of Positive Psychology*, *6*, 119–130.

Donaghue, N., & Fallon, B. J. (2003). Gender role self-stereotyping and the relationship between equity and satisfaction in close relationships. *Sex Roles*, *48*, 217–230.

Duck, S. W. (1982). A topography of relationship disengagement and dissolution. In S. W. Duck (Ed.), *Personal relationships 4: Dissolving personal relationships*. New York: Academic Press.

Ellingson, K. T., & Galassi, J. P. (1995). Testing two theoretical explanations for the attraction-enhancing effects of self-disclosure. *Journal of Counseling and Development*, *73*, 535–541.

Emmers, T. M., & Hart, R. D. (1996). Romantic relationship disengagement and coping rituals. *Communication Research Reports*, *13*, 8–18.

Felmlee, D. H. (1998). "Be careful what you wish for . . .": A quantitative and qualitative investigation of "fatal attractions." *Personal Relationships*, *5*, 235–253.

Geher, G., Bloodworth, R., Mason, J., Stoaks, C., Downey, H. J., Renstrom, K. L., & Romero, J. F. (2005). Motivational underpinnings of romantic partner perceptions: Psychological and physiological evidence. *Journal of Social and Personal Relationships*, *22*, 255–281.

Gibbs, J. L., Ellison, N. B., & Heino, R. D. (2006). Self-presentations in online personals: The role of anticipated future interaction, self-disclosure, and perceived success in Internet dating. *Communication Research*, *33*, 152–177.

Greene, K., Derlega, V. L., & Mathews, A. (2006). Self-disclosure in personal relationships. In A. Vangelisti & D. Perlman (Eds.), *Cambridge handbook of personal relationships* (pp. 409–427). Cambridge: Cambridge University Press.

Hian, L. B., Chuan, S. L., Trevor, T. M. K., Detenber, B. H. (2004). Getting to know you: Exploring the development of relational intimacy in computer-mediated communication. *Journal of Computer-Mediated Communication*, *9*.

Hill, C. T., Rubin, Z., & Peplau, L. A. (1976). Breakups before marriage: The end of 103 affairs. *Journal of Social Issues*, *32*, 147–168.

Honeycutt, J. M., Cantrill, J. G., & Allen, T. (1992). Memory structures for relational decay: A cognitive test of sequencing of de-escalating actions and stages. *Human Communication Research*, *18*, 528–562.

Honeycutt, J. M., Cantrill, J. G., & Greene, R. W. (1989). Memory structures for relational escalation: A cognitive test of the sequencing of relational actions and stages. *Human Communication Research*, *16*, 62–90.

Hubbard, A. S. E. (2001). Conflict between relationally uncertain romantic partners: The influence of relational responsiveness and empathy. *Communication Monographs*, *68*, 400–414.

Hughes, M., Morrison, K., & Asada, K. J. (2005). What's love got to do with it? Exploring the impact of maintenance rules, love attitudes, and network support on friends with benefits. *Western Journal of Communication*, *69*, 49–66.

Ickes, W., Dugosh, J. W., Simpson, J. A., & Wilson, C. L. (2003). Suspicious minds: The motive to acquire relationship threatening information. *Personal Relationships*, *10*, 131–148.

Johnson, A. J., Wittenberg, E., & Haigh, M. (2004). The process of relationship development and deterioration: Turning points in friendships that have terminated. *Communication Quarterly*, *52*, 54–67.

Johnson, A. J., Wittenberg, E., Villagran, M. M., Mazur, M., & Villagran, P. (2003). Relational progression as a dialectic: Examining turning points in communication among friends. *Communication Monographs*, *70*, 230–249.

Kirkpatrick, L. A., & Davis, K. E. (1994). Attachment style, gender, and relationship stability: A longitudinal analysis. *Journal of Personality and Social Psychology*, *66*, 502–512.

Knapp, M. L. (1984). *Interpersonal communication and human relationships*. Boston: Allyn & Bacon.

Knobloch, L. K., & Carpenter-Theune, K. E. (2004). Topic avoidance in developing romantic relationships: Associations with intimacy and relational uncertainty. *Communication Research*, *31*, 173–205.

Knobloch, L. K., & Solomon, D. H. (1999). Measuring the sources and content of relational uncertainty. *Communication Studies*, *50*, 261–278.

Knobloch, L. K., & Solomon, D. H. (2002). Information seeking beyond initial interaction: Negotiating relational uncertainty within close relationships. *Human Communication Research*, *28*, 243–257.

Knobloch, L. K., & Solomon, D. H. (2003). Manifestations of relationship conceptualizations in conversation. *Human Communication Research*, *29*, 482–515.

Knobloch, L. K., Solomon, D. H., & Theiss, J. A. (2006). The role of intimacy in the production and perception of relationship talk within courtship. *Communication Research*, *33*, 211–244.

Koenig Kellas, J., & Manusov, V. (2003). What's in a story? The relationship between narrative completeness and adjustment to relationship dissolution. *Journal of Social and Personal Relationships*, *20*, 285–307.

Kunkel, A. D., Wilson, S. R., Olufowote, J., & Robson, S. (2003). Identity implications of influence goals: Initiating, intensifying, and ending romantic relationships. *Western Journal of Communication*, *67*, 382–412.

Laurenceau, J. P., Felcman Barrett, L., & Petromonaco, P. R. (1998). Intimacy as an interpersonal process: The importance of self-disclosure, partner disclosure, and perceived partner responsiveness in interpersonal exchanges. *Journal of Personality and Social Psychology*, *74*, 1238–1251.

Lewandowski, G. W., Aron, A., Bassis, S., & Kunak, J. (2006). Losing a self-expanding relationship: Implications for the self concept. *Personal Relationships*, *13*, 317–331.

Metts, S. (2004). First sexual involvement in romantic relationships: An empirical investigation of communicative framing, romantic beliefs, and attachment orientation in the passion turning point. In J. H. Harvey, A. Wenzel, & S. Sprecher (Eds.), *Handbook of sexuality in close relationships* (pp. 135–158). Mahwah, NJ: Lawrence Erlbaum.

Metts, S., Cupach, W. R., & Bejlovec, R. A. (1989). "I love you too much to ever start liking you": Redefining romantic relationships. *Journal of Social and Personal Relationships*, *6*, 259–274.

Mongeau, P. A., Ramirez, A., & Vorrell, M. (2003). Friends with benefits: Initial explorations of sexual, non-romantic relationships. Paper presented at the annual meeting of the Western Communication Association, Salt Lake City, UT, February.

Monroe, S. M., Rohde, P., Seeley, J. R., & Lewinsohn, P. M. (1999). Life events and depression in adolescence: Relationship loss as a prospective risk factor for first onset of major depressive disorder. *Journal of Abnormal Psychology*, *108*, 606–614.

Morse, K. A., & Neuberg, S. L. (2004). How do holidays influence relationship processes and outcomes?: Examining the instigating and catalytic effect of Valentine's Day. *Personal Relationships*, *11*, 509–527.

Oswald, D. L., & Clark, E. M. (2003). Best friends forever?: High school best friendships and the transition to college. *Personal Relationships*, *10*, 187–196.

Owen, W. F. (1993). Metaphors in accounts of romantic relationship terminations. In P. J. Kalbfleisch (Ed.), *Interpersonal communication: Evolving interpersonal relationships* (pp. 261–278). Hillsdale, NJ: Lawrence Erlbaum.

Reyns, B. W., Henson, B., & Fisher, B. W. (2012). Stalking in the twilight zone: Extent of cyberstalking victimization and offending among college students. *Deviant Behavior*, *33*, 1–25.

Roloff, M. E., Soule, K. P., & Carey, C. M. (2001). Reasons for remaining in a relationship and responses to relational transgressions. *Journal of Social and Personal Relationships*, *18*, 362–385.

Rose, S., & Serafica, F. C. (1986). Keeping and ending casual, close, and best friendships. *Journal of Social and Personal Relationships*, *3*, 275–288.

Rusbult, C. E., & Buunk, B. P. (1993). Commitment processes in close relationships: An interdependence analysis. *Journal of Social and Personal Relationships*, *10*, 175–204.

Rusbult, C. E., & Martz, J. M. (1995). Remaining in an abusive relationship: An investment model analysis of nonvoluntary dependence. *Personality and Social Psychology Bulletin*, *21*, 558–571.

Sbarra, D. A. (2006). Predicting the onset of emotional recovery following nonmarital relationship dissolution: Survival analyses of sadness and anger. *Personality and Social Psychology Bulletin, 32*, 298–312.

Siegert, J. R., & Stamp, G. H. (1994). "Our first big fight" as a milestone in the development of close relationships. *Communication Monographs, 61*, 345–360.

Sillars, A., Shellen, W., McIntosh, A., Pomegranate, M. (1997). Relational characteristics of language: Elaboration and differentiation in marital conversations. *Western Journal of Communication, 61*, 403–422.

Solomon, D. H., & Knobloch, L. K. (2001). Relationship uncertainty, partner interference, and intimacy within dating relationships. *Journal of Social and Personal Relationships, 18*, 804–820.

Solomon, D. H., & Knobloch, L. K. (2004). A model of relational turbulence: The role of intimacy, relational uncertainty, and interference from partners in appraisals of irritations. *Journal of Social and Personal Relationships, 21*, 795–816.

Spitzberg, B. H. (2002). The tactical topography of stalking victimization and management. *Trauma, Violence, and Abuse, 3*, 261–288.

Spitzberg, B. H., & Veksler, A. E. (2007). The personality of pursuit: Personality attributions of unwanted pursuers and stalkers. *Violence and Victims, 22*, 275–289.

Sprecher, S. (2001). Equity and social exchange in dating couples: Associations with satisfaction, commitment, and stability. *Journal of Marriage and the Family, 63*, 599–613.

Sprecher, S., & Hendrick, S. (2004). Self-disclosure in intimate relationships: Associations with individual and relationship characteristics over time. *Journal of Social and Clinical Psychology, 23*, 857–877.

Sunnafrank, M. (1986). Predicted outcome value during initial interactions: A reformulation of uncertainty reduction theory. *Human Communication Research, 13*, 3–13.

Sunnafrank, M. (1988). Predicted outcome value in initial interactions. *Communication Research Reports, 5*, 169–172.

Sunnafrank, M. (1990). Predicted outcome value and uncertainty reduction theories: A test of competing perspectives. *Human Communication Research, 17*, 76–103.

Sunnafrank, M., & Ramirez, A. (2004). At first sight: Persistent relational effects of get-acquainted conversations. *Journal of Social and Personal Relationships, 21*, 361–379.

Surra, C. A. (1985). Courtship types: Variation in interdependence between partners and social networks. *Journal of Personality and Social Psychology, 49*, 357–375.

Tashiro, T., & Frazier, P. (2003). "I'll never be in a relationship like that again": Personal growth following romantic relationship breakups. *Personal Relationships, 10*, 113–128.

Theiss, J. A., & Solomon, D. H. (2006). A relational turbulence model of communication about irritations in romantic relationships. *Communication Research 33*, 391–418.

Theiss, J. A., & Solomon, D. H. (2007). Communication and the emotional, cognitive, and relational consequences of first sexual experiences in heterosexual dyads. *Communication Quarterly, 55*, 179–206.

Thibaut, J., & Kelley, H. (1959). *The social psychology of groups*. New York: Wiley.

Urberg, K. A., Degirmenciouglu, S. M., Tolson, J. M. (1998). Adolescent friendship selection and termination: The role of similarity. *Journal of Social and Personal Relationships, 15*, 703–710.

Wilmot, W. W., Carbaugh, D. A., & Baxter, L. A. (1985). Communicative strategies used to terminate romantic relationships. *Western Journal of Speech Communication, 49*, 204–216.

10 INTIMACY AND INTERPERSONAL COMMUNICATION

Afifi, W. A., Falato, W. L., & Weiner, J. L. (2001). Identity concerns following a severe relational transgression: The role of discovery method for the relational outcomes of infidelity. *Journal of Social and Personal Relationships, 18*, 291–308.

Agnew, C. R., Van Lange, P. A. M., Rusbult, C. E., & Langston, C. A. (1998). Cognitive interdependence: Commitment and the mental representation of close relationships. *Journal of Personality and Social Psychology, 74*, 939–954.

Aloni, M., & Bernieri, F. J. (2004). Is love blind? The effects of experience and infatuation on the perception of love. *Journal of Nonverbal Behavior, 28*, 287–295.

Aron, A., & Aron, E. N. (1986). *Love as the expansion of self: Understanding attraction and satisfaction.* New York: Hemisphere.

Aron, A., Fisher, H., Mashek, D. J., Strong, G., Haifang, L., & Brown, L. L. (2005). Reward, motivation, and emotion systems associated with early-stage intense romantic love. *Journal of Neurophysiology, 94*, 327–337.

Aylor, B., & Dainton, M. (2004). Biological sex and psychological gender as predictors of routine and strategic relational maintenance. *Sex Roles: A Journal of Research, 50*, 689–697.

Bartholomew, K. (1990). Avoidance of intimacy: An attachment perspective. *Journal of Social and Personal Relationships, 7*, 147–178.

Baumeister, R. F., Wotman, S. R., & Stillwell, A. M. (1993). Unrequited love: On heartbreak, anger, guilt, scriptlessness, and humiliation. *Journal of Personality and Social Psychology, 64*, 377–394.

Baxter, L. A. (1988). A dialectical perspective on communication strategies in relationship development. In S. Duck, D. F. Hay, S. E. Hofball, W. Ickes, & B. M. Montgomery (Eds.), *Handbook of personal relationships: Theory, research, and interventions* (pp. 257–273). Chichester: John Wiley & Sons.

Baxter, L. A., & Montgomery, B. M. (1996). *Relating: Dialogues and dialectics.* New York: Guilford Press.

Berscheid, E., Snyder, M., & Omoto, A. M. (2004). Measuring closeness: The relationship closeness inventory (RCI). In D. J. Mashek & A. P. Aron (Eds.), *Handbook of closeness and intimacy* (pp. 81–101). Mahwah, NJ: Lawrence Erlbaum.

Bippus, A. M., & Rollin, E. (2003). Attachment style differences in relational maintenance and conflict behaviors: Friends' perceptions. *Communication Reports, 16*, 113–123.

Bitzan, J. E., & Kruzich, J. M. (1990). Interpersonal relationships of nursing home residents. *Gerontologist, 30*, 385–390.

Bombar, M. L., & Littig, L. W. (1996). Babytalk as a communication of intimate attachment: An initial study in adult romances and friendships. *Personal Relationships, 3*, 137–158.

Buss, D. M. (1995). Psychological sex differences: Origins through sexual selection. *American Psychologist, 50*, 164–168.

Buss, D. M., & Reeve, H. K. (2003). Evolutionary psychology and developmental dynamics: Comment on Lickliter and Honeycutt (2003). *Psychological Bulletin, 129*, 848–853.

Canary, D. J., & Hause, K. S. (1993). Is there any reason to research sex differences in communication? *Communication Quarterly, 42*, 129–144.

Canary, D. J., & Stafford, L. (1992). Relational maintenance strategies and equity in marriage. *Communication Monographs, 59*, 243–267.

Canary, D. J., Stafford, L., & Semic, B. A. (2002). A panel study of the associations between maintenance strategies and relational characteristics. *Journal of Marriage and Family, 64*, 395–406.

Cann, A., & Baucom, T. R. (2004). Former partners and new rivals as threats to a relationship: Infidelity type, gender, and commitment as factors related to distress and forgiveness. *Personal Relationships, 11*, 305–318.

Collins, N. L., & Read, S. J. (1990). Adult attachment, working models, and relationship quality in dating couples. *Journal of Personality and Social Psychology, 58*, 644–663.

Dainton, M., & Aylor, B. (2002). Routine and strategic maintenance efforts: Behavioral patterns, variations associated with relational length, and the prediction of relational characteristics. *Communication Monographs, 69*, 52–66.

Dainton, M., & Stafford, L. (1993). Routine maintenance behaviors: A comparison of relationship type, partner similarity, and sex differences. *Journal of Social and Personal Relationships, 10*, 255–271.

Dainton, M., Zelley, E., & Langan, E. (2003). Maintaining friendships throughout the lifespan.

In D. J. Canary & M. Dainton (Eds.), *Maintaining relationships through communication* (pp. 79–102). Mahwah, NJ: Lawrence Erlbaum.

Dindia, K., & Canary, D. (1993). Definitions and theoretical perspectives on maintaining relationships. *Journal of Social and Personal Relationships, 10*, 163–173.

Drigotas, S. M., Safstrom, C. A., & Gentilita, T. (1999). An investment model prediction of dating infidelity. *Journal of Personal and Social Psychology, 77*, 509–524.

Feeney, J. A., & Noller, P. (1991). Attachment style and verbal descriptions of romantic partners. *Journal of Social and Personal Relationships, 8*, 187–215.

Fehr, B. (1994). Prototype-based assessment of laypeople's views of love. *Personal Relationships, 1*, 309–331.

Fehr, B. (2004). Intimacy expectations in same-sex friendships: A prototype interaction-pattern model. *Journal of Personality and Social Psychology, 86*, 265–284.

Feldman, S. S., & Cauffman, E. (1999). Your cheatin' heart: Attitudes, behaviors, and correlates of sexual betrayal in late adolescents. *Journal of Research on Adolescents, 9*, 227–252.

Finchum, T. D. (2005). Keeping the ball in the air: Contact in long-distance friendships. *Journal of Women & Aging, 17*, 91–106.

Floyd, K. (1997). Communicating affection in dyadic relationships: An assessment of behavior and expectancies. *Communication Quarterly, 45*, 68–80.

Floyd, K., & Ray, G. B. (2003). Mapping the affectionate voice: Vocalic predictors of perceived affection in initial interaction. *Western Journal of Communication, 67*, 56–73.

Franiuk, R., Cohen, D., & Pomerantz, E. M. (2002). Implicit theories of relationships: Implications for relationship satisfaction and longevity. *Personal Relationships, 9*, 345–367.

Gonzaga, G. C., Turner, R. A., Keltner, D., Campos, B., & Altemus, M. (2006). Romantic love and sexual desire in close relationships. *Emotion, 6*, 163–179.

Gray, D., & Isensee, R. (1996). Balancing autonomy and intimacy in lesbian and gay relationships. In C. J. Alexander (Ed.), *Gay and lesbian mental health: A sourcebook for practitioners* (pp. 95–114). New York: Harrington Park Press.

Gray, J. (1992). *Men are from Mars, women are from Venus.* New York: HarperCollins.

Green, M. C., & Sabini, J. (2006). Gender, socioeconomic status, age, and jealousy: Emotional responses to infidelity in a national sample. *Emotion, 6*, 330–334.

Greene, K., Derlega, V. L., & Mathews, A. (2006). Self-disclosure in personal relationships. In A. Vangelisti & D. Perlman (Eds.), *Cambridge handbook of personal relationships* (pp. 409–427). Cambridge: Cambridge University Press.

Guerrero, L. K. (1997). Nonverbal involvement across interactions with same-sex friends, opposite-sex friends, and romantic partners: Consistency or change? *Journal of Social and Personal Relationships, 14*, 31–58.

Guerrero, L. K., & Andersen, P. A. (1994). Patterns of matching and initiation: Touch behavior and touch avoidance across romantic relationship stages. *Journal of Nonverbal Behavior, 18*, 137–153.

Gupta, V., & Korte, C. (1994). The effects of a confidant and a peer group on the well-being of single elders. *International Journal of Aging and Human Development, 39*, 293–302.

Hall, J. H., & Fincham, F. D. (2006). Relationship dissolution following infidelity: The roles of attributions and forgiveness. *Journal of Social and Clinical Psychology, 25*, 508–522.

Haslett, B. B., & Samter, W. (1997). *Children communicating: The first 5 years.* Mahwah, NJ: Lawrence Erlbaum.

Hazan, C., & Shaver, P. (1987). Romantic love conceptualized as an attachment process. *Journal of Personality and Social Psychology, 52*, 511–524.

Hendrick, C., & Hendrick, S. S. (1990). A relationship-specific version of the Love Attitudes Scale. *Journal of Social Behavior and Personality, 5*, 239–254.

Hendrick, S. S., & Hendrick, C. (2002). Linking romantic love with sex: Development of the perceptions of love and sex scale. *Journal of Social and Personal Relationships, 19*, 361–378.

Ickes, W. (1985). Sex role influences on compatibility in relationships. In W. Ickes (Ed.), *Compatible and incompatible relationships* (pp. 187–208). New York: Springer-Verlag.

Kurdek, L. A. (2006). Differences between partners from heterosexual, gay, and lesbian cohabiting couples. *Journal of Marriage and the Family, 68*, 509–528.

Jankowiak, W. R., & Fischer, E. F. (1992). A cross-cultural perspective on romantic love. *Ethnology, 31*, 149–155.

Kenrick, D. T., Trost, M. R., Sundie, J. M. (2004). Sex roles as adaptations: An evolutionary perspective on gender differences and similarities. In A. H. Eagly, A. E. Beall, & R. J. Sternberg (Eds.), *The psychology of gender* (pp. 65–91). New York: Guilford Press.

Knee, C. R. (1998). Implicit theories of relationships: Assessment and prediction of romantic relationship initiation, coping, and longevity. *Journal of Personality and Social Psychology, 74*, 360–370.

Knobloch, L. K., & Donovan-Kicken, E. (2006). Perceived involvement of network members in courtships: A test of the relational turbulence model. *Personal Relationships, 13*, 281–302.

Knobloch, L. K., & Solomon, D. H. (2002). Information seeking beyond initial interaction: Negotiating relational uncertainty within close relationships. *Human Communication Research, 28*, 243–257.

Knox, D., & Schacht, C., & Zusman, M. E. (1999). Love relationships among college students. *College Student Journal, 33*, 149–151.

Lamke, L., Sollie, D., Durbin, R., & Fitzpatrick, J. (1994). Masculinity, femininity, and relational satisfaction: The mediating role of interpersonal competence. *Journal of Social and Personal Relationships, 11*, 535–554.

Lee, J. W., & Guerrero, L. A. (2001). Types of touch in cross-sex relationships between co-workers: Perceptions of relational and emotional messages, inappropriateness, and sexual harassment. *Journal of Applied Communication Research, 29*, 197–220.

Lewandowski, G. W., & Ackerman, R. A. (2006). Something's missing: Need fulfillment and self-expansion as predictors of susceptibility to infidelity. *Journal of Social Psychology, 146*, 389–403.

McAlister, A. R., Pachana, N., & Jackson, C. J. (2005). Predictors of young dating adults' inclination to engage in extradyadic sexual activities: A multi-perspective study. *British Journal of Psychology, 96*, 331–350.

McClanahan, K. K., Gold, J. A., Lenney, E., Ryckman, R. M., Kulberg, G. E. (1990). Infatuation and attraction to a dissimilar other: Why is love blind? *Journal of Social Psychology, 130*, 433–445.

Meeks, B. S., Hendrick, S. S., & Hendrick, C. (1998). Communication, love and relationship satisfaction. *Journal of Social and Personal Relationships, 15*, 755–773.

Merolla, A. J. (2010). Relational maintenance during military deployment: Perspectives of wives of deployed US soldiers. *Journal of Applied Communication Research, 38*, 4–26.

Mongeau, P. A., & Schulz, B. E. (1997). What he doesn't know won't hurt him (or me): Verbal responses and attributions following sexual infidelity. *Communication Reports, 10*, 143–152.

Morrow, G. D., Clark, E. M., & Brock, K. F. (1995). Individual and partner love styles: Implications for the quality of romantic involvements. *Journal of Social and Personal Relationships, 12*, 363–387.

Murray, S. L., Holmes, J. G., & Griffin, D. W. (1996). The self-fulfilling nature of positive illusions in romantic relationships: Love is not blind, but prescient. *Journal of Personality and Social Pyschology, 71*, 1155–1180.

Noller, P. (1996). What is this thing called love? Defining the love that supports marriage and family. *Personal Relationships, 3*, 97–115.

Noller, P., Feeney, J. A., & Peterson, C. (2001). *Personal relationships across the lifespan.* Philadelphia, PA: Taylor & Francis.

Nussbaum, J. F. (1991). Communication, language and the institutionalised elderly. *Ageing and Society, 11*, 149–166.

Nussbaum, J. F., Hummert, M. L., Williams, A., & Harwood, J. (1996). Communication and older adults. *Communication Yearbook 19* (pp. 1–47). Thousand Oaks, CA: Sage.

Patterson, B. R., Bettini, L., & Nussbaum, J. F. (1993). The meaning of friendship across the lifespan: Two studies. *Communication Quarterly, 41*, 145–160.

Pendell, S. D. (2002). Affection in interpersonal relationships: Not just a "fond and tender feeling." In W. B. Gudykunst (Ed.), *Communication Yearbook 26* (pp. 70–115). Mahwah, NJ: Lawrence Erlbaum.

Rawlins, W. K. (1989). Rehearsing the margins of adulthood: The communicative management of adolescent friendships. In J. F. Nussbaum (Ed.), *Life-span communication: Normative processes* (pp. 137–154). Hillsdale, NJ: Lawrence Erlbaum.

Rawlins, W. K. (2004). Friendships in later life. In J. F. Nussbaum & J. Coupland (Eds.), *Handbook of communication and aging research* (2nd ed., pp. 273–299). Mahwah, NJ: Lawrence Erlbaum.

Regan, P. C. (2000). The role of sexual desire and sexual activity in dating relationships. *Social Behavior and Personality, 28*, 51–59.

Richardson, D. R., Hammock, G. S., Lubben, T., & Mickler, S. (1989). The relationship between love attitudes and conflict responses. *Journal of Social and Clinical Psychology, 8*, 430–441.

Rook, K. S. (1987). Reciprocity of social exchange and social satisfaction among older women. *Journal of Personality and Social Psychology, 52*, 145–154.

Rotenberg, K. J., & Mann, L. (1986). The development of the norm of the reciprocity of self-disclosure and its function in children's attraction to peers. *Child Development, 57*, 1349–1357.

Samter, W. (2003). Friendship interaction skills across the life span. In J. O. Greene & B. R. Burleson (Eds.), *Handbook of communication and social interaction skills* (pp. 637–684). Mahwah, NJ: Lawrence Erlbaum.

Shackelford, T. K., Buss, D. M., & Bennett, K. (2002). Forgiveness or breakup: Sex differences in responses to a partner's infidelity. *Cognition & Emotion, 16*, 299–307.

Shackelford, T. K., LeBlanc, G. J., & Drass, E. (2000). Emotional reactions to infidelity. *Cognition and Emotion, 14*, 643–659.

Shulman, S., & Knafo, D. (1997). Balancing closeness and individuality in adolescent close relationships. *International Journal of Behavioral Development, 21*, 687–702.

Simon, E. P., & Baxter, L. A. (1993). Attachment-style differences in relationship maintenance strategies. *Western Journal of Communication, 57*, 416–430.

Sprecher, S. (1998). Insiders' perspectives on reasons for attraction to a close other. *Social Psychology Quarterly, 61*, 287–300.

Sprecher, S., & Metts, S. (1989). Development of the "romantic beliefs scale" and examination of the effects of gender and gender-role orientation. *Journal of Social and Personal Relationships, 6*, 387–411.

Sprecher, S., & Metts, S. (1999). Romantic beliefs: Their influence on relationships and patterns of change over time. *Journal of Social and Personal Relationships, 16*, 834–851.

Stafford, L., & Canary, D. J. (1991). Maintenance strategies and romantic relationship type, gender, and relational characteristics. *Journal of Social and Personal Relationships, 8*, 217–242.

Stafford, L., Dainton, M., & Haas, S. (2000). Measuring routine and strategic relational maintenance: Scale revision, sex versus gender roles, and the prediction of relational characteristics. *Communication Monographs, 67*, 306–323.

Sternberg, R. J. (1986). A triangular theory of love. *Psychological review, 93*, 119–135.

Tallis, F. (2005). Crazy for you. *Psychologist, 18*, 72–74.

Thompson, S. A., Gold, J. A., & Ryckman, R. M. (2003). The simulated video interaction technique: A new method for inducing infatuation in the laboratory. *Representative Research in Social Psychology, 27*, 32–37.

von Salisch, M., & Vogelgesang, J. (2005). Anger regulation among friends: Assessment and development from childhood to adolescence. *Journal of Social and Personal Relationships, 22*, 837–855.

Wheeless, L. R. (1978). A follow-up study of the relationships among trust, disclosure, and interpersonal solidarity. *Human Communication Research, 4*, 143–157.

Zebrowitz, L. A., Brownlow, S., & Olson, K. (1992). Babytalk to the babyfaced. *Journal of Nonverbal Behavior, 16*, 143–158.

11 COMMUNICATION IN FAMILIES

Afifi, T. D., McManus, T., Hutchinson, S., & Baker, B. (2007). Inappropriate parental divorce disclosures, the factors that prompt them, and their impact on parents' and adolescents' well-being. *Communication Monographs, 74,* 78–102.

Afifi, T. D., & Olson, L. (2005). The chilling effect in families and the pressure to conceal secrets. *Communication Monographs, 72,* 192–216.

Afifi, T. D., Olson, L. N., & Armstrong, C. (2005). The chilling effect and family secrets: Examining the role of self protection, other protection, and communication efficacy. *Human Communication Research, 31,* 564–598.

Baxter, L. A., Braithwaite, D. O., Golish, T. D., & Olson, L. N. (2002). Contradictions of interaction for wives of elderly husbands with adult dementia. *Journal of Applied Communication Research, 30,* 1–26.

Baxter, L. A., & Clark, C. L. (1996). Perceptions of family communication patterns and the enactment of family rituals. *Western Journal of Communication, 60,* 254–268.

Bethea, L. S., Travis, S. S., & Pecchioni, L. (2000). Family caregivers' use of humor in conveying information about caring for dependent older adults. *Health Communication, 12,* 361–376.

Booth, A., & Johnson, D. R. (1994). Declining health and marital quality. *Journal of Marriage and the Family, 56,* 218–223.

Brach, E. L., Camara, K. A., Houser, R. F. (2000). Patterns of dinnertime interaction in divorced and nondivorced families. *Journal of Divorce and Remarriage, 32*(3–4), 125–139.

Brennan, J. L., & Wamboldt, F. S. (1990). From the outside in: Examining how individuals define their experienced family. *Communication Research, 17,* 444–461.

Call, V., Sprecher, S., & Schwartz, P. (1995). The incidence and frequency of marital sex in a national sample. *Journal of Marriage and the Family, 57,* 639–652.

Caughlin, J. P., Golish, T. D., Olson, L. N., Sargent, J. E., Cook, J. S., & Petronio, S. (2000). Intrafamily secrets in various family configurations: A communication boundary management perspective. *Communication Studies, 51,* 116–134.

Cicirelli, V. G. (2006). Caregiving decision making by older mothers and adult children: Process and expected outcomes. *Psychology and Aging, 21,* 209–221.

Dickson, F. C., Christian, A., & Remmo, C. J. (2004). An exploration of the marital and family issues of the later-life adult. In A. Vangelisti (Ed.), *Handbook of family communication* (pp. 153–174). Mahwah, NJ: Lawrence Erlbaum.

Edwards, H., & Noller, P. (1998). Factors influencing caregiver–care receiver communication and its impact on the well-being of older care receivers. *Health Communication, 10,* 317–341.

Feeney, J. A., Hohaus, L., Noller, P., & Alexander, R. P. (2001). *Becoming parents: Exploring the bonds between mothers, fathers, and their infants.* Cambridge: Cambridge University Press.

Fitzpatrick, M. A. (1988) *Between husbands and wives: Communication in marriage.* Newbury Park, CA: Sage.

Fitzpatrick, M. A., Marshall, L. J., Leutwiler, T. J., & Krcmar, M. (1996). The effect of family communication environments on children's social behavior during middle childhood. *Communication Research, 23,* 379–406.

Fitzpatrick, M. A., & Ritchie, L. D. (1994). Communication schemata within the family: Multiple perspectives on family interaction. *Human Communication Research, 20,* 275–301.

Fitzpatrick, M. A., Vangelisti, A. L., & Firman, S. M. (1994). Perceptions of marital interaction and change during pregnancy: A typological approach. *Personal Relationships, 1,* 101–122.

Fitzpatrick, M. A., & Wamboldt, F. S. (1990). Where is all said and done? Toward an integration of intrapersonal and interpersonal models of marital and family communication. *Communication Research, 17,* 421–430.

Floyd, K. (1997). Brotherly love II: A developmental perspective on liking, love, and closeness in the fraternal dyad. *Journal of Family Psychology, 11,* 196–209.

Floyd, K. (2006). Human affection exchange: XII. Affectionate communication is associated with diurnal variation in salivary free cortisol. *Western Journal of Communication, 70,* 47–64.

Floyd, K, & Mikkelson, A. C. (2005). The affectionate communication index. In V. Manusov (Ed.), *The sourcebook of nonverbal measures* (pp. 47–55). Mahwah, NJ: Lawrence Erlbaum.

Floyd, K., Mikkelson, A. C., Hesse, C., & Pauley, P. M. (2007). Affectionate writing reduced total cholesterol: Two randomized, controlled trials. *Human Communication Research*, *33*, 119–142.

Floyd, K., & Morman, M. T. (1998). "I love you man": Overt expressions of affection in male–male interactions. *Sex Roles*, *38*, 871–881.

Floyd, K., Sargent, J. E., & Di Corcia, M. (2004). Human affection exchange: VI. Further tests of reproductive probability as a predictor of men's affection with their adult sons. *Journal of Social Psychology*, *144*, 191–206.

Gagnon, M. D., Hersen, M., Kabacoff, R. I., & Van Hasselt, V. B. (1999). Interpersonal and psychological correlates of marital dissatisfaction in later life: A review. *Clinical Psychological Review*, *19*, 359–378.

Golish, T. D. (2003). Stepfamily communication strengths: Understanding the ties that bind. *Human Communication Research*, *29*, 41–80.

Goodman, C. C., & Silverstein, M. (2006). Grandmothers raising grandchildren: Ethnic and racial differences in well-being among custodial and coparenting families. *Journal of Family Issues*, *27*, 1605–1626.

Gotcher, J. M. (1993). The effects of family communication on psychological adjustment of cancer patients. *Journal of Applied Communication Research*, *21*, 176–188.

Harper, J. M., Schaalje, B. G., & Sandberg, J. G. (2000). Daily hassles, intimacy, and marital quality in later life marriages. *The American Journal of Family Therapy*, *28*, 1–18.

He, W., Sengupta, M., Velkoff, V. A., & DeBarros, K. A. (2005). 65+ in the United States: 2005. *U.S. Census Bureau* (Series P23–P209). Retrieved March 15, 2007, from http://www.census.gov/population/www/socdemo/age.html#elderly.

Hurley, D. (2005). Divorce rate: It's not as high as you think. *New York Times*, April 19.

Huston, T. L., & Holmes, E. K. (2004). Becoming parents. In A. L. Vangelisti (Ed.), *Handbook of family communication* (pp. 105–133). Mahwah, NJ: Lawrence Erlbaum.

Koerner, A. F., & Fitzpatrick, M. A. (1997). Family type and conflict: The impact of conversation orientation and conformity orientation on conflict in the family. *Communication Studies*, *48*, 59–75.

Koerner, A. F., & Fitzpatrick, M. A. (2004). Communication in intact families. In A. L. Vangelisti (Ed.), *Handbook of family communication* (pp. 177–195). Mahwah, NJ: Lawrence Erlbaum.

Kreider, R. M. (2010). Increase in opposite-sex cohabiting couples from 2009 to 2010 in the Annual Social and Economic Supplement (ASEC) to the Current Population Survey (CPS). *Housing and Household Economic Statistics Division Working Paper*, available at: www.census.gov/population/www/socdemo/Inc-Opp-sex-2009-to-2010.pdf, accessed Nov. 23, 2011.

Mather, M. (2010). U.S. children in single mother families. *Population Reference Bureau*, available at: http://www.prb.org/pdf10/single-motherfamilies.pdf, accessed Nov. 23, 2011.

Mather, M., & Lavery, D. (2010). In U.S., proportion married at lowest recorded levels. *Population Reference Bureau*, available at: http://www.prb.org/Articles/2010/usmarriagedecline.aspx, accessed Nov. 23, 2011.

McHale, S. M., & Huston, T. L. (1985). The effect of the transition to parenthood on the marriage relationship: A longitudinal study. *Journal of Family Issues*, *6*, 409–433.

Morman, M. T., & Floyd, K. (2002). A "changing culture of fatherhood": Effects on affectionate communication, closeness, and satisfaction in men's relationships with their fathers and their sons. *Western Journal of Communication*, *66*, 395–411.

Murray, S. L., Holmes, J. G., & Griffin, D. W. (1996). The benefits of positive illusions: Idealization and the construction of satisfaction in close relationships. *Journal of Personality and Social Psychology*, *70*, 79–98.

Petronio, S. (2002). *Boundaries of privacy: Dialectics of disclosure*. Albany, NY: SUNY Press.

Petronio, S. (2010). Communication privacy management theory: What do we know about family privacy regulation? *Journal of Family Theory & Review*, *2*, 175–196.

Ritchie, L. D., & Fitzpatrick, M. A. (1990). Family communication patterns: Measuring interpersonal perceptions of interpersonal relationships. *Communication Research*, *17*, 523–544.

Ruvolo, A. P., & Ruvolo, C. M. (2000). Creating Mr. Right and Ms. Right: Interpersonal ideals and personal change in newlyweds. *Personal Relationships*, 7, 341–363.

Stamp, G. H. (1994). The appropriation of the parental role through communication during the transition to parenthood. *Communication Monographs*, 61, 89–112.

Stamp, G. H., & Banski, M. A. (1992). The communicative management of constrained autonomy during the transition to parenthood. *Western Journal of Communication*, 56, 281–300.

Travis, S. S., Bethea, L. S., & Winn, P. (2000). Medication administration hassles reported by family caregivers of dependent elderly persons. *The Journals of Gerontology*, 55A, M412–M417.

U.S. Census Bureau. (2000). *Household and Family Statistics*. Washington, D.C.: Government Printing Office.

U.S. Department of Health and Human Services (2004). *How many children were adopted in 2000 and 2001*. Washington, DC: Child Welfare Information Gateway.

Van Egeren, L. A., & Barratt, M. S. (2002). The developmental origins of communication: Interactional systems in infancy. In A. L. Vangelisti (Ed.), *Handbook of family communication* (pp. 287–310). Mahwah, NJ: Lawrence Erlbaum.

Vangelisti, A. L. (1994). Family secrets: Forms, functions, and correlates. *Journal of Social and Personal Relationships*, 11, 113–135.

Vangelisti, A. L., & Caughlin, J. P. (1997). Revealing family secrets: The influence of topic, function, and relationships. *Journal of Social and Personal Relationships*, 14, 679–705.

Vangelisti, A. L., Caughlin, J. P., & Timmerman, L. (2001). Criteria for revealing family secrets. *Communication Monographs*, 68, 1–27.

Veroff, J., Douven, E., Orbuch, T. L., Acitelli, L. K. (1998). Happiness in stable marriages: The early years. In T. N. Bradbury (Ed.), *The developmental course of marital dysfunction* (pp. 152–179). New York: Cambridge University Press.

Vinick, B. H., & Ekerdt, D. J. (1990). Retirement: What happens to husband–wife relationship? *Journal of Geriatric Psychiatry*, 24, 23–40.

12 INTERPERSONAL INFLUENCE

Burgoon, J. K., Dunbar, N. E., & Segrin, C. (2002). Nonverbal influence. In J. P. Dillard & M. Pfau (Eds.), *The persuasion handbook* (pp. 445–476). Thousand Oaks, CA: Sage.

Brown, P., & Levinson, S. (1987). *Politeness: Some universals in language use*. New York: Cambridge University Press.

Bylund, C. L. (2000, November). Physicians' and new patients' talk about health risk behaviors: Form, forcefulness, and face. Paper presented at the annual meeting of the National Communication Association, Seattle, WA.

Cai, D., & Wilson, S. R. (2000). Identity implications of influence goals: A cross-cultural comparison on interaction goals and facework. *Communication Studies*, 51, 307–328.

Dillard, J. P. (2008). Goals-plans-action theory of message production: Making influence messages. In L. Baxter & D. Braithewaite (Eds.), *Engaging theories of interpersonal communication: Multiple perspectives*. Thousand Oaks, CA: Sage.

Dillard, J. P., Anderson, J. W., & Knobloch, L. K. (2002). Interpersonal influence. In M. L. Knapp & J. A. Daly (Eds.), *Handbook of interpersonal communication* (3rd ed., pp. 425–474). Thousand Oaks, CA: Sage.

Dillard, J. P., Kinney, T. A., & Cruz, M. G. (1996). Influence, appraisals, and emotions in close relationships. *Communication Monographs*, 63, 105–130.

Dillard, J. P., Segrin, C., & Harden, J. M. (1989). Primary and secondary goals in the production of interpersonal influence messages. *Communication Monographs*, 56, 19–38.

Dillard, J. P., Wilson, S. R., Tusing, K. J., & Kinney, T. A. (1997). Politeness judgments in personal relationships. *Journal of Language and Social Psychology*, 16, 297–325.

Guadagno, R. E., & Cialdini, R. B. (2002). Online persuasion: An examination of gender differences in computer-mediated interpersonal influence. *Group Dynamics: Theory, Research, and Practice, 6*, 38–51.

Hample, D., & Dallinger, J. M. (1998). On the etiology of the rebuff phenomenon: Why are persuasive messages less polite after rebuffs? *Communication Studies, 49*, 305–321.

Ifert, D. E., & Roloff, M. E. (1994). Anticipated obstacles to compliance: Predicting their presence and expression. *Communication Studies, 45*, 120–130.

Ifert, D. E., & Roloff, M. E. (1996). Responding to rejected requests: Persistence and resonse type as functions of obstacles to compliance. *Journal of Language and Social Psychology, 15*, 40–58.

Ifert, D. E., & Roloff, M. E. (1997). Overcoming expressed obstacles to compliance: The role of sensitivity to the expressions of others and ability to modify self-presentation. *Communication Quarterly, 45*, 55–67.

Ifert, D. E., & Roloff, M. E. (1998). Understanding obstacles preventing compliance: Conceptualization and classification. *Communication Research, 25*, 131–153.

Kellermann, K. (2004). A goal-directed approach to gaining compliance: Relating differences among goals to differences in behaviors. *Communication Research, 31*, 397–445.

Knobloch, L. K. (2006). Relational uncertainty and message production within courtship: Features of date request messages. *Human Communication Research, 32*, 244–273.

Kunkel, A. D., Wilson, S. R., Olufowote, J., & Robson, S. (2003). Identity implications of influence goals: Initiating, intensifying, and ending romantic relationships. *Western Journal of Communication, 67*, 382–412.

Marshall, L. J., & Levy, V. M. (1998). The development of children's perceptions of obstacles in compliance-gaining interactions. *Communication Studies, 49*, 342–357.

Paulson, G. D., & Roloff, M. E. (1997). The effect of request form and content on constructing obstacles to compliance. *Communication Research, 24*, 261–290.

Postmes, T., Spears, R., Lee, A. T., & Novak, R. J. (2005). Individuality and social influence in groups: Inductive and deductive routes to group identity. *Journal of Personality and Social Psychology, 89*, 747–763.

Samp, J. A., & Solomon, D. H. (1998). Communicative responses to problematic events in close relationships I: The variety and facets of goals. *Communication Research, 25*, 69–95.

Sanders, R. E., & Fitch, K. L. (2001). The actual practice of compliance seeking. *Communication Theory, 11*, 263–289.

Schrader, D. C., & Dillard, J. P. (1998). Goal structures and interpersonal influence. *Communication Studies, 49*, 276–293.

Solomon, D. H. (1997). A developmental model of intimacy and date request explicitness. *Communication Monographs, 64*, 99–118.

Waldron, V. R. (1999). Communication practices of leaders, members, and protégés: The case of upward influence tactics. In M. E. Roloff (Ed.), *Communication Yearbook 22* (pp. 251–299). Thousand Oaks, CA: Sage.

Wayne, S. J., Liden, R. C., Graf, I. K., & Ferris, G. R. (1997). The role of upward influence tactics in human resource decisions. *Personnel Psychology, 50*, 979–1006.

Wilson, S. R., Cameron, K. A., & Whipple, E. E. (1997). Regulative communication strategies within mother–child interactions: Implications for the study of reflection-enhancing parental communication. *Research on Language and Social Interaction, 30*, 73–92.

Yukl, G., Falbe, C. M., & Youn, J. Y. (1993). Patterns of influence behavior for managers. *Group and Organizational Management, 18*, 5–28.

13 INTERPERSONAL CONFLICT

Afifi, T. D., & Olsen, L. (2005). The chilling effect and the pressure to conceal secrets in families. *Communication Monographs, 72*, 192–216.

Afifi, T. D., Olson, L. N., & Armstrong, C. (2005). The chilling effect and family secrets: Examining the role of self protections, other protection, and communication efficacy. *Human Communication Research, 31*, 564–598.

Allen, T. H., & Berkos, K. M. (2005/2006). Ruminating about symbolic conflict through imagined interactions. *Imagination, Cognition and Personality, 25*, 307–320.

Barki, H., & Hartwick, J. (2004). Conceptualizing the construct of interpersonal conflict. *International Journal of Conflict Management, 15*, 216–244.

Barsky, A. E., & Wood, L. (2005). Conflict avoidance in a university setting. *Higher Education Research & Development, 24*, 249–264.

Baxter, L. A., Wilmot, W. W., Simmons, C. A., & Swartz, A. (1993). Ways of doing conflict: A folk taxonomy of conflict events in personal relationships. In P. J. Kalbfleisch (Ed.), *Interpersonal communication: Evolving interpersonal relationships* (pp. 89–107). Hillsdale, NJ: Lawrence Erlbaum.

Brett, J. M., Shapiro, D. L., & Lytle, A L. (1998). Breaking the bonds of reciprocity in negotiations. *Academy of Management Journal, 41*, 410–424.

Burman, B., Margolin, G., & John, R. S. (1993). America's angriest home videos: Behavioral contingencies observed in home reenactments of marital conflict. *Journal of Consulting and Clinical Psychology, 61*, 28–39.

Caughlin, J. P., & Huston, T. L. (2002). A contextual analysis of the association between demand/withdraw and marital satisfaction. *Personal Relationships, 9*, 95–119.

Caughlin, J. P., & Malis, R. S. (2004a). Demand/withdraw communication between parents and adolescents as a correlate of relational satisfaction. *Communication Reports, 17*, 59–71.

Caughlin, J. P., & Malis, R. S. (2004b). Demand/withdraw communication between parents and adolescents: Connections with self-esteem and substance use. *Journal of Social and Personal Relationships, 21*, 125–148.

Corcoran, K. O., & Mallinckrodt, B. (2000). Adult attachment, self-efficacy, perspective-taking, and conflict resolution. *Journal of Counseling & Development, 78*, 473–483.

Cupuch, W., & Canary, D. J. (2000). *Competence in interpersonal conflict*. Prospect Heights, IL: Waveland Press.

Dersley, I., & Wootton, A. (2000). Complaint sequences within antagonistic argument. *Research on Language and Social Interaction, 33*, 375–406.

de Wied, M., Branje, S. J. T., & Meeus, W. H. J. (2006). Empathy and conflict resolution in friendship relations among adolescents. *Aggressive Behavior, 33*, 48–55.

Ebesu Hubbard, A. S. (2001). Conflict between relational uncertain romantic partners: The influence of relational responsiveness and empathy. *Communication Monographs, 68*, 400–411.

Edelenbos, J., & Klijn, E. (2007). Trust in complex decision-making networks: A theoretical and empirical exploration. *Administration & Society, 39*, 25–50.

Gottman, J. M. (1994). *What predicts divorce?* Hillsdale, NJ: Lawrence Erlbaum.

Gross, M. A., & Guerrero, L. K. (2000). Managing conflict appropriately and effectively: An application of the competence model to Rahim's organizational conflict styles. *International Journal of Conflict Management, 11*, 200–226.

Guerrero, L. K., Trost, M. R, & Yoshimura, S. M. (2005). Romantic jealousy: Emotions and communicative responses. *Personal Relationships, 12*, 233–252.

Hobman, E. V., Bordia, P., Irmer, B., & Chang, A. (2002). The expression of conflict in computer-mediated and face-to-face groups. *Small Group Research, 33*, 439–465.

Holt, J. L., & DeVore, C. J. (2005). Culture, gender, organizational role, and styles of conflict resolution: A meta-analysis. *International Journal of Intercultural Relations, 29*, 165–196.

Janssen, O., & van de Vliert, E. (1996). Concern for the other's goals: Key to (de)escalation of conflict. *International Journal of Conflict Management, 7*, 99–120.

Johnson, K. L., & Roloff, M. E. (2000). Correlates of the perceived resolvability and relational consequences of serial arguing in dating relationships: Argumentative features and the use of coping strategies. *Journal of Social and Personal Relationships, 17*, 676–686.

Keck, K. L., & Samp, J. A. (2007). The dynamic nature of goals and message production as revealed in a sequential analysis of conflict interactions. *Human Communication Research, 33*, 27–47.

Knobloch, L. K. (2005). Evaluating a contextual model of responses to relational uncertainty increasing events: The role of intimacy, appraisals, and emotions. *Human Communication Research, 31*, 60–101.

Makoul, G., & Roloff, M. E. (1998). The role of efficacy and outcome expectations in the decision to withhold relational complaints. *Communication Research, 25*, 5–29.

Malis, R. S., & Roloff, M. E. (2006). Demand/withdraw patterns in serial arguments: Implications for well-being. *Human Communication Research, 32*, 198–216.

O'Leary, K. D., Smith Slep, A. M., & O'Leary, S. G. (2007). Multivariate models of men's and women's partner aggression. *Journal of Consulting and Clinical Psychology, 75*, 752–764.

Rahim, M. A. (1983). A measure of styles of handling interpersonal conflict. *Academy of Management Journal, 26*, 368–376.

Roloff, M. E., & Cloven, D. H. (1990). The chilling effect in interpersonal relationships: The reluctance to speak one's mind. In D. D. Cahn (Ed.), *Intimates in conflict: A communication perspective* (pp. 49–76). Hillsdale, NJ: Lawrence Erlbaum.

Roloff, M. E., & Ifert, D. E. (2000). Conflict management through avoidance: Withholding complaints, suppressing arguments, and declaring topics taboo. In S. Petronio (Ed.), *Balancing the secrets of private disclosures* (pp. 151–163). Mahwah, NJ: Lawrence Erlbaum.

Sabourin, R. C., Infante, D. A., & Rudd, J. E. (1993). Verbal aggression in marraiges : A comparison of violent, distressed but nonviolent, and nodistressed couples. *Human Communication Research, 20*, 245–267.

Sanford, K. (2007). Hard and soft emotion during conflict: Investigating married couples and other relationships. *Personal Relationships, 14*, 65–90.

Schütz, A. (1999). It was your fault! Self-serving biases in autobiographical accounts of conflicts in married couples. *Journal of Social and Personal Relationships, 16*, 193–208.

Siegert, J. R., & Stamp, G. H. (1994). "Our first big fight" as a milestone in the development of close relationship. *Communication Monographs, 61*, 345–360.

Smith Slep, A. M., & O'Leary, S. G. (2007). Multivariate models of mothers' and fathers' aggression toward their children. *Journal of Consulting and Clinical Psychology, 75*, 739–751.

Solomon, D. H., & Samp, J. A. (1998). Power and problem appraisal: Perceptual foundations of the chilling effect in dating relationships. *Journal of Social and Personal Relationships, 15*, 191–209.

Waldron, V. R., & Kelley, D. L. (2005). Forgiving communication as a response to relational transgressions. *Journal of Social and Personal Relationships, 22*, 723–742.

Worcel, S. D., Shields, S. A., & Paterson, C. A. (1999). "She looked at me crazy": Escalation of conflict through telegraphed emotion. *Adolescence, 34*, 689–697.

Zornoza, A., Ripoll, P., & Peiro, J. M. (2002). Conflict management in groups that work in two different communication contexts: Face-to-face and computer-mediated communication. *Small Group Research, 33*, 481–508.

14 COMMUNICATING SUPPORT AND COMFORT

Applegate, J. L., Burleson, B. R., & Delia, J. G. (1992). Reflection-enhancing parenting as an antecedent to children's social-cognitive and communicative development. In I. E. Sigel, A. V. McGillicuddy-DeLisi, & J. J. Goodnow (Eds.), *Parental belief systems: The psychological consequences for children* (pp. 3–39). Hillsdale, NJ: Erlbaum.

Arora, N. K., Rutten, L. J. F., Gustafson, D. H., Moser, R., & Hawkins, R. P. (2007). Perceived helpfulness and impact of social support provided by family, friends, and health care providers to women newly diagnosed with breast cancer. *Psycho-Oncology, 16*, 474–486.

Barbee, A. P., & Cunningham, M. R. (1995). An experimental approach to social support communications: Interactive coping in close relationships. In B. R. Burleson (Ed.), *Communication Yearbook 18* (pp. 381–413). Thousand Oaks, CA: Sage.

Burleson, B. R. (1982). The development of comforting communication skills in childhood and adolescence. *Child Development, 53*, 1578–1588.

Burleson, B. R. (1984). Age, social-cognitive development, and the use of comforting strategies. *Communication Monographs*, *51*, 140–153.

Burleson, B. R. (1994). Comforting messages: Features, functions, and outcomes. In J. A. Daly and J. M. Wiemann (Eds.), *Strategic interpersonal communication* (pp. 135–161). Hillsdale, NJ: Erlbaum.

Burleson, B. R., Delia, J. G., & Applegate, J. L. (1992). Effects of maternal communication and children's social-cognitive and communication skills on children's acceptance by the peer group. *Family Relations*, *41*, 264–272.

Burleson, B. R., & Denton, W. H. (1992). A new look at similarity and attraction in marriage: Similarities in social-cognitive and communication skills as predictors of attraction and satisfaction. *Communication Monographs*, *59*, 268–287.

Burleson, B. R., Kunkel, A. W., Samter, W., & Werking, K. J. (1996). Men's and women's evaluations of communication skills in personal relationships: When sex differences make a difference and when they don't. *Journal of Social and Personal Relationships*, *13*, 201–224.

Burleson, B. R., & Mortenson, S. (2003). Explaining cultural differences in evaluations of emotional support behaviors: Exploring the mediating influences of value systems and interaction goals. *Communication Research*, *30*, 113–146.

Burleson, B. R., & Samter, W. (1985). Consistencies in theoretical and naïve evaluations of comforting messages. *Communication Monographs*, *52*, 103–123.

Chen, W., & Choi, A. S. K. (2011). Internet and social support among Chinese immigrants in Singapore. *New Media and Society*, *13*, 1067–1084.

Clark, L. F. (1993). Stress and the cognitive-conversational benefits of social interaction. *Journal of Social and Clinical Psychology*, *12*, 25–55.

Davidowitz, M., & Myrick, R. D. (1984). Responding to the bereaved: Analysis of "helping" statements. *Death Education*, *8*, 1–10.

Delia, J. G. (1987). Communication research: A history. In C. R. Berger & S. H. Chaffee (Eds.), *Handbook of communication science* (pp. 20–89). Thousand Oaks, CA: Sage.

Elwell, L., Grogan, S., & Coulson, N. (2010). Adolescents living with cancer: The role of computer mediated support groups. *Journal of Health Psychology*, *16*, 236–248.

Feng, B., & MacGeorge, E. L. (2006). Predicting receptiveness to advice: Characteristics of the problem, the advice-giver, and the recipient. *Southern Journal of Communication*, *71*, 67–85.

Hale, J. L., Tighe, M. R., & Mongeau, P. A. (1997). Effects of event type and sex on comforting messages. *Communication Research Reports*, *14*, 214–220.

High, A. C. (2011). The production and reception of verbal person-centered social support in face-to-face and computer-mediated dyadic conversations. Unpublished doctoral dissertation, The Pennsylvania State University, University Park.

High, A. C., & Solomon, D. H. (in press). Locating computer-mediated social support within online communication environments. In K. Wright & L. M. Webb (Eds.), *Computer-mediated communication in personal relationships*.

Hogan, N. S., & DeSantis, L. (1994). Things that help and hinder adolescent sibling bereavement. *Western Journal of Nursing Research*, *16*, 132–153.

Holmstrom, A. J., Burleson, B. R., & Jones, S. M. (2005). Some consequences for helpers who deliver "cold comfort": Why it's worse for women than men to be inept when providing emotional support. *Sex Roles*, *53*, 153–172.

Jones, S. M., & Burleson, B. R. (1997). The impact of situational variables on helpers' perceptions of comforting messages: An attributional analysis. *Communication Research*, *24*, 530–555.

Jones, S. M., & Burleson, B. R. (2003). Effects of helper and recipient sex on the experience and outcomes of comforting messages: An experimental investigation. *Sex Roles*, *48*, 1–19.

Jones, S. M., & Guerrero, L. A. (2001). The effects of nonverbal immediacy and verbal person-centeredness in the emotional support process. *Human Communication Research*, *27*, 567–596.

Jones, S. M., & Wirtz, J. G. (2006). How does the comforting process work? An empirical test of an appraisal-based model of comforting. *Human Communication Research*, *32*, 217–243.

Kaul, M., & Lakey, B. (2003). Where is the support in perceived support? The role of generic relationship satisfaction and enacted support in perceived support's relation to low distress. *Journal of Social and Clinical Psychology, 22,* 59–78.

Lehman, D. R., Ellard, J. H., & Wortman, C. B. (1986). Social support for the bereaved: Recipients' and providers' perspectives on what is helpful. *Journal of Consulting and Clinical Psychology, 54,* 438–446.

Lehman, D. R., & Hemphill, K. J. (1990). Recipients' perceptions of support attempts and attributions for support attempts that fail. *Journal of Social and Personal Relationships, 7,* 563–574.

Marwit, S. J., & Carusa, S. S. (1998). Communicated support following loss: Examining the experiences of parental death and parental divorce in adolescence. *Death Studies, 22,* 237–255.

Mesquita, B. (2001). Emotions in collectivist and individualist cultures. *Journal of Personality and Social Psychology, 80,* 68–74.

Mortenson, S. (2006). Cultural differences and similarities in seeking social support as a response to academic failure: A comparison of American and Chinese college students. *Communication Education, 55,* 127–147.

Mortenson, S., Liu, M., Burleson, B. R., & Liu, Y. (2006). A fluency of feeling: Exploring cultural and individual differences (and similarities) related to skilled emotional support. *Journal of Cross-Cultural Psychology, 37,* 366–385.

Powers, S. R., Buck, R., Kiehl, K., & Schaich-Borg, J. (2007). An fMRI study of neural responses to spontaneous emotional expressions: Evidence for a communicative theory of empathy. Paper presented at the 2007 meeting of the National Communication Association, Chicago, IL.

Priem, J. S., Solomon, D. H., & Steuber, K. R. (2009). Accuracy and bias in perceptions of emotionally supportive communication in marriage. *Personal Relationships, 16,* 531–552.

Rack, J. J., Burleson, B. R., Brodie, G. D., Holmstrom, A. J., & Servaty-Seib, H. (2008). Bereaved adults' evaluations of grief management messages: Effects of message person-centeredness, recipient individual differences, and contextual factors. *Death Studies, 32,* 399–427.

Rains, S. A., & Young, V. (2009). A meta-analysis of research on formal computer-mediated support groups: Examining group characteristics and health outcomes. *Human Communication Research, 35,* 309–336.

Sammarco, A. (2001). Perceived social support, uncertainty, and quality of life of younger breast cancer survivors. *Cancer Nursing, 24,* 212–219.

Samter, W. (2002). How gender and cognitive complexity influence the provision of emotional support: A study of indirect effects. *Communication Reports, 15,* 5–16.

Samter, W., & Burleson, B. R. (1984). Cognitive and motivational influences on spontaneous comforting behavior. *Human Communication Research, 11,* 231–260.

Samter, W., Burleson, B. R., & Badsen-Murphy, L. (1989). Behavioral complexity is in the eye of the beholder: Effects of cognitive complexity and message complexity on impressions of the source of comforting messages. *Human Communication Research, 15,* 612–629.

Samter, W., Burleson, B. R., & Murphy, L. B. (1987). Comforting conversations: Effects of strategy type on evaluations of messages and message producers. *Southern Speech Communication Journal, 52,* 263–284.

Servaty-Seib, H., & Burleson, B. R. (2007). Bereaved adolescents' evaluations of the helpfulness of support-intended statements: Associations with person-centeredness and demographic, personality, and contextual factors. *Journal of Social and Personal Relationships, 24,* 207–223.

Solomon, D. H., Priem, J. S., & Steuber, K. R. (2008). Perceptions of supportive communication in marital interactions: Accuracy, projection, and sentiment override. Paper presented at the meeting of the National Communication Association, San Diego, CA, November.

Trobst, K. K., Collin, R. L., & Embree, J. M. (1994). The role of emotion in social support provision: Gender, empathy, and expressions of distress. *Journal of Social and Personal Relationships, 11,* 45–62.

Uchino, B. N. (2006). Social support and health: A review of physiological processes potentially underlying links to disease outcomes. *Journal of Behavioral Medicine, 29,* 377–387.

Weber, K. M., & Solomon, D. H. (2008). Locating relationship and communication issues among stressors associated with breast cancer. *Health Communication*, *23*, 548–559.

Xu, Y., & Burleson, B. R. (2001). Effects of sex, culture, and support type on perceptions of spousal social support: An assessment of the "support gap" hypothesis in early marriage. *Human Communication Research*, *27*, 535–566.

Index

Page numbers ending in "f" refer to figures and ending in "t" refer to tables.

abstract language 129–31, 129f, 130t
Abu-Rayya, H.M. 85
accenting 172, 173t
action tendencies 187, 188t
active-emphatic listening 213–14, 213t
active listening 219–26, 231–2; asking questions 220–2, 225–6; and attending to detail 225–6; and biased listening 224–5; expressing empathy 222–3, 226; physician and patient listening 221–2; and transcendence 223–4
actor-observer effect 107, 108, 108t, 364
adaptive attributions 109, 110, 110t, 111f, 112
adolescents: communicating with 21; coping with cancer 395; ethnic identity in Israeli 84–5; friendships 281t, 282; identities in transition 88–9; sexual identity 89; supporting identity changes in 91–2
adoption 295, 317
affection: communication within families 298; component of intimacy 268; study of father–son relationships 297–8
affectionate communication index 298
affectionate messages, giving and receiving 13
Afifi, T.D. 17, 302, 303, 366
Afifi, W.A. 11, 72, 257, 286
African Americans: children in single parent households 295; cultural differences 21; ethnic identity 84; stereotyping of 117
age: affecting perception 114; and expression of emotions 194; and

friendships across the lifespan 281–3, 281t; and perceptions of communication competence 21, 23
ageism 290
alcohol and interpersonal encounters 114–16, 120
alcohol myopia theory 115, 116
Alzheimer's disease, coping with 313–14
American Indians, Oklahoma 88
analogic codes 159, 161f
Andersen, P.A. 164, 170, 184, 185, 201, 267
anxiety/uncertainty management theory 59–60, 59f
appraisal theories of emotion 185
appraisals 185–6, 186t, 189–90
appreciative listening 213, 213t
appropriateness of communication 17
arguments 329, 349; demand/withdraw communication in serial 368–9
Armstrong, C,. 302, 366
asking questions 220–2, 225–6
attachment styles 278–9, 278t, 283
attending stage of listening process 210
attraction in interethnic interactions study 57–8
attribution 105–12; biases 107–9, 108t, 120, 364, 371; biases in close relationships 109–11, 110t, 111f, 112; combating attribution biases 111–12; defining 105; dimensions of 105–7, 106t; and escalation of conflict 364–6, 365f, 371, 372, 372t
attributional complexity 114, 115
avoidant conflict strategy 358, 359t
avoiding conflict style 360, 360f

Babad, E. 134
back-channel communication 166–7, 212

Barnett, J.M. 84
Barsky, A.E. 366
basic emotions 183–4
Baxter, L.A. 11, 43, 53, 54, 138, 168, 247, 251, 253, 254, 274, 275, 279, 312, 313, 348
beauty, perceptions of 170
bereavement 396–7
Berger, C. 23, 240
biased listening 224–5
Bisson, M.A. 259
blended families 17, 298, 300f
body movements 157, 165
boundary markers 51–2, 51t
Bradbury, T.N. 103, 107, 109, 110
Braithwaite, D. 53, 54, 313
breadth (of self-disclosure) 246
Brown, P. 144, 337
Burgoon, J. 11, 157, 164, 170, 174, 175, 227, 329
Burleson, B. 19, 170, 190, 191, 195, 209, 379, 380, 381, 383, 387, 390, 391, 392, 397

cancer, coping with 394–6
caretaker relationships 313
cell phones 14f, 46
channels 7–8, 157–9, 157–8t, 162
characteristics of interpersonal communication 7–10, 7f
children: communicating with 21; communication experiences of boys and girls 61–2; family break up and effects on 46, 295, 317; family socialization of 296–7; friendships 281t, 282; interpersonal influence 336–7; labeling by teachers 134, 135; parental strategies to influence 330; perception in 114; teaching cultural values to 45, 297

Chinese language 133
closed families 300, 301f
coercive power 339
cognition 99
cognitive complexity 114, 390–2, 391t, 393–4
cohabitation statistics 46, 295
cold comfort 386
collectivism 47, 48t, 361, 392, 393
comfort, providing 378–89, 394–8; bereavement 396–7; coping with cancer 394–6; expanding toolkit for 387–9; within families 297–8; gendered perceptions of poor comforting 387; ineffective support messages 385, 386–7, 386t; nonverbal support messages 379–80, 380f, 398; preferences for types of support 384; in times of need 397–8; verbal support messages 380–5, 381f, 383t, 385f, 398
comforting behavior, individual differences in 389–94; cognitive complexity 390–2, 391t, 393–4; culture and 392, 393, 398; overcoming obstacles to support 393–4; sex differences 390, 393, 398
communal layer of identity 82
communication accommodation theory 56–7, 56f
communication competence 16–18, 31; and age 21, 23; computer-mediated 21; defining 16; practicing 22–3; promoting 18–20, 20f; and setting 21, 23
communication, defining 4
communication skills 15, 19–20, 21, 22
competing conflict style 358, 360f
complementing 172, 173t
complete/consummate love 269
compliance-seeking messages 328, 328t
comprehensive listening 213, 213t
compromising conflict style 360, 360f
computer-mediated communication 14, 159; competence 21; expressing emotions in 197; gender differences in 143–4; influence messages in 339; organizing information from 102; support networks 52, 378, 379, 395, 395–6
concepts 24–5
concrete language 129–30, 130t, 134–5
conflict 348–54; components of 351–3, 352f; existing at multiple levels

350–1, 351t; forms of 348–50; understanding 353–4
conflict dynamics 364–70, 373; attribution and escalation 364–6, 365f, 371, 372, 372t; avoiding escalation of conflict 365–6, 369, 372, 372t; communication patterns 367–70; demand/withdraw 368–9, 373; and effects of power 366–7, 367f, 371; forgiveness 370, 371t; promoting healthy conflicts 370–2; reciprocity 370
conflict, managing 354–63, 372–3; conflict goals 355–7, 355t, 362–3, 363t; conflict strategies 357–8, 359t, 363t, 373; conflict styles 358–61, 360f, 363, 363t, 373; culture and gender in 361–2; expanding options in 362–3
conformity orientation 310–11
connotative meaning 136, 141
consensual families 311t, 312
consequential, interpersonal communication as 9
content messages 10, 17
contexts 12–14, 21
continuous process of interpersonal communication 7–8
contradicting 172, 173t
controllable/uncontrollable actions 106
conversation orientation 310
cooperative principle 139
Costa Rican cultural norms 193–4
courtship, four trajectories to 239f
cultural institutions 41–2, 41f
cultural norms 40, 41, 193–5
cultural relativism 67
culture 40–50, 65; affecting perception 113; classifying 47–8; and comforting behavior 392, 393, 398; defining 41; dimensions that distinguish 48t; disrespecting another 40; finding common ground for communication 48–50; form and change 44–7, 44f; and gender differences in conflict management 361–2; language related to 132–3; layers of 41–4, 41f; nonverbal behavior differences across 169–70, 171–2; perceptions of communication competence and differences in 21, 23; promoting local 47, 67; transmission of 45, 297
culture and communication 50–5, 65–6; appreciating cultural diversity 54–5;

communication reflecting culture 51–4, 51t; culture shaping communication 50–1; see also intercultural communication
curvilinear association 24f, 25
custody of children after divorce 317

dark side of interpersonal communication 199; see also emotions in close relationships, dark side of
dating: and attraction to others 100; and becoming friends after the relationship 253; communication competence 18; communication differences between men and women 62–3; date refusals research 336; dealing with criticism 228; and effect on use of language 146, 148, 254; feelings causing behaviors 190; happiness levels and perceptions of physical attractiveness 103; homosexual and lesbian 275; and infidelity rates 286; managing conflict 356; online 242, 262; and perceptions of power 366; requests 340–2; terminology 132; touch and intimacy levels research 164
de Vargas, M.C. 194
deception, signs of 173–5, 175f, 177; research into detecting 175
deintensification 164
demand/withdraw communication 368–9, 373
denotative meaning 136
dependence power 366
depression study 86
depth (of self-disclosure) 246
diffusion 47
Dillard, J.P. 166, 185, 190, 192, 228, 229, 323, 325, 328, 329–30, 332, 338, 340
disagreeable communication 349–50
discriminatory listening 213, 213t
disengaged systems 300, 301f
dismiss support strategy 385
display rules 193, 195
distributive conflict strategy 357
divorce 294, 295, 303, 317, 350, 362
Dixon, L.D. 88
doctors: and communication with patients 220–2; labelling patients 134; and patient listening research 221–2; recruiting people for medical

experiments 137; regulating conversation between patients and 166; settings and perceptions of communication competence 21
dominance 329
dominating conflict style 358
drug-use and ethnic identity 84
Duncan, S. 166
dyad 6

effectiveness 17
efficiency 18
elderly 57, 114, 194, 284; friendships 281t, 283, 290; intergenerational communication and negative stereotypes of 117–18, 118f; parents 314–15, 382; women with husbands with Alzheimer's disease 313–14
emblems 169
emerging adulthood 88–9; supporting identity changes 91–2; see also adolescents
emotion-focused coping 395
emotional feelings and communication 190–3; interpretations of messages 191–2
emotional infidelity 286
emotional intelligence 195–6; developing 197–8
emotions 182–90; causes of 185–6, 186t, 189–90; components of 186–8, 188t, 189; nonverbal communication of 163–4, 187, 191, 192; recognizing and communicating 188–90; seeking specific labels for 189; structure of 184f; types of 183–5, 184f, 185f; see also feelings and communication
emotions and communication, factors that affect 193–8; cultural norms 193–5; emotional intelligence 195–6, 197–8; hierarchy of influences 198f; relationship context 196–7
emotions in close relationships, dark side of 198–203, 202f; grief 199–201; hurt 199; jealousy 201, 201–2t, 202f; keeping emotional consequences in check 203
empathic accuracy 223, 226
empathy: in active listening 222–3, 226; brain activation and 380f; and providing comfort 379–80
empty nest 90–1, 92–3
enactment layer of identity 81–2
enmeshed systems 300, 301f

eros 270, 270f
escape support strategy 385
esteem support 383
ethics, interpersonal communication: clarifying 22; communicating ethically 28–30; components for 29, 29f; defining 18; exploring 33, 67, 95, 122, 153, 179, 205, 233, 262, 290, 317, 345, 374, 400; in research 30–1, 33; theory into practice 31
ethnic identity 84–5, 84f, 88, 95
ethnic identity salience scale 44
ethnic stereotypes 117
ethnocentrism 58–9
ethnography 26t
evaluating stage of listening process 211–12
evaluative listening 213, 213t
experiments 26t
expert power 339
explicitness 329
external attribution 105, 107, 108t, 113
eye contact 164
eye movements 157t; when lying 174

face 337
face-threatening acts 337
face threats 252–3, 255
Facebook 46, 190, 238, 301, 379; newsfeeds 197; profile 74; self-disclosure 79; stalking on 256–7; status 247
facial expressions 157t, 160, 160f, 161f, 163, 171; indicating deception 174, 175f; mirroring 379, 380; sympathetic 378, 398
false identities 87
families 294–9; blended 17, 298, 300f; changing face of 295–6; communication in 299–305; defining 296; family secrets 302–3, 304, 304t; family systems 299–300, 300f, 301f, 316; functions of 296–8; improving system operations 303–5; managing communication boundaries 301–2, 303; strengthening bonds in 298–9
families, lifespan of 305–15, 316; coping with changes 315; early years 305–8, 308t; mature families 312–15; raising families 310–12, 311f; transition to parenthood 308–10
family secrets 302–3, 304, 304t
family socialization 296–7
father–son relationships, study of 297–8

fathers 62, 149, 160, 171; after divorce 317
feedback from others 76–7
feelings and communication 190–3; interpretations of messages 191–2
fidelity 16–17
Fincham, F.P. 103, 107, 109, 110, 286
Fiske, D.W. 166
Fitzpatrick, M.A. 176, 296, 306, 309, 310, 311, 312
Floyd, K. 13, 268, 279, 297, 298
folktales 52, 53f
forgiveness 286, 370; forms of 371t
friends-with-benefits 257–9, 258–9t, 258f; study of 259
friendship across lifespan 281–3, 281t, 290
fundamental attribution error 107–8, 108t, 364

Gangestad, S.W. 100
gender: affecting language use 142–4, 147; defining 61; differences and conflict management 361–2; and perceptions of poor comforting study 387
gender-linked language effect 144
gender orientation 280–1, 280t
generalized other 76
Giles, H. 51, 55, 56, 57, 117
goal strain 325
goals: conflict 355–7, 355t, 362–3, 363t; defining 323; see also influence goals
Goldsmith, D. 43, 138, 191
Golish, T. 17, 199, 200–1, 295, 303, 313
grandparents: new 315; study of relationships with grandchildren 83; and talking with grandchildren 17, 56, 57, 83
grave-dressing 254
Greene, J. 223–4
Grice, H.P. 139
grief 199–201; comforting people in 396–7; study of parents with premature babies 200–1
Gudykunst, W. 55, 57, 59, 64
Guerrero, L.K. 72, 100, 164, 165, 171, 185, 201, 267, 268, 357, 361, 379, 381, 390
guilt 190, 191

halo effect 166
Harwood, J. 51, 57, 83, 117, 283

health, interpersonal communication and study of 13–14

hearing 208–9

Hecht, M. 27, 81, 84, 86

Hendrick, C. and S.S. Hendrick 270, 271, 285

Herbers, L. 223–4

Heritage, J. 221

heterosexist language 150, 150f, 151

high stakes episodes 340–2

Holmstrom, A. 195, 387, 397

homophobic abuse 150

Hosman, L. 145

hostile episodes 350

Humphreys, L.R. 224

hurt 199

hurtful comments 8–9, 10; research on 30

identities in transition 88–93, 93–4; emerging adulthood 88–9; empty nest 90–1, 92–3; supporting 91–3

identity 79–88; being true to oneself 87–8; creating 79–81; defining 79; expressing multiple 84–5, 87–8; false 87; gaps 85–6, 87; layers of 81–5, 85–6, 86f, 87–8; non-heterosexual 92; online 79, 81; see also self-concept

idioms 146

Ifert, D.E. 334, 335, 337, 358, 359

immediacy 164–5

impersonal communication 5

independent marriage 306–7, 308t

individualism 45, 47, 48t, 361, 392, 393

infants 61–2, 171, 200

infertility 134, 378, 400

infidelity 286–7, 288

influence goals 322–8, 343; interpersonal 323; managing multiple 325–6, 326t, 327–8; thinking strategically 326–8; types of 323–5, 323t, 324f, 327

influence messages 328–34, 343–4; characteristics 328–30; communication patterns 330–2; crafting effective 332–4; intimacy and 338–9; relationship characteristics and 337–40, 338f; short 332, 333f

informational support 382–3, 395

inhibition conflict 115

insecure attachment 278

instrumental goals 355, 355t

integrating conflict style 359, 360f

integrative conflict strategy 357–8

integrity, communicating with 87

intensification 164

interaction studies 26t

intercultural communication 55–65, 65–6; barriers to 58–61, 58t, 64; defining 55; between men and women 61–3, 62f, 64–5; nature of 55–7; predicting attraction in interethnic interactions 57–8; skills to improve interactions 64–5

intercultural communication apprehension 60

interdependence 248

intergenerational communication 17, 56, 57, 83; stereotypes in 117–18, 118f

internal attribution 105, 108t, 114

interpenetration 85–6, 86f

interpersonal communication 4–15, 31; basic definition 5–6, 5f; characteristics 7–10, 7f; contexts 12–14; correcting misconceptions regarding 11t; thinking critically 15; types of messages 10–12, 12t

interpersonal communication ethics: clarifying 22; communicating ethically 28–30; components for 29, 29f; defining 18; exploring 33, 67, 95, 122, 153, 179, 205, 233, 262, 290, 317, 345, 374, 400; in research 30–1, 33; theory into practice 31

interpersonal communication practice 16–23; communication competence 16–18; culture, setting and age 20–3; promoting communication competence 18–20; theory into practice 22–3

interpersonal communication study 23–8; research 25–7, 26t, 32; theory 23–5, 27, 31–2; theory into practice 27–8

interpersonal conflict 352–3, 352f

interpersonal influence, defining 322

interpersonal influence goals 323

interpersonal influence in action 334–43; date requests 340–2; ethical influence 340–1; high stakes episodes 340–2; overcoming obstacles 334–7, 335t, 336t, 337f, 342; and power 337–8, 339–40; relationship characteristics and influence messages 337–40, 342–3

interpersonal power 366

interpretation stage of listening process 210–11

interpretation stage of perception 102–3, 103f

interviews 26t

intimacy 265–90; attachment styles 278–9, 283–4; components of 266–8, 267t, 268f, 271; embracing 283–4; friendship across lifespan 281–3, 281t; individual differences in 277–84, 289; and influence messages 338–9; keeping your head when falling in love 287–8; language use and 146, 148, 254; love styles 269–71, 269f, 271–2; promoting well-rounded relationships 271–2; relational messages to negotiate 10–11; romantic betrayal 286–7, 288; romantic infatuation 284–5, 285f, 287–8; sex differences and 279–81, 284; triangular theory of love 269–70, 269f

intimate relationships, communication in 272–7, 288–9; coping with tension 274–5, 274t, 276t, 277; maintaining intimacy 272–3; maintaining intimate relationships 274, 276–7

invention 46

investment model 252, 252f

jealousy 184, 196, 201, 201–2t, 202f

Johari Window 72–3, 73f

Johnson, D. 98

Jones, S. 379, 381, 387, 390

Jung, E. 81, 86

Kenny, D.A. 76–7

Kim, Y. 88, 173, 193

Knapp, M.L. 103, 239, 240f

Knobloch, L.K. 146, 186, 190, 247, 248, 254, 274, 323, 341, 357

Korean culture 47

Krieger, J.L. 81, 137

Kulis, S. 84

labels 133–4, 135, 150, 189

laissez-faire families 311t, 312

language, biased 148–50, 152; heterosexist language 150, 150f, 151; job titles 149, 150f; racist language 148–9, 151; sexist language 149–50, 151; using inclusive language 151

language, nature of 128–35; as abstract 129–31, 129f, 130t; and ambiguity 131, 135; as arbitrary 131, 135; as consequential 133–4; defining 129; and harnessing power of language 134–5; as related to culture 132–3 language, rules of 135–42; making conversation 139–41; making meaning 136–8, 136f, 137t, 138t, 141; reducing miscommunication 141–2

language use, factors that affect 142–8; fine-tuning language 146–8; gender 142–4, 147; intimacy 146, 148, 254; power 144–6, 147

Lanutti, P. 116

Lee, C. 57

legitimate power 339

Lerma, M. 100

Levine, T. 101, 174, 259

Levinson, S. 144

Levy, V.M. 337

lies, telling 18, 140, 173, 174, 177

liking, communicating 164–5, 168

linguistic relativity 133

LinkedIn 74, 81, 238

listening 208–19; barriers to effective 215–18, 218–19, 231; defining 209; nonlistening and 217–18, 217t; process 209–12, 209f, 218; styles 214–15, 214f, 218; types of 213–14, 213t; using appropriate strategies 218–19; ways of 212–15; see also active listening

listening for relational meanings 226–30, 229t; framing relational messages 228–9, 229t; making sence of relational messages 230–1; relational messages 227–8, 227t

ludus 270, 270f

Lujan, P. 88

maladaptive attributions 110, 110t, 111f

Malis, R. 368–9

marginalization 58t, 60–1, 92; through language 149, 150, 152

marriage: statistics 46, 295; types of relationship 306–8, 308t

Marshall, L.J. 312, 337

Marsiglia, F.F. 84

masking 164

maxim of manner 140–1, 141f

maxim of quality 139–40

maxim of quantity 139

maxim of relevance 140

Merolla, A. 273

micro-momentary facial expressions 174, 175f

military families: maintaining relationships 273; online forum 52

Miller, C. 130

Miller-Day, M. 84

misconceptions about interpersonal communication 11t

mixed marriage 307, 308t

Monahan, J. 115, 116, 117

monochronic time orientation 169

moods 182, 183f, 191

Mulac, A. 57, 142, 143, 144

mutuality 268

myths 51t, 52–3, 53f, 55–6

negative association 24f, 25

negative face 337

network support 383

noise 215–16

nonlistening 217–18, 217t

nonverbal behavior 169–72, 178; across cultures 169–70, 171–2; defining 156, 157; embracing of differences 171–2; sex differences 170–1, 172

nonverbal communication 156–62, 178; automatic processing 160; being aware of nonverbal cues 162; channels 157–9, 157–8t, 162; characteristics 159–61, 160f, 161f; communication symbol systems 161f; defining 156, 157; potential for universal meaning 159; reducing physical distance 267; simultaneous transmission 160; spontaneous transmission 160; variable intensity 159–60

nonverbal cues, combining verbal and 172–7, 173t, 178; and negotiating sexual intimacy 176–7; in practice 177; signs of deception 173–5, 175f, 177

nonverbal immediacy 165, 379, 387–8

nonverbal leakage 174

nonverbal markers of emotion 187

nonverbal messages, functions of 162–8, 178; communicating emotion 163–4, 187, 191, 192; communicating liking 164–5, 168; communicating power and status 165–6, 168; managing relationships and interactions 168; regulating conversation 166–7, 167f, 168; support messages 379–80, 380f, 398

norm of reciprocity 241–2

norms 40, 41, 193–5; inconsistency with 101

Nussbaum, J.F. 21, 137, 283

obliging conflict style 359–60, 360f

obsessive relational intrusion 256–7

Olson, L. 268, 302, 303, 313, 366

online communication: see computer-mediated communication

online communities 43

online dating 242, 262

online identity 79, 81

open families 300, 301f

openness 267

organization stage of perception 101–2, 102f

Oswald, R.F. 92

other-identity goals 355t, 356

Palomares, N.A. 81

paraphrasing 211

parents: empty nest 90–1, 92–3; parent-child relationship in mature families 314–15; of premature babies study 200–1; transition to parenthood 308–10

Parrott, R.L. 137

Paulson, G. D. 336

Peck, E. 192

perceiving and misperceiving of causes: see attribution

perception, defining 99

perception, factors that affect 113–19, 120; alcohol and interpersonal encounters 114–16, 120; confronting barriers 118–20; individual differences 113–14, 119; stereotyping 116–18, 118f, 119, 120

perception, stages of 98–104, 99f, 104f, 120; directing attention during interpersonal interactions 104; distinguishing between fact and inference 103–4; interpretation 102–3, 103f; organization 101–2, 102f; paying attention to 103–4; selection 99–101

person-centered communication 64, 65

person-centered messages 380–1, 381t, 390–2

person-centeredness 380–1

personal layer of identity 81

personal relevance of information 100

perspective-taking in interpersonal communication 111, 359t, 384, 389

pervasive tension 350

Petronio, S. 191, 301, 303

physiology of emotion 187

pluralistic families 311t, 312

politeness theory 144, 145t, 337
polychronic time orientation 169
positive association 24, 24f
positive face 337
Powell, K. 199, 200–1
power: and conflict dynamics 366–7, 367f, 371; and influence messages 337–8, 338f, 339–40; nonverbal communicating of 165–6, 168; and reaching out to marginalized groups 61; and use of language 144–6, 147
practicing interpersonal communication 16–23; communication competence 16–18; culture, setting and age 20–3; promoting communication competence 18–20; theory into practice 22–3
pragmatic rules 137–8
predicted outcome value 242
premature babies, study of parents of 200–1
primary goals 323, 324f
privacy rules in families 301–2
problem-focused coping 395
process goals 355t, 356
pronouns, use of 146, 151, 152, 254
protective families 311–12, 311t
punitive power 366

questionnaires/surveys 26–7, 26t

racial stereotypes 117
racism 40, 87
racist language 148–9, 151
reciprocity 241–2, 370
referent power 339
reification 134
relational dialectic 274–5, 274t, 276t, 277
relational dialectics theory 274
relational framing 228–9, 229t
relational goals 355, 355t
relational layer of identity 82; study of communication and 83
relational maintenance 272, 273
relational meanings, listening for 226–30, 229t, 231
relational messages 10–12, 17, 227–8; framing 228–9, 229t; making sense of 230–1; paying attention to 15; sources of information about 12t; topics for 227t
relational turbulence model 248

relational uncertainty 246–7; date requests study 341
relationship dissolution 251
relationship talk 247, 250
relationships, beginning 238–44, 260; coping with uncertainty 240–2, 243–4; exploring possibilities 242–3, 244; four trajectories to courtship 239f; Knapp's model of development and dissolution 240f; starting out on the right track 243–4
relationships, escalating 244–50, 260; coordinating behavior 247–8, 250; creating a connection 245–6, 245f, 249; navigating challenges in 249–50; resolving doubts 246–7, 250; striving for equity 248–9
relationships, finishing 251–5, 260–1; coming to terms 254; exiting gracefully 255; making a decision 251–2, 252f, 255; managing face threats 252–3, 255; reasserting independence 253–4
relationships, problems in developing: clarifying and respecting boundaries 260, 261; friends-with-benefits 257–9, 258–9t, 258f; stalking and unrequited love 256–7
remembering stage of listening process 211
research 25–7, 32; ethics in communication 30–1, 33; evaluating 27–8; methods 26t
responding stage of listening process 212
reward power 339
Ritchie, L.D. 311, 312
rituals 51t, 53–4, 55–6
Robinson, J.D. 166, 221–2
Roloff, M. 111, 252, 334, 335, 336, 337, 358, 359, 366, 368–9
romantic betrayal 286–7, 288
romantic infatuation 284–5, 285f, 287–8
routine maintenance 272
rule of distributive justice 249

Sabee, C.M. 19
Safdar, S. 194, 195
Samp, J.A. 224, 228, 272, 356, 357, 358, 367
Samter, W. 21, 282, 283, 380, 381, 390, 391, 392
Sapir-Whorf Hypothesis 133
satisfaction, communication 17, 27
secondary goals 323, 324–5, 324f, 327

secret tests 247, 253
secure attachment 278–9
selection stage of perception 99–101
self-concept 70–9; characteristics of self 71–4, 77–9; defining 71; sources of self-knowledge 74–7, 75f; ways to enhance 77–9
self-disclosure 79; in escalating relationships 246, 249; in forming relationships 240–1, 243–4
self-esteem 71–2, 76; effects of alcohol among women with low 116; enhancing 78–9
self-identity goals 355t, 356
self-perceptions of emotion 186–7
self-reflexive acts 74–5
semantic rules 137
separate marriage 307, 308t
sex: defining 61; differences and intimacy 279–81, 284; differences in communicating comfort and support 390, 393, 398; differences in communication 61–3, 62f, 64–5, 290; differences in nonverbal behavior 170–1, 172; and expression of emotions 194–5; and listening styles 215
sexist language 149–50, 151
sexual behavior, alcohol and risky 115, 116
sexual harassment 63
sexual identity 89, 92, 95
sexual infidelity 286–7, 288
sexual intimacy, negotiating 176–7
Siltanen, S.A. 145
Simpson, J.A. 100, 223, 225, 253
simulation 164
single-parent household statistics 295
small talk 138t, 242–3, 244
social comparison 76
social emotions 185, 185f
social exchange 248–9
social penetration theory 245–6, 245f
social roles 75
social rules 17
socialization 45, 49; family socialization 296–7
solace support strategy 384
Soliz, J. 83
Solomon, D.H. 8, 21, 63, 131, 134, 146, 176, 228, 229, 238, 247, 248, 254, 325, 341, 367, 379, 381, 395, 396
solve support strategy 384
speech acts 137–8, 137t, 138t, 144

speech codes 50, 55
speech codes theory 50–1
speech communities 42–4, 52–3, 55, 64
speech patterns 57, 144, 147
Spitzberg, B. 16, 19, 21, 199, 201, 256, 257
stable/unstable causes of behavior 106–7
stalking 256–7
Stamp, G.H. 224, 309, 355
standpoints 41f, 42
Stephan, W. and C. Stephan 59, 194
stereotyping 116–18, 118f, 119, 120
Sternberg, R.J. 269
Steuber, K.R. 134, 220, 381
storge 270, 270f
strategic maintenance 272, 277
studying interpersonal communication 23–8; research 25–7, 26t, 32; theory 23–5, 27, 31–2; theory into practice 27–8
subcultures 43
substituting 172, 173t
subsystems 299
suicide, male youth 95
support messages: ineffective 385, 386–7, 386t; nonverbal 379–80,

380f, 398; verbal 380–5, 381t, 383t, 385f, 398
supportive communication strategies 384–5
Surra, C.A. 239
surveys/questionnaires 26–7, 26t
symbols 4, 5, 33; fallibility of 15
syntactic rules 136
systems, defining 299
systems theory 299

tangible support 383, 395, 397
Tannen, D. 65
telephone greetings 45
Theiss, J.A. 176, 238, 247
theory 23–5, 27, 31–2
thinking critically 15
time, cultural differences regarding 169
totalizing 133
touch 164, 379
Tracy, K. 79, 82
traditional marriage 306, 308t
transactional model of communication 7, 7f
transcendence 223–4
transmission 47, 297
Twitter 79, 81, 197, 238

uncertainty 240
uncertainty/anxiety management theory 59–60
uncertainty reduction 240
unrequited love 256–7
upward influence 340, 342–3

variable intensity 159–60
verbal support messages 380–5, 381f, 383t, 385f, 398
virtual communities 43
voice cues 163–4, 166, 174

Wilmot, W.W. 11, 247, 254, 348
Wilson, S.R. 19, 142, 252, 323, 328, 330, 340
Wood, L. 366
working self-concept 74
workplace: communication between men and women in 63–4; communication competence in 21; communication satisfaction in 18; interpersonal communication in context of 12–13; power and language use in 145; power and suppression of conflict in 366–7; revealing identity in 80; self-esteem in 72